The purpose of the Cambridge Edition is to offer a translation of the modern German edition of Kant's work in a uniform format suitable for Kant scholars. When complete (fourteen volumes are currently envisaged) the edition will include all of Kant's published writings and a generous selection of his unpublished writings such as the *Opus postumum, handschriftliche Nachlass*, lectures, and correspondence.

This is the first English translation of all of Kant's writings on moral and political philosophy collected in a single volume. No other collection competes with the comprehensiveness of this one. As well as Kant's most famous moral and political writings, the *Groundwork of the Metaphysics of Morals*, the *Critique of Practical Reason*, the *Metaphysics of Morals*, and *Toward Perpetual Peace*, the volume includes shorter essays and reviews, some of which have never been translated before. The translation of the *Metaphysics of Morals* by Mary Gregor appears in a new edition to conform to the guidelines of the Cambridge Edition and to reflect some widely accepted textual emendations adopted in a recent German edition of that work.

The volume has been furnished with a substantial editorial apparatus including translators' introductions and explanatory notes to each text, and a general introduction to Kant's moral and political philosophy by Allen Wood. There is also an English–German and German–English glossary of key terms.

THE CAMBRIDGE EDITION OF THE WORKS
OF IMMANUEL KANT

Theoretical Philosophy, 1755–1770
The Critique of Pure Reason
Theoretical Philosophy After 1781
Practical Philosophy
Aesthetics and Teleology
Religion and Rational Theology
Anthropology, History, and Education
Natural Science
Lectures on Logic
Lectures on Metaphysics
Lectures on Ethics
Opus postumum
Notes and Fragments
Correspondence

IMMANUEL KANT
Practical philosophy

THE CAMBRIDGE EDITION OF THE WORKS OF IMMANUEL KANT

General editors: Paul Guyer and Allen W. Wood

Advisory board: Henry Allison
Lewis White Beck
Reinhard Brandt
Ralf Meerbote
Charles D. Parsons
Hoke Robinson
J. B. Schneewind
Manley P. Thompson

IMMANUEL KANT

Practical philosophy

TRANSLATED AND EDITED BY
MARY J. GREGOR

GENERAL INTRODUCTION BY
ALLEN WOOD
Yale University

CAMBRIDGE
UNIVERSITY PRESS

CAMBRIDGE UNIVERSITY PRESS
Cambridge, New York, Melbourne, Madrid, Cape Town, Singapore, São Paulo, Delhi

Cambridge University Press
32 Avenue of the Americas, New York, NY 10013-2473, USA

www.cambridge.org
Information on this title: www.cambridge.org/9780521654081

© Cambridge University Press 1996

This publication is in copyright. Subject to statutory exception
and to the provisions of relevant collective licensing agreements,
no reproduction of any part may take place without the written
permission of Cambridge University Press.

First published 1996
First paperback edition 1999
12th printing 2008

A catalog record for this publication is available from the British Library.

Library of Congress Cataloging in Publication Data
Kant, Immanuel, 1724–1804
[Selections, English, 1996]
Practical philosophy / Immanuel Kant ; edited by Mary J. Gregor.
p. cm. – (The Cambridge edition of the works of
Immanuel Kant)
Includes bibliographical references and index.
Contents: Review of Schulz's Attempt at an introduction to a
doctrine of morals for all human beings regardless of different
religions – An answer to the question, what is enlightenment? – On
the wrongfulness of unauthorized publication of books – Groundwork
of the metaphysics of morals – Kraus' review of Ulrich's
Eleutheriology – Critique of practical reason – On the common
saying, that may be correct in theory, but is of no use in
practice – Toward perpetual peace – The metaphysics of morals.
On a supposed right to lie from philanthropy.
1. Ethics, Modern – 18th century. I. Gregor, Mary J. II. Title.
III. Series: Kant, Immanuel, 1724–1804. Works. English. 1992.
B27358.G74   1996
170 – dc20   95 – 9656
                                                              CIP

ISBN 978-0-521-37103-2 hardback
ISBN 978-0-521-65408-1 paperback

Cambridge University Press has no responsibility for the persistence or
accuracy of URLs for external or third-party Internet Web sites referred to in
this publication and does not guarantee that any content on such Web sites is,
or will remain, accurate or appropriate. Information regarding prices, travel
timetables, and other factual information given in this work are correct at
the time of first printing, but Cambridge University Press does not guarantee
the accuracy of such information thereafter.

Contents

General editors' preface	page vii
Preface	xi
General introduction	xiii
Review of Schulz's Attempt at an introduction to a doctrine of morals for all human beings regardless of different religions (1783)	1
An answer to the question: What is enlightenment? (1784)	11
On the wrongfulness of unauthorized publication of books (1785)	23
Groundwork of The metaphysics of morals (1785)	37
Review of Gottlieb Hufeland's Essay on the principle of natural right (1786) [translated and edited by Allen Wood]	109
Kraus's review of Ulrich's *Eleutheriology* (1788)	119
Critique of practical reason (1788)	133
On the common saying: That may be correct in theory, but it is of no use in practice (1793)	273
Toward perpetual peace (1795)	311
The metaphysics of morals (1797)	353
On a supposed right to lie from philanthropy (1797)	605
On turning out books (1798) [translated and edited by Allen Wood]	617
Editorial notes	628
Glossary	641
Index of names	661
Index of subjects	664

General editors' preface

Within a few years of the publication of his *Critique of Pure Reason* in 1781, Immanuel Kant (1724–1804) was recognized by his contemporaries as one of the seminal philosophers of modern times – indeed as one of the great philosophers of all time. This renown soon spread beyond German-speaking lands, and translations of Kant's work into English were published even before 1800. Since then, interpretations of Kant's views have come and gone and loyalty to his positions has waxed and waned, but his importance has not diminished. Generations of scholars have devoted their efforts to producing reliable translations of Kant into English as well as into other languages.

There are four main reasons for the present edition of Kant's writings:

1. Completeness. Although most of the works published in Kant's lifetime have been translated before, the most important ones more than once, only fragments of Kant's many important unpublished works have ever been translated. These include the *Opus postumum*, Kant's unfinished *magnum opus* on the transition from philosophy to physics; transcriptions of his classroom lectures; his correspondence; and his marginalia and other notes. One aim of this edition is to make a comprehensive sampling of these materials available in English for the first time.

2. Availability. Many English translations of Kant's works, especially those that have not individually played a large role in the subsequent development of philosophy, have long been inaccessible or out of print. Many of them, however, are crucial for the understanding of Kant's philosophical development, and the absence of some from English-language bibliographies may be responsible for erroneous or blinkered traditional interpretations of his doctrines by English-speaking philosophers.

3. Organization. Another aim of the present edition is to make all Kant's published work, both major and minor, available in comprehensive volumes organized both chronologically and topically, so as to facilitate the serious study of his philosophy by English-speaking readers.

4. Consistency of translation. Although many of Kant's major works have been translated by the most distinguished scholars of their day, some of

GENERAL EDITORS' PREFACE

these translations are now dated, and there is considerable terminological disparity among them. Our aim has been to enlist some of the most accomplished Kant scholars and translators to produce new translations, freeing readers from both the philosophical and literary preconceptions of previous generations and allowing them to approach texts, as far as possible, with the same directness as present-day readers of the German or Latin originals.

In pursuit of these goals, our editors and translators attempt to follow several fundamental principles:

1. As far as seems advisable, the edition employs a single general glossary, especially for Kant's technical terms. Although we have not attempted to restrict the prerogative of editors and translators in choice of terminology, we have maximized consistency by putting a single editor or editorial team in charge of each of the main groupings of Kant's writings, such as his work in practical philosophy, philosophy of religion, or natural science, so that there will be a high degree of terminological consistency, at least in dealing with the same subject matter.

2. Our translators try to avoid sacrificing literalness to readability. We hope to produce translations that approximate the originals in the sense that they leave as much of the interpretive work as possible to the reader.

3. The paragraph, and even more the sentence, is often Kant's unit of argument, and one can easily transform what Kant intends as a continuous argument into a mere series of assertions by breaking up a sentence so as to make it more readable. Therefore, we try to preserve Kant's own divisions of sentences and paragraphs wherever possible.

4. Earlier editions often attempted to improve Kant's texts on the basis of controversial conceptions about their proper interpretation. In our translations, emendation or improvement of the original edition is kept to the minimum necessary to correct obvious typographical errors.

5. Our editors and translators try to minimize interpretation in other ways as well, for example, by rigorously segregating Kant's own footnotes, the editors' purely linguistic notes, and their more explanatory of informational notes; notes in this last category are treated as endnotes rather than footnotes.

We have not attempted to standardize completely the format of individual volumes. Each, however, includes information about the context in which Kant wrote the translated works, an English–German glossary, an index, and other aids to comprehension. The general introduction to each volume includes an explanation of specific principles of translation and, where necessary, principles of selection of works included in that volume. The pagination of the standard German edition of Kant's works, *Kant's Gesammelte Schriften*, edited by the Royal Prussian (later German) Academy of Sciences (Berlin: Georg Reimer, later Walter deGruyter & Co., 1900–   ), is indicated throughout by means of marginal numbers.

GENERAL EDITORS' PREFACE

Our aim is to produce a comprehensive edition of Kant's writings, embodying and displaying the high standards attained by Kant scholarship to the English-speaking world during the second half of the twentieth century, and serving as both an instrument and a stimulus for the further development of Kant studies by English-speaking readers in the century to come. Because of our emphasis on literalness of translation and on information rather than interpretation in editorial practices, we hope our edition will continue to be usable despite the inevitable evolution and occasional revolutions in Kant scholarship.

PAUL GUYER
ALLEN W. WOOD

Preface

The manuscript for this book was virtually complete only a few months before the death of Mary J. Gregor on October 31, 1994. She had finished not only nearly all of the texts themselves, but also the introductions and editorial notes accompanying the individual works. Only two short essays remained to be translated. Apart from minor revisions (to which she had agreed), the only other editorial work left to be done was the General Introduction and the glossaries. Some corrections in the translations were due to the helpful comments of B. Sharon Byrd, Thomas McCarthy, and Georg Geismann.

Gregor's translations of Kant are characterized not only by meticulous linguistic accuracy and scholarly erudition but also by an unfailing sense of style and an uncanny ability to render Kant's meaning into readable and even elegant English. Over a period of more than thirty years, she produced excellent English versions of Kant's writings: *The Doctrine of Virtue* (1964), *Anthropology from a Pragmatic Standpoint* (1974), *The Conflict of the Faculties* (1979), "On the Philosopher's Medicine of the Body" (1985), and the whole of the *Metaphysics of Morals* (1991). Her translations of all these works are being used as the basis of the Cambridge Edition versions.

In addition to her accomplishments as a translator, Gregor made significant contributions to Kant scholarship. She wrote articles on Kant's moral and political philosophy, and her book *Laws of Freedom* (1963) was almost alone at the time in stressing the indispensability of the *Metaphysics of Morals* for a proper understanding of Kant's ethical theory. Today the importance of Kant's last great ethical work is universally acknowledged among students of Kantian ethics.

This comprehensive edition of all Kant's published writings on practical philosophy, brought together in a single volume for the first time, should be the definitive English version of all Kant's moral and political writings for many years to come. As Gregor's greatest and most lasting contribution to Kant studies, it speaks more eloquently about her scholarly accomplishments than any eulogy.

Ithaca: February, 1995   A.W.W.

General introduction

Kant was drawn to philosophy through his interest in natural science, not through moral or political concerns. His systematic interests in practical philosophy were slow in developing, and in the beginning his theoretical discussions of morality were governed less by his substantive moral convictions than by concerns about the grounding of knowledge and the architectonic structure of a system of philosophy. Yet from early in his career, Kant did have distinctive and deeply held moral beliefs, formed partly, no doubt, by his pietistic religious upbringing, but profoundly influenced by modern Enlightenment culture and especially by the writings of Jean-Jacques Rousseau. In the end, Kant's mature thought was grounded on the primacy of the practical, and the critical philosophy is at least as much a moral outlook as it is a position on matters of knowledge, theory, or speculative metaphysics.

Among the works Kant published during the last decade of his life, the emphasis was heavily on practical topics – morality, religion, politics, education, pragmatic anthropology, the final end and historical destiny of the human species. Kant's critical writings on practical philosophy, here collected for the first time in a single volume, are equal in importance and influence to anything else in his philosophy, even the *Critique of Pure Reason*.

THE FOUNDATIONS OF MORAL THEORY: 1762–81

At the end of 1762 Kant submitted to the Prussian Royal Academy of Sciences a prize essay, *Inquiry concerning the Distinctness of the Principles of Natural Theology and Morals* (in the competition it finished second to an essay by Moses Mendelssohn). Kant's prize essay was concerned mainly with the foundations of metaphysical knowledge and especially with the difference between metaphysical and mathematical cognition. But its final section briefly compared the theoretical sciences with morality, as regards the nature and sources of their first principles. In it, Kant complains that the fundamental principles of morality are not yet certain enough to ground a science because even the fundamental concept of moral obligation has not been clarified sufficiently. Anticipating his later distinction between hypothetical and categorical imperatives, Kant asserts that the word "ought," which expresses the practical necessity of an action, is capable of two distinct meanings. Either I ought to do something merely as a means to some further end, or I ought immediately to do something (as itself an end). An obligation, he says, is truly present only where "ought" has the latter meaning (AK 2:298).[1] Obligations, then, depend on ends that are immediately necessary in themselves, and whose goodness cannot be demonstrated, but must be apprehended directly.

Kant's account of this direct awareness of goodness appears to have been influenced by his recent acquaintance with the moral sense theory of the Scottish philosopher Francis Hutcheson. He distinguishes the faculty of *cognition*, as the capacity to represent *truth*, from the faculty of experiencing *goodness*, which is *feeling*. "If the good is simple, then the judgment: 'This is good,' will be completely indemonstrable. This judgment will be an immediate effect of the consciousness of the feeling of pleasure combined with the representation of the object" (AK 2:299). Kant claims that there are many simple feelings of the good to be found in us, which provide the basis for indemonstrable principles, "which, as postulates, contain the foundations of all the other practical principles" (AK 2:300). Both Kant's unpublished reflections and his lecture transcriptions of this period indicate that he was prepared to claim that human beings possess a universal and unanimous capacity for moral feeling, distinct from reason, which is to be regarded as the final moral criterion and the ground of all moral principles and judgments (R6581 AK 19:931; AK 27:4–6).

Yet the final sentence of the prize essay itself, after apparently endorsing moral sense theory, renews the claim that moral concepts are not yet precise enough and infers from this to a more tentative estimate of the sources of moral principles.

> The ultimate fundamental concepts of obligation need first of all to be determined more reliably. And in this respect, practical philosophy is even more defective than speculative philosophy, for it has yet to be determined whether it is merely the faculty of cognition, or whether it is feeling (the first inner ground of the faculty of desire) which decides its first principles. (AK 2:300)

It was not long before Kant began to back away from the theory of moral feeling. *Observations on the Feeling of the Beautiful and Sublime*, completed by October 1764, claims that there is "a feeling for the beauty and dignity of human nature" that is universal among human beings (AK 2:217). But then just a few pages later Kant insists that "it is impossible to reach a common agreement on feelings, because feeling is by no means uniform" (AK 2:226; cf. AK 20:49–50). This variability of feeling is subsequently

---

[1]. Kant's writings will be cited from the Berlin Academy Edition (abbreviated as "AK") by volume:page number, except in the case of the *Critique of Pure Reason*, which will be cited by the standard A/B page numbers.

cited as a reason why it cannot serve as a criterion of what is objectively good, since this must necessarily be the same for all (AK 19:124, 149; 4:442; 5:25). But Kant later comes to argue also that even if people were unanimous in their moral feelings, the necessity of moral obligation could never rest on such a merely empirical foundation (AK 19:116–17, 120, 149; 4:408; 5:26).[2]

In his notes on *Observations on the Feeling of the Beautiful and Sublime*, Kant had already suggested that freedom is the object of our moral interest and the basis of feelings of dignity. In that sense, the normative basis for his mature ethics was already emerging, although he still needed to find the right metaethics and metaphysics in which to imbed his normative ideal. By 1765 Kant had decided that moral philosophy required metaphysical foundations (AK 10:56), and by 1768 he claimed to be at work on a book concerned with the "metaphysics of morals" (AK 10:74). At this point, however, that title appears to refer only to knowledge arising from the analysis of concepts, as distinct from knowledge derived from the immediacy of feelings, and does not necessarily imply that the principles of morality must not be of empirical origin. It was not until the Inaugural Dissertation of 1770 that Kant further specified that "metaphysics" deals only with a priori cognitions originating in the understanding; and it was only in § 9 of that work that he first inferred that a metaphysics of morals, as the foundation of moral philosophy, must not include any empirical principles (AK 2:396).

During the 1770s, when Kant published very little, he continued to promise a philosophical system whose practical part, resting on a priori principles, was to be given the title "Metaphysics of Morals" (AK 10:97, 132, 144).[3] During this period he contemplated the possibility that if the formal principle of morality is a priori, it might be constituted merely by the idea of universality and systematicity, which could be applied to empirical material to form a system of happiness (R6820 AK 19:172, R7029 AK 19:230, R7202 AK 19:276–82).[4] But it was also during Kant's "silent decade" that he first began to associate the metaphysical foundations of moral philosophy with the metaphysical idea of the will's freedom (R6725 AK 19:141–2; R5441 AK 18:182–3; 27:110–12).

According to the first edition of the *Critique of Pure Reason* (1781), there is a pure science of ethics (A480/B508), whose principles are a priori and based on the transcendental freedom of every rational being (A15/B29,

---

2. See Dieter Henrich, *The Unity of Reason*, ed. R. Velkley, trans. J. Edwards, L. Hunt, M. Kuehn, and G. Zöller (Cambridge, Mass.: Harvard University Press, 1994), pp. 55–87.
3. See Lewis White Beck, *A Commentary on Kant's "Critique of Practical Reason"* (Chicago: University of Chicago Press, 1960), pp. 7–9.
4. These reflections will be included in Paul Guyer, ed., *Notes and Fragments*, in the present edition of Kant's writings.

A802/B830, A807/B835, A840/B868). As part of the system of philosophy, a "metaphysics of morals" parallels the "metaphysics of nature," since the former is grounded on "laws of freedom" just as the latter is based on laws of nature (A841/B869). But Kant excludes moral theory from "transcendental philosophy," on the ground that the concept of duty, involving as it does the representation of subjective obstacles to be overcome, depends on empirical concepts as well as a priori principles (A15/B29). Morality is presented chiefly as the source of practical *ideas*, which are held to be the ground of the experience of the good (A318/B375).

Morality as practical cognition, however, enters the system of the *Critique* itself only "methodologically," in the form of a "Canon of Pure Reason," a "sum total of the principles of [reason's] correct use." Kant tells us that there is no canon for the speculative use of reason, but one only for its practical use (A796/B824), and that moral laws alone belong to the canon of pure reason (A800/B828). Yet this canon is concerned chiefly not with the formulation of moral principles and duties, but with systematizing rational ends in the concept of a highest good and with the moral belief (or faith) in its possibility (A804–31/B832–59). In the first *Critique*, the closest Kant comes to a formula of the moral law is the claim that the "idea of a moral world" is that of "a *corpus mysticum* of the rational beings in it, insofar as the free will of each, under moral laws, is in complete systematic unity with itself and with the freedom of every other" (A808/B836).

In moral philosophy, as elsewhere in Kant's thought, the traditional division between "precritical" and "critical" is misleading if it is taken to refer to a basic difference in attitude or outlook. It is more accurate to see Kant simply as undergoing a long period of exploration and preparation, which eventually bore fruit in the shape of the critical system only after Kant was well into middle age. The exploration did not cease even then, of course, but lasted the rest of Kant's life. The critical philosophy itself was modified in the second edition of the *Critique of Pure Reason* (1787), when Kant decided to write a second critique (of practical reason), and it was reshaped again when he wrote the *Critique of Judgment* (1790). Its foundations were rethought once again in the *Opus postumum*, until Kant's restless search was broken off by old age and death. In the case of Kant's writings and reflections on morality, the first *Critique* is not a turning point of any unique significance. Kant's precritical thought investigates the concept of moral obligation and the sources of our knowledge of moral principles. By 1781 he had assembled all the principal materials for a theory of morality, but this theory was to receive its first real formulation only in the *Groundwork* of 1785.[5]

---

5. See Josef Schmucker, *Die Ursprünge der Ethik Kants in seinen vorkritischen Schriften und Reflexionen* (Meisenheim am Glan: Verlag Anton Heim, 1961). This is the best existing study of Kant's early ethical thought. An older (now widely disputed) account can be found in Paul

GENERAL INTRODUCTION

THE DIGNITY OF HUMANITY

Alongside Kant's reflections on moral *theory*, his precritical writings and reflections also record some substantive moral *convictions* that equally shape Kant's mature moral thought and are perhaps even more important for understanding both its content and its lasting influence. We have already seen evidence of it in Kant's claim that there is in all human beings a universal feeling for "the beauty and dignity of human nature" (AK 2:217). This remark is one evidence of the fact that Kant's earliest period of intense reflection on morality coincides with his reading of Rousseau's *Of the Social Contract* and *Émile* around 1764. A striking (and often quoted) reflection from the mid-1760s documents the profound change that Rousseau effected in Kant's outlook on life:

> I am an inquirer by inclination. I feel a consuming thirst for knowledge, the unrest which goes with the desire to progress in it, and satisfaction at every advance in it. There was a time when I believed this constituted the honor of humanity, and I despised the people, who know nothing. Rousseau set me right about this. This binding prejudice disappeared. I learned to honor humanity, and I would find myself more useless than the common laborer if I did not believe that this attitude of mine can give worth to all others in establishing the rights of humanity. (AK 20:44)

Perhaps the most striking thing about Kant's outlook here is its unqualified egalitarianism. People tend to judge themselves to be better than others on various grounds, such as birth, wealth, honor, power, or – in Kant's case – learning. But these judgments are always mere opinions, without truth, and all social inequalities are therefore founded on falsehood and deception: "The opinion of inequality makes people unequal. Only the teaching of M. R[ousseau] can bring it about that even the most learned philosopher with his knowledge holds himself, uprightly and without the help of religion, no better than the common human being" (AK 20:176). The reason that Kant's egalitarianism is unqualified is that the worth of every human being is a "dignity" – that is, an absolute and incomparable value, a worth for which nothing else can be substituted as its equivalent (AK 4:434).

One might think that Kant would qualify his egalitarianism at least by admitting that people can differ in worth on *moral* grounds – that the morally better or more virtuous person would have more worth than the bad or vicious, the person of good will more value than the person of evil will. Kant does allow that the morally good person has greater "inner" worth – that is, worth as measured by comparison with the person's own

---

Arthur Schilpp, *Kant's Pre-Critical Ethics* (Evanston, Ill.: Northwestern University Press, 1938). A discussion in English that disputes Schilpp's account is Keith Ward, *The Development of Kant's View of Ethics* (Oxford: Oxford University Press, 1972).

self-given moral law or idea of virtue. When I am conscious of doing my duty, therefore, I feel an inner self-contentment (AK 5:88, 117; 6:387, 391), while transgressions of duty occasion "self-contempt and inner abhorrence" (AK 4:426). But Kant does not regard these judgments of self-worth in comparison with the moral law as legitimating any comparisons between people: "Moral self-esteem, which is grounded in the worth of humanity, should not be derived from comparison with others, but from comparison with the moral law" (AK 27:349). Hence they do not disturb the fundamental equality of self-worth that follows from the dignity of humanity present in every human being: "All human beings are equal to one another, and only he who is morally good has a superior inner worth" (AK 27:462). Kant even reinterprets the admiration we show for the merits of another so that it involves no moral comparisons between people, only a comparison between myself and my own duty, of which the example of the upright person serves merely as a reminder (AK 5:76–7).

The other noteworthy feature of Kant's conviction about the worth of humanity is one that seems clearly at odds with his initial disposition toward Hutcheson's moral sense theory, hence one that probably played a role in his early separation from views of that kind. Kant sees the worth of humanity not in the guise of something likeable or attractive, hence not as something that appeals to our feelings of love, sympathy, or generosity, but rather as a ground of rational esteem or respect, which makes demands on us that we are not entitled to refuse, however reluctant our *feelings* may be to acknowledge them. Thus Rousseau's teaching, as Kant understands it, asserts not the natural goodness (amiability or sympathy) of human nature, but rather concerns the *rights* of humanity, which we are obligated to respect regardless of our feelings. Kant's early reflections thus focus on human rights and justice, and they display a decided mistrust toward the common moralist's enthusiasm for love of humanity and virtue understood as warmhearted generosity: "One always talks so much of virtue. One must, however, abolish injustice before one can be virtuous. One must set aside comforts, luxuries and everything that oppresses others while elevating myself, so that I am not one of those who oppress their species. Without this conclusion, all virtue is impossible" (AK 20:151). The beneficence on which the wealthy and strong pride themselves, Kant insists, is often nothing but a cover for their oppression of the poor and weak, and a way of excusing their refusal to acknowledge the equality of others founded on human dignity:

> Many people take pleasure in doing good actions, but consequently do not want to stand under obligations toward others. If one only comes to them submissively, they will do everything; they do not want to subject themselves to the rights of people, but to view them simply as objects of their magnanimity. It is not all the

same under what title I get something. What properly belongs to me must not be accorded me as something I beg for. (AK 19:145)[6]

Like Rousseau, Kant regards all rational beings as of equal worth and infers from this that the social inequalities between people, inequalities of honor, power, and above all of wealth, are fundamentally unjust. What appears in our society as benevolence is therefore merely a partial restitution made to the victims of this general injustice by those who profit from it.

In accordance with [benevolence], people are merciful to others and show beneficence to them after they have earlier taken from them, even though they are conscious of no injustice to anyone. But one can participate in the general injustice, even if one does no one any injustice according to the civil laws and institutions. Now if one shows beneficence to a wretch, then one has not given him anything gratuitously, but has given him only what one had earlier helped to take from him through the general injustice. For if no one took more of the goods of life than another, then there would be no rich and no poor. Accordingly, even acts of generosity are acts of duty and indebtedness, which arise from the rights of others. (AK 27:416)

The "general injustice" of which Kant speaks here is, in his view, consistent with the principles of right that are coercively enforceable (though they do give rise to a social obligation of beneficence to the poor, which the state is entitled to discharge, AK 6:325–7).[7] Consequently, he does not think the "civil equality" to which people are entitled as citizens of a state is inconsistent with large disparities of wealth (AK 8:291). But Kant does hold that the general injustice attaching to existing social relations produces a systematic deception in regard to people's benevolent feelings.

In our present condition, when general injustice is firmly entrenched, the natural rights of the lowly cease. They are therefore only debtors, the superiors owe them nothing. Therefore, these superiors are called "gracious lords." But he who needs nothing from them but justice can hold them to their debts and does not need to be submissive. (AK 20:140–1)

The wealthy, therefore, should not regard their charity as meritorious, since it is really nothing but the discharging of a debt, which the general injustice of society falsely presents to us as a beneficence freely given (AK 6:454).

It is in this same light that we must understand Kant's insistence, which scandalizes many of his readers, that there is moral worth in an act

---

6. See J. B. Schneewind, "Autonomy, Obligation and Virtue," in P. Guyer, ed., *The Cambridge Companion to Kant* (New York: Cambridge University Press, 1991), p. 311.
7. See Allen Rosen, *Kant's Theory of Justice* (Ithaca, N.Y.: Cornell University Press, 1992), ch. 6.

of charity done reluctantly, by a person who is naturally coldhearted or weighed down by his own sorrows, but no such worth in a similar act done with pleasure by a person of sympathetic disposition who loves spreading joy around (AK 4:398–9). For Kant, warmhearted benevolence deserves less esteem than sentimental moralists are wont to accord it because it is to be seen only as a device of nature, a way of compensating for the "general injustice" prevailing in human society (AK 27:416).

KANT'S FIRST STATEMENT OF THE MATURE THEORY

Before 1781 Kant repeatedly claimed to be writing a work entitled "The Metaphysics of Morals," but this work was again and again postponed. Even when Kant did begin to formulate his mature moral theory in the mid-1780s, fulfillment of the promise was again deferred: "Intending to publish some day a metaphysics of morals, I issue this groundwork in advance" (AK 4:391). We might wonder why Kant did not directly formulate his metaphysics of morals, but once again felt the need to engage in a preliminary inquiry as a propadeutic to moral theory proper. On the other hand, we might equally ask what had happened by 1785 that finally put him in a position to make some headway with a project he had delayed so long. One possibility suggests itself if we attend to some of the shorter essays Kant was writing in the middle of the 1780s. In February 1784 an article appeared written by Kant's colleague and follower Johann Schulze which contained the following cryptic remark:

> A favorite idea of Professor Kant is that the final end of the human race is the attainment of the most perfect political constitution, and he wishes that a philosophical historian would undertake to provide us in this respect with a history of humanity, and to show how far humanity has approached this final end in different ages, or how far it has been from it, and what is yet to be done to attain it. (AK 8:468)

Kant made good on Schulze's hint in an essay published in the *Berlinische Monatschrift* in November of the same year: "Idea toward a Universal History with a Cosmopolitan Aim" (AK 8:15–31). It dealt with the philosophy of history from the standpoint of the idea of the historical development and progress of the human species, and the social and political conditions required for it. In the December issue of the same journal he published another article, "Answer to the Question: What Is Enlightenment?" (AK 8:33–42), which also dealt with the theme of human progress and specifically with the essential role of free public discussion in such progress – a topic on which he had earlier expressed himself in the *Critique of Pure Reason* (A738–69/B766–97).

One likely stimulus to Kant's thinking on these topics was the first

GENERAL INTRODUCTION

volume of *Ideas for a Philosophy of the History of Humanity* by Kant's erstwhile student J. G. Herder, which was published in July of 1784 and reviewed by Kant early in 1785. Kant regarded Herder's postulation of spiritual forces and entelechies in nature as metaphysically extravagant, and his use of arguments from analogy as uncritical and far-fetched; the tone of the review was condescending. The second volume of Herder's *Ideas*, which appeared in the summer of 1785, contained an explicit attack on Kant's "Idea toward a Universal History." Kant had argued that human history can be understood in terms of devices employed by nature to induce or compel individuals to promote the collective ends of the species. More specifically, he had argued, on essentially Rousseauian grounds, that human beings in society are naturally in conflict with one another, and that nature uses this conflict to compel them to submit themselves to the discipline of a law-governed civil society. Herder regarded this view of history as denigrating to the worth of human individuals (his reaction anticipates many of the moral objections later raised by "methodological individualists" against any theory of history that employs the notion of a collectivist teleology). Herder was particularly offended by Kant's "evil principle" that "The human being is an animal who needs a master" (AK 8:23). Kant replied to these criticisms in his review of Herder's second volume, published in November 1785. Thereafter he declined to review further installments of Herder's *Ideas*, but did write a brilliant satire on Herder's attempt, in Book 10 of the *Ideas*, to use the book of Genesis to speculate about the historical origins of the human species. Kant's "Conjectural Beginning of Human History" appeared in January 1786.

Herder and Kant can be regarded as developing an essentially Rousseauian conception of the human condition in two different directions. Herder's view of human nature is optimistic: Human beings are destined by nature to be happy and to live harmoniously with one another, and they do so as long as their mode of life is grounded in their whole humanity, their reason assuming its rightful place alongside the life of natural feeling, poetic inspiration, and religious sensibility, which furnish them with an extrarational divine guidance. They become wicked and unhappy when their reason cuts itself off from these spiritual moorings and attempts to chart its own course. Hence if we employ the term "enlightenment" in its Kantian sense, to refer to the human being's exit from tutelage (whether of nature or tradition) and the resolve to think for oneself, then Herder identifies the principle of enlightenment as the source of human evil and unhappiness. Along with Rousseau, Herder is one of the earliest thinkers to display an attraction for older, simpler, more exotic, and more distant ways of life based on feeling, tradition, and religion, and that ambivalence toward modernity, with its ideals of reason, science, and endless progress, that has become one of modernity's own most persistent cultural features.

Kant does not deny that reason's independent development sooner leads to discontent than to happiness, that animals living under the guidance of instinct are free of most of the cares and sorrows that beset human beings, and that peoples who live a life of thoughtless indolence, guided by nature or tradition rather than by their own thinking, will have lives that are happier and less plagued by vices and social conflicts than modern civilized peoples, who have set out on a self-directed path that is both uncharted and beset with dangers. Kant's counterclaim is that even our discontent is nature's device for developing the capacities of our species, enabling it to fulfill its destiny, and that self-direction through reason enables individual human beings to give themselves a worth far greater than any happiness they might enjoy. The sweet fantasy of returning to a simpler life – the life of innocent shepherds or carefree South Sea Islanders – is nothing but a delusion, a symptom of the inevitable discontents of civilization, through which nature spurs us on (AK 8:122). Even if people could realize this dream, their lives would then have no more meaning than those of the innocent, happy sheep and cattle they tended (AK 8:21, 65).

The *Groundwork*, published in March 1785 (AK 4:626–8), is not only a step in fulfilling Kant's project of a metaphysics of morals, but also an eloquent defense of enligthenment and self-directing reason against Herder's doubts and objections. According to its opening pages, nature gave us reason not in order to make us happy (an end to which unthinking instinct would in any case have better directed us) but for a far higher end – the good will, the only thing in the world or beyond it that can be conceived good without qualification. The good will, moreover, consists in acting solely from respect for the moral law of reason, even in opposition to our benevolent natural feelings and in complete disregard of happiness, whose worth, like that of all goods other than a good will, is merely conditional and dependent on being combined with a good will (AK 4:392–9). Reason commands us not to be content with lives of idleness and pleasure, but to develop all the faculties of our species so as to honor our humanity as an end in itself (AK 4:4, 422–3, 430). The moral law is the only conceivable source of obligation because it is a principle of *autonomy*, which recognizes no law except what rational beings give themselves a priori through their own reason – a reason that is entirely self-directing, free of any guidance by natural impulse, social tradition, religious revelation, or poetic inspiration. It is this capacity to be unconditionally legislative that constitutes the dignity (absolute and incomparable worth) of humanity (AK 4:434). The principle of autonomy is also a principle of *enlightenment*, because it locates the source of moral legislation in the reason of human individuals who think for themselves, locating the ultimate criterion of morality in "the moral judgment of every human being insofar as he makes the effort to think [the moral law] clearly" (A807/B835).

GENERAL INTRODUCTION

THE BASIS OF KANT'S PRACTICAL PHILOSOPHY

As its name implies, the *Groundwork of the Metaphysics of Morals* provides the foundation for all Kant's subsequent writings on practical philosophy. Its avowed aim is "nothing more than the search for and establishment of the *supreme principle of morality*" (AK 4:392). In its first section, Kant begins from "common rational moral cognition" and moves to "philosophical cognition" by deriving a formulation of the moral principle by relating the idea of the good will to that of duty, and the latter to the idea of acting from respect for a universal law. The first formulation is the Formula of Universal Law (FUL):

FUL: "I ought never to act except in such a way that I could also will that my maxim should become a universal law." (AK 4:402)[8]

In the second section, Kant derives FUL "philosophically" from the concepts of a finite rational will and of a categorical imperative (AK 4:421). From this he derives the first *applicable* form of the moral principle, the Formula of the Law of Nature (FLN):

FLN: "Act as if the maxim of your action were to become by your will a *universal law of nature.*" (AK 4:421)

This formula is then applied to four examples, illustrating the taxonomy of duties as duties to oneself and duties to others, and as perfect and imperfect duties (AK 4:421–3).

At this point, however, Kant is still far from the completion of his task. For he still has not formulated the moral principle from the standpoint of the motive through which a will could be determined by it. He proceeds to identify this motive as the objective worth of rational nature (or humanity) regarded as an end in itself. This leads to his second main formulation, the Formula of Humanity (FH):

FH: "So act that you use humanity, whether in your own person or in the person of any other, always at the same time as an end, never merely as a means." (AK 4:429)

---

8. The closest thing to a standard classification of the *Groundwork*'s formulations of the supreme principle of morality is found in H. J. Paton, *The Categorical Imperative* (New York: Harper, 1947), Book III, pp. 129–98. Paton identifies the three main formulations with roman numerals, and the principal variants of the first and third formulations by appending a lowercase "a" to the corresponding numeral. Thus the abbreviations used here correspond to Paton's abbreviations as follows:

   I   = Formula of Universal Law (FUL)
   Ia = Formula of the Law of Nature (FLN)
   II = Formula of Humanity as End in Itself (FH)
   III = Formula of Autonomy (FA)
   IIIa = Formula of the Kingdom of Ends (FKE)

This formula is illustrated with the same four examples (AK 4:429–30). Kant then proceeds to combine the idea of universal law with that of the value of rational nature by viewing "the will of every rational being as a will giving universal law" (AK 4:431). This leads to the idea of *autonomy* or self-legislation as the only possible ground of moral obligation, and to the third main formulation of the moral law, the Formula of Autonomy (FA):

FA: "Act so that [your] will could regard itself as giving universal law through all its maxims." (AK 4:434)

FA seems difficult at first to distinguish from FUL. But there is an important difference between the two. FUL proposes a test for maxims, for any given maxim taken severally and singly, which is to be used in determining whether that maxim accords with universally valid moral laws. But FA proposes to identify the common source for such laws (namely, the will of every rational being as autonomous or self-legislative), and it tells us to conform all our maxims to the *system* of laws that is legislated by such a will. FA thus leads naturally to the thought of all rational beings as constituting a moral community under a common legislation, whose source is the rational volition they all share. This idea has great affinity with Kant's closest approximation to a formulation of the law in the *Critique of Pure Reason*, which was that the "idea of a moral world" is that of "a *corpus mysticum* of the rational beings in it, insofar as the free will of each, under moral laws, is in complete systematic unity with itself and with the freedom of every other" (A808/B836). Using the *Groundwork*'s conception of every rational being as an end in itself, Kant now represents the community of rational beings as an ideal "kingdom" (AK 4:433) and subsequently presents the moral law as the Formula of the Kingdom of Ends (FKE):

FKE: "Act in accordance with the maxims of a member giving universal laws for a merely possible kingdom of ends." (AK 4:439)

Kant then presents all three formulas, FUL, FH, and FA (formulated in terms of FKE), as a system of formulations of one and the same law, but viewed from three different standpoints (AK 4:436–7). This system of formulas ends Kant's "search" for the supreme principle of morality. In the third section of the *Groundwork*, Kant proceeds with the task of "establishing" the principle, employing FA for this purpose. Kant's argument is that FA is binding on the will of a rational being if and only if this will is free, and although the will's freedom cannot be theoretically proved, it must be presupposed from a practical standpoint if we are to understand ourselves as the subjects even of our acts of judgment (AK 4:445–8). As in the first *Critique*, Kant argues that we may consistently regard ourselves as free from a practical standpoint by considering ourselves as members of an intelligible or noumenal world (AK 4:452–3).

GENERAL INTRODUCTION

THE SECOND AND THIRD *CRITIQUES*

Kant did not set out to write three "critiques." *The Critique of Pure Reason* had recognized the possibility of a metaphysics of nature and a metaphysics of morals as parts of the system of philosophy, but appeared to regard a single critique of pure reason as a sufficient ground for both (A841/B869).9 The third section of the *Groundwork* is entitled "Transition from Metaphysics of Morals to the Critique of Pure Practical Reason" (AK 4:446). But at the time Kant clearly had no intention of writing a work with the latter title. In the Preface to the *Groundwork*, he promised to write a "Metaphysics of Morals," but disavowed the intention to write a separate critique of reason in its practical use for two reasons: first, practical reason is not dialectical (or deceptive) in the way theoretical reason is, and second, the main task of a critique of practical reason would be to display the unity of reason (which is one and the same in both theory and practice), and this would be a digression from the main task of developing moral philosophy proper (AK 4:391).10

In 1786 Kant dealt with the metaphysics of nature in the *Metaphysical First Grounds of Natural Science* (AK 4:465–565). In line with this, his next natural step after the *Groundwork* would have been to proceed to the long-promised *Metaphysics of Morals* itself. He may have intended something like this in April 1786, when he wrote of a plan to produce a "System of Practical Philosophy" encompassing both an a priori metaphysics of morals and a practical anthropology (AK 10:441). But apparently Kant's plans changed as he worked on a new and expanded second edition of the *Critique of Pure Reason*. In November he announced through his publisher that "To the Critique of pure speculative reason contained in the first edition, in the second there will be appended a critique of practical reason" (AK 3:556; cf. 10:471). We do not know precisely when Kant abandoned this proposal in favor of writing a separate *Critique of Practical Reason*, but the decision may have been taken even before the publisher's announcement appeared, and it had clearly been made before he wrote the preface to the second edition of the first *Critique* in April 1787. The *Critique of Practical Reason*, written quite hurriedly for a major Kantian text, was probably completed in the middle of 1787 and was published in 1788 (AK 5:497).

Aside from the unwieldiness of a *Critique of Pure Reason* with a practical "appendix," Kant had several good reasons for writing a separate book. He clearly wanted to reply to critics of his moral philosophy, such as J. F.

9. Beck, *A Commentary to Kant's "Critique of Practical Reason,"* p. 9.
10. On the changes in Kant's views about what a system of practical philosophy should be like, see Georg Anderson, "Kants Metaphysik der Sitten – ihre Idee und ihre Verhältnis zur Ethik der Wolffischen Schule," *Kant-Studien* 28 (1923): 41–61.

GENERAL INTRODUCTION

Flatt, H. A. Pistorius, G. A. Tittel, and Thomas Wizenmann.[11] He also wanted to clarify the concept of transcendental freedom and its relation to the moral law. Instead of arguing that freedom is a practical presupposition of reason and deriving the moral law from it, as he had done in the *Groundwork*, Kant now argues that the presupposition of freedom derives solely from the moral law, which is given us as a "fact of reason" (AK 5:30–32). More generally, Kant wanted to defend (especially against the objections of Pistorius) the consistency of his doctrine of the practical postulates with his critical constraints on cognition of the transcendent, which he did through an extensive reformulation of the former doctrine in the Dialectic of Pure Practical Reason (AK 5:106–61). He also wanted to clarify both the application of the moral law (to the setting of ends) and his theory of moral motivation in Chapters II and III of the Anlaytic (AK 5:57–89).

According to the *Groundwork*, however, the principal aim of any "critique of practical reason" is the establishment of the unity of reason in its theoretical and practical uses. This certainly is a recurrent theme in the *Critique of Practical Reason* (see AK 5:3–4, 50–7, 89–106, 134–48). But there is reason to think that he was not entirely contented with the second *Critique* in this regard, since only two years later he wrote the *Critique of Judgment* with the avowed aim of employing judgment as a way of mediating between the theoretical legislation of the understanding and the practical legislation of reason (AK 5:176–9).

The third *Critique* is not specifically a work in practical philosophy, but it has important implications for Kant's practical thought. In it Kant aims to bridge the "immeasurable gulf" between the domain of sensible nature and supersensible freedom (AK 5:175–6). He does this by relating the moral view of the world both to aesthetic feeling and to the teleology of nature, so as to give an empirical content to moral experience.[12] In the Methodology of Teleological Judgment, however, he also gives morality a new focus, drawing on themes in his writings on the philosophy of history and formulating morality as a system of ends, grounded on humanity as the ultimate end of nature and the moral discipline of the will as the final end of the world (AK 5:425–36). The collective pursuit of these ends by the human species in history becomes an important theme in a series of writings that Kant produced in the early 1790s.

---

11. On these critics and the replies to them, see Beck, *A Commentary to Kant's "Critique of Practical Reason,"* pp. 58–60, 353–6, and Frederick C. Beiser, *The Fate of Reason* (Cambridge, Mass.: Harvard University Press, 1987), pp. 111–18, 184–5, 188–92.
12. On this theme, see Paul Guyer, *Kant and the Experience of Freedom* (New York: Cambridge University Press, 1993).

GENERAL INTRODUCTION

MORALITY, RELIGION, AND POLITICS

The death of Frederick the Great in 1786 brought to the Prussian throne Frederick William II, whose views and policies concerning religion and education differed sharply from those of his predecessor. Frederick, a patron of enlightenment, had tolerated and even encouraged religious freethinkers, who had come to occupy a number of pulpits and university chairs of philosophy and theology. The new monarch, a Rosicrucian and religious conservative, was alarmed by the growth of heterodoxy among his subjects and surrounded himself with ministers who were determined to put a stop to it. In July 1788, J. C. Wöllner, the minister of ecclesiastical and educational affairs, issued an edict providing both for the dismissal of preachers and professors who deviated from the creed of the established church, and for oaths and examinations to ensure that only orthodoxy would be taught by the new candidates for such posts.

Kant regarded these measures as accomplishing nothing except to add hypocrisy and mendacity to the indispensable qualifications for appointment to any civil office pertaining to religious affairs. Kant's first published protest came in an appendix to his 1791 essay "On the Miscarriage of All Philosophical Trials in Theodicy" (AK 8:253–71). Two years later, Kant infuriated the censors when he evaded their authority and published *Religion within the Boundaries of Mere Reason* by submitting it to the faculty of philosophy at his university. The *Religion*'s first part, on the radical evil in human nature, provides a new and distinctively modern interpretation of the Christian doctrine of original sin, while the second moralizes and secularizes the doctrine of justification. The third part connects religion of Kant's philosophy of history, by identifying the church or "ethical community" as an indispensable vehicle of humanity's moral progress. But the fourth part attacks "priestcraft" and the "counterfeit service of God" in existing ecclesiastical faiths, advancing Kant's severe moral criticisms of such things as faith in miracles, formal creeds, formal liturgy, and petitionary prayer.

The first part of the *Religion* also makes significant contributions to Kant's moral philosophy itself, especially to his moral psychology and to his account of free agency. Kant here makes clear (what readers of the *Groundwork* have often found murky) how the will can be subject to moral laws, hence morally accountable, while freely choosing not to obey them. He also makes it explicit that moral evil is not to be located in natural inclinations themselves but in a freely chosen maxim of the will, inverting the proper rational order of the incentives of morality and self-love (AK 6:21–2, 34–7). The ground of evil, on this account, is a product of freedom, hence metaphysically inscrutable, though Kant, like Rousseau, does relate it to the propensity to competitive self-valuation that belongs to our nature as members of a society beset with all kinds of inequality (AK 6:27–34, 93–8).

Kant had already heard of plans to silence him on religious topics before he published the bitterly satirical essay "The End of All Things" (1794), in which he warned that when Christianity abandons a liberal way of thinking for policies of coercion, then it forfeits its moral authority, which is founded on the way it puts love in the service of the moral law (AK 8:336–9). The letter of reprimand, signed by Wöllner in the king's name, was finally sent in October 1794. In his reply, Kant promised the king not to write or teach on matters of religion – a promise he kept until the death of Frederick William II in 1797. Thereafter he published *The Conflict of the Faculties* (1798), dealing prominently with the relations between philosophy and theology, not only as faculties within the legal structure of the university but also as ways of thinking in relation to the progressive destiny of the human species.

It may have been partly Kant's uneasy relation to this regressive and unfriendly political regime, but it may also have been simply the need of a philosopher approaching seventy years of age to address questions of universal human concern, that spurred Kant in the early to middle 1790s to write two important popular essays dealing with political subjects. *On the Common Saying: That May Be Correct in Theory, But It Is of No Use in Practice* (1793) is actually a combination of three essays. The first is about personal morality, a reply to Christian Garve's criticism of Kant's conceptions of the good will and moral faith (AK 8:278–89). The second is the first articulation of Kant's theory of political right, which was later to be developed in the *Metaphysics of Morals*. It defends (ostensibly against Hobbes) the proposition that subjects have rights against the ruler in a state, but also holds these rights to be unenforceable, thus denying to subjects any right of revolution and requiring them to obey even unjust commands of those in power (which provided beforehand a rationale for Kant's decision to comply with the demands Wöllner was later to make of him) (AK 8:289–306). The third essay defends (this time ostensibly against the more pessimistic views of Moses Mendelssohn) the theory of history Kant had espoused nearly a decade earlier in "Idea toward a Universal History," arguing that on practical grounds we are entitled to hold that on the whole the human race is progressing in history, and that this progress, though it may be interrupted from time to time, can never finally be broken off (AK 8:307–13).

From the 1780s onward, one of the chief tenets of Kant's historical optimism was always the hope that political states would unite in a free federation to maintain between them a permanent condition of peace (AK 8:24–26, 310–12). Kant made this hope the subject of his best-known popular essay, *Toward Perpetual Peace* (1795) (AK 8:341–86). The continuing interest of the essay is deserved on account of its uncanny farsightedness. The earlier projects by the Abbé de Saint Pierre and Rousseau, on which Kant's was modeled, had proposed a federation of the Christian states of Europe, but Kant's project is not limited in this way and even condemns European states for their wrongful and arrogant conduct toward peoples in other parts of the world (AK 8:357–60). Even more original are the relationships Kant sees between the goal of peace in the external relations between states with their internal economic and political constitution. In "Idea to a Universal History," Kant argued that a just civil constitution can be achieved only along with peace among nations, because internal justice is impossible in a state founded on its capacity to make war (AK 8:24–6). In *Perpetual Peace,* he maintains as an article of perpetual peace that states should have a republican constitution, on the ground that the advantages of war accrue to a military aristocracy while the burdens fall on the general population, and therefore peaceful policies are more likely to be chosen in states with representative institutions (AK 8:349–54). Even more striking is Kant's reason for claiming that our goal ought to be a permanent law-governed condition of perpetual peace, and not merely the cessation of open warfare between nations. Kant regards the condition of constant military preparedness as wasting, distorting, and repressing the economic powers and social energies of a people. The economic effects of a perpetual arms race, he thinks, are, in the long run, even more dangerous to humanity's fulfillment of its historical destiny than the devastation and bloodshed of actual wars themselves (AK 8:345; cf. 8:24, 121, 312).

In Kant's popular political essays, he quite self-consciously adopts the role of the abstract philosophical theorist and moralist, which he contrasts with that of the practical politician, to whom he attributes a tendency to expediency and opportunism, along with cynicism, shortsightedness, and lack of principle. He adopts the same persona in his (infamous) late essay "On a Supposed Right to Lie from Philanthropy" (AK 8:423–30), in which he replies to Benjamin Constant's defense of untruth as an acceptable means to achieve good ends.

Kant's consistent message is that the best political practice is always that informed by moral principle. Philosophers, like other citizens, must always obey the powers that be, but on the other hand, philosophers are always the best advisors to princes. From this we can see how Kant reconciled views in political philosophy that many have found jointly paradoxical and even have charged with inconsistency. Though Kant's moral convictions and his historical hopes for the human species are both in many respects quite radical, many of the political policies he advocates strike some readers as excessively cautious and even objectionably conservative.[13] While confessing to a "wishful participation approaching enthusiasm" for the French Revolution,

---

13. For example, see Frederick C. Beiser, *Enlightenment, Revolution, Romanticism* (Cambridge, Mass.: Harvard University Press, 1991), ch. 2.

GENERAL INTRODUCTION

Kant nevertheless sees revolutionary social upheavals as both wrongful and counterproductive. Progressive reform, he maintains, is most effective when it proceeds gradually and is instituted from above (AK 7:85, 92-3; 8:368-80). The historical future, as Kant sees it, will belong to republican government and representative institutions. But in regard to his own time, which is still an age of absolutism, Kant's vision of the relation between philosophy and politics is best summed up in the words of Frederick the Great: "It pertains to philosophers to be the teachers of the world and the leaders of princes; they must think consequently, and it pertains to us to act consequently; they must discover, we must carry it out."[14]

THE FINAL FORM OF KANT'S PRACTICAL PHILOSOPHY

It was in 1768 that Kant first claimed to be writing a "metaphysics of morals"; he promised he would complete it within a year (AK 10:74). Thirty years passed before be published a work with that title. One measure of the distance he covered during those years is that there is much in the *Metaphysics of Morals* that ought to surprise even a reader of the *Groundwork* and the *Critique of Practical Reason* (and accordingly, much that is at odds with the common image of Kantian ethics, which is drawn from those works).

The *Groundwork* asserts that moral philosophy is divided into two main parts: (1) a "metaphysics of morals," as a system of moral principles that are a priori and wholly independent of anything pertaining to the empirical nature of human beings, and (2) a "practical anthropology," drawn from experience, to which the metaphysical principles are applied (AK 4:388). But Kant never wrote a "practical anthropology"; the closest thing to an attempt to do so is found in some of his lectures on anthropology from a pragmatic standpoint, delivered in the 1780s.[15] By the late 1790s, Kant appears to have abandoned this whole way of looking at the relation between metaphysics and anthropology in moral philosophy.

The Introduction to *The Metaphysics of Morals* claims that a metaphysics of morals itself "cannot dispense with principles of application, and we shall often have to take as our object the particular *nature* of human beings, which is known only by experience" (AK 6:217).[16] Kant now

---

14. Quoted by Friedrich Paulsen, "Aufklärung und Aufklärungspädagogik" (1903), in F. Köpitsch, ed., *Aufklärung, Absolutismus und Bürgertum in Deutschland* (Munich, 1976), p. 280. I am grateful to Arthur Strum for bringing this quotation to my attention.
15. The transcriptions from these lectures are still unpublished even in German. I am grateful to Brian Jacobs for calling them to my attention.
16. This change in Kant's conception of a metaphysics of morals is noted by Ludwig Siep, "Wozu Metaphysik der Sitten?," in O. Höffe, ed., *Grundlegung zur Metaphysik der Sitten: Ein koöperativer Kommentar* (Frankfurt: Klostermann, 1989), pp. 31-44.

GENERAL INTRODUCTION

contrasts a metaphysics of morals on the one hand to an empirical science of human nature that deals with "the subjective conditions in human nature that hinder human beings or help them in *fulfilling* the metaphysics of morals" (AK 6:217) and on the other to a system of duties that depend not on human nature in general but on people's particular circumstances and social relationships (AK 6:468–9). This means that although Kant's practical philosophy is always based on a priori or metaphysical principles, its final form recognizes such principles only insofar as they have already been applied to human nature in general.

A second surprise concerns the division of the *Metaphysics of Morals* into a Doctrine of Right and a Doctrine of Virtue. A reader of the *Groundwork* or the second *Critique* has been told that practical philosophy rests on a single fundamental principle of morality, which is synthetic a priori and reciprocally implied by the postulate of transcendental freedom (AK 4:445–63; 5:28–33). In the *Metaphysics of Morals*, however, right is presented prior to ethics and grounded on a principle of its own (AK 6:231), which is said to be analytic, in contrast to the principle of the doctrine of virtue, which is synthetic (AK 6:396). This would seem to imply that the principle of right, and the entire part of practical philosophy on which it rests, is *independent* of the categorical imperative, though it is admittedly unclear whether this is truly Kant's intention, and also difficult to see how this could supply him with a defensible doctrine.

Finally, readers of the *Groundwork* usually get the impression that moral deliberation in the Kantian system consists chiefly of formulating the maxims of actual or proposed actions and testing them for universalizability according to FUL. Kantian ethics is also usually thought to be oriented exclusively toward the moral rightness of actions in contrast to one that is concerned either with the goodness of ends or the cultivation of virtues of character. The *Metaphysics of Morals*, however, is organized around a taxonomy of duties (duties to oneself and to others, narrow and wide duties). This was, to be sure, anticipated in the *Groundwork*'s division of duties (AK 4:421–3, 429–30); but the *Groundwork* has usually given its readers the impression that each duty, on each occasion, is to be derived from some formula of the universal principle of morality, typically by testing one's maxim against FUL or FLN (see AK 4:421–3, 436–7).

The Doctrine of Virtue, however, uses moral principles only to derive general classes of duties. Throughout the *Metaphysics of Morals* Kant seldom cites FUL in deriving the different classes of duties; overwhelmingly, the formula most often appealed to is FH and the dignity of humanity as an end in itself.[17] Further, the Doctrine of Virtue represents moral

---

17. Kant glosses Ulpian's principle of natural right, *honeste vive*, as "asserting one's worth as a human being in relation to others, a duty expressed by the saying: 'Do not make yourself a mere means for others but be at the same time an end for them' " (AK 6:237). The innate

deliberation not as querying the universalizability of maxims but as the weighing of duties against one another. The theory allows for a good deal of latitude or *Spielraum* (in the case of wide ethical duties) and leaves it up to individuals (within the constraints imposed by narrow duties) to determine the projects and commitments around which they will structure their lives (AK 6:390–5).

Kant's conception of moral reasoning in the Doctrine of Virtue is also strikingly teleological in orientation and oriented toward the cultivation of virtuous traits of character rather than toward the performance of individually right actions. "Duties of virtue" are defined as "ends which are also duties" (AK 6:382–6). This means that what agents weigh in ethical deliberation proper is not so much the weight of binding moral rules but the value of morally constraining *ends* (which fall under the twin headings of "one's own perfection" and "the happiness of others") (AK 6:386–8). Since Kant understands "virtue" as the strength of will in fulfilling duty, he sees different virtues as corresponding to the different ends of morality ("duties of virtue") and views the principal task of the moral life as the *cultivation* of the virtues (that is, of the traits of character

---

right to freedom is said to "belong to every human being in virtue of his humanity" (AK 6:237). There are fourteen ethical duties explicitly enumerated by Kant. Of these, only (1) the duty of beneficence to others is grounded on FUL (AK 6:389, 451, 453). Nine of the remaining thirteen are explicitly based on FH, and the other four are based on it by implication. The emphasis on FH is strongest in the case of duties to oneself. (2) The duty against suicide is based on the fact that "disposing of oneself as a mere means to some discretionary end is debasing humanity in one's person" (AK 6:423); (3) the duty against carnal self-degradation on the fact that it "violates humanity in one's own person" (AK 6:425); (4) that against drunkenness on the fact that the drunkard is "like a mere animal" and cannot be "treated as a human being" (AK 6:427). (5) Lying "violates the dignity of humanity in one's own person" (AK 6:429), and (6) the self-respect opposed to servility is a duty "with reference to the dignity of humanity within us" (AK 6:436). (7) The human being's duty to develop his natural perfection is one "he owes himself (as a rational being)" because it is "bound up with the end of humanity in our own person" (AK 6:444, 392). (8) Violation of the duty of gratitude is "a rejection of one's own humanity" (AK 6:454) based on "pride in the dignity of humanity in one's own person" (AK 6:459), while (9) the duty to sympathize with others holds insofar as "the human being is regarded not merely as a rational being but as an animal endowed with reason" (AK 6:456). (10) All duties of respect to others are grounded on "the dignity in other human beings" (AK 6:462). There is no explicit appeal to any formula in the case of four duties: (11) our duty to ourselves not to be avaricious (AK 6:432), (12) our duty as self-judge (AK 6:437–40), (13) our duty to increase our moral perfection (AK 6:446–7), or (14) our duty to ourselves regarding nonrational beings (AK 6:442–443). But (12)–(14) are all duties relating to our acting from the motive of duty, which (as we have just seen) is explicitly grounded on our dignity as rational beings: and (11) our duty to avoid avarice is defended on the ground that it impairs our rational nature in respect of the use of money (self-impairment is also used as the basis for (4)). Reference to FH also grounds Kant's discussion of five of the six enumerated vices opposed to duties to others: envy, ingratitude, arrogance, defamation, ridicule (AK 6:458–61, 465–67); no explicit appeal to any formula occurs regarding the vice of malice (AK 6:460).

that strengthen the promotion of these ends) (AK 6:403–9). Kant's taxonomy of duties thus regularly takes the form of a taxonomy of *virtues* and the *vices* opposed to them (AK 6:429–37, 458–60, 465–8).

No doubt Kant's approach to the determination of moral ends and the Kantian conception of virtues and vices of character differ sharply from those of the ethical theories commonly called "teleological" or "virtue ethics." But only by entirely disregarding the *Metaphysics of Morals* can anyone say that Kant ignores the role of ends and virtues in morality, or even that he underemphasizes their importance.

Thus Kant's final and most extensive treatise on practical philosophy also makes it clear how inaccurate it is to take Kant's discussion of the famous four examples in the *Groundwork* as typical of the kind of moral reasoning his theory recommends. But then we should have known better than to think that a philosopher's first provisional attempts to illustrate the fundamental principle of his theory (in its initial and most abstract formulation) would be the best place to look for his account of the kind of deliberation in which he thinks ordinary moral agents should normally engage. It is to be hoped that a comprehensive collection of all Kant's ethical writings in a single volume will help correct the false (often grotesque) images of his ethical theory that have been formed by reading only the foundational works (the *Groundwork* and second *Critique*) and neglecting Kant's far more extensive writings that deal with the interpretation and application of the fundamental principles.[18]

ALLEN W. WOOD

18. I am grateful to Paul Guyer for thoughtful comments and suggestions on a draft of this General Introduction.

Review of Schulz's
Attempt at an introduction to a doctrine
of morals for all human beings regardless
of different religions

Introduction

Kant's review of Part I of Johann Heinrich Schulz's work (the full title of which is given in the text of the review) was published in a Königsberg journal, *Rässonirenden Bücherverzeichnis*. Part I of Schulz's work, like Kant's review of it, appeared in 1783. Part II was published in the same year, whereas Parts III and IV did not appear until 1790. The dates are of interest.

As for Kant's review, it is worth noting that he wrote it shortly before the *Groundwork of the Metaphysics of Morals*. A reviewer, Kant says, should first present briefly the author's position and then judge the work as a whole. Kant's judgment might profitably be compared with Part III of the *Groundwork*.

Schulz's career is of interest in the context of political events in Prussia. He was a preacher, in Gielsdorf, whose defiance of the ecclesiastical establishment extended from his personal appearance to his views on the relevance of orthodox religion to the relation of subject and sovereign. His refusal to wear a wig while preaching to his congregation earned him the nickname *Zopfschulz* ("pigtail-Schulz"). Such behavior was symptomatic of the philosophic position that made him suspect to the church authorities. Frederick the Great had protected Schulz from prosecution by the Brandenburg Consistory, but he was brought to court under the religious edict drawn up by Frederick William II and his minister Wöllner. Although the judges found Schulz not guilty of contradicting the teachings of Christianity, the king reversed their verdict, fined the judges, and dismissed Schulz from his appointment.

Kant, too, would eventually be censured by the authorities for his own unorthodox view of the relation of religion to morality. Such concerns are, however, rather tangential to Schulz's principles and to Kant's judgment of them. What is at issue, in this review, is the more fundamental question of moral agency.

Review of
Schulz's
Attempt at introduction to a doctrine of morals for all human beings regardless of different religions
Part I

Attempt at an introduction to a doctrine of morals[a] for all human beings regardless of different religions, including an appendix of capital punishment. Part I. (Berlin, Stahlbaum, 1783)

This first part is supposed to be only an introduction to a new moral system, setting forth the psychological principles to be built upon subsequently: principles about the place a human being occupies in the scale of beings, about his sensitive,[b] thinking, and volitionally active[c] nature, about freedom and necessity, about life, death, and a future life. It is a work that – because of its candor and, still more, because of the good intentions of its independently thinking author,[1] which are evident even in its many striking paradoxes – must raise in every reader impatient expectations as to how a doctrine of morals based on such premises will turn out.

A reviewer will first trace briefly the course of the author's thought and conclude by adding his judgment on the whole.

At the very beginning the concept of vital force is extended in such a way as to apply to all creatures indiscriminately; that is to say, it becomes simply the concept *of the sum of all forces present in a creature and belonging to its nature.* From this follows a law of the *continuity* of all beings, such that on the great ladder each is aligned[d] above and below another but in such a way that every species[e] of creature remains between limits, which creatures cannot overstep as long as they remain fellow members of the same species. Hence nothing is really inanimate but is only less animate, and what distinguishes one species from another is only its degree of vital force. A soul, as a being distinct from the body, is a mere creation of the imagination; the most exalted seraph and a tree are both artful[f] machines. So much for the nature of the soul.

The same sort of graduated connection is present in all cognitions. Error and truth are not specifically different but differ only as the lesser from the greater: there is no absolute error; instead, every cognition, *at the time* it arises in a human being, is true *for him.* Its correction is only the addition of representations that were previously wanting, and what was once truth is subsequently changed into error by the mere progress of cognition. Our cognition is sheer error in comparison with that of an angel. Reason cannot err: every force is assigned its track. Reason's criti-

---

[a] *zur Sittenlehre*
[b] *empfindenden*
[c] *durch Willen tätigen*
[d] *hat seinen Nebenmann*
[e] *Gattung*
[f] *künstliche*

cism of itself[g] does not take place in judging but afterwards, when one is already in another place and has acquired more information. I should not say that a child errs but rather that he does not yet understand so well as he will understand in the future, that this is a lesser judgment. Wisdom and folly, science and ignorance, do not, therefore, deserve either praise or censure; they are to be regarded merely as the gradual progress of nature, with respect to which I am not free. As for the will: all inclinations and impulses are included in a single one, namely *self-love*, though with respect to this every human being has his particular frame of mind,[h] which can still never deviate from a general frame of mind. Self-love is always determined by all our sensations[i] together, but in such a way that either the more obscure or the more distinct sensations have the greatest part in it. *There is, therefore, no free will:* the will is subject to the strict law of necessity; however, if self-love is determined by no distinct representations at all but merely by sensation this is called an *unfree* action. All *remorse*[j] is idle and absurd; for a wrongdoer appraises his deed[k] not from his former but from his present frame of mind which, if it had existed in him then, would certainly have prevented the deed, though the supposition that it also ought to have prevented the deed is false because it was not actually present in his former state. Remorse is merely a misunderstood representation of how one could *act better in the future*, and in fact nature has no other purpose in it than the end of improvement. Resolution of the difficulty, how God could be the author of sin. *Virtue and vices are not essentially different.* (So here again what is otherwise taken as a *specific* difference is changed into a mere *difference in terms of degrees*.) Virtue cannot exist without vices, and these are only occasioning grounds[l] for becoming better (hence for rising a step higher). Human beings cannot compare themselves in regard to what they call virtue except in regard to that without which no human welfare is possible, that is, *general virtue;* but it is absolutely impossible for a human being to deviate from this, and one who does deviate from it is not vicious but out of his mind.[m] A human being who practiced a general vice would act contrary to self-love, and this is impossible. Accordingly the path of general virtue is so even, so straight, and so fenced in on both sides that all human beings absolutely must remain on it. What makes a difference among human beings in general virtue is nothing other than the particular frame of mind of each; were they to exchange their positions, one of them would act just as the other.

[g] *Die Verurteilung der Vernunft durch sich selbst*
[h] *Stimmung*
[i] *Empfindungen*
[j] *Reue*
[k] Or "action," *Tat*
[l] *Gelegenheitsgründe*
[m] *aberwitzig*

Moral good or evil signifies nothing more than a higher or lower degree of perfection. Human beings are vicious in comparison with angels, as are angels in comparison with God. Accordingly, since there is no freedom all retributive punishments are unjust, especially capital punishments; in place of them, only restitution and improvement, but by no means mere admonition, must constitute the purpose of penal laws. To bestow *praise* because of a useful deed indicates but little knowledge of human beings: the human being was just as much determined and moved to it as was the arsonist to set fire to a house. The only purpose of praise is to encourage the author and others to similar good deeds.

The author calls this doctrine of necessity a *blessed doctrine* and maintains that by it the doctrine of morals obtains for the first time its real worth; in this context he remarks incidentally that, with regard to wrongdoing, certain teachers who depict how easy it is *to make one's peace with God* should lay claim to it. In this one cannot fail to recognize our author's good intentions. He wants to do away with mere painful and idle remorse, which is nevertheless so often commended as in itself propitiating, and to put in its place firm resolutions to lead a better life; he seeks to vindicate the wisdom and kindness of God through the progress of all his creatures toward perfection and eternal happiness though on various paths, to lead religion back from unproductive beliefs to deeds, and finally also to make civil punishments more humane and more useful for the particular as well as for the common good." Moreover, the audacity of his speculative assertions will not seem so frightful to one acquainted with what Priestley[2] – an English theologian esteemed as much for his piety as for his insight – has said in unison with our author and expressed even more boldly, and what several clergymen of this country, though far beneath him in talent, are already repeating unreservedly – indeed, what Professor Ehlers[3] just recently put forward as a concept of free will, namely that of the faculty of thinking beings to act in keeping with the *existing state of their ideas*.

However, no impartial reader, especially if he is sufficiently practiced in this sort of speculation, will fail to note that the general fatalism which is the most prominent principle in this work and the most powerful one, affecting all morality, turns all human conduct into a mere puppet show and thereby does away altogether with the concept of obligation; that, on the other hand, the "ought" or the imperative that distinguishes the practical law from the law of nature also puts us in idea⁰ altogether beyond the chain of nature, since unless we think of our will as free this imperative is impossible and absurd and what is left us is only to await and observe what sort of decisions God will effect in us by means of natural causes, but not what we can and ought to do *of ourselves*, as authors. From this must arise

---
" *Beste*
⁰ *in der Idee*

IMMANUEL KANT

the grossest enthusiasm,[p] which does away with any influence of sound reason, even though the author has taken pains to maintain its rights. In fact, the practical concept of freedom has nothing to do with the speculative concept, which is abandoned entirely to metaphysicians. For I can be quite indifferent as to the origin of my state[q] in which I am now to act; I ask only what I now have to do, and then freedom is a necessary practical presupposition and an idea under which alone I can regard commands of reason as valid. Even the most obstinate skeptic grants that, when it comes to acting, all sophistical scruples about a universally deceptive illusion[r] must come to nothing.

In the same way, the most confirmed fatalist, who is a fatalist as long as he gives himself up to mere speculation, must still, as soon as he has to do with wisdom and duty, always act *as if he were free*, and this idea also actually produces the deed that accords with it and can alone produce it. It is hard to cease altogether to be human. The author, having justified every human action, however bad it may seem to others, on the basis of one's particular frame of mind, says on page 137: "May I lose everything, absolutely and without exception everything, that can make me happy temporally and eternally (a daring expression), if you would not have acted just as badly as the other had you only been in his position." Still, according to what he himself affirms, the greatest conviction in one point of time can provide no assurance that in another point of time, cognition having progressed further, what was formerly truth will not afterwards become error: How would that extremely risky protestation look then? Although he would not himself admit it, he has assumed in the depths of his soul that understanding is able to determine his judgment in accordance with objective grounds that are always valid and is not subject to the mechanism of merely subjectively determining causes, which could subsequently change; hence he always admits freedom to think, without which there is no reason. In the same way he must also assume freedom of the will in acting, without which there would be no morals, when – as I have no doubt – he wants to proceed in his righteous conduct in conformity with the eternal laws of duty and not to be a plaything of his instincts and inclinations, though at the same time he denies himself this freedom because he is not otherwise able to bring his practical principles into harmony with speculative principles. But even if no one were to succeed in this, in fact not much would be lost.

[p] *Schwärmerei*
[q] *woher mir ursprünglich der Zustand . . . gekommen sei*
[r] *Schein*

*An answer to the question:
What is enlightenment?*

Introduction

Since the eighteenth century was the "Age of Enlightenment," it was appropriate to ask "What is Enlightenment?" Kant's answer to the question appeared in the December 1784 issue of the *Berlinische Monatsschrift*. As his concluding note indicates, the September issue, which Kant had not yet received, contained an essay on the same topic by Moses Mendelssohn. The occasion for both replies to the question could have been an essay in the December 1783 issue, "Is It Advisable to Sanction Marriage through Religion?" by Johann Friedrich Zöllner, which contained the passage "*What is Enlightenment?* The question, which is almost as important as the question *What is truth?*, should be answered before one begins to enlighten others. And yet I have never found it answered anywhere."

As might be expected, Kant's answer and Mendelssohn's were not in agreement. Consistently with his eudaimonism, Mendelssohn had located enlightenment in the cultivation of what Kant would call the theoretical, as distinguished from the practical, use of one's intellectual powers. To this extent, Kant's reply to Garve in "Theory and Practice" would serve against Mendelssohn as well.

Kant's insistence upon freedom of the press, in the present context as the instrument of enlightenment, reappears in virtually all his political writings. A number of points introduced here – Kant's distinction between the public and the private use of reason, his principles of scriptural exegesis, his views about what kind of sect a government could sanction consistently with its own interest – were elaborated in a treatise written in 1794, which had to be withheld from publication because of the repressive measures of Frederick the Great's nephew and successor. In 1798, after the death of Frederick William II, it was published as Part I of *The Conflict of the Faculties*.

*An answer to the question:
What is enlightenment?*

Enlightenment is the human being's emergence from his self-incurred minority.[a] *Minority* is inability to make use of one's own understanding without direction from another. This minority is *self-incurred* when its cause lies not in lack of understanding but in lack of resolution and courage to use it without direction from another. *Sapere aude!*[b] Have courage to make use of your *own* understanding! is thus the motto of enlightenment.

It is because of laziness and cowardice that so great a part of humankind, after nature has long since emancipated them from other people's direction (*naturaliter maiorennes*), nevertheless gladly remains minors for life, and that it becomes so easy for others to set themselves up as their guardians. It is so comfortable to be a minor! If I have a book that understands for me, a spiritual advisor who has a conscience for me, a doctor who decides upon a regimen for me, and so forth, I need not trouble myself at all. I need not think, if only I can pay; others will readily undertake the irksome business for me. That by far the greatest part of humankind (including the entire fair sex) should hold the step toward majority to be not only troublesome but also highly dangerous will soon be seen to by those guardians who have kindly taken it upon themselves to supervise them; after they have made their domesticated animals dumb and carefully prevented these placid creatures from daring to take a single step without the walking cart[c] in which they have confined them, they then show them the danger that threatens them if they try to walk alone. Now this danger is not in fact so great, for by a few falls they would eventually learn to walk; but an example of this kind makes them timid and usually frightens them away from any further attempt.

Thus it is difficult for any single individual to extricate himself from the minority that has become almost nature to him. He has even grown fond of it and is really unable for the time being to make use of his own understanding, because he was never allowed to make the attempt. Precepts and formulas, those mechanical instruments of a rational use, or rather misuse, of his natural endowments, are the ball and chain of an everlasting minority. And anyone who did throw them off would still make only an uncertain leap over even the narrowest ditch, since he would not be accustomed to free movement of this kind. Hence there are only a few who have succeeded, by their own cultivation of their spirit, in extricating themselves from minority and yet walking confidently.

But that a public should enlighten itself is more possible; indeed this is almost inevitable, if only it is left its freedom. For there will always be a few independent thinkers, even among the established guardians of the great masses, who, after having themselves cast off the yoke of minority,

---

[a] *Unmündigkeit*
[b] Horace *Epodes* 1.2, 40. Literally, "dare to be wise."
[c] A *Gängelwagen* was a device used by parents and nurses to provide support for young children while they were learning to walk.

will disseminate the spirit of a rational valuing of one's own worth and of the calling of each individual to think for himself. What should be noted here is that the public, which was previously put under this yoke by the guardians, may subsequently itself compel them to remain under it, if the public is suitably stirred up by some of its guardians who are themselves incapable of any enlightenment; so harmful is it to implant prejudices, because they finally take their revenge on the very people who, or whose predecessors, were their authors. Thus a public can achieve enlightenment only slowly. A revolution may well bring about a falling off of personal despotism and of avaricious or tyrannical oppression, but never a true reform in one's way of thinking; instead new prejudices will serve just as well as old ones to harness the great unthinking masses.

For this enlightenment, however, nothing is required but *freedom*, and indeed the least harmful of anything that could even be called freedom: namely, freedom to make *public use* of one's reason in all matters. But I hear from all sides the cry: *Do not argue!* The officer says: Do not argue but drill! The tax official: Do not argue but pay! The clergyman: Do not argue but believe! (Only one ruler in the world says: *Argue* as much as you will and about whatever you will, *but obey!*) Everywhere there are restrictions on freedom. But what sort of restriction hinders enlightenment, and what sort does not hinder but instead promotes it? – I reply: The *public* use of one's reason must always be free, and it alone can bring about enlightenment among human beings; the *private use* of one's reason may, however, often be very narrowly restricted without this particularly hindering the progress of enlightenment. But by the public use of one's own reason I understand that use which someone makes of it *as a scholar* before the entire public of the *world of readers*. What I call the private use of reason is that which one may make of it in a certain *civil* post or office with which he is entrusted. Now, for many affairs conducted in the interest of a commonwealth a certain mechanism is necessary, by means of which some members of the commonwealth must behave merely passively, so as to be directed by the government, through an artful[d] unanimity, to public ends (or at least prevented from destroying such ends). Here it is, certainly, impermissible to argue; instead, one must obey. But insofar as this part of the machine also regards himself as a member of a whole commonwealth, even of the society of citizens of the world, and so in his capacity of a scholar who by his writings addresses a public in the proper sense of the word, he can certainly argue without thereby harming the affairs assigned to him in part as a passive member. Thus it would be ruinous if an officer, receiving an order from his superiors, wanted while on duty to engage openly in subtle reasoning about its appropriateness[e] or utility; he

---

[d] *künstliche*
[e] *Zweckmäßigkeit*

must obey. But he cannot fairly[f] be prevented, as a scholar, from making remarks about errors in the military service and from putting these before his public for appraisal. A citizen cannot refuse to pay the taxes imposed upon him; an impertinent censure of such levies when he is to pay them may even be punished as a scandal (which could occasion general insubordination). But the same citizen does not act against the duty of a citizen when, as a scholar, he publicly expresses his thoughts about the inappropriateness or even injustice of such decrees. So too, a clergyman is bound to deliver his discourse to the pupils in his catechism class and to his congregation in accordance with the creed of the church he serves, for he was employed by it on that condition. But as a scholar he has complete freedom and is even called upon to communicate to the public all his carefully examined and well-intentioned thoughts about what is erroneous in that creed and his suggestions for a better arrangement of the religious and ecclesiastical body. And there is nothing in this that could be laid as a burden on his conscience. For what he teaches in consequence of his office as carrying out the business of the church, he represents as something with respect to which he does not have free power to teach as he thinks best, but which he is appointed to deliver as prescribed and in the name of another. He will say: Our church teaches this or that; here are the arguments it uses. He then extracts all practical uses for his congregation from precepts to which he would not himself subscribe with full conviction but which he can nevertheless undertake to deliver because it is still not altogether impossible that truth may lie concealed in them, and in any case there is at least nothing contradictory to inner religion present in them. For if he believed he had found the latter in them, he could not in conscience hold his office; he would have to resign from it. Thus the use that an appointed teacher makes of his reason before his congregation is merely a *private use;* for a congregation, however large a gathering it may be, is still only a domestic gathering; and with respect to it he, as a priest, is not and cannot be free, since he is carrying out another's commission. On the other hand as a scholar, who by his writings speaks to the public in the strict sense, that is, the world – hence a clergyman in the *public use* of his reason – he enjoys an unrestricted freedom to make use of his own reason and to speak in his own person. For that the guardians of the people (in spiritual matters) should themselves be minors is an absurdity that amounts to the perpetuation of absurdities.

But should not a society of clergymen, such as an ecclesiastical synod or a venerable classis (as it calls itself among the Dutch), be authorized to bind itself by oath to a certain unalterable creed, in order to carry on an unceasing guardianship over each of its members and by means of them over the people, and even to perpetuate this? I say that this is quite

[f] *billigermaßen*

impossible. Such a contract, concluded to keep all further enlightenment away from the human race forever, is absolutely null and void, even if it were ratified by the supreme power, by imperial diets and by the most solemn peace treaties. One age cannot bind itself and conspire to put the following one into such a condition that it would be impossible for it to enlarge its cognitions (especially in such urgent matters) and to purify them of errors, and generally to make further progress in enlightenment. This would be a crime against human nature, whose original vocation lies precisely in such progress; and succeeding generations are therefore perfectly authorized to reject such decisions as unauthorized and made sacrilegiously. The touchstone of whatever can be decided upon as law for a people lies in the question: whether a people could impose such a law upon itself. Now this might indeed be possible for a determinate short time, in expectation as it were of a better one, in order to introduce a certain order; during that time each citizen, particularly a clergyman, would be left free, in his capacity as a scholar, to make his remarks publicly, that is, through writings, about defects in the present institution; meanwhile, the order introduced would last until public insight into the nature of these things had become so widespread and confirmed that by the union of their voices (even if not all of them) it could submit a proposal to the crown, to take under its protection those congregations that have, perhaps in accordance with their concepts of better insight, agreed to an altered religious institution, but without hindering those that wanted to acquiesce in the old one. But it is absolutely impermissible to agree, even for a single lifetime, to a permanent religious constitution not to be doubted publicly by anyone and thereby, as it were, to nullify a period of time in the progress of humanity toward improvement and make it fruitless and hence detrimental to posterity. One can indeed, for his own person and even then only for some time, postpone enlightenment in what it is incumbent upon him to know; but to renounce enlightenment, whether for his own person or even more so for posterity, is to violate the sacred right of humanity and trample it underfoot. But what a people may never decide upon for itself, a monarch may still less decide upon for a people;[1] for his legislative authority rests precisely on this, that he unites in his will the collective will of the people. As long as he sees to it that any true or supposed improvement is consistent with civil order, he can for the rest leave it to his subjects to do what they find it necessary to do for the sake of their salvation;[2] that is no concern of his, but it is indeed his concern to prevent any one of them from forcibly hindering others from working to the best of their ability to determine and promote their salvation. It even infringes upon his majesty if he meddles in these affairs by honoring with governmental inspection the writings in which his subjects attempt to clarify their insight, as well as if he does this from his own supreme insight, in which case he exposes himself to the reproach *Caesar non est super grammaticos,*[g] but much more so if he demeans his supreme authority so far as to support the spiritual despotism of a few tyrants within his state against the rest of his subjects.

If it is now asked whether we at present live in an *enlightened* age, the answer is: No, but we do live in an *age of enlightenment*. As matters now stand, a good deal more is required for people on the whole to be in the position, or even able to be put into the position, of using their own understanding confidently and well in religious matters, without another's guidance. But we do have distinct intimations that the field is now being opened for them to work freely in this direction and that the hindrances to universal enlightenment or to humankind's emergence from its self-incurred minority are gradually becoming fewer. In this regard this age is the age of enlightenment or the century of Frederick.

A prince who does not find it beneath himself to say that he considers it his *duty* not to prescribe anything to human beings in religious matters but to leave them complete freedom, who thus even declines the arrogant name of *tolerance*, is himself enlightened and deserves to be praised by a grateful world and by posterity as the one who first released the human race from minority, at least from the side of government, and left each free to make use of his own reason in all matters of conscience. Under him, venerable clergymen, notwithstanding their official duties, may in their capacity as scholars freely and publicly lay before the world for examination their judgments and insights deviating here and there from the creed adopted, and still more may any other who is not restricted by any official duties. This spirit of freedom is also spreading abroad, even where it has to struggle with external obstacles of a government which misunderstands itself. For it shines as an example to such a government that in freedom there is not the least cause for anxiety about public concord and the unity of the commonwealth. People gradually work their way out of barbarism of their own accord if only one does not intentionally contrive to keep them in it.

8:41

I have put the main point of enlightenment, of people's emergence from their self-incurred minority, chiefly in *matters of religion* because our rulers have no interest in playing guardian over their subjects with respect to the arts and sciences and also because that minority, being the most harmful, is also the most disgraceful of all. But the frame of mind of a head of state who favors the first goes still further and sees that even with respect to his *legislation* there is no danger in allowing his subjects to make *public* use of their own reason and to publish to the world their thoughts about a better way of formulating it, even with candid criticism of that already given; we have a shining example of this, in which no monarch has yet surpassed the one whom we honor.

---

[g] Caesar is not above the grammarians

But only one who, himself enlightened, is not afraid of phantoms, but at the same time has a well-disciplined and numerous army ready to guarantee public peace, can say what a free state*h* may not dare to say: *Argue as much as you will and about what you will; only obey!* Here a strange, unexpected course is revealed in human affairs, as happens elsewhere too if it is considered in the large, where almost everything is paradoxical. A greater degree of civil freedom seems advantageous to a people's freedom of *spirit* and nevertheless puts up insurmountable barriers to it; a lesser degree of the former, on the other hand, provides a space for the latter to expand to its full capacity. Thus when nature has unwrapped, from under this hard shell, the seed for which she cares most tenderly, namely the propensity and calling to *think* freely, the latter gradually works back upon the mentality*i* of the people (which thereby gradually becomes capable of *freedom* in acting) and eventually even upon the principles of *government*, which finds it profitable to itself to treat the human being, *who is now more than a machine,j* in keeping with his dignity.*

Königsberg in Prussia, 30th September, 1784

*Today, on September 30th, I read in *Büschings³ Wöchentliche Nachrichten* of 13th September a notice concerning this month's *Berlinische Monatsschrift*, which mentions Mendelssohn's answer to the same question. I have not yet seen this journal; otherwise I should have held back the present essay, which may now stand only in order to find out to what extent chance may bring about agreement in thoughts.
h Freistaat
i Sinnesart
j der nun mehr als Maschine ist

On the wrongfulness of unauthorized publication of books

Introduction

Kant's essay "On the Wrongfulness of Unauthorized Publication of Books" was first published in the *Berlinische Monatsschrift* in May 1785. On June 5 the editor of the journal, Johann Erich Biester, wrote to Kant about other matters and, in passing, expressed the hope that Kant would soon use "our mouth, in order to deliver your speech to the public by means of us." Apart from the fact that, as the opening paragraph of this essay indicates, the topic of literary piracy was being discussed at the time, nothing definite is known about the occasion for this essay. Perhaps Kant's discussion of the subject twelve years later, in Part I of *The Metaphysics of Morals*, was an attempt to substantiate his assertion that the case he makes is "undoubtedly to be found in the elementary concepts of natural right" and to provide "the requisite eloquence of Roman legal scholarship," insofar as this could be done within the limits of metaphysical first principles.

Kant himself was eventually involved in legal difficulties because of the cavalier way in which questions of copyright were treated. Had Kant given J. H. Tieftrunk permission to include, in his proposed collection of Kant's minor writings, all three parts of *Der Streit der Fakultäten*? Tieftrunk assumed that he had and published all three, though not in serial order. The authorized publisher of the book, C. F. Nicolovius, brought a lawsuit against Tieftrunk, who cited as his evidence Kant's failure to object when proofs for the collection were sent to him. As might be expected, Kant's concern is not with rules of evidence but with the kind of right involved in publishing (though his discussion, in *The Metaphysics of Morals*, of "Acquisition That Is Dependent Subjectively upon the Decision of a Public Court of Justice" [§§ 36–42, AK 6:296–310] would be relevant to the former).

*On the wrongfulness of unauthorized
publication of books*

Some regard the publication of a book as a use of property in a copy 8:79
(whether the copy has come to the possessor as a manuscript from the
author or as a print of the manuscript from an already existing publisher)
and then want, nevertheless, to restrict the use of this right by the reservation of certain rights, either of the author or of the publisher appointed by
him, so that unauthorized publication of it would not be permitted; they
can never succeed in this. For the author's property in his thought (even if
one grants that there is such a thing in terms of external rights) is left to
him regardless of the unauthorized publication; and, since there cannot
reasonably be an *express consent* of one who buys a book to such a restriction of his property,* how much less will a merely *presumed* consent suffice
for his obligation?

But I believe there are grounds for regarding publication not as dealing
with a commodity *in one's own name*, but as *carrying on an affair in the name*
of another, namely the author, and that in this way I can easily and clearly
show the wrongfulness of unauthorized publication.[1] My argument is
contained in a syllogism[a] that establishes the *right of a publisher*, upon
which follows a second syllogism that should refute the *claim of an unauthorized publisher*.

I
DEDUCTION OF THE RIGHT OF A PUBLISHER
AGAINST AN UNAUTHORIZED PUBLISHER

*Someone who carries on another's affairs in his name but against his will is held
to cede to him or to the agent he has empowered any profits that might accrue to* 8:80
*him from this and to compensate the former or the latter for any loss that may
arise from it.*

Now, an unauthorized publisher is someone who [carries on] another's (the
author's) affair, and so forth.

Therefore he is held [to cede] to the author or to the agent he has
empowered (his publisher), and so forth.

Proof of the major premise

Since an agent who forces himself upon [another] acts in the other's name
in a way that is not permitted, he has no claim to the profits that may arise
from this affair; instead, the one in whose name he carries on the affair, or

---

*Would a publisher really venture to bind everyone buying the book he publishes to the
condition that the buyer would be prosecuted for misappropriating another's goods entrusted to him if the copy sold were used for unauthorized publication, whether intentionally
or even by negligence? Someone would hardly agree to this, since he would thereby leave
himself open to all sorts of difficulties regarding investigation and responsibility. Publishing
would therefore remain a burden to him.

[a] *in einem Vernunftschluße*

another, empowered agent to whom the latter has delegated it, possesses the right to appropriate these profits as the fruit of his property. Furthermore, because this agent violates the possessor's right by his unauthorized meddling in another's affair, he has to make good all damages. This is undoubtedly present in the elementary concepts of natural right.

Proof of the minor premise

The first point of the minor premise is that *a publisher carries on another's affair by publishing*. Here everything comes down to the concept of a book or of a writing in general, as a work of an author, and to the concept of a publisher in general (whether empowered or not): in other words, whether a book is a commodity that the author, either directly or by means of someone else, can trade with the public, so that he can alienate it with or without the reservation of certain rights, or whether it is, instead, a mere *use of his powers* (*opera*), which he can indeed *grant* to others (*concedere*) but can never *alienate* (*alienare*); further, whether a publisher carries on his affairs in his own name or carries on someone else's affairs in another's name.

In a book, as a writing, the author *speaks* to his reader; and the one who has printed the book *speaks*, by his copy, not for himself but simply and solely in the author's name. He presents the author as speaking publicly and only mediates delivery of his speech to the public. It does not matter to whom the copy of this speech belongs, whether it is in the author's handwriting or in print; to make use of it for oneself or to carry on trade with it is still an affair that every owner of it can carry on *in his own name* and at his discretion. However, *to let someone speak publicly*, to bring his speech as such to the public – that is, to let him speak in his own name and, as it were, to say to the public: "Through me a writer will by means of letters[b] have you informed of this or that, instruct you, and so forth. I am not responsible for anything, not even for the freedom which the author assumes to speak publicly through me: I am only the medium by which it reaches you" – that is undoubtedly an affair that someone can execute only in another's name and never in his own name (as publisher). He indeed provides in his own name *the mute instrument for delivering the author's speech to the public;** but to *bring his speech to the public* by printing it, and so to show himself as the one *through whom the author speaks* to the public, is something he can do only in the name of another.

---

*A book is the instrument for delivering a *speech* to the public, not merely a thought, as is, for example, a picture, a symbolic representation of some idea or event. This is what is essential here: that what is thereby delivered is not a *thing* but an *opera*, namely *speech*, and indeed by letters. By calling it a mute instrument I distinguish it from one that delivers speech by sounds, such as a megaphone or even the *mouth* of another.

[b] *buchstäblich*

The second point of the minor premise is that an *unauthorized publisher* not only takes upon himself, without any permission of the owner, the affair (of the author) but does so even *against his will.* The reason he is an unauthorized publisher is that he attacks in his affairs another *who has been empowered* to publish by the author himself; so the question arises, whether the author could confer this same authorization on someone else besides and consent to it. But it is clear that, because in this case each of the two, the first publisher and the one who afterwards arrogates publication (the unauthorized publisher) would carry on the author's affair with one and the same entire public, the work of one of them would have to make that of the other unprofitable and injurious to each of them; thus it would not be possible for an author to make a contract with one publisher with the reservation that he might allow someone besides to publish his work; hence the author is not authorized to give anyone else (an unauthorized publisher) permission to publish his book, and the latter can therefore never presume the former's permission; consequently, unauthorized publication is an affair undertaken quite contrary to what the owner *can permissibly will* and yet an affair undertaken in his name.

From this argument it also follows that it is not the author but the publisher empowered by him who is wronged. For, because the former has given over to the publisher, completely and without any reservation about making further arrangements from another quarter, his right to carry on his affair with the public, the publisher is sole owner of this agency,[e] and an unauthorized publisher violates the publisher's right, not the author's.

But because this right to carry on affairs – something that another can do just as well, just as promptly and accurately – is not to be regarded as in itself *inalienable* (*ius personalissimum*), unless there is some special arrangement about it the publisher is authorized to grant someone else his right to publish, since he owns the empowerment; and because the author must consent to this, the one who takes over the affair at second hand is not an unauthorized publisher but one legitimately empowered, that is, one to whom the publisher appointed by the author has made over his empowerment.

II

REFUTATION OF THE PRETENDED RIGHT OF AN UNAUTHORIZED PUBLISHER AGAINST THE PUBLISHER

The following question has still to be answered: when a publisher *alienates* to the public the work of his author, does not ownership of a copy involve

[e] *Geschäftsführung*

the consent of the publisher (and so too of the author, who empowered him to do this) to [the owner's] making whatever use of it he pleases and so to his publishing it without authorization, however disagreeable this may be to the publisher? Perhaps the latter was attracted by profit to undertake the affair of publishing at this risk, without excluding the buyer from doing it by an express contract, since this might have put an end to his affairs. I now prove by the following syllogism that ownership of a copy does not furnish this right.

> *A positive right against another person*[d] *can never be inferred solely from ownership of a thing.*
> *But the right to publish is a positive right against a person.*
> *Therefore, it can never be inferred solely from ownership of a thing (a copy).*[2]

Proof of the major premise

There is indeed bound up with ownership of a thing the negative right to deny something,[e] to resist anyone who wants to hinder me in my use of it as I please; but a *positive right against a person*, to require of him that he perform something or render me some service, cannot follow from mere ownership of a thing. This latter right can be attached, by a special agreement, to a contract by which I acquire property from someone, that, for example, when I buy some goods the seller is also to send them post-free to a certain place. But in that case my right against a person, to make him do something for me, does not follow from my mere ownership of the thing I have purchased but from a separate contract.

Proof of the minor premise

If someone can *in his own name* dispose of something as he pleases, he has a right to a thing in regard to it. But if he can do something *only in another's name*, he carries on this affair in such a way that by it the other is bound as if he were doing it himself. (*Quod quis facit per alium, ipsa fecisse putandus est.*)[f] Hence my right to carry on some affair in another name is a positive right against a person, that is, to compel[g] the author of this affair to perform something, namely to look after whatever he has had done through me or to which he has bound himself through me. Now, publication is speech to the public (through printing) in the name of the author and hence an affair carried on in another's name. A right to do it is therefore a right of the publisher against a person: it is not merely a right

---

[d] *Ein persönliches bejahendes Recht auf ein andern.* Perhaps "a right against a person, a positive right against another."
[e] *das verneinende Recht*
[f] That which he does by another, the same is imputed [to him] as done.
[g] *nötigen*

of the publisher to defend himself against him in regard to using his property as he pleases, but to compel him to acknowledge as his own and be responsible for a certain affair that the publisher carries on in his name. It is therefore a positive right against a person.

The copy that the publisher has had printed is a *work* of the author (*opus*) and belongs entirely to the publisher, once he has negotiated for the manuscript or a printed copy, so that he can do whatever he wants with it that can be done *in his own name;* for that is requisite to a full right to a thing, that is, to property. But such use as he can make of it only *in the name of another* (namely, of the author) is a *affair* (*opera*) that this other carries on through the owner of the copy, and for this a separate contract is required, besides the one in regard to property.[h]

Now, publication of a book is an affair that can be carried on only in the name of another (namely, of the author), whom the publisher presents to the public as speaking through him; hence the right to publish cannot be included in the rights that depend upon ownership of a copy; it can become rightful only by a separate contract with the author. One who publishes without such a contract with the author (or, if the author has already granted this right to another as his real[i] publisher, without a contract with him) is an unauthorized publisher, who therefore wrongs the real publisher and must compensate him for all damages.

General remark

That a publisher carries on his affair of publishing not merely in his own name but in the name of another* (namely, the author), and cannot carry it on at all without the author's consent is confirmed by certain obligations that are generally admitted to be connected with this affair. Were the author to die after he has given his manuscript to the publisher for printing and the latter has bound himself to print it, the publisher is not at liberty to hold the manuscript back as his property; instead, if the author has no heirs, the public has a right to compel him either to publish or to turn the manuscript over to someone else who offers to do so. For it was once an affair that the author wanted to carry on with the public through him and for which he offered himself as the agent. It is not necessary for the public to know of the author's promise or to accept it: it obtains this

---

*If the publisher is at the same time the author as well, the two affairs are still distinct, and he publishes in his capacity as a merchant what he has written in his capacity as a scholar. However, we can set aside this case and limit our discussion to the case in which the publisher is not at the same time the author; afterwards it will be easy to extend the results to the first case as well.

[h] *ausser dem Eigentum*
[i] *eigentlichen*

right against the publisher (to perform something) by law alone. For the publisher possesses the manuscript only under the condition that he make use of it for the author's affair with the public, and this obligation to the public remains even if the obligation to the author has ceased through his death. It is not a right of the public to the manuscript but to an affair with the author that is the basis for this. If, after the author's death, the publisher were to put out his work in an abridged or falsified form, or in an edition smaller than the demand for it, the public would be authorized to compel him to correct or enlarge the edition or, failing this, to provide for someone else to do so. All this could not happen unless the publisher's right were derived from an affair that he carries on between the author and the public *in the author's name.*

But to this obligation of the publisher, which will presumably be granted, there must be a correlative right based on it, namely the right to everything necessary for him to fulfill that obligation. This is, that he has exclusive right to publish it,[j] since others' engaging in his affair[k] would make it practically impossible for him to carry it on.

On the other hand, *works of art*, as things, can be copied or cast from a copy that has been rightfully acquired, and the copies of it can be traded publicly without the consent of the artist who made the original,[l] or of the foreman he employed to realize his idea, being required. A drawing that someone has made or has had someone else engrave for him or execute in stone, metal, or plaster, can be molded or cast and so traded publicly by one who buys this product; as always, what someone can do with his thing *in his own name* does not require the consent of another. Anyone who possesses Lippert's *Dactology*[3] can, if he knows how, copy it and put it up for sale, without its inventor being able to complain about intrusion into his affairs. For it is a work (*opus*, not *opera alterius*), which anyone who possesses it can alienate without even having to mention the name of the originator;[m] hence he can also copy it and make use of the copies for public trade in his own name, as what is his. But another's writing is the *speech* of a person (*opera*), and one who publishes it can speak to the public only in the name of this other and can say no more of himself than that the author through him (*Impensis Bibliopolae*) delivers the following speech to the public. For it is a contradiction to deliver *in one's own name* a speech that, by one's own announcement and in keeping with the public's demand, is to be the *speech of another.* This, then, is the reason that all works of art of another may be copied for sale to the public whereas books that

---

[j] *dass er das Verlagsrecht ausschliesslich ausübe*
[k] *anderer Concurrenz zu seinem Geschäfte*
[l] *des Urhebers ihres Originals*
[m] *Urheber*

already have their appointed publisher may not be reprinted:*n* the first are *works* (*opera*), whereas the second are *actions* (*operae*): the former can exist on their own, as things,*o* whereas the latter can have their existence only in a person. Hence these latter belong exclusively to the person of the author,* and the author has in them an inalienable right (*ius personalissimum*)*p* always *himself* to speak through anyone else, the right, that is, that no one may deliver the same speech to the public other than in his (the author's) name. But if someone so alters another's book (abridges it, adds to it, or revises it) that it would even be a wrong to pass it off any longer in the name of the author of the original, then the revision in the editor's own name is not unauthorized publication and therefore not impermissible. For here another author, through his publisher, carries on with the public a different affair from the first, and therefore does not interfere with him in his affair with the public; he does not represent the first author as speaking through him, but another one. Again, translation into a foreign language cannot be taken as unauthorized publication; for it is not the same speech of the author, even though the thoughts might be precisely the same.

8:87

If the idea of publication of a book as such, on which this is based, were firmly grasped and (as I flatter myself it could be) elaborated with the requisite eloquence of Roman legal scholarship, complaints against unauthorized publishers could indeed be taken to court without it being necessary first to wait for a new law.

---

*The author and someone who owns a copy can both, with equal right, say of the same book, "it is my book," but in different senses. The former takes the book as writing or speech, the second merely as the mute instrument of delivering speech to him or the public, i.e., as a copy. This right of the author is, however, not a right to the thing, namely to the copy (for the owner can burn it before the author's eyes), but an innate right in his own person, namely, to prevent another from having him speak to the public without his consent, which consent certainly cannot be presumed because he has already given it exclusively to someone else.

n nachgedruckt
o als für sich selbst existierende Dinge . . . ihr Dasein haben können
p The most personal right

Groundwork of The metaphysics of morals

Introduction

Kant's short treatise *Groundwork of the Metaphysics of Morals* is by far the best known of his writings in moral philosophy. Its influence has been out of all proportion to its size; so too has been the amount of commentary, interpretation, criticism, and debate to which it has given rise. Yet we have little historical evidence about Kant's decision to write this treatise. Like the *Critique of Practical Reason*, it seems to have been almost a by-product of his plan to write a "metaphysics of morals," the vicissitudes of which are outlined in the editorial introduction to *The Metaphysics of Morals*. Early in 1784 Kant's friends and associates began to mention in their correspondence his work on a "Prodromus" or "Prolegomena" to his metaphysics of morals. In September of that year Hamann reported that Kant had sent off the manuscript of his *Grundlegung zur Metaphysik der Sitten*, and in April 1785 that he had received four copies of the book from his publisher in Halle.

Kant's reasons for writing a treatise preliminary to his metaphysics of morals are adequately explained within the *Groundwork* itself. Before the supreme principle of morality is applied to human nature it should be exhibited in its purity. Three years earlier, in the *Critique of Pure Reason* and in his lectures on ethics roughly contemporaneous with it, Kant had recognized that the principle for appraising actions as duties is the formal principle expressed in "the categorical imperative." However, he had not yet seen that the thought of this principle could provide a motive for acting or, as he put it in the *Groundwork*, that our moral judgments assume autonomy as a property of the will. This was a radically new conception, and one that would influence profoundly the subsequent derivation of duties. If all other systems of moral philosophy assume that the human will can be determined only by some motive having its origin in "human nature" – if, that is to say, they assume heteronomy as a property of the will – it would be advisable to present this new conception in a treatise devoted solely to "the supreme principle of morality."

Moreover, as Kant insisted repeatedly, disagreements among philosophers, especially in such matters as the foundations of moral philosophy, are not merely intellectual exercises for the faculty of a university. Through "popular moral philosophers" and "teachers of virtue" they influence the public. Even as Kant's analysis of what is implicit in the judgments of "common human understanding" moves to the highest level of abstraction, he interpolates reminders of the need for distinguishing the source of moral concepts and principles. Whether the supreme principle of morality has an empirical or a purely rational source is not an academic quibble but a matter of practical importance. It is, in other words, the most fundamental question of practical philosophy.

Groundwork of
The metaphysics of morals

Preface

Ancient Greek philosophy was divided into three sciences: **physics, ethics,** and **logic.** This division is perfectly suitable to the nature of the subject and there is no need to improve upon it except, perhaps, to add its principle, partly so as to insure its completeness and partly so as to be able to determine correctly the necessary subdivisions.

All rational cognition is either *material* and concerned with some object, or *formal* and occupied only with the form of the understanding and of reason itself and with the universal rules of thinking in general, without distinction of objects. Formal philosophy is called **logic,** whereas material philosophy, which has to do with determinate objects and the laws to which they are subject, is in turn divided into two. For these laws are either laws of **nature** or laws of **freedom.** The science of the first is called **physics,** that of the other is **ethics**; the former is also called the doctrine of nature, the latter the doctrine of morals.^a

Logic can have no empirical part, that is, no part in which the universal and necessary laws of thinking would rest on grounds taken from experience; for in that case it would not be logic, that is, a canon for the understanding or for reason, which holds for all thinking and which must be demonstrated. On the other hand natural as well as moral philosophy^b can each have its empirical part, since the former must determine laws of nature as an object of experience, the latter, laws of the human being's will insofar as it is affected by nature – the first as laws in accordance with which everything happens, the second as laws in accordance with which everything ought to happen, while still taking into account the conditions under which it very often does not happen.

All philosophy insofar as it is based on grounds of experience can be called *empirical;* but insofar as it sets forth its teachings simply from a priori principles it can be called *pure* philosophy. When the latter is merely formal it is called *logic;* but if it is limited to determinate objects of the understanding it is called *metaphysics.*

In this way there arises the idea of a twofold metaphysics, a *metaphysics*

---

^a *Naturlehre . . . Sittenlehre.* According to the *Critique of Judgment,* the doctrinal (*doktrinal*), as distinguished from the critical, part of philosophy is the metaphysics of nature and of morals (5:170).
^b *Weltweisheit,* a common eighteenth-century word for *Philosophie*

of nature and a *metaphysics of morals*. Physics will therefore have its empirical part but it will also have a rational part; so too will ethics, though here the empirical part might be given the special name *practical anthropology*, while the rational part might properly be called *morals*.[c]

All trades, crafts, and arts have gained by the division of labor, namely when one person does not do everything but each limits himself to a certain task that differs markedly from others in the way it is to be handled, so as to be able to perform it most perfectly and with greater facility. Where work is not so differentiated and divided, where everyone is a jack-of-all-trades, there trades remain in the greatest barbarism. Whether pure philosophy in all its parts does not require its own special man might in itself be a subject not unworthy of consideration, and it might be worth asking whether the whole of this learned trade would not be better off if a warning were given to those who, in keeping with the taste of the public, are in the habit of vending the empirical mixed with the rational in all sorts of proportions unknown to themselves, who call themselves "independent thinkers,"[d] and others, who prepare the rational part only, "hair-splitters":[e] the warning not to carry on at the same time two jobs which are very distinct in the way they are to be handled, for each of which a special talent is perhaps required, and the combination of which in one person produces only bunglers. Here, however, I ask only whether the nature of science does not require that the empirical part always be carefully separated from the rational part, and that a metaphysics of nature be put before physics proper (empirical physics) and a metaphysics of morals before practical anthropology, with metaphysics carefully cleansed of everything empirical so that we may know how much pure reason can accomplish in both cases and from what sources it draws this a priori teaching of its own[f] – whether the latter job be carried on by all teachers of morals (whose name is legion) or only by some who feel a calling to it.

Since my aim here is directed properly to moral philosophy, I limit the question proposed only to this: is it not thought to be of the utmost necessity to work out for once a pure moral philosophy, completely cleansed of everything that may be only empirical and that belongs to anthropology? For, that there must be such a philosophy is clear of itself from the common idea of duty and of moral laws. Everyone must grant that a law, if it is to hold morally, that is, as a ground of an obligation, must carry with it absolute necessity; that, for example, the command "thou

---

[c] *eigentlich Moral*, perhaps, "morals strictly speaking." *Moral* and *Sitten* are translated as "morals," *Moralität* and *Sittlichkeit* as "morality," *sittliche Weltweisheit* and *Moralphilosophie* as "moral philosophy," and *Sittenlehre* as "the doctrine of morals." Kant occasionally uses *Moral* in the sense of "moral philosophy."

[d] *Selbstdenker*

[e] *Grübler*

[f] *sie selbst diese ihre Belehrung a priori schöpfe*

shalt not lie" does not hold only for human beings, as if other rational beings did not have to heed it, and so with all other moral laws properly so called; that, therefore, the ground of obligation here must not be sought in the nature of the human being or in the circumstances of the world in which he is placed, but a priori simply in concepts of pure reason; and that any other precept, which is based on principles of mere experience – even if it is universal in a certain respect – insofar as it rests in the least part on empirical grounds, perhaps only in terms of a motive,[g] can indeed be called a practical rule but never a moral law.

Thus, among practical cognitions, not only do moral laws, along with their principles, differ essentially from all the rest,[h] in which there is something empirical, but all moral philosophy is based entirely on its pure part; and when it is applied to the human being it does not borrow the least thing from acquaintance with him (from anthropology) but gives to him, as a rational being, laws a priori, which no doubt still require a judgment sharpened by experience, partly to distinguish in what cases they are applicable and partly to provide them with access[i] to the will of the human being and efficacy for his fulfillment of them;[j] for the human being is affected by so many inclinations that, though capable of the idea of a practical pure reason, he is not so easily able to make it effective *in concreto* in the conduct of his life.

A metaphysics of morals is therefore indispensably necessary, not merely because of a motive to speculation – for investigating the source of the practical basic principles[k] that lie a priori in our reason – but also because morals themselves remain subject to all sorts of corruption as long as we are without that clue[l] and supreme norm by which to appraise them correctly. For, in the case of what is to be morally good it is not enough that it *conform* with the moral law but it must also be done *for the sake of the law;* without this, that conformity is only very contingent and precarious, since a ground that is not moral will indeed now and then produce actions in conformity with the law, but it will also often produce actions contrary to the

4:390

---

[g] *Bewegungsgründe.* Kant subsequently (4:427) distinguishes this from an "incentive" (*Triebfeder*), and the force of some passages depends upon this distinction. However, he does not abide by the distinction, and no attempt has been made to bring his terminology into accord with it. He occasionally uses *Bewegursache*, in which case "motive," which seems to be the most general word available, has been used.

[h] Here, as elsewhere, the difference between German and English punctuation creates difficulties. It is not altogether clear from the context whether the clause "in which there is something empirical" is restrictive or nonrestrictive.

[i] Or "entry," "admission," *Eingang*

[j] *Nachdruck zur Ausübung*

[k] *Grundsätze.* Kant does not draw a consistent distinction between *Grundsatz* and *Prinzip* and often uses one where the other would seem more appropriate. *Prinzip* is always, and *Grundsatz* often, translated as "principle."

[l] *Leitfaden*

law. Now the moral law in its purity and genuineness (and in the practical this is what matters most) is to be sought nowhere else than in a pure philosophy; hence this (metaphysics) must come first, and without it there can be no moral philosophy at all. That which mixes these pure principles with empirical ones does not even deserve the name of philosophy (for what distinguishes philosophy from common rational cognition is just that it sets forth in separate sciences what the latter comprehends only mixed together); much less does it deserve the name of a moral philosophy, since by this very mixture it even infringes upon*ᵐ* the purity of morals themselves and proceeds contrary to its own end.

Let it not be thought, however, that what is here called for already exists in the celebrated Wolff's¹ propaedeutic to his moral philosophy, namely in what he called *universal*ⁿ *practical philosophy*, and that we do not therefore have to break into an entirely new field. Just because it was to be a universal practical philosophy it took into consideration, not a will of any special kind, such as one that would be completely determined from a priori principles without any empirical motives and that could be called a pure will, but rather volition generally,*ᵒ* with all the actions and conditions that belong to it in this general*ᵖ* sense; and by this it differs from a metaphysics of morals in the same way that general logic, which sets forth the actions and rules of thinking *in general*, differs from transcendental philosophy, which sets forth the special actions and rules of **pure** thinking, that is, of thinking by which objects are cognized completely a priori. For, the metaphysics of morals has to examine the idea and the principles of a possible *pure* will and not the actions and conditions of human volition generally, which for the most part are drawn from psychology. That this universal practical philosophy also discusses (though without any warrant)*ᑫ* moral laws and duties is no objection to my assertion. For the authors of that science remain true to their idea of it in this too; they do not distinguish motives that, as such, are represented completely a priori by reason alone and are properly moral from empirical motives, which the understanding raises to universal concepts merely by comparing experiences; instead they consider motives only in terms of the greater or smaller amount of them, without paying attention to the difference of their sources (since all of them are regarded as of the same kind); and this is how they form their concept*ʳ* of *obligation*, which is anything but moral,

---

ᵐ Abbruch tut. For Kant's explanation of this term, taken from the context of rights, see *The Metaphysics of Morals* (6:429).

ⁿ allgemeinen

ᵒ überhaupt

ᵖ allgemeinen

ᑫ Or "authorization," *Befugnis.* For an explanation of this term in its moral use, see *The Metaphysics of Morals* (6:222).

ʳ und machen sich dadurch ihren Begriff

although the way it is constituted is all that can be desired in a philosophy that does not judge at all about the *origin* of all possible practical concepts, whether they occur only a posteriori or a priori as well.

Intending to publish some day a metaphysics of morals,[2] I issue this groundwork in advance. Indeed there is really no other foundation for a metaphysics of morals than the critique of a *pure practical reason*, just as that of metaphysics is the critique of pure speculative reason, already published. But in the first place the former is not of such utmost necessity as the latter, because in moral matters human reason can easily be brought to a high degree of correctness and accomplishment, even in the most common understanding, whereas in its theoretical but pure use it is wholly dialectical; and in the second place I require that the critique of a pure practical reason, if it is to be carried through completely, be able at the same time to present the unity of practical with speculative reason in a common principle, since there can, in the end, be only one and the same reason, which must be distinguished merely in its application. But I could not yet bring it to such completeness here without bringing into it considerations of a wholly different kind and confusing the reader. Because of this I have made use of the title *Groundwork of the Metaphysics of Morals* instead of *Critique of Pure Practical Reason*.

But in the third place, since a metaphysics of morals, despite its intimidating title, is yet capable of a great degree of popularity and suitability for the common understanding, I find it useful to separate from it this preliminary work of laying its foundation, so that in the future I need not add subtleties, which are unavoidable in it, to teachings more easily grasped.

4:392

The present groundwork is, however, nothing more than the search for and establishment of the *supreme principle of morality*, which constitutes by itself a business that in its purpose is complete and to be kept apart from every other moral investigation. No doubt my assertions on this important and central question, discussion of which has till now been far from satisfactory, would receive a great deal of light from the application of the same principle to the whole system, and of confirmation through the adequacy that it would everywhere show; but I had to forgo this advantage, which would be after all more gratifying to me than commonly useful since the facility with which a principle can be used and its apparent adequacy furnish no quite certain proof of its correctness but, instead, awaken a certain bias against rigorously investigating and weighing it in itself and without any regard for what follows from it.

I have adopted in this work the method that is, I believe, most suitable if one wants to proceed analytically from common cognition to the determination of its supreme principle, and in turn synthetically from the examination of this principle and its sources back to the common cognition in which we find it used. Accordingly, the division turns out as follows:

1. *First section:* Transition from common rational to philosophic moral cognition.
2. *Second section:* Transition from popular moral philosophy to metaphysics of morals.
3. *Third section:* Final step from metaphysics of morals to the critique of pure practical reason.

Section I
Transition from common rational to philosophic moral cognition

It is impossible to think of anything at all in the world, or indeed even beyond it, that could be considered good without limitation except a **good will**. Understanding, wit, judgment³ and the like, whatever such *talents* of mind*ˢ* may be called, or courage, resolution, and perseverance in one's plans, as qualities of *temperament*, are undoubtedly good and desirable for many purposes,*ᵗ* but they can also be extremely evil and harmful if the will which is to make use of these gifts of nature, and whose distinctive constitution*ᵘ* is therefore called *character*, is not good. It is the same with *gifts of fortune*. Power, riches, honor, even health and that complete well-being and satisfaction*ᵛ* with one's condition called *happiness*, produce boldness and thereby often arrogance*ʷ* as well unless a good will is present which corrects the influence of these on the mind and, in so doing, also corrects the whole principle of action and brings it into conformity with universal ends*ˣ* – not to mention that an impartial rational spectator can take no delight in seeing the uninterrupted prosperity of a being graced with no feature of a pure and good will, so that a good will seems to constitute the indispensable condition even of worthiness to be happy.

Some qualities are even conducive*ʸ* to this good will itself and can

---

ˢ Geistes. Compare Kant's use of *Geist* in *Anthropology from a Pragmatic Point of View* (7:225) and of *Geisteskräfte* in *The Metaphysics of Morals* (6:445).

ᵗ in mancher Absicht, perhaps "in many respects"

ᵘ Beschaffenheit, occasionally translated as "character." "Constitution" is also used to translate *Einrichtung* and sometimes *Anlage*, which is used rather loosely in the *Groundwork*.

ᵛ Kant uses a great variety of words for what could be called "pleasure" (*Lust*) in the most general sense. Although he later draws broad distinctions among pleasures in terms of their origins (e.g., between the pleasure of taste and that of sensation, and between both of these and moral pleasure), these distinctions still leave a number of words problematic. Within the *Groundwork* (4:396) he suggests a distinction between *Zufriedenheit* or "satisfaction" in general and reason's own kind of *Zufriedenheit*, which in that context I have translated as "contentment." However, his vocabulary is not consistent, and I have not attempted to make it so.

ʷ Mut . . . Übermut

ˣ allgemein-zweckmäßig mache

ʸ beförderlich. Compare *The Metaphysics of Morals* (6:407–9). *Befördern* is usually translated as "to further" or "to promote."

make its work much easier; despite this, however, they have no inner unconditional worth but always presuppose a good will, which limits the esteem one otherwise rightly has for them and does not permit their being taken as absolutely good. Moderation in affects and passions, self-control, and calm reflection are not only good for all sorts of purposes but even seem to constitute a part of the *inner* worth of a person; but they lack much that would be required to declare them good without limitation (however unconditionally they were praised by the ancients); for, without the basic principles of a good will they can become extremely evil, and the coolness of a scoundrel makes him not only far more dangerous but also immediately more abominable in our eyes than we would have taken him to be without it.

A good will is not good because of what it effects or accomplishes, because of its fitness to attain some proposed end, but only because of its volition, that is, it is good in itself and, regarded for itself, is to be valued incomparably higher than all that could merely be brought about by it in favor of some inclination and indeed, if you will, of the sum of all inclinations. Even if, by a special disfavor of fortune or by the niggardly provision of a stepmotherly nature, this will should wholly lack the capacity to carry out its purpose – if with its greatest efforts it should yet achieve nothing and only the good will were left (not, of course, as a mere wish but as the summoning of all means insofar as they are in our control) – then, like a jewel, it would still shine by itself, as something that has its full worth in itself. Usefulness or fruitlessness can neither add anything to this worth nor take anything away from it. Its usefulness would be, as it were, only the setting to enable us to handle it more conveniently in ordinary commerce or to attract to it the attention of those who are not yet expert enough, but not to recommend it to experts or to determine its worth.

There is, however, something so strange in this idea of the absolute worth of a mere will, in the estimation of which no allowance is made for any usefulness, that, despite all the agreement even of common understanding with this idea, a suspicion must yet arise that its covert basis is perhaps mere high-flown fantasy and that we may have misunderstood the purpose of nature in assigning reason to our will as its governor. Hence we shall put this idea to the test from this point of view.

In the natural constitution of an organized being, that is, one constituted purposively for life,[z] we assume as a principle that there will be found in it no instrument for some end other than what is also most appropriate to that end and best adapted to it. Now in a being that has reason and a will, if the proper end of nature were its *preservation*, its *welfare*, in a word its *happiness*, then nature would have hit upon a very bad

---

[z] *zweckmäßig zum Leben eingerichteten. Zweck* is translated as "end" except when it occurs as part of *zweckmäßig, Zweckmäßigkeit,* and *zwecklos.*

arrangement in selecting the reason of the creature to carry out this purpose. For all the actions that the creature has to perform for this purpose, and the whole rule of its conduct, would be marked out for it far more accurately by instinct, and that end would have thereby been attained much more surely than it ever can be by reason; and if reason should have been given, over and above, to this favored creature, it must have served it only to contemplate the fortunate constitution of its nature, to admire this, to delight in it, and to be grateful for it to the beneficent cause, but not to submit its faculty of desire[a] to that weak and deceptive guidance and meddle with nature's purpose. In a word, nature would have taken care that reason should not break forth into *practical use* and have the presumption, with its weak insight, to think out for itself a plan for happiness and for the means of attaining it. Nature would have taken upon itself the choice not only of ends but also of means and, with wise foresight, would have entrusted them both simply to instinct.

And, in fact, we find that the more a cultivated reason purposely occupies itself with the enjoyment of life and with happiness, so much the further does one get away from true satisfaction; and from this there arises in many, and indeed in those who have experimented most with this use of reason, if only they are candid enough to admit it, a certain degree of *misology*, that is, hatred of reason; for, after calculating all the advantages they draw – I do not say from the invention of all the arts of common luxury, but even from the sciences (which seem to them to be, at bottom, only a luxury of the understanding) – they find that they have in fact only brought more trouble upon themselves instead of gaining in happiness; and because of this they finally envy rather than despise the more common run of people, who are closer to the guidance of mere natural instinct and do not allow their reason much influence on their behavior. And to this extent we must admit that the judgment of those who greatly moderate, and even reduce below zero, eulogies extolling the advantages that reason is supposed to procure for us with regard to the happiness and satisfaction of life is by no means surly or ungrateful to the goodness of the government of the world; we must admit, instead, that these judgments have as their covert basis the idea of another and far worthier purpose of one's existence, to which therefore, and not to happiness, reason is properly destined,[b] and to which, as supreme condition, the private purpose of the human being must for the most part defer.

Since reason is not sufficiently competent to guide the will surely with

4:396

---

[a] *Begehrungsvermögen.* For Kant's definition of this term see *Critique of Practical Reason* (5:8 n) and *The Metaphysics of Morals* (6:211). *Vermögen* by itself is sometimes translated as "capacity" or "ability."
[b] *bestimmt.* Except when it has this sense of "vocation," *Bestimmung* and its cognates are translated in terms of "determination."

regard to its objects and the satisfaction of all our needs (which it to some extent even multiplies) – an end to which an implanted natural instinct would have led much more certainly; and since reason is nevertheless given to us as a practical faculty, that is, as one that is to influence the *will;* then, where nature has everywhere else gone to work purposively in distributing its capacities,[c] the true vocation of reason must be to produce a will that is good, not perhaps *as a means* to other purposes, but *good in itself,* for which reason was absolutely necessary. This will need not, because of this, be the sole and complete good, but it must still be the highest good and the condition of every other, even of all demands for happiness. In this case it is entirely consistent with the wisdom of nature if we perceive that the cultivation of reason, which is requisite to the first and unconditional purpose, limits in many ways – at least in this life – the attainment of the second, namely happiness, which is always conditional; indeed it may reduce it below zero without nature proceeding unpurposively in the matter, because reason, which cognizes its highest practical vocation in the establishment of a good will, in attaining this purpose is capable only of its own kind of satisfaction, namely from fulfilling an end which in turn only reason determines, even if this should be combined with many infringements upon the ends of inclination.

4:397
We have, then, to explicate[d] the concept of a will that is to be esteemed in itself and that is good apart from any further purpose, as it already dwells in natural sound understanding and needs not so much to be taught as only to be clarified – this concept that always takes first place in estimating the total worth of our actions and constitutes the condition of all the rest. In order to do so, we shall set before ourselves the concept of **duty,** which contains that of a good will though under certain subjective limitations and hindrances, which, however, far from concealing it and making it unrecognizable, rather bring it out by contrast and make it shine forth all the more brightly.

I here pass over all actions that are already recognized as contrary to duty, even though they may be useful for this or that purpose; for in their case the question whether they might have been done *from duty* never arises, since they even conflict with it. I also set aside actions that are really in conformity with duty but to which human beings have *no inclination* immediately[e] and

---

[c] *Anlagen*

[d] *entwickeln.* In the context of organisms generally, and more specifically with reference to man's talents and capacities, this is translated as "to develop." However, in the context of analytic and synthetic propositions, see the Jäsche *Logik* (9:111, *Anmerkung* 1), where it is said that in an implicitly identical proposition (as distinguished from a tautology), a predicate that lies *unentwickelt* (*implicite*) in the concept of the subject is made clear by means of *Entwickelung* (*explicatio*).

[e] *unmittelbar.* Kant occasionally uses *direkt* as a synonym; no temporal reference is intended.

which they still perform because they are impelled[f] to do so through another inclination. For in this case it is easy to distinguish whether an action in conformity with duty is done *from duty* or from a self-seeking purpose. It is much more difficult to note this distinction when an action conforms with duty and the subject has, besides, an *immediate* inclination to it. For example, it certainly conforms with duty that a shopkeeper not overcharge an inexperienced customer, and where there is a good deal of trade a prudent merchant does not overcharge but keeps a fixed general price for everyone, so that a child can buy from him as well as everyone else. People are thus served *honestly;* but this is not nearly enough for us to believe that the merchant acted in this way from duty and basic principles of honesty; his advantage required it; it cannot be assumed here that he had, besides, an immediate inclination toward his customers, so as from love, as it were, to give no one preference over another in the matter of price. Thus the action was done neither from duty nor from immediate inclination but merely for purposes of self-interest.

On the other hand, to preserve one's life is a duty, and besides everyone has an immediate inclination to do so. But on this account the often anxious care that most people take of it still has no inner worth and their maxim has no moral content. They look after their lives *in conformity with duty* but not *from duty.* On the other hand, if adversity and hopeless grief have quite taken away the taste for life; if an unfortunate man, strong of soul and more indignant about his fate than despondent or dejected, wishes for death and yet preserves his life without loving it, not from inclination or fear but from duty, then his maxim has moral content.

To be beneficent[g] where one can is a duty, and besides there are many souls so sympathetically attuned that, without any other motive of vanity or self-interest they find an inner satisfaction in spreading joy around them and can take delight in the satisfaction of others so far as it is their own work. But I assert that in such a case an action of this kind, however it may conform with duty and however amiable it may be, has nevertheless no true moral worth but is on the same footing with other inclinations, for example, the inclination to honor, which, if it fortunately lights upon what is in fact in the common interest and in conformity with duty and hence honorable, deserves praise and encouragement but not esteem; for the maxim lacks moral content, namely that of doing such actions not from inclination but *from duty.* Suppose, then, that the mind of this philanthropist were overclouded by his own grief, which extinguished all sympathy with the fate of others, and that while he still had the means to benefit

4:398

---

[f] *getrieben. Antrieb* is translated as "impulse."

[g] *Wohltätig sein.* In view of Kant's distinction between *Wohltun* and *Wohlwollen* (6:393, 450 ff.), *Wohltun* and its cognates are translated in terms of "beneficence" and *Wohlwollen* in terms of "benevolence."

others in distress their troubles did not move him because he had enough to do with his own; and suppose that now, when no longer incited to it by any inclination, he nevertheless tears himself out of this deadly insensibility and does the action without any inclination, simply from duty; then the action first has its genuine moral worth. Still further: if nature had put little sympathy in the heart of this or that man; if (in other respects an honest[h] man) he is by temperament cold and indifferent to the sufferings of others, perhaps because he himself is provided with the special gift of patience and endurance toward his own sufferings and presupposes the same in every other or even requires it; if nature had not properly fashioned such a man (who would in truth not be its worst product) for a philanthropist, would he not still find within himself a source from which to give himself a far higher worth than what a mere good-natured temperament might have? By all means! It is just then that the worth of character comes out, which is moral and incomparably the highest, namely that he is beneficent not from inclination but from duty.

4:399

To assure one's own happiness is a duty (at least indirectly); for, want of satisfaction with one's condition, under pressure from many anxieties and amid unsatisfied needs, could easily become a great *temptation to transgression of duty*. But in addition, without looking to duty here, all people have already, of themselves, the strongest and deepest inclination to happiness because it is just in this idea that all inclinations unite in one sum. However, the precept of happiness is often so constituted that it greatly infringes upon some inclinations, and yet one can form no determinate and sure concept of the sum of satisfaction of all inclinations under the name of happiness. Hence it is not to be wondered at that a single inclination, determinate both as to what it promises and as to the time within which it can be satisfied, can often outweigh a fluctuating idea, and that a man – for example, one suffering from gout – can choose to enjoy what he likes and put up with what he can since, according to his calculations, on this occasion at least he has not sacrificed the enjoyment of the present moment to the perhaps groundless expectation of a happiness that is supposed to lie in health. But even in this case, when the general[i] inclination to happiness did not determine his will; when health, at least for him, did not enter as so necessary into this calculation, there is still left over here, as in all other cases, a law, namely to promote his happiness not from inclination but from duty; and it is then that his conduct first has properly moral worth.

It is undoubtedly in this way, again, that we are to understand the

---

[h] *ehrlicher*. I have translated this as "honest" because Kant gives the Latin *honestas* as a parenthetical equivalent of such derivatives of *Ehre* as *Ehrbarkeit*. However, the context often makes it clear that he is not thinking of "honesty" in the narrow sense.
[i] *allgemeine*

passages from scripture in which we are commanded to love our neighbor, even our enemy. For, love as an inclination cannot be commanded, but beneficence from duty – even though no inclination impels us to it and, indeed, natural and unconquerable aversion opposes it – is *practical* and not *pathological*[j] love, which lies in the will and not in the propensity of feeling,[k] in principles of action and not in melting sympathy; and it alone can be commanded.

The second proposition is this: an action from duty has its moral worth not in the *purpose* to be attained by it but in the maxim in accordance with which it is decided upon, and therefore does not depend upon the realization of the object of the action but merely upon the *principle of volition* in accordance with which the action is done without regard for any object of the faculty of desire. That the purposes we may have for our actions, and their effects as ends and incentives of the will, can give actions no unconditional and moral worth is clear from what has gone before. In what, then, can this worth lie, if it is not to be in the will in relation to the hoped for effect of the action? It can lie nowhere else *than in the principle of the will* without regard for the ends that can be brought about by such an action. For, the will stands between its a priori principle, which is formal, and its a posteriori incentive, which is material, as at a crossroads; and since it must still be determined by something, it must be determined by the formal principle of volition as such when an action is done from duty, where every material principle has been withdrawn from it.

The third proposition, which is a consequence of the two preceding, I would express as follows: *duty is the necessity of an action from respect for law.* For an object as the effect of my proposed action I can indeed have *inclination* but *never respect*, just because it is merely an effect and not an activity of a will. In the same way I cannot have respect for inclination as such, whether it is mine or that of another; I can at most in the first case approve it and in the second sometimes even love it, that is, regard it as favorable to my own advantage. Only what is connected with my will merely as ground and never as effect, what does not serve my inclination but outweighs it or at least excludes it altogether from calculations in making a choice[l] – hence the mere law for itself – can be an object of respect and so a command. Now, an action from duty is to put aside entirely the influence of inclination and with it every object of the will; hence there is left for the will nothing that could determine it except

---

[j] *pathologische*, i.e., dependent upon sensibility
[k] *Empfindung*. In the *Critique of Judgment* (5:206) Kant distinguishes an "objective sensation" (e.g., green) from a "subjective sensation" (e.g., pleasure) and suggests that misunderstanding could be avoided if "feeling" (*Gefühl*) were used for the latter. I have followed his suggestion, while indicating the German word in a note.
[l] *bei der Wahl*

objectively the *law* and subjectively *pure respect* for this practical law, and so the maxim* of complying with such a law even if it infringes upon all my inclinations.

Thus the moral worth of an action does not lie in the effect expected from it and so too does not lie in any principle of action that needs to borrow its motive from this expected effect. For, all these effects (agreeableness of one's condition, indeed even promotion of others' happiness) could have been also brought about by other causes, so that there would have been no need, for this, of the will of a rational being, in which, however, the highest and unconditional good alone can be found. Hence nothing other than the *representation of the law* in itself, *which can of course occur only in a rational being*, insofar as it and not the hoped-for effect is the determining ground of the will, can constitute the preeminent good we call moral, which is already present in the person himself who acts in accordance with this representation and need not wait upon the effect of his action.†

But what kind of law can that be, the representation of which must determine the will, even without regard for the effect expected from it, in order for the will to be called good absolutely and without limitation? Since I have deprived the will of every impulse that could arise for it from obeying some law, nothing is left but the conformity of actions as such with universal law,ᵐ which alone is to serve the will as its principle, that is,

---

*A *maxim* is the subjective principle of volition; the objective principle (i.e., that which would also serve subjectively as the practical principle for all rational beings if reason had complete control over the faculty of desire) is the practical *law*.

†It could be objected that I only seek refuge, behind the word *respect*, in an obscure feeling, instead of distinctly resolving the question by means of a concept of reason. But though respect is a feeling, it is not one *received* by means of influence; it is, instead, a feeling *self-wrought* by means of a rational concept and therefore specifically different from all feelings of the first kind, which can be reduced to inclination or fear. What I cognize immediately as a law for me I cognize with respect, which signifies merely consciousness of the *subordination* of my will to a law without the mediation of other influences on my sense. Immediate determination of the will by means of the law and consciousness of this is called *respect*, so that this is regarded as the *effect* of the law on the subject, and not as the *cause* of the law. Respect is properly the representation of a worth that infringes upon my self-love. Hence there is something that is regarded as an object neither of inclination nor of fear, though it has something analogous to both. The *object* of respect is therefore simply the *law*, and indeed the law that we impose upon *ourselves* and yet as necessary in itself. As a law we are subject to it without consulting self-love; as imposed upon us by ourselves it is nevertheless a result of our will; and in the first respect it has an analogy with fear, in the second with inclination. Any respect for a person is properly only respect for the law (of integrity and so forth) of which he gives us an example. Because we also regard enlarging our talents as a duty, we represent a person of talents also as, so to speak, an *example of the law* (to become like him in this by practice), and this is what constitutes our respect. All so-called moral *interest* consists simply in *respect* for the law.

ᵐ *die allgemeine Gesetzmäßigkeit der Handlungen überhaupt*

I ought never to act except in such a way that I could also will that my maxim should become a universal law. Here mere conformity to law as such, without having as its basis some law determined for certain actions, is what serves the will as its principle, and must so serve it, if duty is not to be everywhere an empty delusion and a chimerical concept. Common human reason also agrees completely with this in its practical appraisals and always has this principle before its eyes. Let the question be, for example: may I, when hard pressed, make a promise with the intention not to keep it? Here I easily distinguish two significations the question can have: whether it is prudent or whether it is in conformity with duty to make a false promise. The first can undoubtedly often be the case. I see very well that it is not enough to get out of a present difficulty by means of this subterfuge but that I must reflect carefully whether this lie may later give rise to much greater inconvenience for me than that from which I now extricate myself; and since, with all my supposed *cunning*, the results cannot be so easily foreseen but that once confidence in me is lost this could be far more prejudicial to me than all the troubles[a] I now think to avoid, I must reflect whether the matter might be handled *more prudently* by proceeding on a general maxim and making it a habit to promise nothing except with the intention of keeping it. But it is soon clear to me that such a maxim will still be based only on results feared. To be truthful from duty, however, is something entirely different from being truthful from anxiety about detrimental results, since in the first case the concept of the action in itself already contains a law for me while in the second I must first look about elsewhere to see what effects on me might be combined with it. For, if I deviate from the principle of duty this is quite certainly evil; but if I am unfaithful to my maxim of prudence this can sometimes be very advantageous to me, although it is certainly safer to abide by it. However, to inform myself in the shortest and yet infallible way about the answer to this problem, whether a lying promise is in conformity with duty, I ask myself: would I indeed be content that my maxim (to get myself out of difficulties by a false promise) should hold as a universal law (for myself as well as for others)? and could I indeed say to myself that every one may make a false promise when he finds himself in a difficulty he can get out of in no other way? Then I soon become aware that I could indeed will the lie, but by no means a universal law to lie; for in accordance with such a law there would properly be no promises at all, since it would be futile to avow my will with regard to my future actions to others who would not believe this avowal or, if they rashly did so, would pay me back in like coin; and thus my maxim, as soon as it were made a universal law, would have to destroy itself.

I do not, therefore, need any penetrating acuteness to see what I have

---

[a] *alles Übel.* Übeln is translated as "troubles" or "ills." "Evil" is reserved for *Böse*.

to do in order that my volition be morally good. Inexperienced in the course of the world, incapable of being prepared for whatever might come to pass in it, I ask myself only: can you also will that your maxim become a universal law? If not, then it is to be repudiated, and that not because of a disadvantage to you or even to others forthcoming from it but because it cannot fit as a principle into a possible giving of universal law,[o] for which lawgiving reason, however, forces[p] from me immediate respect. Although I do not yet see[q] what this respect is based upon (this the philosopher may investigate), I at least understand this much: that it is an estimation of a worth that far outweighs any worth of what is recommended by inclination, and that the necessity of my action from *pure* respect for the practical law is what constitutes duty, to which every other motive must give way because it is the condition of a will good *in itself*, the worth of which surpasses all else.

Thus, then, we have arrived, within the moral cognition of common human reason, at its principle, which it admittedly does not think so abstractly in a universal form[r] but which it actually has always before its eyes and uses as the norm for its appraisals. Here it would be easy to show how common human reason, with this compass in hand, knows very well how to distinguish in every case that comes up what is good and what is evil, what is in conformity with duty or contrary to duty, if, without in the least teaching it anything new, we only, as did Socrates, make it attentive to its own principle; and that there is, accordingly, no need of science and philosophy to know what one has to do in order to be honest and good, and even wise and virtuous. We might even have assumed in advance that cognizance of what is incumbent upon everyone to do, and so also to know, would be the affair of every human being, even the most common.

---

[o] *allgemeine Gesetzgebung.* This phrase, which recurs frequently throughout Kant's works in practical philosophy, presents a number of difficulties, First, it is not always clear whether, within the compound word *Gesetzgebung,* "universal" is intended to modify "law" or "giving." If the context suggests the latter, I have used "universal lawgiving" and indicated the phrase in a footnote. Second, Kant distinguishes between positive law, which is *willkürlich* ("chosen" by the *Gesetzgeber*) and *zufällig* ("contingent"), and natural law, which can be known *a priori.* See *The Metaphysics of Morals* (6:224 and 227). Since "legislation" and "legislator" suggest "making" laws or enacting positive laws, I have reserved these words for the context of "public right," which is distinguished from "private right" by the existence of legislative, executive, and judicial authorities.

[p] *abzwingt.* In *The Metaphysics of Morals,* where the concept of *Zwang* comes to the foreground in the context of moral constraint, Kant sometimes gives *Nötigung* as a parenthetical equivalent of *Zwang.* There *Nötigung* is translated as "necessitation," *Zwang* as "constraint," and (*äußere*) *Zwang* as "external constraint" or "coercion." In more general contexts, however, *nötigen* and *zwingen* are sometimes translated as "forced" or "constrained" or "compelled."

[q] Or "have insight into," *einsehe.* On the whole Kant seems to use *einsehen* informally. But see below 4:446, note q.

[r] *so in einer allgemeinen Form abgesondert. Absondern* is sometimes translated as "to separate" or "to set aside."

58

Yet we cannot consider without admiration how great an advantage the practical faculty of appraising*ʳ* has over the theoretical in common human understanding. In the latter, if common reason ventures to depart from laws of experience and perceptions of the senses it falls into sheer incomprehensibilities*ˢ* and self-contradictions, at least into a chaos of uncertainty, obscurity, and instability. But in practical matters, it is just when common understanding excludes all sensible incentives from practical laws that its faculty of appraising first begins to show itself to advantage. It then becomes even subtle, whether in quibbling tricks with its own conscience or with other claims regarding what is to be called right, or in sincerely wanting to determine the worth of actions for its own instruction; and, what is most admirable, in the latter case it can even have as good a hope of hitting the mark as any philosopher can promise himself; indeed, it is almost more sure in this matter, because a philosopher, though he cannot have any other principle than that of common understanding, can easily confuse his judgment by a mass of considerations foreign and irrelevant to the matter and deflect it from the straight course. Would it not therefore be more advisable in moral matters to leave the judgment of common reason as it is and, at most, call in philosophy only to present the system of morals all the more completely and apprehensibly*ᵘ* and to present its rules in a form more convenient for use (still more for disputation), but not to lead common human understanding, even in practical matters,*ᵛ* away from its fortunate simplicity and to put it, by means of philosophy, on a new path of investigation and instruction?

There is something splendid about innocence; but what is bad about it, in turn, is that it cannot protect itself very well and is easily seduced. 4:405 Because of this, even wisdom – which otherwise consists more in conduct than in knowledge – still needs science, not in order to learn from it but in order to provide access and durability for its precepts. The human being feels within himself a powerful counterweight to all the commands of duty, which reason represents to him as so deserving of the highest respect – the counterweight of his needs and inclinations, the entire satisfaction of which he sums up under the name happiness. Now reason issues its precepts unremittingly,*ʷ* without thereby promising anything to the inclinations, and so, as it were, with disregard and contempt for those claims, which are so impetuous and besides so apparently equitable (and refuse to be neutralized by any command). But from this there arises a *natural dialectic,* that is, a propensity to rationalize against those strict laws

---

ʳ Beurteilungsvermögen
ˢ Unbegreiflichkeiten
ᵘ faßlicher
ᵛ in praktischer Absicht
ʷ gebietet die Vernunft . . . unnachlaßlich . . . ihre Vorschriften

of duty and to cast doubt upon their validity, or at least upon their purity and strictness, and, where possible, to make them better suited to our wishes and inclinations, that is, to corrupt them at their basis and to destroy all their dignity – something that even common practical reason cannot, in the end, call good.

In this way *common human reason* is impelled, not by some need of speculation (which never touches it as long as it is content to be mere sound reason), but on practical grounds themselves, to go out of its sphere and to take a step into the field of *practical philosophy*, in order to obtain there information and distinct instruction regarding the source of its principle and the correct determination of this principle in comparison with maxims based on need and inclination, so that it may escape from its predicament about claims from both sides and not run the risk of being deprived of all genuine moral principles through the ambiguity[x] into which it easily falls. So there develops unnoticed in common practical reason as well, when it cultivates itself, a *dialectic* that constrains it to seek help in philosophy, just as happens in its theoretical use; and the first will, accordingly, find no more rest than the other except in a complete critique of our reason.

[x] *Zweideutigkeit*

Section II
Transition from popular moral philosophy to metaphysics of morals

If we have so far drawn our concept of duty*ʸ* from the common use of our practical reason, it is by no means to be inferred from this that we have treated it as a concept of experience. On the contrary, if we attend to experience of people's conduct we meet frequent and, as we ourselves admit, just complaints that no certain example can be cited of the disposition to act from pure duty; that, though much may be done *in conformity with* what *duty* commands, still it is always doubtful whether it is really done *from duty* and therefore has moral worth. Hence there have at all times been philosophers who have absolutely denied the reality*ᶻ* of this disposition in human actions and ascribed everything to more or less refined self-love. They did not, on account of this, call into doubt the correctness of the concept of morality but rather spoke with deep regret of the frailty and impurity of human nature, which is indeed noble enough to take as its precept an idea so worthy of respect but at the same time is too weak to follow it, and uses reason, which should serve it for giving law, only to look after the interests of the inclinations, whether singly or, at most, in their greatest compatibility with one another.

In fact, it is absolutely impossible by means of experience to make out with complete certainty a single case in which the maxim of an action otherwise in conformity with duty rested simply on moral grounds and on the representation of one's duty. It is indeed sometimes the case that with the keenest self-examination we find nothing besides the moral ground of duty that could have been powerful enough to move us to this or that good action and to so great a sacrifice; but from this it cannot be inferred with certainty that no covert impulse of self-love, under the mere pretense of that idea, was not actually the real determining cause of the will; for we like to flatter ourselves by falsely attributing to ourselves a nobler motive, whereas in fact we can never, even by the most strenuous self-examination, get entirely behind our covert incentives, since, when moral worth is at

---
ʸ unsern bisherigan Begriff der Pflicht
ᶻ Wirklichkeit and its cognates are translated indifferently in terms of "reality" or "actuality."

issue, what counts is not actions,[a] which one sees, but those inner principles of actions that one does not see.

Moreover, one cannot better serve the wishes of those who ridicule all morality as the mere phantom of a human imagination overstepping itself[b] through self-conceit than by granting them that concepts of duty must be drawn solely from experience (as, from indolence, people like to persuade themselves is the case with all other concepts as well); for then one prepares a sure triumph for them. From love of humankind I am willing to admit that even most of our actions are in conformity with duty; but if we look more closely at the intentions and aspirations in them we everywhere come upon the dear self, which is always turning up; and it is on this that their purpose is based, not on the strict command of duty, which would often require self-denial. One need not be an enemy of virtue but only a cool observer, who does not take the liveliest wish for the good straightaway as its reality, to become doubtful at certain moments (especially with increasing years, when experience has made one's judgment partly more shrewd and partly more acute in observation) whether any true virtue is to be found in the world. And then nothing can protect[c] us against falling away completely from our ideas of duty and can preserve in our soul a well-grounded respect for its law than the clear conviction that, even if there never have been actions arising from such pure sources, what is at issue here is not whether this or that happened; that, instead, reason by itself and independently of all appearances commands what ought to happen; that, accordingly, actions of which the world has perhaps so far given no example, and whose very practicability[d] might be very much doubted by one who bases everything on experience, are still inflexibly commanded by reason; and that, for example, pure sincerity in friendship can be no less required of everyone even if up to now there may never have been a sincere friend, because this duty – as duty in general – lies, prior to all experience, in the idea of a reason determining the will by means of a priori grounds.

If we add further that, unless we want to deny to the concept of morality any truth and any relation to some possible object, we cannot dispute that its law is so extensive in its import that it must hold not only for human beings but for all *rational beings as such*, not merely under contingent conditions and with exceptions but with *absolute necessity*, then it is clear that no experience could give occasion to infer even the possibility of such apodictic laws. For, by what right could we bring into unlimited respect, as a universal precept for every rational nature, what is perhaps

---

[a] *es nicht auf die Handlungen ankommt*
[b] *sich selbst übersteigenden*
[c] *bewahren*
[d] *Tunlichkeit*

valid only under the contingent conditions of humanity? A[ll]
laws of the determination of *our* will be taken as laws of th[e ...]
of the will of rational beings as such, and for ours only a[s ...]
if they were merely empirical and did not have their o[rigin a]
priori in pure but practical reason?

Nor could one give worse advice to morality than by wanting [to derive] it from examples. For, every example of it represented to me must itself first be appraised in accordance with principles of morality, as to whether it is also worthy to serve as an original example, that is, as a model; it can by no means authoritatively provide the concept of morality. Even the Holy One of the Gospel must first be compared with our ideal of moral perfection before he is cognized as such; even he says of himself: why do you call me (whom you see) good? none is good (the archetype of the good) but God only (whom you do not see).ᵉ But whence have we the concept of God as the highest good? Solely from the *idea* of moral perfection that reason frames a priori and connects inseparably with the concept of a free will. Imitation has no place at all in matters of morality, and examples serve only for encouragement, that is, they put beyond doubt the practicability of what the law commands and make intuitiveᶠ what the practical rule expresses more generally, but they can never justify setting aside their true original, which lies in reason, and guiding oneself by examples.

4:409

If there is, then, no genuine supreme basic principle of morality that does not have to rest only on pure reason independently of all experience, I believe it unnecessary even to ask whether it is a good thing to set forth in their generalityᵍ (*in abstracto*) these concepts as they, along with the principles belonging to them, are fixed a priori, if this cognition is to be distinguished from the common and called philosophic. But in our day it may well be necessary to ask this. For if votes were collected as to which is to be preferred – pure rational cognition separated from anything empirical, hence metaphysics of morals, or popular practical philosophy – one can guess at once on which side the preponderance would fall.

This descending to popular concepts is certainly very commendable, provided the ascent to the principles of pure reason has first taken place and has been carried through to complete satisfaction. That would mean that the doctrine of morals is first *grounded* on metaphysics and afterwards, when it has been firmly established, is provided with *access* by means of popularity. But it is quite absurd to want to comply with popularity in the first investigation, on which all correctness of basic principles depends. Not only can this procedure never lay claim to the very rare merit of a true *philosophic popular-*

ᵉ Matthew 19:17
ᶠ *machen ... anschaulich*
ᵍ *im Allgemeinen*

ity, since there is no art in being commonly understandable if one thereby renounces any well-grounded insight; it also produces a disgusting hodgepodge of patchwork observations and half-rationalized principles, in which shallow pates revel because it is something useful for everyday chitchat, but the insightful, feeling confused and dissatisfied without being able to help themselves, avert their eyes – although philosophers, who see quite well through the deception, get little hearing when they call [moralists] away for a time from this alleged popularity, so that they may be rightly popular only after having acquired determinate insight.

One need only look at attempts at morality in that popular taste. One will find now the special determination[h] of human nature (but occasionally the idea of a rational nature as such along with it), now perfection, now happiness, here moral feeling, there fear of God, a bit of this and also a bit of that in a marvellous mixture, without its occurring to them to ask whether the principles of morality are to be sought at all in acquaintance with human nature (which we can get only from experience) and, if this is not the case – if these principles are to be found altogether a priori, free from anything empirical, solely in pure rational concepts and nowhere else even to the slightest extent – instead to adopt the plan[i] of quite separating this investigation as pure practical philosophy or (if one may use a name so decried) as metaphysics of morals,* of bringing it all by itself to its full completeness, and of putting off the public, which demands popularity, pending the outcome of this undertaking.

But such a completely isolated metaphysics of morals, mixed with no anthropology, theology, physics, or hyperphysics and still less with occult qualities (which could be called hypophysical), is not only an indispensable substratum of all theoretical and surely determined cognition of duties; it is also a desideratum of utmost importance to the actual fulfillment of their precepts. For, the pure thought of duty and in general of the moral law, mixed with no foreign addition of empirical inducements, has by way of reason alone (which with this first becomes aware that it can of itself also be practical) an influence on the human heart so much more powerful than all other incentives,† which may be summoned from the

---

*One can, if one wants to, distinguish pure philosophy of morals (metaphysics) from applied (namely to human nature), (just as pure mathematics is distinguished from applied, and pure logic from applied). By using this name one is also reminded at once that moral principles are not based on what is peculiar to human nature but must be fixed[j] a priori by themselves, while from such principles it must be possible to derive practical rules for every rational nature, and accordingly for human nature as well.

†I have a letter from the late excellent Sulzer[4] in which he asks me what the cause might be that the teachings of virtue, however much they contain that is convincing to reason, accom-

[h] *Bestimmung*
[i] *den Anschlag zu fassen*
[j] *besteheud sein müssen*

empirical field, that reason, in the consciousness of its dignity, despises the latter and can gradually become their master; on the other hand a mixed doctrine of morals, put together from incentives of feeling and inclination and also of rational concepts, must make the mind waver between motives that cannot be brought under any principle, that can lead only contingently to what is good and can very often also lead to what is evil.

From what has been said it is clear that all moral concepts have their seat and origin completely a priori in reason, and indeed in the most common reason just as in reason that is speculative in the highest degree; that they cannot be abstracted from any empirical and therefore merely contingent cognitions; that just in this purity of their origin lies their dignity, so that they can serve us as supreme practical principles; that in adding anything empirical to them one subtracts just that much from their genuine influence and from the unlimited worth of actions; that it is not only a requirement of the greatest necessity for theoretical purposes, when it is a matter merely of speculation, but also of the greatest practical importance to draw its concepts and laws from pure reason, to set them forth pure and unmixed, and indeed to determine the extent of this entire practical or pure rational cognition, that is, to determine the entire faculty of pure practical reason; and in so doing, it is of the greatest practical importance not to make its principles dependent upon the special nature of human reason – as speculative philosophy permits and even at times finds necessary – but instead, just because moral laws are to hold for every rational being as such, to derive them from the universal concept of a rational being as such, and in this way to set forth completely the whole of morals, which needs anthropology for its *application* to human beings, at first independently of this as pure philosophy, that is, as metaphysics (as can well be done in this kind of quite separated cognitions);[l] [for we are] well aware that, unless we are in possession of this, it would be – I will not say futile to determine precisely for speculative appraisal the moral element of duty in all that conforms with duty, but – impossible to base

4:412

---

plish so little. By trying to prepare a complete answer I delayed too long. However, my answer is simply that the teachers themselves have not brought their concepts to purity, but, since they want to do too well by hunting everywhere for motives to moral goodness, in trying to make their medicine really strong they spoil it. For the most ordinary observation shows that if we represent, on the one hand, an action of integrity[k] done with steadfast soul, apart from every view to advantage of any kind in this world or another and even under the greatest temptations of need or allurement, it leaves far behind and eclipses any similar act that was affected in the least by an extraneous incentive; it elevates the soul and awakens a wish to be able to act in like manner oneself. Even children of moderate age feel this impression, and one should never represent duties to them in any other way.

[k] *Rechtschaffenheit*

[l] The structure of this sentence, from the semicolon to "impossible to base morals," has been slightly modified.

morals on their genuine principles even for common and practical use, especially that of moral instruction, and thereby to bring about pure moral dispositions and engraft them onto people's minds for the highest good in the world.*ᵐ*

However, in order to advance by natural steps in this study – not merely from common moral appraisal (which is here very worthy of respect) to philosophic, as has already been done, but – from a popular philosophy, which goes no further than it can by groping with the help of examples, to metaphysics (which no longer lets itself be held back by anything empirical and, since it must measure out the whole sum of rational cognition of this kind, goes if need be all the way to ideas, where examples themselves fail us), we must follow and present distinctly the practical faculty of reason, from its general rules of determination to the point where the concept of duty arises from it.

Everything in nature works in accordance with laws. Only a rational being has the capacity to act *in accordance with the representation* of laws, that is, in accordance with principles, or has a *will*. Since *reason* is required for the derivation of actions from laws, the will is nothing other than practical reason. If reason infallibly determines the will, the actions of such a being that are cognized as objectively necessary are also subjectively necessary, that is, the will is a capacity to choose *only that* which reason independently of inclination cognizes as practically necessary, that is, as good. However, if reason solely by itself does not adequately determine the will; if the will is exposed*ⁿ* also to subjective conditions (certain incentives) that are not always in accord with the objective ones; in a word, if the will is not *in itself* completely in conformity with reason (as is actually the case with human beings), then actions that are cognized as objectively necessary are subjectively contingent, and the determination of such a will in conformity with objective laws is *necessitation:* that is to say, the relation of objective laws to a will that is not thoroughly good is represented as the determination of the will of a rational being through grounds of reason, indeed, but grounds to which this will is not by its nature necessarily obedient.

The representation of an objective principle, insofar as it is necessitating for a will, is called a command (of reason), and the formula of the command is called an **imperative**.

All imperatives are expressed by an *ought* and indicate by this the relation of an objective law of reason to a will that by its subjective constitution is not necessarily determined by it (a necessitation). They say that to do or to omit something would be good, but they say it to a will that does not always do something just because it is represented to it that it

---

ᵐ zum höchsten Weltbesten
ⁿ unterworfen

would be good to do that thing. Practical good, however, is that which determines the will by means of representations of reason, hence not by subjective causes but objectively, that is, from grounds that are valid for every rational being as such. It is distinguished from the *agreeable,* as that which influences the will only by means of feeling*ᵒ* from merely subjective causes, which hold only for the senses of this or that one, and not as a principle of reason, which holds for everyone.*

A perfectly good will would, therefore, equally stand under objective laws (of the good), but it could not on this account be represented as *necessitated* to actions in conformity with law since of itself, by its subjective constitution, it can be determined only through the representation of the good. Hence no imperatives hold for the *divine* will and in general for a *holy* will: the "ought" is out of place here, because volition*ᵖ* is of itself necessarily in accord with the law. Therefore imperatives are only formulae expressing the relation of objective laws of volition in general to the subjective imperfection of the will of this or that rational being, for example, of the human will.

4:414

Now, all imperatives command either *hypothetically* or *categorically.* The former represent the practical necessity of a possible action as a means to achieving something else that one wills (or that it is at least possible for one to will). The categorical imperative would be that which represented an action as objectively necessary of itself, without reference to another end.

Since every practical law represents a possible action as good and thus as necessary for a subject practically determinable by reason, all imperatives are formulae for the determination of action that is necessary in accordance with the principle of a will which is good in some way. Now, if the action would be good merely as a means *to something else* the imperative is *hypothetical;* if the action is represented as *in itself* good, hence as necessary in a will in itself conforming to reason, as its principle, *then it is categorical.*

---

*The dependence of the faculty of desire upon feelings is called inclination, and this accordingly always indicates a *need.* The dependence of a contingently determinable will on principles of reason, however, is called an *interest.* This, accordingly, is present only in the case of a dependent will, which is not of itself always in conformity with reason; in the case of the divine will we cannot think of any interest. But even the human will can *take an interest* in something without therefore *acting from interest.* The first signifies *practical* interest in the action, the second, *pathological* interest in the object of the action. The former indicates only dependence of the will upon principles of reason *in themselves;* the second, dependence upon principles of reason for the sake of inclination, namely where reason supplies only the practical rule as to how to remedy the need of inclination. In the first case the action interests me; in the second, the object of the action (insofar as it is agreeable to me). We have seen in the first Section that in the case of an action from duty we must look not to interest in the object but merely to that in the action itself and its principle in reason (the law).

ᵒ Empfindung
ᵖ das Sollen . . . das Wollen

The imperative thus says which action possible by me would be good, and represents a practical rule in relation to a will that does not straightaway do an action just because it is good, partly because the subject does not always know that it is good, partly because, even if he knows this, his maxims could still be opposed to the objective principles of a practical reason.

Hence the hypothetical imperative says only that the action is good for some *possible* or *actual* purpose. In the first case it is a **problematically** practical principle, in the second an **assertorically** practical principle. The categorical imperative, which declares the action to be of itself objectively necessary without reference to some purpose, that is, even apart from any other end, holds as an **apodictically** practical principle.

One can think of what is possible only through the powers of some rational being as also a possible purpose of some will; accordingly, principles of action, insofar as this is represented as necessary for attaining some possible purpose to be brought about by it, are in fact innumerable. All sciences have some practical part, consisting of problems [which suppose] that some end is possible for us and of imperatives as to how it can be attained. These can therefore be called, in general, imperatives of **skill**. Whether the end is rational and good is not at all the question here, but only what one must do in order to attain it. The precepts for a physician to make his man healthy in a well-grounded way, and for a poisoner to be sure of killing his, are of equal worth insofar as each serves perfectly to bring about his purpose. Since in early youth it is not known what ends might occur to us in the course of life, parents seek above all to have their children learn *a great many things* and to provide for *skill* in the use of means to all sorts of *discretionary* ends,[q] about none of which can they determine whether it might in the future actually become their pupil's purpose, though it is always *possible* that he might at some time have it; and this concern is so great that they commonly neglect to form and correct their children's judgment about the worth of the things that they might make their ends.

There is, however, *one* end that can be presupposed as actual in the case of all rational beings (insofar as imperatives apply to them, namely as dependent beings), and therefore one purpose that they not merely *could* have but that we can safely presuppose they all actually *do have* by a natural necessity, and that purpose is *happiness*. The hypothetical imperative that represents the practical necessity of an action as a means to the promotion of happiness is **assertoric**. It may be set forth not merely as necessary to some uncertain, merely possible purpose but to a purpose that can be presupposed surely and a priori in the case of every human being, because it belongs to his essence. Now, skill in the choice of means

---

[q] *beliebigen Zwecken*

to one's own greatest well-being can be called *prudence** in the narrowest sense. Hence the imperative that refers to the choice of means to one's own happiness, that is, the precept of prudence, is still always *hypothetical;* the action is not commanded absolutely but only as a means to another purpose.

Finally there is one imperative that, without being based upon and having as its condition' any other purpose to be attained by certain conduct, commands this conduct immediately. This imperative is **categorical**. It has to do not with the matter of the action and what is to result from it, but with the form and the principle from which the action itself follows; and the essentially good in the action' consists in the disposition, let the result be what it may. This imperative may be called the imperative **of morality.**

Volition in accordance with these three kinds of principles is also clearly distinguished by *dissimilarity'* in the necessitation of the will. In order to make this dissimilarity evident, I think they would be most suitably named in their order by being said to be either *rules* of skill, or *counsels* of prudence, or *commands* (*laws*) of morality. For, only law brings with it the concept of an *unconditional* and objective and hence universally valid *necessity,* and commands are laws that must be obeyed, that is, must be followed even against inclination. *Giving counsel* does involve necessity, which, however, can hold only under a subjective and contingent condition, whether this or that man counts this or that in his happiness; the categorical imperative, on the contrary, is limited by no condition and, as absolutely although practically necessary, can be called quite strictly a command. The first imperative could also be called *technical* (belonging to art), the second pragmatic† (belonging to welfare), the third moral (belonging to free conduct as such, that is, to morals).

Now the question arises: how are all these imperatives possible? This question does not inquire how the performance of the action that the

4:417

---

*The word "prudence" is taken in two senses: in the one it may bear the name of "knowledge of the world,"5 in the other that of "private prudence." The first is a human being's skill in influencing others so as to use them for his own purposes. The second is the insight to unite all these purposes to his own enduring advantage. The latter is properly that to which the worth even of the former is reduced, and if someone is prudent in the first sense but not in the second, we might better say of him that he is clever and cunning but, on the whole, nevertheless imprudent.

†It seems to me that the proper meaning of the word *pragmatic* can be most accurately determined in this way. For *sanctions* are called "pragmatic" that do not flow strictly from the right of *states* as necessary laws but from *provision* for the general welfare. A *history* is composed pragmatically when it makes us *prudent,* that is, instructs the world how it can look after its advantage better than, or at least as well as, the world of earlier times.

' *als Bedingung zum Grunde zu legen*
' *das Wesentlich-Gute derselben*
' *Ungleichheit*

imperative commands can be thought, but only how the necessitation of the will, which the imperative expresses in the problem, can be thought. How an imperative of skill is possible requires no special discussion. Whoever wills the end also wills (insofar as reason has decisive influence on his actions) the indispensably necessary means to it that are within his power. This proposition is, as regards the volition, analytic; for in the volition of an object as my effect, my causality as acting cause, that is, the use of means, is already thought, and the imperative extracts the concept of actions necessary to this end merely from the concept of a volition of this end (synthetic propositions no doubt belong to determining the means themselves to a purpose intended, but they do not have to do with the ground for actualizing[u] the act of will but for actualizing the object). That in order to divide a line into two equal parts on a sure principle I must make two intersecting arcs from its ends, mathematics admittedly teaches only by synthetic propositions; but when I know that only by such an action can the proposed effect take place, then it is an analytic proposition that if I fully[v] will the effect I also will the action requisite to it; for, it is one and the same thing to represent something as an effect possible by me in a certain way and to represent myself as acting in this way with respect to it.

If only it were as easy to give a determinate concept of happiness, imperatives of prudence would agree entirely with those of skill and would be just as[w] analytic. For it could be said, here just as there: who wills the end also wills (necessarily in conformity with reason) the sole means to it that are within his control. But it is a misfortune that the concept of happiness is such an indeterminate concept that, although every human being wishes to attain this, he can still never say determinately and consistently with himself what he really wishes and wills. The cause of this is that all the elements that belong to the concept of happiness are without exception empirical, that is, they must be borrowed from experience, and that nevertheless for the idea of happiness there is required an absolute whole, a maximum of well-being in my present condition and in every future condition. Now, it is impossible for the most insightful and at the same time most powerful but still finite being to frame for himself a determinate concept of what he really wills here. If he wills riches, how much anxiety, envy and intrigue might he not bring upon himself in this way! If he wills a great deal of cognition and insight, that might become only an eye all the more acute to show him, as all the more dreadful, ills that are now concealed from him and that cannot be avoided, or to burden

---

[u] *wirklich zu machen*
[v] *vollständig*
[w] *eben sowohl*

his desires,[x] which already give him enough to do, with still more needs. If he wills a long life, who will guarantee him that it would not be a long misery? If he at least wills health, how often has not bodily discomfort kept someone from excesses into which unlimited health would have let him fall, and so forth. In short, he is not capable of any principle by which to determine with complete certainty what would make him truly happy, because for this omniscience would be required. One cannot therefore act on determinate principles for the sake of being happy, but only on empirical counsels, for example, of a regimen,[y] frugality, courtesy, reserve and so forth, which experience teaches are most conducive to well-being on the average. From this it follows that imperatives of prudence cannot, to speak precisely, command at all, that is, present actions objectively as practically *necessary;* that they are to be taken as counsels (*consilia*) rather than as commands (*praecepta*) of reason; that the problem of determining surely and universally which action would promote the happiness of a rational being is completely insoluble, so that there can be no imperative with respect to it that would, in the strict sense, command him to do what would make him happy; for happiness is not an ideal of reason but of imagination, resting merely upon empirical grounds, which it is futile to expect should determine an action by which the totality of a series of results in fact infinite would be attained. This imperative of prudence would, nevertheless, be an analytic practical proposition if it is supposed that the means to happiness can be assigned with certainty; for it is distinguished from the imperative of skill only in this: that in the case of the latter the end is merely possible, whereas in the former it is given; but since both merely command the means to what it is presupposed one wills as an end, the imperative that commands volition of the means for him who wills the end is in both cases analytic. Hence there is also no difficulty with respect to the possibility of such an imperative.

On the other hand, the question of how the imperative of *morality* is possible is undoubtedly the only one needing a solution, since it is in no way hypothetical and the objectively represented necessity can therefore not be based on any presupposition, as in the case of hypothetical imperatives. Only we must never leave out of account, here, that it cannot be made out *by means of any example,* and so empirically, whether there is any such imperative at all, but it is rather to be feared that all imperatives which seem to be categorical may yet in some hidden way be hypothetical. For example, when it is said "you ought not to promise anything deceitfully," and one assumes that the necessity of this omission is not giving

---

[x] *Begierden.* According to *The Metaphysics of Morals* (6:212), *Begierde* must always be preceded by a feeling of pleasure.
[y] *Diät*

counsel for avoiding some other ill – in which case what is said would be "you ought not to make a lying promise lest if it comes to light you destroy your credit" – but that an action of this kind must be regarded as in itself evil and that the imperative of prohibition is therefore categorical: one still cannot show with certainty in any example that the will is here determined merely through the law, without another incentive, although it seems to be so; for it is always possible that covert fear of disgrace, perhaps also obscure apprehension of other dangers, may have had an influence on the will. Who can prove by experience the nonexistence of a cause when all that experience teaches is that we do not perceive it? In such a case, however, the so-called moral imperative, which as such appears to be categorical and unconditional, would in fact be only a pragmatic precept that makes us attentive to our advantage and merely teaches us to take this into consideration.

We shall thus have to investigate entirely a priori the possibility of a *categorical* imperative, since we do not here have the advantage of its reality being given in experience, so that the possibility would be necessary not to establish it but merely to explain it.² In the meantime, however, we can see this much: that the categorical imperative alone has the tenor of*ᵃ* a practical **law**; all the others can indeed be called *principles* of the will but not laws, since what it is necessary to do merely for achieving a discretionary purpose can be regarded as in itself contingent and we can always be released from the precept if we give up the purpose; on the contrary, the unconditional command leaves the will no discretion*ᵇ* with respect to the opposite, so that it alone brings with it that necessity which we require of a law.

Second, in the case of this categorical imperative or law of morality the ground of the difficulty (of insight into its possibility) is also very great. It is an a priori synthetic practical proposition;* and since it is so difficult to see the possibility of this kind of proposition in theoretical cognition, it can be readily gathered that the difficulty will be no less in practical cognition.

In this task we want first to inquire whether the mere concept of a categorical imperative may not also provide its formula containing the

---

*I connect the deed with the will, without a presupposed condition from any inclination, a priori and hence necessarily (though only objectively, i.e., under the idea of a reason having complete control over all subjective motives).ᶜ This is, therefore, a practical proposition that does not derive the volition of an action analytically from another volition already presupposed (for we have no such perfect will), but connects it immediately with the concept of the will of a rational being as something that is not contained in it.

² *und also die Möglichkeit nicht zur Festsetzung, sondern bloss zur Erklärung nötig wäre*
ᵃ *als . . . laute*
ᵇ *dem Willen kein Belieben . . . frei läßt*
ᶜ *Bewegursachen*

proposition which alone can be a categorical imperative. For, how such an absolute command is possible, even if we know its tenor, will still require special and difficult toil, which, however, we postpone to the last section.

When I think of a *hypothetical* imperative in general I do not know beforehand what it will contain; I do not know this until I am given the condition. But when I think of a *categorical* imperative I know at once what it contains. For, since the imperative contains, beyond the law, only the necessity that the maxim* be in conformity with this law, while the law contains no condition to which it would be limited, nothing is left with which the maxim of action is to conform but the universality of a law as such; and this conformity alone is what the imperative properly represents as necessary.

There is, therefore, only a single categorical imperative and it is this: *act only in accordance with that maxim through which you can at the same time will that it become a universal law.*

Now, if all imperatives of duty can be derived from this single imperative as from their principle, then, even though we leave it undecided whether what is called duty is not as such an empty concept, we shall at least be able to show what we think by it and what the concept wants to say.

Since the universality of law in accordance with which effects take place constitutes what is properly called *nature* in the most general sense (as regards its form) – that is, the existence of things insofar as it is determined in accordance with universal laws – the universal imperative of duty can also go as follows: *act as if the maxim of your action were to become by your will a* **universal law of nature.**

We shall now enumerate a few duties in accordance with the usual division of them into duties to ourselves and to other human beings and into perfect and imperfect duties.†

1) Someone feels sick of life because of a series of troubles that has grown to the point of despair, but is still so far in possession of his reason that he can ask himself whether it would not be contrary to his duty to

4:421

4:422

---

*A *maxim* is the subjective principle of acting, and must be distinguished from the *objective* principle, namely the practical law. The former contains the practical rule determined by reason conformably with the conditions of the subject (often his ignorance or also his inclinations), and is therefore the principle in accordance with which the subject *acts;* but the law is the objective principle valid for every rational being, and the principle in accordance with which he *ought to act,* i.e., an imperative.

†It must be noted here that I reserve the division of duties entirely for a future *Metaphysics of Morals,* so that the division here stands only as one adopted at my discretion (for the sake of arranging my examples). For the rest, I understand here by a perfect duty one that admits no exception in favor of inclination, and then I have not merely external but also internal *perfect duties;* although this is contrary to the use of the work adopted in the schools, I do not intend to justify it here, since for my purpose it makes no difference whether or not it is granted me.

himself to take his own life. Now he inquires whether the maxim of his action could indeed become a universal law of nature. His maxim, however, is: from self-love I make it my principle to shorten my life when its longer duration threatens more troubles than it promises agreeableness. The only further question is whether this principle of self-love could become a universal law of nature. It is then seen at once that a nature whose law it would be to destroy life itself by means of the same feeling whose destination[d] is to impel toward the furtherance of life would contradict itself and would therefore not subsist[e] as nature; thus that maxim could not possibly be a law of nature and, accordingly, altogether opposes the supreme principle of all duty.

2) Another finds himself urged by need to borrow money. He well knows that he will not be able to repay it but sees also that nothing will be lent him unless he promises firmly to repay it within a determinate time. He would like to make such a promise, but he still has enough conscience to ask himself: is it not forbidden and contrary to duty to help oneself out of need in such a way? Supposing that he still decided to do so, his maxim of action would go as follows: when I believe myself to be in need of money I shall borrow money and promise to repay it, even though I know that this will never happen. Now this principle of self-love or personal advantage is perhaps quite consistent with my whole future welfare, but the question now is whether it is right. I therefore turn the demand of self-love into a universal law and put the question as follows: how would it be if my maxim became a universal law? I then see at once that it could never hold as a universal law of nature and be consistent with itself, but must necessarily contradict itself. For, the universality of a law that everyone, when he believes himself to be in need, could promise whatever he pleases with the intention of not keeping it would make the promise and the end one might have in it itself impossible, since no one would believe what was promised him but would laugh at all such expressions as vain pretenses.

3) A third finds in himself a talent that by means of some cultivation could make him a human being useful for all sorts of purposes. However, he finds himself in comfortable circumstances and prefers to give himself up to pleasure than to trouble himself with enlarging and improving his fortunate natural predispositions.[f] But he still asks himself whether his maxim of neglecting his natural gifts, besides being consistent with his propensity to amusement, is also consistent with what one calls duty. He now sees that a nature could indeed always subsist with such a universal law, although (as with the South Sea Islanders) the human being should

---

[d] *Bestimmung*
[e] *bestehen*
[f] *Naturanlagen*

let his talents rust and be concerned with devoting his life merely to idleness, amusement, procreation – in a word, to enjoyment; only he cannot possibly **will** that this become a universal law or be put in us as such by means of natural instinct. For, as a rational being he necessarily wills that all the capacities in him be developed, since they serve him and are given to him for all sorts of possible purposes.

Yet a *fourth*, for whom things are going well while he sees that others (whom he could very well help) have to contend with great hardships, thinks: what is it to me? let each be as happy as heaven wills or as he can make himself; I shall take nothing from him nor even envy him; only I do not care to contribute anything to his welfare or to his assistance in need! Now, if such a way of thinking were to become a universal law the human race could admittedly very well subsist, no doubt even better than when everyone prates about sympathy and benevolence and even exerts himself to practice them occasionally, but on the other hand also cheats where he can, sells the right of human beings or otherwise infringes upon it. But although it is possible that a universal law of nature could very well subsist in accordance with such a maxim, it is still impossible to **will** that such a principle hold everywhere as a law of nature. For, a will that decided this would conflict with itself, since many cases could occur in which one would need the love and sympathy[g] of others and in which, by such a law of nature arisen from his own will, he would rob himself of all hope of the assistance he wishes for himself.

These are a few of the many actual duties, or at least of what we take to be such, whose derivation[h] from the one principle cited above is clear. We must *be able to will* that a maxim of our action become a universal law: this is the canon of moral appraisal of action in general. Some actions are so constituted that their maxim cannot even be *thought* without contradiction as a universal law of nature, far less could one *will* that it *should* become such. In the case of others that inner impossibility is indeed not to be found, but it is still impossible to *will* that their maxim be raised to the universality of a law of nature because such a will would contradict itself. It is easy to see that the first is opposed to strict or narrower (unremitting)[i] duty, the second only to wide (meritorious) duty; and so all duties, as far as the kind of obligation (not the object of their action) is concerned, have by these examples been set out completely in their dependence upon the one principle.

4:424

If we now attend to ourselves in any transgression of a duty, we find that we do not really will that our maxim should become a universal law, since that is impossible for us, but that the opposite of our maxim should

---

[g] *Teilnehmung*
[h] reading *Ableitung* instead of *Abteilung*, "classification"
[i] *unnachlaßlich*

instead remain a universal law, only we take the liberty of making an *exception* to it for ourselves (or just for this once) to the advantage of our inclination. Consequently, if we weighed all cases from one and the same point of view, namely that of reason, we would find a contradiction in our own will, namely that a certain principle be objectively necessary as a universal law and yet subjectively not hold universally but allow exceptions. Since, however, we at one time regard our action from the point of view of a will wholly conformed with reason but then regard the very same action from the point of view of a will affected by inclination, there is really no contradiction here but instead a resistance[j] of inclination to the precept of reason (*antagonismus*), through which the universality of the principle (*universalitas*) is changed into mere generality (*generalitas*) and the practical rational principle is to meet the maxim half way. Now, even though this cannot be justified in our own impartially rendered judgment, it still shows that we really acknowledge the validity of the categorical imperative and permit ourselves (with all respect for it) only a few exceptions that, as it seems to us, are inconsiderable and wrung from us.

We have therefore shown at least this much: that if duty is a concept that is to contain significance and real lawgiving for our actions it can be expressed only in categorical imperatives and by no means in hypothetical ones; we have also – and this is already a great deal – set forth distinctly and as determined for every use the content of the categorical imperative, which must contain the principle of all duty (if there is such a thing at all). But we have not yet advanced so far as to prove a priori that there really is such an imperative, that there is a practical law, which commands absolutely of itself and without any incentives, and that the observance of this law is duty.

For the purpose of achieving this it is of the utmost importance to take warning that we must not let ourselves think of wanting to derive the reality of this principle from the *special property of human nature*. For, duty is to be practical unconditional necessity of action and it must therefore hold for all rational beings (to which alone an imperative can apply at all) and *only because of this* be also a law for all human wills. On the other hand, what is derived from the special natural constitution of humanity – what is derived from certain feelings and propensities and even, if possible, from a special tendency that would be peculiar to human reason and would not have to hold necessarily for the will of every rational being – that can indeed yield a maxim for us but not a law; it can yield a subjective principle on which we might act if we have the propensity and inclination,[k] but not an objective principle on which we would be *directed* to act even though every propensity, inclination, and natural tendency of ours were

---
[j] *Widerstand*
[k] *nach welchem wir handeln zu dürfen Hang und Neigung haben*

against it – so much so that the sublimity and inner dignity of the command in a duty is all the more manifest the fewer are the subjective causes in favor of it and the more there are against it, without thereby weakening in the least the necessitation by the law or taking anything away from its validity.

Here, then, we see philosophy put in fact in a precarious position, which is to be firm even though there is nothing in heaven or on earth from which it depends or on which it is based. Here philosophy is to manifest its purity as sustainer of its own laws, not as herald of laws that an implanted sense or who knows what tutelary nature whispers to it, all of which – though they may always be better than nothing at all – can still never yield basic principles that reason dictates and that must have their source entirely and completely a priori and, at the same time, must have their commanding authority from this: that they expect nothing from the inclination of human beings but everything from the supremacy of the law and the respect owed it or, failing this, condemn the human being to contempt for himself and inner abhorrence.

Hence everything empirical, as an addition[l] to the principle of morality, is not only quite inept for this; it is also highly prejudicial to the purity of morals, where the proper worth of an absolutely good will – a worth raised above all price – consists just in the principle of action being free from all influences of contingent grounds, which only experience can furnish. One cannot give too many or too frequent warnings against this laxity, or even mean cast of mind, which seeks its principle among empirical motives and laws; for, human reason in its weariness gladly rests on this pillow and in a dream of sweet illusions (which allow it to embrace a cloud instead of Juno) it substitutes for morality a bastard patched up from limbs of quite diverse ancestry, which looks like whatever one wants to see in it but not like virtue for him who has once seen virtue in her true form.*

The question is therefore this: is it a necessary law *for all rational beings* always to appraise their actions in accordance with such maxims as they themselves could will to serve as universal laws? If there is such a law, then it must already be connected (completely a priori) with the concept of the will of a rational being as such. But in order to discover this connection we must, however reluctantly, step forth, namely into metaphysics, although into a domain[m] of it that is distinct from speculative philosophy, namely

4:426

4:427

---

*To behold virtue in her proper form is nothing other than to present morality stripped of any admixture of the sensible and of any spurious adornments of reward or self-love. By means of the least effort of his reason everyone can easily become aware of how much virtue then eclipses everything else that appears charming to the inclinations, provided his reason is not altogether spoiled for abstraction.

[l] *Zutat*, literally "an ornament"
[m] *Gebiet*

into metaphysics of morals. In a practical philosophy, where we have to do not with assuming*ⁿ* grounds for what *happens* but rather laws for what *ought to happen* even if it never does, that is, objective practical laws, we do not need to undertake an investigation into the grounds on account of which something pleases or displeases; how the satisfaction of mere sensation differs from taste, and whether the latter differs from a general satisfaction of reason; upon what the feeling of pleasure of displeasure rests, and how from it desires and inclinations arise, and from them, with the cooperation of reason, maxims; for, all that belongs to an empirical doctrine of the soul,*ᵒ* which would constitute the second part of the doctrine of nature when this is regarded as *philosophy of nature* insofar as it is based *on empirical laws*. Here, however, it is a question of objective practical laws and hence of the relation of a will to itself insofar as it determines itself only by reason; for then everything that has reference to the empirical falls away of itself, since if reason entirely by itself determines conduct (and the possibility of this is just what we want now to investigate), it must necessarily do so a priori.

The will is thought as a capacity to determine itself to acting in conformity with the *representation of certain laws*. And such a capacity can be found only in rational beings. Now, what serves the will as the objective ground of its self-determination is an end, and this, if it is given by reason alone, must hold equally for all rational beings. What, on the other hand, contains merely the ground of the possibility of an action the effect of which is an end is called a *means*. The subjective ground of desire is an *incentive;* the objective ground of volition is a *motive;* hence the distinction between subjective ends, which rest on incentives, and objective ends, which depend on motives, which hold for every rational being. Practical principles are *formal* if they abstract from all subjective ends, whereas they are *material* if they have put these, and consequently certain incentives, at their basis. The ends that a rational being proposes at his discretion as *effects* of his actions (material ends) are all only relative; for only their mere relation to a specially constituted*ᵖ* faculty of desire on the part of the subject gives them their worth, which can therefore furnish no universal principles, no principles valid and necessary for all rational beings and also for every volition, that is, no practical laws. Hence all these relative ends are only the ground of hypothetical imperatives.

But suppose there were something the *existence of which in itself* has an absolute worth, something which as *an end in itself* could be a ground of determinate laws; then in it, and in it alone, would lie the ground of a possible categorical imperative, that is, of a practical law.

ⁿ anzunehmen
ᵒ Seelenlehre
ᵖ geartetes

Now I say that the human being and in general every rational being *exists* as an end in itself, *not merely as a means* to be used by this or that will at its discretion; instead he must in all his actions, whether directed to himself or also to other rational beings, always be regarded *at the same time as an end*. All objects of the inclinations have only a conditional worth; for, if there were not inclinations and the needs based on them, their object would be without worth. But the inclinations themselves, as sources of needs, are so far from having an absolute worth, so as to make one wish to have them,^q that it must instead be the universal wish of every rational being to be altogether free from them. Thus the worth of any object *to be acquired* by our action is always conditional. Beings the existence of which rests not on our will but on nature, if they are beings without reason, still have only a relative worth, as means, and are therefore called *things*,^r whereas rational beings are called *persons* because their nature already marks them out as and end in itself, that is, as something that may not be used merely as a means, and hence so far limits all choice (and is an object of respect). These, therefore, are not merely subjective ends, the existence of which as an effect of our action has a worth *for us*, but rather *objective ends*, that is, beings^s the existence of which is in itself an end, and indeed one such that no other end, to which they would serve *merely* as means, can be put in its place, since without it nothing of *absolute worth* would be found anywhere; but if all worth were conditional and therefore contingent, then no supreme practical principle for reason could be found anywhere.

If, then, there is to be a supreme practical principle and, with respect to the human will, a categorical imperative, it must be one such that, from the representation of what is necessarily an end for everyone because it is an *end in itself,* it constitutes an *objective* principle of the will and thus can serve as a universal practical law.^t The ground of this principle is: *rational nature exists as an end in itself.* The human being necessarily represents his own existence in this way; so far it is thus a *subjective* principle of human actions. But every other rational being also represents his existence in this way consequent on^u just the same rational ground that also holds for me;* thus it is at the same time an *objective* principle from which, as a supreme

4:429

---

*Here I put forward this proposition as a postulate. The grounds for it will be found in the last Section.
^q *um sie selbst zu wünschen*
^r *Sachen*
^s *Dinge*. Although both *Sache* and *Ding* would usually be translated as "thing," *Sache* has the technical sense of something usable that does not have free choice, i.e., "*Sache ist ein Ding*" to which nothing can be imputed (*The Metaphysics of Morals* 6:223).
^t *ausmacht, mithin zum allgemeinen praktischen Gesetz dienen kann.* It is not clear, grammatically, whether the subject of "can serve" is "end in itself" or "objective principle."
^u *zufolge*

practical ground, it must be possible to derive all laws of the will. The practical imperative will therefore be the following: *So act that you use humanity, whether in your own person or in the person of any other, always at the same time as an end, never merely as a means.* We shall see whether this can be carried out.

To keep to the preceding examples:

First, as regards the concept of necessary duty to oneself, someone who has suicide[v] in mind will ask himself whether his action can be consistent with the idea of humanity *as an end in itself.* If he destroys himself in order to escape from a trying condition he makes use of a person *merely as a means* to maintain a tolerable condition up to the end of life. A human being, however, is not a thing and hence not something that can be used *merely* as a means, but must in all his actions always be regarded as an end in itself. I cannot, therefore, dispose of a human being in my own person by maiming, damaging or killing him. (I must here pass over a closer determination of this principle that would prevent any misinterpretation, e.g., as to having limbs amputated in order to preserve myself, or putting my life in danger in order to preserve my life, and so forth; that belongs to morals proper.)

Second, as regards necessary duty to others or duty owed[w] them, he who has it in mind to make a false promise to others sees at once that he wants to make use of another human being *merely as a means,* without the other at the same time containing in himself the end. For, he whom I want to use for my purposes by such a promise cannot possibly agree to my way of behaving toward him, and so himself contain the end of this action. This conflict with the principle of other human beings is seen more distinctly if examples of assaults on the freedom and property of others are brought forward. For then it is obvious that he who transgresses the rights of human beings intends to make use of the person of others merely as means, without taking into consideration that, as rational beings, they are always to be valued at the same time as ends, that is, only as beings who must also be able to contain in themselves the end of the very same action.*

Third, with respect to contingent (meritorious) duty to oneself, it is not enough that the action does not conflict with humanity in our person as an

---

*Let it not be thought that the trite *quod tibi non vis fieri* etc.[x] can serve as norm of principle here. For it is, though with various limitations, only derived from the latter. It can be no universal law because it contains the ground neither of duties to oneself nor of duties of love to others (for many a man would gladly agree that others should not benefit him if only he might be excused from showing them beneficence), and finally it does not contain the ground of duties owed to others; for a criminal would argue on this ground against the judge punishing him, and so forth.

[v] *Selbstmorde,* perhaps "murdering himself." In *The Metaphysics of Morals, Selbstmord (homocidium dolosum),* is carefully distinguished from *Selbstentleibung (suicidium)* (6:421–4).

[w] *schuldige*

[x] what you do not want others to do to you, etc. [i.e., don't do the same to them].

end in itself; it must also *harmonize with it*. Now there are in humanity predispositions[y] to greater perfection, which belong to the end of nature with respect to humanity in our subject; to neglect these might admittedly be consistent with the *preservation* of humanity as an end in itself but not with the *furtherance* of this end.

Fourth, concerning meritorious duty to others, the natural end that all human beings have is their own happiness. Now, humanity might indeed subsist if no one contributed to the happiness of others but yet did not intentionally withdraw anything from it; but there is still only a negative and not a positive agreement with *humanity as an end in itself* unless everyone also tries, as far as he can, to further the ends of others. For, the ends of a subject who is an end in itself must as far as possible be also *my* ends, if that representation is to have its *full* effect in me.

This principle of humanity, and in general of every rational nature, *as an end in itself* (which is the supreme limiting condition of the freedom of action of every human being) is not borrowed from experience; first because of its universality, since it applies to all rational beings as such and no experience is sufficient to determine anything about them; second because in it humanity is represented not as an end of human beings (subjectively), that is, not as an object that we of ourselves actually make our end, but as an objective end that, whatever ends we may have, ought as law to constitute the supreme limiting condition of all subjective ends, so that the principle must arise from pure reason. That is to say, the ground of all practical lawgiving lies (in accordance with the first principle) *objectively in the rule* and the form of universality which makes it fit to be a law (possibly[z] a law of nature); *subjectively*, however, it lies in the *end;* but the subject of all ends is every rational being as an end in itself (in accordance with the second principle); from this there follows now the third practical principle of the will, as supreme condition of its harmony with universal practical reason, the idea *of the will of every rational being as a will giving universal law*.

4:431

In accordance with this principle all maxims are repudiated that are inconsistent with the will's own giving of universal law. Hence the will is not merely subject to the law but subject to it in such a way that it must be viewed as also giving the law to itself[a] and just because of this as first subject to the law (of which it can regard itself as the author).[b]

Imperatives as they were represented above – namely in terms of the conformity of actions with universal law similar to a *natural order* or of the universal *supremacy as ends*[c] of rational beings in themselves – did exclude

---

[y] *Anlagen*
[z] *allenfalls*
[a] Or "as itself lawgiving," *als selbstgesetzgebend*
[b] *Urheber*
[c] *Zweckvorzuges*

from their commanding authority any admixture of interest as incentive, just by their having been represented as categorical; but they were only *assumed*[d] to be categorical because we had to make such an assumption if we wanted to explain the concept of duty. But that there are practical propositions which command categorically could not itself be proved,[e] any more than it could be proved either here or anywhere else in this section; one thing, however, could still have been done: namely, to indicate in the imperative itself the renunciation of all interest, in volition from duty, by means of some determination the imperative contains, as the specific mark distinguishing[f] categorical from hypothetical imperatives; and this is done in the present third formula of the principle, namely the idea of the will of every rational being as a *will giving universal law*.

For when we think a will of this kind, then although a will that *stands under law* may be bound to this law by means of some interest, a will that is itself the supreme lawgiver cannot possibly, as such, depend upon some interest; for, a will that is dependent in this way would itself need yet another law that would limit the interest of its self-love to the condition of a validity for universal law.

Thus the *principle* of every human will as *a will giving universal law through all its maxims*,* provided it is otherwise correct, would be very *well suited* to be the categorical imperative by this: that just because of the idea of giving universal law *it is based on no interest* and therefore, among all possible imperatives, can alone be *unconditional;* or still better, by converting the proposition, if there is a categorical imperative (i.e., a law for every will of a rational being) it can only command that everything be done from the maxim of one's will as a will that could at the same time have as its object itself as giving universal law; for only then is the practical principle, and the imperative that the will obeys, unconditional, since it can have no interest as its basis.

If we look back upon all previous efforts that have ever been made to discover the principle of morality, we need not wonder now why all of them had to fail. It was seen that the human being is bound to laws by his duty, but it never occurred to them that he is subject *only to laws given by himself but still universal* and that he is bound only to act in conformity with his own will, which, however, in accordance with nature's end[g] is a will giving universal law. For, if one thought of him only as subject to a law (whatever it may be), this law had to carry with it some interest by way of

---

*I may be excused from citing examples to illustrate this principle, since those that have already illustrated the categorical imperative and its formula can all serve for the same end here.

[d] *angenommen*
[e] *bewiesen werden*
[f] *Unterscheidungszeichen*
[g] *dem Naturzwecke nach*

attraction or constraint, since it did not as a law arise from *his* will; in order to conform with the law, his will had instead to be constrained by *something else* to act in a certain way.*ʰ* By this quite necessary consequence, however, all the labor to find a supreme ground of duty was irretrievably lost. For, one never arrived at duty but instead at the necessity of an action from a certain interest. This might be one's own or another's interest. But then the imperative had to turn out always conditional and could not be fit for a moral command. I will therefore call this basic principle the principle of the **autonomy** of the will in contrast with every other, which I accordingly count as **heteronomy**.

The concept of every rational being as one who must regard himself as giving universal law through all the maxims of his will, so as to appraise himself and his actions from this point of view, leads to a very fruitful concept dependent upon it,*ⁱ* namely that *of a kingdomʲ of ends*.

By a *kingdom* I understand a systematic union of various rational beings through common laws. Now since laws determine ends in terms of their universal validity, if we abstract from the personal differences of rational beings as well as from all the content of their private ends we shall be able to think of a whole of all ends in systematic connection (a whole both of rational beings as ends in themselves and of the ends of his own that each may set himself), that is, a kingdom of ends, which is possible in accordance with the above principles.

For, all rational beings stand under the *law* that each of them is to treat himself and all others *never merely as means* but always *at the same time as ends in themselves*. But from this there arises a systematic union of rational beings through common objective laws, that is, a kingdom, which can be called a kingdom of ends (admittedly only an ideal) because what these laws have as their purpose is just the relation of these beings to one another as ends and means.

A rational being belongs as a *member* to the kingdom of ends when he gives universal laws in it but is also himself subject to these laws. He belongs to it *as sovereignᵏ* when, as lawgiving, he is not subject to the will of any other.

A rational being must always regard himself as lawgiving in a kingdom of ends possible through freedom of the will, whether as a member or as sovereign. He cannot, however, hold the position of sovereign merely by the maxims of his will but only in case he is a completely independent being, without needs and with unlimited resources*ˡ* adequate to his will.

4:434

ʰ sondern dieser gesetzmässig von etwas anderm genötigt wurde, auf gewisse Weise zu handeln
ⁱ Or "attached to it," *ihm anhangenden*
ʲ Reich, which could also be translated "commonwealth"
ᵏ als Oberhaupt
ˡ Vermögen

Morality consists, then, in the reference of all action to the lawgiving by which alone a kingdom of ends is possible. This lawgiving must, however, be found in every rational being himself and be able to arise from his will, the principle of which is, accordingly: to do no action on any other maxim than one such that it would be consistent with it to be a universal law, and hence to act only *so that the will could regard itself as at the same time giving universal law through its maxim.* Now, if maxims are not already of their nature in agreement with this objective principle of rational beings as givers of universal law, the necessity of an action in accordance with this principle is called practical necessitation, that is, *duty.* Duty does not apply to the sovereign in the kingdom of ends, but it does apply to every member of it and indeed to all in equal measure.

The practical necessity of acting in accordance with this principle, that is, duty, does not rest at all on feelings, impulses, and inclinations but merely on the relation of rational beings to one another, in which the will of a rational being must always be regarded as at the same time *lawgiving,* since otherwise it could not be thought as an *end in itself.* Reason accordingly refers every maxim of the will as giving universal law to every other will and also to every action toward oneself, and does so not for the sake of any other practical motive or any future advantage but from the idea of the *dignity* of a rational being, who obeys no law other than that which he himself at the same time gives.

In the kingdom of ends everything has either a *price* or a *dignity.*[m] What has a price can be replaced by something else as its *equivalent;* what on the other hand is raised above all price and therefore admits of no equivalent has a dignity.

What is related to general human inclinations and needs has a *market price;* that which, even without presupposing a need, conforms with a certain taste, that is, with a delight[n] in the mere purposeless[o] play of our mental powers, has a *fancy price;*[p] but that which constitutes the condition under which alone something can be an end in itself has not merely a relative worth, that is, a price, but an inner worth, that is, *dignity.*

Now, morality is the condition under which alone a rational being can be an end in itself, since only through this is it possible to be a lawgiving member in the kingdom of ends. Hence morality, and humanity insofar as it is capable of morality, is that which alone has dignity. Skill and diligence in work have a market price; wit, lively imagination and humor have a fancy price; on the other hand, fidelity in promises and benevolence from basic principles (not from instinct) have an inner worth. Nature, as well as

---

[m] *Würde*
[n] *Wohlgefallen*
[o] *zwecklosen*
[p] *Affectionspreis*

art, contains nothing that, lacking these, it could put in their place; for their worth does not consist in the effects arising from them, in the advantage and use they provide, but in dispositions,*q* that is, in maxims of the will that in this way are ready to manifest themselves through actions, even if success does not favor them. Such actions also need no recommendation from any subjective disposition*r* or taste, so as to be looked upon with immediate favor and delight, nor do they need any immediate propensity or feeling for them; they present the will that practices them as the object of an immediate respect, and nothing but reason is required to *impose* them upon the will, not to *coax* them from it, which latter would in any case be a contradiction in the case of duties. This estimation therefore lets the worth of such a cast of mind be cognized as dignity and puts it infinitely above all price, with which it cannot be brought into comparison or competition at all without, as it were, assaulting its holiness.*s*

And what is it, then, that justifies a morally good disposition, or virtue, in making such high claims? It is nothing less than the *share* it affords a rational being *in the giving of universal laws*, by which it makes him fit to be a member of a possible kingdom of ends, which he was already destined to be by his own nature as an end in itself and, for that very reason, as lawgiving in the kingdom of ends – as free with respect to all laws of nature, obeying only those which he himself gives and in accordance with which his maxims can belong to a giving of universal law (to which at the same time he subjects himself). For, nothing can have a worth other than that which the law determines for it. But the lawgiving itself, which determines all worth, must for that very reason have a dignity, that is, an unconditional, incomparable worth; and the word *respect* alone provides a becoming expression for the estimate of it that a rational being must give. *Autonomy* is therefore the ground of the dignity of human nature and of every rational nature.

4:436

The above three ways of representing the principle of morality are at bottom only so many formulae of the very same law, and any one of them of itself unites the other two in it. There is nevertheless a difference among them, which is indeed subjectively rather than objectively practical, intended namely to bring an idea of reason closer to intuition (by a certain analogy) and thereby to feeling. All maxims have, namely,

1) a *form*, which consists in universality; and in this respect the formula of the moral imperative is expressed thus: that maxims must be chosen*t* as if they were to hold as universal laws of nature;
2) a *matter*, namely an end, and in this respect the formula says that a

---

q Gesinnungen
r Disposition
s Heiligkeit
t so müssen gewählt werden

rational being, as an end by its nature and hence as an end in itself, must in every maxim serve as the limiting condition of all merely relative and arbitrary*u* ends;

3) *a complete determination* of all maxims by means of that formula, namely that all maxims from one's own lawgiving are to harmonize with a possible kingdom of ends as with a kingdom of nature.* A progression takes place here, as through the categories of the *unity* of the form of the will (its universality), the *plurality* of the matter (of objects, i.e., of ends), and the *allness*^v or totality of the system of these. But one does better always to proceed in moral *appraisal* by the strict method and put at its basis the universal formula of the categorical imperative: *act in accordance with a maxim that can at the same time make itself a universal law.* If, however, one wants also to provide *access* for the moral law, it is very useful to bring one and the same action under the three concepts mentioned above and thereby, as far as possible, bring it closer to intuition.

We can now end where we set out from at the beginning, namely with the concept of a will unconditionally good. *That will is absolutely good* which cannot be evil, hence whose maxim, if made a universal law, can never conflict with itself. This principle is, accordingly, also its supreme law: act always on that maxim whose universality as a law you can at the same time will; this is the sole condition under which a will can never be in conflict with itself, and such an imperative is categorical. Since the validity of the will as a universal law for possible actions has an analogy with the universal connection of the existence of things in accordance with universal laws, which is the formal aspect of nature in general, the categorical imperative can also be expressed thus: *act in accordance with maxims that can at the same time have as their object themselves as universal laws of nature.* In this way, then, the formula of an absolutely good will is provided.

Rational nature is distinguished from the rest of nature by this, that it sets itself an end. This end would be the matter of every good will. But since, in the idea of a will absolutely good without any limiting condition (attainment of this or that end) abstraction must be made altogether from every end to be *effected* (this would make every will only relatively good), the end must here be thought not as an end to be effected but as an *independently existing*^w end, and hence thought only negatively, that is, as

---

*Teleology considers nature as a kingdom of ends, *morals* considers a possible kingdom of ends as a kingdom of nature. In the former the kingdom of ends is a theoretical idea for explaining what exists. In the latter, it is a practical idea for the sake of bringing about, in conformity with this very idea, that which does not exist but which can become real by means of our conduct.

^u *willkürlichen*
^v *Allheit*
^w *selbstständiger*

that which must never be acted against and which must therefore in every volition be estimated never merely as a means but always at the same time as an end. Now, this end can be nothing other than the subject of all possible ends itself, because this subject is also the subject of a possible absolutely good will; for, such a will cannot without contradiction be subordinated to any other object. The principle, so act with reference to every rational being (yourself and others) that in your maxim it holds at the same time as an end in itself, is thus at bottom the same as the basic principle, act on a maxim that at the same time contains in itself its own universal validity for every rational being. For, to say that in the use of means to any end I am to limit my maxim to the condition of its universal validity as a law for every subject is tantamount to saying that the subject of ends, that is, the rational being itself, must be made the basis of all maxims of actions, never merely as a means but as the supreme limiting condition in the use of all means, that is, always at the same time as an end.

4:438

Now, from this it follows incontestably that every rational being, as an end in itself, must be able to regard himself as also giving universal laws with respect to any law whatsoever to which he may be subject; for, it is just this fitness of his maxims for giving universal law that marks him out as an end in itself; it also follows that this dignity (prerogative) he has over all merely natural beings brings with it that he must always take his maxims from the point of view of himself, and likewise every other rational being, as lawgiving beings (who for this reason are also called persons). Now in this way a world of rational beings (*mundus intelligibilis*)[x] as a kingdom of ends is possible, through the giving of their own laws[y] by all persons as members. Consequently, every rational being must act as if he were by his maxims at all times a lawgiving member of the universal kingdom of ends. The formal principle of these maxims is, act as if your maxims were to serve at the same time as a universal law (for all rational beings). A kingdom of ends is thus possible only by analogy with a kingdom of nature; the former, however, is possible only through maxims, that is, rules imposed upon oneself, the latter only through laws of externally necessitated efficient causes. Despite this, nature as a whole, even though it is regarded as a machine, is still given the name "a kingdom of nature" insofar as and because it has reference to[z] rational beings as its ends. Now, such a kingdom of ends would actually come into existence through maxims whose rule the categorical imperative prescribes to all rational beings *if they were universally followed.* It is true that, even though a rational being scrupulously follows this maxim himself, he cannot for that reason

---

[x] intelligible world
[y] *durch die eigene Gesetzgebung*

count upon every other to be faithful to the same maxim nor can he count upon the kingdom of nature and its purposive order to harmonize with him, as a fitting member, toward a kingdom of ends possible through himself, that is, upon its favoring his expectation of happiness; nevertheless that law, act in accordance with the maxims of a member giving universal laws for a merely possible kingdom of ends, remains in its full force because it commands categorically. And just in this lies the paradox that the mere dignity of humanity as rational nature, without any other end or advantage to be attained by it – hence respect for a mere idea – is yet to serve as an inflexible precept of the will, and that it is just in this independence of maxims from all such incentives that their sublimity consists, and the worthiness of every rational subject to be a lawgiving member in the kingdom of ends; for otherwise he would have to be represented only as subject to the natural law of his needs. Even if the kingdom of nature as well as the kingdom of ends were thought as united under one sovereign, so that the latter would no longer remain a mere idea but would obtain true reality, it would no doubt gain the increment of a strong incentive but never any increase of its inner worth; for, even this sole absolute lawgiver would, despite this, still have to be represented as appraising the worth of rational beings only by their disinterested conduct, prescribed to themselves merely from that idea. The essence of things is not changed by their external relations; and that which, without taking account of such relations, alone constitutes the worth of a human being is that in terms of which he must also be appraised by whoever does it, even by the supreme being. *Morality* is thus the relation of actions to the autonomy of the will, that is, to a possible giving of universal law through its maxims. An action that can coexist with the autonomy of the will is *permitted;* one that does not accord with it is *forbidden.* A will whose maxims necessarily harmonize with the laws of autonomy is a *holy,* absolutely good will. The dependence upon the principle of autonomy of a will that is not absolutely good (moral necessitation) is *obligation.* This, accordingly, cannot be attributed to a holy being. The objective necessity of an action from obligation is called *duty.*

From what has just been said it is now easy to explain how it happens that, although in thinking the concept of duty we think of subjection to the law, yet at the same time we thereby represent a certain sublimity and *dignity* in the person who fulfills all his duties. For there is indeed no sublimity in him insofar as he is *subject* to the moral law, but there certainly is insofar as he is at the same time *lawgiving* with respect to it and only for that reason subordinated to it. We have also shown above how neither fear nor inclination but simply respect for the law is that incentive which can give actions a moral worth. Our own will insofar as it would act only under the condition of a possible giving of universal law through its maxims – this will possible for us in idea – is the proper object of respect; and the dignity of humanity consists just in this capacity to give universal law, though with the condition of also being itself subject to this very lawgiving.

AUTONOMY OF THE WILL
AS THE SUPREME PRINCIPLE OF MORALITY

Autonomy of the will is the property*a* of the will by which it is a law to itself (independently of any property of the objects of volition). The principle of autonomy is, therefore: to choose only in such a way that the maxims of your choice*b* are also included*c* as universal law in the same volition. That this practical rule is an imperative, that is, that the will of every rational being is necessarily bound to it as a condition, cannot be proved by mere analysis*d* of the concepts to be found in it, because it is a synthetic proposition; one would have to go beyond cognition of objects to a critique of the subject, that is, of pure practical reason, since this synthetic proposition, which commands apodictically, must be capable of being cognized completely a priori. This business, however, does not belong in the present section. But that the above principle of autonomy is the sole principle of morals can well be shown by mere analysis of the concepts of morality. For, by this analysis we find that its principle must be a categorical imperative, while this commands neither more nor less than just this autonomy.

HETERONOMY OF THE WILL 4:441
AS THE SOURCE OF ALL SPURIOUS PRINCIPLES OF MORALITY

If the will seeks the law that is to determine it *anywhere else* than in the fitness of its maxims for its own giving of universal law – consequently if, in going beyond itself, it seeks this law in a property of any of its objects – *heteronomy* always results. The will in that case does not give itself the law; instead the object, by means of its relation to the will, gives the law to it. This relation, whether it rests upon inclination or upon representations of reason, lets only hypothetical imperatives become possible: I ought to do something *because I will something else.* On the contrary, the moral and therefore categorical imperative says: I ought to act in such or such a way even though I have not willed anything else. For example, the former says: I ought not to lie if I will to keep my reputation; but the latter says: I ought

---

a Beschaffenheit
b zu wählen also so, dass die Maximen seiner Wahl. Kant has apparently not yet drawn the distinction between *Wille* ("the will") and *Willkür* ("choice" or "the power of choice") so prominent in *The Metaphysics of Morals.*
c mit begriffen seien
d Zergliederung

not to lie even though it would not bring me the least discredit. The latter must therefore abstract from all objects to this extent: that they have no *influence* at all on the will, so that practical reason (the will) may not merely administer an interest not belonging to it,[c] but may simply show its own commanding authority as supreme lawgiving. Thus, for example, I ought to try to further the happiness of others, not as if its existence were of any consequence to me (whether because of immediate inclination or because of some indirect agreeableness through reason), but simply because a maxim that excludes this cannot be included as a universal law in one and the same volition.

DIVISION
OF ALL POSSIBLE PRINCIPLES OF MORALITY TAKEN FROM HETERONOMY ASSUMED AS THE BASIC CONCEPT

Here, as everywhere else, human reason in its pure use, as long as it lacks a critique, first tries all possible wrong ways before it succeeds in finding the only true way.

All principles that can be taken from this point of view are either *empirical* or *rational*. The **first**, taken from the principle of *happiness*, are built upon physical or moral feeling; the second, taken from the principle of *perfection*, are built either upon the rational concept of perfection as a possible effect of our will or upon the concept of an independently existing perfection (the will of God) as the determining cause of our will.

Empirical principles are not at all fit to be the ground of moral laws. For, the universality with which these are to hold for all rational beings without distinction – the unconditional practical necessity which is thereby imposed upon them – comes to nothing if their ground is taken from the *special constitution of human nature* or the contingent circumstances in which it is placed. The principle of *one's own happiness*, however, is the most objectionable, not merely because it is false and experience contradicts the pretense that well-being always proportions itself to good conduct, nor yet merely because it contributes nothing at all to the establishment of morality, since making someone happy is quite different from making him good, or making him prudent and sharp-sighted for his own advantage is quite different from making him virtuous; it is the most objectionable because it bases morality on incentives that undermine it and destroy all its sublimity, since they put motives to virtue and those to vice in one class and only teach us to calculate better, but quite obliterate

---

[c] *fremdes Interesse. Fremd* is also translated as "alien," "foreign," or "another's."

the specific difference between virtue and vice. On the other hand, moral feeling – this supposed special sense,* (however superficial the appeal to it is, inasmuch as those who cannot *think* believe they can help themselves out by feeling in what has to do merely with universal law,[f] and however little feelings, which by nature differ infinitely from one another in degree, can furnish a uniform standard of good and evil, and one cannot judge validly for others by means of one's feeling) – nevertheless remains closer to morality and its dignity inasmuch as it shows virtue the honor of ascribing to her *immediately* the delight[g] and esteem we have for her and does not, as it were, tell her to her face that it is not her beauty but only our advantage that attaches us to her.

4:443

Among the *rational* grounds of morality or those based on reason,[h] the ontological concept of *perfection* (however empty, however indeterminate and hence useless it is for finding, in the immeasurable field of possible reality, the greatest sum appropriate to us; and however much, in trying to distinguish specifically the reality here in question from every other, it has an unavoidable propensity to get involved in a circle and cannot avoid covertly presupposing the morality which it is supposed to explain) is nevertheless better than the theological concept, which derives morality from a divine, all-perfect will; it is better not merely because we cannot intuit the perfection of this will but can only derive it from our concepts, among which that of morality is foremost, but because if we do not do this (and to do it would be a grossly circular explanation), the concept of his will still left to us, made up of the attributes[i] of desire for glory and dominion combined with dreadful representations of power and vengefulness, would have to be the foundation for a system of morals that would be directly opposed to morality.

But if I had to choose between the concept of the moral sense and that of perfection generally (both of which at least do not infringe upon morality, even though they are not at all fit to support it as its foundation), then I should decide[j] for the latter; for, since it at least withdraws the decision of the question from sensibility and brings it to the court of pure reason,

---

*I count the principle of moral feeling under that of happiness because every empirical interest promises to contribute to our well-being by the agreeableness that something affords, whether this happens immediately and without a view to advantage or with regard for it. One must likewise, with Hutcheson,[6] count the principle of sympathy with the happiness of others under the moral sense assumed by him.

[f] It is not altogether clear whether the clause "in what has to do merely with universal law" modifies "think" or "feeling."

[g] *Wohlgefallen*

[h] *Unter den rationalen oder Vernunftgründen*

[i] *Eigenschaften*

[j] *bestimmen*

even though it decides nothing there it still preserves the indeterminate idea (of a will good in itself) unfalsified, for closer determination.

For the rest, I believe I may be excused from a lengthy refutation of all these doctrines.[k] That is so easy, and is presumably so well seen even by those whose office requires them to declare themselves for one of these theories (because their hearers would not tolerate suspension of judgment), that it would be merely superfluous labor. But what interests us more here is to know that all these principles set up nothing other than heteronomy of the will as the first ground of morality, and just because of this they must necessarily fail in their end.

Wherever an object of the will has to be laid down as the basis for prescribing the rule that determines the will, there the rule is none other than heteronomy; the imperative is conditional, namely: *if* or *because* one wills this object, one ought to act in such or such a way; hence it can never command morally, that is, categorically. Whether the object determines the will by means of inclination, as in the principle of one's own happiness, or by means of reason directed to objects of our possible volition in general, as in the principle of perfection, the will never determines itself *immediately*, just by the representation of an action, but only by means of an incentive that the anticipated effect of the action has upon the will: *I ought to do something on this account, that I will something else,* and here yet another law must be put as a basis in me, the subject, in accordance with which I necessarily will this something else, which law in turn needs an imperative that would limit this maxim. For, because the impulse that the representation of an object possible through our powers is to exert on the will of the subject in accordance with his natural constitution belongs to the nature of the subject – whether to his sensibility (inclination and taste) or to his understanding and reason, which by the special constitution of their nature employ themselves with delight[l] upon an object – it would, strictly speaking, be nature that gives the law; and this, as a law of nature, must not only be cognized and proved by experience – and is therefore in itself contingent and hence unfit for an apodictic practical rule, such as moral rules must be – but it is *always only heteronomy* of the will; the will would not give itself the law but a foreign impulse would give the law to it by means of the subject's nature, which is attuned to be receptive to it.

An absolutely good will, whose principle must be a categorical imperative, will therefore, indeterminate with respect to all objects, contain merely the *form* of *volition* as such and indeed as autonomy; that is, the fitness of the maxims of every good will to make themselves into universal law is itself the sole law that the will of every rational being imposes upon

---

[k] *Lehrbegriffe*
[l] *Wohlgefallen*

itself, without having to put underneath it some incentive or interest as a basis.

How such a synthetic practical proposition is possible a priori and why it is necessary is a problem whose solution does not lie within the bounds of metaphysics of morals, and we have not here affirmed its truth, much less pretended to have a proof of it in our power. By explicating the generally received concept of morality we showed only that an autonomy of the will unavoidably depends upon it,*ᵐ* or much rather lies at its basis. Thus whoever holds morality to be something and not a chimerical idea without any truth must also admit the principle of morality brought forward. This section then, like the first, was merely analytic. That morality is no phantom – and this follows if the categorical imperative, and with it the autonomy of the will, is true and absolutely necessary as an a priori principle – requires a possible *synthetic use of pure practical reason*, which use, however, we cannot venture upon without prefacing it by a *critique* of this rational faculty itself, the main features of which we have to present, sufficiently for our purpose, in the last section.

4:445

ᵐ anhänge, perhaps "is attached to it"

4:446

Section III
Transition from metaphysics of morals to the critique of pure practical reason

THE CONCEPT OF FREEDOM IS THE KEY TO THE EXPLANATION[n] OF THE AUTONOMY OF THE WILL

Will is a kind of causality of living beings insofar as they are rational, and *freedom* would be that property[o] of such causality that it can be efficient independently of alien causes *determining it*, just as *natural necessity* is the property of the causality of all nonrational beings to be determined to activity by the influence of alien causes.

The preceding definition[p] of freedom is *negative* and therefore unfruitful for insight into[q] its essence; but there flows from it a *positive* concept of freedom, which is so much the richer and more fruitful. Since the concept of causality brings with it that of laws in accordance with which, by something that we call a cause, something else, namely an effect, must be posited, so freedom, although it is not a property of the will in accordance with natural laws, is not for that reason lawless but must instead be a causality in accordance with immutable laws but of a special kind; for otherwise a free will would be an absurdity.[r] Natural necessity was a heteronomy of efficient causes, since every effect was possible only in accordance with the law that something else determines the efficient cause to causality; what, then, can freedom of the will be other than autonomy, that is, the will's property of being a law to itself? But the proposition, the will is in all its actions a law to itself, indicates only the principle, to act on no other maxim than that which can also have as object itself as a universal law. This, however, is precisely the formula of the

4:447

---

[n] *Erklärung*
[o] *Eigenschaft*
[p] *Erklärung*. On the translation of *Erklärung* see *The Metaphysics of Morals* (6:226).
[q] *einzusehen*. As was noted above, Kant seems on the whole to use *einsehen* informally. In the Jäsche *Logik* (9: 64–65), however, he distinguishes seven levels of *Erkenntnis* in the general sense, the sixth of which is *einsehen (perspicere)*, i.e., to cognize through reason or a priori, and the seventh *begreifen (comprehendere)*, which adds to *einsehen* "sufficiently for our purpose." Some passages in Section III, notably 4:459 and 460, suggest that he has this distinction in mind.
[r] *Unding*

94

categorical imperative and is the principle of morality; hence a free will and a will under moral laws are one and the same.

If, therefore, freedom of the will is presupposed, morality together with its principle follows from it by mere analysis of its concept. But the principle of morality – that an absolutely good will is that whose maxim can always contain itself regarded as a universal law – is nevertheless always a synthetic proposition; for, by analysis of the concept of an absolutely good will that property of its maxim cannot be discovered. Such synthetic propositions are possible only in this way: that the two cognitions are bound together*^t* by their connection with a third in which they are both to be found. The *positive* concept of freedom provides this third cognition, which cannot be, as in the case of physical causes, the nature of the sensible world (in the concept of which the concepts of something as cause in relation to *something else* as effect come together). What this third cognition is, to which freedom points us and of which we have an idea a priori, cannot yet be shown here and now; nor can the deduction of the concept of freedom from pure practical reason, and with it the possibility of a categorical imperative as well, as yet be made comprehensible; instead, some further preparation is required.

FREEDOM MUST BE PRESUPPOSED AS A PROPERTY OF THE WILL OF ALL RATIONAL BEINGS

It is not enough that we ascribe freedom to our will on whatever ground, if we do not have sufficient ground for attributing it also to all rational beings. For, since morality serves as a law for us only as rational beings, it must also hold for all rational beings; and since it must be derived solely from the property of freedom, freedom must also be proved*^t* as a property of all rational beings; and it is not enough to demonstrate*^u* it from certain supposed experiences of human nature (though this is also absolutely impossible and it can be demonstrated only a priori), but it must be proved as belonging to the activity of all beings whatever that are rational and endowed with a will. I say now: every being that cannot act otherwise than *under the idea of freedom* is just because of that really free in a practical respect, that is, all laws that are inseparably bound up with freedom hold for him just as if his will had been validly pronounced*^v* free also in itself and in theoretical philosophy.* Now I assert that to every rational being

4:448

---
^t *untereinander verbunden werden*
^t *bewiesen*
^u *darzutun*
^v *gültig für frei erklärt würde*
*I follow this route – that of assuming freedom, sufficiently for our purpose, only as laid down by rational beings merely *in idea* as a ground for their actions – so that I need not be

having a will we must necessarily lend the idea of freedom also, under which alone he acts. For in such a being we think of a reason that is practical, that is, has causality with respect to its objects. Now, one cannot possibly think of a reason that would consciously receive direction from any other quarter with respect to its judgments, since the subject would then attribute the determination of his judgment not to his reason but to an impulse. Reason must regard itself as the author of its principles independently of alien influences; consequently, as practical reason or as the will of a rational being it must be regarded of itself as free, that is, the will of such a being cannot be a will of his own except under the idea of freedom, and such a will must in a practical respect*ˣ* thus be attributed to every rational being.

OF THE INTEREST ATTACHING *ʸ* TO THE IDEAS OF MORALITY

We have finally traced the determinate concept of morality back to the idea of freedom; but we could not even prove the latter as something real in ourselves and in human nature; we saw only that we must presuppose it if we want to think of a being as rational and endowed with consciousness of his causality with respect to actions, that is, with a will, and so we find that on just the same grounds we must assign to every being endowed with reason and will this property of determining himself to action under the idea of his freedom.

But there also flowed from the presupposition of this idea consciousness of a law for acting: that subjective principles of actions, that is, maxims, must always be so adopted that they can also hold as objective, that is, hold universally as principles, and so serve for our own giving of universal laws. But why, then, ought I to subject myself to this principle and do so imply as a rational being, thus also subjecting to it all other beings endowed with reason? I am willing to admit that no interest *impels* me to do so, for that would not give a categorical imperative; but I must still necessarily *take* an interest in it and have insight into how this comes about; for this "ought" is strictly speaking a "will"*ᶻ* that holds for every rational being under the condition that reason in him is practical without hindrance; but for beings

4:449

ʷ bound to prove freedom in its theoretical respect*ʷ* as well. For even if the latter is left unsettled, still the same laws hold for a being that cannot act otherwise than under the idea of its own freedom as would bind a being that was actually free. Thus we can escape here from the burden that weighs upon theory.

ʷ Absicht

ˣ in praktischer Absicht. The subject of "must be attributed" could be either "this idea" or "such a will."

ʸ welches den Ideen . . . anhängt

ᶻ dieses Sollen ist eigentlich ein Wollen

like us – who are also affected by sensibility, by incentives of a different kind, and in whose case that which reason by itself would do is not always done – that necessity of action is called only an "ought," and the subjective necessity is distinguished from the objective.

It seems, then, that in the idea of freedom we have actually only presupposed the moral law, namely the principle of the autonomy of the will itself, and could not prove by itself its reality and objective necessity; and in that case we should still have gained something considerable by at least determining the genuine principle more accurately than had previously been done, but we should have got no further with respect to its validity and the practical necessity of subjecting oneself to it; for, if someone asked us why the universal validity of our maxim as a law must be the limiting condition of our actions, and on what we base the worth we assign to this way of acting – a worth so great that there can be no higher interest anywhere – and asked us how it happens that a human being believes that only through this does he feel his personal worth, in comparison with which that of an agreeable or disagreeable condition[a] is to be held as nothing, we could give him no satisfactory answer.

We do indeed find that we can take an interest in a personal characteristic[b] that brings with it no interest at all in a condition, if only the former makes us fit to participate in the latter in case reason were to effect the distribution, that is, that mere worthiness to be happy, even without the motive of participating in this happiness, can interest us of itself; but this judgment is in fact only the result of the importance we have already supposed belongs to the moral law (when by the idea of freedom we detach ourselves from all empirical interest); but we cannot yet see, in this way, that we ought to detach ourselves from such interest, that is, to regard ourselves as free in acting and so to hold ourselves yet subject to certain laws in order to find merely in our own person a worth that can compensate us for the loss of everything that provides a worth to our condition; and we cannot yet see how this is possible, and hence *on what grounds*[c] *the moral law is binding.*

It must be freely admitted that a kind of circle comes to light here from which, as it seems, there is no way to escape. We take ourselves as free in the order of efficient causes in order to think ourselves under moral laws in the order of ends; and we afterwards think ourselves as subject to these laws because we have ascribed to ourselves freedom of will; for, freedom and the will's own lawgiving are both autonomy and hence reciprocal concepts, and for this very reason one cannot be used to explain the other or to furnish a ground for it but can at most be used only for the logical

4:450

---

[a] *Zustand*
[b] *Beschaffenheit*
[c] *woher*

purpose of reducing apparently different representations of the same object to one single concept (as different fractions of equal value are reduced to their lowest expression).

One resource, however, still remains to us, namely to inquire whether we do not take a different standpoint when by means of freedom we think ourselves as causes efficient a priori than when we represent ourselves in terms of our actions as effects that we see before our eyes.

No subtle reflection is required to make the following remark, and one may assume that the commonest understanding can make it, though in its own way, by an obscure discrimination of judgment which it calls feeling: that all representations which come to us involuntarily[d] (as do those of the senses) enable us to cognize objects only as they affect us and we remain ignorant of what they may be in themselves so that, as regards representations of this kind, even with the most strenuous attentiveness and distinctness that the understanding can ever bring to them we can achieve only cognition *of appearances,* never of *things in themselves.* As soon as this distinction has once been made (perhaps merely by means of the difference noticed between representations given us from somewhere else and in which we are passive, and those that we produce simply from ourselves and in which we show our activity), then it follows of itself that we must admit and assume behind appearances something else that is not appearance, namely things in themselves, although, since we can never become acquainted with them but only with how they affect us, we resign ourselves to being unable to come any closer to them or ever to know what they are in themselves. This must yield a distinction, although a crude one, between a *world of sense* and the *world of understanding,* the first of which can be very different according to the difference of sensibility in various observers of the world while the second, which is its basis, always remains the same. Even as to himself, the human being cannot claim to cognize what he is in himself through the cognizance he has by inner sensation. For, since he does not as it were create himself and does not get his concept a priori but empirically, it is natural that he can obtain information even about himself only through inner sense and so only through the appearance of his nature and the way in which his consciousness is affected — although beyond this constitution of his own subject, made up of nothing but appearances, he must necessarily assume something else lying at their basis, namely his ego as it may be constituted in itself; and thus as regards mere perception and receptivity to sensations he must count himself as belonging to the *world of sense,* but with regard to what there may be of pure activity in him (what reaches consciousness immediately and not through affection of the senses) he must count himself as belonging to the *intellectual world,* of which however he has no further cognizance.

[d] *ohne unsere Willkür*

A reflective human being must come to a conclusion of this kind about all the things that present themselves to him; presumably it is also to be found even in the most common understanding, which, as is well known, is very much inclined to expect behind the objects of the senses something else invisible and active of itself – but it spoils this again by quickly making this invisible something sensible in turn, that is, wanting to make it an object of intuition, so that it does not thereby become any the wiser.

Now, a human being really finds in himself a capacity by which he distinguishes himself from all other things, even from himself insofar as he is affected by objects, and that is *reason.* This, as pure self-activity, is raised even above the *understanding* by this: that though the latter is also self-activity and does not, like sense, contain merely representations that arise when we are *affected* by things (and are thus passive), yet it can produce from its activity no other concepts than those which serve merely *to bring sensible representations under rules* and thereby to unite them in one consciousness, without which use of sensibility it would think nothing at all; but reason, on the contrary, shows in what we call "ideas" a spontaneity so pure that it thereby goes far beyond anything that sensibility can ever afford it, and proves its highest occupation in distinguishing the world of sense and the world of understanding from each other and thereby marking out limits for the understanding itself.

Because of this a rational being must regard himself *as intelligence* (hence not from the side of his lower powers) as belonging not to the world of sense but to the world of understanding; hence he has two standpoints from which he can regard himself and cognize laws for the use of his powers and consequently for all his actions; *first,* insofar as he belongs to the world of sense, under laws of nature (heteronomy); *second,* as belonging to the intelligible world, under laws which, being independent of nature, are not empirical but grounded merely in reason.

As a rational being, and thus as a being belonging to the intelligible world, the human being can never think of the causality of his own will otherwise than under the idea of freedom; for, independence from the determining causes of the world of sense (which reason must always ascribe to itself) is freedom. With the idea of freedom the concept of *autonomy* is now inseparably combined, and with the concept of autonomy the universal principle of morality, which in idea is the ground of all actions of *rational beings,* just as the law of nature is the ground of all appearances.

The suspicion that we raised above is now removed, the suspicion that a hidden circle was contained in our inference from freedom to autonomy and from the latter to the moral law – namely that we perhaps took as a ground the idea of freedom only for the sake of the moral law, so that we could afterwards infer the latter in turn from freedom, and that we were thus unable to furnish any ground at all for the moral law but could put it forward only as a *petitio principii*[e] disposed souls would gladly grant us, but never as a demonstrable[f] proposition. For we now see that when we think of ourselves as free we transfer ourselves into the world of understanding as members of it and cognize autonomy of the will along with its consequence, morality; but if we think of ourselves as put under obligation[g] we regard ourselves as belonging to the world of sense and yet at the same time to the world of understanding.

HOW IS A CATEGORICAL IMPERATIVE POSSIBLE?

A rational being counts himself, as intelligence, as belonging to the world of understanding, and only as an efficient cause belonging to this does he call his causality a *will*. On the other side he is also conscious of himself as a part of the world of sense, in which his actions are found as mere appearances of that causality; but their possibility from that causality of which we are not cognizant cannot be seen; instead, those actions as belonging to the world of sense must be regarded as determined by other appearances, namely desires and inclinations. All my actions as only a member of the world of understanding would therefore conform perfectly with the principle of autonomy of the pure will; as only a part of the world of sense they would have to be taken to conform wholly to the natural law of desires and inclinations, hence to the heteronomy of nature. (The former would rest on the supreme principle of morality, the latter on that of happiness.) But because *the world of understanding contains the ground of the world of sense and so too of its laws*, and is therefore immediately lawgiving with respect to my will (which belongs wholly to the world of understanding) and must accordingly also be thought as such, it follows that I shall cognize myself as intelligence, though on the other side as a being belonging to the world of sense, as nevertheless subject to the law of the world of understanding, that is, of reason, which contains in the idea of freedom the law of the world of understanding, and thus cognize myself as subject to the autonomy of the will; consequently the laws of the world of understanding must be regarded as imperatives for me, and actions in conformity with these as duties.

And so categorical imperatives are possible by this: that the idea of freedom makes me a member of an intelligible world and consequently, if I were only this, all my actions *would* always be in conformity with the autonomy of the will; but since at the same time I intuit myself as a member of the world of sense, they *ought* to be in conformity with it; and this *categorical* ought represents a synthetic proposition a priori, since to my will affected

---

[e] *Erbittung des Prinzips*
[f] *erweislichen*
[g] *als verpflichtet*

by sensible desires there is added the idea of the same will but belonging to the world of the understanding – a will pure and practical of itself, which contains the supreme condition, in accordance with reason, of the former will; this is roughly like the way in which concepts of the understanding, which by themselves signify nothing but lawful form in general, are added to intuitions of the world of sense and thereby make possible synthetic propositions a priori on which all cognition of a nature rests.

The practical use of common human reason confirms the correctness of this deduction. There is no one – not even the most hardened scoundrel, if only he is otherwise accustomed to use reason – who, when one sets before him examples of honesty of purpose, of steadfastness in following good maxims, of sympathy and general benevolence (even combined with great sacrifices of advantage and comfort), does not wish that he might also be so disposed. He cannot indeed bring this about in himself, though only because of his inclinations and impulses; yet at the same time he wishes to be free from such inclinations, which are burdensome to himself. Hence he proves, by this, that with a will free from impulses of sensibility he transfers himself in thought into an order of things altogether different from that of his desires in the field of sensibility, since from that wish he can expect no satisfaction of his desires and hence no condition[h] that would satisfy any of his actual or otherwise imaginable inclinations (for if he expected this, the very idea which elicits that wish from him would lose its preeminence); he can expect only a greater inner worth of his person. This better person, however, he believes himself to be when he transfers himself to the standpoint of a member of the world of understanding, as the idea of freedom, that is, of independence from *determining* causes of the world of sense, constrains him involuntarily[i] to do; and from this standpoint he is conscious of a good will that, by his own acknowledgments, constitutes the law for his evil will as a member of the world of sense – a law of whose authority he is cognizant even while he transgresses it. The moral "*ought*" is then his own necessary "*will*" as a member of an intelligible world, and is thought by him as "ought" only insofar as he regards himself at the same time as a member of the world of sense.

4:455

ON THE EXTREME BOUNDARY OF ALL PRACTICAL PHILOSOPHY

All human beings think of themselves as having free will.[j] From this come all judgments upon actions as being such that they *ought to have been done even though they were not done.* Yet this freedom is no concept of experi-

---
[h] *Zustand*
[i] *unwillkürlich*
[j] *denken sich dem Willen nach als frei*

ence, and moreover cannot be one, since it always remains even though experience shows the opposite of those requirements that are represented as necessary under the presupposition of freedom. On the other side, it is equally necessary that everything which takes place should be determined without exception in accordance with laws of nature; and this natural necessity is also no concept of experience, just because it brings with it the concept of necessity and hence of an a priori cognition. But this concept of a nature is confirmed by experience and must itself unavoidably be presupposed if experience, that is, coherent cognition of objects of the senses in accordance with universal laws, is to be possible. Hence freedom is only an *idea* of reason, the objective reality of which is in itself doubtful, whereas nature is a *concept of the understanding* that proves, and must necessarily prove, its reality in examples from experience.

From this there arises a dialectic of reason since, with respect to the will, the freedom ascribed to it seems to be in contradiction with natural necessity; and at this parting of the ways reason *for speculative purposes* finds the road of natural necessity much more traveled and more usable than that of freedom; yet *for practical purposes* the footpath of freedom is the only one on which it is possible to make use of our reason in our conduct; hence it is just as impossible for the most subtle philosophy as for the most common human reason to argue freedom away. Philosophy must therefore assume that no true contradiction will be found between freedom and natural necessity in the very same human actions, for it cannot give up the concept of nature any more than that of freedom.

Nevertheless, this seeming contradiction must be removed in a convincing way, even though we shall never be able to comprehend how freedom is possible. For if even the thought of freedom contradicts itself or contradicts nature, which is equally necessary, it would have to be given up altogether in favor of natural necessity.

It would, however, be impossible to escape this contradiction if the subject who seems to himself free thought of himself *in the same sense* or *in the very same relation* when he calls himself free as when he takes himself to be subject to the law of nature with regard to the same action. Hence it is an indispensable task of speculative philosophy at least to show that its illusion[k] about the contradiction rests on our thinking of the human being in a different sense and relation when we call him free and when we hold him, as a part of nature, to be subject to its laws, and to show that both not only *can* very well coexist but also must be thought as *necessarily united* in the same subject; for otherwise no ground could be given why we should burden reason with an idea which, though it may *without contradiction* be united with another that is sufficiently established, yet entangles us in a business that brings reason into difficult straits in its theoretical use. This

---

[k] *Täuschung*

duty, however, is incumbent upon speculative philosophy only so that it may clear the way for practical philosophy. Hence it is not left to the philosopher's discretion whether he wants to remove the seeming conflict or leave it untouched; for, in the latter case the theory about this would be *bonum vacans*,[1] into possession of which the fatalist could justifiably enter and chase all morals from its supposed property, as occupying it without title.

Nevertheless it cannot yet be said here that the boundary of practical philosophy begins. For, the settlement of that controversy does not belong to it; instead it only requires of speculative reason that it put an end to the discord in which it entangles itself in theoretical questions, so that practical reason may have tranquillity and security from the external attacks that could make the land on which it wants to build a matter of dispute.

4:457

But the rightful claim[m] to freedom of will made even by common human reason is based on the consciousness and the granted presupposition of the independence of reason from merely subjectively determining causes, all of which together constitute what belongs only to feeling[n] and hence come under the general name of sensibility. The human being, who this way regards himself as an intelligence, thereby puts himself in a different order of things and in a relation to determining grounds of an altogether different kind when he thinks of himself as an intelligence endowed with a will, and consequently with causality, than when he perceives himself as a phenomenon in the world of sense (as he also really is) and subjects his causality to external determination in accordance with laws of nature. Now he soon becomes aware that both can take place at the same time, and indeed must do so. For, that a *thing in appearance* (belonging to the world of sense) is subject to certain laws from which *as a thing* or a being *in itself* it is independent contains not the least contradiction; that he must represent and think of himself in this twofold way, however, rests as regards the first on consciousness of himself as an object affected through the senses and as regards the second on consciousness of himself as an intelligence, that is, as independent of sensible impressions in the use of reason (hence as belonging to the world of understanding).

So it is that the human being claims for himself a will which lets nothing be put to his account that belongs merely to his desires and inclinations, and on the contrary thinks as possible by means of it – indeed as necessary – actions that can be done only by disregarding all desires and sensible incitements. The causality of such actions lies in him as intelligence and in the laws of effects and actions in accordance with principles of an intelligible world, of which he knows nothing more than

---

[1] i.e., something that belongs to no one
[m] *Rechtsanspruch*
[n] *Empfindung*

that in it reason alone, and indeed pure reason independent of sensibility, gives the law, and, in addition, that since it is there, as intelligence only, that he is his proper self (as a human being he is only the appearance of himself), those laws apply to him immediately and categorically, so that what inclinations and impulses (hence the whole nature of the world of sense) incite him to cannot infringe upon the laws of his volition as intelligence; indeed, he does not hold himself accountable for the former or ascribe them to his proper self, that is, to his will, though he does ascribe to it the indulgence he would show them if he allowed them to influence his maxims to the detriment of the rational laws of his will.

By *thinking* itself into a world of understanding practical reason does not at all overstep its boundaries, but it would certainly do so if it wanted to *intuit* or *feel itself* into it.° That is only a negative thought with respect to the world of sense: it gives reason no laws for determining the will and is positive only in this single point: that freedom as a negative determination is combined with a (positive) capacity as well, and indeed with a causality of reason that we call a will, a capacity so to act that the principle of actions conforms with the essential constitution of a rational cause, that is, with the condition of universal validity of a maxim as a law. But if practical reason were to fetch in addition an *object of the will*, that is, a motive, from the world of understanding, then it would overstep its bounds and pretend to be cognizant of something of which it knows nothing. The concept of a world of understanding is thus only a *standpoint* that reason sees itself constrained to take outside appearances *in order to think of itself as practical*, as would not be possible if the influences of sensibility were determining for the human being but is nevertheless necessary insofar as he is not to be denied consciousness of himself as an intelligence and consequently as a rational cause active by means of reason, that is, operating freely.ᵖ This thought admittedly brings with it the idea of another order and another lawgiving than that of the mechanism of nature, which has to do with the sensible world; and it makes necessary the concept of an intelligible world (i.e., the whole of rational beings as things in themselves), but without the least pretense to think of it further than in terms merely of its *formal* condition, that is, of the universality of maxims of the will as law and so of the autonomy of the will, which alone is compatible with its freedom; on the contrary, all laws that are determined with reference to an object give heteronomy, which can be found only in laws of nature and also can have to do only with the world of sense.

But reason would overstep all its bounds if it took it upon itself to *explain how* pure reason can be practical, which would be exactly the same task as to explain *how freedom is possible.*

° *hineinschauen, hineinempfinden*
ᵖ *als vernünftige und durch Vernunft tätige, d.i. frei wirkende*

GROUNDWORK OF THE METAPHYSICS OF MORALS

For we can explain nothing but what we can reduce to laws the object of which can be given in some possible experience. Freedom, however, is a mere idea, the objective reality of which can in no way be presented in accordance with laws of nature and so too cannot be presented in any possible experience; and because no example of anything analogous[q] can ever be put under it, it can never be comprehended or even only seen.[r] It holds only as a necessary presupposition of reason in a being that believes itself to be conscious of a will, that is, of a faculty distinct from a mere faculty of desire (namely, a faculty of determining itself to action as an intelligence and hence in accordance with laws of reason independently of natural instincts). Now, where determination by laws of nature ceases, there all *explanation* ceases as well, and nothing is left but *defense*, that is, to repel the objections of those who pretend to have seen deeper into the essence of things and therefore boldly declare that freedom is impossible. We can only point out to them that the supposed contradiction they have discovered in it lies nowhere else than in this: in order to make the law of nature hold with respect to human actions they must necessarily regard the human being as an appearance; and now when they are required to think of him, as an intelligence, as also a thing in itself they nevertheless continue to regard him as appearance here too; in that case the separation[s] of his causality (i.e., of his will) from all the natural laws of the world of sense in one and the same subject would be a contradiction; but this would come to nothing if they were willing to reflect and to acknowledge, as is equitable, that things in themselves (though hidden) must lie behind appearances as their ground and that one cannot insist that the laws of their operation[t] should be the same as those under which their appearances stand.

The subjective impossibility of *explaining* the freedom of the will is the same as the impossibility of discovering and making comprehensible[u] an *interest* which the human being can take in moral laws;* and yet he does

4:460

---

*An interest is that by which reason becomes practical, i.e., becomes a cause determining the will. Hence only of a rational being does one say that he takes an interest in something; nonrational creatures feel only sensible impulses. Reason takes an immediate interest in an action only when the universal validity of the maxim of the action is a sufficient determining ground of the will. Only such an interest is pure. But if it can determine the will only by means of another object of desire[v] or on the presupposition of a special feeling of the subject, then reason takes only a mediate interest in the action, and since reason all by itself, without experience, can discover neither objects of the will nor a special feeling lying at its basis, this latter interest would be only empirical and not a pure rational interest. The logical interest of reason (to further its insights) is never immediate but presupposes purposes for its use.

[q] *niemals nach irgend einer Analogie*
[r] *niemals begriffen, oder auch nur eingesehen werden kann*
[s] *Absonderung*
[t] *Wirkungsgesetzen*
[u] *ausfindig und begreiflich zu machen*
[v] *des Begehrens*

really take an interest in them, the foundation of which in us we call moral feeling, which some have falsely given out as the standard for our moral appraisal whereas it must rather be regarded as the *subjective* effect that the law exercises on the will, to which reason alone delivers the objective grounds.

In order for a sensibly affected rational being to will that for which reason alone prescribes the "ought," it is admittedly required that his reason have the capacity to *induce a feeling of pleasure* or of delight in the fulfillment of duty, and thus there is required a causality of reason to determine sensibility in conformity with its principles. But it is quite impossible to see, that is, to make comprehensible a priori,[w] how a mere thought which itself contains nothing sensible produces a feeling[x] of pleasure or displeasure; for that is a special kind of causality about which, as about any causality, we can determine nothing whatever a priori but must for this consult experience alone. But since this cannot provide us with any relation of cause to effect except between two objects of experience – whereas here pure reason, by means of mere ideas (which yield no object at all for experience), is to be the cause of an effect that admittedly lies in experience – it follows that for us human beings it is quite impossible to explain how and why the *universality of a maxim as law* and hence morality interests us. This much only is certain: it is not *because the law interests* us that it has validity for us (for that is heteronomy and dependence of practical reason upon sensibility, namely upon a feeling lying at its basis, in which case it could never be morally lawgiving); instead, the law interests because it is valid for us as human beings, since it arose from our will as intelligence and so from our proper self; *but what belongs to mere appearance is necessarily subordinated by reason to the constitution of the thing in itself.*

Thus the question, how a categorical imperative is possible, can indeed be answered to the extent that one can furnish the sole presupposition on which alone it is possible, namely the idea of freedom, and that one can also see the necessity of this presupposition, which is sufficient for the *practical use* of reason, that is, for the conviction of the *validity of this imperative* and so also of the moral law; but how this presupposition itself is possible can never be seen by any human reason. On the presupposition of the freedom of the will of an intelligence, however, its *autonomy*, as the formal condition under which alone it can be determined, is a necessary consequence. Moreover, to presuppose this freedom of the will is (as speculative philosophy can show) not only quite *possible* (without falling into contradiction with the principle of natural necessity in the connection of appearances in the world of sense); it is also practically *necessary* – that is, necessary in idea, without any further condition – for a rational being

---

[w] *einzusehen, d.e. a priori begreiflich zu machen*
[x] *Empfindung*

GROUNDWORK OF THE METAPHYSICS OF MORALS

who is conscious of his causality through reason and so of a will (which is distinct from desires) to put it under all his voluntary[y] actions as their condition. But it is quite beyond the capacity of any human reason to explain *how* pure reason, without other incentives that might be taken from elsewhere, can be of itself practical, that is, how the mere *principle of the universal validity of all its maxims as laws* (which would admittedly be the form of a pure practical reason), without any matter (object) of the will in which one could take some interest in advance, can of itself furnish an incentive and produce an interest that would be called purely *moral;* it is impossible for us to explain, in other words, *how pure reason can be practical,* and all the pains and labor of seeking an explanation of it are lost.

It is just the same as if I tried to fathom how freedom itself as the causality of a will is possible. For then I leave the philosophic ground of explanation behind and I have no other. I might indeed revel[z] in the intelligible world, the world of intelligences, which is still left to me; but even though I have an *idea* of it, which has its good grounds, yet I have not the least *cognizance* of it nor can I ever attain this by all the efforts of my natural faculty of reason. It signifies only a "something" that is left over when I have excluded from the determining grounds of my will everything belonging to the world of sense, merely in order to limit the principle of motives from the field of sensibility by circumscribing this field and showing that it does not include everything within itself[a] but that there is still more beyond it; but of this something more I have no further cognizance. As for pure reason, which thinks this ideal: after its isolation from all matter, that is, cognition of objects, nothing is left for me but the form of it – namely the practical law of the universal validity of maxims – and to think of reason, conformably with this, with reference to a pure world of understanding as a possible efficient cause, that is, a cause determining the will. Here an incentive must be quite lacking; for this idea of an intelligible world would itself have to be the incentive or that in which reason originally takes an interest; but to make this comprehensible is precisely the problem that we cannot solve.

4:462

Here, then, is the highest[b] limit of all moral inquiry; and it is already of great importance to determine it just so that reason may not, on the one hand, to the detriment of morals search about in the world of sense for the supreme motive and a comprehensible but empirical interest, and that it may not, on the other hand, impotently flap its wings without moving from the spot in the space, which is empty for it, of transcendent concepts

---

[y] *willkürlichen*
[z] *herumschwärmen*
[a] *Alles in Allem in sich fasse*
[b] *oberste.* Given the heading of the division beginning on 455, one would have expected *äußerste,* "extreme."

called the intelligible world, and so lose itself among phantoms. Moreover, the idea of a pure world of understanding as a whole of all intelligences, to which we ourselves belong as rational beings (though on the other side we are also members of the world of sense), remains always a useful and permitted idea for the sake of a rational belief, even if all knowledge stops at its boundary – useful and permitted for producing in us a lively interest in the moral law by means of the noble ideal of a universal kingdom of *ends in themselves* (rational beings) to which we can belong as members only when we carefully conduct ourselves in accordance with maxims of freedom as if they were laws of nature.

CONCLUDING REMARK

The speculative use of reason *with respect to nature* leads to the absolute necessity of some supreme cause of the *world:* the practical use of reason *with regard to freedom* leads also to an absolute necessity, but only *of laws of actions* of a rational being as such. Now, it is an essential *principle* of every use of our reason to push its cognition to consciousness of its *necessity* (for without this it would not be cognition on the part of reason). It is, however, an equally essential *limitation* of this same reason that it can see neither the *necessity* of what is and what happens nor the necessity of what ought to happen unless a *condition* under which it is and happens or ought to happen is put at the basis of this. In this way, however, by constant inquiry after the condition, the satisfaction of reason is only further and further postponed. Hence it restlessly seeks the unconditionally necessary and sees itself constrained to assume it without any means of making it comprehensible to itself, fortunate enough if it can discover only the concept that is compatible with this presupposition. It is therefore no censure of our deduction of the supreme principle of morality, but a reproach that must be brought against human reason in general, that it cannot make comprehensible as regards its absolute necessity an unconditional practical law (such as the categorical imperative must be); for, that it is unwilling to do this through a condition – namely by means of some interest laid down as a basis – cannot be held against it, since then it would not be the moral law, that is, the supreme law of freedom. And thus we do not indeed comprehend the practical unconditional necessity of the moral imperative, but we nevertheless comprehend its *incomprehensibility;* and this is all that can fairly be required of a philosophy that strives in its principles to the very boundary of human reason.

Review of Hufeland's
Essay on the principle of natural right

Introduction

In October 1785 Gottlieb Hufeland (1760–1817), then a twenty-five-year-old scholar with doctorates in philosophy and law at the University of Jena, sent Kant a copy of his book on natural right (see AK 10:388–389, 412–413). Kant was requested to review it for the *Jenaer Allegemeine Literaturzeitung* (see AK 10:398–399), and the review appeared on April 18, 1786 (AK 13:173).

Hufeland's approach to ethics is Wolffian, basing ethics in general on the striving for perfection. He attempts to derive the individual's right from the obligation to pursue one's own perfection, arguing that it entails the authorization to use coercion to defend one's perfection and to act so as to increase it. Kant's review praises the thoroughness and scholarship of Hufeland's book, and expresses optimism about Hufeland's future contributioon to this and other areas of philosophy.

In his review Kant emphasizes the points on which he and Hufeland agree, such as the apriority of principles of right, but criticizes Hufeland's derivation of right from an obligation, arguing that this leads to the paradox that people have no rights they may not press to the full, and also leaves indeterminate the extent of an individual's rights. Kant's own approach, already present in the *Critique of Pure Reason*, is to base right on the conditions of everyone's external freedom under universal laws (A316/B373).

I am grateful to Paul Guyer for helpful suggestions on the translation.

Review of Hufeland's
Essay on the principle of natural right

Essay on the principle of natural right – with an appendix, by Gottlieb Hufeland, Doctor of Philosophy[a] and both Laws. Leipzig: G. J. Göschen, 1785

In sciences whose object must be thought through pure[b] rational concepts, such as those which constitute practical philosophy,[c] one must not merely go back to the primary basic concepts and principles, but rather because these can easily lack accessibility and objective reality, due to the insufficiency of their principles for individuality occurring cases, which is still not sufficiently proven, therefore it is a praiseworthy undertaking to seek their sources in the faculty of reason itself, to which Mr. Hufeland has here submitted himself in regard to natural right. He presents, in ten sections, the object of natural right, the development of the concept of right, the necessary properties of its principle, and then the various systems concerning it and their examination, the former with historical completeness, the latter with critical precision; one encounters the principles of Grotius, Hobbes, Pufendorf, Thomasius, Heinrich and Samuel Cocceji, Wolff, Gundling, Beyer, Treuer, Köhler, Claproth, Schmauss, Achenwall, Sulzer, Feder, Eberhard, Platner, Mendelssohn, Garve, Höpfner, Ulrich, Zöllner, Hamann, Selle, Flatt, and Schlettwein;[1] and one will not easily find anything missing, which is an agreeable alleviation of the task of anyone who would survey or undertake a general review of the whole of what has occurred in this field. He investigates the causes of this *variety in principles*; establishes on them the formal conditions of natural right, derives its principle in a theory thought out by himself, more precisely determines what is obligatory in natural right and completes this work by drawing consequences from it; in the appendix, a few more particular applications of those concepts and principles are added.

To make remarks about individual points in such a great manifold of materials would be just as tedious as it is unsuitable.[d] Thus it may be sufficient to extract from the eighth section the principle on which is erected the proper system characterizing this work, and to indicate its source as well as its function.[e] The author, namely, does not hold principles[f] of a free will, regardless of its object, to be sufficient to prescribe practical laws, and therefore to derive their obligatoriness. Hence for

[a] *Weltweisheit*
[b] *lauter*
[c] *Weltweisheit*
[d] *unzweckmäßig*
[e] *Bestimmung*
[f] *Principien*

those formal rules he seeks a material, i.e. an object,^g which as the highest end of rational being, which the nature of things prescribes to him, can be assumed as a postulate, and he posits it in the perfecting of *this end*.[2] Hence the supreme practical principle is: Further the perfection of all sensing^h beings, chiefly of rational beings – hence also your own perfection; from which, then, we get the proposition: Prevent the diminution of perfection in others – but chiefly in you yourself (insofar as others might be the cause of it), which latter proposition obviously includes in itself a resistance, hence a coercion.

Now what is most characteristic of our author's system consists in the fact that he posits the ground of all natural right and all authorizationⁱ in a prior natural obligation, and that the human being is therefore authorized to coerce others because he is obligated to do so (according to the last part of the principle); otherwise, he believes, the authorization to use coercion cannot be explained. Although he grounds the whole science of natural rights on obligations, he nevertheless warns us not to misunderstand by this the obligation of others to perform what satisfies our right (Hobbes already remarks that where coercion accompanies our claims, an obligation of others to submit to this coercion can no longer be thought).[3] From this he infers that the doctrine of obligation in natural right is superfluous, and can often mislead. In this the reviewer gladly agrees with the author. For here the question is only under what conditions I can exercise the coercion without coming into conflict with the universal principles of right; whether the other may comport himself passively, or react according to the very same principles, is his business to investigate – as long, namely, as everything is being considered in the state of nature; for in the civil state there is, corresponding to the judicial verdict which recognizes the right of one party, always an obligation of the opposing party. This remark also has a great utility in natural right, that of not confusing the proper ground of right by mixing in ethical questions. Yet that even the authorization to coerce must always have as its ground an obligation laid on us by nature itself – to the reviewer this does not seem to be clear, chiefly because the ground contains more than what is necessary for that consequence. For it seems to follow from it that one *can cede nothing*^j of one's right as permitting coercion, because this permission rests on an inner obligation in every case to obtain the contested perfection for ourselves, if necessary with force. It also appears that on the assumed standard for authorization, the estimation of that to which I have a right, even in the commonest cases of life, must turn out to be so artificial that even the

---

^g*Object*
^h*empfindende*, which could also be translated 'feeling'
ⁱ*Befugnis*
^j*nichts nachlassen könne*

most practiced understanding must find itself in continual bewilderment, if not in a downright impossible position, when it tries to make out how far its right might reach. – On the right of *compensation*⁴ the author asserts that in a mere state of nature it does not occur as a right of coercion, yet he admits that he has abandoned it merely because he does not believe he can prove it. In the same state he also allows for no *imputation*, because no judge is present there.⁵ – The author gives a few pointers regarding application in his appendix, where he treats of first acquisition, of acquisition through contracts, of constitutional right and the right of nations, and finally proposes a new necessary science which could fill in the gap between natural and positive right. One cannot deny that in this work there is contained much that is new, deeply thought out and at the same time true, even that everywhere there is something well-prepared and suggestive for discovering the criteria of truth in the principles^k of natural right and for determing the boundaries of its proper terrain. Yet the reviewer also counts very much on the further use the author will make of his principles in future lectures. For in no species of cognition from mere concepts is this kind of experiment^l more necessary and yet at the same time more feasible than in questions about right, which rest on mere reason; but no one is better capable of setting about such an attempt^m in a more manifold and complete manner than he who has had the opportunity to put his assumed principle to the test in the case of many conclusions that his whole system, so frequently gone through, has offered. It would be appropriate to propose objections against a treatise grounded on the particular system which the reviewer has constructed about the same object; his authority^n extends no further than to testing the agreement with one another of the propositions which the author has presented, or their agreement with such truths as the reviewer can assume the author will concede. Hence we can add nothing further except that the present treatise demonstrates the lively and searching spirit of the author, from which much is to be expected in the sequel; and that a similar treatment in this as in other sciences of reason, carefully correcting the principles,^o is well suited to the taste and perhaps the vocation^p of this age, and hence is to be universally praised.

8:130

^k*Sätzen*
^l*Experiment*
^m*Versuch*. This word could also be translated as "experiment"; but it is in addition the word translated as "essay" in the title of Hufeland's treatise.
^n*Befugnis*
^o*Principien*
^p*Berufe*

Kraus's review of Ulrich's Eleutheriology

Introduction

The present Introduction to this review will simply paraphrase the Introduction of the editor by the Academy Edition, Paul Menzer. The review was included as an appendix in AK 8 because Kraus testifies that he has made use of a short essay by Kant. On this basis Vaihinger had the review published (in volume 16 of *Philosophische Monatschefte*, 1880, pp. 193–208) under the title "A Hitherto Unknown Essay by Kant on Freedom" and attempted a reconstruction of Kant's contribution to it. Menzer forgoes such a reconstruction but thinks that Vaihinger's opinion that the beginning of the review in particular may be traced to Kant may be correct. Kant's notes for the review are to be found in 23:79–81 (*Vorarbeit zur Ulrich Rezension*).

Kraus's review invites comparison with Kant's own review, in 1783 (8:9–14), of the book by Schulz to which Kraus refers. A translation of Kant's review is included in this volume.

I am indebted to Sharon Byrd and Jan Jörden for their assistance with an earlier draft of this translation.

Kraus's review of Ulrich's Eleutheriology

Johann August Heinrich Ulrich: *Eleutheriology, or On freedom and necessity* (Cröker, Jena, 1788)

8:453

There is a distinction between the physical and the moral in the human being that is familiar to the most common reason: on the one hand, as a subject of nature, he feels the constant influence of its causes and is directed by his understanding itself to calculate all actions in advance and to explain them afterwards in accordance with its determined laws; on the other hand, as in command of nature, he credits himself with a spontaneity[a] independent of nature and gives himself his own laws, in accordance with which despite all alien influence, he cognizes it as an indispensable command to order future actions and inexorably approves or condemns past actions according to the verdicts of a judge within him;[b] and indeed, if common reason wanted not to recognize this distinction or wanted to cast doubt on it, it would have to do what it neither can nor may do, cease to distinguish what is and does happen from what ought to be and ought to happen. But insofar as he is to think the very same actions not only in accordance with relations of determined natural necessity but also in reference to an unconditional spontaneity, and indeed both together, the nexus of the physical and the moral in the human being surpasses what his spirit can grasp, which, depending on whether it tries to take these actions either as determined by nature, in conformity with the need of understanding, or as produced through freedom, in conformity with the requirement of morality, soon realizes[c] that in the first case it would have to give up the essence of morality and in the other the use of understanding; and since neither of these can be given up, it becomes aware that it is in the presence of a mystery.[d] What is left for reflection to do in regard to this mystery? Only, first to put the essential distinction between the natural and the moral in the brightest light and in complete assurance and certainty against all the doubts and objections that inquisitiveness opposes to it, and then, by a critical investigation of our whole cognitive faculty, to seek a satisfying clarification of why the nexus of both[e] is incomprehensible and in what respect it can still be thought without contradiction that both actually exist united in the human being (though the way in which nature and freedom are joined in him cannot be fathomed). That indeed seems to be very little, and is certainly less than our greedy desire for knowledge demands, though it is still as much as the ends of life may ever require. But if, through the investigation that fully affords us that clarifica-

8:454

[a] *Selbsttätigkeit*
[b] *in seinem Inneren*
[c] *einsieht*
[d] *Geheimnis*
[e] *der Zusammenhang jener beiden Verknüpfungen*

tion, it were disclosed and proved that, by the very limitation of its knowledge, reason, which otherwise is self-defeating in its speculations about the theoretical and the practical, arrived at the most perfect harmony with regard to both and that, by the very discussion of its incapacity to join nature and morality with each other, our spirit won the most gratifying view into a world of understanding different from the world of sense and the most desired clarification of its vocation and dignity; then it would be short-sighted indeed to complain about the limitation of our knowledge and the incapacity of our spirit, and folly to refuse to acknowledge what is nevertheless undeniable: namely, that the most important and absorbing of all reason's problems is insoluble for us here below. However, no matter how clearly all this may be shown, it will not prevent attempts from time to time to solve the problem. For this is how it is with the human being: in matters of reflection, especially about objects that are obscure and, just because of this, attractive, the last thing he arrives at is cognition of his ignorance, and he will do anything more readily than prevail upon himself to admit his incapacity; and so it must indeed be, since attempts of this kind – unlike such attempts in, say, mathematics, where highflown inventions come from novices and bunglers in the science – often originate in men whose insights and learning can hardly lead to the suspicion that they misunderstand what is really at issue in the problem or mistake a masking of the difficulties for a real solution of them, which however is always the case. The present writing provides a proof of this in all respects. The author, who is as acute as he is learned, strives to set forth the system of thoroughgoing natural necessity of all human manifestations of force,[f] under the name of *determinism*, as the only correct one and, in regard to morality, not only to explain it as compatible with morality but also to commend it as conducive to morality. To require new, if only turns of expression[g] and methods, not to mention grounds and proofs in the matter, would mean failing to know of the object of the project on which the human spirit has worked and exhausted itself for millennia. Thus on the one side, regarding the correctness of this doctrine itself, everything turns out *as usual:* whatever can be perceived by outer or inner sense, insofar as it is to be comprehended by the understanding, is also necessarily determined in conformity with the requirements of the understanding and excluding chance, so that the human being as a natural being must be subject to natural laws (a proposition that is certainly irrefutable but still leaves open the question at issue, whether the human being is to be really regarded only as a natural being); on the other side, as regards the relation of physical necessity to morality, except for certain logical formalities everything again turns out *much as it did,* in particular in the well-known

[f] *Kraftäußerungen*
[g] *Wendungen*

Attempt at a Doctrine of Morals for All Human Beings, resulting in a fatalism that does not allow the genuine concepts of obligation and imputation to further exist.[h] No one versed in the matter will be surprised by that; what did surprise us is, in part, the author's insinuation (page 8) "that he has allowed himself no reservation and intentionally sophistical ambiguity or vagueness," and in part the confidence with which, in the dedication directed to *the darlings of his soul*, that is, his most valued readers, "he wants nothing more than that they might find in this doctrine of his all the tranquillity and contentment that he himself has experienced from it, and calls upon them to show by their example that determinism correctly understood (i.e., as he has set it forth here) does not nullify morality but rather supports it." In fact, the two of these, compared with the diction and content of the writing, make a somewhat astonishing contrast with each other, and it will certainly be a kindness to the reader to cast more light on this by the following elucidation of the main thought. That is to say, since *ought* presupposes *can*, and hence the ought that is independent of all that actually happens presupposes the can that is likewise independent of all that actually happens – or, moral obligation presupposes the original spontaneity that is really what has to be thought as *freedom* and yet cannot be comprehended – the author instead tries to find a transition from can to ought to evade this incomprehensibility. Now, there certainly is a can that is also called freedom and is still quite understandable, insofar as the human being is causal[i] by thoughts and not by impact like a machine or by feeling like an animal and insofar as all thoughts that might at all come to be present to the human being by means of inner sense and offer themselves to perception must be comprehensible and explainable in the same way as all other phenomena of the sensible world in regard to the way they arise, disappear and return, grow and diminish in clarity, vividness and force – in short, in regard to their appearing and changing. And it is from this that the author sets out explaining freedom, among other ways (p. 59), through the improvability of our practical cognition, and enumerates the causes on which the acquisition and development of practical cognition depends, for example, on the causes of opportunity, the causes of learning from experience and in part on the causes of deliberate reflection, deliberate attention, practice and so forth. In regard to the latter he candidly adds throughout, especially on page 62, "that whatever is deliberate itself depends in turn upon a thousand different circumstances that lie in the whole connection (of physical causes)." His system, however, indeed requires this admission, inasmuch as the psychological, with regard to its explicability as object of perception, is annexed to the series of the mechanical, chemical and organic and thereby as so many

8:456

---

[h] *weiter keinen Bestand lässt*
[i] *wirksam ist*

particular secondary species forms the chief genus of the *physical.*[j] But what of the transition from this nominal freedom, which is nothing other than *natural necessity,* to morality, which is altogether cut off from it, or from this dependent can to the absolute ought? The transition? Instead of pointing out the transition, on which everything really depended, the author complains on page 17, "the concept of the absolute ought (which is indeed the real thorn in the side for empirical moralists) is one of the most difficult concepts in the whole of moral philosophy, and he will reserve investigating it to another time"; he asks his audience, on page 38, "to recall that they have heard about the absolute ought in moral lectures, when the idea of duty was laboriously explicated"[k] – unfortunately the reader knows nothing about this; he bargains and haggles to save the correctness of at least half his theory, in regard to the future, even if not in regard to the past; at the very end, among the emendations and appendices on the next to the last page, love of truth coaxes from him the naive question: "What difference would it make if everything moral could finally be reduced to something physical?" What difference would it make? Only that there would then, after all, be nothing moral, and along with the distinction of the physical and the moral would disappear the distinction between what is or happens and what ought to be or to happen. But that is precisely the theory that the author called upon the darlings of his soul to refute by their conduct. As was said, however, the author moved, among other things, to halve his proposal. "The human being ought" (it is said on pages 63, 82, etc.) "to become other or better, and he can become so: *however, no human being as of now can be other or better than he is.*" Hence: not, however, *as of now* and *up till now.*[l] But what if they always arose from the *now* flowing onward, as a line arises from a point flowing onward, and if the now were valid for every position of future and past time just as a point is valid for every place of a line taken upwards and downwards? In fact, if everything future will some day be present just as everything past has already been present, then if human conduct *up till now* is always determined once and for all by necessity, it must in the same way also be determined for all time to come to infinity, inasmuch as the now, taken as the boundary of necessity, must proceed serially through that time to come to infinity. Or, if the author should want to deny that, he would have to maintain that, for example, now, after the end of the year, the people of Jena's conduct during the preceding year absolutely had to be just as it was, whereas before the beginning of the year it did not have to be as it was, and in the same way all actions of all people in all

8:457

---

[j] *und damit als eben so viel besondere Nebenarten die Hauptgattung des Physischen bildet*
[k] *bei der mühsahmen Entwickelung*
[l] " . . . *nur kein Mensch kann schon jetzt anders oder besser sein, als er ist."Also nur schon jetzt und bis jetzt nicht.*

chronological sequences, when viewed retrospectively from B to A could not have been other than they were, but when viewed prospectively from A to B, could have been quite different than they were; according to this, one and the same judgment about one and the same thing, taken objectively, would be both true and false at the same time,^m an incomprehensibility greater than that which was to be avoided by the detour around moral freedom; and not just the author has fallen into it by an oversight: anyone who takes the same path must, in the end, inevitably get entangled in it, despite all precautions. And so, once the deception played with the *now* and *as of now* and *once* is removed, it becomes apparent that the author's main thought is simply untenable and that his writing, despite the confidence he put in it, is nothing other than a superfluous contribution to the proof of the proposition – which is clear of itself – *that freedom* insofar as it is the basis of morality *cannot be comprehended,* and insofar as it can be comprehended it cannot serve as the foundation of morality; what the writing aims at is, rather, to change the whole moral world of understanding, which rests on one's personal control over oneself,^n into a physical sensible world, where everything proceeds in accordance with a natural necessity that is determined from elsewhere and unalterable, and where (insofar as [page 90] no one has really contributed or could have contributed anything to the given state of his moral worth or lack of worth by his deliberate efforts), neither a human being, who is only a cause and not an author, can find anything at all to censure in his own or another's conduct nor can even the deity, who sees in everything his own work and only himself acting, find anything to censure in all of us together, and where there can be no more talk of duties and obligations but only of facts^o and occurrences, no more talk of merit and demerit,^p virtue and vice, but only of good luck and misfortune, enjoyment and suffering; in such a world, in regard to which there is nothing left other than letting deceptive and dizzying reason^q be rocked to sleep by fantasy, this bothersome comforter, into the wild dream of a providence which – on the natural chain of necessary causes, some of the results of which, by virtue of a beneficent delusion, seem to us to be free actions – mechanically moves all human beings and all rational beings or persons, like so many actual automata, toward a common final goal of happiness, some of them later by the

8:458

---

^m *zugleich*
^n *auf persönlicher Selbstmacht*
^o Or "actions," *Taten.* In *The Metaphysics of Morals* (6:227), Kant defines "*Tat*" or "deed" as follows: "*Imputation* (*imputatio*) in the moral sense is the *judgment* by which someone is regarded as the author (*causa libera*) of an action, which is then called a *deed* (*factum*) and stands under laws." In the present passage Kraus is apparently using the common distinction between *actiones liberae* and *actiones non liberae.*
^p *Schuld*
^q *schwindelnde Vernunft*

detour of so-called vice, others earlier by the straight path of putative virtue. How a system of this kind could afford complete contentment is in itself strange (though there may well be no reflective human being to whom it has not occurred at one time or another); but it is altogether odd on the part of the author, since he himself expressed considerable doubt about it. Namely, in the polemical part of his writing, which is directed against the Kantian theory of freedom (a theory worthy of a genuine philosopher, who insists upon scientific certitude where it is to be had at all but also frankly acknowledges ignorance where it cannot be remedied, and of which the initial main features were laid down at the beginning of this review),[r] Ulrich straightway admits (p. 33) that this theory would be irrefutable if one took for granted the proposition that time is a merely subjective form of appearances; from this there follows quite clearly the scruple that if one could neither overthrow this proposition itself nor refute the proof on which it rests, this theory must be correct, and then the contentment the author has extracted from the system opposed to it must have been a mere delusion. He can secure himself against this concern in only one way: by proving clearly the complete inadmissibility of that proposition or, strictly speaking, of the thought expressed by it; should he succeed in this undertaking, he would have the gratitude of the opponents of Kantian philosophy as well as of its connoisseurs, and of its author himself; the former would thank him because it would provide the means for them to disregard the antinomies of reason, which up to now, as it seems, can be resolved only by means of that proposition, and to flatter themselves with the hope of a perfect victory; the latter, because by it they would win unexpected disclosures about human cognition, such as are more welcome to them than any system, which they cherish only insofar as it affords them indispensable and wished for disclosures. However, nothing is effected against that proposition by mere counterdeclarations (as on page 33, "Say what one will, that proposition has not yet been thoroughly proved and what has been said about it so often by me as well[s] has not yet been answered") or by mere challenges to it, especially if these challenges either result in vain misunderstanding or concern only the elucidation of the proposition and not the proposition itself. Several objections of both kinds are advanced here. So it is said among other things (page 34): "If one maintains an original spontaneity of the pure faculty of reason, how will one avoid the question of why this faculty is employed in certain actions and not in others? For there must either be a ground for its employment in one case and omission in the other, or not, so that in the

---

[r] *und von welcher die ersten Grundzüge zum Eingange dieser Recension dargelegt sind*

[s] *auch von ihm.* Although the parenthetical material is enclosed in quotation marks, it is really an indirect quotation. The relevant part of Schulz's original sentence, quoted by the *Akademie* editor, Paul Menzer, reads "*und dasjenige, was darüber so oft, auch von mir gesagt worden.*"

first case necessity enters, and in the other, chance." This and all similar questions, which assume that one should know about freedom not only *that it is real* but also *how it is constituted*, are quite truly avoided by the admission that one can know nothing with regard to the latter; for freedom does not reveal itself through sense perception, although one can assign determining grounds for its *results* insofar as these offer themselves to our perception, as one can for all other phenomena that result in time, and so in this respect that question need not be avoided. It is the same with the other objection (page 38), where it is said that Kant himself admits that our reason is not practical without obstacles and hence that our spontaneity is not effective without restraint; for these restraints and obstacles, which become present to us through sense perception, again hold only for what *can be sensibly perceived in us,* but not for what, withdrawn from such a perception,[t] *can only be thought.* And so it is with several further objections, which demand explanation of a concept although nothing like it can be found in the whole realm of experience and although its object, freedom, is such that speculative philosophy (dispensing with insight into its constitution) must be content with being able to cognize that it is contradictory neither in itself nor in conjunction with the natural necessity of its phenomena, that is, our actions, but can instead be thought as coexistent in man in accordance with the twofold manner of his existence, in the chronological order and beyond all temporal determinations.

8:460

---

[t] *einer solchen Wahrnehmung entnommen*

Critique of practical reason

Introduction

In his Preface to the *Groundwork of the Metaphysics of Morals* Kant stated his intention of writing a book to be called *The Metaphysics of Morals.* There is no indication that he intended to produce a work entitled the *Critique of Practical Reason.* Metaphysics, he explained, has two parts, metaphysics of nature and metaphysics of morals, and just as a critique of pure speculative reason is the only foundation for a metaphysics of nature, so a critique of pure practical reason is the only foundation for a metaphysics of morals. However, what it was necessary and feasible to do could be done in the course of laying the foundation for the metaphysics of morals. Section III of the *Groundwork*, the transition to a "critique of pure practical reason, " would suffice.

By April 1786 Kant had begun his extensive revisions for the second edition of the *Critique of Pure Reason* and, early in the course of making them, apparently entertained the thought of adding to it a critique of practical reason. In November 1786 the *Allgemeine Literaturzeitung,* announcing the forthcoming publication of the new edition, said that in it a critique of pure practical reason would be appended to the critique of pure speculative reason contained in the first edition (AK 3:556). However, no such addition was made. In April 1787 Kant had completed his revisions, and his only extensive rewriting beyond the Transcendental Analytic was in the Dialectic's chapter on "The Paralogisms of Pure Reason," a part having no direct bearing on moral philosophy.

Although Kant's decision not to append a critique of practical reason to the 1787 edition of the *Critique of Pure Reason* could have been justified by the sheer length of the book even without such an addition, there were philosophic issues involved. By its resolution of the third antinomy, the supposed contradiction between natural necessity and a causal activity not determined by temporal conditions, the *Critique of Pure Reason* had established the logical possibility of a free causality. But as Kant continued to reflect on practical or moral matters, his concern with the question of freedom, and specifically with the freedom of the human will, took on a new dimension. The *Groundwork*'s analysis of what is implicit in the moral appraisals of "common human understanding" ended with the assumption of autonomy as a property of the will, a concept that provides a definite law for the exercise of free causality. To deal with this "positive concept of freedom" – not to mention the subsidiary issues involved when it is applied to the human will – would have required more time and space than a new edition of the *Critique of Pure Reason* allowed. A new Preface to the second edition indicated Kant's continuing concern with the concept of freedom and his intention to get on with his metaphysics of morals.

However, in a letter dated June 25, 1787 (10:490), Kant told his correspondent Schütz that he had almost finished a work called the *Critique of Practical Reason*, which would be sent to the publisher in Halle within a week. By September it had been delivered to the publisher (10:494), although, because of technical delays, the official publication date was 1788. The speed with which Kant produced the work is less surprising than his decision to write a second critique. Paul Natorp, the Academy editor of the *Critique of Practical Reason*, suggests that Kant's Preface provides a clue to his decision.

In the Preface Kant remarks that the most considerable objections he has seen to the *Critique of Pure Reason* turn about two points: the objective reality of the categories applied to noumena, which is denied in theoretical cognition and affirmed in practical cognition, and the related distinction between the noumenal and phenomenal with regard to the self. H. A. Pistorius, in his review of the *Groundwork*, had found such an inconsistency between the theoretical and the practical use of pure reason. So too had a number of other critics for whom Kant had less regard than for the "astute" Pistorius, whom he describes as "devoted to truth" and therefore worthy of respect. Only a detailed *Critique of Practical Reason*, not piecemeal answers to such objections, "can remove all this misinterpretation." Kant did not, apparently, think that he had accomplished what the *Groundwork* said would be required of a complete critique of practical reason, namely that it show the unity of practical and theoretical reason in a common principle. However, his thorough critique of reason in its practical use goes beyond the specific issue raised by his critics and attempts to show not only the consistency between speculative and practical reason but their interdependence and mutual support.

Critique
of
practical reason

Preface

Why this *Critique*[a] is not entitled a *Critique of Pure Practical Reason* but simply a *Critique of Practical Reason* generally, although its parallelism with the speculative seems to require the first, is sufficiently explained in this treatise. It has merely to show *that there is pure practical reason,* and for this purpose it criticizes reason's entire *practical faculty.* If it succeeds in this it has no need to criticize the *pure faculty itself* in order to see whether reason is merely making a claim in which it presumptuously *oversteps* itself (as does happen with speculative reason). For, if as pure reason it is really practical, it proves its reality and that of its concepts by what it does,[b] and all subtle reasoning against the possibility of its being practical is futile.

With this faculty transcendental *freedom* is also established, taken indeed in that absolute sense in which speculative reason needed it, in its use of the concept of causality, in order to rescue itself from the antinomy into which it unavoidably falls when it wants to think the *unconditioned* in the series of causal connection; this concept, however, it could put forward only problematically, as not impossible to think, without assuring it objective reality, and only lest the supposed impossibility of what it must at least allow to be thinkable call its being into question and plunge it into an abyss of skepticism.

Now, the concept of freedom, insofar as its reality is proved by an apodictic law of practical reason, constitutes the *keystone* of the whole structure of a system of pure reason, even of speculative reason; and all other concepts (those of God and immortality), which as mere ideas remain without support in the latter, now attach themselves to this concept and with it and by means of it get stability and objective reality, that is, their *possibility* is *proved* by this: that freedom is real, for this idea reveals itself through the moral law.

But among all the ideas of speculative reason freedom is also the only one the possibility of which we *know* a priori, though without having

---

[a] *Kritik.* I have adopted the convention of using *Critique* when Kant seems to refer to a book or its content, even if the book does not have the title Kant uses, e.g., "the *Critique* of speculative reason." Otherwise, "critique" or "critical examination" or occasionally "critical philosophy" is used.
[b] *durch die Tat,* possibly "by a deed." See AK 5:98 note a and 5:118 note a.

insight*c* into it, because it is the condition* of the moral law, which we do know. The ideas of *God* and *immortality*, however, are not conditions of the moral law but only conditions of the necessary object of a will determined by this law, that is, of the mere practical use of our pure reason; hence with respect to those ideas we cannot affirm that we *cognize* and *have insight into* – I do not merely say the reality but even the possibility of them. But they are, nevertheless, conditions of applying the morally determined will to its object given to it a priori (the highest good). Consequently their possibility in this practical relation can and must be *assumed*, although we cannot theoretically cognize and have insight into them. For practical purposes it is sufficient for this assumption*e* that they contain no intrinsic impossibility (contradiction). Here there is a ground of assent that is, in comparison with speculative reason, merely *subjective* but that is yet *objectively* valid for a reason equally pure but practical; by means of the concept of freedom objective reality is given to the ideas of God and immortality and a warrant,*f* indeed a subjective necessity (a need of pure reason) is provided to assume them, although reason is not thereby extended in theoretical cognition and, instead, all that is given is that their possibility, which was hitherto only a *problem*, here becomes an *assertion* and so the practical use of reason is connected with the elements of the theoretical. And this need is not a hypothetical one for some *discretionary* purpose of speculation, where one must assume something if one *wants* to ascend to the completion of the use of reason in speculation, but rather a *need having the force of law*,*g* to assume something without which that cannot happen which one *ought* to set unfailingly as the aim of one's conduct.

It would certainly be more satisfying to our speculative reason to solve those problems for itself without this circuit and to have put them aside as insight for practical use; but, as matters stand, our faculty of speculation is not so well off. Those who boast of such high cognition should not keep it back but should present it publicly to be tested and esteemed. They want to *prove:* very well, let them prove, and the critical philosophy lays all its

---

*Lest anyone suppose that he finds an *inconsistency* when I now call freedom the condition of the moral law and afterwards, in the treatise, maintain that the moral law is the condition under which we can first *become aware* of freedom, I want only to remark*d* that whereas freedom is indeed the *ratio essendi* of the moral law, the moral law is the *ratio cognoscendi* of freedom. For, had not the moral law *already* been distinctly thought in our reason, we should never consider ourselves justified in *assuming* such a thing as freedom (even though it is not self-contradictory). But were there no freedom, the moral law would *not be encountered* at all in ourselves.

c einzusehen. See note 9 to *Groundwork of the Metaphysics of Morals* 4:446.
d erinnern
e Für die letztere Forderung
f Or "authorization," *Befugnis*
g gesetzliches

weapons at their feet as the victors. *Quid statis? Nolint. Atqui licet esse beatis.*[h] Since they then do not in fact want to, presumably because they cannot, we must take up these weapons again in order to seek in the moral use of reason and to base on it the concepts of *God, freedom,* and *immortality,* for the *possibility* of which speculation does not find sufficient guarantee.

Here, too, the enigma of the critical philosophy is first explained: how one can *deny* objective *reality* to the supersensible *use of the categories* in speculation and yet *grant* them this *reality* with respect to the objects of pure practical reason; for this must previously have seemed *inconsistent,* as long as such a practical use is known only by name. But now one becomes aware, by a thorough analysis of the latter, that the reality thought of here does not aim at any theoretical *determination of the categories* and extension of cognition to the supersensible but that what is meant by it is only that in this respect an *object* belongs to them, because they are either contained in the necessary determination of the will a priori or else are inseparably connected with the object of its determination; hence that inconsistency disappears because one makes a different use of those concepts than speculative reason requires. On the contrary, there is now disclosed a very satisfying confirmation of the speculative *Critique*'s *consistent way of thinking* – one which was hardly to be expected before – inasmuch as it insisted on letting objects of experience as such, including even our own subject, hold only as *appearances* but at the same time on putting things in themselves at their basis and hence on not taking everything supersensible as a fiction and its concept as empty of content; now practical reason of itself, without any collusion with speculative reason, furnishes reality to a supersensible object of the category of causality, namely to *freedom* (although, as a practical concept, only for practical use), and hence establishes by means of a fact what could there only be *thought.* By this, the strange though incontestable assertion of the speculative *Critique, that even the thinking subject is* in inner intuition *a mere appearance to itself,* gets its full confirmation in the *Critique of Practical Reason,* and that so thoroughly that one would have to arrive at it even if the former had never proved this proposition at all.*

5:6

By this I also understand why the most considerable objections to the *Critique* that have so far come to my attention turn about just these two points: namely, *on the one side* the objective reality of the categories applied

---

*The union of causality as freedom with causality as natural mechanism, the first of which is established by the moral law, the second by the law of nature, and indeed in one and the same subject, the human being, is impossible without representing him with regard to the first as a being in itself but with regard to the second as an appearance, the former in *pure*, the latter in *empirical* consciousness. Otherwise the contradiction of reason with itself is unavoidable.

[h] In Horace *Satires* 1.1.19, a god, having given men the opportunity to change places with each other, says "What are you waiting for? They are not willing. Yet they might be happy."

to noumena, denied in theoretical cognition and affirmed in practical, and *on the other side* the paradoxical requirement to make oneself as subject of freedom a noumenon but at the same, with regard to nature, a phenomenon in one's own empirical consciousness; for, as long as one had as yet formed no determinate concepts of morality and freedom, one could not conjecture, on the one side, what one was to put as a noumenon at the basis of the alleged appearance and, on the other side, whether it was at all possible even to form a concept of it, since all the concepts of the pure understanding in its theoretical use had already been assigned exclusively to mere appearances. Only a detailed *Critique of Practical Reason* can remove all this misinterpretation and put in a clear light the consistent way of thinking that constitutes its greatest merit.

So much by way of justifying [the fact] that in this work the concepts and principles[i] of pure speculative reason, which have already undergone their special critique, are now and again subjected to examination; although this would not elsewhere be appropriate to the systematic procedure for constructing a science (since matters that have been decided should only be referred to and not raised again), it was *here allowed* and indeed necessary because reason is considered in transition to a quite different use of those concepts from what it made of them *there*. Such a transition makes it necessary to compare the old use with the new, in order to distinguish well the new path from the previous one and at the same time to draw attention to their connection. Accordingly, considerations of this kind, including those that are once more directed to the concept of freedom, though in the practical use of pure reason, should not be regarded as interpolations which might serve only to fill up gaps in the critical system of speculative reason (for this is complete for its purpose), or as like the props and buttresses that are usually added afterwards to a hastily constructed building, but as true members that make the connection of the system plain, so that concepts which could there be represented only problematically can now be seen in their real presentation. This reminder is especially relevant to the concept of freedom, with regard to which one cannot help observing with surprise that so many boast of being quite well able to understand[j] it and to explain its possibility while they consider it only in its psychological context, whereas if they had earlier pondered it carefully in its transcendental context they would have cognized its *indispensability* as a problematic concept in the complete use of speculative reason as well as its complete *incomprehensibility*;[k] and if they afterwards proceeded with it to practical use, they would have had to

---

[i] *Grundsätze*. Here again, as in the *Groundwork of the Metaphysics of Morals*, Kant draws no consistent distinction between *Grundsatz* and *Prinzip*. *Prinzip* is always, and *Grundsatz* often, translated as "principle."

[j] *einzusehen*

[k] *Unbegreiflichkeit*

arrive by themselves at the very same determination of it with respect to its principles that they are now so unwilling to agree to. The concept of freedom is the stumbling block for all *empiricists,* but also the key to the most sublime practical principles for *critical* moralists, who thereby see that they must necessarily proceed *rationally.* For this reason I beg the reader not to pass lightly over what is said about this concept at the conclusion of the Analytic. 5:8

I must leave it to connoisseurs of a work of this kind to estimate whether such a system of pure practical reason as is here developed from the *Critique* of it has cost much or little trouble, especially so as not to miss the right point of view from which the whole can be correctly traced out. It presupposes, indeed, the *Groundwork of the Metaphysics of Morals,* but only insofar as this constitutes preliminary acquaintance with the principle of duty and provides and justifies a determinate formula of it;* otherwise, it stands on its own. That the *complete classification*[l] of all practical sciences was not added, such as the *Critique* of speculative reason carried out, has a valid ground in the constitution[m] of this practical rational faculty itself. For, the special determination of duties as human duties, with a view to classifying them, is possible only after the subject of this determination (the human being) is cognized as he is really constituted, though only to the extent necessary with reference to duty generally; this, however, does not belong to a *Critique of Practical Reason* as such, which has only to give a complete account of the principles of its possibility, of its extent, and of its limits, without special reference to human nature. Here, accordingly, the classification belongs to the system of science, not to the system of critique.

In the second chapter of the Analytic I have, I hope, dealt adequately with the objection of a certain reviewer[2] of the *Groundwork of the Metaphysics of Morals,* one who is devoted to truth and astute and therefore always worthy of respect: that *there the concept of the good was not established before the moral principle* (as, in his opinion, was necessary).† I have also taken 5:9

---

*A reviewer[1] who wanted to say something censuring this work hit the mark better than he himself may have intended when he said that no new principle of morality is set forth in it but only a *new formula.* But who would even want to introduce a new principle of all morality and, as it were, first invent it? Just as if, before him, the world had been ignorant of what duty is or in thoroughgoing error about it. But whoever knows what a *formula* means to a mathematician, which determines quite precisely what is to be done to solve a problem and does not let him miss it, will not take a formula that does this with respect to all duty in general as something that is insignificant and can be dispensed with.

†The further objection could have been put to me, why have I not previously explicated the concept of the *faculty of desire* or of the *feeling of pleasure,* although this reproach would be unfair because this explication as given in psychology could reasonably be presupposed. However, the definition there could admittedly be so framed that the feeling of pleasure

[l] *Einteilung*
[m] *Beschaffenheit*

143

into consideration many other objections that have reached me from men who show that they have at heart the discovery of truth, and I shall continue to do so (for, those who have only their old system before their eyes and who have already settled what is to be approved or disapproved do not desire any discussion that might stand in the way of their private purpose).

When it is a matter of determining a particular faculty of the human soul as to its sources, its contents, and its limits, then, from the nature of human cognition, one can begin only with the *parts*, with an accurate and complete presentation of them (complete as far as is possible in the present situation of such elements as we have already acquired). But there is a second thing to be attended to, which is more philosophic and *architectonic:* namely, to grasp correctly the *idea of the whole* and from this idea to see all those parts in their mutual relation by means of their derivation from the concept of that whole in a pure rational faculty. This examination and guarantee is possible only through the most intimate acquaintance with the system; and those who find the first inquiry too irksome and hence do not think it worth their trouble to attain such an acquaintance cannot reach the second stage, namely the overview, which is a synthetic return to what had previously been given analytically; and it is no wonder that they find inconsistencies everywhere, although the gaps they suppose they find are not in the system itself but only in their own incoherent train of thought.

---

would ground the determination of the faculty of desire (as is in fact commonly done), and thus the supreme principle of practical philosophy would necessarily turn out to be *empirical*, although this has to be settled first and in the present *Critique* is altogether refuted. I will, therefore, give this explication here in the way it must be given in order, as is reasonable, to leave this contested point undecided at the beginning – **Life** is the faculty of a being to act in accordance with laws of the faculty of desire. The **faculty of desire** is a being's *faculty to be by means of its representations the cause of the reality of the objects of these representations.* Pleasure is the *representation of the agreement of an object or of an action with the* subjective *conditions of life,* i.e., with the faculty of the *causality of a representation with respect to the reality of its object* (or with respect to the determination of the powers of the subject to action in order to produce the object). For the purposes of this *Critique* I have no further need of concepts borrowed from psychology; the *Critique* itself supplies the rest. It is easily seen that the question whether pleasure must always be put at the basis of the faculty of desire or whether under certain conditions pleasure only follows upon its determination, is left undecided by this exposition; for it is composed only of marks belonging to the pure understanding, i.e., categories, which contain nothing empirical. Such a precaution – namely, not to anticipate one's judgments by definitions ventured before complete analysis of the concept, which is often achieved very late – is to be highly recommended throughout philosophy, and yet is often neglected. It may be observed throughout the course of the critical philosophy (of theoretical as well as practical reason) that many opportunities are presented to make up for defects in the old dogmatic procedure of philosophy and to correct errors that are not noticed until one makes such a use of concepts of reason as is directed to the whole.

I have no fear, with respect to this treatise, of the reproach that I want to introduce a *new language,* because here the kind of cognition itself approaches popularity. This reproach with respect to the first *Critique* could also not have occurred to anyone who had thought it through and not merely turned over the pages. To invent new words where the language already has no lack of expressions for given concepts is a childish effort to distinguish oneself from the crowd, if not by new and true thoughts yet by new patches on an old garment. If, therefore, the readers of that work know of more popular expressions that are still just as suitable to the thought as the ones I used seem to me, or if they think they can show the nullity of these thoughts themselves and so too of the expressions signifying them, they would by the first very much oblige me, for I only desire to be understood; but with respect to the second, they would deserve well of philosophy. However, as long as these thoughts stand, I very much doubt that expressions suitable for them and yet more common can be found.*

In this way the a priori principles of two faculties of the mind, the

---

*Here I am less worried (about that unintelligibility) than about occasional misinterpretation with respect to some expressions that I have sought out with the greatest care in order that the concepts to which they point may not be missed. Thus, in the table of categories of *practical* reason under the heading Modality, the *permitted* and the *forbidden* (the practically objectively possible and impossible), have almost the same sense in the common use of language as the immediately following categories, *duty* and *contrary to duty;* here, however, the *first* mean that which harmonizes or conflicts with a merely *possible* practical precept (as, say, the solution of all problems of geometry and mechanics), the *second,* that which is similarly related to a law *actually* present in reason as such; and this distinction in meaning is not altogether foreign even to the common use of language, although it is somewhat unusual. Thus, for example, it is *forbidden* to an orator, as such, to forge new words or constructions; this is to some extent *permitted* to a poet; in neither case is there any thought of duty. For if anyone is willing to forfeit his reputation as an orator, no one can prevent him. We have here to do only with the distinction of *imperatives* under *problematic, assertoric,* and *apodictic* determining grounds. So too, in the note where I compared the moral ideas of practical perfection in different philosophic schools, I distinguished the idea of *wisdom* from that of *holiness,* although I explained them as identical in their ground and objectively. In that place, however, I understood by wisdom only that wisdom to which the human being (the Stoic) lays claim, and thus took it *subjectively,* as an attribute ascribed to the human being. (Perhaps the expression *virtue,* which the Stoic also made much of, could better indicate what is characteristic of his school.) But the expression, a *postulate* of pure practical reason, could most of all occasion misinterpretation if confused with the meaning that postulates of pure mathematics have, which bring with them apodictic certainty. The latter, however, postulate the *possibility of an action,* the object of which has been previously theoretically cognized a priori with complete certitude as *possible.* But the former postulate the possibility of an *object* itself (God and the immortality of the soul) from apodictic *practical* laws, and therefore only on behalf of a practical reason, so that this certainty of the postulated possibility is not at all theoretical, hence also not apodictic, i.e., it is not a necessity cognized with respect to the object but is, instead, an assumption necessary with respect to the subject's observance of its objective but practical laws, hence merely a necessary hypothesis. I could find no better expression for this subjective but nevertheless unconditional rational necessity.

faculty of cognition and that of desire, would be found and determined as to the conditions, extent, and boundaries of their use, and a firm basis would thereby be laid for a scientific system of philosophy, both theoretical and practical.

Nothing worse could happen to these labors than that someone should make the unexpected discovery that there is and can be no a priori cognition at all.[3] But there is no danger of this. It would be tantamount to someone's wanting to prove by reason that there is no reason. For, we say that we cognize something by reason only when we are aware that we could have known it even if it had not presented itself to us as it did in experience; hence rational cognition and cognition a priori are one and the same. It is an outright contradiction to want to extract necessity from an empirical proposition (*ex pumice aquam*)[a] and to give a judgment, along with necessity, true universality (without which there is no rational inference and so not even inference from analogy, which is at least a presumed universality and objective necessity and therefore presupposes it). To substitute subjective necessity, that is, custom, for objective necessity, which is to be found only in a priori judgments, is to deny to reason the ability to judge an object, that is, to cognize it and what belongs to it; it is to deny, for example, that when something often or always follows upon a certain prior state one could *infer* it from that (for this would mean objective necessity and the concept of an a priori connection) and to say only that we may expect similar cases (just as animals do), that is, to reject the concept of cause fundamentally as false and a mere delusion of thought. As for wanting to remedy this lack of objective and hence universal validity by saying that one sees no ground for attributing to other rational beings a different way of representing things:[b] if that yielded a valid inference then our ignorance would render us greater service in enlarging our cognition than all our reflection. For, merely because of our not knowing rational beings other than human beings, we would have a right to assume them to be constituted just as we cognize ourselves to be, that is, we would really know them. I do not even mention here that universality of assent does not prove the objective validity of a judgment (i.e., its validity as cognition) but only that, even if universal assent should happen to be correct, it could still not yield a proof of agreement with the object; on the contrary, only objective validity constitutes the ground of a necessary universal agreement.

Hume would be quite content with this system of universal empiricism of principles; for, as is well known, he asked nothing more than that a merely subjective meaning of necessity, namely custom, be assumed in place of any objective meaning of necessity in the concept of cause, so as

---

[a] "water from a pumice stone." Plautus, *The Persians* 1.1.42.
[b] *Vorstellungsart*

to deny to reason any judgment about God, freedom, and immortality: and, if once his principles were granted, he certainly knew very well how to draw conclusions from them with all logical validity. But Hume himself did not make empiricism so universal as to include mathematics.[4] He held its propositions to be analytic, and if this were correct they would in fact be apodictic also: but from this no inference could be drawn to reason's ability to make apodictic judgments in philosophy as well, namely judgments that would be synthetic (as the proposition of causality is). However, if one assumes a *universal* empiricism of principles, then mathematics will be included.

Now, if mathematics comes into conflict with a reason that admits only empirical principles, as inevitably happens in the antinomy where mathematics proves incontestably the infinite divisibility of space, which empiricism cannot allow, then the greatest possible evidence of demonstration is in manifest contradiction with the alleged inferences from empirical principles, and one has to ask, like Cheselden's blind man, "Which deceives me, sight or touch?"[5] (For empiricism is based on a necessity *felt*, but rationalism on a necessity *seen*.)*p* And thus universal empiricism reveals itself as genuine skepticism, which in this unlimited sense has been falsely ascribed to Hume,* since he left at least one certain touchstone of experience in mathematics, whereas genuine skepticism admits no such touchstone at all (which can only be found in a priori principles), although experience consists not of feelings only but also of judgments.

Since, however, in this philosophic and critical age such empiricism can scarcely be taken seriously, and it is presumably put forward only as an exercise for judgment and in order to put the necessity of rational a priori principles in a clearer light by contrast, one can only be grateful to those who are willing to trouble themselves with this otherwise uninstructive work.

---

*Names that designate the followers of a sect have always been accompanied with a good deal of injustice;[6] this would be much the case if someone said, *N is an idealist*. For, although he not only admits but even insists that real objects, external things, correspond to our representations of external things, he nevertheless holds that the form of intuition of them does not depend on them but only on the human mind.

p *eingesehenen*

Introduction
On the idea of a critique of practical reason

The theoretical use of reason was concerned with objects of the cognitive faculty only, and a critique of it with regard to this use really dealt only with the *pure* cognitive faculty, since this raised the suspicion, which was afterwards confirmed, that it might easily lose itself beyond its boundaries, among unattainable objects or even among contradictory concepts. It is quite different with the practical use of reason. In this, reason is concerned with the determining grounds of the will, which is a faculty either of producing objects corresponding to representations or of determining itself to effect such objects (whether the physical power is sufficient or not), that is, of determining its causality. For, in that, reason can at least suffice to determine the will and always has objective reality insofar as volition alone is at issue. The first question here, then, is whether pure reason of itself alone suffices to determine the will or whether it can be a determining ground of the will only as empirically conditioned. Now there enters here a concept of causality justified by the *Critique of Pure Reason* although not capable of being presented empirically, namely that of *freedom;* and if we can now discover grounds for proving that this property does in fact belong to the human will (and so to the will of all rational beings as well), then it will not only be shown that pure reason can be practical but that it alone, and not reason empirically limited, is unconditionally practical. Consequently, we shall not have to do a critique of *pure practical* reason but only of *practical* reason as such. For, pure reason, once it is shown to exist, needs no critique. It is pure reason that itself contains the standard for the critical examination of every use of it. It is therefore incumbent upon the *Critique of Practical Reason* as such to prevent empirically conditioned reason from presuming that it, alone and exclusively, furnishes the determining ground of the will. If it is proved that there is pure reason, its use is alone immanent; the empirically conditioned use, which lays claim to absolute rule,[q] is on the contrary transcendent and expresses itself in demands and commands that go quite beyond its

---

[q] *Alleinherrschaft*

CRITIQUE OF PRACTICAL REASON

sphere – precisely the opposite relation from what could be said of pure reason in its speculative use.

Since, however, it is still pure reason whose cognition here lies at the basis of its practical use, the division of a *Critique of Practical Reason* must in its general outline be arranged in conformity with that of the speculative. We shall therefore have to have a *Doctrine of Elements*[r] and a *Doctrine of Method* for it; and within the former, an *Analytic*, as the rule of truth, as the first part, and a *Dialectic*, as the exposition and resolution of illusion[s] in the judgments of practical reason. However, the order in the subdivision of the Analytic will be the reverse of that in the *Critique* of pure speculative reason. For, in the present *Critique* we shall begin with *principles* and proceed to *concepts*, and only then, where possible, from them to the senses, whereas in the case of speculative reason we had to begin with the senses and end with principles. The ground for doing so lies, again, in this: that now we have to do with a will and have to consider reason not in its relation to objects but in relation to this will and its causality; thus the principles of empirically unconditioned causality must come first, and only afterward can the attempt be made to establish our concepts of the determining ground of such a will, of their application to objects and finally to the subject and its sensibility. Here the law of causality from freedom, that is, some pure practical rational principle, constitutes the unavoidable beginning and determines the objects to which alone it can be referred.

---

[r] *Elementarlehre*. On "doctrine" in its strict sense, see the text from the *Critique of Judgment* (5:170) referred to in the note to *The Metaphysics of Morals* (6:205).
[s] *Schein*

*The
critique of practical reason
Part one*

*Doctrine of the elements
of
pure practical reason*

Book one
The analytic of pure practical reason

Chapter I
On the Principles of Pure Practical Reason

1.
DEFINITION[t]

Practical *principles* are propositions that contain a general determination of the will, having under it several practical rules. They are *subjective* or *maxims*, when the condition is regarded by the subject as holding only for his will; but they are *objective* or practical *laws*, when the condition is cognized as objective, that is, as holding for the will of every rational being.

Remark

If it is assumed that *pure* reason can contain within itself a practical ground, that is, one sufficient to determine the will, then there are practical laws; otherwise all practical principles will be mere maxims. Within a pathologically[u] affected will of a rational being there can be found a conflict of maxims with the practical laws cognized by himself. For example, someone can make it his maxim to let no insult pass unavenged and yet at the same time see that this is no practical law but only his maxim – that, on the contrary, as being in one and the same maxim a rule for the will of every rational being it could not harmonize with itself. In cognition of nature[v] the principles of what happens (e.g., the principle of equality of action and reaction in the communication of motion) are at the same time laws of nature; for there the use of reason is theoretical and determined by the constitution of the object. In practical cognition – that is, cognition having to do only with determining grounds of the will – the principles that one makes for oneself are not yet laws to which one is unavoidably

---

[t] *Erklärung.* See *Critique of Pure Reason* (A:730; B:758), and note *m* to *The Metaphysics of Morals* (6:226).
[u] *pathologisch.* Kant uses "pathological" in the sense of "dependent upon sensibility."
[v] *Naturekenntnis*

subject, because reason, in the practical, has to do with the subject, namely with his faculty of desire, which by its special constitution can make various adjustments to the rule.*" A practical rule is always a product of reason because it prescribes action as a means to an effect, which is its purpose. But for a being in whom reason quite alone is not the determining ground of the will, this rule is an *imperative,* that is, a rule indicated by an "ought," which expresses objective necessitation to the action and signifies that if reason completely determined the will the action would without fail take place in accordance with this rule. Imperatives, therefore, hold objectively and are quite distinct from maxims, which are subjective principles. But the former either determine the conditions of the causality of a rational being as an efficient cause merely with respect to the effect and its adequacy to it or they determine only the will, whether or not it is sufficient for the effect. The first would be hypothetical imperatives and would contain mere precepts of skill; the second, on the contrary, would be categorical and would alone be practical laws. Thus maxims are indeed *principles* but not *imperatives.* But imperatives themselves, when they are conditional – that is, when they do not determine the will simply as will but only with respect to a desired effect, that is, when they are hypothetical imperatives – are indeed practical *precepts* but not *laws.* The latter must sufficiently determine the will as will even before I ask whether I have the ability required for a desired effect or what I am to do in order to produce it, and must thus be categorical: otherwise they are not laws because they lack the necessity which, if it is to be practical, must be independent of conditions that are pathological and therefore only contingently connected with the will. Tell someone, for example, that he must work and save in his youth in order not to want in his old age; this is a correct and also important practical precept of the will. But it is readily seen that here the will is directed to something *else* which it is presupposed that it desires; and as to this desire, it must be left to the agent himself whether he foresees other resources than means acquired by himself, or does not hope to live to old age, or thinks that in case of future need he can make do with little. Reason, from which alone can arise any rule that is to contain necessity, does indeed put necessity even into this precept (for otherwise it would not be an imperative), though it is only a subjectively conditioned necessity and cannot be presupposed in the same degree in all subjects. But it is requisite to reason's lawgiving that it should need to presuppose only *itself,* because a rule is objectively and universally valid only when it holds without the contingent, subjective conditions that distinguish one rational being from another. Now tell someone that he ought never to make a lying promise; this is a rule that has to do only with his will, regardless of whether the purposes the human being may have can be thereby attained; the mere volition is that which is to be determined

---

" sich die Regel vielfältig richten kann

completely a priori by this rule. If, now, it is found that this rule is practically correct, then it is a law because it is a categorical imperative. Thus practical laws refer only to the will, without regard to what is attained by its causality, and one may abstract from this letter (as belonging to the world of sense) so as to have them pure.

2.
THEOREM I

All practical principles that presuppose an *object* (matter) of the faculty of desire as the determining ground of the will are, without exception, empirical and can furnish no practical laws.

By "the matter of the faculty of desire" I understand an object whose reality is desired. Now, when desire for this object precedes the practical rule and is the condition of its becoming a principle, then I say (*first*) that this principle is in that case always empirical. For, the determining ground of choice[x] is then the representation of an object and that relation of the representation to the subject by which the faculty of desire is determined to realize the object. Such a relation to the subject, however, is called *pleasure* in the reality of an object. This would therefore have to be presupposed as a condition of the possibility of the determination of choice. But it cannot be cognized a priori of any representation of an object, whatever it may be, whether it will be connected with *pleasure* or *displeasure* or be *indifferent*. Hence in such a case the determining ground of choice must always be empirical, and so too must be the practical material principle that presupposes it as a condition.

Now (*second*) a principle that is based only on the subjective condition of receptivity to a pleasure or displeasure (which can always be cognized only empirically and cannot be valid in the same way for all rational beings) can indeed serve as his *maxim* for the subject who possesses this receptivity but not as a *law* even for him (because it is lacking in objective necessity, which must be cognized a priori); such a principle can, accordingly, never furnish a practical law.

3.
THEOREM II

All material practical principles as such are, without exception, of one and the same kind and come under the general principle of self-love or one's own happiness.

Pleasure arising from the representation of the existence[y] of a thing,

---
[x] *Willkür*. See *The Metaphysics of Morals* (6: 213–14, 226). *Wahl* is translated as "a choice" and *wählen* as "to choose."

[y] *Existenz*. The word translated as "existence" later in this clause is *Dasein*.

insofar as it is to be a determining ground of desire for this thing, is based on the *receptivity* of the subject, since it *depends* upon the existence of an object; hence it belongs to sense (feeling) and not to the understanding, which expresses a relation of a representation *to an object* by concepts, not to the subject by feelings. It is, then, practical only insofar as the feeling[z] of agreeableness that the subject expects from the reality of an object determines the faculty of desire. Now, a rational being's consciousness of the agreeableness of life uninterruptedly accompanying his whole existence is *happiness,* and the principle of making this the supreme determining ground of choice is the principle of self-love. Thus all material principles, which place the determining ground of choice in the pleasure or displeasure to be felt in the reality of some object, are wholly *of the same kind* insofar as they belong without exception to the principle of self-love or one's own happiness.

Corollary

All *material* practical rules put the determining ground of the will in the *lower faculty of desire,* and were there no *merely formal* laws of the will sufficient to determine it, then neither could *any higher faculty of desire* be admitted.

Remark I

It is surprising that men, otherwise acute, believe they can find a distinction between the *lower* and the *higher* faculty of desire according to whether the **representations** that are connected with the feeling of pleasure have their origin *in the senses* or in the *understanding.* For when one inquires about the determining grounds of desire and puts them in the agreeableness expected from something or other, it does not matter at all where the *representation* of this pleasing object comes from but only how much it *pleases.* If a representation, even though it may have its seat and origin in the understanding, can determine choice only by presupposing a feeling of pleasure in the subject, its being a determining ground of choice is wholly dependent upon the nature of inner sense, namely that this can be agreeably affected by the representation. However dissimilar representations of objects may be – they may be representations of the understanding or even of reason, in contrast to representations of sense – the feeling

---

[z] *Empfindung.* On Kant's use of *Empfindung* and *Gefühl,* see note k to the *Groundwork of the Metaphysics of Morals,* (4:399). In order to avoid excessive annotation, in the present context "feeling" is used for both *Empfindung* and *Gefühl* unless the sense of *Empfindung* seems doubtful.

of pleasure by which alone they properly constitute the determining ground of the will (the agreeableness, the gratification[a] expected from the object, which impels activity to produce it) is nevertheless of one and the same kind not only insofar as it can always be cognized only empirically but also insofar as it affects one and the same vital force that is manifested in the faculty of desire, and in this respect can differ only in degree from any other determining ground. Otherwise, how could one make a comparison in *magnitude* between two determining grounds quite different as to the kind of representation, so as to prefer the one that most affects the faculty of desire? The same human being can return unread an instructive book that he cannot again obtain, in order not to miss a hunt; he can leave in the middle of a fine speech in order not to be late for a meal; he can leave an intellectual conversation, such as he otherwise values highly, in order to take his place at the gaming table; he can even repulse a poor man whom at other times it is a joy for him to benefit because he now has only enough money in his pocket to pay for his admission to the theater. If the determination of his will rests on the feeling of agreeableness or disagreeableness that he expects from some cause, it is all the same to him by what kind of representation he is affected. The only thing that concerns him, in order to decide upon a choice, is how intense, how long, how easily acquired, and how often repeated this agreeableness is. Just as, to someone who wants money to spend it is all the same whether the material in it, the gold, was dug out of a mountain or washed out of sand provided it is accepted everywhere at the same value, so no one asks, when he is concerned only with the agreeableness of life, whether representations belong to the understanding or to the senses but only *how much* and *how great* satisfaction they will furnish him for the longest time. Only those who would like to deny to pure reason the ability to determine the will without some feeling being presupposed could deviate so far from their own definition[b] as to explain[c] as quite heterogeneous what they have themselves previously brought under one and the same principle. Thus it is found, for example, that we can find satisfaction in the mere *exercise of our powers*, in consciousness of our strength of soul in overcoming obstacles opposed to our plans, in cultivating our talents of spirit, and so forth, and we correctly call these joys and delights *more refined* because they are more under our control than others, do not wear out but rather strengthen feeling for further enjoyment of them, and while they delight they at the

5:24

---

[a] See note v to the *Groundwork of the Metaphysics of Morals* (4:393). In the following pages Kant again uses a variety of words for "pleasure," and no attempt has been made to distinguish, in particular, between *Zufriedenheit* and *Vergnügen*.
[b] *Erklärung*
[c] *erklären*

same time cultivate. But as for passing them off, on this account, as a different way of determining the will then merely through sense, even though they presuppose for the possibility of that satisfaction a feeling for it implanted in us as the first condition of this pleasure: this is just as when ignorant people who would like to dabble in metaphysics think of matter so refined, so superrefined, that they make themselves giddy with it and then believe that in this way they have devised a *spiritual* and yet extended being. If, with Epicurus, we have virtue determine the will only by means of the gratification it promises, we cannot afterward find fault with him for holding that this is of exactly the same kind as those of the coarsest senses; for we have no ground at all to charge him with ascribing the representations by which this feeling is excited in us to the bodily senses only. As far as can be conjectured, he sought the source of many of them in the use of the higher cognitive faculty; but this did not and could not prevent him from holding, in accordance with the principle mentioned above, that the satisfaction itself which those intellectual representations afford us and by which alone they can be determining grounds of the will is of exactly the same kind. *Consistency* is the greatest obligation[d] of a philosopher and yet the most rarely found. The ancient Greek schools give us more examples of it than we find in our *syncretistic* age, in which a certain *coalition system* of contradictory principles, replete with dishonesty and shallowness, is contrived, because it commends itself better to a public that is satisfied with knowing something of everything and nothing as a whole, so that it can turn its hand to anything. The principle of one's own happiness, however much understanding and reason may be used in it, still contains no determining ground for the will other than such as is suitable to the *lower* faculty of desire; and thus either there is no higher faculty of desire at all or else *pure reason* must be practical of itself and alone, that is, it must be able to determine the will by the mere form of a practical rule without presupposing any feeling and hence without any representation of the agreeable or disagreeable as the matter of the faculty of desire, which is always an empirical condition of principles. Then only, insofar as reason of itself (not in the service of the inclinations) determines the will, is reason a true *higher* faculty of desire, to which the pathologically determinable is subordinate, and then only is reason really, and indeed *specifically*, distinct from the latter, so that even the least admixture of the latter's impulses infringes upon its strength and superiority, just as anything at all empirical as a condition in a mathematical demonstration degrades and destroys its dignity and force. In a practical law reason determines the will immediately, not by means of an intervening feeling of pleasure or displeasure, not even in this law; and that it can as pure reason be practical is what alone makes it possible for it to *be lawgiving*.

[d] *Obliegenheit*

Remark II

To be happy is necessarily the demand of every rational but finite being and therefore an unavoidable determining ground of its faculty of desire. For, satisfaction with one's whole existence is not, as it were, an original possession and a beatitude,' which would presuppose a consciousness of one's independent self-sufficiency, but is instead a problem imposed upon him by his finite nature itself, because he is needy and this need is directed to the matter of his faculty of desire, that is, something related to a subjective feeling of pleasure or displeasure underlying it by which is determined what he needs in order to be satisfied with his condition. But just because this material determining ground can be cognized only empirically by the subject, it is impossible to regard this problem as law, since a law, as objective, must contain the *very same determining ground* of the will in all cases and for all rational beings. For, although the concept of happiness *everywhere* underlies the practical relation of *objects* to the faculty of desire, it is still only the general name for subjective determining grounds, and it determines nothing specific about it although this is all that matters in this practical problem and without such determination the problem cannot be solved at all. That is to say, in what each has to put his happiness comes down to the particular feeling of pleasure and displeasure in each and, even within one and the same subject, to needs that differ as this feeling changes; and a law that is *subjectively necessary* (as a law of nature) is thus *objectively* a very *contingent* practical principle, which can and must be very different in different subjects, and hence can never yield a law because, in the desire for happiness, it is not the form of lawfulness that counts but simply the matter, namely whether I am to expect satisfaction from following the law, and how much. Principles of self-love can indeed contain universal rules of skill (for finding means to one's purposes), but in that case they are only theoretical principles* (such as, e.g., how someone who would like to eat bread has to construct a mill). But practical precepts based on them can never be universal because the determining ground of the faculty of desire is based on the feeling of pleasure or displeasure, which can never be assumed to be universally directed to the same objects.

But suppose that finite rational beings were thoroughly agreed with respect to what they had to take as objects of their feelings of pleasure and

---

*Propositions that in mathematics or physics are called *practical* should properly be called *technical*. For in these teachings it is not at all a question of the determination of the will; they only point out the manifold of the possible action that is sufficient to produce a certain effect, and are thus as theoretical as any proposition that asserts the connection of a cause with an effect. Whoever approves the effect must also be willing to approve the cause.

' *eine Seligkeit*

pain and even with respect to the means they must use to obtain the first and avoid the other; even then they could by no means pass off the *principle of self-love* as *a practical law;* for, this unanimity itself would still be only contingent. The determining ground would still be only subjectively valid and merely empirical and would not have that necessity which is thought in every law, namely objective necessity from a priori grounds, unless one had to say that this necessity is not practical at all but only physical, namely that the action is as unavoidably forced from us by our inclination as is yawning when we see others yawn. It would be better to maintain that there are no practical laws at all but only *counsels* on behalf of our desires than to raise merely subjective principles to the rank of practical laws, which absolutely must have objective and not merely subjective necessity and which must be cognized a priori by reason, not by experience (however empirically universal this may be). Even the rules of uniform appearances are called laws of nature (e.g., mechanical laws) only when they are either cognized really a priori or (as in the case of chemical laws) when it is assumed that they would be cognized a priori from objective grounds if our insight went deeper. But in the case of merely subjective practical principles it is expressly made a condition that they must have as their basis not objective but subjective conditions of choice, and hence that they must always be represented as mere maxims, never as practical laws. This latter remark seems at first glance to be mere cavilling at words; but it defines the terms[f] of the most important distinction that can ever be considered in practical investigations.

4.
THEOREM III

If a rational being is to think of his maxims as practical universal laws, he can think of them only as principles that contain the determining ground of the will not by their matter but only by their form.

The matter of a practical principle is the object of the will. This is either the determining ground of the will or it is not. If it is the determining ground of the will, then the rule of the will is subject to an empirical condition (to the relation of the determining representation to the feeling of pleasure or displeasure), and so is not a practical law. Now, all that remains of a law if one separates from it everything material, that is, every object of the will (as its determining ground), is the mere *form* of giving universal law. Therefore, either a rational being cannot think of *his* subjectively practical principles, that is, his maxims, as being at the same time universal laws or he must assume that their mere form, by which *they are fit for a giving of universal law*, of itself and alone makes them practical laws.

---

[f] *sie ist die Wortbestimmung*

Remark

The most common understanding can distinguish without instruction what form in a maxim makes it fit for a giving of universal law and what does not. I have, for example, made it my maxim to increase my wealth by every safe means. Now I have a *deposit* in my hands, the owner of which has died and left no record of it. This is, naturally, a case for my maxim. Now I want only to know whether that maxim could also hold as a universal practical law. I therefore apply the maxim to the present case and ask whether it could indeed take the form of a law, and consequently whether I could through my maxim at the same time give such a law as this: that everyone may deny a deposit which no one can prove has been made. I at once become aware that such a principle, as a law, would annihilate itself since it would bring it about that there would be no deposits at all. A practical law that I cognize as such must qualify for a giving of universal law: this is an identical proposition and therefore self-evident. Now, if I say that my will is subject to a practical *law*, I cannot cite my inclination (e.g., in the present case my avarice) as the determining ground of my will appropriate to a universal practical law; for this is so far from being qualified for a giving of universal law that in the form of a universal law it must instead destroy itself.

5:28

It is, therefore, strange that intelligent men could have thought of passing off the desire for happiness as a universal *practical law* on the ground that the desire, and so too the *maxim* by which each makes this desire the determining ground of his will, is universal. For whereas elsewhere a universal law of nature makes everything harmonious, here, if one wanted to give the maxim the universality of a law, the most extreme opposite of harmony would follow, the worst conflict, and the complete annihilation of the maxim itself and its purpose. For then the will of all has not one and the same object but each has his own (his own welfare), which can indeed happen to accord with the purposes of others who are likewise pursuing their own but which is far from sufficing for a law because the exceptions that one is warranted in making upon occasion are endless and cannot be determinately embraced in a universal rule. In this way there results a harmony like that which a certain satirical poem depicts in the unanimity between a married couple bent on going to ruin: "*O marvellous harmony, what he wants she wants too*" and so forth, or like what is said of the pledge of King Francis I to the Emperor Charles V: "What my brother Charles would have (Milan), that I would also have." Empirical determining grounds are not fit for any universal external legislation[g] and are no more fit for internal lawgiving; for each puts at the basis of inclination his subject – another, another subject – and even within each subject now the

---

[g] *allgemeinen äußern Gesetzgebung*

influence of one inclination preponderates and now that of another. To discover a law that under this condition would govern them all – that is to say, with omnilateral concord – is quite impossible.

5.
PROBLEM I

Supposing that the mere lawgiving form of maxims is the only sufficient determining ground of a will: to find the constitution of a will that is determinable by it alone.

Since the mere form of a law can be represented only by reason and is therefore not an object of the senses and consequently does not belong among appearances, the representation of this form as the determining ground of the will is distinct from all determining grounds of events in nature in accordance with the law of causality, because in their case the determining grounds must themselves be appearances. But if no determining ground of the will other than that universal lawgiving form can serve as a law for it, such a will must be thought as altogether independent of the natural law of appearances in their relations to one another, namely the law of causality. But such independence is called *freedom* in the strictest, that is, in the transcendental, sense. Therefore, a will for which the mere lawgiving form of a maxim can alone serve as a law is a free will.

6.
PROBLEM II

Supposing that a will *is free:* to find the law that alone is competent to determine it necessarily.

Since the matter of a practical law, that is, an object of maxim, can never be given otherwise than empirically whereas a free will, as independent of empirical conditions (i.e., conditions belonging to the sensible world), must nevertheless be determinable, a free will must find a determining ground in the law but independently of the *matter* of the law. But, besides the matter of the law, nothing further is contained in it than the lawgiving form. The lawgiving form, insofar as this is contained in the maxim, is therefore the only thing that can constitute a determining ground of the will.

Remark

Thus freedom and unconditional practical law reciprocally imply each other.[h] Now I do not ask here whether they are in fact different or whether

---

[h] *weisen . . . wechselsweise auf einander zurück.* In the *Groundwork of the Metaphysics of Morals* (4:450), Kant said that freedom and the lawgiving of one's own will are both autonomy and hence *Wechselbegriffe.*

it is not much rather the case that an unconditional law is merely the self-consciousness of a pure practical reason, this being identical with the positive concept of freedom; I ask instead from what our *cognition* of the unconditionally practical *starts*, whether from freedom or from the practical law. It cannot start from freedom, for we can neither be immediately conscious of this, since the first concept of it is negative, nor can we conclude to it from experience, since experience lets us cognize only the law of appearances and hence the mechanism of nature, the direct opposite of freedom. It is therefore the *moral law*, of which we become immediately conscious (as soon as we draw up maxims of the will for ourselves), that *first* offers itself to us and, inasmuch as reason presents it as a determining ground not to be outweighed by any sensible conditions and indeed quite independent of them, leads directly to the concept of freedom. But how is consciousness of that moral law possible? We can become aware of pure practical laws just as we are aware of pure theoretical principles, by attending to the necessity with which reason prescribes them to us and to the setting aside of all empirical conditions to which reason directs us. The concept of a pure will arises from the first, as consciousness of a pure understanding arises from the latter. That this is the true subordination of our concepts and that morality first discloses to us the concept of freedom, so that it is *practical reason* which first poses to speculative reason, with this concept, the most insoluble problem so as to put it in the greatest perplexity, is clear from the following: that, since nothing in appearances can be explained by the concept of freedom and there the mechanism of nature must instead constitute the only guide; since, moreover, the antinomy of pure reason when it wants to ascend to the unconditioned in the series of causes gets it entangled in incomprehensibilities on one side as much as on the other, whereas the latter (mechanism) is at least useful in the explanation of appearances, one would never have ventured to introduce freedom into science had not the moral law, and with it practical reason, come in and forced this concept upon us. But experience also confirms this order of concepts in us. Suppose someone asserts of his lustful inclination that, when the desired object and the opportunity are present, it is quite irresistible to him; ask him whether, if a gallows were erected in front of the house where he finds this opportunity and he would be hanged on it immediately after gratifying his lust, he would not then control his inclination. One need not conjecture very long what he would reply. But ask him whether, if his prince demanded, on pain of the same immediate execution, that he give false testimony against an honorable man whom the prince would like to destroy under a plausible pretext, he would consider it possible to overcome his love of life, however great it may be. He would perhaps not venture to assert whether he would do it or not, but he must admit without hesitation that it would be possible for him. He judges, therefore, that he can do something because he is aware that he ought to do it and cognizes freedom within him, which, without the moral law, would have remained unknown to him.

7.
FUNDAMENTAL LAW OF PURE PRACTICAL REASON

So act that the maxim of your will could always hold at the same time as a principle in a giving of universal law.

Remark

Pure geometry has postulates as practical propositions which, however, contain nothing further than the presupposition that one *could* do something if it were required that one should do it, and these are the only propositions of pure geometry that concern an existing thing.[i] They are thus practical rules under a problematic condition of the will. Here, however, the rule says: one ought absolutely to proceed in a certain way. The practical rule is therefore unconditional and so is represented a priori as a categorical practical proposition by which the will is objectively determined absolutely and immediately (by the practical rule itself, which accordingly is here a law). For, pure reason, *practical of itself,* is here immediately lawgiving. The will is thought as independent of empirical conditions and hence, as a pure will, as determined *by the mere form of law,* and this determining ground is regarded as the supreme condition of all maxims. The thing is strange enough, and has nothing like it in all the rest of our practical cognition. For, the a priori thought of a possible giving of universal law, which is thus merely problematic, is unconditionally commanded as a law without borrowing anything from experience or from some external will. But it is also not a precept in accordance with which an action by which a desired effect is possible should be done (for then the rule would always be physically conditioned); it is instead a rule that determines the will a priori only with respect to the form of its maxims; and so it is at least not impossible to think of a law that serves only for the *subjective* form of principles as yet a determining ground through the *objective* form of a law as such. Consciousness of this fundamental law may be called a fact of reason because one cannot reason it out from antecedent data of reason, for example, from consciousness of freedom (since this is not antecedently given to us) and because it instead forces itself upon us of itself as a synthetic a priori proposition that is not based on any intuition, either pure or empirical, although it would be analytic if the freedom of the will were presupposed; but for this, as a positive concept, an intellectual intuition

---

[i] *ein Dasein*

would be required, which certainly cannot be assumed here. However, in order to avoid misinterpretation in regarding this law as *given*, it must be noted carefully that it is not an empirical fact but the sole fact of pure reason which, by it, announces itself as originally lawgiving (*sic volo, sic jubeo*).^j

Corollary

Pure reason is practical of itself alone and gives (to the human being) a universal law which we call the *moral law*.

Remark

The fact mentioned above is undeniable. One need only analyze the judgment that people pass on the lawfulness of their actions in order to find that, whatever inclination may say to the contrary, their reason, incorruptible and self-constrained, always holds the maxim of the will in an action up to the pure will, that is, to itself inasmuch as it regards itself as a priori practical. Now this principle of morality, just on account of the universality of the lawgiving that makes it the formal supreme determining ground of the will regardless of all subjective differences, is declared by reason to be at the same time a law for all rational beings insofar as they have a will, that is, the ability^k to determine their causality by the representation of rules, hence insofar as they are capable of actions in accordance with principles and consequently also in accordance with a priori practical principles (for these alone have that necessity which reason requires for a principle). It is, therefore, not limited to human beings only but applies to all finite beings that have reason and will and even includes the infinite being as the supreme intelligence. In the first case, however, the law has the form of an imperative, because in them, as rational beings, one can presuppose a *pure* will but, insofar as they are beings affected by needs and sensible motives, not a *holy* will, that is, such a will as would not be capable of any maxim conflicting with the moral law. Accordingly the moral law is for them an *imperative* that commands categorically because the law is unconditional; the relation of such a will to this law is *dependence* under the name of obligation, which signifies a *necessitation*, though only by reason and its objective law, to an action which is called *duty* because a choice that is pathologically affected (though not thereby determined, hence still free) brings with it a wish arising from *subjective* causes, because of which it can often be opposed to the pure objective determining ground and thus needs a resistance of practical reason which, as moral necessita-

^j What I will, I command. Juvenal *Satire* 6.
^k *Vermögen*

tion, may be called an internal but intellectual constraint. In the supremely self-sufficient intelligence, choice is rightly represented as incapable of any maxim that could not at the same time be objectively a law, and the concept of *holiness*, which on that account belongs to it, puts it, not indeed above all practically restrictive laws and so above obligation and duty. This holiness of will is nevertheless a practical *idea*, which must necessarily serve as a *model* to which all finite rational beings can only approximate without end and which the pure moral law, itself called holy because of this, constantly and rightly holds before their eyes; the utmost that finite practical reason can effect is to make sure of this unending progress of one's maxims toward this model and of their constancy in continual progress, that is, virtue; and virtue itself, in turn, at least as a naturally acquired ability, can never be completed, because assurance in such a case never becomes apodictic certainty and, as persuasion, is very dangerous.

8.

THEOREM IV

Autonomy of the will is the sole principle of all moral laws and of duties in keeping with them; *heteronomy* of choice, on the other hand, not only does not ground any obligation at all but is instead opposed to the principle of obligation and to the morality of the will. That is to say, the sole principle of morality consists in independence from all matter of the law (namely, from a desired object) and at the same time in the determination of choice through the mere form of giving universal law that a maxim must be capable of. That *independence*, however, is freedom in the *negative* sense, whereas this *lawgiving of its own*[1] on the part of pure and, as such, practical reason is freedom in the *positive* sense. Thus the moral law expresses nothing other than the *autonomy* of pure practical reason, that is, freedom, and this is itself the formal condition of all maxims, under which alone they can accord with the supreme practical law. If, therefore, the matter of volition, which can be nothing other than the object of a desire that is connected with the law, enters into the practical law **as a condition of its possibility**, there results heteronomy of choice, namely dependence upon the natural law of following some impulse or inclination, and the will does not give itself the law but only the precept for rationally following pathological law; but a maxim which, in this way, can never contain within it the form of giving universal law not only establishes no obligation but is itself opposed to the principle of a *pure* practical reason and so also to the moral disposition, even though the action arising from it may be in conformity with the law.

[1] *diese eigene Gesetzgebung*

Remark I

Thus a practical precept that brings with it a material (hence empirical) condition must never be reckoned a practical law. For, the law of the pure will, which is free, puts the will in a sphere quite different from the empirical, and the necessity that the law expresses, since it is not to be a natural necessity, can therefore consist only in the formal conditions of the possibility of a law in general. All the matter of practical rules rests always on subjective conditions, which afford it no universality for rational beings other than a merely conditional one (in case I *desire* this or that, what I would then have to do in order to make it real), and they all turn on the principle *of one's own happiness*. Now it is indeed undeniable that every volition must also have an object and hence a matter; but the matter is not, just because of this, the determining ground and condition of the maxim; for if it is, then the maxim cannot be presented in the form of giving universal law, since expectation of the existence of the object would then be the determining cause of choice, and the dependence of the faculty of desire upon the existence of some thing would have to be put at the basis of volition; and since this dependence can be sought only in empirical conditions, it can never furnish the basis for a necessary and universal rule. Thus, the happiness of other beings can be the object of the will of a rational being. But if it were the determining ground of the maxim, one would have to presuppose that we find not only a natural satisfaction in the well-being of others but also a need, such as a sympathetic sensibility[m] brings with it in human beings. But I cannot presuppose this need in every rational being (not at all in God). Thus the matter of the maxim can indeed remain, but it must not be the condition of the maxim since the maxim would then not be fit for a law. Hence the mere form of a law, which limits the matter, must at the same time be a ground for adding this matter to the will but not for presupposing it. Let the matter be, for example, my own happiness. This, if I attribute it to each (as, in the case of finite beings, I may in fact do) can become an *objective* practical law only if I include in it the happiness of others. Thus the law to promote the happiness of others arises not from the presupposition that this is an object of everyone's choice but merely from this: that the form of universality, which reason requires as the condition of giving to a maxim of self-love the objective validity of a law, becomes the determining ground of the will; and so the object (the happiness of others) was not the determining ground of the pure will; this was, instead, the mere lawful form alone, by which I limited my maxim based on inclination in order to afford it the universality of a law and in this way to make it suitable for pure practical reason; only from this limitation, and not from the addition of an external

---

[m] *Sinnesart*

incentive,"ⁿ could there arise the concept of *obligation* to extend the maxim of my self-love to the happiness of others as well.

Remark II

The direct opposite of the principle of morality is the principle of *one's own* happiness made the determining ground of the will; and, as I have shown above, whatever puts the determining ground that is to serve as a law anywhere else than in the lawgiving form of the maxim must be counted in this. This conflict, however, is not merely logical, like that between empirically conditioned rules that one might nevertheless want to raise to necessary principles of cognition; it is instead practical and would ruin morality altogether were not the voice of reason in reference to the will so distinct, so irrepressible, and so audible even to the most common human beings; thus it can maintain itself only in the perplexing speculations of the schools, which are brazen enough to shut their ears to that heavenly voice in order to support a theory they need not break their heads over.

Suppose that an acquaintance whom you otherwise liked tried to justify to you his having given false testimony by first pleading what he asserts to be the sacred duty of his own happiness and then by recounting all the advantages he had acquired by doing so, pointing out the prudence he had observed in order to be secure from discovery even by yourself, to whom he reveals the secret only because he can deny it at any time; and suppose he were then to affirm, in all seriousness, that he has fulfilled a true human duty: you would either laugh in his face or shrink back from him with disgust, even though, if someone has directed his principles solely to his own advantage, you would not have the least objection to bring against these measures. Or suppose that someone recommends to you as steward a man to whom you could blindly trust all your affairs and, in order to inspire you with confidence, extols him as a prudent human being with masterly understanding of his own advantage and also as an indefatigably active one, who lets pass no opportunity to advance it; and finally, lest any concern about a vulgar selfishness in him stand in the way, the recommender praises his understanding of how to live with refinement, seeking his satisfaction not in making money or in coarse luxury but in enlarging his knowledge, in select and instructive society, and even in beneficence to the needy, while as to the means (which of course derive all their worth or lack of it from the end) he is not particular and is ready to use other people's money and goods for his end as if they were his own, provided he knows that he can do so without being discovered or thwarted; you would

---

ⁿ *Triebfeder.* It subsequently becomes clear that Kant does not maintain the distinction drawn between *Triebfeder* and *Bewegungsgrund* in the *Groundwork of the Metaphysics of Morals* (4:427).

believe either that the recommender was making a fool of you or that he had lost his mind. So distinctly and sharply drawn are the boundaries of morality and self-love that even the most common eye cannot fail to distinguish whether something belongs to the one or the other. The few remarks that follow may seem superfluous where the truth is so evident, but they may serve at least to afford the judgement of common human reason somewhat greater distinctness.

The principle of happiness can indeed furnish maxims, but never such as would be fit for laws of the will, even if *universal* happiness were made the object. For, because cognition of this rests on sheer data of experience, each judgement about it depending very much upon the opinion of each which is itself very changeable, it can indeed give *general* rules but never *universal* rules, that is, it can give rules that on the average are most often correct but not rules that must hold always and necessarily; hence no practical *laws* can be based on it. Just because an object of choice is here put at the basis of its rule and must therefore precede it, the rule can be referred to and can be based upon nothing other than what one approves,[o] and so it refers to and is based upon experience, and then the variety of judgment must be endless. This principle, therefore, does not prescribe the very same practical rules to all rational beings, even though the rules come under a common heading,[p] namely that of happiness. The moral law, however, is thought as objectively necessary only because it is to hold for everyone having reason and will.

The maxim of self-love (prudence) merely *advises;* the law of morality *commands.* But there is a great difference between that which we are *advised* to do and that to which we are *obligated.*

What is to be done in accordance with the principle of the autonomy of choice is seen quite easily and without hesitation by the most common understanding; what is to be done on the presupposition of heteronomy of choice is difficult to see and requires knowledge of the world; in other words, what *duty* is, is plain of itself to everyone, but what brings true lasting advantage, if this is to extend to the whole of one's existence, is always veiled in impenetrable obscurity, and much prudence is required to adapt the practical rule in accordance with it to the ends of life even tolerably, by making appropriate exceptions. But the moral law commands compliance from everyone, and indeed the most exact compliance. Appraising what is to be done in accordance with it must, therefore, not be so difficult that the most common and unpracticed understanding should not know how to go about it, even without worldly prudence.

To satisfy the categorical command of morality is within everyone's power at all times; to satisfy the empirically conditioned precept of happi- 5:37

---

[o] *empfiehlt*. Hartenstein reads *empfindet* (feels).
[p] *Titel*

ness is but seldom possible and is far from being possible for everyone even with respect to only a single purpose. The reason is that in the first case it is a question only of the maxim, which must be genuine and pure, whereas in the latter case it is also a question of one's powers and one's physical ability to make a desired object real. A command that everyone should seek to make himself happy would be foolish, for one never commands of someone what he unavoidably wants already. One would have to command of him only the measures – or, better, provide him with them, since he cannot do all that he wants to do. But to command morality under the name of duty is quite reasonable; for, first, it is not the case that everyone willingly obeys its precept when it is in conflict with his inclinations; and as for the measures – how he can comply with it – here these need not be taught; for in regard to this, what he wills to do, that he also can do.

He who has *lost* at play can indeed be *chagrined* with himself and his imprudence; but if he is conscious of having *cheated* at play (although he has gained by it), he must *despise* himself as soon as he compares himself with the moral law. This must, therefore, be something other than the principle of one's own happiness. For, to have to say to himself "I am a *worthless* man[q] although I have filled my purse," he must have a different criterion of judgment from that by which he commends himself and says "I am a *prudent* man,[r] for I have enriched my cash box."

Finally there is in the idea of our practical reason something further that accompanies the transgression of a moral law, namely its *deserving punishment*. Now, becoming a partaker in happiness cannot be combined with the concept of a punishment as such. For, although he who punishes can at the same time have the kindly intention of directing the punishment to this end as well, yet it must first be justified in itself as punishment, that is, as mere harm,[s] so that he who is punished, if it stopped there and he could see no kindness hidden behind this harshness, must himself admit that justice was done to him[t] and that what was allotted him was perfectly suited to his conduct. In every punishment as such there must first be justice,[u] and this constitutes what is essential in this concept. Kindness can, indeed, be connected with it, but the one who deserves punishment for his conduct has not the least cause to count on this. Thus punishment is a physical harm that, even if it is not connected with moral wickedness as a *natural* consequence, would still have to be connected with it as a

---

[q] *Unwürdiger*

[r] *Mensch*

[s] Or "ill-being," *Übel*. In the following passage *Böse* is translated as "wickedness." On the distinction between *Übel* and *Böse* see AK5:59–60.

[t] *es sei ihm Recht geschehen*

[u] *Gerechtigkeit*

consequence in accordance with the principles of a moral lawgiving. Now if every crime, even without regard to the physical consequence with respect to the agent, is of itself punishable – that is, forfeits happiness (at least in part) – it would obviously be absurd to say that the crime consisted just in his having brought a punishment upon himself and thereby infringed upon his own happiness (which, in accordance with the principle of self-love, would have to be the proper concept of all crime). The punishment would in this way be the ground for calling something a crime, and justice would have to consist instead in omitting all punishment and even warding off that which is natural; for then there would no longer be any wickedness in the action, since the harm that would otherwise follow upon it and on account of which alone the action would be called wicked would now be prevented. But to look upon all punishments and rewards as mere machinery in the hands of a higher power, serving only to put rational beings into activity toward their final purpose (happiness) is so patently a mechanism which does away with the freedom of their will that it need not detain us here.

5:38

More refined, though equally untrue, is the pretense of those who assume a certain special moral sense which, instead of reason, determines the moral law and in accordance with which consciousness of virtue is immediately connected with satisfaction and pleasure, and consciousness of vice with mental unease and pain, so that everything is still reduced to desire for one's own happiness. Without repeating what has been said above, I want only to note the deception[v] going on here. In order to represent someone vicious as tormented with mental unease by consciousness of his offenses they must first represent him as morally good, at least to some degree, in what is most basic to his character, just as they must represent someone who is delighted by consciousness of his dutiful actions as already virtuous. The concept of morality and duty would therefore have to precede any regard for this satisfaction and cannot be derived from it. Now, one must first value the importance of what we call duty, the authority of the moral law, and the immediate worth that compliance with it gives a person in his own eyes, in order to feel that satisfaction in consciousness of one's conformity with it and bitter remorse if one can reproach oneself with having transgressed it. Thus one cannot feel such satisfaction or mental unease prior to cognition of obligation and cannot make it the basis of the latter. Someone must be at least half way toward being an honest man even to frame for himself a representation of those feelings. For the rest, as the human will is by virtue of its freedom immediately determinable by the moral law, I certainly do not deny that frequent practice in conformity with this determining ground can finally produce subjectively a feeling of satisfaction with oneself; on the contrary, to estab-

[v] *Täuschung*

lish and to cultivate this feeling, which alone deserves to be called moral feeling strictly speaking, itself belongs to duty; but the concept of duty cannot be derived from it – otherwise we should have to think of a feeling of a law as such*ʷ* and make what can only be thought by reason an object of sensation;*ˣ* and this, if it is not to be a flat contradiction, would quite do away with any concept of duty and put in its place merely a mechanical play of refined inclinations sometimes contending with the coarser.

If we now compare our *formal* supreme principle of pure practical reason (as that of an autonomy of the will) with all previous *material* principles of morality, we can set forth all the rest, as such, in a table in which all possible cases are actually exhausted, except the one formal principle; and thus we can prove visually that it is futile to look around for any other principle than that now presented. That is to say, all possible determining grounds of the will are either merely *subjective* and therefore empirical or also *objective* and rational; and both are either *external* or *internal*.

Practical Material Determining Grounds[7]
in the principle of morality are
Subjective

External	*Internal*
Of education	Of physical feeling
(according to Montaigne)	(according to Epicurus)
Of the civil constitution	Of moral feeling
(according to Mandeville)	(according to Hutcheson)

Objective

Internal	*External*
Of perfection	Of the will of God
(according to Wolff	(according to Crusius and other theo-
and the Stoics)	logical moralists)

Those in the first group*ʸ* are without exception empirical and obviously not at all qualified for the universal principle of morality. But those in the second group are based on reason (for, perfection as a *characteristic*ᶻ of things, and the supreme perfection represented in *substance*, i.e. God, are both to be thought only by means of rational concepts). However, the first concept, namely that of *perfection*, can be taken either in the *theoretical* sense, and then it signifies nothing other than the completeness of each thing in its kind (transcendental perfection) or of a thing merely as a thing in general (metaphysical perfection), and we are not concerned with that here. But the concept of perfection in the *practical* sense is the fitness or

---

ʷ *ein Gefühl eines Gesetzes als eines solchen*
ˣ Empfindung
ʸ "on the left side," as the table is set up in the Academy edition, i.e., the "subjective principles."
ᶻ Beschaffenheit

adequacy of a thing for all sorts of ends. This perfection, as a *characteristic* of the human being and so as internal is nothing other than *talent* and what strengthens or completes this, *skill.* The supreme perfection in *substance* – that is, God – and so as external (from a practical point of view) is the adequacy of this being to all ends in general. Now, if ends must first be given to us, in relation to which alone the concept of *perfection* (whether internal in ourselves or external in God) can be the determining ground of the will; and if an end as an *object* which must precede the determination of the will by a practical rule and contain the ground of the possibility of such a determination – hence as the *matter* of the will taken as its determining ground – is always empirical; then it can serve as the Epicurean principle of the doctrine of happiness but never as the pure rational principle of the doctrine of morals and of duty (so too, talents and their development only because they contribute to the advantages of life, or the will of God if agreement with it is taken as the object of the will without an antecedent practical principle independent of this idea, can become motives of the will only by means of the happiness we expect from them); from this it follows, *first,* that all the principles exhibited here are *material*; *second,* that they include all possible material principles; and, finally, the conclusion from this, that since material principles are quite unfit to be the supreme moral law (as has been proved), the *formal practical principle* of pure reason (in accordance with which the mere form of a possible giving of universal law through our maxims must constitute the supreme and immediate determining ground of the will) is the *sole* principle that can *possibly* be fit for categorical imperatives, that is, practical laws (which make actions duties), and in general for the principle of morality, whether in appraisals or in application to the human will in determining it.

I.

ON THE DEDUCTION OF THE PRINCIPLES
OF PURE PRACTICAL REASON

This Analytic shows that pure reason can be practical – that is, can of itself, independently of anything empirical, determine the will – and it does so by a fact in which pure reason in us proves itself actually practical, namely autonomy in the principle of morality by which reason determines the will to deeds. At the same time it shows that this fact is inseparably connected with, and indeed identical with, consciousness of freedom of the will, whereby the will of a rational being that, as belonging to the sensible world cognizes itself as, like other efficient causes, necessarily subject to laws of causality, yet in the practical is also conscious of itself on another side, namely as a being in itself, conscious of its existence as determinable in an intelligible order of things – conscious of this not, indeed, by a special intuition of itself but according to certain dynamic laws that can determine its causality in the sensible world; for it has been sufficiently proved elsewhere[8] that freedom, if it is attributed to us, transfers us into an intelligible order of things.

If we compare with this Analytic the analytical part of the *Critique* of pure speculative reason, we see a contrast between them worth noting. Not principles but instead pure sensible *intuition* (space and time) was there the first datum that made a priori cognition possible and, indeed, only for objects of the senses. Synthetic principles from mere concept without intuition were impossible; instead, such principles could be had only with reference to intuition, which was sensible, and so only with reference to objects of possible experience, since the concepts of the understanding joined with such intuition alone make possible that cognition which we call experience. Speculative reason was quite rightly denied anything positive for *cognition* beyond objects of experience, hence of things as noumena. Nevertheless, speculative reason went so far as to secure the concept of noumena – that is, the possibility and indeed the necessity of thinking them – and, for example, to preserve against all objections the assumption of freedom, regarded negatively, as quite compatible with those principles and limitations of pure theoretical reason, though without letting us cognize anything determinate and enlarging about such objects, inasmuch as it instead cut off altogether any prospect of that.

On the other hand, the moral law, even though it gives no *prospect*, nevertheless provides a fact absolutely inexplicable from any data of the sensible world and from the whole compass of our theoretical use of reason, a fact that points to a pure world of the understanding and, indeed, even *determines* it *positively* and lets us cognize something of it, namely a law.

This law is to furnish the sensible world, as a *sensible nature* (in what concerns rational beings), with the form of a world of the understanding, that is, of a *supersensible* nature, though without infringing upon the mechanism of the former. Now, nature in the most general sense is the existence of things under laws. The sensible nature of rational beings in general is their existence under empirically conditioned laws and is thus, for reason, *heteronomy*. The supersensible nature of the same beings, on the other hand, is their existence in accordance with laws that are independent of any empirical condition and thus belong to the *autonomy* of pure reason. And since the laws by which the existence of things depends on cognition are practical, supersensible nature, so far as we can make for ourselves a concept of it, is nothing other than *a nature under the autonomy of pure practical reason*. The law of this autonomy, however, is the moral law, which is therefore the fundamental law of a supersensible nature and of a pure world of the understanding, the counterpart of which is to exist in the sensible world but without infringing upon its laws. The former could be called the *archetypal world (natura archetypa)* which we cognize only in reason, whereas the latter could be called the *ectypal world (natura ectypa)* because it contains the possible effect of the idea of the former as the determining ground of the will. For, the moral law in fact transfers us, in idea,[a] into a nature in which pure reason, if it were accompanied with suitable physical power, would produce the highest good, and it determines our will to confer on the sensible world the form of a whole of rational beings.

The most ordinary attention to oneself confirms that this idea is really, as it were, the pattern for the determinations of our will.

When the maxim on which I intend to give testimony is tested by practical reason, I always consider what it would be if it were to hold as a universal law of nature. It is obvious that in this way everyone would be necessitated to truthfulness. For it cannot hold with the universality of a law of nature that statements should be allowed as proof and yet be intentionally untrue. Similarly, the maxim that I adopt with respect to disposing freely of my life is at once determined when I ask myself what it would have to be in order that a nature should maintain itself in accordance with such a law. It is obvious that in such a nature no one could end his life *at will*,[b] for such an arrangement would not be an enduring natural order. And so in all other cases. But in actual nature, insofar as it is an object of experience, the free will is not of itself determined to such maxims as could of themselves establish a nature in accordance with universal laws, or even to such maxims as could of themselves fit into a nature arranged in accordance with them; they are, instead, private inclinations which do constitute a natural whole in accordance with pathological (physical) laws but not a nature that would be possible only through our will in accordance with pure practical laws. Yet we are conscious through reason of a law to which all our maxims are subject, as if a natural order must at the same time arise from our will. This law must therefore be the idea of a nature not given empirically and yet possible through freedom, hence a supersensible nature to which we give objective reality at least in a practical respect, since we regard it as an object of our will as pure rational beings.

5:44

Hence the difference between the laws of a nature to which *the will is subject* and of a *nature which* is subject *to a will* (as far as the relation of the will to its free actions is concerned) rests on this: that in the former the objects must be the causes of the representations that determine the will, whereas in the latter the will is to be the cause of the objects, so that its causality has its determining ground solely in the pure faculty of reason, which can therefore also be called a pure practical reason.

There are, accordingly, two very different problems: how, *on the one*

---

[a] *der Idee nach*
[b] *willkürlich*

side, pure reason can *cognize* objects a priori and how, *on the other side*, it can be an immediate determining ground of the will, that is, of the causality of a rational being with respect to the reality of objects (merely through the thought of the universal validity of its own maxims as law).

The first, as belonging to the *Critique* of pure speculative reason, requires that it first be explained how intuitions, without which no object at all can be given and without which, therefore, none can be cognized synthetically, are possible a priori; and its solution turns out to be that these are without exception sensible only and therefore do not make possible any speculative cognition that would go further than possible experience reaches and, consequently, that all principles of that pure speculative reason do no more than make experience possible, either of given objects or of those that may be given to us ad infinitum but are never completely given.

The second, which belongs to the *Critique of Practical Reason*, requires no explanation of how objects of the faculty of desire are possible, for that, as a problem of theoretical cognition of nature, is left to the *Critique* of speculative reason, but only how reason can determine maxims of the will, whether this takes place only by means of empirical representations as determining grounds of whether pure reason might also be practical and might be a law of a possible order of nature not empirically cognizable. The possibility of such a supersensible nature, the concept of which can also be the ground of its reality through our free will, requires no a priori intuition (of an intelligible world), which in this case, as supersensible, would also have to be impossible for us. For it is a question only of the determining ground of volition in maxims of volition, whether it is empirical or whether it is a concept of pure reason (of its lawfulness in general), and how it can be the latter. Whether the causality of the will is adequate for the reality of the objects or not is left to the theoretical principles of reason to estimate, this being an investigation into the possibility of objects of volition, the intuition of which is accordingly no component of the practical problem. It is here a question only of the determination of the will and of the determining ground of its maxims as a free will, not of its result. For, provided that the will conforms to the law of pure reason, then its power in execution[c] may be as it may, and a nature may or may not actually arise in accordance with these maxims of giving law for a possible nature; the *Critique* which investigates whether and how reason can be practical, that is, whether and how it can determine the will immediately, does not trouble itself with this.

In this undertaking the *Critique* can therefore not be censured for beginning with pure practical laws and their reality, and it must begin there. Instead of intuition, however, it takes as its basis those laws, the

[c] *Vermögen . . . in der Ausführung*

concept of their existence in the intelligible world, namely the concept of freedom. For this concept means nothing else, and those laws are possible only in relation to the freedom of the will; but on the presupposition of freedom they are necessary or, conversely, freedom is necessary because those laws are necessary, as practical postulates. How this consciousness of moral laws or, what is the same thing, this consciousness of freedom is possible cannot be further explained; its admissibility can, however, be defended in the theoretical *Critique*.

The *exposition* of the supreme principle of practical reason is now finished, that is, it has been shown, first, what it contains, that it stands of itself[d] altogether a priori and independently of empirical principles, and then what distinguishes it from all other practical principles. With the *deduction*, that is, the justification of its objective and universal validity and the discernment[e] of the possibility of such a synthetic proposition a priori, one cannot hope to get on so well as was the case with the principles of the pure theoretical understanding. For, these referred to objects of possible experience, namely appearances, and it could be proved that these appearances could be *cognized* as objects of experience only by being brought under the categories in accordance with these laws and consequently that all possible experience must conform to these laws. But I cannot not take such a course in the deduction of the moral law. For, the moral law is not concerned with cognition of the constitution of objects that may be given to reason from elsewhere but rather with a cognition insofar as it can itself become the ground of the existence of objects and insofar as reason, by this cognition, has causality in a rational being, that is, pure reason, which can be regarded as a faculty immediately determining the will.

But all human insight is at an end as soon as we have arrived at basic powers or basic faculties;[f] for there is nothing through which their possibility can be conceived, and yet it may not be invented and assumed at one's discretion. Therefore, in the theoretical use of reason only experience can justify us in assuming them. But this substitute, adducing empirical proofs in place of a deduction from sources of cognition a priori, is also denied us here with respect to the pure practical faculty of reason. For, whatever needs to draw the evidence for its reality from experience must be dependent for the grounds of its possibility upon principles of experience, whereas pure but practical reason, by its very concept, cannot possibly be held to be dependent in this way. Moreover the moral law is given, as it were, as a fact of pure reason of which we are a priori conscious and which is apodictically certain, though it be granted that no example of exact observance of it can be found in experience. Hence the objective reality of

5:47

---

[d] *für sich bestehe*
[e] *Einsicht*
[f] *Grundkräften oder Grundvermögen*

the moral law cannot be proved by any deduction, by any efforts of theoretical reason, speculative or empirically supported, so that, even if one were willing to renounce its apodictic certainty, it could not be confirmed by experience and thus proved a posteriori; and it is nevertheless firmly established of itself.

But something different and quite paradoxical[g] takes the place of this vainly sought deduction of the moral principle, namely that the moral principle, conversely itself serves as the principle of the deduction of an inscrutable faculty which no experience could prove but which speculative reason had to assume as at least possible (in order to find among its cosmological ideas what is unconditioned in its causality, so as not to contradict itself), namely the faculty of freedom, of which the moral law, which itself has no need of justifying grounds, proves not only the possibility but the reality in beings who cognize this law as binding upon them. The moral law is, in fact, a law of causality through freedom and hence a law of the possibility of a supersensible nature, just as the metaphysical law of events in the sensible world was a law of the causality of sensible nature; and the moral law thus determines that which speculative philosophy had to leave undetermined, namely the law for a causality the concept of which was only negative in the latter, and thus for the first time provides objective reality to this concept.

5:48 This kind of credential of the moral law – that it is itself laid down as a principle of the deduction of freedom as a causality of pure reason – is fully sufficient in place of any a priori justification, since theoretical reason was forced *to assume* at least the possibility of freedom in order to fill a need of its own. For, the moral law proves its reality, so as even to satisfy the *Critique* of speculative reason, by adding a positive determination to a causality thought only negatively, the possibility of which was incomprehensible to speculative reason, which was nevertheless forced to assume it; it adds, namely, the concept of a reason determining the will immediately (by the condition of a universal lawful form of its maxims), and thus is able for the first time to give objective though only practical reality to reason, which always became extravagant when it wanted to proceed speculatively with its ideas, and changes its *transcendent* use into an *immanent* use (in which reason is by means of ideas itself an efficient cause in the field of experience).

The determination of the causality of beings in the sensible world can as such never be unconditioned, and yet for every series of conditions there must necessarily be something unconditioned and so too a causality that is altogether self-determining. Hence the idea of freedom as a faculty of absolute spontaneity was not a need but, *as far as its possibility is concerned*, an analytic principle of pure speculative reason. It is, however,

[g] *Widersinnisches*

absolutely impossible to give anywhere in experience an example of it, since among the causes of things as appearances no determination of causality that would be absolutely unconditioned can be found; hence we could *defend* the *thought* of a freely acting cause, when we apply this to a being in the sensible world, only insofar as this being is also regarded on the other side as a noumenon, by showing that it is not self-contradictory to regard all its actions as physically conditioned insofar as they are appearances and yet also to regard their causality as physically unconditioned insofar as the acting being is a being of the understanding,[h] and thus making the concept of freedom a regulative principle of reason; by it I do not cognize at all the object to which such causality is attributed – what the object may be – but I nevertheless remove the obstacle inasmuch as on the one side, in the explanation of events in the world and so too of the actions of rational beings, I grant the mechanism of natural necessity the justice of going back from the conditioned to the condition ad infinitum, while on the other side I keep open for speculative reason the place which for it is vacant, namely the intelligible, in order to transfer the unconditioned into it. But I could not *realize* this *thought*, that is, could not convert it into *cognition* of a being acting in this way, not even of its mere possibility. Pure practical reason now fills this vacant place with a determinate law of causality in an intelligible world (with freedom), namely the moral law. By this, speculative reason does not gain anything with respect to its insight but it still gains something only with respect to the *security* of its problematic concept of freedom, which is here afforded *objective* and, though only practical, undoubted *reality*. Even the concept of causality, which has application and so too significance strictly speaking[i] only in reference to appearances, in order to connect them into experiences (as the *Critique of Pure Reason* proves) is not enlarged in such a way as to extend its use beyond the boundaries mentioned. For, if reason sought to do this it would have to try to show how the logical relation of ground and consequence could be used synthetically with a kind of intuition different from the sensible, that is, how a *causa noumenon* is possible; this it cannot do, but as practical reason it does not even concern itself with this inasmuch as it only puts the *determining ground* of the causality of the human being as a sensible being (which is given) *in pure reason* (which is therefore called practical), and accordingly uses the concept of cause itself – from whose application to objects for theoretical cognition it can here abstract altogether (since this concept is always found a priori in the understanding, even independently of any intuition) – not in order to cognize objects but to determine causality with respect to objects in general, and so for none other than a practical purpose; and thus it can transfer the determin-

5:49

---

[h] *Verstandeswesen*
[i] *dessen Anwendung, mithin auch Bedeutung eigentlich nur . . . stattfindet*

ing ground of the will into the intelligible order of things inasmuch as it readily admits at the same time that it does not understand how the concept of cause might be determined for cognition of these things. It must, of course, cognize in a determinate way causality with respect to the actions of the will in the sensible world, since otherwise practical reason could not actually produce any deed. But as for the concept which it makes of its own causality as noumenon, it need not determine it theoretically with a view to cognition of its supersensible existence and so need not be able to give it significance in this way. For, the concept receives significance apart from this – though only for practical use – namely, through the moral law. Even regarded theoretically it always remains a pure concept of the understanding given a priori, which can be applied to objects whether they are given sensibly or not sensibly, although in the latter case it has not determinate theoretical significance or application but is merely the understanding's formal though still essential thought of an object in general. The significance which reason furnishes it through the moral law is solely practical, namely that the idea of the law of a causality (of the will) itself has causality or is its determining ground.

II.
ON THE WARRANT OF PURE REASON IN ITS PRACTICAL USE TO AN EXTENSION WHICH IS NOT POSSIBLE TO IT IN ITS SPECULATIVE USE

In the moral principle we have presented a law of causality which puts the determining ground of the latter above all conditions of the sensible world; and as for the will and hence the subject of this will (the human being),[j] we have not merely *thought* it, as it is determinable inasmuch as it belongs to an intelligible world, as belonging to a world of pure understanding though in this relation unknown to us (as can happen according to the *Critique* of speculative reason): we have also *determined* it with respect to its causality by means of a law that cannot be counted as any natural law of the sensible world; and thus we have *extended* our cognition beyond the boundaries of the latter, a claim that the *Critique of Pure Reason* declared void in all speculation. How, then, is the practical use of pure reason here to be united[k] with its theoretical use with respect to determining the boundaries of its competence?[l]

David Hume, who can be said to have really begun all the assaults on the rights of pure reason which made a thorough investigation of them

---

[j] I take the pronouns in the rest of this sentence to refer to "the will," although "the human being" is a possible referent.
[k] *vereinigt*, perhaps *"reconciled"*
[l] *ihres Vermögens*

CRITIQUE OF PRACTICAL REASON

necessary, concluded as follows. The concept of *cause* is a concept that contains the *necessity* of the connection of the existence of what is different just insofar as it is different, so that if A is posited I cognize that something altogether different from it, B, must necessarily also exist. But necessity can be attributed to a connection only insofar as the connection is cognized a priori; for, experience would enable us to cognize of such a conjunction[m] only that it is, not that it is necessarily so. Now it is impossible, he says, to cognize a priori and as necessary the connection between one thing and *another* (or between one determination and another altogether different from it) if they are not given in perception. Therefore the concept of a cause is itself fraudulent and deceptive and, to speak of it in the mildest way, an illusion to be excused insofar as the *custom*[n] (a *subjective* necessity) of perceiving certain things or their determinations as often associated along with or after one another in their existence is insensibly taken for an *objective* necessity of putting such a connection in the objects themselves; and thus the concept of a cause is acquired surreptitiously and not rightfully – indeed, it can never be acquired or certified because it demands a connection in itself void, chimerical, and untenable before reason, one to which no object can ever correspond. So, with respect to all cognition having to do with the existence of things (mathematics thus remaining excepted) *empiricism* was first introduced as the sole source of principles, but along with it the most rigorous *skepticism* with respect to the whole of natural science (as philosophy). For, on such principles we can never *infer* a consequence from the given determinations of things as existing (since for this the concept of a cause, which contains the necessity of such a connection, would be required) but can only expect, by the rule of imagination, cases similar to preceding ones, though this expectation is never secure however often it is fulfilled. Of no event could one say: something *must* have preceded it, upon which it *necessarily followed, that is, it must have a cause;* and thus, however frequent the cases one knew of in which there was such an antecedent, so that a rule could be derived from them, one could still not, on account of this, assume it as always and necessarily happening in this way, and one would also have to give blind chance its right, with which all use of reason ceases; and this firmly grounds and makes irrefutable skepticism with respect to inferences rising from effects to causes.

5:51

5:52

Mathematics escaped well so far because Hume held that its propositions were all analytic, that is, proceeded from one determination to another by virtue of identity and consequently by the principle[o] of contradiction (but this is false since they are instead all synthetic; and although,

---
[m] *Verbindung*
[n] Or "habit," *Gewohnheit*
[o] *Satze*

e.g., geometry does not have to do with the existence of things but only with their determination a priori in a possible intuition, it nevertheless passes, just as through the causal concept, from one determination (A) to another altogether different one (B) as still necessarily connected with the former). But in the end that science, so highly esteemed for its apodictic certainty, must also succumb to *empiricism in principles* on the same ground on which Hume put custom in the place of objective necessity in the concept of cause; despite all its pride, it must consent to lower its bold claims commanding a priori assent and expect approval of the universal validity of its propositions from the kindness of observers who, as witnesses, would not refuse to admit that what the geometer propounds as principles they have always perceived as well, and who would therefore allow it to be expected in the future even though it is not necessary. In this way Hume's empiricism in principles also leads unavoidably to skepticism even with respect to mathematics and consequently in every *scientific* theoretical use of reason (for this belongs either to philosophy or to mathematics). I leave each to appraise for himself whether (in view of such a terrible downfall of the chief branches of cognition) the common use of reason will come through any better and will not instead become irretrievably entangled in this same destruction of all science, so that from the same principles a *universal* skepticism will have to follow (though it would, admittedly, concern only the learned).

As for my labor in the *Critique of Pure Reason*, which was occasioned by that Humean skeptical teaching but went much further and included the whole field of pure theoretical reason in its synthetic use and so too the field of what is generally called metaphysics, I proceeded as follows with respect to the doubt of the Scottish philosopher concerning the concept of causality. When Hume took objects of experience as things in themselves (as is done almost everywhere) he was quite correct in declaring the concept of cause to be deceptive and a false illusion; for, as to things in themselves and the determinations of them as such, it cannot be seen why, because something, A, is posited, something else, B, must necessarily be posited also, and thus he could certainly not admit such an a priori cognition of things in themselves. Still less could this acute man grant an empirical origin of this concept, since this directly contradicts the necessity of the connection that constitutes what is essential in the concept of causality; hence the concept was proscribed and into its place stepped custom in observation of the course of perceptions.

From my investigations, however, it resulted that the objects with which we have to do in experience are by no means things in themselves but only appearances and that, although in the case of things in themselves it is not to be understood and is indeed impossible to see[p] how, if A

---

[p] *nicht abzusehen ist, ja unmöglilch ist einzusehen*

is posited it should be *contradictory* not to posit B which is quite different from A (the necessity of the connection between A as cause and B as effect), yet it can very well be thought that as appearances they must necessarily be connected *in one experience* in a certain way (e.g., with respect to temporal relations) and cannot be separated without *contradicting* that connection by means of which this experience is possible, in which they are objects and in which alone they are cognizable by us. And it was found to be so in fact as well; and thus I was able not only to prove the objective reality of the concept of cause with respect to objects of experience but also to *deduce* it as an a priori concept because of the necessity of the connection that it brings with it, that is, to show its possibility from pure understanding without empirical sources; and thus, after removing empiricism from its origin, I was able to overthrow the unavoidable consequence of empiricism, namely skepticism first with respect to natural science and then, because skepticism in mathematics follows from just the same grounds, with respect to mathematics as well, both of which sciences have reference to objects of possible experience; in this way I was able to eradicate total doubt of whatever theoretical reason professes to have insight into.

But how is it with the application of this category of causality (and so too of all the others, for without them no cognition can be had of what exists) to things that are not objects of possible experience but lie beyond its boundaries? For I was able to deduce the objective reality of these concepts only with respect to *objects of possible experience.* But what gives them a place in the pure understanding, from which they are referred to objects in general (whether sensible or not) is just this: that I also saved them only in case I proved that objects may nevertheless be *thought* through them although not determined a priori. If anything is still wanting, it is the condition *for the application* of these categories and especially that of causality to objects, namely intuition; where this is not given, application with *a view to theoretical cognition* of an object as a noumenon is made impossible, so that such cognition, when someone ventures upon it, is altogether forbidden (as also happens in the *Critique of Pure Reason*), while the objective reality of the concept (of causality) nevertheless remains and can be used even of noumena, although this concept cannot be theoretically determined in the least and thereby produce a cognition. For, that this concept, even in relation to an object, contains nothing impossible was proved by this: that in any application to objects of the senses, its seat in the pure understanding was secured; and even though, when it might subsequently be referred to things in themselves (which cannot be objects of experience), it is not capable of being determined so as to represent *a determinate object* for the sake of theoretical cognition, yet for the sake of something else (the practical, perhaps) it could be capable of being determined for its application; and this would not be the case if, as

5:54

Hume maintained, this concept of causality contained something that it is always impossible to think.

In order now to discover this condition of the application of the concept in question to noumena, we need only recall *why we are not satisfied with its application to objects of experience* but would like to use it of things in themselves as well. For then it soon becomes apparent that it is not a theoretical but a practical purpose that makes this a necessity for us. Even if we were successful in this application we would still have made no true acquisition for speculation, in cognition of nature or, in general, with respect to any objects that might be given to us; instead we would at most have taken a long step from the sensibly conditioned (and we already have enough to do to remain in it and diligently go through the chain of causes) to the supersensible, in order to complete our cognition on the side of grounds and to fix its boundary, although an infinite gulf between that boundary and what we know remains always unfilled and we would have listened to a frivolous curiosity rather than a solid desire for knowledge.

However, besides the relation in which the *understanding* stands to object (in theoretical cognition) it has also a relation to the faculty of desire, which is therefore called the will and is called the pure will insofar as the pure understanding (which in this case is called reason) is practical through the mere representation of a law. The objective reality of a pure will or, what is the same thing, of a pure practical reason is given a priori in the moral law, as it were by a fact – for so we may call a determination of the will that is unavoidable even though it does not rest upon empirical principles. In the concept of a will, however, the concept of causality is already contained, and thus in the concept of a pure will there is contained the concept of a causality with freedom, that is, a causality that is not determinable in accordance with laws of nature and hence not capable of any empirical intuition as proof of its reality, but that nevertheless perfectly justifies its objective reality a priori in the pure practical law, though not (as is easily seen) with a view to the theoretical use of reason but only to its practical use. Now, the concept of a being that has free will is the concept of a *causa noumenon;* and one is already assured that this concept does not contradict itself since the concept of a cause, as having arisen wholly from the pure understanding, also has its objective reality with respect to objects in general assured by the deduction inasmuch as, being in its origin independent of all sensible conditions and so of itself not restricted to phenomena (unless one should want to make a determinate theoretical use of it), the concept could certainly be applied to things as beings of the pure understanding. But because no intuition, which can only be sensible, can be put under this application, *causa noumenon* with respect to the theoretical use of reason is, though a possible, thinkable concept, nevertheless an empty one. But I do not now claim *to know theoretically* by this concept the constitution of a being *insofar as* it has a *pure* will; it is enough for me to thereby only designate it as such a being and hence only to connect the concept of causality with that of freedom (and with what is inseparable from it, the moral law as its determining ground); and I am certainly authorized to do so by virtue of the pure, not empirical origin of the concept of cause, inasmuch as I consider myself authorized to make no other use of it than with regard to the moral law which determines its reality, that is, only a practical use.

Had I, with Hume, deprived the concept of causality of objective reality in its practical[q] use not only with respect to things in themselves (the supersensible) but also with respect to objects of the senses, it would be declared devoid of all meaning and, as a theoretically impossible concept, quite unusable; and since no use at all can be made of what is nothing,[r] the practical use of a concept *theoretically null* would have been absurd. Now, however, the concept of an empirically unconditioned causality is indeed theoretically empty (without any intuition appropriate to it) but it is nevertheless possible and refers to an undetermined object; in place of that, however, the concept is given significance in the moral law and consequently in its practical reference; thus I have, indeed, no intuition that would determine its objective theoretical reality for it, but it has nonetheless a real application which is exhibited *in concreto* in dispositions or maxims, that is, it has practical reality which can be specified; and this is sufficient to justify it even with regard to noumena.

But this objective reality of a pure concept of the understanding in the field of the supersensible, once introduced, gives all the other categories objective reality as well, though only insofar as they stand in *necessary* connection with the determining ground of the pure will (the moral law) – an objective reality which is, however, of only practical applicability and has not the least influence on theoretical cognition of these objects, as insight into their nature by pure reason, so as to extend this. As we shall also find in the sequel, these categories have reference only to beings as *intelligences*, and in them only to the relation of *reason* to the *will* and consequently always to the *practical* only, and beyond this they lay claim to no cognition of these beings; as for whatever other properties, belonging to the theoretical way of representing such supersensible things, may be brought forward in connection with these categories, these are without exception to be counted not as knowledge but only as a warrant (for practical purposes, however, a necessity) to admit and presuppose them, even where supersensible beings (such as God) are assumed by analogy, that is, by a purely rational relation of which we make a practical use with respect to what is sensible; and so, by this application to the supersensible

5:57

---

[q] Vorländer amends this to read *im theoretischen Gebrauche*, "in its theoretical use."
[r] *von Nichts*

but only for practical purposes, pure theoretical reason is not given the least encouragement to fly into the transcendent.[s]

The analytic of practical reason
Chapter II
On the concept of an object of pure practical reason

By a concept of an object of practical reason I understand the representation of an object as an effect possible through freedom. To be an object of practical cognition so understood signifies, therefore, only the relation of the will to the action by which it or its opposite would be made real, and to appraise whether or not something is an object of *pure* practical reason is only to distinguish the possibility or impossibility of *willing* the action by which, if we had the ability to do so (and experience must judge about this), a certain object would be made real. If the object is taken as the determining ground of our faculty of desire, the *physical possibility* of it by the free use of our powers must precede our appraisal of whether it is an object of practical reason or not. On the other hand, if the a priori law can be regarded as the determining ground of the action, and this, accordingly, can be regarded as determined by pure practical reason, then the judgment whether or not something is an object of pure practical reason is quite independent of this comparison with our physical ability, and the question is only whether we could *will* an action which is directed to the existence of an object if the object were within our power;[t] hence the *moral possibility* of the action must come first, since in this case the determining ground of the will is not the object but the law of the will.

The only objects of a practical reason are therefore those of the *good* and the *evil.* For by the first is understood a necessary object of the faculty of desire, by the second, of the faculty of aversion,[u] both, however, in accordance with a principle of reason.

If the concept of the good is not to be derived from an antecedent practical law but, instead, is to serve as its basis, it can be only the concept of something whose existence promises pleasure and thus determines the causality of the subject, that is, the faculty of desire, to produce it. Now because it is impossible to see a priori which representation will be accompanied with *pleasure* and which with *displeasure,* it would be up to experience alone to make out what is immediately good or evil. The property of the

---

[s] *zum Schwärmen ins Überschwengliche*
[t] *in unserer Gewalt*
[u] *des Begehrungs-* . . . *des Verabscheuungsvermögen*

subject, with reference to which alone this experience can be had, is the *feeling*[v] of pleasure and displeasure, as a receptivity belonging to inner sense, and thus the concept of that which is immediately good would be directed only to that with which the feeling of *gratification*[w] is immediately connected, and the concept of the simply evil would have to be referred only to that which immediately excites *pain*. But since this is opposed even to the use of language, which distinguishes the *agreeable* from the *good* and the *disagreeable* from the *evil* and requires that good and evil always be appraised by reason and hence through concepts, which can be universally communicated, not through mere feeling, which is restricted to individual subjects and their receptivity; and since, nevertheless, pleasure or displeasure cannot of themselves be connected a priori with any representation of an object, a philosopher who believed that he had to put a feeling of pleasure at the basis of his practical appraisal would have to call *good* that which is a *means* to the agreeable, and *evil* that which is a cause of disagreeableness and of pain; for, appraisal of the relation of means to ends certainly belongs to reason. But, although reason alone is capable of discerning the connection of means with their purposes (so that the will could also be defined as the faculty of ends, inasmuch as these are always determining grounds of the faculty of desire in accordance with principles), the practical maxims that would follow from the above concept of the good merely as a means would never contain as the object of the will anything good in itself, but always only good *for something;* the good would always be merely the useful, and that for which it is useful would always have to lie outside the will, in feeling. Now if the latter, as agreeable feeling, had to be distinguished from the concept of the good, then there would be nothing at all immediately good, and the good would have to be sought, instead, only in the means to something else, namely some agreeableness.

5:59

There is an old formula of the schools, *nihil appetimus, nisi sub ratione boni; nihil aversamur, nisi sub ratione mali;*[x] and it has a use which is often correct but also often very detrimental to philosophy, because the expressions *boni* and *mali* contain an ambiguity,[y] owing to the poverty of the language, by which they are capable of a double sense and thus unavoidably involve practical laws in ambiguities;[z] and the philosophy which, in using them, becomes aware of the difference of concepts in the same word but can still find no special expressions for them is forced into

---

[v] *Gefühl*

[w] *Empfindung des Vergnügens*. Throughout this paragraph, in which *Gefühl* and *Empfindung* are both translated as "feeling," Kant uses the two words interchangeably.

[x] We desire nothing except under the form of the good; nothing is avoided except under the form of the bad.

[y] *Zweideutigkeit*

[z] *auf Schrauben stellen*

187

subtle distinctions about which there is subsequently no agreement inasmuch as the difference cannot be directly indicated by any suitable expression.*

The German language has the good fortune to possess expressions which do not allow this difference to be overlooked. For that which the Latins denominate with a single word, *bonum,* it has two very different concepts and equally different expressions as well: for *bonum* it has *das Gute*[a] and *das Wohl,*[b] for *malum* it has *das Böse*[c] and *das Übel*[d] (or *Weh*),[e] so that there are two very different appraisals of an action depending upon whether we take into consideration the *good* and *evil* of it or our *well-being* and *woe* (ill-being). From this it already follows that the above psychological proposition is at least very doubtful if it is translated: we desire nothing except with a view to our *well-being* or *woe*, whereas if it is rendered: we will nothing under the direction of reason except insofar as we hold it to be good or evil, it is indubitably certain and at the same time quite clearly expressed.

Well-being or *ill-being* always signifies only a reference to our state of *agreeableness* or *disagreeableness*, of gratification or pain, and if we desire or avoid an object on this account we do so only insofar as it is referred to our sensibility and to the feeling of pleasure or displeasure it causes. But *good* or *evil* always signifies a reference to the *will* insofar as it is determined by the *law of reason* to make something its object; for, it is never determined directly by the object and the representation of it, but is instead a faculty of making a rule of reason the motive of an action (by which an object can become real). Thus good or evil is, strictly speaking, referred to actions, not to the person's state of feeling, and if anything is to be good or evil absolutely (and in every respect and without any further condition), or is to be held to be such, it would be only the way of acting, the maxim of the will, and consequently the acting person himself as a good or evil human being, that could be so called, but not a thing.

Thus one may always laugh at the Stoic who in the most intense pains

---

*Moreover, the expression *sub ratione boni* is also ambiguous. For it may mean: we represent to ourselves something as good when and *because we desire* (will) *it*, or also: we desire something *because we represent it to ourselves as good*, so that either desire is the determining ground of the concept of the object as a good, or the concept of the good is the determining ground of desire (of the will); so in the first case *sub ratione boni* would mean, we will something *under the idea* of the good; in the second, we will something *in consequence of this idea*, which must precede volition as its determining ground.
[a] good
[b] well-being
[c] evil
[d] ill-being
[e] woe

of gout cried out: Pain, however you torment me I will still never admit that you are something evil (κακον, *malum*)!; nevertheless, he was correct. He felt that the pain was an ill, and his cry betrayed that; but he had no cause whatever to grant that any evil attached to him because of it, for the pain did not in the least diminish the worth of his person but only the worth of his condition. A single lie of which he had been aware would have had to strike down his pride,[f] but the pain served only as an occasion to raise it when he was aware that he had not incurred it by any wrongful action and thereby made himself deserving of punishment.

What we are to call good must be an object of the faculty of desire in the judgment of every reasonable human being, and evil an object of aversion in the eyes of everyone; hence for this appraisal reason is needed, in addition to sense. So it is with truthfulness as opposed to lying, with justice as opposed to violence, and so forth. But we can call something an ill which everyone must yet at the same time pronounce good, sometimes mediately but sometimes even immediately. Someone who submits to a surgical operation feels it no doubt as an ill, but through reason he and everyone else pronounce it good. But if someone who likes to vex and disturb peace-loving people finally gets a sound thrashing for one of his provocations, this is certainly an ill, yet everyone would approve of it and take it as good in itself even if nothing further resulted from it; indeed, even the one who received it must in his reason recognize that justice was done to him,[g] because he sees the proportion between well-being and acting well, which reason unavoidably holds before him, here put into practice exactly.

Certainly, our well-being and woe count for a *very great deal* in the appraisal of our practical reason and, as far as our nature as sensible beings is concerned, *all* that counts is our *happiness* if this is appraised, as reason especially requires, not in terms of transitory feeling but of the influence this contingency has on our whole existence and our satisfaction with it; but happiness is not *the only thing* that counts. The human being is a being with needs, insofar as he belongs to the sensible world, and to this extent his reason certainly has a commission from the side of his sensibility which it cannot refuse, to attend to its interest and to form practical maxims with a view to happiness in this life and, where possible, in a future life as well. But he is nevertheless not so completely an animal as to be indifferent to all that reason says on its own and to use reason merely as a tool for the satisfaction of his needs as a sensible being. For, that he has reason does not at all raise him in worth above mere animality if reason is to serve him only for the sake of what instinct accomplishes

5:61

---

[f] *Mut*
[g] *das ihm Recht geschehe*

for animals; reason would in that case be only a particular mode*ʰ* nature had used to equip the human being for the same end to which it has destined*ⁱ* animals, without destining him to a higher end. No doubt once this arrangement of nature has been made for him he needs reason in order to take into consideration at all times his well-being and woe; but besides this he has it for a higher purpose:*ʲ* namely, not only to reflect upon what is good or evil in itself as well – about which only pure reason, not sensibly interested at all, can judge – but also to distinguish the latter appraisal altogether from the former and to make it the supreme condition of the former.

In this appraisal of what is good and evil in itself, as distinguished from what can be called so only with reference to well-being or ill-being, it is a question of the following points. Either a rational principle is already thought as in itself the determining ground of the will without regard to possible objects of the faculty of desire (hence through the mere lawful form of the maxim), in which case that principle is a practical law a priori and pure reason is taken to be practical of itself. In that case the law determines the will *immediately*, the action in conformity with it is *in itself good*, and a will whose maxim always conforms with this law is *good absolutely, good in every respect* and the *supreme condition of all good*. Or else a determining ground of the faculty of desire precedes the maxim of the will, which presupposes an object of pleasure or displeasure and hence something that *gratifies* or *pains*, and the maxim of reason to pursue the former and avoid the latter determines actions which are good with reference to our inclination and hence good only mediately (relatively to a further end, as means to it), and such maxims can in that case never be called laws but can still be called rational practical precepts. The end itself, the gratification that we seek, is in the latter case not a *good* but a *well-being*, not a concept of reason but an empirical concept of an object of feeling; but the use of means to it, that is, the action, is nevertheless called good (because rational reflection is required for it), not, however, good absolutely but only with reference to our sensibility, with respect to its feeling of pleasure and displeasure; but the will whose maxim is affected by it is not a pure will, which is directed only to that by which pure reason can of itself be practical.

This is the place to explain the paradox of method in a *Critique of Practical Reason, namely, that the concept of good and evil must not be determined before the moral law (for which, as it would seem, this concept would have to be made the basis) but only (as was done here) after it and by means of it.* That is to say: even if we did not know that the principle of morality is a pure

---

ʰ Manier
ⁱ bestimmt hat
ʲ Behuf

law determining the will a priori, we would at least have to leave it *undecided* in the beginning whether the will has only empirical or also pure determining grounds a priori, in order not to assume principles quite gratuitously (*gratis*); for, it it is contrary to all basic rules of philosophic procedure to assume as already decided the foremost question to be decided. Suppose that we wanted to begin with the concept of the good in order to derive from it laws of the will: then this concept of an object (as a good object) would at the same time supply this as the sole determining ground of the will. Now, since this concept had no practical a priori law for its standard, the criterion of good or evil could be placed in nothing other than the agreement of the object with our feeling of pleasure or displeasure, and the use of reason could only consist partly in determining this pleasure or displeasure in connection with all the feelings of my existence and partly in determining the means for providing myself with the object of such feelings. Now, since what is in keeping with the feeling of pleasure can be made out only through experience, and since the practical law is nevertheless, by hypothesis, to be based on this as its condition, the possibility of a priori practical laws would be at once excluded, because it was thought to be necessary first of all to find an object for the will, the concept of which, as that of a good, would have to constitute the universal though empirical determining ground of the will. But what it was necessary to investigate first was whether there is not also an a priori determining ground of the will (which could never be found elsewhere than in a pure practical law, and indeed insofar as it prescribes to maxims only their lawful form without regard to an object). Since, however, an object in accordance with concepts of the good and evil had already been made the basis of all practical laws, while the former, without a law preceding it, could be thought only by empirical concepts, the possibility of even thinking of a pure practical law was already removed in advance; on the other hand, if the latter had first been investigated analytically it would have been found that, instead of the concept of the good as an object determining and making possible the moral law, it is on the contrary the moral law that first determines and makes possible the concept of the good, insofar as it deserves this name absolutely.

5:64

This remark, which concerns only the method of ultimate moral investigations, is important. It explains at once the occasioning ground of all the errors of philosophers with respect to the supreme principle of morals. For they sought an object of the will in order to make it into the matter and the ground of a law (which was thus to be the determining ground of the will not immediately but rather by means of that object referred to the feeling of pleasure or displeasure), whereas they should first have searched for a law that determined the will a priori and immediately, and only then determined the object conformable to the will. Now, whether they placed this object of pleasure, which was to yield the supreme concept of good, in happiness, in perfection, in moral feeling, or in the will of God, their principle was in every case heteronomy and they had to come unavoidably upon empirical conditions for a moral law, since they could call their object, as the immediate determining ground of the will, good or evil only by its immediate relation to feeling, which is always empirical. Only a formal law, that is, one that prescribes to reason nothing more than the form of its universal lawgiving as the supreme condition of maxims, can be a priori a determining ground of practical reason. The ancients revealed this error openly by directing their moral investigation entirely to the determination of the concept of the *highest good,* and so of an object which they intended afterwards to make the determining ground of the will in the moral law, an object which can much later – when the moral law has first been established by itself and justified as the immediate determining ground of the will – be represented as object to the will, now determined a priori in its form; and this we will undertake in the Dialectic of pure practical reason. The moderns, with whom the question of the highest good seems to have gone out of use or at least to have become a secondary matter, hide the above error (as in many other cases) behind indeterminate words; but one can still see it showing through their systems, since it always reveals heteronomy of practical reason, from which an a priori moral law commanding universally can never arise.

Now, since the concepts of good and evil, as consequences of the a priori determination of the will, presuppose also a pure practical principle and hence a causality of pure reason, they do not refer originally to objects (as, say, determinations of the synthetic unity of the manifold of given intuitions in one consciousness), as do the pure concepts of the understanding or categories of reason used theoretically; instead, they presuppose these objects as given; they are rather, without exception, *modi* of a single category, namely that of causality, insofar as the determining ground of causality consists in reason's representation of a law of causality which, as the law of freedom, reason gives to itself and thereby proves itself a priori to be practical. However, since actions *on the one side* indeed belong under a law which is no law of nature but a law of freedom, and consequently belong to the conduct of intelligible beings, but *on the other side* as also events in the sensible world yet belong to appearances, the determinations of a practical reason can take place only with reference to the latter and therefore, indeed, conformably with the categories of the understanding, but not with a view to a theoretical use of the understanding, in order to bring a priori the manifold of (sensible) *intuition* under one consciousness, but only in order to subject a priori the manifold of *desires* to the unity of consciousness of a practical reason commanding in the moral law, or of a pure will.

These *categories of freedom* – for this is what we are going to call them in

CRITIQUE OF PRACTICAL REASON

contrast to those theoretical concepts which are categories of nature – have an obvious advantage over the latter inasmuch as the latter are only forms of thought which, by means of universal concepts, designate only indeterminately objects in general for every intuition possible for us; the former, on the contrary, are directed to the determination of a free choice[k] (to which indeed no fully corresponding intuition can be given but which – as does not happen in the case of any concepts of the theoretical use of our cognitive faculty – has as its basis a pure practical law a priori); hence, instead of the form of intuition (space and time), which does not lie in reason itself but must be drawn from elsewhere, namely from sensibility, these, as practical elementary concepts, have as their basis the *form of a pure will* as given within reason and therefore within the thinking faculty itself; by this it happens that, since all precepts of pure practical reason have to do only with the *determination of the will*, not with the natural conditions (of practical ability) for *carrying out its purpose*, the practical a priori concepts in relation to the supreme principle of freedom at once become cognitions and do not have to wait for intuitions in order to receive meaning; and this happens for the noteworthy reason that they themselves produce the reality of that to which they refer (the disposition of the will), which is not the business of theoretical concepts. But one must note well that these categories concern only practical reason in general and so proceed in their order from those which are as yet morally undetermined and sensibly conditioned to those which, being sensibly unconditioned, are determined only by the moral law.

5:66

TABLE
of the categories of freedom with respect to the concepts of the good and evil

1.
Of quantity
Subjective, in accordance with maxims (*intentions of the will*[l] of the individual)
Objective, in accordance with principles (*precepts*)
A priori objective as well as subjective principles of freedom (*laws*)

2.	3
Of quality	Of relation
Practical rules of *commission*	To *personality*
(*praeceptivae*)	To the *condition*[m] of the person

---

[k] *freien Willkür*
[l] *Willensmeinungen*
[m] or "state," *Zustand*

Practical rules of *omission*   Reciprocally, of one person
   (*prohibitivae*)   to the condition of others
Practical rules of *exceptions*
   (*exceptivae*)

4.
Of modality
The *permitted* and the *forbidden*
Duty and what is *contrary to duty*
Perfect and *imperfect* duty

One quickly sees that in this table freedom is regarded as a kind of causality – which, however, is not subject to empirical grounds of determination – with respect to actions possible through it as appearances in the sensible world, and that consequently it is referred to the categories of their natural possibility,[n] while yet each category is taken so universally that the determining ground of that causality can be taken to be also outside the sensible world in freedom as the property of an intelligible being, until the categories of modality introduce, but only *problematically*, the transition from practical principles in general to those of morality, which can only afterwards be presented *dogmatically* through the moral law.

I add nothing further here to elucidate the present table, since it is intelligible enough in itself. A division of this kind, drawn up in accordance with principles, is very useful in any science, for the sake of thoroughness as well as intelligibility. Thus, for example, one knows at once from the above table and its first number where one has to set out from in practical considerations: from the maxims that each bases on his inclination, from the precepts that hold for a species[o] of rational beings insofar as they agree in certain inclinations, and finally from the law that holds for all without regard for their inclinations, and so forth. In this way one surveys the whole plan of what has to be done, every question of practical philosophy that has to be answered, and also the order that is to be followed.

OF THE TYPIC OF PURE PRACTICAL JUDGMENT[p]

The concepts of good and evil first determine an object for the will. They themselves, however, stand under a practical rule of reason which, if it is pure reason, determines the will a priori with respect to its object. Now, whether an action possible for us in sensibility is or is not a case that

---
[n] *ihrer Naturmöglichkeit*. Abbot translates the phrase as "its [freedom's] physical possibility."
[o] *Gattung*
[p] *Urteilskraft*, i.e., "the faculty of judgment"

stands under the rule requires practical judgment, by which what is said in the rule universally (*in abstracto*) is applied to an action *in concreto*. But a practical rule of pure reason *first*, as *practical*, concerns the existence of an object, and *second*, as a *practical rule* of pure reason, brings with it necessity with respect to the existence of an action and is thus a practical law, not a natural law through empirical grounds of determination but a law of freedom in accordance with which the will is to be determinable independently of anything empirical (merely through the representation of a law in general and its form); however, all cases of possible actions that occur can be only empirical, that is, belong to experience and nature; hence, it seems absurd to want to find in the sensible world a case which, though as such it stands only under the law of nature, yet admits of the application to it of a law of freedom and to which there could be applied the supersensible idea of the morally good, which is to be exhibited in it *in concreto*. Thus the judgment of pure practical reason is subject to the very same difficulties as that of pure theoretical reason, though the latter had means at hand of escaping from these difficulties, namely that with respect to its theoretical use it depended upon intuitions to which pure concepts of the understanding could be applied, and such intuitions (though only of objects of the senses) can be given a priori and thus, as far as the connection of the manifold in them is concerned, given a priori (as *schemata*) conformably with pure concepts of the understanding. On the other hand, the morally good as an object is something supersensible, so that nothing corresponding to it can be found in any sensible intuition; and judgment under laws of pure practical reason seems, therefore, to be subject to special difficulties having their source in this: that a law of freedom is to applied to actions as events that take place in the sensible world and so, to this extent, belong to nature.

But here again a favorable prospect opens for pure practical judgment. Subsumption of an action possible to me in the sensible world under a *pure practical law* does not concern the possibility of the *action* as an event in the sensible world; for, it belongs to the theoretical use of reason to appraise that possibility in accordance with the law of causality, a pure concept of the understanding for which reason has a *schema* in sensible intuition. Physical causality, or the condition under which it takes place, belongs among concepts of nature, whose schema transcendental imagination sketches. Here, however, we have to do not with the schema of a case in accordance with laws but with the schema of a law itself (if the word schema is appropriate here), since the *determination of the will* (not the action with reference to its result) through the law alone without any other determining ground connects the concept of causality to conditions quite other than those which constitute natural connection.

To a natural law, as a law to which objects of sensible intuition as such are subject, there must correspond a schema, that is, a universal procedure of the imagination (by which it presents a priori to the senses the pure concept of the understanding which the law determines). But no intuition can be put under the law of freedom (as that of a causality not sensibly conditioned) – and hence under the concept of the unconditioned good as well – and hence no schema on behalf of its application *in concreto*. Thus the moral law has no cognitive faculty other than the understanding (not the imagination) by means of which it can be applied to objects of nature, and what the understanding can put under an idea of reason is not a *schema* of sensibility but a law, such a law, however, as can be presented *in concreto* in objects of the senses and hence a law of nature, though only as to its form; this law is what the understanding can put under an idea of reason on behalf of judgment, and we can, accordingly, call it the *type* of the moral law.

The rule of judgment under laws of pure practical reason is this: ask yourself whether, if the action you propose were to take place by a law of the nature of which you were yourself a part, you could indeed regard it as possible through your will. Everyone does, in fact, appraise actions as morally good or evil by this rule. Thus one says: if *everyone* permitted himself to deceive when he believed it to be to his advantage, or considered himself authorized to shorten his life as soon as he was thoroughly weary of it, or looked with complete indifference on the need of others, and if you belonged to such an order of things, would you be in it with the assent of your will? Now everyone knows very well that if he permits himself to deceive secretly it does not follow that everyone else does so, or that if, unobserved, he is hard-hearted[q] everyone would not straightaway be so toward him; accordingly, this comparison of the maxim of his actions with a universal law of nature is also not the determining ground of his will. Such a law is, nevertheless, a *type* for the appraisal of maxims in accordance with moral principles. If the maxim of the action is not so constituted that it can stand the test as to the form of a law of nature in general, then it is morally impossible. This is how even the most common understanding judges; for the law of nature always lies at the basis of its most ordinary judgments, even those of experience. Thus it has the law of nature always at hand, only that in cases where causality from freedom is to be appraised it makes that *law of nature* merely the type of a *law of freedom*, because without having at hand something which it could make an example in a case of experience, it could not provide use in application for the law of a pure practical reason.

Hence it is also permitted to use *the nature of the sensible world* as the *type* of an *intelligible nature*, provided that I do not carry over into the latter

---

[q] *lieblos*

intuitions and what depends upon them but refer to it only the *form of lawfulness* in general (the concept of which occurs even in the most common use of reason, although it cannot be determinately cognized a priori for any purpose other than the pure practical use of reason). For to this extent laws as such are the same, no matter from what they derive their determining grounds.

Furthermore, since of all the intelligible absolutely nothing [is cognized] except freedom (by means of the moral law), and even this only insofar as it is a presupposition inseparable from that law; and since, moreover, all intelligible objects to which reason might lead us under the guidance of that law have in turn no reality for us except on behalf of that law and of the use of pure practical reason, although reason is entitled and even required to use nature (in the understanding's pure form of nature) as the *type* of judgment; the present remark will serve to prevent reckoning among concepts themselves that which belongs only to the *typic* of concepts. This, then, as the typic of judgment, guards against *empiricism* of practical reason, which places the practical concepts of good and evil merely in experiential consequences (so-called happiness), although happiness and the endless useful consequences of a will determined by self-love, if this will at the same time made itself into a universal law of nature, can certainly serve as a quite suitable type for the morally good but is still not identical with it. The same typic also guards against *mysticism* of practical reason, which makes what served only as a *symbol* into a *schema*, that is, puts under the application of moral concepts real but not sensible intuitions (of an invisible kingdom of God) and strays into the transcendent. Only *rationalism* of judgment is suitable for the use of moral concepts, since it takes from sensible nature nothing more than what pure reason can also think for itself, that is, conformity with law, and transfers into the supersensible nothing but what can, conversely, be really exhibited by actions in the sensible world in accordance with the formal rule of a law of nature in general. However, it is much more important and advisable to guard against *empiricism* of practical reason, since *mysticism* is still compatible with the purity and sublimity of the moral law and, besides, it is not natural and not in keeping with the common way of thinking to strain one's imagination to supersensible intuitions, so that the danger from this side is not so general; empiricism, on the contrary, destroys at its roots the morality of dispositions (in which, and not merely in actions, consists the high worth that humanity can and ought to procure for itself through morality), and substitutes for it something quite different, namely in place of duty an empirical interest, with which the inclinations generally are secretly leagued; and empiricism, moreover, being on this account allied with all the inclinations, which (no matter what fashion they put on) degrade humanity when they are raised to the dignity of a supreme practical principle and which are, nevertheless, so favorable to everyone's way of feeling,[r] is for that reason much more dangerous than any enthusiasm, which can never constitute a lasting condition of any great number of people.[s]

Chapter III
On the incentives of pure practical reason

What is essential to any moral worth of actions is *that the moral law determine the will immediately*. If the determination of the will takes place *conformably* with the moral law but only by means of a feeling, of whatever kind, that has to be presupposed in order for the law to become a sufficient determining ground of the will, so that the action is not done *for the sake of the law*, then the action will contain *legality* indeed but not *morality*.

5:72 Now, if by *incentive (elater animi)* is understood the subjective determining ground of the will of a being whose reason does not by its nature necessarily conform with the objective law, then it will follow: first; that no incentives at all can be attributed to the divine will but that the incentive of the human will (and of the will of every created rational being) can never be anything other than the moral law; and thus that the objective determining ground must always and quite alone be also the subjectively sufficient determining ground of action if this is not merely to fulfill the *letter* of the law without containing its *spirit*.*

For the sake of the law and in order to give it influence on the will one must not, then, look for some other incentive by which that of the moral law itself might be dispensed with, because this would produce sheer hypocrisy without substance,[t] and it is even hazardous to let any other incentive (such as that of advantage) so much as cooperate *alongside* the moral law; so nothing further remains than to determine carefully in what way the moral law becomes the incentive and, inasmuch as it is, what happens to the human faculty of desire as an effect of that determining ground upon it. For, how a law can be of itself and immediately a determining ground of the will (though this is what is essential in all morality) is for human reason an insoluble problem and identical with that of how a free will is possible. What we shall have to show a priori is, therefore, not the ground from which[u] the moral law in itself supplies an incentive but rather

---

*Of every action that conforms to the law but is not done for the sake of the law, one can say that it is morally good only in accordance with the *letter* but not the *spirit* (the disposition).
[r] *Sinnesart*
[s] The construction of the last part of this sentence is, as Natorp remarks, "difficult, but with Kant perhaps still possible." With minor changes I have reproduced Abbott's construction.
[t] *ohne Bestand*
[u] *woher*

what it effects (or, to put it better, must effect) in the mind insofar as it is an incentive.

What is essential in every determination of the will by the moral law is that, as a free will – and so not only without the cooperation of sensible impulses but even with rejection of all of them and with infringement upon all inclinations insofar as they could be opposed to that law – it is determined solely by the law. So far, then, the effect of the moral law as incentive is only negative, and as such this incentive can be cognized a priori. For, all inclination and every sensible impulse is based on feeling, and the negative effect on feeling (by the infringement upon the inclinations that takes place) is itself feeling. Hence we can see a priori that the moral law, as the determining ground of the will, must by thwarting all our inclinations produce a feeling that can be called pain; and here we have the first and perhaps the only case in which we can determine a priori from concepts the relation of a cognition (here the cognition of a pure practical reason) to the feeling of pleasure or displeasure. All the inclinations together (which can be brought into a tolerable system and the satisfaction of which is then called one's own happiness) constitute regard for oneself[v] (*solipsismus*). This is either the self-regard of *love for oneself,* a predominant *benevolence* toward oneself (*Philautia*), or that of *satisfaction with oneself* (*Arrogantia*). The former is called, in particular, *self-love;*[w] the latter, *self-conceit.*[x] Pure practical reason merely *infringes upon* self-love, inasmuch as it only restricts it, as natural and active in us even prior to the moral law, to the condition of agreement with this law, and then it is called *rational self-love.* But it *strikes down* self-conceit altogether, since all claims to esteem for oneself that precede accord with the moral law are null and quite unwarranted because certainty of a disposition in accord with this law is the first condition of any worth of a person (we shall soon make this more distinct), and any presumption prior to this is false and opposed to the law. Now, the propensity to self-esteem, so long as it rests only on sensibility, belongs with the inclinations which the moral law infringes upon. So the moral law strikes down self-conceit. But since this law is still something in itself positive – namely the form of an intellectual causality, that is, of freedom – it is at the same time an object of *respect* inasmuch as, in opposition to its subjective antagonist, namely the inclinations in us, it *weakens* self-conceit; and inasmuch as it even *strikes down* self-conceit, that is, humiliates it, it is an object of the greatest *respect* and so too the ground of a positive feeling that is not of empirical origin and is cognized a priori. Consequently, respect for the moral law is a feeling that is produced by

5:73

---

[v] *Selbstsucht*
[w] *Eigenliebe*
[x] *Eigendünkel*

an intellectual ground, and this feeling is the only one that we can cognize completely a priori and the necessity of which we can have insight into.

In the preceding chapter we have seen that anything which presents itself as an object of the will *prior to* the moral law is excluded from the determining grounds of the will called the unconditionally good by that law itself as the supreme condition of practical reason, and that the mere practical form, which consists in the fitness of maxims for giving universal law, first determines what is good in itself and absolutely and grounds the maxims of a pure will, which alone is good in every respect. Now, however, we find our nature as sensible beings so constituted that the matter of the faculty of desire (objects of inclination, whether of hope or fear) first forces itself upon us, and we find our pathologically determinable self, even though it is quite unfit to give universal law through its maxims, nevertheless striving antecedently to make its claims primary and originally valid, just as if it constituted our entire self. This propensity to make oneself as having subjective determining grounds of choice[y] into the objective determining ground of the will in general can be called *self-love;* and if self-love makes itself lawgiving and the unconditional practical principle, it can be called *self-conceit.* Now the moral law, which alone is truly objective (namely objective in every respect), excludes altogether the influence of self-love on the supreme practical principle and infringes without end upon self-conceit, which prescribes as laws the subjective conditions of self-love. Now, what in our own judgment infringes upon our self-conceit humiliates. Hence the moral law unavoidably humiliates every human being when he compares with it the sensible propensity of his nature. If something represented *as a determining ground of our will* humiliates us in our self-consciousness, it awakens *respect* for itself insofar as it is positive and a determining ground. Therefore the moral law is even subjectively a ground of respect. Now, all that is found in self-love belongs to inclination, while all inclination rests on feeling, so that what infringes upon all the inclinations in self-love has, just by this, a necessary influence on feeling; thus we conceive how it is possible to see a priori that the moral law can exercise an effect on feeling, inasmuch as it excludes the inclinations and the propensity to make them the supreme practical condition, that is, self-love, from all participation in the supreme lawgiving – an effect which on the one side is merely *negative* but on the other side, and indeed with respect to the restricting ground of pure practical reason, is *positive;* and for this no special kind of feeling need be assumed, under the name of a practical or moral feeling preceding the moral law and serving as its basis.

The negative effect upon feeling (disagreeableness) is *pathological*, as is every influence on feeling and every feeling in general. As the effect of

---

[y] *sich selbst nach den subjectiven Bestimmungsgründen seiner Willkür*

consciousness of the moral law, and consequently in relation to an intelligible cause, namely the subject of pure practical reason as the supreme lawgiver, this feeling of a rational subject affected by inclinations is indeed called humiliation (intellectual contempt); but in relation to its positive ground, the law, it is at the same time called respect for the law; there is indeed no feeling for this law, but inasmuch as it moves resistance out of the way, in the judgment of reason this removal of a hindrance is esteemed equivalent to a positive furthering of its causality. Because of this, this feeling can now also be called a feeling of respect for the moral law, while on both grounds together it can be called a *moral feeling.*

Thus the moral law, since it is a formal determining ground of action through practical pure reason and since it is also a material but only objective determining ground of the objects of action under the name of good and evil, is also a subjective determining ground – that is, an incentive – to this action inasmuch as it has influence on the sensibility of the subject and effects a feeling conducive to the influence of the law upon the will. There is here no *antecedent* feeling in the subject that would be attuned to morality: that is impossible, since all feeling is sensible whereas the incentive of the moral disposition must be free from any sensible condition. Instead, sensible feeling, which underlies all our inclinations, is indeed the condition of that feeling we call respect, but the cause determining it lies in pure practical reason; and so this feeling, on account of its origin, cannot be called pathologically effected but must be called *practically effected,* and is effected as follows: the representation of the moral law deprives self-love of its influence and self-conceit of its illusion, and thereby the hindrance to pure practical reason is lessened and the representation of the superiority of its objective law to the impulses of sensibility is produced and hence, by removal of the counterweight, the relative weightiness of the law (with regard to a will affected by impulses) in the judgment of reason. And so respect for the law is not the incentive to morality; instead it is morality itself subjectively considered as an incentive inasmuch as pure practical reason, by rejecting all the claims of self-love in opposition with its own, supplies authority to the law, which now alone has influence. With regard to this it should be noted that, since respect is an effect on feeling and hence on the sensibility of a rational being, it presupposes this sensibility and so too the finitude of such beings on whom the moral law imposes respect, and that respect for the *law* cannot be attributed to a supreme being or even to one free from all sensibility, in whom this cannot be an obstacle to practical reason.

5:76

This feeling (under the name of moral feeling) is therefore produced solely by reason. It does not serve for appraising actions and certainly not for grounding the objective moral law itself, but only as an incentive to make this law its maxim. But what name could one more suitably apply to this singular feeling which cannot be compared to any pathological feeling? It is of such a peculiar kind that it seems to be at the disposal[z] only of reason, and indeed of practical pure reason.

Respect is always directed only to persons, never to things. The latter can awaken in us *inclination* and even *love* if they are animals (e.g., horses, dogs, and so forth), or also *fear*, like the sea, a volcano, a beast of prey, but never *respect*. Something that comes nearer to this feeling is *admiration*, and this as an affect, amazement, can be directed to things also, for example, lofty mountains, the magnitude, number, and distance of the heavenly bodies, the strength and swiftness of many animals, and so forth. But none of this is respect. A human being can also be an object of my love, fear, or admiration even to amazement and yet not be an object of respect. His jocular humor, his courage and strength, the power he has by his rank among others, could inspire me with feelings of this kind even though inner respect toward him is lacking. Fontenelle[9] says, "*I bow before an eminent man, but my spirit does not bow.*" I can add: before a humble common man[a] in whom I perceive uprightness of character in a higher degree than I am aware of in myself *my spirit bows*, whether I want it or whether I do not and hold my head ever so high, that he may not overlook my superior position. Why is this? His example holds before me a law that strikes down my self-conceit when I compare it with my conduct, and I see observance of that law and hence its *practicability* proved before me in fact. Now, I may even be aware of a like degree of uprightness in myself, and yet the respect remains. For, since in human beings all good is defective, the law made intuitive by an example still strikes down my pride, the standard being furnished by the man I see before me whose impurity,[b] such as it may be, is not so well known to me as is my own who therefore appears to me in a purer light. *Respect* is a *tribute* that we cannot refuse to pay to merit, whether we want to or not; we may indeed withhold it outwardly but we still cannot help feeling it inwardly.

So little is respect a feeling of *pleasure* that we give way to it only reluctantly with regard to a human being. We try to discover something that could lighten the burden of it for us, some fault in him to compensate us for the humiliation that comes upon us through such an example. Even the dead are not always safe from this critical examination, especially if their example appears inimitable. Even the moral law itself in its *solemn majesty* is exposed to this striving to resist respect for it. Can it be thought that any other cause can be assigned for our being so ready to demean it to our familiar inclination, or that there is any other cause of our taking such trouble to make it out to be the popular precept of our own advantage well

---

[z] *zu Gebote*

[a] *niedrigen, bürgerlich gemeinen Mann*

[b] *Unlauterkeit.* See *Religion within the Boundaries of Mere Reason* (6:29–30). Later in the sentence "purer" is used to translate *reinerem*.

understood, than that we want to be free from the intimidating respect that shows us our own unworthiness with such severity? But, in turn, *so little displeasure* is there in it that, once one has laid self-conceit aside and allowed practical influence to that respect, one can in turn never get enough of contemplating the majesty of this law, and the soul believes itself elevated in proportion as it sees the holy elevated above itself and its frail nature. No doubt, great talents and activity proportioned to them can also produce respect or a feeling analogous to it, and it is also quite proper to offer it; and then it seems as if admiration were the same as that feeling. But if one looks more closely one will notice that, since it always remains uncertain how much was contributed to someone's competence by native talent and how much by his industry in cultivating it, reason represents it to us as presumably the fruit of cultivation and so as merit, and this noticeably reduces our self-conceit and either casts a reproach on us or imposes on us the following of such an example in the way suitable to us. This respect, then, which we show to such a person (strictly speaking to the law that his example holds before us) is not mere admiration, as is also confirmed by this: that when the common run of admirers believes it has somehow learned the badness of character of such a man (such as Voltaire) it gives up all respect for him, whereas the true scholar still feels it at least with regard to his talents, because he is himself engaged in a business and a calling that make imitation of such a man to some extent a law for him.

5:78

Respect for the moral law is therefore the sole and also the undoubted moral incentive, and this feeling is also directed to no object except on this basis. First, the moral law determines the will objectively and immediately in the judgment of reason; but freedom, the causality of which is determinable only through the law, consists just in this: that it restricts all inclinations, and consequently the esteem of the person himself, to the condition of compliance with its pure law. This restriction now has an effect on feeling and produces the feeling of displeasure which can be cognized a priori from the moral law. It is, however, so far a *negative* effect which, as arising from the influence of a pure practical reason, mainly infringes upon the activity of the subject so far as inclinations are his determining grounds and hence upon the opinion of his personal worth (which, in the absence of agreement with the moral law, is reduced to nothing), so that the effect of this law on feeling is merely humiliation, which we can thus discern a priori though we cannot cognize in it the force of the pure practical law as incentive but only the resistance to incentives of sensibility. But the same law is yet objectively – that is, in the representation of pure reason – an immediate determining ground of the will, so that this humiliation takes place only relatively to the purity of the law; accordingly, the lowering of pretensions to moral self-esteem – that is, humiliation on the sensible side – is an elevation of the moral – that is, practical – esteem

5:79

for the law itself on the intellectual side; in a word, it is respect for the law, and so also a feeling that is positive in its intellectual cause, which is known a priori. For, whatever diminishes the hindrances to an activity is a furthering of this activity itself. Recognition of the moral law is, however, consciousness of an activity of practical reason from objective grounds, which fails to express its effect in actions only because subjective (pathological) causes hinder it. Therefore respect for the moral law must be regarded as also a positive though indirect effect of the moral law on feeling insofar as the law weakens the hindering influence of the inclinations by humiliating self-conceit, and must therefore be regarded as a subjective ground of activity – that is, as the incentive to compliance with the law – and as the ground for maxims of a course of life in conformity with it. From the concept of an incentive arises that of an *interest*, which can never be attributed to any being unless it has reason and which signifies an *incentive* of the will insofar as it is *represented by reason*. Since in a morally good will the law itself must be the incentive, the *moral interest* is a pure sense-free interest of practical reason alone. On the concept of an interest is based that of a *maxim*. A maxim is therefore morally genuine only if it rests solely on the interest one takes in compliance with the law. All three concepts, however – that of an *incentive*, of an *interest* and of a *maxim* – can be applied only to finite beings. For they all presuppose a limitation of the nature of a being, in that the subjective constitution of its choice does not of itself accord with the objective law of a practical reason; they presuppose a need to be impelled to activity by something because an internal obstacle is opposed to it. Thus they cannot be applied to the divine will.

There is something so singular in the boundless esteem for the pure moral law stripped of all advantage – as practical reason, whose voice makes even the boldest evildoer tremble and forces him to hide from its sight, presents it to us for obedience – that one cannot wonder at finding this influence of a mere intellectual idea on feeling quite impenetrable for speculative reason and at having to be satisfied that one can yet see a priori this much: that such a feeling is inseparably connected with the representation of the moral law in every finite rational being. If this feeling of respect were pathological and hence a feeling of *pleasure* based on the inner *sense*, it would be futile to [try to] discover a priori a connection of it with any idea. But it is a feeling which is directed only to the practical and which depends on the representation of a law only as to its form and not on account of any object of the law; thus it cannot be reckoned either as enjoyment or as pain, and yet it produces an *interest* in compliance with the law which we call *moral* interest, just as the capacity to take such an interest in the law (or respect for the moral law itself) is *the moral feeling* properly speaking.

The consciousness of a *free* submission of the will to the law, yet as combined with an unavoidable constraint put on all inclinations though only by one's own reason, is respect for the law. The law that demands this respect and also inspires it is, as one sees, none other than the moral law (for no other excludes all inclinations from immediate influence on the will). An action that is objectively practical in accordance with this law, with the exclusion of every determining ground of inclination, is called *duty*, which, because of that exclusion, contains in its concept practical *necessitation*, that is, determination to actions however *reluctantly* they may be done. The feeling that arises from consciousness of this necessitation is not pathological, as would be a feeling produced by an object of the senses, but practical only, that is, possible through a preceding (objective) determination of the will and causality of reason. As *submission* to a law, that is, as a command (indicating constraint for the sensibly affected subject), it therefore contains in it no pleasure but instead, so far, displeasure in the action. On the other hand, however, since this constraint is exercised only by the lawgiving of his *own* reason, it also contains something *elevating*, and the subjective effect on feeling, inasmuch as pure practical reason is the sole cause of it,ᶜ can thus be called *self-approbation* with reference to pure practical reason, inasmuch as he cognized himself as determined to it solely by the law and without any interest, and now becomes conscious of an altogether different interest subjectively produced by the law, which is purely practical and *free;* and his taking this interest in a dutiful action is not advised by any inclination; instead, reason through the practical law absolutely commands it and also actually produces it, because of which it has a quite special name, that of respect.

5:81

The concept of duty, therefore, requires of the action *objective* accord with the law but requires of the maxim of the action *subjective* respect for the law, as the sole way of determining the will by the law. And on this rests the distinction between consciousness of having acted *in conformity with duty* and *from duty*, that is, respect for the law, the first of which (legality) is possible even if the inclinations alone have been the determining grounds of the will whereas the second (*morality*), moral worth, must be placed solely in this: that the action takes place from duty, that is, for the sake of the law alone.*

It is of the greatest importance in all moral appraisals to attend with the utmost exactness to the subjective principle of all maxims, so that all the

---

*If one examines accurately the concept of respect for persons, as it has already been set forth, one becomes aware that it always rests on consciousness of a duty which an example holds before us, and that, accordingly, respect can never have any but a moral ground; and it is very good and even, from a psychological point of view, very useful for knowledge of human beings that whenever we use this expression we should attend to the hidden and wonderful, yet often recurring, regard which the human being in his appraisals has for the moral law.

ᶜ *der letzteren.* "Something elevating" (literally, "elevation") is grammatically possible.

morality of actions is placed in their necessity *from duty* and from respect for the law, not from love and liking[d] for what the actions are to produce. For human beings and all created rational beings moral necessity is necessitation, that is, obligation, and every action based on it is to be represented as duty, not as a kind of conduct which we already favor of our own accord or could come to favor – as if we could ever bring it about that without respect for the law, which is connected with fear or at least apprehension of transgressing it, we of ourselves, like the Deity raised beyond all dependence, could come into possession of *holiness* of will by an accord of will with the pure moral law becoming, as it were, our nature, an accord never to be disturbed (in which case the law would finally cease to be a command for us, since we could never be tempted to be unfaithful to it).

The moral law is, in other words, for the will of a perfect being a law of *holiness*, but for the will of every finite rational being a law of *duty*, of moral necessitation and of the determination of his actions through *respect* for this law and *reverence*[e] for his duty. No other subjective principle must be assumed as incentive, for then the action can indeed turn out as the law prescribes, but since, though in conformity with duty it was not done from duty, the disposition to the action is not moral; and in this lawgiving it is really the disposition that matters.

It is very beautiful to do good to human beings from love for them and from sympathetic benevolence, or to be just from love of order; but this is not yet the genuine moral maxim of our conduct, the maxim befitting our position among rational beings as *human beings*, when we presume with proud conceit, like volunteers, not to trouble ourselves about the thought of duty and, as independent of command, to want to do of our own pleasure what we think we need no command to do. We stand under a *discipline* of reason, and in all our maxims must not forget our subjection to it or withdraw anything from it or by an egotistical illusion detract anything from the authority of the law (although our own reason gives it), so as to put the determining ground of our will, even though it conforms with the law, anywhere else than in the law itself and in respect for this law. Duty and what is owed[f] are the only names that we must give to our relation to the moral law. We are indeed lawgiving members of a kingdom of morals possible through freedom and represented to us by practical reason for our respect; but we are at the same time subjects in it, not its sovereign, and to fail to recognize our inferior position as creatures and to deny from self-conceit the authority of the holy law is already to defect from it in spirit, even though the letter of the law is fulfilled.

[d] *Zuneigung*
[e] *Ehrfurcht*
[f] *Schuldigkeit*

The possibility of such a commandment[g] as *Love God above all, and your neighbor as yourself* agrees with this very well.* For, as a commandment it requires respect for a law that *commands*[h] love and does not leave it to one's discretionary choice to make this one's principle. But love for God as inclination (pathological love) is impossible, for he is not an object of the senses. The same thing toward human beings is indeed possible but cannot be commanded, for it is not within the power of any human being to love someone merely on command.[i] It is, therefore, only *practical love* that is understood in that kernel of all laws. To love God means, in this sense, to do what He commands *gladly;* to love one's neighbor means to practice all duties toward him *gladly*. But the command that makes this a rule cannot command us to *have* this disposition in dutiful actions but only to *strive* for it. For, a command that one should do something gladly is in itself contradictory because if we already know of ourselves what it is incumbent upon us to do and, moreover, were conscious of liking to do it, a command about it would be quite unnecessary; and if we did it without liking to do it but only from respect for the law, a command that makes this respect the incentive of our maxim would directly counteract the disposition commanded. That law of all laws, therefore, like all the moral precepts of the Gospel, presents the moral disposition in its complete perfection, in such a way that as an ideal of holiness it is not attainable by any creature but is yet the archetype which we should strive to approach and resemble in an uninterrupted but endless progress. That is to say, if a rational creature could ever reach the stage of thoroughly *liking* to fulfill all moral laws, this would mean that there would not be in him even the possibility of a desire that would provoke him to deviate from them; for, to overcome such a desire always costs the subject some sacrifice and therefore requires self-constraint, that is, inner necessitation to what one does not altogether like to do. But no creature can ever reach this stage of moral disposition. For, being a creature and thus always dependent with regard to what he requires for complete satisfaction with his condition, he can never be altogether free from desires and inclinations which, because they rest on physical causes, do not of themselves accord with the moral law, which has quite different sources; and consequently, with reference to those desires, it is always necessary for him to base the disposition of his maxims on moral necessitation, not on ready fidelity but on respect, which *demands* compliance with the law even though this is done reluc-

5:84

---

*The principle of one's own happiness, which some would make the supreme principle of morality, is in striking contrast to this law. The former would go as follows: *Love yourself above all, but God and your neighbor for your own sake.*
[g] *Gebots*
[h] *befiehlt*
[i] *auf Befehl*

tantly; not on love, which is not anxious about any inner refusal of the will toward the law, even though it is necessary for him to make this latter – namely, mere love for the law (which would then cease to be a *command*, and morality, having passed subjectively into holiness, would cease to be *virtue*) – the constant though unattainable goal of his striving. For, in the case of what we highly esteem but yet dread (because of consciousness of our weakness), through increased facility in satisfying it the most reverential dread changes into liking and respect into love; at least this would be the consummate perfection of a disposition devoted to the law, if it were possible for a creature to attain it.

This consideration is intended not so much to bring to clear concepts the evangelical command just cited, in order to prevent *religious enthusiasm* in regard to love of God, but to determine accurately the moral disposition directly, in regard to our duties toward human beings as well, and to check, or where possible prevent, a *merely moral* enthusiasm which infects many people. The moral level on which a human being (and, as far as we can see, every rational creature as well) stands is respect for the moral law. The disposition incumbent upon him to have in observing it is to do so from duty, not from voluntary liking nor even from an endeavor he undertakes unbidden, gladly and of his own accord; and his proper moral condition, in which he can always be, is *virtue*, that is, moral disposition *in conflict*, and not *holiness* in the supposed *possession* of a complete *purity* of dispositions of the will. By exhortation to actions as noble, sublime, and magnanimous, minds are attuned to nothing but moral enthusiasm and exaggerated self-conceit; by such exhortations they are led into the delusion that it is not duty – that is, respect for the law whose yoke (though it is a mild one because reason itself imposes it on us) they must bear, even if reluctantly – which constitutes the determining ground of their actions, and which always humbles them inasmuch as they observe the law (*obey* it), but that it is as if those actions are expected from them, not from duty but as bare merit. For, when they imitate such deeds – namely, from such a principle – not only have they quite failed to fulfill the spirit of the law, which consists in the disposition subjecting itself to the law, not in the lawfulness of the action (whatever the principle may be); not only do they locate the incentive *pathologically* (in sympathy or self-love), not *morally* (in the law); but they produce in this way a frivolous, high-flown, fantastic cast of mind, flattering themselves with a spontaneous goodness of heart[j] that needs neither spur nor bridle and for which not even a command is necessary and thereby forgetting their obligation,[k] which they ought to think of rather than merit. Actions of others that are done with great sacrifice and for the sake of duty alone may indeed be praised by calling

---

[j] *freiwillige Gutartigkeit ihrer Gemüts*
[k] *Schuldigkeit*

them *noble* and *sublime* deeds, but only insofar as there are traces suggesting that they were done wholly from respect for duty and not from ebullitions of feeling. But if one wants to represent these to someone as examples to be imitated, respect for duty (which is the only genuine moral feeling) must be used as the incentive – this earnest, holy precept that does not leave it to our vain self-love to dally with pathological impulses (as far as they are analogous to morality) and to credit ourselves with *meritorious* worth. If only we search carefully we shall find for all actions that are praiseworthy a law of duty, which *commands* and does not leave it to our discretion to choose what may be agreeable to our propensity. This is the only way of representing them that educates the soul morally, because it alone is capable of firm and accurately determined principles.

If *enthusiasm* in the most general sense is an overstepping of the bounds of human reason undertaken on principles, then *moral enthusiasm* is such an overstepping of the bounds that practical pure reason sets to humanity, thereby forbidding us to place the subjective determining ground of dutiful actions – that is, their moral motive – anywhere else than in the law itself or to place the disposition which is thereby brought into the maxims anywhere else than in respect for this law, and so commanding us to make the thought of duty, which strikes down all *arrogance* as well as vain *self-love*, the supreme *life-principle* of all morality in human beings.

If this is so, then not only novelists and sentimental educators (even though they may be strongly opposed to sentimentalism) but sometimes even philosophers – and even the most austere of all, the Stoics – have ushered in *moral enthusiasm* instead of a sober but wise moral discipline, though the enthusiasm of the latter was more heroic while that of the former is of a more insipid and languishing character; and one can, without hypocrisy, say quite truly of the moral teaching of the Gospel that, by the purity of its moral principle but at the same time by the suitability of this principle to the limitations of finite beings, it first subjected all good conduct of man to the discipline of a duty laid before his eyes, which does not allow them to rove among fancied moral perfections, and set limits of humility (i.e., self-knowledge) to self-conceit as well as to self-love, both of which are ready to mistake their boundaries.

Duty! Sublime and mighty name that embraces nothing charming or insinuating but requires submission, and yet does not seek to move the will by threatening anything that would arouse natural aversion or terror in the mind but only holds forth a law that of itself finds entry into the mind and yet gains reluctant reverence (though not always obedience), a law before which all inclinations are dumb, even though they secretly work against it; what origin is there worthy of you, and where is to be found the root of your noble descent which proudly rejects all kinship with the inclinations, descent from which is the indispensable condition of that worth which human beings alone can give themselves?

5:86

It can be nothing less than what elevates a human being above himself (as a part of the sensible world), what connects him with an order of things that only the understanding can think and that at the same time has under it the whole sensible world and with it the empirically determinable existence of human beings in time and the whole of all ends (which is alone suitable to such unconditional practical laws as the moral). It is nothing other than *personality*, that is, freedom and independence from the mechanism of the whole of nature, regarded nevertheless as also a capacity of a being subject to special laws – namely pure practical laws given by his own reason, so that a person as belonging to the sensible world is subject to his own personality insofar as he also belongs to the intelligible world; for, it is then not to be wondered at that a human being, as belonging to both worlds, must regard his own nature in reference to his second and highest vocation only with reverence, and its laws with the highest respect.

On this origin are based many expressions that indicate the worth of objects according to moral ideas. The moral law is *holy* (inviolable). A human being is indeed unholy enough but the *humanity* in his person must be holy to him. In the whole of creation everything one wants and over which one has any power can also be used *merely as a means*; a human being alone, and with him every rational creature, is an *end in itself*: by virtue of the autonomy of his freedom he is the subject of the moral law, which is holy. Just because of this every will, even every person's own will directed to himself, is restricted to the condition of agreement with the *autonomy* of the rational being, that is to say, such a being is not to be subjected to any purpose that is not possible in accordance with a law that could arise from the will of the affected[1] subject himself; hence this subject is to be used never merely as a means but as at the same time an end. We rightly attribute this condition even to the divine will with respect to the rational beings in the world as its creatures, inasmuch as it rests on their *personality*, by which alone they are ends in themselves.

This idea of personality, awakening respect by setting before our eyes the sublimity of our nature (in its vocation) while at the same time showing us the lack of accord of our conduct with respect to it and thus striking down self-conceit, is natural even to the most common human reason and is easily observed. Has not every even moderately honorable man sometimes found that he has abstained from an otherwise harmless lie by which he could either have extricated himself from a troublesome affair or even procured some advantage for a beloved and deserving friend, solely in order not to have to despise himself secretly in his own eyes? When an upright man is in the greatest distress, which he could have avoided if he could only have disregarded duty, is he not sustained by the consciousness that he has maintained humanity in its proper dignity in his own person

---

[1] *leidenden*

and honored it, that he has no cause to shame himself in his own eyes and to dread the inward view of self-examination? This consolation is not happiness, not even the smallest part of it. For, no one would wish the occasion for it on himself, or perhaps even a life in such circumstances. But he lives and cannot bear to be unworthy of life in his own eyes. This inner tranquility is therefore merely negative with respect to everything that can make life pleasant; it is, namely, only warding off the danger of sinking in personal worth, after he has given up completely the worth of his condition. It is the effect of a respect for something quite different from life, something in comparison and contrast with which life with all its agreeableness has no worth at all. He still lives only from duty, not because he has the least taste for living.

This is how the genuine moral incentive of pure practical reason is constituted; it is nothing other than the pure moral law itself insofar as it lets us discover the sublimity of our own supersensible existence and subjectively effects respect for their higher vocation in human beings, who are at the same time conscious of their sensible existence and of the dependence, connected with it, on their pathologically affected nature. Now, so many charms and attractions of life may well be connected with this incentive that even for their sake alone the most prudent choice of a reasonable Epicurean, reflecting on the greatest well-being of life, would declare itself for moral conduct; and it can even be advisable to connect this prospect of a cheerful enjoyment of life with that motive which is supreme and already sufficiently determining of itself; but this connection should be made only to counterbalance the allurements that vice does not fail to display on the opposite side, and not so as to place in this the proper moving force, not even the smallest part of it, when it is a question of duty. For that would be tantamount to wanting to taint the pure moral disposition in its source. The majesty of duty has nothing to do with the enjoyment of life; it has its own law and also its own court, and even though one might want to shake both of them together thoroughly, so as to give them blended, like medicine, to the sick soul, they soon separate of themselves; if they do not, the former will effect nothing at all, and though physical life might gain some force, the moral life would fade away irrecoverably.

CRITICAL ELUCIDATION OF THE ANALYTIC OF PURE PRACTICAL REASON

By the critical elucidation of a science, or of a portion of it that constitutes a system by itself, I understand the investigation and justification of why it must have precisely this and no other systematic form when it is compared with another system having a similar cognitive faculty as its basis. Now, practical reason has as its basis the same cognitive faculty as does speculative reason so far as both are *pure reason*. Therefore the difference in the systematic form of the one from that of the other must be determined by a comparison of the two, and the ground of this difference must be assigned.

The Analytic of pure theoretical reason had to do with cognition of such objects as could be given to the understanding; it thus had to begin from *intuition* and consequently (since this is always sensible) from sensibility, and only then progress to concepts (of the objects of this intuition), and could end with *principles* only after preparation by way of both these. Practical reason, on the contrary, since it does not have to do with objects for the sake of *cognizing* them but with its own ability *to make them real* (conformably with cognition of them), that is, with a *will* that is a causality inasmuch as reason contains its determining ground; since, accordingly, it does not have to provide an object of intuition but, as practical reason, *only a law* for such an object (because the concept of causality always contains reference to a law that determines the existence of a manifold in relation to one another); it follows that a critique of the Analytic of reason, insofar as it is to be a practical reason (and this is the real problem), must begin from the *possibility of practical principles* a priori. Only from these could it proceed to *concepts* of objects of a practical reason, namely, to the concepts of the simply good and evil, in order first to give them in keeping with those principles (for, prior to those principles these cannot possibly be given as good and evil by any cognitive faculty), and only then could the last chapter conclude this part, namely the chapter about the relation of pure practical reason to sensibility and about its necessary influence upon sensibility to be cognized a priori, that is, about *moral feeling*. Thus the Analytic of practical pure reason divides the whole sphere of all the conditions of its use quite analogously with that of theoretical reason, but in reverse order. The Analytic of theoretical pure reason was divided into transcendental Aesthetic and transcendental Logic; that of practical reason, reversely, into Logic and Aesthetic of pure practical reason (if I may be allowed, merely by an analogy, to use these terms, which are not altogether suitable); the Logic in turn was there divided into Analytic of concepts and Analytic of principles, here into that of principles and concepts. The Aesthetic there had two parts, because of the twofold kind of sensible intuition; here sensibility is not regarded as a capacity for intuition at all but only as feeling (which can be a subjective ground of desire), and with respect to it pure practical reason admits no further division.

As to why this division into two parts with their subdivision was not actually undertaken here (as one might initially have been induced to attempt by the example of the first *Critique*), this is easily seen. For, since it is *pure reason* that is here considered in its practical use, and consequently as proceeding from a priori principles and not from empirical determining grounds, the division of the Analytic of pure practical reason must turn out like that of a syllogism, namely, proceeding from the universal in the *major premise* (the moral principle), through undertaking in a *minor premise* a subsumption of possible actions (as good or evil) under the former, to the *conclusion*, namely, the subjective determination of the will (an interest in the practically possible good and in the maxim based on it). For someone who has been able to convince himself of the propositions presented in the Analytic such comparisons will be gratifying; for they rightly occasion the expectation of perhaps being able some day to attain insight into the unity of the whole pure rational faculty (theoretical as well as practical) and to derive everything from one principle – the undeniable need of human reason, which finds complete satisfaction only in a complete systematic unity of its cognitions.

5:91

But if we now consider also the content of the cognition that we can have of a pure practical reason and by means of it, as the Analytic of pure practical reason presents this content, there is found, along with a remarkable analogy between it and the theoretical, no less remarkable differences. With respect to the theoretical, the *faculty of a pure rational cognition* a priori could be quite easily and evidently proved through examples from the sciences (in which, since they put their principles to the test in so many ways by methodic use, one need not fear so much as in common cognition a secret mixture of empirical grounds of cognition). But that pure reason, without the admixture of any empirical determining ground, is practical of itself alone: this one had to be able to show from the *most common practical use of reason*, by confirming the supreme practical principle as one that every natural human reason cognizes – a law completely a priori and independent of any sensible data – as the supreme law of its will. It was necessary first to establish and justify the purity of its origin even *in the judgment of this common reason* before science would take it in hand in order to make use of it, so to speak, as a fact that precedes all subtle reasoning about its possibility and all the consequences that may be drawn from it. But this circumstance can also be very well explained from what has just been said; it is because practical pure reason must necessarily begin from principles, which must therefore, as the first data, be put at the basis of all science and cannot first arise from it. But for this reason the justification of moral principles as principles of a pure reason could also be carried out very well and with sufficient certainty by a mere appeal to the judgment of common human understanding, because anything empirical that might slip into our maxims as a determining ground of the will *makes itself known* at once by the feeling of gratification or pain that necessarily attaches to it insofar as it arouses desire, whereas pure practical reason directly *opposes* taking this feeling into its principle as a condition. The dissimilarity of determining grounds (empirical and rational) is made known by this resistance of a practically lawgiving reason to every meddling inclination, by a special kind of *feeling*, which, however, does not precede the lawgiving of practical reason but is instead produced only by it and indeed as a constraint, namely, through the feeling of a respect such

5:92

as no human being has for inclinations of whatever kind but does have for the law; and it is made known so saliently and so prominently that no one, not even the most common human understanding, can fail to see at once, in an example presented to him, that he can indeed be advised by empirical grounds of volition to follow their charms but that he can never be expected to *obey* anything but the pure practical law of reason alone.

The distinction of the *doctrine of happiness* from the *doctrine of morals*, in the first of which empirical principles constitute the whole foundation whereas in the second they do not make even the smallest addition to it, is the first and most important business incumbent upon the Analytic of pure practical reason, in which it must proceed as *precisely* and, so to speak, as *scrupulously* as any geometer in his work. A philosopher, however, has greater difficulties to contend with here (as always in rational cognition through mere concepts without construction of them), because he cannot put any intuition (a pure noumenon) at its basis. He has, however, the advantage that, almost like a chemist, he can at any time set up an experiment with every human practical reason in order to distinguish the moral (pure) determining ground from the empirical, namely, by adding the moral law (as a determining ground) to the empirically affected will (e.g., that of someone who would gladly lie because he can gain something by it). When an analyst adds alkali to a solution of calcareous earth in hydrochloric acid, the acid at once releases[m] the lime and unites with the alkali, and the lime is precipitated. In just the same way, if a man who is otherwise honest (or who just this once puts himself only in thought in the place of an honest man) is confronted with the moral law in which he cognizes the worthlessness of a liar, his practical reason (in its judgment of what he ought to do) at once abandons[n] the advantage, unites with what maintains in him respect for his own person (truthfulness), and the advantage, after it has been separated and washed from every particle of reason (which is altogether on the side of duty), is weighed by everyone, so that it can enter into combination with reason in other cases, only not where it could be opposed to the moral law, which reason never abandons but unites with most intimately.

But this *distinction* of the principle of happiness from that of morality is not, for this reason, at once an *opposition* between them, and pure practical reason does not require[o] that one should *renounce* claims to happiness but only that as soon as duty is in question one should *take no account* of them. It can even in certain respects be a duty to attend to one's happiness, partly because happiness (to which belong skill, health, wealth) contains means for the fulfillment of one's duty and partly because lack of it (e.g.,

---

[m] *verläßt*
[n] *verläßt*
[o] *will nicht*

poverty) contains temptations to transgress one's duty. However, it can never be a direct duty to promote one's happiness, still less can it be a principle of all duty. Now, because all determining grounds of the will except the one and only pure practical law of reason (the moral law) are without exception empirical and so, as such, belong to the principle of happiness, they must without exception be separated from the supreme moral principle and never be incorporated with it as a condition, since this would destroy all moral worth just as any empirical admixture to geometrical principles would destroy all mathematical evidence, which (in Plato's judgment) is the most excellent thing in mathematics, surpassing even its utility.

But instead of the deduction of the supreme principle of pure practical reason – that is, the explanation of the possibility of such a cognition a priori – nothing more could be adduced than that, if one had insight into the possibility of freedom of an efficient cause, one would also have insight into not merely the possibility but even the necessity of the moral law as the supreme practical law of rational beings, to whom one attributes freedom of the causality of their will; for, the two concepts are so inseparably connected that one could even define practical freedom through independence of the will from anything other than the moral law alone. But no insight can be had into the possibility of the freedom of an efficient cause, especially in the sensible world: we are fortunate if only we can be sufficiently assured that there is no proof of its impossibility, and are now forced to assume it and are thereby justified in doing so by the moral law, which postulates it. For, there are many who believe that they can nevertheless explain this freedom in accordance with empirical principles, like any other natural ability, and regard it as a *psychological* property, the explanation of which simply requires a more exact investigation of the *nature of the soul* and of the incentives of the will, and not as a *transcendental* predicate of the causality of a being that belongs to the sensible world (although this is all that is really at issue here); and they thus deprive us of the grand disclosure brought to us through practical reason by means of the moral law, the disclosure, namely of an intelligible world through realization of the otherwise transcendent concept of freedom, and with this deprive us of the moral law itself, which admits absolutely no empirical determining ground. It will therefore be necessary to add something here as a protection against this delusion, and to show *empiricism* in all its bare superficiality.

The concept of causality as *natural necessity*, as distinguished from the concept of causality as *freedom*, concerns only the existence of things insofar as it is *determinable in time* and hence as appearances, as opposed to their causality as things in themselves. Now, if one takes the determinations of the existence of things in time for determinations of things in themselves (which is the most usual way of representing them), then the necessity in the causal relation can in no way be united with freedom;

5:94

instead they are opposed to each other as contradictory. For, from the first it follows that every event, and consequently every action that takes place at a point of time, is necessary under the condition of what was in the preceding time. Now, since time past is no longer within my control, every action that I perform must be necessary by determining grounds *that are not within my control*, that is, I am never free at the point of time in which I act. Indeed, even if I assume that my whole existence is independent from any alien cause (such as God), so that the determining grounds of my causality and even of my whole existence are not outside me, this would not in the least transform that natural necessity into freedom. For, at every point of time I still stand under the necessity of being determined to action by *that which is not within my control*, and the series of events infinite a parte priori which I can only continue in accordance with a predetermined order would never begin of itself: it would be a continuous natural chain, and therefore my causality would never be freedom.

If, then, one wants to attribute freedom to a being whose existence is determined in time, one cannot, so far at least, except this being from the law of natural necessity as to all events in its existence and consequently as to its actions as well; for, that would be tantamount to handing it over to blind chance. But since this law unavoidably concerns all causality of things so far as *their existence in time* is determinable, if this were the way in which one had to represent also the *existence of these things in themselves* then freedom would have to be rejected as a null and impossible concept. Consequently, if one still wants to save it, no other path remains than to ascribe the existence of a thing so far as it is determinable in time, and so too its causality in accordance with the law of *natural necessity, only to appearance, and to ascribe freedom to the same being as a thing in itself.* This is certainly unavoidable if one wants to maintain both these mutually repellent concepts together; but in application, when one wants to explain them as united in one and the same action, and so to explain this union itself, great difficulties come forward, which seem to make such a unification unfeasible.*ᵖ*

If I say of a human being who commits a theft that this deed is, in accordance with the natural law of causality, a necessary result of determining grounds in preceding time, then it was impossible that it could have been left undone; how, then, can appraisal in accordance with the moral law make any change in it and suppose that it could have been omitted because the law says that it ought to have been omitted? That is, how can that man be called quite free at the same point of time and in regard to the same action in which and in regard to which he is nevertheless subject to an unavoidable natural necessity? It is a wretched subterfuge to seek to evade this by saying that the *kind* of determining grounds of his causality in accordance with

ᵖ untunlich

natural law agrees with a *comparative* concept of freedom (according to which that is sometimes called a free effect, the determining natural ground of which lies *within* the acting being, e.g., that which a projectile accomplishes when it is in free motion, in which case one uses the word "freedom" because while it is in flight it is not impelled from without; or as we also call the motion of a clock a free motion because it moves the hands itself, which therefore do not need to be pushed externally; in the same way the actions of the human being, although they are necessary by their determining grounds which preceded them in time, are yet called free because the actions are caused from within, by representations produced by our own powers, whereby desires are evoked on occasion of circumstances and hence actions are produced at our own discretion). Some still let themselves be put off by this subterfuge and so think they have solved, with a little quibbling about words, that difficult problem on the solution of which millennia have worked in vain and which can therefore hardly be found so completely on the surface. That is to say, in the question about that freedom which must be put at the basis of all moral laws and the imputation appropriate to them, it does not matter whether the causality determined in accordance with a natural law is necessary through determining grounds lying *within* the subject or *outside* him, or in the first case whether these determining grounds are instinctive or thought by reason, if, as is admitted by these men themselves, these determining representations have the ground of their existence in time and indeed in the *antecedent state,* and this in turn in a preceding state, and so forth, these determinations may be internal and they may have psychological instead of mechanical causality, that is, produce actions by means of representations and not by bodily movements; they are always *determining grounds* of the causality of a being insofar as its existence is determinable in time and therefore under the necessitating conditions of past time, which are thus, when the subject is to act, *no longer within his control* and which may therefore bring with them psychological freedom (if one wants to use this term for a merely internal chain of representations in the soul) but nevertheless natural necessity; and they therefore leave no *transcendental freedom,* which must be thought as independence from everything empirical and so from nature generally, whether it is regarded as an object of inner sense in time only or also of outer sense in both space and time; without this freedom (in the latter and proper sense), which alone is practical a priori, no moral law is possible and no imputation in accordance with it. Just for this reason, all necessity of events in time in accordance with the natural law of causality can be called the *mechanism* of nature, although it is not meant by this that the things which are subject to it must be really material *machines*. Here one looks only to the necessity of the connection of events in a time series as it develops in accordance with natural law, whether the subject in which this development takes place is called *automaton materiale,* when the machinery is driven by matter, or with Leibniz *spirituale*, when it is driven by representations; and if the freedom of our will were none other than the latter (say, psychological and comparative but not also transcendental, i.e., absolute), then it would at bottom be nothing better than the freedom of a turnspit, which, when once it is wound up, also accomplishes its movements of itself.

Now, in order, in the case at hand, to remove the apparent contradiction between the mechanism of nature and freedom in one and the same action, one must recall what was said in the *Critique of Pure Reason* or follows from it: that the natural necessity which cannot coexist with the freedom of the subject attaches merely to the determinations of a thing which stands under conditions of time and so only to the determinations of the acting subject as appearance, and that, accordingly, the determining grounds of every action of the subject so far lie in what belongs to past time and *is no longer within his control* (in which must be counted his past deeds and the character as a phenomenon thereby determinable for him in his own eyes). But the very same subject, being on the other side conscious of himself as a thing in itself, also views his existence *insofar as it does not stand under conditions of time* and himself as determinable only through laws that he gives himself by reason; and in this existence of his nothing is, for him, antecedent to the determination of his will, but every action – and in general every determination of his existence changing conformably with inner sense, even the whole sequence of his existence as a sensible being – is to be regarded in the consciousness of his intelligible existence as nothing but the consequence and never as the determining ground of his causality as a *noumenon*. So considered, a rational being can now rightly say of every unlawful action he performed that he could have omitted it even though as appearance it is sufficiently determined in the past and, so far, is inevitably necessary; for this action, with all the past which determines it, belongs to a single phenomenon of his character, which he gives to himself and in accordance with which he imputes to himself, as a cause independent of all sensibility, the causality of those appearances.

The judicial sentences of that wonderful capacity in us which we call conscience are in perfect agreement with this. A human being may use what art he will to paint some unlawful conduct he remembers as an unintentional fault,[q] – as a mere oversight which one can never avoid altogether, and so as something in which he was carried away by the stream of natural necessity – and to declare himself innocent of it; he nevertheless finds that the advocate who speaks in his favor can by no means reduce to silence the prosecutor within him, if only he is aware that at the time he did this wrong he was in his senses, that is, had the use of his freedom; and while he *explains* his misconduct by certain bad habits,

---

[q] *Versehen*

CRITIQUE OF PRACTICAL REASON

which by gradual neglect of attention he has allowed to grow in him to such a degree that he can regard his misconduct as their natural consequence, yet this cannot protect him from the reproach and censure he casts upon himself. This is also the ground of repentance for a deed long past at every recollection of it, a painful feeling aroused by the moral disposition, which is empty in a practical way to the extent that it cannot serve to undo what has been done and would even be absurd (and Priestley,[10] a genuine *fatalist* proceeding consistently, declares it absurd; and for this candor he deserves more applause than those who, while maintaining the mechanism of the will in deeds[r] but its freedom in words, yet want it to be thought that they include it in their syncretistic system, though without making the possibility of such imputation comprehensible); but repentance, as pain, is still quite legitimate because reason, when it is a question of the law of our intelligible existence (the moral law), recognizes no distinction of time and asks only whether the event belongs to me as a deed and, if it does, then always connects the same feeling with it morally, whether it was done just now or long ago. For, the *sensible life* has, with respect to the *intelligible* consciousness of its existence (consciousness of freedom), the absolute unity of a phenomenon, which, so far as it contains merely appearances of the disposition that the moral law is concerned with (appearances of the character), must be appraised not in accordance with the natural necessity that belongs to it as appearance but in accordance with the absolute spontaneity of freedom. One can therefore grant that if it were possible for us to have such deep insight into a human being's cast of mind, as shown by inner as well as outer actions, that we would know every incentive to action, even the smallest, as well as all the external occasions affecting them, we could calculate a human being's conduct for the future with as much certainty as a lunar or solar eclipse and could nevertheless maintain that the human being's conduct is free. If, that is to say, we were capable of another view, namely an intellectual intuition of the same subject (which is certainly not given to us and in place of which we have only the rational concept), then we would become aware that this whole chain of appearances, with respect to all that the moral law is concerned with, depends upon the spontaneity of the subject as a thing in itself, for the determination of which no physical explanation can be given. In default of this intuition, the moral law assures us of this difference between the relation of our actions as appearances to the sensible being of our subject and relation by which this sensible being is itself referred to the intelligible substratum in us. From this perspective, which is natural to our reason though inexplicable, appraisals can be justified which, though made in all conscientiousness, yet seem at first glance quite contrary to all equity. There are cases in which human beings, even with

5:99

---

[r] *in der Tat.* For a definition of "deed" see *The Metaphysics of Morals* (6:224).

the same education that was profitable to others, yet show from childhood such early wickedness*s* and progress in it so continuously into their adulthood that they are taken to be born villains and quite incapable of improvement as far as their cast of mind is concerned; and nevertheless they are so judged for what they do or leave undone that they are censured as guilty of their crimes; indeed, they themselves (the children) find these censures as well founded as if, despite the hopeless natural constitution of mind*t* ascribed to the, they remained as accountable as any other human being. This could not happen if we did not suppose that whatever arises from one's choice (as every action intentionally performed undoubtedly does) has as its basis a free causality, which from early youth expresses its character in its appearances (actions); these actions, on account of the uniformity of conduct, make knowable a natural connection that does not, however, make the vicious*u* constitution of the will necessary but is instead the consequence of the evil and unchangeable principles freely*v* adopted, which make it only more culpable and deserving of punishment.

But a difficulty still awaits freedom insofar as it is to be united with the mechanism of nature in a being that belongs to the sensible world, a difficulty which, even after all the foregoing has been agreed to, still threatens freedom with complete destruction. In this danger there is at the same time, however, a circumstance that offers hope of an outcome still favorable to maintaining freedom, namely that the same difficulty presses much more strongly (in fact, as we shall presently see, presses only) upon the system in which existence determinable in time and space is held to be the existence of things in themselves; hence it does not force us to give up our main supposition of the ideality of time as a mere form of sensible intuition and so as merely a way of representing things that is proper to the subject as belonging to the sensible world; and thus the difficulty only requires us to unite this supposition with the idea of freedom.

That is to say: if it is granted us that the intelligible subject can still be free with respect to a given action, although as a subject also belonging to the sensible world, he is mechanically conditioned with respect to the same action, it nevertheless seems that, as soon as one admits that *God* as universal original being *is the cause also of the existence of substance* (a proposition that can never be given up without also giving up the concept of God as the being of all beings and with it his all-sufficiency, on which everything in theology depends), one must admit that a human being's actions have their determining ground in *something altogether beyond his control,* namely in the causality of a supreme being which is distinct from him and

---

s *Bosheit*
t *Naturbeschaffenheit ihres Gemüts*
u *arge*
v *freiwillig*

upon which his own existence and the entire determination of his causality absolutely depend. In fact, if a human being's actions insofar as they belong to his determinations in time were not merely determinations of him as appearance but as a thing in itself, freedom could not be saved. A human being would be a marionette or an automaton, like Vaucanson's,[11] built and wound up by the supreme artist; self-consciousness would indeed make him a thinking automaton, but the consciousness of his own spontaneity, if taken for freedom, would be mere delusion inasmuch as it deserves to be called freedom only comparatively, because the proximate determining causes of its motion and a long series of their determining causes are indeed internal but the last and highest is found entirely in an alien hand. Therefore I do not see how those who insist on regarding time and space as determinations belonging to the existence of things in themselves would avoid fatalism of actions; or if (like the otherwise acute Mendelssohn)[12] they flatly allow both to be conditions necessarily belonging only to the existence of finite and derived beings but not to that of the infinite original being, I do not see how they would justify themselves in making such a distinction, whence they get a warrant to do so, or even how they would avoid the contradiction they encounter when they regard existence in time as a determination attaching necessarily to finite things in themselves, while God is the cause of this existence but cannot be the cause of time (or space) itself (because this must be presupposed as a necessary a priori condition of the existence of things); and consequently his causality with respect to the existence of these things must be conditioned and even temporally conditioned; and this would unavoidably have to bring in all that is contradictory to the concept of his infinity and independence. On the other hand, it is quite easy for us to distinguish between the determination of the divine existence as independent of all temporal conditions and that of a being of the sensible world, the distinction being that between *the existence of a being in itself* and that of a *thing in appearance*. Hence, if this ideality of time and space is not adopted, nothing remains but Spinozism, in which space and time are essential determinations of the original being itself, while the things dependent upon it (ourselves, therefore, included) are not substances but merely accidents inhering in it; for, if these things exist merely as its effects *in time,* which would be the condition of their existence itself, then the actions of these beings would have to be merely its actions that it performs in any place and at any time. Thus Spinozism, despite the absurdity of its fundamental idea, argues more consistently than the creation theory can when beings assumed to be substances and *in themselves existing in time* are regarded as effects of a supreme cause and yet as not belonging to him and his action but as substances in themselves.

5:102

The difficulty mentioned above is resolved briefly and clearly as follows. If existence *in time* is only a sensible way of representing things which belongs to thinking beings in the world and consequently does not apply to them as things in themselves, then the creation of these beings is a creation of things in themselves, since the concept of a creation does not belong to the sensible way of representing existence or causality but can only be referred to noumena. Consequently, if I say of beings in the sensible world that they are created, I so far regard them as noumena. Just as it would thus be a contradiction to say that God is a creator of appearances, so it is also a contradiction to say that as creator he is the cause of actions in the sensible world and thus of actions as appearances, even though he is the cause of the existence of the acting beings (as noumena). If it is now possible to affirm freedom without compromising the natural mechanism of actions as appearances (by taking existence in time to be something that holds only of appearances, not of things in themselves), then it cannot make the slightest difference that the acting beings are creatures, since creation has to do with their intelligible but not their sensible existence and therefore cannot be regarded as the determining ground of appearances; but it would turn out quite differently if the beings in the world as things in themselves existed *in time*, since the creator of substance would also be the author of the entire mechanism in this substance.

Of such great importance is the separation of time (as well as space) from the existence of things in themselves that was accomplished in the *Critique* of pure speculative reason.

It will be said that the solution to the difficulty given here involves even greater difficulty and is hardly susceptible of a lucid presentation. But is any other solution that has been attempted, or that may be attempted, easier and more apprehensible? One might rather say that the dogmatic teachers of metaphysics have shown more shrewdness than sincerity in keeping this difficult point out of sight as much as possible, in the hope that if they said nothing about it no one would be likely to think of it. If a science is to be advanced, all difficulties must be *exposed* and we must even *search* for those, however well hidden, that lie in its way; for, every difficulty calls forth a remedy that cannot be found without science gaining either in extent or in determinateness, so that even obstacles become means for promoting the thoroughness of science. On the contrary, if the difficulties are purposely concealed or removed merely through palliatives, then sooner or later they break out in incurable troubles that bring science to ruin in a complete skepticism.

· ·

Since it is really the concept of freedom that, among all the ideas of pure speculative reason, alone provides such a great extension in the field of the supersensible, though only with respect to practical cognition, I ask myself *why it exclusively has such great fruitfulness* whereas the others indeed indicate the vacant place for possible beings of the pure understanding but cannot determine the concept of them by anything. I soon see that, since I can think nothing without a category, a category must first be sought in reason's idea of freedom with which I am now concerned, which is here the category of *causality;* and I see that, even though no corresponding intuition can be put under the *rational concept* of freedom, which is a transcendent concept, nevertheless a sensible intuition must first be given for the *concept of the understanding* (of causality) – for the synthesis of which the *rational concept of freedom* requires the unconditioned – by which it is first assured objective reality. Now, all the categories are divided into two classes: the *mathematical,* which are directed merely to the unity of synthesis in the representation of objects, and the *dynamical,* which are directed to the unity of synthesis in the representation of the existence of objects. The former (those of quantity and quality) always contain a synthesis of the *homogeneous,* in which the unconditioned can never be found for the conditioned in space and time given in sensible intuition since it itself belongs in turn to space and time and must thus in turn always be conditioned; hence in the Dialectic of pure theoretical reason the two opposed ways of finding the unconditioned and the totality of the conditions for it were both false. The categories of the second class (those of the causality and of the necessity of a thing) did not at all require this homogeneity (of the conditioned and the condition in the synthesis) since what was to be represented here was not how the intuition is formed from a manifold within it but only how the existence of the conditioned object corresponding to it was to be added to the existence of the condition (added in the understanding, as connected with it), and there it was permitted to place in the intelligible world the unconditioned for the altogether conditioned in the sensible world (with regard to the causality as well as to the contingent existence of things themselves), although this unconditioned otherwise remained indeterminate, and permitted to make the synthesis transcendent; hence it was also found in the Dialectic of pure speculative reason that the two seemingly opposed ways of finding the unconditioned for the conditioned – in the synthesis of causality, for example, to think for the conditioned in the series of causes and effects of the sensible world a causality that is not further sensibly conditioned – did not in fact contradict each other, and that the same action which, as belonging to the sensible world, is always sensibly conditioned – that is, mechanically necessary – can at the same time, as belonging to the causality of an acting being so far as it belongs to the intelligible world, have as its basis a sensibly unconditioned causality and so be thought as free. Then, the only point at issue was whether this *can* be changed into *is,* that is, whether one could show in an actual case, as it were by a fact, that certain actions presuppose such a causality (intellectual, sensibly unconditioned causality), whether such actions are actual or only commanded, that is, objectively practically necessary. We could not hope to meet with

5:104

5:105 this connection in actions actually given in experience as events of the sensible world, since causality through freedom must always be sought outside the sensible world in the intelligible world. But other things, things outside the sensible world, are not given to perception and observation. Hence nothing remained but that there might be found an incontestable and indeed an objective principle of causality that excludes all sensible conditions from its determination, that is, a principle in which reason does not call upon something *else* as the determining ground with respect to its causality but already itself contains this determining ground by that principle, and in which it is therefore as *pure reason* itself practical. Now, this principle does not need to be searched for or devised; it has long been present in the reason of all human beings and incorporated in their being, and is the principle of *morality*. Therefore, that unconditioned causality and the capacity for it, freedom, and with it a being (I myself) that belongs to the sensible world but at the same time to the intelligible world, is not merely *thought* indeterminately and problematically (speculative reason could already find this feasible) but is even *determined with respect to the law* of its causality and *cognized* assertorically; and thus the reality of the intelligible world is given to us, and indeed as *determined* from a practical perspective, and this determination, which for theoretical purposes would be *transcendent* (extravagant), is for practical purposes *immanent*. We could not, however, take a similar step with respect to the second dynamical idea, namely that of a *necessary being*. We could not rise to it from the sensible world without the mediation of the first dynamical idea. For, if we wanted to attempt it we would have had to venture the leap of leaving all that is given to us and bounding into that of which nothing is given to us by which we could mediate the connection of such an intelligible being with the sensible world (because the necessary being is to be cognized as given *outside us*); on the other hand this is quite possible, as is now clear, with respect to *our own* subject inasmuch as we cognize ourselves *on the one side* as intelligible beings determined by the moral law (by virtue of freedom), and *on the other side* as active in the sensible world in accordance with this determination. The concept of freedom alone allows us to find the unconditioned and intelligible for the conditioned and sensible without going outside ourselves. For, it is our reason itself which by means of

5:106 the supreme and unconditional practical law cognizes itself and the being that is conscious of this law (our own person) as belonging to the pure world of understanding and even determines the way in which, as such, it can be active. In this way it can be understood why in the entire faculty of reason *only the practical* can provide us with the means for going beyond the sensible world and provide cognitions of a supersensible order and connection, which, however, just because of this can be extended only so far as is directly necessary for pure practical purposes.

On this occasion permit me to call attention to one thing, namely, that every step one takes with pure reason, even in the practical field where one does not take subtle speculation into consideration, nevertheless fits with all the moments[w] of the *Critique* of theoretical reason as closely, and indeed of itself, as if each step had been thought out with deliberate foresight merely to provide this confirmation. Such a precise agreement – in no way sought but offering itself (as anyone can convince himself if he will only carry moral considerations up to their principles) – of the most important propositions of practical reason with the remarks of the *Critique* of speculative reason, which often seemed overly subtle and unnecessary, occasions surprise and astonishment, and strengthens the maxim already cognized and praised by others: in every scientific investigation to pursue one's way with all possible exactness and candor, to pay no heed to offense that might be given outside its field but, as far as one can, to carry it through truly and completely by itself. Frequent observation has convinced me that when such an undertaking has been carried through to its end, that which, halfway through it, seemed to me at times very dubious in view of other, extraneous doctrines was at the end found to harmonize perfectly, in an unexpected way, with what had been discovered independently, without the least regard for those doctrines and without any partiality or prejudice for them, provided I left this dubiousness out of sight for a while and attended only to the business at hand until I had brought it to completion. Writers would save themselves many errors and much labor lost (because spent on a delusion) if they could only resolve to go to work with somewhat more candor.

[w] *Momente*

Book II
Dialectic of pure practical reason

Chapter I
On a dialectic of pure practical reason in general

Pure reason always has its dialectic, whether it is considered in its speculative or in its practical use; for it requires the absolute totality of conditions for a given conditioned, and this can be found only in things in themselves. Since, however, all concepts of things must be referred to intuitions which, for us human beings cannot be other than sensible and hence do not let objects be cognized as things in themselves but only as appearances, in whose series of the conditioned and conditions the unconditioned can never be found, an unavoidable illusion[x] arises from the application of this rational idea of the totality of conditions (and so of the unconditioned) to appearances as if they were things in themselves (for, in the absence of a warning critique they are always held to be such), an illusion which, however, would never be noticed as deceptive if it were not revealed by a *conflict* of reason with itself in the application to appearance of its basic principle of presupposing the unconditioned for everything conditioned. By this, however, reason is forced to investigate this illusion – whence it arises and how it can be removed – and this can be done only through a complete critical examination of the whole pure faculty of reason; thus the antinomy of pure reason, which becomes evident in its dialectic, is in fact the most beneficial error into which human reason could ever have fallen, inasmuch as it finally drives us to search for the key to escape from this labyrinth; and when this key is found, it further discovers what we did not seek and yet need, namely a view into a higher, immutable order of things in which we already are and in which we can henceforth be directed, by determinate precepts, to carry on our existence in accordance with the highest vocation of reason.

How that natural dialectic in the speculative use of pure reason is to be resolved and how the error arising from an otherwise natural illusion is to be avoided can be found in detail in the *Critique* of that faculty. But reason in its practical use is no better off. As pure practical reason it likewise seeks the unconditioned for the practically conditioned (which rests on inclinations and natural needs), not indeed as the determining ground of the will, but even when this is given (in the moral law), it seeks the

---
[x] *Schein*

unconditioned totality of the object of pure practical reason, under the name of the *highest good.*

To determine this idea practically – that is, sufficiently for the maxims of our rational conduct – is the *doctrine of wisdom,* and this in turn, as a *science, is philosophy* in the sense in which the word was understood by the ancients, for whom it was a direction to the concept in which the highest good was to be placed and to the conduct by which it was to be acquired. We would do well to leave this word in its ancient sense, as a *doctrine of the highest good* so far as reason strives to bring it to *science.* For, on the one hand, the restrictive condition attached would suit the Greek expression (which signifies love of *wisdom*) while yet sufficing to embrace under the name of philosophy love of *science* and so of all speculative rational cognition insofar as it is serviceable to reason for that concept as well as for the practical determining ground, without letting us lose sight of the chief end on account of which alone it can be called doctrine of wisdom. On the other hand, it would do no harm to discourage the self-conceit of someone who ventures to claim the title of philosopher if one holds before him, in the very definition, a standard for self-estimation that would very much lower his pretension. For, to be a *teacher of wisdom* would mean something more than to be a student who has not yet come so far as to guide himself, and still less to guide others, with assured expectation of so high an end; it would mean to be a *master in the knowledge of wisdom,* which says more than a modest man would himself claim; and philosophy, as well as wisdom, would itself always remain an ideal, which objectively is represented completely only in reason alone, whereas subjectively, for a person, it is only the goal of his unceasing endeavors; and no one would be justified in professing to be in possession of it, so as to assume the name of philosopher, unless he could also show its infallible effect in his own person as an example (in mastery of himself and the unquestioned interest that he preeminently takes in the general good), which the ancients also required for deserving that honorable title.

5:109

We have only one further preliminary remark[y] to make with respect to the dialectic of pure practical reason in determining the concept *of the highest good* (a successful resolution of which would lead us to expect, as with the dialectic of theoretical reason, the most beneficial result, inasmuch as the self-contradictions of pure practical reason, honestly stated and not concealed), force us to undertake a complete critical examination of its own capacity.

The moral law is the sole determining ground of the pure will. But since this is merely formal (that is to say, it requires only that the form of a maxim be universally lawgiving), it abstracts as determining ground from all matter and so from every object of volition. Hence, though the highest

---

[y] Or "reminder," *Erinnerung*

good may be the whole *object* of a pure practical reason, that is, of a pure will, it is not on that account to be taken as its *determining ground*, and the moral law alone must be viewed as the ground for making the highest good and its realization or promotion the object. This reminder is important in so delicate a case as the determination of moral principles, where even the slightest misinterpretation corrupts dispositions. For, it will have been seen from the Analytic that if one assumes any object under the name of a good as a determining ground of the will prior to the moral law and then derives from it the supreme practical principle, this would always produce heteronomy and supplant the moral principle.

It is, however, evident that if the moral law is already included as supreme condition in the concept of the highest good, the highest good is then not merely *object:* the concept of it and the representation of its existence as possible by our practical reason are at the same time the *determining ground* of the pure will because in that case the moral law, already included and thought in this concept, and no other object, in fact determines the will in accordance with the principle of autonomy. This order of concepts of the determination of the will must not be lost sight of, since otherwise we misunderstand ourselves and believe that we are contradicting ourselves even where everything stands together in the most perfect harmony.

Chapter II
On the dialectic of pure reason in determining the concept of the highest good

The concept of the *highest* already contains an ambiguity[z] that, if not attended to, can occasion needless disputes. The highest can mean either the supreme *(supremum)* or the complete *(consummatum)*. The first is that condition which is itself unconditioned, that is, not subordinate to any other *(originarium)*; the second is that whole which is not part of a still greater whole of the same kind *(perfectissimum)*. That *virtue* (as worthiness to be happy) is the *supreme condition* of whatever can even seem to us desirable and hence of all our pursuit of happiness and that it is therefore the *supreme* good has been proved in the Analytic. But it is not yet, on that account, the whole and complete good as the object of the faculty of desire of rational finite beings; for this, *happiness* is also required, and that not merely in the partial eyes of a person who makes himself an end but even in the judgment of an impartial reason, which regards a person in the world generally as an end in itself. For, to need happiness, to be also

---
[z] *Zweideutigkeit*

worthy of it, and yet not to participate in it cannot be consistent with the perfect volition of a rational being that would at the same time have all power, even if we think of such a being only for the sake of the experiment. Now, inasmuch as virtue and happiness together constitute possession of the highest good in a person, and happiness distributed in exact proportion to morality (as the worth of a person and his worthiness to be happy) constitutes the *highest good* of a possible world, the latter means the whole, the complete good, in which, however, virtue as the condition is always the supreme good, since it has no further condition above it, whereas happiness is something that, though always pleasant to the possessor of it, is not of itself absolutely and in all respects good but always presupposes morally lawful conduct as its condition.

Two determinations *necessarily* combined in one concept must be connected as ground and consequent, and so connected that this *unity* is considered either as *analytic* (logical connection) or as synthetic (real *connection*), the former in accordance with the law of identity, the latter in accordance with the law of causality. The connection of virtue with happiness can therefore be understood in one of two ways: either the endeavor to be virtuous and the rational pursuit of happiness are not two different actions but quite identical, in which case no maxim need be made the ground of the former other than that which serves for the latter; or else that connection is found in virtue's producing happiness as something different from the consciousness of virtue, as a cause produces an effect.

Of the ancient Greek schools there were, strictly speaking, only two, which in determining the concept of the highest good followed one and the same method insofar as they did not let virtue and happiness hold as two different elements of the highest good and consequently sought the unity of the principle in accordance with the rule of identity; but they differed, in turn, in their choice of which of the two was to be the fundamental concept. The Epicurean said: to be conscious of one's maxim leading to happiness is virtue; the Stoic said: to be conscious of one's virtue is happiness. For the first, *prudence* was equivalent to morality; for the second, who chose a higher designation for virtue, *morality* alone was true wisdom.

One must regret that the acuteness of these men (whom one must, nevertheless, admire for having in such early times already tried all conceivable paths of philosophic conquest) was unfortunately applied in searching out identity between extremely heterogeneous concepts, that of happiness and that of virtue. But it was in keeping with the dialectical spirit of their times, which sometimes misleads subtle minds even now, to suppress essential and irreconcilable differences in principle by trying to change them into disputes about words and so to devise a specious unity of concept under merely different names; and this usually occurs in cases where the unification of heterogeneous grounds lies so deep or so high, or would require so complete a transformation of the doctrines assumed in the rest of the philosophic system, that they are afraid to penetrate deeply into the real difference and prefer to treat it as a diversity merely in formulae.

While both schools tried to search out the sameness of the practical principles of virtue and happiness, they were not agreed as to how they would force this identity but separated infinitely from each other inasmuch as one put its principle on the aesthetic side[a] and the other on the logical side, the former in consciousness of sensible need, the other in the independence of practical reason from all sensible determining grounds. According to the Epicurean the concept of virtue was already present in the maxim of promoting one's own happiness; according to the Stoic, on the other hand, the feeling of happiness was already contained in consciousness of one's virtue. What is contained in another concept, however, is indeed identical with a part of the concept containing it but not identical with the whole, and two wholes can, moreover, be specifically different from each other although they consist of the same material,[b] if, namely, the two parts are combined into a whole in quite different ways. The Stoic maintained that virtue is the *whole highest good,* and happiness only the consciousness of this possession as belonging to the state of the subject. The Epicurean maintained that happiness is the *whole highest good,* and virtue only the form of the maxim for seeking to obtain it, namely, the rational use of means to it.

Now, it is clear from the Analytic that the maxims of virtue and those of one's own happiness are quite heterogeneous with respect to their supreme practical principle; and, even though they belong to one highest good, so as to make it possible, yet they are so far from coinciding that they greatly restrict and infringe upon each other in the same subject. Thus the question, *how is the highest good practically possible?* still remains an unsolved problem despite all the *attempts at coalition* that have hitherto been made. The Analytic has, however, shown what it is that makes the problem difficult to solve, namely that happiness and morality are two specifically quite *different elements* of the highest good and that, accordingly, their combination cannot be cognized *analytically* (as if someone who seeks his own happiness should find, by mere resolution[c] of his concepts, that in so acting he is virtuous, or as if someone who follows virtue should in the consciousness of such conduct find that he is already happy *ipso facto*); it must instead be a *synthesis* of concepts. But because this combination is cognized as a priori – thus as practically necessary and not as derived from experience –

---

[a] *ästhetischen ... Seite,* i.e., on the side of feeling. See *The Metaphysics of Morals* (6:399–403, 471).
[b] *Stoffe*
[c] *Auflösung*

and because the possibility of the highest good therefore does not rest on any empirical principles, it follows that the *deduction* of this concept must be *transcendental.* It is a priori (morally) necessary *to produce the highest good through the freedom of the will:* the condition of its possibility must therefore rest solely on a priori grounds of cognition.

I.
THE ANTINOMY OF PRACTICAL REASON

In the highest good which is practical for us, that is, to be made real through our will, virtue and happiness are thought as necessarily combined, so that the one cannot be assumed by pure practical reason without the other also belonging to it. Now, this combination is (like every other) either *analytic* or *synthetic.* Since, as has already been shown, the given combination cannot be analytic, it must be thought synthetically and, indeed, as the connection of cause and effect, because it concerns a practical good, that is, one that is possible through action. Consequently, either the desire for happiness must be the motive to maxims of virtue or the maxim of virtue must be the efficient cause of happiness. The first is *absolutely* impossible because (as was proved in the Analytic) maxims that put the determining ground of the will in the desire for one's happiness are not moral at all and can be the ground of no virtue. But the second is *also impossible* because any practical connection of causes and effects in the world, as a result of the determination of the will, does not depend upon the moral dispositions of the will but upon knowledge of the laws of nature and the physical ability to use them for one's purposes; consequently, no necessary connection of happiness with virtue in the world, adequate to the highest good, can be expected from the most meticulous observance of moral laws. Now, since the promotion of the highest good, which contains this connection in its concept, is an a priori necessary object of our will and inseparably bound up with the moral law, the impossibility of the first must also prove the falsity of the second. If, therefore, the highest good is impossible in accordance with practical rules, then the moral law, which commands us to promote it, must be fantastic and directed to empty imaginary ends and must therefore in itself be false.

5:114

II.
CRITICAL RESOLUTION*ᵈ* OF THE ANTINOMY OF PRACTICAL REASON

In the antinomy of pure speculative reason there is a similar conflict between natural necessity and freedom in the causality of events in the world. It was resolved by showing that there is no true conflict if the

---
ᵈ Aufhebung

events and even the world in which they occur are regarded (and they should also be so regarded) merely as appearances; for, one and the same acting being as *appearance* (even to his own inner sense) has a causality in the world of sense that always conforms to the mechanism of nature, but with respect to the same event, insofar as the acting person regards himself at the same time as *noumenon* (as pure intelligence, in his existence that cannot be temporally determined), he can contain a determining ground of that causality in accordance with laws of nature which is itself free from all laws of nature.

It is just the same with the foregoing antinomy of pure practical reason. The first of the two propositions, that the endeavor after happiness produces a ground for a virtuous disposition, is *absolutely false;* but the second, that a virtuous disposition necessarily produces happiness, is false *not absolutely* but only insofar as this disposition is regarded as the form of causality in the sensible world, and consequently false only if I assume existence in the sensible world to be the only kind of existence of a rational being; it is thus only *conditionally false.* But since I am not only warranted in thinking of my existence also as a noumenon in a world of the understanding but even have in the moral law a purely intellectual determining ground of my causality (in the sensible world), it is not possible that morality of disposition should have a connection, and indeed a necessary connection,' as cause with happiness as effect in the sensible world, if not immediately yet mediately (by means of an intelligible author of nature), a connection which, in a nature that is merely an object of the senses, can never occur except contingently and cannot suffice for the highest good.

Thus, despite this seeming conflict of a practical reason with itself, the highest good is the necessary highest end of a morally determined will and is a true object of that will; for it is practically possible, and the maxims of such a will, which refer to it as regards their matter, have objective reality, which at first was threatened by that antinomy in the combination of morality with happiness in accordance with a universal law, but only from a misinterpretation, because the relation between appearances was held to be a relation of things in themselves to those appearances.

When we find ourselves compelled to go so far, namely to the connection with an intelligible world, to seek the possibility of the highest good which reason points out to all rational beings as the goal of all their moral wishes, it must seem strange that philosophers both of ancient and modern times could nevertheless have found happiness in precise proportion to virtue already in *this life* (in the sensible world), or persuaded themselves that they were conscious of it. For, Epicurus as well as the Stoics extolled above all the happiness that arises from consciousness of living

---

' *einen . . . Zusammenhang . . . habe*

virtuously; and the former was not so base in his practical precepts as one might infer from the principles of his theory, which he used for explanation and not for action, or as they were interpreted by many who were misled by his use of the expression "pleasure"*f* for "contentment";*g* on the contrary, he reckoned the most disinterested practice of the good among the ways of enjoying the most intimate delight*h* and included in his scheme of pleasure*i* (by which he meant a constantly cheerful heart)*j* such moderation and control of the inclinations as the strictest moral philosopher might require; his chief divergence from the Stoics consisted only in his placing the motive in this pleasure, which they quite rightly refused to do. For, on the one hand, the virtuous Epicurus – like many morally well-disposed men of this day who nevertheless do not reflect deeply enough on their principles – fell into the error of presupposing the virtuous *disposition* in the persons for whom he wanted first of all to provide the incentive to virtue (and in fact an upright man cannot be happy if he is not first conscious of his uprightness; for, with such a disposition, the censure that his own cast of mind would force him to bring against himself in case of a transgression, and his moral self-condemnation would deprive him of all enjoyment of the agreeableness that his state might otherwise contain). But the question is, how is such a disposition and cast of mind in estimating the worth of one's existence possible in the first place, since prior to this no feeling at all for moral worth as such would be found in the subject? If a human being is virtuous he will certainly not enjoy life unless he is conscious of his uprightness in every action, however fortune may favor him in the physical state of life; but in order to make him virtuous in the first place, and so before he esteems the moral worth of his existence so highly, can one commend to him the peace of mind that would arise from consciousness of an uprightness for which he as yet has no sense?

5:116

But on the other hand, there is always present here the ground of an error of subreption *(vitium subreptionis)* and, as it were, of an optical illusion in the self-consciousness of what one *does* as distinguished from what one *feels* – an illusion that even the most practiced cannot altogether avoid. The moral disposition is necessarily connected with consciousness of the determination of the will *directly by the law*. Now, consciousness of a determination of the faculty of desire is always the ground of a satisfaction*k* in the action produced by it; but this pleasure, this satisfaction with oneself, is not the determining ground of the action: instead, the determi-

---

f *Wollust*
g *Zufriedenheit.* See *Groundwork of the Metaphysics of Morals* (4:393 note v) and *The Metaphysics of Morals* (6:375).
h *mit zu den Genußarten der innigste Freude*
i *Vergnügens*
j Compare *The Metaphysics of Morals* (6:485)
k *Wohlgefallens*

nation of the will directly by reason alone is the ground of the feeling of pleasure, and this remains a pure practical, not aesthetic, determination of the faculty of desire. Now, since this determination has exactly the same inward effect, that of an impulse to activity, as a feeling of the agreeableness expected from the desired action would have produced, we easily look upon what we ourselves do as something that we merely passively feel and take the moral incentive for a sensible impulse, just as always happens in so-called illusion of the senses (in this case, inner sense). It is something very sublime in human nature to be determined to actions directly by a pure rational law, and even the illusion that takes the subjective side of this intellectual determinability of the will as something aesthetic and the effect of a special sensible feeling (for an intellectual feeling would be a contradiction) is sublime. It is also of great importance to take notice of this property of our personality and to cultivate as much as possible the effect of reason on this feeling. But one must also be on guard against demeaning and deforming the real and genuine incentive, the law itself – as it were, by means of a false foil – by such spurious praise of the moral determining ground as incentive as would base it on feelings of particular joys (which are nevertheless only results). Respect, and not the gratification or enjoyment of happiness, is thus something for which there can be no feeling *antecedent* to reason and underlying it (for this would always be aesthetic and pathological): respect as consciousness of direct necessitation of the will by the law is hardly an analogue of the feeling of pleasure, although in relation to the faculty of desire it does the same thing but from different sources; only by this way of representing things, however, can one attain what one seeks, namely that actions be done not merely in conformity with duty (as a result of pleasant feelings) but from duty, which must be the true end of all moral cultivation.

Have we not, however, a word that does not denote enjoyment, as the word happiness does, but that nevertheless indicates a satisfaction with one's existence, an analogue of happiness that must necessarily accompany consciousness of virtue? Yes! This word is *contentment with oneself*,[1] which in its strict meaning always designates only a negative satisfaction with one's existence, in which one is conscious of needing nothing. Freedom, and the consciousness of freedom as an ability to follow the moral law with an unyielding disposition, is *independence from the inclinations*, at least as motives determining (even if not as *affecting*) our desire, and so far as I am conscious of this freedom in following my moral maxims, it is the sole source of an unchangeable contentment, necessarily combined with it and resting on no special feeling, and this can be called intellectual contentment. Aesthetic contentment (improperly so called), which rests on satisfaction of the inclinations, however refined they may be made out to

---

[1] *Selbstzufriedenheit*

be, can never be adequate to what is thought about contentment. For the inclinations change, grow with the indulgence one allows them, and always leave behind a still greater void than one had thought to fill. Hence they are always *burdensome* to a rational being, and though he cannot lay them aside, they wrest from him the wish to be rid of them. Even an inclination to what conforms with duty (e.g., to beneficence) can indeed greatly facilitate the effectiveness of *moral* maxims but cannot produce any. For in these everything must be directed to the representation of the law as determining ground if the action is to contain not merely *legality* but also *morality*. Inclination is blind and servile, whether it is kindly or not; and when morality is in question, reason must not play the part of mere guardian to inclination but, disregarding it altogether, must attend solely to its own interest as pure practical reason. Even this feeling of compassion and tender sympathy,*ᵐ* if it precedes consideration of what is duty and becomes the determining ground, is itself burdensome to right-thinking persons, brings their considered maxims into confusion, and produces the wish to be freed from them and subject to lawgiving reason alone.

From this we can understand how consciousness of this ability of a pure practical reason (virtue)*ⁿ* can in fact produce consciousness of mastery over one's inclinations, hence of independence from them and so too from the discontent that always accompanies them, and thus can produce a negative satisfaction with one's state, that is, *contentment*, which in its source is contentment with one's person. Freedom itself becomes in this way (namely indirectly) capable of an enjoyment, which cannot be called happiness because it does not depend upon the positive concurrence of a feeling; nor is it, strictly speaking, *beatitude*, since it does not include complete independence from inclinations and needs; but it nevertheless resembles the latter, at least insofar as one's determination of one's will can be held free from their influence and so, at least in its origin, it is analogous to the self-sufficiency that can be ascribed only to the supreme being.

5:119

From this resolution of the antinomy of practical pure reason it follows that in practical principles a natural and necessary connection between the consciousness of morality and the expectation of a happiness proportionate to it as its result can at least be thought as possible (though certainly not, on this account, cognized and understood);*ᵒ* that, on the other hand, principles of the pursuit of happiness cannot possibly produce morality;

ᵐ der Mitleids und der weichherzigen Teilnehmung. See *The Metaphysics of Morals* (6:456–7).
ⁿ wie das Bewußtsein dieses Vermögens . . . durch Tat (die Tugend); perhaps "how consciousness of this ability of a pure practical reason through a deed (virtue)." According to *The Metaphysics of Morals* (6:394), virtue is a *Vermögen*. Although it would be inaccurate to call virtue a deed (see 6:224), this sentence allows that construal. Compare AK 5:3 note b, and 5:98, note b.
ᵒ einsehen

that, accordingly, the *supreme* good (as the first condition of the highest good) is morality, whereas happiness constitutes its second element but in such a way that it is only the morally conditioned yet necessary result of the former. Only with this subordination is the *highest good* the whole object of pure practical reason, which must necessarily represent it as possible since it commands us to contribute everything possible to its production. But since the possibility of such a connection of the conditioned with its condition belongs wholly to the supersensible relation of things and cannot be given in accordance with the laws of the sensible world, although the practical results of this idea – namely actions that aim at realizing the highest good – belong to the sensible world, we shall try to set forth the grounds of that possibility, first with respect to what is *immediately* within our power and then, secondly, in that which is not in our power but which reason presents to us, as the supplement to our inability, for the possibility of the highest good (which is necessary in accordance with practical principles).

III.
ON THE PRIMACY OF PURE PRACTICAL REASON IN ITS CONNECTION WITH SPECULATIVE REASON

By primacy among two or more things connected by reason I understand the prerogative of one to be the first determining ground of the connection with all the rest. In a narrower practical sense it signifies the prerogative of the interest of one insofar as the interest of the others is subordinated to it (and it cannot be inferior to any other). To every faculty of the mind one can attribute an *interest,* that is, a principle that contains the condition under which alone its exercise is promoted. Reason, as the faculty of principles, determines the interest of all the powers of the mind but itself determines its own. The interest of its speculative use consists in the *cognition* of the object up to the highest a priori principles; that of its practical use consists in the determination of the *will* with respect to the final and complete end. That which is required for the possibility of any use of reason as such, namely, that its principles and affirmations must not contradict one another, constitutes no part of its interest but is instead the condition of having reason at all; only its extension, not mere consistency with itself, is reckoned as its interest.

If practical reason may not assume and think as given anything further than what *speculative* reason of itself could offer it from its insight, the latter has primacy. Supposing, however, that practical reason has of itself original a priori principles with which certain theoretical positions are inseparably connected, while these are withdrawn from any possible insight of speculative reason (although they must not contradict it): then the question is, which interest is supreme (not, which must give way, for one does not necessarily conflict with the other)? Whether speculative reason, which knows nothing about all that which practical reason offers for its acceptance, must accept these propositions and, although they are transcendent for it, try to unite them, as a foreign possession handed over to it, with its own concepts, or whether it is justified in obstinately following its own separate interest and, in accordance with the canon of Epicurus, rejecting as empty subtle reasoning everything that cannot accredit its objective reality by manifest examples to be shown in experience, however much it might be interwoven with the interest of the practical (pure) use of reason and in itself not contradict the theoretical, merely because it actually infringes upon the interest of speculative reason to the extent that it removes the bounds which the latter has set itself and hands it over to every nonsense or delusion of imagination?

In fact, to the extent that practical reason is taken as dependent upon pathological conditions, that is, as merely regulating the inclinations by the sensible principle of happiness, this demand could not be made on speculative reason. Mohammed's paradise or the fusion with the Deity of the theosophists and mystics would obtrude their monstrosities on reason according to the taste[p] of each, and one might as well have no reason at all as surrender it in such a way to all sorts of dreams. But if pure reason of itself can be and really is practical, as the consciousness of the moral law proves it to be, it is still only one and the same reason which, whether from a theoretical or a practical perspective, judges according to a priori principles; and then it is clear that, even if from the first perspective its capacity does not extend to establishing certain propositions affirmatively, although they do not contradict it, *as soon as these same propositions belong inseparably to the practical interest* of pure reason it must accept them – indeed as something offered to it from another source, which has not grown on its own land but yet is sufficiently authenticated – and try to compare and connect them with everything that it has within its power as speculative reason, being mindful, however, that these are not its insights but are yet extensions of its use from another, namely a practical perspective; and this is not in the least opposed to its interest, which consists in the restriction of speculative mischief.

Thus, in the union of pure speculative with pure practical reason in one cognition,[q] the latter has primacy, assuming that this union is not *contingent* and discretionary but based a priori on reason itself and therefore *necessary*. For, without this subordination a conflict of reason with itself would arise, since if they were merely juxtaposed (coordinate), the first would of itself close its boundaries strictly and admit nothing from

5:121

---

[p] *Sinn*
[q] *Verbindung . . . zu einem Erkenntnisse*

the latter into its domain, while the latter would extend its boundaries over everything and, when its need required, would try to include the former within them. But one cannot require pure practical reason to be subordinate to speculative reason and so reverse the order, since all interest is ultimately practical and even that of speculative reason is only conditional and is complete in practical use alone.

IV.
THE IMMORTALITY OF THE SOUL AS A POSTULATE OF PURE PRACTICAL REASON

The production of the highest good in the world is the necessary object of a will determinable by the moral law. But in such a will the *complete conformity*[r] of dispositions with the moral law is the supreme condition of the highest good. This conformity must therefore be just as possible as its object is, since it is contained in the same command to promote the object. Complete conformity of the will with the moral law is, however, *holiness*, a perfection of which no rational being of the sensible world is capable at any moment[s] of his existence. Since it is nevertheless required as practically necessary, it can only be found in an *endless progress*[t] toward that complete conformity, and in accordance with principles of pure practical reason it is necessary to assume such a practical progress as the real object of our will.

This endless progress is, however, possible only on the presupposition of the *existence* and personality of the same rational being continuing *endlessly* (which is called the immortality of the soul). Hence the highest good is practically possible only on the presupposition of the immortality of the soul, so that this, as inseparably connected with the moral law, is a **postulate** of pure practical reason (by which I understand a *theoretical* proposition, though one not demonstrable as such, insofar as it is attached inseparably to an a priori unconditionally valid *practical* law).

The proposition about the moral vocation of our nature, that only in an endless progress can we attain complete conformity with the moral law, is of the greatest usefulness, not merely in regard to the present supplement to the incapacity of speculative reason but also with respect to religion. In default of it, one either quite degrades the moral law from its *holiness* by making it out to be *lenient* (indulgent) and thus conformed to our convenience, or else strains ones's calling as well as ones's expectation to an unattainable vocation, namely to a hoped-for full acquisition of holiness of

---

[r] or "fitness," *Angemessenheit*
[s] *Zeitpunkte*
[t] Or "a progress to infinity," *ins Unendliche gehend*

will, and so gets lost in enthusiastic *theosophical* dreams that quite contradict self-knowledge;" in both cases, constant *effort* to observe precisely and fully a strict and inflexible command of reason, which is yet not ideal but true, is only hindered. For a rational but finite being only endless progress from lower to higher stages of moral perfection is possible. *The eternal being,*ᵛ to whom the temporal condition is nothing, sees in what is to us an endless series the whole of conformity with the moral law, and the holiness that his command inflexibly requires in order to be commensurable with his justice in the share he determines for each in the highest good is to be found whole in a single intellectual intuition of the existence of rational beings. All that a creature can have with respect to hope for this share is consciousness of his tried disposition, so that, from the progress he has already made from the worse to the morally better and from the immutable resolution he has thereby come to know, he may hope for a further uninterrupted continuance of this progress, however long his existence may last, even beyond this life;* and thus he cannot hope, either here or in any foreseeable future moment of his existence, to be fully adequate to God's will (without indulgence or dispensation, which do not harmonize with justice); he can hope to be so only in the endlessness of his duration (which God alone can survey).

V.

THE EXISTENCE OF GOD AS A POSTULATE
OF PURE PRACTICAL REASON

In the preceding analysis the moral law led to a practical task that is set by pure reason alone and without the aid of any sensible incentives, namely that of the necessary completeness of the first and principal part of the

---

*Conviction of the immutability of one's disposition in progress toward the good seems, nevertheless, to be in itself impossible for a creature. Because of this the Christian religious doctrine has it come only from the same spirit that works sanctification, i.e., this firm resolution and with it consciousness of steadfastness in moral progress. But even in a natural way, someone who is aware of having persisted through a long portion of his life up to its end in progress to the better, and this from genuine moral motives, may very well have the comforting hope, though not certitude, that even in an existence continuing beyond this life he will persevere in these principles; and although he is never justified here in his own eyes, and can never hope to be justified even given the future increase of natural perfection to which he looks forward – but with it of his duties as well – nevertheless in this progress which, though it has to do with a goal endlessly postponed, yet holds for God as possession, he can have a prospect of a future of *beatitude;* for this is the expression that reason employs to designate complete *well-being* independent of all contingent causes in the world, which, like *holiness,* is an idea that can be contained only in an endless progress and its totality, and hence is never fully attained by a creature.

" *Selbsterkenntniss*
ᵛ Or "The Infinite Being," *Der Unendliche*

highest good, **morality**; and, since this can be fully accomplished only in an eternity, it led to the postulate of *immortality*. The same law must also lead to the possibility of the second element of the highest good, namely **happiness** proportioned to that morality, and must do so as disinterestedly as before, solely from impartial reason; in other words, it must lead to the supposition of the existence of a cause adequate to this effect, that is, it must postulate the *existence of God* as belonging necessarily to the possibility of the highest good (which object of our will is necessarily connected with the moral lawgiving of pure reason). We shall present this connection in a convincing manner.

Happiness is the state of a rational being in the world in the whole of whose existence *everything goes according to his wish and will*, and rests, therefore, on the harmony of nature with his whole end as well as with the essential determining ground of his will. Now, the moral law as a law of freedom commands through determining grounds that are to be quite independent of nature and of its harmony with our faculty of desire (as incentives); the acting rational being in the world is, however, not also the cause of the world and of nature itself. Consequently, there is not the least ground in the moral law for a necessary connection[w] between the morality and the proportionate happiness of a being belonging to the world as part of it and hence dependent upon it, who for that reason cannot by his will be a cause of this nature and, as far as his happiness is concerned, cannot by his own powers make it harmonize thoroughly with his practical principles. Nevertheless, in the practical task of pure reason, that is, in the necessary pursuit of the highest good, such a connection is postulated as necessary: we *ought* to strive to promote the highest good (which must therefore be possible). Accordingly, the existence of a cause of all nature, distinct from nature, which contains the ground of this connection, namely of the exact correspondence of happiness with morality, is also *postulated*. However, this supreme cause is to contain the ground of the correspondence of nature not merely with a law of the will of rational beings but with the representation of this *law*, so far as they make it the *supreme determining ground of the will*, and consequently not merely with morals in their form but also with their morality as their determining ground, that is, with their moral disposition. Therefore, the highest good in the world is possible only insofar as a supreme cause of nature having a causality in keeping with the moral disposition is assumed. Now, a being capable of actions in accordance with the representation of laws is *an intelligence* (a rational being), and the causality of such a being in accordance with this representation of laws is his *will*. Therefore the supreme cause of nature, insofar as it must be presupposed for the highest good, is a being that is the cause of nature by *understanding* and *will* (hence its

---
[w] *Zusammenhang*

author), that is, **God**. Consequently, the postulate of the possibility of the *highest derived good* (the best world) is likewise the postulate of the reality of a *highest original good,* namely of the existence of God. Now, it was a duty for us to promote the highest good; hence there is in us not merely the warrant but also the necessity, as a need connected with duty, to presuppose the possibility of this highest good, which, since it is possible only under the condition of the existence of God, connects the presupposition of the existence of God inseparably with duty; that is, it is morally necessary to assume the existence of God.

It is well to note here that this moral necessity *is subjective,* that is, a need, and not *objective,* that is, itself a duty; for, there can be no duty to assume the existence of anything (since this concerns only the theoretical use of reason). Moreover, it is not to be understood by this that it is necessary to assume the existence of God *as a ground of all obligation in general* (for this rests, as has been sufficiently shown, solely on the autonomy of reason itself). What belongs to duty here is only the striving to produce and promote the highest good in the world, the possibility of which can therefore be postulated, while our reason finds this thinkable only on the presupposition of a supreme intelligence; to assume the existence of this supreme intelligence is thus connected with the consciousness of our duty, although this assumption itself belongs to theoretical reason; with respect to theoretical reason alone, as a ground of explanation, it can be called a *hypothesis;* but in relation to the intelligibility of an object given us by the moral law (the highest good), and consequently if a need for practical purposes, it can be called *belief*[x] and, indeed, a pure *rational belief* since pure reason alone (in its theoretical as well as in its practical use) is the source from which it springs.

5:126

From this *deduction* it now becomes comprehensible why the *Greek* schools could never solve their problem of the practical possibility of the highest good: it was because they made the rule of the use which the human will makes of its freedom the sole and sufficient ground of this possibility, without, as it seemed to them, needing the existence of God for it. They were indeed correct in establishing the principle of morals by itself, independently of this postulate and solely from the relation of reason to the will, so that they made it the *supreme* practical condition of the highest good; but this principle was not on this account the *whole* condition of its possibility. The Epicureans had indeed assumed an altogether false principle of morals as supreme, namely that of happiness, and had substituted for a law a maxim of each choosing as he pleased according to his inclination;[y] they proceeded, however, *consistently* enough in this by demeaning their highest good in the same way, namely in proportion to

---

[x] Or "faith," *Glaube*
[y] *der beliebigen Wahl nach jedes seiner Neigung*

the meanness of their principle, and expecting no greater happiness than can be acquired by human prudence (including temperance and moderation of the inclinations), which,*ᶻ* as we know, has to be paltry enough and turn out very differently according to circumstances, not to mention the exceptions which their maxims had to constantly admit and which made them unfit for laws. The Stoics, on the contrary, had chosen their supreme practical principle quite correctly, namely virtue, as the condition of the highest good; but inasmuch as they represented the degree of virtue required by its pure law as fully attainable in this life, they not only strained the moral capacity of the *human being,* under the name of a *sage,* far beyond all the limits of his nature and assumed something that contradicts all cognition of the human being, but also and above all they would not let the second *component* of the highest good, namely happiness, hold as a special object of the human faculty of desire but made their *sage,* like a divinity in his consciousness of the excellence of his person, quite independent of nature (with respect to his own contentment), exposing him indeed to the ills of life but not subjecting him to them (at the same time representing him as also free from evil); and thus they really left out the second element of the highest good, namely one's own happiness, placing it solely in acting and in contentment with one's personal worth and so including it in consciousness of one's moral cast of mind – though in this they could have been sufficiently refuted by the voice of their own nature.

The doctrine of Christianity,* even if it is not regarded as a religious

---

*It is commonly held that the Christian precept of morals has no advantage with respect to its purity over the moral concepts of the Stoics; but the difference between them is nonetheless very obvious. The Stoic system made consciousness of strength of soul the pivot on which all moral dispositions were to turn; and although its disciples spoke of duties and even determined them quite well, yet they put the incentive and proper determining ground of the will in an elevation of one's cast of mind above the lower incentives of the senses, which have power only through weakness of soul. With them therefore, virtue was a certain heroism of the *sage,* who, raising himself above the animal nature of the human being, is sufficient to himself, and through the discourses on duties to others is himself raised above them and is not subject to any temptation to transgress the moral law. All this, however, they could not have done if they had represented this law in all its purity and strictness, as the precept of the Gospel does. If I understand by an *idea* a perfection to which nothing adequate can be given in experience, the moral ideas are not, on that account, something transcendent, that is, something of which we cannot even determine the concept sufficiently or of which it is uncertain whether there is any object corresponding to it at all, as is the case with the ideas of speculative reason; instead, the moral ideas, as archetypes of practical perfection, serve as the indispensable rule of moral conduct and also as the *standard of comparison.* Now, if I consider *Christian morals* on their philosophic side, then, compared with the ideas of the Greek schools they would appear as follows: the ideas of the *Cynics,* the *Epicureans,* the *Stoics,* and the *Christians* are *natural simplicity, prudence, wisdom,* and *holiness.* With respect to the path for attaining them, what distinguished the Greek schools from one another was that the Cynics found *common human understanding* sufficient, the others the path of *science* alone; but

ᶻ It is not clear whether *die* refers to "happiness" or to "prudence."

doctrine, gives on this point a concept of the highest good (of the kingdom of God) which alone satisfies the strictest demand of practical reason. The moral law is holy (inflexible) and demands holiness of morals, although all the moral perfection that a human being can attain is still only virtue, that is, a disposition conformed with law *from respect* for law, and thus consciousness of a continuing propensity to transgression or at least impurity, that is, an admixture of many spurious (not moral) motives to observe the law, hence a self-esteem combined with humility; and so, with respect to the holiness that the Christian law demands, nothing remains for a creature but endless progress, though for that very reason he is justified in hoping for his endless duration. The *worth* of a disposition *completely* conformed with the moral law is infinite, since all possible happiness in the judgment of a wise and all-powerful distributor of it has no restriction other than rational beings' lack of conformity with their duty. But the moral law of itself still does not *promise* any happiness, since this is not necessarily connected with observance of the law according to our concepts of a natural order as such. The Christian doctrine of morals now supplements this lack (of the second indispensable component of the highest good) by representing the world in which rational beings devote themselves with their whole soul to the moral law as a *kingdom of God*, in which nature and morals come into a harmony, foreign to each of them of itself, through a holy author who makes the derived highest good possible. *Holiness* of morals is prescribed to them as a rule even in this life, while the well-being proportioned to it, namely *beatitude*, is represented as attainable only in an eternity; for, the *former* must always be the archetype of their conduct in every state, and progress toward it is already possible and necessary in this life, whereas the *latter*, under the name of happiness, cannot be attained at all in this world (so far as our own capacity is concerned) and is therefore made solely an object of hope. Nevertheless, the Christian principle of *morals* itself is not theological (and so heteronomy); it is instead autonomy of pure practical reason by itself, since it does not make cognition of God and his will the basis of these laws but only of the attainment of the highest good subject to the condition of observing these laws, and since it places even the proper *incentive* to observing them not in the results wished for but in the representation of duty alone, faithful observance of which alone constitutes worthiness to acquire the latter.

In this way the moral law leads through the concept of the highest good,

---

both found the mere *use of natural powers* sufficient for it. Christian morals, because it frames its precept so purely and inflexibly (as must be done), deprives the human being of confidence that he can be fully adequate to it, at least in this life, but again sets it up by enabling us to hope that if we act as well as is within our *power*, then what is not within our power will come to our aid from another source, whether or not we know in what way. Aristotle and Plato differed only with respect to the *origin* of our moral concepts.

as the object and final end of pure practical reason, *to religion, that is, to the recognition*[a] *of all duties as divine commands, not as sanctions – that is, chosen and in themselves contingent ordinances of another's will* – but as essential *laws* of every free will in itself, which must nevertheless be regarded as commands of the supreme being because only from a will that is morally perfect (holy and beneficent[b]) and at the same time all-powerful, and so through harmony with this will, can we hope to attain the highest good, which the moral law makes it our duty to take as the object of our endeavors. Here again, then, everything remains disinterested and grounded only on duty, and there is no need to base it on incentives of fear and hope, which if they became principles would destroy the whole moral worth of actions. The moral law commands me to make the highest possible good in a world the final object of all my conduct. But I cannot hope to produce this except by the harmony of my will with that of a holy and beneficent author of the world; and although in the concept of the highest good, as that of a whole in which the greatest happiness is represented as connected in the most exact proportion with the greatest degree of moral perfection (possible in creatures), *my own happiness* is included, this is nevertheless not the determining ground of the will that is directed to promote the highest good; it is instead the moral law (which, on the contrary, limits by strict conditions my unbounded craving for happiness).

For this reason, again, morals[c] is not properly the doctrine of how we are to *make* ourselves happy but of how we are to become *worthy* of happiness. Only if religion is added to it does there also enter the hope of some day participating in happiness to the degree that we have been intent upon not being unworthy of it.

Someone is *worthy* of possessing a thing or a state when it harmonizes with the highest good that he is in possession of it. It can now be readily seen that all worthiness depends upon moral conduct, since in the concept of the highest good this constitutes the condition of the rest (which belongs to one's state), namely, of one's share of happiness. Now, from this it follows that *morals* in itself must never be treated as a *doctrine of happiness*, that is, as instruction in how to become happy; for morals has to do solely with the rational condition *(conditio sine qua non)* of happiness and not with the means of acquiring it. But when morals (which merely imposes duties and does not provide rules for selfish wishes) has been set forth completely, then – after the moral wish, based on a law, to promote the highest good (to bring the kingdom of God to us) has been awakened, which could not previously have arisen in any selfish soul, and for the sake of this wish the step to religion has been taken – then for the first time can this

---

[a] *Erkenntnis*
[b] *gütigen*
[c] Or "moral philosophy," *die Moral*

ethical doctrine also be called a doctrine of happiness, because it is only with religion that the *hope* of happiness first arises.

From this it can also be seen that if one asks about *God's final end* in creating the world, one must not name the *happiness* of the rational beings in it but *the highest good,* which adds a condition to that wish of such beings, namely the condition of being worthy of happiness, that is, the *morality* of these same rational beings, which condition alone contains the standard in accordance with which they can hope to participate in the former at the hands of a *wise* author. For, since *wisdom* considered theoretically signifies *cognition of the highest good,* and practically *the fitness of the will for the highest good,* one cannot attribute to a highest independent wisdom an end that would be based merely on beneficence.*d* For one cannot conceive the effect of this beneficence (with respect to the happiness of rational beings) as befitting the highest original good except under the limiting conditions of harmony with the *holiness* of his will.* Hence those who put the end of creation in the glory*e* of God (provided this is not thought anthropomorphically, as inclination to be praised) perhaps hit upon the best expression. For, nothing glorifies God more than what is most estimable in the world, respect for his command, observance of the holy*f* duty that his law lays upon us, when there is added to this his magnificent plan of crowning such a beautiful order with corresponding happiness. If the latter (to speak humanly) makes him worthy of love, by the former he is an object of worship (adoration). Human beings themselves can acquire love by beneficence, but by it alone they can never acquire respect, so that the greatest beneficence procures them honor*g* only when it is exercised in accordance with worthiness.

It now follows of itself that in the order of ends the human being (and with him every rational being) is an *end in itself,* that is, can never be used merely as a means by anyone (not even by God) without being at the same time himself an end, and that humanity in our person must, accordingly,

---

*In passing, and to make what is proper to these concepts distinguishable, I add only this remark. Although one ascribes to God various attributes the quality of which is found appropriate to creatures as well except that in him they are raised to the highest degree, e.g., power, knowledge, presence, goodness, and so forth, calling them omnipotence, omniscience, omnipresence, all-goodness, and so forth, there are still three that are ascribed to God exclusively and yet without the addition of greatness, and all of them are moral: he is the *only holy,* the *only blessed,* the *only wise,* because these concepts already imply the absence of limitation. According to the order of these attributes he is also the *holy lawgiver* (and creator), the *beneficent governor* (and preserver), and the *just judge* – three attributes which include everything by which God is the object of religion and in conformity with which the metaphysical perfections are added of themselves in reason.

d Gütigkeit
e Ehre
f Or "sacred," *heiligen*
g ihnen . . . Ehre macht, perhaps "does them honor"

be *holy*[h] to ourselves: for he is the *subject of the moral law* and so of that which is holy in itself, on account of which and in agreement with which alone can anything be called holy. For, this moral law is based on the autonomy of his will, as a free will which, in accordance with its universal laws, must necessarily be able at the same time *to agree* to that to which it is to *subject* itself.

VI.
ON THE POSTULATES OF PURE PRACTICAL REASON IN GENERAL

All of them proceed from the principle of morality, which is not a postulate but a law by which reason determines the will immediately; and this will, just because it is so determined as a pure will, requires these necessary conditions for observance of its precept. These postulates are not theoretical dogmas but *presuppositions* having a necessarily practical reference[i] and thus, although they do not indeed extend speculative cognition, they give objective reality to the ideas of speculative reason in *general* (by means of their reference to what is practical) and justify its holding concepts even the possibility of which it could not otherwise presume to affirm.

These postulates are those of *immortality*, of *freedom* considered positively (as the causality of a being insofar as it belongs to the intelligible world), and of the *existence of God*. The *first* flows from the practically necessary condition of a duration befitting the complete fulfillment of the moral law; the *second* from the necessary presupposition of independence from the sensible world and of the capacity to determine one's will by the law of an intelligible world, that is, the law of freedom; the *third* from the necessity of the condition for such an intelligible world to be the highest good, through the presupposition of the highest independent good, that is, of the existence of God.

Aiming at the highest good, made necessary by respect for the moral law, and the presupposition flowing from this of its objective reality lead through the postulates of practical reason to concepts that speculative reason could indeed present as problems but could never solve. Thus it leads to 1: the problem in the solution of which speculative reason could do nothing but commit *paralogisms* (namely, the problem of immortality) because it lacked the mark of permanence by which to supplement the psychological concept of an ultimate subject, necessarily ascribed to the soul in self-consciousness, so as to make it the real representation of a substance; this mark practical reason furnishes by the postulate of a duration required for conformity with the moral law in the highest good as the

---
[h] Or "sacred," *heilig*
[i] *in notwendig praktischer Rucksicht*

whole end of practical reason. 2. It leads to the concept with regard to which speculative reason contained nothing but an *antinomy*, the resolution of which it could base only on a concept that was indeed problematically thinkable but not demonstrable or determinable as to its objective reality, namely the *cosmological* idea of an intelligible world and consciousness of our existence in it; it leads to this by means of the postulate of freedom (the reality of which it lays down through the moral law and with it the law of an intelligible world as well, to which speculative reason could only point but could not determine its concept). 3. As for that which speculative reason had to think but to leave undetermined as mere transcendental *ideal*, the *theological* concept of the original being, it furnishes significance to this (for practical purposes, i.e., as a condition of the possibility of the object of a will determined by that law), as the supreme principle of the highest good in an intelligible world, by means of moral lawgiving accompanied by power[j] in it.

But is our cognition really extended in this way by pure practical reason, and is what was *transcendent* for speculative reason *immanent* in practical reason? Certainly, but only *for practical purposes*. For we thereby cognize neither the nature of our souls, nor the intelligible world, nor the supreme being as to what they are in themselves, but have merely unified the concepts of them in the *practical* concept *of the highest good* as the object of our will, and have done so altogether a priori through pure reason but only by means of the moral law and, moreover, only in reference to it, with respect to the object it commands. But how freedom is even possible and how this kind of causality has to be represented theoretically and positively is not thereby seen; that there is such a causality is only postulated by the moral law and for the sake of it. It is the same with the remaining ideas, the possibility of which no human understanding will ever fathom although no sophistry will ever convince even the most common human being that they are not true concepts.

VII.
HOW IS IT POSSIBLE TO THINK OF AN EXTENSION OF PURE REASON FOR PRACTICAL PURPOSES WITHOUT THEREBY ALSO EXTENDING ITS COGNITION AS SPECULATIVE?

In order not to be too abstract, we are going to answer this question at once in its application to the present case. In order to extend a pure cognition *practically* there must be a *purpose* given a priori, that is, an end as object (of the will) that, independently of all theoretical principles, is represented as practically necessary by an imperative determining the will

---

[j] durch gewalthabende moralische Gesetzgebung

immediately (a categorical imperative), and in this case that is the *highest good*. This, however, is not possible without presupposing three theoretical concepts (for which, because they are only pure rational concepts, no corresponding intuition can be found and consequently, by the theoretical path, no objective reality): namely, freedom, immortality, and God. Thus by the practical law that commands the existence of the highest good possible in a world, the possibility of those objects of pure speculative reason, the objective reality which the latter could not assure them, is postulated; by this the theoretical cognition of pure reason certainly receives an increment, but it consists only in this: that those concepts, otherwise problematic (merely thinkable) for it, are now declared[k] assertorically to be concepts to which real objects belong, because practical reason unavoidably requires the existence of them for the possibility of its object, the highest good, which is absolutely necessary practically, and theoretical reason is thereby justified in assuming them. But this extension of theoretical reason is no extension of speculation, that is, no positive use can now be made of it for *theoretical purposes*. For, since nothing further is accomplished in this by practical reason than that those concepts are real and really have their (possible) objects, but nothing is thereby given us by way of intuition of them (which can also not be demanded), no synthetic proposition is possible by this reality granted them. Hence this disclosure does not help us in the least for speculative purposes, although with respect to the practical use of pure reason it does help us to extend this cognition of ours.[l] The above three ideas of speculative reason are in themselves still not cognitions; nevertheless they are (transcendent) *thoughts* in which there is nothing impossible. Now they receive objective reality through an apodictic practical law, as necessary conditions of the possibility of what it commands us *to make an object*, that is, we are instructed by it *that they have objects*, although we are not able to show how their concept refers to an object, and this is not yet cognition *of these objects;* for one cannot thereby judge synthetically about them at all or determine their application theoretically; hence one can make no theoretical rational use[m] of them at all, in which use all speculative cognition of reason properly consists. Nevertheless, theoretical cognition, *not indeed of these objects* but of reason in general, is extended by this insofar as *objects were given* to those ideas by the practical postulates, a merely problematic thought having by this means first received objective reality. There was therefore no extension of the cognition *of given supersensible objects*, but there was nevertheless an extension of theoretical reason and of its cognition with respect to the supersensible in general, inasmuch as theoretical

---

[k] *erklärt werden*
[l] It is not clear from the text whether the phrase *zur Erweiterung dieses unseres Erkenntnisses* should be placed here or after *in speculativer Absicht*.
[m] *keinen theoretischen Gebrauch der Vernunft machen*

reason was forced to grant *that there are such objects,* though it cannot determine them more closely and so cannot itself extend this cognition of the objects (which have now been given to it on practical grounds and, moreover, only for practical use); for this increment, then, pure theoretical reason, for which all those ideas are transcendent and without objects, has to thank its practical capacity only. In this they become *immanent* and *constitutive* inasmuch as they are grounds of the possibility of *making real the necessary object* of pure practical reason (the highest good), whereas apart from this they are *transcendent* and merely *regulative* principles of speculative reason, which do not require it to assume a new object beyond experience but only to bring its use in experience nearer to completeness. But when once reason is in possession of this increment, it will, as speculative reason, go to work with these ideas in a negative way (really, only to secure its practical use), that is, not extending but purifying, so as on one side to ward off *anthropomorphism* as the source of *superstition* or specious extension of those concepts by supposed experience, and on the other side *fanaticism,* which promises such an extension by means of supersensible intuition or feelings – all of which are hindrances to the practical use of pure reason, so that the removal of them certainly belongs to an extension of our cognition for practical purposes, without contradicting the admission that for speculative purposes reason has not in the least gained by this.

5:136

Every use of reason with respect to an object requires pure concepts of the understanding *(categories),* without which no object can be thought. These can be applied for the theoretical use of reason, that is, for cognition of that kind, only insofar as intuition (which is always sensible) is also put under them, and therefore merely in order to represent by means of them an object of possible experience. But here *ideas* of reason, which cannot be given in any experience at all, are what I would have to think by means of categories in order to cognize an object. Here, however, our concern with these ideas is not for the sake of theoretical cognition of their objects but only with whether they have objects at all. Pure practical reason provides this reality, and theoretical reason has nothing further to do in this than merely *to think* those objects through categories, and this, as we have elsewhere clearly shown, can be done quite well without needing intuition (whether sensible or supersensible) because the categories have their seat and origin in the pure understanding solely as the faculty of thinking, independently of and prior to any intuition, and they always signify only an object in general, *in whatever way it may be given to us.* Now, insofar as the categories are to be applied to these ideas, it is not possible to give them any object in intuition; but *that an object really exists,* so that a category as a mere form of thought is here not empty but has significance, is sufficiently assured them by an object that practical reason presents beyond doubt in the concept of the highest good, namely the *reality of the concepts* that are required for the possibility of the highest good, without, however, effecting by this increment the least extension of cognition in accordance with theoretical principles.

If these ideas of God, of an intelligible world (the kingdom of God), and of immortality are determined more closely by predicates drawn from our own nature, this determination cannot be regarded as either a *sensualizing*" of those pure rational ideas (anthropomorphism) or as a transcendent cognition of *supersensible* objects; for these predicates are no others than understanding and will, considered moreover in the relation to each other in which they must be though in the moral law, and hence only to the extent that a pure practical use is made of them. As for all the rest that is added to these concepts psychologically – that is, insofar as we observe these faculties of ours empirically *in their exercise* (for example, that human understanding is discursive so that its representations are not intuitions but thoughts, that these follow one another in time, that the human will is always dependent for its satisfaction upon the existence of its object, and so forth, which cannot be the case in the supreme being) – this is abstracted from in that case, and then what remains of the concepts by which we think of a pure intelligence*º* is nothing more than what is required for the possibility of thinking of a moral law; thus there is indeed a cognition of God but only with practical reference, and if we attempt to extend it to a theoretical cognition we find an understanding that does not think but *intuits,* a will that is directed to objects upon the existence of which its satisfaction does not in the least depend (not to mention the transcendental predicates, as, e.g., a magnitude of existence, i.e., duration, which, however, is not in time, the only possible means we have of representing existence as magnitude). All of these are attributes of which we can form no concept fit for *cognition* of the object, and we learn from this that they can never be used for a *theory* of supersensible beings, so that on this side they are quite unable to ground a speculative cognition and their use is, instead, limited solely to the practice of the moral law.

This last is so obvious, and can be proved so clearly by fact, that one can confidently challenge all supposed *natural theologians*ᵖ (a singular name)* to cite (over and above the merely ontological predicates) even

---

*Learning*ᑫ is, strictly speaking, only the sum total of the *historical* sciences. Consequently only the teacher of revealed theology can be called a theologian. If, however, one wants to call someone who is in possession of the rational sciences (mathematics and philosophy) *learned,* even though this could conflict with the meaning of the word (which always counts as learning only that which must be *taught*ʳ and which, therefore, one cannot of oneself discover by reason), the philosopher, with his cognition of God as a positive science, would cut too poor a figure to let himself be called on that account a *learned* man.

ⁿ *Versinnlichung*
º *Verstandeswesen*
ᵖ *Gottesgelehrten*
ᑫ *Gelehrsamkeit*
ʳ *gelehrt*

one property, say of the understanding or the will, determining this object of theirs, of which it could not be shown incontestably that if everything anthropomorphic is separated from it nothing would remain to us but the mere word, without our being able to combine with it the least concept by which we could hope for an extension of theoretical cognition. But with respect to the practical there still remains to us, of the properties of understanding and will, the concept of a relation to which the practical law (which precisely determines a priori this relation of the understanding to the will) furnishes objective reality. Once this is done, reality is given to the concept of the object of a morally determined will (that of the highest good) and with it to the conditions of its possibility, the ideas of God, freedom, and immortality, but always only with reference to the practice of the moral law (not for any speculative purpose).

After these reminders[s] it is now easy to find the answer to the important question: *whether the concept of God is a concept belonging to physics* (and therefore also to the metaphysics, which only contains the pure a priori principles of the former in their universal meaning) *or to morals*. If, in order to *explain* the arrangements of nature or their changes, one has recourse to God as the author of all things, this is at least no physical explanation and is a complete confession that one has come to an end of one's philosophy; for, one is forced to assume something of which in itself one otherwise has no concept, in order to be able to frame a concept of the possibility of what one sees before one's eyes. But it is impossible through metaphysics to proceed *by sure inferences* from knowledge of this world to the concept of God and to the proof of his existence, for this reason: that in order to say that this world was possible only through a *God* (as we must think this concept) we would have to cognize this world as the most perfect whole possible and, in order to do so, cognize all possible worlds as well (so as to be able to compare them with this one), and would therefore have to be omniscient. Finally,[t] however, it is absolutely impossible to cognize the existence of this being from mere concepts, because every existential proposition – that is, every proposition that says, of a being of which I frame a concept, that it exists – is a synthetic proposition, that is, one by which I go beyond that concept and say more about it than was thought in the concept, namely, that to this concept *in the understanding* there corresponds an object *outside the understanding*, which it is absolutely impossible to elicit by any inference. Thus there remains for reason only one single procedure by which to arrive at this cognition, namely, as pure reason to start from the supreme principle of its pure practical use (inasmuch as this is always directed simply to the *existence* of something as a result of reason) and determine its object. And then, in its unavoidable

---
[s] Or "According to these remarks," *Nach diesen Erinnerungen*
[t] *Vollends,* perhaps "to cognize completely"

problem, namely that of the necessary direction of the will to the highest good, there is shown not only the necessity of assuming such an original being in relation to the possibility of this good in the world but – what is most remarkable – something that was quite lacking in the progress of reason on the path of nature, *a precisely determined concept of this original being.* Since we can know only a small part of this world and can still less compare it with all possible worlds, we can well infer from its order, purposiveness, and magnitude a *wise, beneficent, powerful,* and so forth author of it, but not his *omniscience, all-beneficence, omnipotence,* and so forth. It may even very well be granted that one is authorized[u] to supplement this unavoidable defect by a permitted, quite reasonable hypothesis, namely, that when wisdom, beneficence and so forth are displayed in all the parts that offer themselves to our closer cognition, it is just the same in all the rest, and that it would therefore be reasonable to ascribe all possible perfection to the author of the world; but these are not *inferences* in which we can pride ourselves on our insight, but only liberties[v] which can be overlooked but still need further recommendation before we can make use of them. Thus the concept of God always remains, on the path of empirical inquiry (physics), a concept of the perfection of the first being not determined precisely enough to be held adequate to the concept of a deity (but with metaphysics in its transcendental part nothing at all is to be accomplished.)

5:140 When I now try to bring this concept into relation with the object of practical reason, I find that the moral principle admits it as possible only on the presupposition of an author of the world possessed of the *highest perfection.* He must be *omniscient* in order to cognize my conduct even to my inmost disposition in all possible cases and throughout the future, *omnipotent* in order to bestow results appropriate to it, and so too *omnipresent, eternal,* and so forth. Thus the moral law, by means of the concept of the highest good as the object of a pure practical reason, determines the concept of the original being as the *supreme being,* something that the physical (and, pursued higher, the metaphysical) and so the whole speculative course of reason could not effect. The concept of God, then, is one belonging originally not to physics, that is, to speculative reason, but to morals, and the same can be said of the other concepts of reason which we treated above as postulates of reason in its practical use.

If in the history of Greek philosophy we find no clear traces of a pure rational theology earlier than Anaxagoras, the reason is not that the older philosophers had not enough understanding or insight to raise themselves to it by the path of speculation, at least with the aid of a quite reasonable

[u] *befugt*
[v] *Befugnisse*

hypothesis; what could have been easier, what more natural, than the thought that occurs of itself to everyone, to assume a single rational cause of the world having *all perfection* in place of indeterminate degrees of perfection of several causes? But the ills in the world seemed to them to be much too important objections to consider themselves justified in such a hypothesis. Thus they showed understanding and insight precisely in not permitting themselves this hypothesis and instead looked about among natural causes to see if they could not find among them the character[w] and capacity required for original beings. But once this acute people had advanced so far in their investigations as to treat philosophically even moral objects, about which other peoples had never done more than prate, they then first found a new need, namely a practical one, which did not fail to give them the determined concept of the original being; and in this speculative reason had the role of a spectator, or at best had the merit of embellishing a concept that had not grown on its own land and of furthering, by a train of confirmations from the study of nature which now came forward for the first time, not indeed its authority (which was already established) but only its display, with a supposed theoretical insight of reason.

5:141

By these reminders the readers of the *Critique* of pure speculative reason will be perfectly convinced how extremely necessary, how salutary for theology and morals that laborious *deduction* of the categories was. For, if they are placed in the pure understanding it is only by this deduction that we can be prevented from taking them, with Plato, to be innate and basing on them extravagant pretensions and theories of the supersensible to which we can see no end, thereby making theology a magic lantern of chimeras; but if they are taken to be acquired, this deduction prevents us from restricting, with Epicurus, all and every use of them, even for practical purposes, merely to objects and determining grounds of the senses. But now that the *Critique* has shown by that deduction, *first* that they are not of empirical origin but have their seat and source a priori in the pure understanding, and *second* that, since they are referred *to objects in general* independently of intuition of these objects, they indeed bring about *theoretical cognition* only in application to *empirical* objects but still, applied to an object given by pure practical reason, also serve for a *determined thought of the supersensible*, yet only to the extent that this is determined merely through such predicates as necessarily belong to the pure *practical purpose* given a priori and to its possibility. Speculative restriction of pure reason and its practical extension first bring it into that *relation of equality* in which reason in general can be used purposively, and this example shows better than any other that the path *to wisdom*, if it is to be assured and not impassible or misleading, must for us human beings unavoidably pass

[w] *Beschaffenheit*

through science; but it is not till science is completed that we can be convinced that it leads to that goal.

VIII.
ON ASSENT[x] FROM A NEED OF PURE REASON

A need of pure reason in its speculative use leads only to hypotheses, that of pure practical reason, however, to postulates; for in the first case I ascend from the derived as high *as I will* in the series of grounds and do not need an original ground[y] in order to give objective reality to what is derived (e.g., to the causal connection of things and changes in the world), but only in order to satisfy completely my inquiring reason with respect to it. Thus I see before me order and purposiveness in nature, and need not proceed to speculation in order to assure myself of their *reality;* instead, it is only in order *to explain* them that I need *to presuppose a Deity* as their cause; but, since an inference from an effect to a determined cause, especially to a cause so precise and so completely determined as we have to think in God, is always uncertain and doubtful, such a presupposition cannot be brought further than the degree of being the most reasonable opinion for us human beings.* On the other hand, a need *of pure practical* reason is based on a *duty,* that of making something (the highest good) the object of my will so as to promote it with all my powers; and thus I must suppose its possibility and so too the conditions for this, namely God, freedom, and immortality, because I cannot prove these by my speculative reason, although I can also not refute them. This duty is based on something that is indeed quite independent of these suppositions and of itself apodictically certain, namely the moral law; and so far it needs no further support by theoretical opinions as to the inner character of things, the secret aim of the order of the world,[z] or a ruler presiding over it, in order to bind us most perfectly to actions unconditionally conformed to the law. But the subjective effect of this law, namely the disposition conformed with it and also made necessary by it to promote the practically possible highest good, nevertheless presupposes at least that the latter is *possible;* in the contrary case it would be practically impossible to strive for the object

---

*But even here we could not allege a need *of reason* if we had not before our eyes a problematic but yet unavoidable concept of reason, namely that of an absolutely necessary being. This concept now wants to be determined, and this, when the drive toward extension is added, is the objective ground of a need of speculative reason, namely, to determine more closely the concept of a necessary being that is to serve as the original ground of others and so to make this recognizable by some means. Without such prior necessary problems there are no *needs,* at least *not of pure reason;* the rest are needs of inclination.

[x] *Fürwahrhalten,* literally "holding to be true"
[y] *Urgrund*
[z] *Abzweckung der Weltordnung*

CRITIQUE OF PRACTICAL REASON

of a concept that would be, at bottom, empty and without an object. Now, the above-mentioned postulates concern only the physical or metaphysical conditions – in a word, those which lie in the nature of things – of the *possibility* of the highest good, not, however, for the sake of a discretionary speculative purpose but of a practically necessary end of a pure rational will, which does not here *choose;* instead, it *obeys* an inflexible command of reason that has its ground *objectively* in the character of things as they must be appraised universally by pure reason and is not based upon, say, *inclination,* which is by no means justified in at once assuming, for the sake of what we *wish* on merely *subjective* grounds, that the means to it are possible or that its object is real. This is, accordingly, a *need from an absolutely necessary point of view* and justifies its presupposition not merely as a permitted hypothesis but as a postulate from a practical point of view; and, granted that the pure moral law inflexibly binds everyone as a command (not as a rule of prudence), the upright man may well say: I *will* that there be a God, that my existence in this world be also an existence in a pure world of the understanding beyond natural connections, and finally that my duration be endless; I stand by this, without paying attention to rationalizations, however little I may be able to answer them or to oppose them with others more plausible, and I will not let this belief be taken from me; for this is the only case in which my interest, because I *may* not give up anything of it, unavoidably determines my judgment.*

∴

In order to prevent misinterpretations in the use of a concept as yet so unusual as that of a pure practical rational belief, I may add one more remark. It might almost seem as if this rational belief is here announced as itself a *command,* namely to assume the highest good as possible. But a belief that is commanded is an absurdity. If, however, one recalls from the

5:144

---

*In the *Deutsches Museum,* February 1787, there is a treatise by a very subtle and clearheaded man, the late Wizenmann,[13] whose early death is to be lamented, in which he disputes the authorization to conclude from a need to the objective reality of its object and illustrates the point by the example of a *man in love,* who, having fooled himself into an idea of beauty that is merely a chimera of his own brain, would like to conclude that such an object really exists somewhere. I grant that he is perfectly correct in this, in all cases where the need is based upon *inclination,* which cannot necessarily postulate the existence of its object even for the one affected by it, much less can it contain a requirement valid for everyone, and therefore it is a *merely subjective* ground of the wish. But in the present case it is *need of reason* arising from an *objective* determining ground of the will, namely the moral law, which necessarily binds every rational being and therefore justifies him a priori in presupposing in nature the conditions befitting it and makes the latter inseparable from the complete practical use of reason. It is a duty to realize the highest good to the utmost of our capacity; therefore it must be possible; hence it is also unavoidable for every rational being in the world to assume what is necessary for its objective possibility. The assumption is as necessary as the moral law, in relation to which alone it is valid.

preceding explanation what is required to be assumed in the concept of the highest good, one will become aware that the assumption of this possibility cannot be commanded, and that no practical disposition requires one to *grant* it but that speculative reason must concede it without being asked, since no one can want to maintain that a worthiness of rational beings in the world to be happy in conformity with the moral law combined with a possession of this happiness proportioned to it is *impossible* in itself. Now, with respect to the first element of the highest good, namely that which concerns morality, the moral law gives merely a command, and to doubt that possibility of that component would be tantamount to calling in question the moral law itself. But as for what concerns the second part of that object, namely happiness in thorough conformity with that worthiness, there is no need of a command to grant its possibility in general, since theoretical reason has nothing to say against it; but *the way* in which *we* are to think such a harmony of the laws of nature with those of freedom has in it something with respect to which we have a *choice*, since theoretical reason decides nothing with apodictic certainty about it, and with respect to this there can be a moral interest which turns the scale.

I said above that in accordance with a mere course of nature in the world happiness in exact conformity with moral worth is not to be expected and is to be held impossible, and that therefore the possibility of the highest good on this side can be granted only on the presupposition of a moral author of the world. I deliberately postponed the restricting of this judgment to the subjective conditions of our reason so as not to make use of it until the manner of its assent had been determined more closely. In fact, the impossibility referred to is *merely subjective,* that is, our reason finds it *impossible for it* to conceive, in the mere course of nature, a connection so exactly proportioned and so thoroughly purposive[a] between events occurring in the world in accordance with such different laws, although, as with everything else in nature that is purposive, it nevertheless cannot prove – that is, set forth sufficiently on objective grounds – the impossibility of it in accordance with universal laws of nature.

Now, however, a deciding ground of a different kind comes into play so as to turn the scale in this irresolution of speculative reason. The command to promote the highest good is based objectively (in practical reason); its possibility in general is likewise objectively based (in theoretical reason, which has nothing against it). But as for the way we are to represent this possibility, whether in accordance with universal laws of nature without a wise author presiding over nature or only on the supposition of such an author, reason cannot decide this objectively. Now a *subjective* condition of reason enters into this, the only way in which it is theoreti-

---

[a] *zweckmäßig*

cally possible for it to think the exact harmony of the realm*ᵇ* of nature with the realm of morals as the condition of the possibility of the highest good, and at the same time the only way that is conducive to morality (which is subject to an *objective* law of reason). Now, since the promotion of the highest good, and therefore the supposition of its possibility, is *objectively* necessary (though only as a consequence of practical reason), while at the same time the manner, the way in which we would think it as possible rests with our choice, in which a free interest of pure practical reason decides for the assumption of a wise author of the world, it follows that the principle that determines our judgment about it, though it is *subjective* as a need, is yet, as the means of promoting what is *objectively* (practically) necessary, the ground of a maxim of assent for moral purposes, that is, *a pure practical rational belief.* This, then, is not commanded but – being a voluntary*ᶜ* determination of our judgment, conducive to the moral (commanded) purpose and moreover harmonizing with the theoretical need of reason to assume that existence and to make it the basis of the further use of reason – it has itself arisen from the moral disposition; it can therefore often waver even in the well-disposed but can never fall into unbelief.

IX.
ON THE WISE ADAPTATION OF THE HUMAN BEING'S COGNITIVE FACULTIES TO HIS PRACTICAL VOCATION

If human nature is called to strive for the highest good, it must also be assumed that the measure of its cognitive faculties, especially their relation to one another, is suitable to this end. Now, the *Critique* of pure *speculative* reason proves its utter insufficiency for solving, conformably with this end, the most important problems that are proposed to it, although the *Critique* does not fail to recognize the natural hints of this same reason, which are not to be overlooked, nor the great steps that it can take to approach this great goal that is set before it, which, however, it can never reach of itself, even with the aid of the greatest cognition of nature. Nature then seems here to have provided for us only in a stepmotherly fashion with the faculty needed for our end.

Assuming now that nature had here complied with our wish and given us that capacity for insight or that enlightenment*ᵈ* which we would like to possess or which some believe erroneously they actually do possess, what would, as far as we can tell, be the result of it? Unless our whole nature were at the same time changed, the *inclinations*, which always have the first

---
ᵇ Reichs
ᶜ freiwillig
ᵈ Erleuchtung

word, would first demand their satisfaction and, combined with reasonable reflection, their greatest possible and most lasting satisfaction under the name of *happiness;* the moral law would afterward speak, in order to keep them within their proper limits and even to subject them all to a higher end which has no regard to inclination. But instead of the conflict that the moral disposition now has to carry on with the inclinations, in which, though after some defeats, moral strength of soul is to be gradually acquired, *God and eternity with their awful majesty* would stand unceasingly *before our eyes* (for what we can prove perfectly holds as much certainty for us as what we are assured of by our sight). Transgression of the law would, no doubt, be avoided: what is commanded would be done; but because the *disposition* from which actions ought to be done cannot be instilled by any command, and because the spur to activity in this case would be promptly at hand and *external,* reason would have no need to work itself up so as to gather strength to resist the inclinations by a lively representation of the dignity of the law: hence most actions conforming to the law would be done from fear, only a few from hope, and none at all from duty, and the moral worth of actions, on which alone in the eyes of supreme wisdom the worth of the person and even that of the world depends, would not exist at all. As long as human nature remains as it is, human conduct would thus be changed into mere mechanism in which, as in a puppet show, everything would *gesticulate* well but there would be *no life* in the figures. Now, when it is quite otherwise with us; when with all the effort of our reason we have only a very obscure and ambiguous view into the future; when the governor of the world allows us only to conjecture his existence and his grandeur, not to behold them or prove them clearly; when, on the other hand, the moral law within us, without promising or threatening anything with certainty, demands of us disinterested respect; and when, finally, this respect alone, become active and ruling, first allows us a view into the realm of the supersensible, though only with weak glances; then there can be a truly moral disposition, devoted immediately to the moral law, and a rational creature can become worthy of the highest good in conformity with the moral worth of his person and not merely with his actions. Thus what the study of nature and of the human being teaches us sufficiently elsewhere may well be true here also: that the inscrutable wisdom by which we exist is not less worthy of veneration in what it has denied us than in what it has granted us.

*The
critique of practical reason
Part two*

*Doctrine of the method
of
pure practical reason*

The *doctrine of the method* of pure *practical* reason cannot be understood as 5:151
the way to proceed (in reflection as well as in exposition) with pure
practical principles with a view to scientific *cognition* of them, which alone
is properly called method elsewhere, in the *theoretical* (for popular cognition needs a *manner*[e] but science a *method*, i.e., a procedure *in accordance with principles* of reason by which alone the manifold of a cognition can become a *system*). Here the doctrine of method is understood, instead, as the way in which one can provide the laws of pure practical reason with *access* to the human mind and *influence* on its maxims, that is, the way in which one can make objectively practical reason *subjectively* practical as well.

It is now clear that those determining grounds of the will which alone make maxims properly moral and give them a moral worth – the immediate representation of the law and the objectively necessary observance of it as duty – must be represented as the proper incentives to action, since otherwise *legality* of actions would be produced but not *morality* of dispositions. But it is not so clear, and on the contrary must at first glance seem to everyone quite improbable, that even subjectively that presentation of pure virtue can have *more power* over the human mind and can provide a far stronger incentive to effect even that legality of actions and to bring forth stronger resolutions to prefer the law to every other consideration, from pure respect for it, than all the deceptive allurements[f] of enjoyment and, in general, everything that may be counted as happiness, or even all threats of pain and troubles can produce. But it is really so, and if human 5:152
nature were not so constituted, no way of representing the law by circumlocutions and by means recommending it[g] would ever bring forth morality of disposition. Everything would be sheer hypocrisy; the law would be hated or even despised, though still observed for the sake of one's own advantage. The letter of the law (legality) would be found in our actions, but the spirit of it in our dispositions (morality) would not be found at all; and since with all our efforts we could not altogether free ourselves from reason in our judgment, we would unavoidably have to appear worthless, depraved human beings in our own eyes, even if we sought to compensate ourselves for this mortification before the inner court by enjoying the pleasure that, in our delusion, we suppose a natural or divine law has connected with the machinery of its police, guided only by what was done without troubling itself about the motives from which it was done.

It certainly cannot be denied that in order to bring either a mind that is still uncultivated or one that is degraded onto the track of the morally good in the first place, some preparatory guidance is needed to attract it

[e] *Art*
[f] *Anlockungen aus Vorspiegelungen*
[g] *empfehlende Mittel*

by means of its own advantage or to alarm it by fear of harm; but as soon as this machinery, these leading strings have had even some effect, the pure moral motive must be brought to bear on the soul, the motive which – not only because it is the only one that can ground a character (a consistent practical cast of mind in accordance with unchangeable maxims) but also because it teaches the human being to feel his own dignity – gives his mind power, unexpected even by himself, to tear himself away from all sensible attachments so far as they want to rule over him and to find a rich compensation for the sacrifice he makes in the independence of his rational nature and the greatness of soul to which he sees that he is called. We will therefore show, by observations anyone can make, that this property of our minds, this receptivity to a pure moral interest and hence the moving force of the pure representation of virtue, when it is duly brought to bear on the human heart is the most powerful incentive to the good and the only one when an enduring and meticulous observance of moral maxims is in question. It must, however, be remembered that if these observations show only the reality of such a feeling but not any moral improvement brought about by it, this takes nothing away from[h] the only method there is for making the objectively practical laws of pure reason subjectively practical merely through the pure representation of duty, as if it were an empty fantasy. For, since this method has never yet been widely practiced experience can say nothing of its result; instead one can only ask for proofs of the receptivity to such incentives, which I will now present briefly and then sketch in a few words the method of founding and cultivating genuine moral dispositions.

If one attends to the course of conversation in mixed companies consisting not merely of scholars and subtle reasoners but also of business people or women, one notices that their entertainment includes, besides storytelling and jesting, arguing; for storytelling, if it is to have novelty and with it interest, is soon exhausted and jesting easily becomes insipid. Now, of all arguments there are none that more excite the participation of persons who are otherwise soon bored with subtle reasoning and that bring a certain liveliness into the company than arguments about the *moral worth* of this or that action by which the character of some person is to be made out. Those for whom anything subtle and refined in theoretical questions is dry and irksome soon join in when it is a question of how to make out the moral import of a good or evil action that has been related, and to an extent one does not otherwise expect of them on any object of speculation they are precise, refined, and subtle in thinking out everything that could lesson or even just make suspect the purity of purpose and consequently the degree of virtue in it. In these appraisals one can often see revealed the character of the person himself who judges others: some, in exercising

---

[h] *keinen Abbruch tue*

CRITIQUE OF PRACTICAL REASON

their judicial office especially upon the dead, seem inclined chiefly to defend the goodness that is related of this or that deed against all injurious charges of impurity and ultimately to defend the whole moral worth of the person against the reproach of dissimulation and secret wickedness; others, on the contrary, are more prone to contest this worth by accusations and fault-finding. One cannot always, however, attribute to the latter the intention of arguing away all virtue from examples of human beings in order to make it an empty name: often it is, instead, only well-meant strictness in determining genuine moral import in accordance with an uncompromising law, comparison with which, instead of with examples, greatly lowers self-conceit in moral matters, and humility is not only taught but felt by anyone when he examines himself strictly. Nevertheless, one can for the most part see, in those who defend the purity of intention in given examples, that where there is a presumption of uprightness they would like to remove even the least spot from the determining ground lest, if the truthfulness of all examples were disputed and the purity of all human virtue denied, human virtue might in the end be held a mere phantom, and so all striving toward it would be deprecated as vain affectation and delusive self-conceit.

5:154

I do not know why educators of young people have not long since made use of this propensity of reason to enter with pleasure upon even the most subtle examination of the practical questions put to them and why they have not, after first laying the foundation in a purely moral catechism, searched through the biographies of ancient and modern times in order to have at hand instances for the duties presented, in which, especially by comparison of similar actions under different circumstances, they could well activate their pupils' appraisal in marking the lesser or greater moral import of such actions; they would find that even someone very young, who is not yet ready for speculation, would soon become very acute and thereby not a little interested, since he would feel the progress of his faculty of judgment; and, what is most important, they could hope with confidence that frequent practice in knowing good conduct in all its purity and approving it and, on the other hand, marking with regret or contempt the least deviation from it, even though it is carried on only as a game of judgment in which children can compete with one another, yet will leave behind a lasting impression of esteem on the one hand and disgust on the other, which by mere habituation,[i] repeatedly looking on such actions as deserving approval or censure, would make a good foundation for uprightness in the future conduct of life. But I do wish that educators would spare their pupils examples of so-called *noble* (supermeritorious) actions, with which our sentimental writings so abound, and would expose them all[j] only to

5:155

[i] *Gewohnheit*
[j] *alles ... auszusetzen*, perhaps "refer everything"

263

duty and to the worth that a human being can and must give himself in his own eyes by consciousness of not having transgressed it; for, whatever runs up into empty wishes and longings for inaccessible perfection produces mere heroes of romance who, while they pride themselves on their feeling for extravagant greatness, release themselves in return from the observance of common and everyday obligation,[k] which then seems to them insignificant and petty.*

But if one asks: What, then, really is *pure* morality, by which as a touchstone one must test the moral content of every action? I must admit that only philosophers can make the decision of this question doubtful, for it is long since decided in common human reason, not indeed by abstract general formulae but by habitual use, like the difference between the right and the left hand. We will, accordingly, first show in an example the mark by which pure virtue is tested and, representing it as set before, say, a ten-year-old boy for his appraisal, see whether he must necessarily judge so of himself, without being directed to it by a teacher. One tells him the story of an honest man whom someone wants to induce to join the calumniators of an innocent but otherwise powerless person (say, Anne Boleyn, accused by Henry VIII of England). He is offered gain, that is, great gifts or high rank; he rejects them. This will produce mere approval and applause in the listener's soul, because it is gain. Now threats of loss begin. Among these calumniators are his best friends, who now refuse him their friendship; close relatives, who threaten to disinherit him (he is not wealthy); powerful people, who can pursue and hurt him in all places and circumstances; a prince who threatens him with loss of freedom and even of life itself. But, so that the measure of suffering may be full and he may also feel the pain that only a morally good heart can feel very deeply, represent his family, threatened with extreme distress and poverty, as *imploring him to yield* and himself, though upright, yet with a heart not hard or insensible[m] either to compassion or to his own distress; represent him at a moment when he wishes that he had never lived to see the day that exposed him to such unutterable pain and yet remains firm in his resolu-

---

*It is quite advisable to praise actions in which a great, unselfish, sympathetic disposition or humanity is manifested. But in this case one must call attention not so much to the *elevation of soul*, which is very fleeting and transitory, as to the *subjection of the heart* to *duty*, from which a more lasting impression can be expected, because this brings principles with it (but the former, only ebullitions).[l] One need only reflect a little and one will always find a debt that he has somehow incurred with respect to the human race (even if it were only that, by the inequality of human beings in the civil constitution, one enjoys advantages on account of which others must all the more do without), which will prevent the self-complacent image of *merit* from supplanting the thought of *duty*.

[k] *Schuldigkeit*
[l] *Aufwallungen*
[m] *doch eben nicht von festen, unempfindlichen Organen das Gefühl*

tion to be truthful, without wavering or even doubting; then my young listener will be raised step by step from mere approval to admiration, from that to amazement, and finally to the greatest veneration and a lively wish that he himself could be such a man (though certainly not in such circumstances); and yet virtue is here worth so much only because it costs so much, not because it brings any profit. All the admiration, and even the endeavor to resemble this character, here rests wholly on the purity of the moral principle, which can be clearly represented only if one removes from the incentive to action everything that people may reckon only to happiness. Thus morality must have more power over the human heart the more purely it is presented. From this it follows that if the law of morals and the image of holiness and virtue are to exercise any influence at all on our soul, they can do so only insofar as they are laid to heart in their purity as incentives, unmixed with any view to one's welfare, for it is in suffering that they show themselves most excellently. But that which, by being removed strengthens the effect of a moving force must have been a hindrance. Consequently every admixture of incentives taken from one's own happiness is a hindrance to providing the moral law with influence on the human heart. I maintain, further, that even in that admired action, if the motive from which it was done was esteem for one's duty, then it is just this respect for the law that straightaway has the greatest force on the mind of a spectator, and not, say, any pretension to inner magnanimity and a noble cast of mind; consequently duty, not merit, must have not only the most determinate influence on the mind but, when it is represented in the correct light of its inviolability, the most penetrating influence as well.

5:157

In our times, when one hopes to have more influence on the mind through melting, tender feelings or high-flown, puffed-up pretensions, which make the heart languid instead of strengthening it, than by a dry and earnest representation of duty, which is more suited to human imperfection and to progress in goodness, it is more necessary than ever to direct attention to this method. It is altogether contrapurposive to set before children, as a model, actions as noble, magnanimous, meritorious, thinking that one can captivate them by inspiring enthusiasm for such actions. For, since they are still so backward in observance of the commonest duty and even in correct estimation of it, this is tantamount to soon making them fantasizers. But even with the instructed and experienced part of humankind this supposed incentive has, if not a prejudicial effect on the heart, at least no genuine moral one, though this is what one wanted to bring about by means of it.

All *feelings*, especially those that are to produce unusual exertions, must accomplish their effect at the moment they are at their height and before they calm down; otherwise they accomplish nothing because the heart naturally returns to its natural moderate vital motion and accordingly falls back into the languor that was proper to it before, since something was applied that indeed stimulated it but nothing that strengthened it. *Principles* must be built on concepts; on any other foundation there can be only seizures, which can give a person no moral worth and not even confidence in himself, without which the consciousness of one's moral disposition and of a character of this kind, the highest good in human beings, cannot come to exist. Now, if these concepts are to become subjectively practical they must stop short with objective laws or morality, to be admired and esteemed with reference to humanity: the representation of them must be considered in relation to human beings and to the individual human being; for then this law appears in a form that, though indeed highly deserving of respect, is not so pleasing as if it belonged to the element to which he is naturally accustomed but instead as it constrains him to leave this element, often not without self-denial, and to go to a higher element in which he can maintain himself only with effort and with unceasing apprehension of relapsing. In a word, the moral law demands obedience from duty and not from a predilection that cannot and ought not to be presupposed at all.

Let us now see in an example whether there is more subjective moving force as an incentive if an action is represented as a noble and magnanimous one than if it is represented merely as duty in relation to the earnest moral law. The action by which someone tries with extreme danger to his life to rescue people from a shipwreck, finally losing his own life in the attempt, will indeed be reckoned, on one side, as duty but on the other and even for the most part as a meritorious action; but our esteem for it will be greatly weakened by the concept of *duty to himself,* which seems in this case to suffer some infringement. More decisive is someone's magnanimous sacrifice of his life for the preservation of his country; and yet there still remains some scruple as to whether it is so perfect a duty to devote oneself to this purpose of one's own accord and unbidden, and the action has not in itself the full force of a model and impulse to imitation. But if it is an essential[n] duty, transgression of which violates the moral law in itself and without regard to human welfare and, as it were, tramples on its holiness (such as are usually called duties to God because in him we think the ideal of holiness in a substance), then we give the most perfect esteem to compliance with it at the sacrifice of everything that could ever have value for our dearest inclinations, and we find our soul strengthened and elevated by such an example when we can convince ourselves, in it, that human nature is capable of so great an elevation above every incentive that nature can oppose to it. Juvenal presents such an example in a climax that makes the reader feel vividly the force of the incentive present in the pure law of duty, as duty:

[n] *unerlaßliche*

*Esto bonus miles, tutor bonus, arbiter idem Integer; ambiguae si quando citabere testis
Incertaeque rei, Phalaris licet imperet, ut sis Falsus, et admoto dictet periuria tauro,
Summum crede nefas animam praeferre pudori, Et propter vitam vivendi perdere causas.*[o]

When we can bring any flattering thought of merit into our action, then the incentive is already somewhat mixed with self-love and thus has some assistance from the side of sensibility. But to put everything below the holiness of duty alone and become aware that one *can* do it because our own reason recognizes this as its command and says that one *ought* to do it: this is, as it were, to raise oneself altogether above the sensible world,[p] and this consciousness of the law as also an incentive is inseparably combined with consciousness of a power *ruling over sensibility*, even if not always with effect; yet frequent engagement with it and the initially minor attempts at using it give hope of its effectiveness, so that gradually the greatest, but purely moral, interest in it may be produced in us.

Accordingly, the method takes the following course. *At first* it is only a question of making appraisal of actions by moral laws a natural occupation and, as it were, a habit accompanying all our own free actions as well as our observation of those of others, and of sharpening it by asking first whether the action objectively *conforms with the moral law*, and with which law; by this, attention to such law as provides merely a *ground* of obligation is distinguished from that which is in fact *obligatory (leges obligandi a legibus obligantibus)*[q] (e.g., the law of what the *need* of human beings requires of me as contrasted with what their *right* requires, the latter of which prescribes essential duties whereas the former prescribes only nonessential[r] duties), and thus one teaches how to distinguish different duties that come together in an action. The other point to which attention must be directed is the question whether the action was also done (subjectively) *for the sake of the moral law*, so that it has not only moral correctness as a deed but also moral worth as a disposition by its maxim. Now, there is no doubt that this exercise and the consciousness of a cultivation of our reason in judging merely about the practical, arising from this exercise, must gradually produce a certain interest in reasons's law itself and hence in morally good actions. For, we finally come to like something the contemplation of which lets us feel a more extended use of our cognitive powers, which is especially furthered by that in which we find moral correctness, since only

5:159

5:160

---

[o] Be a good soldier, a good guardian, and an incorruptible judge; if summoned to bear witness in some dubious and uncertain cause, though Phalaris[14] himself should dictate that you perjure yourself and bring his bull to move you, count it the greatest of all iniquities to prefer life to honor and to lose, for the sake of living, all that makes life worth living. (Juvenal *Satire* 8.79–84).
[p] The remainder of this sentence is grammatically difficult.
[q] Compare *The Metaphysics of Morals* (6:224).
[r] *außerwesentliche*

in such an order of things can reason, with its capacity to determine a priori in accordance with principles what ought to be done, find satisfaction. Even an observer of nature finally comes to like objects that at first offended his senses when he discovers in them the great purposiveness of their organization, so that his reason delights in contemplating them, and Leibniz spared an insect that he had carefully examined with a microscope and replaced it on its leaf because he had found himself instructed by his view of it and had, as it were, received a benefit from it.

But this employment of the faculty of judgment, which lets us feel our own cognitive powers, is not yet interest in actions and in their morality itself. It merely brings someone to like to entertain himself with such an appraisal and gives to virtue or the cast of mind according to moral laws a form of beauty, which is admired but not yet on that account sought *(laudatur et alget);*[s] it is the same with everything whose contemplation produces subjectively a consciousness of the harmony of our powers of representation and in which we feel our entire cognitive faculty (understanding and imagination) strengthened: it produces a satisfaction that can also be communicated to others, while nevertheless the existence of the object remains indifferent to us, inasmuch as the object is viewed only as the occasion of our becoming aware of the tendency of talents[t] in us which are elevated above animality. Now, however, the *second* exercise begins its work, namely to draw attention, in the lively presentation of the moral disposition in examples, to the purity of will, first only as a negative perfection of the will insofar as in an action from duty no incentives of inclination have any influence on it as determining grounds; by this, however, the pupil's attention is fixed on the consciousness of his *freedom* and, although this renunciation excites an initial feeling of pain, nevertheless, by its withdrawing the pupil from the constraint of even true needs, there is made known to him at the same time a deliverance from the manifold dissatisfaction in which all those needs entangle him and his mind is made receptive to the feeling of satisfaction from other sources. The heart is freed and relieved of a burden that always secretly presses upon it, when in pure moral resolutions, examples of which are set before him, there is revealed to the human being an inner capacity not otherwise correctly known by himself, the *inner freedom* to release himself from the impetuous importunity of inclinations so that none of them, not even the dearest, has any influence on a resolution for which we are now to make use of our reason. In a case where *I alone* know that the wrong is on my side and, although a free confession of it and an offer of satisfaction are strongly opposed by vanity, selfishness, and even an otherwise not illegitimate antipathy to him whose right I have detracted from, I am neverthe-

---

[s] [Honesty] is praised and starves. (Juvenal *Satire* 1.74).
[t] *Anlage der Talente*

less able to disregard all these considerations; and this includes consciousness of an independence from inclinations and from circumstances and of the possibility of being sufficient to myself, which is salutary to me in general, in other respects as well. And now the law of duty, through the positive worth that observance of it lets us feel, finds easier access through the *respect for ourselves* in the consciousness of our freedom. When this is well established, when a human being dreads nothing more than to find, on self-examination, that he is worthless and contemptible in his own eyes, then every good moral disposition can be grafted onto it, because this is the best, and indeed the sole, guard to prevent ignoble and corrupting impulses from breaking into the mind.

I have intended, here, only to point out the most general maxims of the doctrine of the method of moral cultivation and exercise. Since the variety of duties requires further special determinations for each kind of duty and would thus constitute a lengthy affair, I shall be excused if in a work such as this, which is only preparatory, I go no further than these outlines.

Conclusion

Two things fill the mind with ever new and increasing admiration and reverence,"[u] the more often and more steadily one reflects on them: *the starry heavens above me and the moral law within me.* I do not need to search for them and merely conjecture them as though they were veiled in obscurity or in the transcendent region[v] beyond my horizon; I see them before me and connect them immediately with the consciousness of my existence. The first begins from the place I occupy in the external world of sense and extends the connection in which I stand into an unbounded magnitude with worlds upon worlds and systems of systems, and moreover into the unbounded times of their periodic motion, their beginning and their duration. The second begins from my invisible self, my personality, and presents me in a world which has true infinity but which can be discovered only by the understanding, and I cognize that my connection with that world (and thereby with all those visible worlds as well) is not merely contingent, as in the first case, but universal and necessary. The first view of a countless multitude of worlds annihilates, as it were, my importance as an *animal creature,* which after it has been for a short time provided with vital force (one knows not how) must give back to the planet (a mere speck in the universe) the matter from which it came. The second, on the contrary, infinitely raises my worth as an *intelligence* by my

5:162

---

[u] *Ehrfurcht*
[v] *im Überschwenglichen*

personality, in which the moral law reveals to me a life independent of animality and even of the whole sensible world, at least so far as this may be inferred from the purposive determination[w] of my existence by this law, a determination not restricted to the conditions and boundaries of this life but reaching into the infinite.

But though admiration and respect can indeed excite to inquiry, they cannot supply the want of it. What, then, is to be done in order to enter upon inquiry in a way that is useful and befitting the sublimity of the object? Examples may serve in this for warning but also for imitation. Consideration of the world began from the noblest spectacle that can ever be presented to the human senses and that our understanding can bear to follow in its broad extent, and it ended – in astrology. Morals began with the noblest property of human nature, the development and cultivation of which looked to infinite use, and it ended – in enthusiasm or in superstition. So it is with all crude attempts in which the principal part of the business depends upon the use of reason, which does not come of itself, like the use of the feet, by frequent exercise, especially when it has to do with properties that cannot be directly exhibited in common experience. But after there had come into vogue, though late, the maxim of carefully reflecting beforehand on all the steps that reason proposed to take and not letting it proceed otherwise than on the track of a previously well-considered method, then appraisal of the structure of the universe obtained quite a different direction and along with it an incomparably happier outcome. The fall of a stone, the motion of a sling, resolved into their elements and the forces manifested in them and treated mathematically, produced at last that clear and henceforth unchangeable insight into the structure of the world which, with continued observation, one can hope will always be extended while one need never fear having to retreat.

This example can recommend that we take the same path in treating of the moral predispositions[x] of our nature and can give us hope of a similarly good outcome. We have at hand examples of reason judging morally. We can analyze them into their elementary concepts and, in default of *mathematics*, adopt a procedure similar to that of *chemistry* – the *separation*, by repeated experiments on common human understanding, of the empirical from the rational that may be found in them – and come to know both of them *pure* and what each can accomplish of itself; and in this way we can prevent on the one hand the errors of a still *crude*, unpracticed appraisal and on the other hand (what is far more necessary) the *leaps of genius* by which, as happens with the adepts of the philosopher's stone, without any methodical study or knowledge of nature visionary treasures are promised and true ones are thrown away. In a word, science (critically

---

[w] *zweckmäßigen Bestimmung*
[x] *Anlagen*

sought and methodically directed) is the narrow gate that leads to the *doctrine of wisdom,* if by this is understood not merely what one ought *to do* but what ought to serve *teachers* as a guide to prepare well and clearly the path to wisdom which everyone should travel, and to secure others against taking the wrong way; philosophy must always remain the guardian of this science, and though the public need take no interest[y] in its subtle investigations it has to take an interest in the *doctrines*[z] which, after being worked up in this way, can first be quite clear to it.

[y] *keinen Anteil . . . zu nehmen hat*
[z] *Lehren*

On the common saying: That may be correct in theory, but it is of no use in practice

Introduction

On July 30, 1792, Kant wrote to Johann Erich Biester, editor of the *Berlinische Monatsschrift*, requesting that he return "as soon as possible" a manuscript, the four parts of which were to have appeared in four successive issues of the journal (AK 11:336). The manuscript was eventually published as *Religion within the Boundaries of Mere Reason*. Biester had obtained the Berlin censors' imprimatur for the treatise that became Book I of *Religion* but, despite his appeal from their decision, had been firmly denied permission to publish the treatise that became Book II. As Kant pointed out, the first treatise, without the others, could cut an "odd figure" in the journal. In place of it he offered to provide a strictly "moral" treatise, dealing with Christian Garve's criticism of Kant's moral principle in Part I of his *Essays on Various Topics from Morals, Literature and Social Life* (1792).

The treatise, as Kant first described it, never appeared. Instead, the reply to Garve became Part I of Kant's essay "On the Common Saying: That May Be True in Theory, but It Is of No Use in Practice," which was published in the *Berlinische Monatsschrift* in 1793. Since Garve's criticism was, in part, that Kant's formal principle could not provide a motive for action, it could well be brought under the "common saying." So too could Kant's contention against Hobbes, in Part II, that subjects have noncoercive rights against their sovereign, and his objection, in Part III, to Moses Mendelssohn's view that the human race will never make moral progress. As to why Kant chose to focus on this common saying and extend it, there is no hard evidence. There is, however, room for conjecture, especially with regard to Part II.

Kant's interest in the French Revolution, with its "Declaration of the Rights of Men and of Citizens" in 1789, was, of course, shared by others. Edmund Burke's *Reflections on the Revolution in France* (1790) contemptuously dismissed the subtle "political metaphysics" of theorists who object to any state not established on their principles. On the other hand, August Wilhelm Rehberg's *Examination of the French Revolution*, published at the beginning of 1793, declared that "metaphysics" had brought about the revolution, something never heard of before. In his preliminary notes to the present essay (AK 23:127) Kant mentions the recent charge, never heard of before, that metaphysics can cause a revolution, and questions whether this gives it undeserved honor or undeserved blame, since "men of affairs" have long made it their principle to banish metaphysics to the schools. Kant's contention, here as in Part I, is that metaphysics or a priori principles can be put into practice. Although he denies that subjects have a right to rebel, he insists upon a sovereign's duty to give laws in conformity with their right to freedom, equality, and independence and so to realize a civil society that approaches reason's idea of a civil union. The objection that this cannot be done is based, like Garve's, on the futile attempt to base theory on empirical grounds.

Of the three goals included in the motto "Liberty, Equality, Fraternity," the first two have traditionally claimed the lion's share of attention. Kant's political writings are no exception. In Part III of the present essay, however, Kant takes issue with Moses Mendelssohn's view that the human race will never make moral progress. If this were the case, Kant maintains, we should be unable to fulfill our duty of philanthropy. Although it need only be shown that the moral improvement of the human race is not impossible, another essay, apparently written in 1795, finds evidence of its improvement. Entitled "An Old Question Raised Again: Is the Human Race Constantly Progressing?" it was published in 1798 as Part II of *The Conflict of the Faculties*. The next treatise in the present volume, *Toward Perpetual Peace*, returns to the political questions raised with regard to the "common saying."

*On the common saying:
That may be correct in theory,
but it is of no use in practice*

A sum of rules, even of practical rules, is called *theory* if those rules are thought as principles having a certain generality,[a] so that abstraction is made from a multitude of conditions that yet have a necessary influence on their application. Conversely, not every doing[b] is called *practice*, but only that effecting of an end which is thought as the observance of certain principles of procedure represented in their generality.

It is obvious that between theory and practice there is required, besides, a middle term connecting them and providing a transition from one to the other, no matter how complete a theory may be; for, to a concept of the understanding, which contains a rule, must be added an act of judgment by which a practitioner distinguishes whether or not something is a case of the rule; and since judgment cannot always be given yet another rule by which to direct its subsumption (for this would go on to infinity), there can be theoreticians who can never in their lives become practical because they are lacking in judgment, for example, physicians or jurists who did well during their schooling but who are at a loss when they have to give an expert opinion. But even where this natural talent is present there can still be a deficiency in premises, that is, a theory can be incomplete and can, perhaps, be supplemented only by engaging in further experiments and experiences, from which the recently schooled physician, agriculturalist, or economist can and should abstract new rules for himself and make his theory complete. In such cases it was not the fault of theory if it was of little use in practice, but rather of there having been *not enough* theory, which the man in question should have learned from experience and which is true theory even if he is not in a position to state it himself and, as a teacher, set it forth systematically in general propositions, and so can make no claim to the title of theoretical physician, agriculturalist and the like. Thus no one can pretend to be practically proficient in a science and yet scorn theory without declaring that he is an ignoramus in his field, inasmuch as he believes that by groping about in experiments and experiences, without putting together certain principles (which really constitute what is called theory) and without having thought out some whole relevant to his business[c] (which, if one proceeds methodically in it, is called a system), he can get further than theory could take him.

Yet it is easier to put up with an ignorant man who declares that theory is unnecessary and dispensable in his supposed practice than with a would-be expert who concedes it and its value in schools (perhaps only to exercise the mind) but at the same time maintains that matters are quite different in practice; that when one goes from school into the world one becomes aware that one has been pursuing empty ideals and philosophic

---

[a] *Allgemeinheit*
[b] *Hantirung*
[c] *ein Ganzes . . . über sein Geschäft*

dreams; in short, that what sounds good in theory has no validity for practice. (This is often expressed as, this or that proposition does indeed hold *in thesi*, but not *in hypothesi*.) Now if an empirical engineer tried to disparage general mechanics, or an artilleryman the mathematical doctrine of ballistics, by saying that whereas the theory of it is nicely thought out it is not valid in practice since, when it comes to application, experience yields quite different results than theory, one would merely laugh at him (for, if the theory of friction were added to the first and the theory of the resistance of air to the second, hence if only still more theory were added, these would accord very well with experience). However, it is quite different with a theory having to do with objects of intuition than with a theory in which objects are represented only by means of concepts (with objects of mathematics and objects of philosophy); the latter objects could perhaps be *thought* quite well and irreproachably (on the part of reason), but perhaps they could not be *given* at all but might well be mere empty ideas, of which either no use at all would be made in practice or even a use that would be detrimental to it. That common saying could, therefore, still be correct in such cases.

But in a theory that is based on the *concept of duty*, concern about the empty ideality of this concept quite disappears. For it would not be a duty to aim at a certain effect of our will if this effect were not also possible in experience (whether it be thought as completed or as always approaching completion); and it is theory of this kind only that is at issue in the present treatise. For, to the scandal of philosophy, it is not uncommonly alleged of this theory that what may be correct in it is yet invalid in practice; and this is said in a lofty, disdainful tone, full of the presumption of wanting to reform reason by experience even in that in which reason puts its highest honor, and in a wisdom that can see farther and more clearly with its dim moles' eyes fixed on experience than with the eyes belonging to a being that was made to stand erect and look at the heavens.

This maxim, which has become very common in our times, so full of talk and empty of deeds, does the greatest harm when it has to do with something moral (duties of virtue or duties of right). For here it is a matter of the canon of reason (in the practical), where the worth of practice rests entirely on its conformity with the theory underlying it, and all is lost if the empirical and hence contingent conditions of carrying out the law are made conditions of the law itself, so that a practice calculated with reference to an outcome probable in accordance with *previous* experience is given authority to control a self-sufficient theory.

I divide this treatise according to the three different standpoints from which the worthy gentleman[1] who so boldly disparages theories and systems usually appraises his objects, and so in his three capacities[d] 1) as a *private*

---

[d] *in dreifacher Qualität*

individual who is still a *man of affairs*, 2) as a *statesman*, 3) as a *man of the world* (or citizen of the world generally). These three persons are at one in attacking the *academic*, who works on theory on behalf of them all and for their benefit; since they fancy that they understand matters better than he, they seek to banish him to his school *(illa se iactet in aula!),*[e] as a scholar who, spoiled for practice, only stands in the way of their experienced wisdom.

We shall therefore present the relation of theory to practice in three parts: *first* in *morals*[f] generally (with a view to the well-being[g] of every human being), *second* in *politics* (with reference to the well-being of *states*), *third* from a *cosmopolitan* perspective (with a view to the well-being of the *human race* as a whole and insofar as it is conceived as progressing toward its well-being in the series of generations of all future times). The titles of the parts will, on grounds arising from the treatise itself, be expressed as the relation of theory to practice in *morals*, in the *right of a state*, and in the *right of nations*.

8:278

I.
ON THE RELATION OF THEORY OF PRACTICE IN MORALS GENERALLY

(In reply to some objections by Professor Garve*)

Before I come to the real point of controversy over what, in the use of one and the same concept, may be valid in theory only or in practice, I must compare my theory, as I have elsewhere represented it, with the representation of it that Garve gives, in order to see in advance whether we even understand each other.

A. I explained morals provisionally as the introduction to a science that teaches, not how we are to become happy, but how we are to become worthy of happiness.† In doing so I did not fail to remark that the human

---

Versuche über verschiedne Gegenstände aus der Moral und Literatur, von Ch. Garve. Erster Theil, S. 111 bis 116. [Essays on Various Topics from Morals and Literature, by Christian Garve, Part I, pp. 111–16].[2] I call this worthy man's contesting of my propositions *objections* to matters in which (as I hope) he wishes to reach agreement with me, not attacks, which, as disparaging assertions, should provoke a defense; this is not the place to defend them nor am I inclined to do so here.

†Worthiness to be happy is that quality of a person, based upon the subject's own will, such that a reason giving universal laws (for nature as well as for free will) would harmonize with all the ends of this person. It is therefore quite different from skill in acquiring some happiness.[h] For he is not even worthy of this skill and of the talents nature has lent him for it if he has a will which does not harmonize with that will which alone is adapted to a universal legislation of reason and which cannot be included in it (i.e., which conflicts with morality).

[e] Let him lord it there in his own court! Virgil *Aeneid* 1.140.

[f] *Moral.* Although I have translated *Moral* throughout this essay as "morals," in some passages Kant uses it in the sense of "moral philosophy."

[g] *das Wohl*

[h] *ein Glück*

being is not thereby required to *renounce* his natural end, happiness, when it is a matter of complying with his duty; for that he cannot do, just as no finite rational being whatever can; instead, he must *abstract* altogether from this consideration when the command of duty arises; he must on no account make it the *condition* of his compliance with the law prescribed to him by reason; indeed he must, as far as is possible for him, strive to become aware that no *incentive* derived from that gets mixed, unnoticed, into the determination of duty, and this is effected by his representing duty as connected with the sacrifices its observance (virtue) costs us rather than with the advantages it yields us, so as to represent the command of duty in all its authority, as requiring unconditional obedience, sufficient in itself and in need of no other influences.

a. Now, the way Garve expresses this proposition of mine is that "I had maintained that observance of the moral law, without any regard for happiness at all, is the *sole final end* for the human being, that is must be considered the creator's sole end." (According to my theory, neither human morality by itself nor human happiness by itself is the creator's sole end, but rather the highest good possible in the world, which consists of the union and harmony of the two.)

B. I remarked further that this concept of duty does not have to be grounded on any particular end but rather *introduces* another end for the human being's will, namely to work to the best of one's ability[i] toward the *highest good* possible in the world (universal happiness combined with and in conformity with the purest morality throughout the world), which, since it is within our control from one quarter but not from both taken together, exacts from reason belief, *for practical purposes*, in a moral ruler of the world and in a future life. It is not as if the universal concept of duty first gets "support and stability" only on the presupposition of both, that is, gets a sure basis and the requisite strength of an *incentive*, but rather that only in that ideal of pure reason does it also get an *object*.* For, in itself

---

*The need to assume, as the final end of all things, a good that is the *highest good* in the world and also possible through our cooperation is a need [arising] not from a deficiency in moral incentives but from a deficiency in the external relations within which alone an object as end in itself (as moral *final end*) can be produced in conformity with these incentives. For without some end there can be no *will*, although, if it is a question only of lawful necessitation of actions, one must abstract from any end and the law alone constitutes its determining ground. But not every end is moral (e.g., that of one's own happiness is not), but this must rather be an unselfish one; and the need for a final end assigned by pure reason and comprehending the whole of all ends under one principle (a world as the highest good and possible through our cooperation) is a need of an unselfish will *extending* itself beyond observance of the formal law to production of an object (the highest good). This is a special kind of determination of the will, namely through the idea of the whole of all ends, the basis of which is that *if* we stand in certain moral relations to things in the world we must everywhere obey the moral law, and beyond this there is added the duty to bring it about as

[i] *nach allem Vermögen*

duty is nothing other than the *limitations* of the will to the condition of a giving of universal law possible through a maxim adopted, whatever the object of the will or the end may be (thus happiness as well), from which, as well as from every end one may have, we here abstract altogether. In the question of the *principle* of morals the doctrine of the *highest good*, as the final end of a will determined by this doctrine and conformed with its laws, can be completely passed over and set aside (as episodic); and it will also become apparent in what follows, when it comes to the real point of controversy, that this is not taken into consideration at all but only morals in general.

b. Garve expresses this proposition as follows: "that the virtuous person can never lose sight of that perspective (his own happiness) nor may he do so, since otherwise he would lose altogether passage into the invisible world, to conviction of the existence of God and of immortality, which is yet, according to this theory, absolutely necessary *to give the moral system support and stability*"; and he then concludes by briefly summing up the assertions he attributes to me: "The virtuous person, according to those principles, strives unceasingly to be worthy of happiness but never, *insofar as* he is truly virtuous, to be happy." (The words *insofar as* create an ambiguity here, which must be settled at the outset. They can mean, *in the act* by which, as virtuous he subjects himself to his duty, in which case this proposition is perfectly in accord with my theory. Or they can mean that just by his being virtuous generally, and so even when it is not a matter of duty and there would be no conflict with it, a virtuous person should still have no regard at all for happiness; and this quite contradicts my assertions.)

These objections are therefore nothing but misunderstandings (for I do not care to take them as misrepresentations), and their possibility would have to be astonishing, did not the human propensity to follow one's accustomed course of thought even in appraising the thoughts of others, and thus to carry the former over into the latter, adequately explain such a phenomenon.

Upon this polemical treatment of the above moral principle there now

8:281

---

far as we can *that* such a relation (a world in keeping with the moral highest ends) exists. In this the human being thinks of himself by analogy with the Deity who, although subjectively in need of no external thing, still cannot be thought to shut himself up within himself but rather to be determined to produce the highest good beyond himself just by his consciousness of his complete self-sufficiency; and this necessity in the supreme being (which in the human being is a duty) can be represented *by us* only as a moral need. With the human being too, accordingly, the incentive which is present in the idea of the highest good possible in the world by his cooperation is not his own happiness thereby intended but only this idea as end in itself, and hence compliance with it as duty. For it contains no prospect of happiness absolutely, but only of a proportion between it and the worthiness of a subject, whatever that may be. But a determination of will which limits itself and its aim of belonging to such a whole to this condition is *not selfish*.

follows a dogmatic assertion of the opposite. Garve concludes analytically as follows: "In the ordering of *concepts*, perception and distinction of states,[j] whereby one of them is given *preference* over the other, must precede the choice[k] of one of them and hence the determination in advance[l] of a certain end. But a state that a being endowed with consciousness of himself and of his state *prefers* to other ways of being, when this state is present and perceived by him, is a *good* state; and a series of such good states is the most general concept expressed by the word *happiness*." Further, "A law supposes motives, while motives suppose an already perceived distinction of a worse state from a better one. This perceived distinction is the element of the concept of happiness, and so forth." Further, "*From happiness* in the most general sense of the word *arises* the motives *for every effort* and so too for observance of the moral law. I must first know in general that something is good before I can ask whether fulfillment of moral duties belongs under the heading of the good; the human being must have an *incentive*, which puts him in motion, *before* one can set him a *goal*,* toward which this motion is to be directed."

This argument is nothing more than a play upon the ambiguity of the word *the good;* for this [can be taken to mean] either what is good in itself and unconditionally, as opposed to what is evil in itself, or else what is only conditionally good, as compared with what is a lesser or greater good, since the state chosen[m] in the latter case can be a state that is relatively better but in itself evil. The maxim of unconditional observance of a categorically commanding law of free choice[n] (i.e., of duty), without having regard for any end at all put at its basis, is essentially different, that is, different *in kind*, from the maxim in which the motive for acting in a certain way is to pursue the end assigned us by nature itself (which is called happiness in general). For the first maxim is in itself good, the second by no means; in case of a collision with duty it can be quite evil. On the other hand, if a certain end is laid down as a basis, so that no law commands unconditionally (but only under the condition of this end), then two opposing actions can both be conditionally good but one better

---

*This is precisely what I insist upon. The incentive which the human being can have before a goal (end) is set for him can obviously be nothing other than the law itself through the respect that it inspires (without its being determined what end one may have and may attain by complying with it). For the law with respect to what is formal in choice is indeed all that remains when I have left out of consideration the matter of choice (the goal, as Garve calls it).

[j] *Zustande.* In Part I of this essay, where there is no need to distinguish *Zustand* from *Staat*, *Zustand* in translated as "state."
[k] *Wahl*
[l] *Vorausbestimmung*
[m] *der Zustand der Wahl*
[n] *der freien Willkür*

than the other (the latter of which could then be called relatively evil); for they are different from each other not *in kind* but merely *in degree*. And this is how it is with all actions the motive of which is not the unconditional law of reason (duty) but an end that we have by choice*ᵒ* made their basis; for this belongs to the sum of all ends the attainment of which is called happiness, and one action can contribute more, another less to my happiness and so be better or worse than the other. But the *preference* of one state of determination of the will to another is merely an act of freedom *(res merae facultatis,*³ as jurists say), in regard to which no account at all is taken of whether this (determination of the will) is good or evil in itself, and is thus indifferent with respect to both.

A state of being bound up with a certain *given end* that I prefer to any other *of the same kind* is a relatively better state, namely in the sphere of happiness (which is recognized *by reason* as *good* only conditionally, so far as one is worthy of it). But that state in which I am aware that, in case of a collision of certain of my ends with the moral law of duty, I prefer the latter is not merely a better state but the only one that is good in itself; it is a good from another sphere altogether, where ends that may present themselves to me (and so too their sum, happiness) are not taken into consideration at all and where it is not the matter of choice (an object put at its basis) but the mere form of the universal lawfulness of its maxims that constitutes its determining ground. Thus it can by no means be said that I account to my happiness any state that I *prefer* to be in than any other kind. For I must first be sure that I am not acting against my duty; only afterwards am I permitted to look around for happiness, to the extent that I can unite the state of being happy with that morally (not naturally) good state of mine.*

Certainly, the will must have *motives;* but these are not certain objects proposed as ends related to *natural feeling*, but nothing other than the unconditional *law* itself; and the will's receptivity to finding itself subject to the law as unconditional necessitation is called *moral feeling*, which is therefore not the cause but the effect of the determination of the will, and

8:283

---

*Happiness contains all (and also not more than) that which nature provides us; but virtue contains what no one other than the human being can give himself or take away from himself. If someone wanted to retort that by deviating from the latter a human being can at least bring upon himself reproach and purely moral self-censure and hence dissatisfaction, so that he can make himself unhappy, that may certainly be granted. But only a virtuous man or one who is on his way to being virtuous is susceptible to*ᵖ* this purely moral dissatisfaction (not from disadvantageous results of his action but from its unlawfulness itself). His dissatisfaction is consequently not the cause but only the effect of his being virtuous; and the motive for being virtuous could not be derived from such unhappiness (if one wants to give this name to the pain resulting from a misdeed).

ᵒ willkürlich
ᵖ fähig

we would not have the least perception of it within ourselves if that necessitation were not already present within us. Thus the old refrain, that this feeling and hence a pleasure that we make an end for ourselves is the first cause of the determination of the will, so that happiness (to which it belongs as an element) still constitutes the basis of all objective necessity in acting and hence of all obligation, is a piece of sophistical *trifling*.[q] That is to say, if one cannot cease asking, even after a cause has been cited for a certain effect, one finally makes the effect its own cause.

I now come to the point that really concerns us here, namely to illustrate with examples and to test the supposed conflicting interests of theory and of practice in philosophy. Garve gives the best example of it in his treatise cited above. He says first (speaking of the distinction I find between a doctrine of how we are to become *happy* and one of how we are to become *worthy* of happiness): "For my own part, I confess that I very well conceive this division of ideas in my *head*, but that I do not find this division of wishes and strivings in my *heart*, and that it is even inconceivable to me how any one can become aware of having detached himself altogether from his desire for happiness and hence aware of having performed his duty quite unselfishly."

I shall first reply to the latter. I readily grant that no one can become aware with certainty of *having performed his duty* quite unselfishly; for that belongs to inner experience, and to this consciousness of his state of soul there would have to belong a perfectly clear representation of all the associated representations[r] and considerations attached to the concept of duty by imagination, habit, and inclination, which cannot be required in any case; and, in general, the nonexistence of something (and so too of a covertly thought advantage) cannot be an object of experience. But that the human being *ought to perform* his duty quite unselfishly and that he *must* altogether separate his craving for happiness from the concept of duty, in order to have this concept quite pure: of that he is aware with the utmost clarity or, should he believe that he is not, it can be required of him that he be so, as far as he can; for the true worth of morality is to be found precisely in this purity, and he must therefore also be capable of it. Perhaps no one has ever performed quite unselfishly (without admixture of other incentives) the duty he cognizes and also reveres; perhaps no one will ever succeed in doing so, however hard he tries. But insofar as, in examining himself most carefully, he can perceive not only no such cooperating motive but instead self-denial with respect to many motives opposing the idea of duty, he can become aware of a maxim of striving for such purity; that he is capable of, and that is also sufficient for his observance of duty. On the other hand, to make it his maxim to foster the influence of

---

[q] *unter die vernünftelnden Tändelein gehört*
[r] *Nebenvorstellungen*

such motives, on the pretext that human nature does not admit of such purity (though this, again, he cannot assert with certainty) is the death of all morality.

As for Garve's avowal, just cited, that he does not find such a division (strictly speaking, separation) in his *heart*, I have no hesitation in contradicting his self-accusation outright and in championing his heart against his head. He, a man of integrity, has actually *found* this separation in his heart every time (in his determination of will), only it would not be reconciled in his head* – for the sake of speculation and of comprehending what is incomprehensible (inexplicable), namely the possibility of categorical imperatives (such as those of duty are) – with the usual principles of psychological explanation (all of which have the mechanism of natural necessity as their basis).

But I must loudly and zealously contradict Garve when he concludes by saying: "Such fine distinctions among ideas already become *obscure* in *reflecting* upon particular objects; but they *disappear completely* when it comes to *acting*, when they are to be applied to desires and purposes. The more simple, rapid and *stripped of clear representations* is the step by which we pass from considering motives to actually acting, so much the less is it possible to cognize precisely and surely the determinate weight that each motive contributed to guiding the step in this and in no other way."

The concept of duty in its complete purity is not only incomparably simpler, clearer and, for practical use, more readily grasped and more natural to everyone than any motive derived from happiness, or mixed with it and with regard for it (which always requires much art[s] and reflection); it is also, even in the judgment of the most common human reason – if only the concept is presented in its purity to a human will, separated from and even in opposition to the latter – far *more powerful*, forceful, and promising of results than all motives borrowed from the latter, selfish principle. Take the case, for example, that someone is holding in trust something belonging to another *(depositum)*, the owner of which has died, and that the owner's heirs know nothing about it and can

---

*Professor Garve (in his notes to Cicero's book on duties [*De Officiis*], 1783 edition, p. 69) makes the following admission, notable and worthy of his acuteness: "Freedom, according to his innermost conviction, will always remain unresolved and will never be explained." A proof of its reality can absolutely not be found either in an immediate or in a mediate experience; and yet one also cannot accept it without any proof. Since a proof of its reality cannot be derived from merely theoretical grounds (for these would have to be sought in experience) and must therefore be derived from practical rational propositions only – but not from technically practical ones (since these would in turn require experiential grounds) – and can consequently be derived only from morally practical propositions, one has to wonder why Garve did not have recourse to the concept of freedom, so as at least to save the possibility of such imperatives.

[s] *Kunst*

never come to know of it. We submit this case even to a child some eight or nine years old, and add that the holder of this deposit suffers at this very time (through no fault of his own) a complete reversal of his fortune and sees around him a miserable family of wife and children oppressed by want that he could relieve in a moment by appropriating this deposit; we add further that he is philanthropic and beneficent whereas those heirs are wealthy, hard-hearted and, besides, so thoroughly given to luxury and wastefulness that adding anything to their resources would be equivalent to throwing it into the sea. And we now ask whether, under such circumstances, it can be considered permissible for him to put this deposit to his own use. The one being questioned will undoubtedly answer, No! and, in place of any grounds, will be able to say only, *It is wrong!* – that is, it conflicts with duty. Nothing is clearer than this, though it is surely not clear that the trustee would be furthering his own *happiness* by giving up the deposit. For, if he expected to determine his decision in view of the latter he could, for example, think as follows: "If you give up the other's goods you have to the true owners without being called upon to do so, they will presumably reward you for your honesty; or if that does not happen, you will acquire a good reputation at large, which can be very lucrative. But all this is most uncertain. Many doubts also arise about the opposite course: If you embezzle the deposit so as to get out of your depressed circumstances at one stroke, by making quick use of it you will incur suspicion as to how and by what means you had so soon bettered your circumstances; but if you put it to work slowly, your poverty will meanwhile increase so much it would come to be beyond remedy." By the maxim of happiness a will thus vacillates between its incentives as to what it should decide upon; for it looks to the outcome and this is highly uncertain; a good head is required to find a way out of the crush of arguments and counterarguments without cheating oneself in the total reckoning. On the other hand, if he asks himself what his duty is in this matter, he is not at all perplexed about what answer to give but certain on the spot what he has to do. He even feels, if the concept of duty counts for something with him, a revulsion merely at calculating the advantages he could gain by transgressing it, as if he still had a choice[1] in the matter.

That these distinctions (which, as we have just shown, are not so fine as Garve thinks but are inscribed on the human soul in the broadest and most legible characters), as he says, *disappear altogether when it comes to acting* thus contradicts even his own experience. Admittedly, it does not contradict the experience that the *history* of maxims drawn from the one or the other principle presents; such experience proves, regrettably, that maxims for the most part flow from the latter principle (of selfishness);

---

[1] *Wahl*

but it does contradict the experience, which can only be inward,*a* that no idea so elevates the human mind and animates it even to inspiration as that of a pure moral disposition, revering duty above all else, struggling with the countless ills of life and even with its most seductive allurements and yet overcoming them (as we may rightly assume that one is capable of doing). That the human being is aware that he can do this because he ought to discloses within him a depth of divine predispositions and lets him feel, as it were, a holy awe at the greatness and sublimity of his true vocation. And if this attention were drawn to it more often and he became used to ridding virtue completely of all the rich booty of advantages to be amassed through the observance of duty and to representing it in all its purity; if it became a principle of private and public instruction always to make use of this (a method of inculcating duties that has almost always been neglected), human morality would soon be better off. That historical experience up to now has still not proved the success of the doctrine of virtue may well be the fault of just the false presupposition that the incentive derived from the idea of duty in itself is much too fine for the common concept whereas the coarser incentive drawn from certain advantages to be expected, in this world or even in a future one, from compliance with the law (without regard for the law itself as the incentive) would work more powerfully on the mind, and that up to now it has been made a principle of education and homiletics to give preference to the aspiration for happiness over that which reason makes the supreme condition of this, namely worthiness to be happy. For *precepts* as to how one can make oneself happy or at least avoid what is disadvantageous are not *commands.* They do not bind anyone absolutely; having been warned, one may choose*v* what he thinks good, if he is prepared to suffer the consequences. He has no cause to regard as punishments such troubles as might issue from his failure to follow the advice he was given; for punishments happen only to a will that is free but contrary to the law; nature and inclination, however, cannot give laws to freedom. It is quite different with the idea of duty, someone's transgression of which, even without his considering the disadvantages to himself resulting from it, works immediately upon his mind and makes him reprehensible and punishable in his own eyes.

8:288

Here, then, is a clear proof that everything in moral philosophy that is correct for theory must also hold for practice. Everyone in his capacity as a human being, a being subjected by his own reason to certain duties, is accordingly a *man of affairs;* and since, as a man, he never outgrows the school of wisdom, he cannot with proud contempt, as someone supposedly better instructed by experience about what a human being is and what can be required of him, send the adherent of theory back to school.

a innerlich
v wählen

8:289 For all this experience does not help him at all to escape the precept of theory, but at most only helps him to learn how theory could be better and more generally put to work, after one has adopted it into one's principles; but we are not speaking here of such pragmatic skill but only of principles.

II.
ON THE RELATION OF THEORY TO PRACTICE IN THE RIGHT OF A STATE

(Against Hobbes)

Among all the contracts by which a multitude of people unites into a society *(pactum sociale)*, the contract establishing a *civil constitution* among them *(pactum unionis civilis)* is of such a distinctive kind that, although with respect to its *application*[w] it has much in common with any other (which is likewise directed to some discretionary[x] end to be promoted by common effort), it is essentially different from every other in the principle of its institution *(constitutionis civilis)*. The union of many for some (common) end (that all of them *have*) is to be found in any social contract; but that union which is in itself an end (that each *ought to have*) and which is therefore the unconditional and first duty in any external relation of people in general, who cannot help mutually affecting one another, is to be found in a society only insofar as it is in the civil condition,[y] that is, constitutes a commonwealth. Now the end that, in such an external relation, is in itself duty and even the supreme formal condition[z] *(conditio sine qua non)* of all other external duties is the *right* of human beings under *public coercive laws*, by which what belongs to each can be determined for him and secured against encroachment by any other.

But the concept of an external right as such proceeds entirely from the concept of *freedom* in the external relation of people to one another and has nothing at all to do with the end that all of them naturally have (their aim of happiness) and with the prescribing of means for attaining it; hence too the latter absolutely must not intrude in the laws of the former as their

8:290 determining ground. *Right* is the limitation of the freedom of each to the condition of its harmony with the freedom of everyone insofar as this is possible in accordance with a universal law; and *public* right is the sum of *external laws* which make such a thoroughgoing harmony possible. Now, since any limitation of freedom through another's choice[a] is called coercion, it follows that a civil constitution is a relation of *free* human beings

---

[w] *Ausführung*
[x] *beliebigen*
[y] *Zustand*
[z] *Bedingung*
[a] *Willkür*

who (without prejudice to their freedom within the whole of their union with one another) are nevertheless subject to coercive laws; for reason itself wills it so, and indeed pure reason giving laws a priori, which has no regard for any empirical ends (all of which are comprehended under the general name happiness); for, since people differ in their thinking about happiness and how each would have it constituted, their wills with respect to it cannot be brought under any common principle and so under any external law harmonizing with everyone's freedom.

Thus the civil condition, regarded merely as a rightful condition, is based a priori on the following principles:

1. The *freedom* of every member of the society as a human being.
2. His *equality* with every other as a *subject*.
3. The *independence* of every member of a commonwealth as a *citizen*.

These principles are not so much laws given by a state already established as rather principles in accordance with which alone the establishment of a state is possible in conformity with pure rational principles of external human right. Accordingly,

1. As for the *freedom* [of every member of a state] as a human being I express its principle for the constitution of a commonwealth in the following formula: No one can coerce me to be happy in his way (as he thinks of the welfare*b* of other human beings); instead, each may seek his happiness in the way that seems good to him, provided he does not infringe upon that freedom of others to strive for a like end which can coexist with the freedom of everyone in accordance with a possible universal law (i.e., does not infringe upon this right of another). A government established on the principle of benevolence toward the people like that of a *father* toward his children – that is, a *paternalistic government (imperium paternale)*, in which the subjects, like minor children who cannot distinguish between what is truly useful or harmful to them, are constrained to behave only passively, so as to wait only upon the judgment of the head of state as to how they *should be* happy and, as for his also willing their happiness, only upon his kindness – is the greatest *despotism* thinkable (a constitution that abrogates all the freedom of the subjects, who in that case have no rights at all). Not a *paternalistic* but a *patriotic* government *(imperium non paternale, sed patrioticum)* is the only one that can be thought for human beings, who are capable*c* of rights, and also with reference to the benevolence of the ruler. In a *patriotic* way of thinking everyone in a state (its head not excepted) regards the commonwealth as the maternal womb, or the country as the paternal land, from which and on which he has arisen and which he must also leave behind as a cherished pledge, only so as to consider himself

8:291

b *Wohlsein*
c *fähig*

authorized to protect its rights by laws of the common will but not to subject the use of it to his unconditional discretion. This right of freedom belongs to him, a member of a commonwealth, as a human being namely insofar as he is a being that is, as such, capable of rights.

2. The *equality* [of each member of a state] as a subject, the formula of which can read: Each member of a commonwealth has coercive rights against every other, the only exception being the head of state (since he is not a member of the commonwealth but its creator or preserver), who alone is authorized to coerce without himself being subject to a coercive law. But whoever is *subject* to laws[d] is a subject[e] within a state and is thus subjected[f] to coercive right equally with all the other members of the commonwealth; only one (physical or moral person), the head of state, by whom alone any rightful coercion can be exercised, is excepted. For if he could also be coerced he would not be the head of state and the sequence of subordination would ascend to infinity. But if there were two of them (uncoercible persons), neither would be subject to coercive laws and one could do the other no wrong; and that is impossible.

But this thoroughgoing equality of individuals within a state, as its subjects, it quite consistent with the greatest inequality in terms of the quantity and degree of their possessions, whether in physical or mental superiority over others or in external goods[g] and in rights generally (of which there can be many) relatively to others; thus the welfare of one is very much dependent upon the will of another (that of the poor on the rich); thus one must obey (as a child its elders or a wife her husband) and the other directs; thus one serves (a day laborer) and the other pays him, and so forth. But *in terms of right* (which, as the expression of the general will, can be only one and which concerns the form of what is laid down as right[h] not the matter or the object in which I have a right), they are nevertheless all equal to one another as subjects; for, no one of them can coerce any other except through public law (and its executor, the head of state), through which every other also resists him in like measure; but no one can lose this authorization to coerce (and so to have a right against others) except by his own crime, and he cannot give it away of his own accord, that is, by a contract, and so bring it about by a rightful action[i] that he has no rights but only duties; for he would thereby deprive himself of the right to make a contract and thus the contract would nullify itself.

From this idea of the equality of human beings as subjects within a

---

[d] *unter Gesetzen steht*
[e] *Untertan*
[f] *unterworfen*
[g] *Glücksgütern*
[h] *Rechtens*
[i] *rechtliche Handlung*

commonwealth there also issues the following formula: Every member of a commonwealth must be allowed to attain any level of rank within it (that can belong to a subject) to which his talent, his industry and his luck can take him; and his fellow subjects may not stand in his way by means of a *hereditary* prerogative (privileges [reserved] for a certain rank), so as to keep him and his descendants forever beneath the rank.

For all right consists merely in the limitation of the freedom of every other to the condition[j] that it can coexist with my freedom in accordance with a universal law, and public right (within a commonwealth) is merely the condition[k] of an actual legislation in conformity with this principle and joined with power, by virtue of which all those belonging to a people as subjects are in a rightful condition *(status iuridicus)* as such, namely a condition of equality of action and reaction of a choice limiting one another[l] in conformity with a universal law of freedom (which is called the civil condition); hence the *innate right* of each in this condition (i.e., his right prior to any rightful deed) is altogether *equal* with respect to the authorization to coerce every other to remain always within the bounds of the consistency of the use of his freedom with mine. Now since birth is not a *deed* of the one who is born, he cannot incur by it any inequality of rightful condition and any other subjection to coercive laws than merely that which is common to him along with all others, as subjects of the sole supreme legislative power; hence there can be no innate prerogative of one member of a commonwealth over another as fellow subjects, and no one can bequeath to his descendants the prerogative of the *rank* which he has within a commonwealth and so also cannot, as if qualified by birth for the ruling rank, coercively prevent others from attaining by their own merit the higher levels of subordination (of *superior* and *inferior*, in which no one, however, is *imperans* and the other *subiectus*). He may bequeath anything else, whatever is a thing (not pertaining to personality) and can be acquired as property and also alienated by him, and so in a series of generations produce a considerable inequality of financial circumstances among the members of a commonwealth (of hireling and hirer, landowners[m] and agricultural laborers, and so forth); but he may not prevent their being authorized to raise themselves to like circumstances if their talent, their industry, and their luck make this possible for them. For otherwise he could coerce without others in turn being able to coerce him by their reaction, and would rise above the level of a fellow subject. Again, no one living in a rightful condition of a commonwealth can fall from this equality otherwise than by his own crime, never by a contract or by military force

8:293

---

[j] *Bedingung*
[k] *Zustand*
[l] *einer . . . einander einschränkenden Willkür*
[m] *Gutseigentümers*

(occupatio bellica); for he cannot, by means of any rightful deed (whether his own or another's) cease to be in rightful possession of himself*ⁿ* and enter the class of domestic animals, which are used for any service as one wants and are kept in it without their consent as long as one wants, even though with the restriction (sometimes sanctioned by religion, as with the Indians) not to maim or kill them. He can be considered happy*ᵒ* in that condition provided he is aware that, if he does not reach the same level as others, the fault lies only in himself ([his lack of] ability or earnest will) or in circumstances for which he cannot blame any other, but not in the irresistible will of others who, as his fellow subjects in this condition, have no advantage over him as far as right is concerned.*

3. The *independence* (*sibisufficientia*) of a member of a state as a *citizen*, that is, as a colegislator. As for legislation itself, it is not the case that all who are free and equal under already existing public laws are to be held equal with regard to the right to give these laws. Those who are not qualified*ᵗ* for this right are still, as members of the commonwealth, subject to compliance with these laws and thereby enjoy protection in accordance with them, not, however, as *citizens* but as *cobeneficiaries of this protection.*ᵘ All right, that is to say, depends upon laws. But a public law that determines for everyone what is to be rightfully permitted or forbidden him is

---

*If we want to connect with the word *gracious* a determinate concept (distinct from kind, beneficent, protective and the like), it can be assigned only to him against whom there is *no coercive* right. Hence only the head of *public administration*ᵖ who brings about and bestows whatever good is possible in accordance with public laws (for the *sovereign*, which gives laws, is, as it were invisible; it is the personified law itself, not its agent) can be entitled *gracious lord*, as the only one against whom there is no coercive right. So even in an aristocracy, as in Venice, for example, the *Senate* is the only gracious lord; all the nobles who comprise it, not excluding the *Doge* himself, are subjects (for only the *Grand Council* is the sovereign) and, as far as the exercise of right*ᑫ* is concerned, are equal to all others, that is a coercive right against each of them belongs to a subject. Princes (i.e., persons to whom there belongs a hereditary right to government) are, however, called gracious lords (by courtly etiquette, *par courtoisie*) only prospectively and because of that claim; but in terms of their status of possession*ʳ* they are still fellow subjects, and even the least of their servants must have a coercive right against them by means of the head of state. Thus there can be no more than a single gracious lord within a state. But as for gracious (strictly speaking, distinguished) ladies, they can be regarded as justified [in their claim to] this title by their *rank* together with their *sex* (thus only against the *male sex*), and this by virtue of a refinement of manners*ˢ* (called gallantry) by which the male sex believes that it honors itself in proportion as it grants the fair sex precedence over itself.

ⁿ *Eigner seiner selbst zu sein*
ᵒ *für glücklich*
ᵖ *Staatsverwaltung*
ᑫ *Rechtsausübung*
ʳ *Besitzstand*
ˢ *Sitten*
ᵗ *fähig*
ᵘ *Schutzgenossen*

the act of a public will, from which all right proceeds and which must therefore itself be incapable of doing wrong to anyone. But this is possible through no other will than that of the entire people (since all decide about all, hence each about himself); for it is only to oneself that one can never do wrong. But if it is another, then the mere will of one distinct from him can decide nothing about him that could not be wrong, and the law of this will would, accordingly, require yet another law that would limit its legislation; hence no particular will can be legislative for a commonwealth. (Strictly speaking, the concepts of external freedom, equality, and the *unity* of the will of *all* come together in order to constitute this concept, and if the first two are taken together, independence is the condition of the last where voting is required.)[v] This basic law, which can arise only from the general (united) will of the people, is called the *original contract.*

He who has the right to vote in this legislation is called a *citizen* (*citoyen*, i.e., *citizen of a state*, not of a town, *bourgeois*). The quality requisite to this, apart from the *natural* one (of not being a child or a woman), is only that of *being one's own master (sui iuris)*, hence having some *property* (and any art, craft, fine art, or science can be counted as property) that supports him – that is, if he must acquire from others in order to live, he does so only by *alienating* what *is his** and not by giving others permission to make use of his powers – and hence [the requisite quality is] that, in the strict sense of the word, he *serves* no one other than the commonwealth. Here craftsmen and large (or small) landowners are all equal, namely each is entitled to only one vote. For in regard to the latter – without even raising the question, how it could with right have come about that someone received as his own more land than he could himself make use of with his own hands (for acquisition by military seizure is not first acquisition), and how it came about that many human beings who could otherwise have acquired a lasting status of possession were thereby reduced merely to serving him in order to be able to live? – it would already conflict with the above principle of equality if a law were to grant them such a privileged rank that either

---

*Someone who makes an *opus* can convey it to someone else by *alienating* it, just as if it were his property. But *praestatio operae*[+] is not alienating something. A domestic servant, a shop clerk, a day laborer, or even a barber are merely *operarii*, not *artifices* (in the wider sense of the word) and not members of the state, and are thus also not qualified to be citizens. Although a man to whom I give my firewood to chop and a tailor to whom I give my cloth to make into clothes both seem to be in a quite similar relation to me, still the former differs from the latter, as a barber from a wigmaker (even if I have given him the hair for the wig) and hence as a day laborer from an artist or craftsman, who makes a work that belongs to him until he is paid for it). The latter, in pursuing his trade, thus exchanges his property with another (*opus*), the former, the use of his powers, which he grants[w] to another (*operam*). It is, I admit, somewhat difficult to determine what is required in order to be able to claim the rank of a human being who is his own master.

[v] *zu welcher letzteren, da Stimmgebung erfordert wird . . . Selbstständigkeit die Bedingung ist*
[w] *bewilligt*

their descendants should always remain large (feudal) landowners, whose estates could not be sold or divided by inheritance and thus be used by more of the people, or else that, if there were such a division, no one other than those belonging to a certain class of people decreed at will[x] could acquire something of it. That is to say, a great landowner[y] eliminates as many smaller owners and their votes as could take his place; thus he does not vote in their name and accordingly has only one vote. Since it must therefore be left dependent only upon the ability, industry, and good fortune of each member of a commonwealth for each at some time to acquire a part of it and all to acquire the whole, but this distinction cannot be taken into account in the universal legislation, the number of those qualified to vote in legislation must be appraised by the number of those in the status of possession, not by the size of their possessions.

But *all* who have this right to vote must agree to this law of public justice; for otherwise there would be a dispute about rights[z] between those who do not agree to it and the first, and yet another higher principle of right would be needed to decide it. Thus if the first cannot be expected of an entire people, so that a majority of votes – and indeed not of those voting directly (in a large people) but only of those delegated to do so as representatives of the people – is all that can be foreseen as attainable, the very principle of letting such a majority be sufficient, adopted as with universal agreement and so by a contract, must be the ultimate basis on which a civil constitution is established.

Conclusion

Now this is an *original contract*, on which alone a civil and hence thoroughly rightful constitution among human beings can be based and a commonwealth established. But it is by no means necessary that this contract (called *contractus originarius* or *pactum sociale*), as a coalition of every particular and private will within a people into a common and public will (for the sake of a merely rightful legislation), be presupposed as a *fact* (as a fact it is indeed not possible) – as if it would first have to be proved from history that a people, into whose rights and obligations we have entered as descendants, once actually carried out such an act, and that it must have left some sure record or instrument of it, orally or in writing, if one is to hold oneself bound to an already existing civil constitution. It is instead *only an idea* of reason, which, however, has its undoubted practical reality, namely to bind every legislator to give his laws in such a way that they *could* have arisen from the united will of a whole people and to regard

---

[x] *willkürlich*
[y] *Gutsbesitzer*
[z] *Rechtstreit*

each subject, insofar as he wants to be a citizen, as if he has joined in voting for such a will. For this is the touchstone of any public law's conformity with right. In other words, if a public law is so constituted that a whole people *could not possibly* give its consent to it (as, e.g., that a certain class of *subjects* should have the hereditary privilege of *ruling rank*), it is unjust;[a] but if it is *only possible* that a people could agree to it, it is a duty to consider the law just, even if the people is at present in such a situation or frame of mind that, if consulted about it, it would probably refuse its consent.*

But this limitation obviously holds only for the judgment of the legislator, not that of a subject. Thus if a people now subject to a certain actual legislation were to judge that in all probability this is detrimental to its happiness, what is to be done about it? Should the people not resist it? The answer can only be that, on the part of the people, there is nothing to be done about it but to obey. For what is under discussion here is not the happiness that a subject may expect from the institution or administration of a commonwealth but above all merely the right that is to be secured for each by means of it, which is the supreme principle for which all maxims having to do with a commonwealth must proceed and which is limited by no other principle. With respect to the former (happiness) no universally valid principle for laws can be given. For both the circumstances of the times and the highly conflicting but always changing illusion[b] in which someone places his happiness (though no one can prescribe to him in what he should place it) make any fixed principle impossible and [happiness] in itself unfit to be a principle of legislation. The saying *Salus publica suprema civitatis lex est*[c] remains undiminished in its worth and authority; but the public well-being[d] that must *first* be taken into account is precisely that lawful constitution which secures everyone his freedom by laws, whereby each remains at liberty to seek his happiness in whatever way seems best to him, provided he does not infringe upon that universal freedom in conformity with law and hence upon the right of other fellow subjects.

---

*If, e.g., a war tax were imposed proportionately on all subjects, they could not, because they found it oppressive, say that it is unjust because in their opinion the war may be unnecessary; for they are not entitled to appraise this but instead, because it is still always *possible* that the war is unavoidable and the tax indispensable, the tax must hold in a subject's judgment as in conformity with right. But if, during such a war, certain landowners were burdened with levies while others of the same rank were exempted, it is easily seen that a whole people could not agree to a law of this kind, and it is authorized at least to make representations against it, since it cannot take this unequal distribution of burdens to be just.

[a] *nicht gerecht*
[b] *Wahn*
[c] The public well-being is the supreme law of the state
[d] *Heil*

If the supreme power gives laws that are directed chiefly to happiness (the prosperity of the citizens, increased population and the like), this is not done as the end for which a civil constitution is established but merely as means for *securing* a *rightful condition*, especially against a people's external enemies. A head of state must be authorized to judge for himself and alone whether such laws pertain to the commonwealth's flourishing, which is required to secure its strength and stability both internally and against external enemies, not in order, as it were, to make the people happy against its will but only to make it exist as a commonwealth.* Now the legislator can indeed err in his appraisal of whether those measures are adopted *prudently*, but not when he asks himself whether the law also harmonizes with the principle of right; for there he has that idea of the original contract at hand as an infallible standard, and indeed has it a priori (and need not, as with the principle of happiness, wait for experience that would first have to teach him whether his means are suitable). For, provided it is not self-contradictory that an entire people should agree to such a law, however bitter they might find it, the law is in conformity with right. But if a public law is in conformity with this, and so beyond reproach (*irresprehensibel*) with regard to right, then there is also joined with it authorization to coerce and, on the other's part, a prohibition against actively resisting the will of the legislator; that is, the power within a state that gives effect to the law is also unopposable (*irresistibel*), and there exists no rightful commonwealth that can hold its own without a force of this kind that puts down all internal resistance, since each resistance would take place in conformity with a maxim that, made universal, would annihilate any civil constitution and eradicate the condition in which alone people can be in possession of rights generally.

From this it follows that any resistance to the supreme legislative power, any incitement to have the subjects' dissatisfaction become active, any insurrection that breaks out in rebellion, is the highest and most punishable crime within a commonwealth, because it destroys its foundation. And this prohibition is *unconditional*, so that even if that power or its agent, the head of state, has gone so far as to violate the original contract and has thereby, according to the subjects' concept, forfeited the right to be legislator inasmuch as he has empowered the government to proceed quite violently (tyrannically), a subject is still not permitted any resistance by way of counteracting force. The ground of this is that in an already existing civil constitution the people's judgment to determine how the

---

*Certain restrictions on imports are included among these laws, so that the means of acquiring livelihood will promote the subjects' interests and not the advantage of foreigners or encouragement of others' industry, since a state, without the prosperity of the people, would not possess enough strength to resist foreign enemies or to maintain itself as a commonwealth.

constitution should be administered is no longer valid.^e For suppose that the people can so judge, and indeed contrary to the judgment of the actual head of state; who is to decide on which side the right is? Neither can make the decision as judge in its own suit. Hence there would have to be another head above the head of state, that would decide between him and the people; and this is self-contradictory. Nor could a right of necessity (*ius in casu necessitatis*), which, as a supposed *right* to do *wrong* when in extreme (physical) need, is in any case an absurdity,* enter here and provide a way to raise the barrier limiting the people's despotic power.^h For, the head of state can as well urge that his harsh behavior toward his subjects is justified by their recalcitrance as they can urge that their rebellion is justified by their complaints against him of their undeserved suffering; and who is to decide the issue? Only he who possesses the supreme administration of public right can do so, and that is precisely the head of state; and no one within a commonwealth can, accordingly, have a right to contest his possession of it.

Yet I find estimable men who maintain that under certain circumstances a subject is authorized to use force against his superiors; the only one of them I want to cite here is Achenwall,†5 who is very cautious, definite, and modest in his teachings on natural right. He says: "If the danger that threatens a commonwealth as a result of continuing to endure the injustice of the head of state is greater than the danger to be feared from taking up arms against him, then the people can resist him, for the sake of this right^i withdraw from its contract of subjection, and dethrone

8:301

---

*There is no *casus necessitatis* except in a case where duties, namely an *unconditional duty* and a (perhaps very important yet) *conditional duty*, conflict with each other, e.g., if it is a matter of preventing some catastrophe to the state by betraying a man who might stand in the relationship to another of father and son. This prevention of trouble to the former is an unconditional duty, whereas preventing misfortune to the latter is only a conditional duty (namely, insofar as he has not made himself guilty of a crime against the state). One of the relatives might report the other's plans to the authorities with the utmost reluctance, but he is compelled by necessity (namely, moral necessity) – but if it is said of someone who, in order to preserve his own life, pushes another survivor of a shipwreck from his plank, that he has a right to do so by his (physical) necessity, that is quite false. For to preserve my life is only a conditional duty (if it can be done without a crime); but not to take the life of another who is committing no offense against me^f and does not even *lead* me into the danger of losing my life is an unconditional duty. Yet teachers of general civil right proceed quite consistently in conceding rightful authorization for such extreme measures.^g For the authorities can connect no *punishment* with the prohibition, since this punishment would have to be death. But it would be an absurd law to threaten someone with *death* if he did not voluntarily deliver himself up to *death* in dangerous circumstances.

†*Ius Naturae. Editio Vta. Pars posterior*, §203–6.

^e *das Volk kein zu Recht beständiges Urteil mehr hat*
^f *der mich nicht beleidigt*
^g *Nothülfe*
^h *die Eigenmacht des Volks*
^i *zum Behuf dieses Rechts*

him as a tyrant." From this he concludes: "In this way the people (in relation to its previous ruler) returns to the state of nature."

I readily believe that neither Achenwall nor any of the worthy men who have reasoned subtly in agreement with him on this would ever have given their advice or assent to such a dangerous undertaking in any case at hand; and it is hardly to be doubted that if those uprisings by which Switzerland or the United Netherlands or even Great Britain won its constitution, now considered so fortunate, had failed, those who read the history of them would see in the execution of their now celebrated authors nothing but the deserved punishment of great political criminals. For the outcome usually mingles in our appraisal of the rightful grounds,[j] though the former was uncertain and the latter certain. But it is clear that, as far as the latter is concerned – even if it is granted that by such an uprising no wrong is done to a ruler (perhaps one who had violated a *joyeuse entrée*,[6] an actual basic contract[k] with the people – nevertheless the people did wrong in the highest degree by seeking their rights in this way; for this way of doing it (adopted as a maxim) would make every rightful constitution insecure and introduce a condition of complete lawlessness (*status naturalis*), in which all rights cease, at least to have effect. In view of this propensity of so many well-meaning authors to take the people's part (to its own ruin), I want to remark only that the cause of their doing so is in part the common mistake, when the principle of right is under discussion, of substituting the principle of happiness for it in their judgments, and in part that, where there is to be found no instrument of an actual contract submitted to the commonwealth, accepted by its head, and sanctioned by both, they take the idea of an original contract, which is always present in reason as the basis [of a commonwealth], as something that must *actually* have taken place, and so think they can always save for the people authorization to withdraw from the contract as it sees fit if, though by its own appraisal, the contract has been grossly violated.*

Here it is obvious what evil the principle of happiness (which is really not fit for any determinate principle at all) gives rise to in the right of a

---

*Even if an actual contract of the people with the ruler has been violated, the people cannot react at once *as a commonwealth* but only as a mob.[l] For the previously existing constitution has been torn up by the people, while their organization into a new commonwealth has not yet taken place. It is here that the condition of anarchy arises with all the horrors that are at least possible by means of it; and the wrong that is done here is that which each faction in the people inflicts on the other, as is also clear from the example cited, where the rebellious subjects of that state finally wanted to thrust upon one another by force a constitution which would have been far more oppressive than the one they abandoned: they would, namely, have been devoured by ecclesiastics and aristocrats, instead of being able to expect greater equality in the distribution of political burdens under one head of state ruling over all.

[j] *Rechtsgründe*
[k] *zum Grunde liegenden Vertrag*
[l] *durch Rottierung*

state, just as it does in morals, despite the best intentions of those who teach it. The sovereign wants to make the people happy in accordance with his concepts and becomes a despot; the people are not willing to give up their universal human claim to their own happiness and become rebels. Had it first been asked what is laid down as right (where principles stand firm a priori and no empiricist can bungle them), then the idea of the social contract would remain in its incontestable authority, not however as a fact (as Danton would have it, apart from which he declares null and void all rights and all property to be found in the actually existing civil constitution[7]) but only as a rational principle for appraising any public rightful constitution. And it would then be seen that before the general will exists the people possesses no coercive right at all against its commander[m] since it can rightfully use coercion only through him; but if the general will exists, there is likewise no coerion to be exercised by it against him, since otherwise the people itself would be the supreme commander; hence the people never has a coercive right against the head of state (insubordination in word or deed).

We also see this theory adequately confirmed in practice. In the constitution of Great Britain – where the people carry on about their constitution as if it were the model for the whole world – we nevertheless find that it is quite silent about the authorization belonging to the people in case the monarch should transgress the contract of 1688,[8] so that if he wanted to violate the constitution, there being no law about such a case, the people secretly reserves to itself rebellion against him. For, that the constitution should contain a law for such a case authorizing the overthrow of the existing constitution, from which all particular laws proceed (even supposing the contract violated) is an obvious contradiction; for then it would also have to contain a *publicly constituted** opposing power, so that there would have to be a second head of state to protect the people's rights against the first, and then yet a third to decide between the two, which of them had right on its side. Moreover, those leaders (or, if you will, guardians) of the people, being concerned about such an accusation should their undertaking fail, preferred *to attribute* a voluntary abdication of government to the monarch they frightened away than to claim the right to depose him, whereby they would have put the constitution in obvious contradiction with itself.

I will surely not be reproached, because of these assertions, with flatter-

---

*No right within a state can be concealed, treacherously as it were, by a secret reservation, least of all the right that the people claims for itself as one belonging to the constitution; for all laws of the constitution must be thought as arising out of a public will. Thus if the constitution permitted insurrection, it would have to declare publicly the right to it and in what way use is to be made of it.

[m] *Gebieter*

ing monarchs too much by such inviolability; so, I hope, I will also be spared the reproach of overstating the case in favor of the people when I say that the people too has its inalienable rights against the head of state, although these cannot be coercive rights.

Hobbes is of the opposite opinion. According to him (*de Cive*, Chap. 7, §14), a head of state has no obligation to the people by the contract and cannot do a citizen any wrong (he may make what arrangements he wants about him). This proposition would be quite correct if a wrong were taken to mean an injury that gives the injured party a *coercive right* against the one who wronged him; but stated so generally, the proposition is appalling.

A nonrecalcitrant subject must be able to assume that his ruler does not *want* to do him any wrong. Accordingly, since every human being still has his inalienable rights, which he can never give up even if he wanted to and about which he is authorized to judge for himself, while, on that assumption, the wrong that in his opinion is done to him occurs only from the supreme power's error or ignorance of certain consequences of his laws, a citizen must have, with the approval of the ruler himself, the authorization to make known publicly his opinions about what it is in the ruler's arrangements that seems to him to be a wrong against the commonwealth. For, to assume that the head of state could never err or be ignorant of something would be to represent him as favored with divine inspiration and raised above humanity. Thus *freedom of the pen* – kept within the limits of esteem and love for the constitution within which one lives by the subjects' liberal way of thinking, which the constitution itself instills in them (and pens themselves also keep one another within these limits, so that they do not lose their freedom) – is the sole palladium of the people's rights. For to want to deny them this freedom is not only tantamount to taking from them any claim to a right with respect to the supreme commander (according to Hobbes), but is also to withhold from the latter – whose will gives order to the subjects as citizens only by representing the general will of the people – all knowledge of matters that he himself would change if he knew about them and to put him in contradiction with himself. But to instill in a head of state concern that unrest in the state might be aroused by [the subjects'] thinking independently and aloud is tantamount to awakening in him mistrust of his own power or even hatred of his people.

But the universal principle by which a people has to appraise its rights *negatively* – that is, appraise merely what may be regarded as *not ordained* by the supreme legislation, as with its best will – is contained in the proposition: *What a people cannot decree for itself, a legislator also cannot decree for a people.*

Thus if the question is, for example: Can a law prescribing that a certain ecclesiastical constitution, once arranged, is to continue permanently, be regarded as issuing from the real[n] will of the legislator (his intention)? then it will first be asked: *May* a people itself make it a law that certain articles of faith and forms of external religion, once adopted, are to remain forever? And so: *May* a people hinder itself, in its posterity, from making further progress in religious insight or from at some time correcting old errors? It then becomes clear that an original contract of the people that made this a law would in itself be null and void because it conflicts with the vocation and end of humanity; hence a law given about this is not to be regarded as the real will of the monarch, to whom counterrepresentations can accordingly be made. In all cases, however, where something of this sort was nevertheless arranged by the supreme legislation, general and public judgments could be passed on it, but resistance to it in word or deed could never be summoned.

In every commonwealth there must be *obedience* under the mechanism of the state constitution to coercive laws (applying to the whole), but there must also be a *spirit of freedom*, since each, in what has to do with universal human duties, requires to be convinced by reason that this coercion is in conformity with right, lest he fall into contradiction with himself. The former without the latter is the occasioning cause[o] of all *secret societies*. For it is a natural calling of humanity to communicate with one another, especially in what concerns people generally; hence those societies would disappear if such freedom were favored. And how else, again, could the government get the knowledge it requires for its own essential purpose than by letting the spirit of freedom, so worthy of respect in its origin and in its effects, express itself?

. .

Nowhere does a practice that ignores all pure rational principles deny theory so arrogantly as in the question of what is required for a good constitution of a state. The cause is that a lawful constitution of long standing gradually accustoms the people to a rule of appraising its happiness as well as its rights in terms of the condition[p] in which everything up to now has followed its quiet course, but not, conversely, to evaluate that condition in terms of the concepts of both provided by reason; instead [it leads the people] always to prefer that passive condition to the dangerous situation of seeking a better one (what Hippocrates told physicians to take to heart holds here: *iudicium anceps, experimentum periculosum*).[q] Now, all constitutions of sufficiently long standing, whatever deficiencies they may have and for all their differences, give the same result, namely being

---

[n] *eigentlichen*
[o] *veranlassende Ursache*
[p] *Zustand*
[q] judgment is uncertain and experiments are dangerous

satisfied with the constitution one is in; so, if one looks to the *people's welfare*, no theory at all is really valid, but everything rests on a practice docile to experience.

But if there is in reason something that can be expressed by the words *right of a state*, and if this concept has binding force for people opposed to one another in the antagonism of their freedom, and hence has objective (practical) reality irrespective of the well-being or ill-being that may arise from it (knowledge of which rests only on experience), then the right of a state is based on a priori principles (for experience cannot teach what right is),[r] and there is a *theory* of the right of a state, no practice being valid unless it accords with this.

The only objection that can be raised to this is that, although people have in their heads the idea of rights belonging to them, they would still be unqualified and unworthy to be treated in accord with them because of the hardness of their hearts, so that a supreme power proceeding merely in accordance with rules of prudence may and must keep them in order. But this desperate leap (*salto mortale*) is of such a kind that, once the issue is not that of right but only of force, the people may also try out its own force and thus make every lawful constitution insecure. If there is not something that through reason compels immediate respect (such as the rights of human beings), then all influences on the choice of human beings are incapable of restraining their[s] freedom; but if, alongside benevolence, right speaks out loudly, human nature does not show itself too depraved to listen deferentially to its voice. (*Tum pietate gravem meritisque si forte virum quem Conspexere, silent arrectisque auribus adstant.* Virgil.)[t]

8:307

III.
ON THE RELATION OF THEORY TO PRACTICE IN THE RIGHT OF NATIONS CONSIDERED FROM A UNIVERSALLY PHILANTHROPIC, THAT IS, COSMOPOLITAN POINT OF VIEW*

(Against Moses Mendelssohn)[9]

Is the human race as a whole to be loved, or is it an object such that one must regard it with vexation, for which one indeed wishes everything good

---

*It is not at once obvious how a universally *philanthropic* presupposition can point the way to a *cosmopolitan* constitution, and this in turn to the foundation of a *right of nations* as a condition in which alone the predispositions belonging to humanity that make our species worthy of love can be developed. But the conclusion of this part will make this connection clear.

[r] *was Recht sei*

[s] Or perhaps "its freedom," *derselben* referring to *Willkür*

[t] If they catch sight of a man respected for his virtue and services, they are silent and stand close with ears alert. Virgil *Aeneid* 1.151–2.

(so as not to become misanthropic) but of which one must never expect this, so that one must prefer to avert one's eyes from it? The reply to this question rests upon the answer one gives to another: Are there in human nature predispositions from which one can gather that the race will always progress toward what is better and that the evil of present and past times will disappear in the good of future times? For in that case we could still love the race, at least in its constant approach to the good; otherwise, we should have to hate or despise it, whatever might be said to the contrary by the affectations of universal philanthropy (which would then be at most only a love of benevolence, not of delight).[10] For, however one may try to exact love from oneself, one cannot avoid hating what is and remains evil, especially in deliberate mutual violation of the most sacred human rights not exactly so as to inflict troubles upon him but still so as to have as little as possible to do with him.

Moses Mendelssohn was of the latter opinion (*Jerusalem* Section II, pp. 44–47), which he opposed to his friend Lessing's hypothesis of a divine education of the human race.[11] It is, to him, a fantasy "that the whole, humanity here below, should in the course of time always move forward and perfect itself." "We see," he said, "the human race as a whole make small oscillations, and it never takes a few steps forward without soon afterward sliding back twice as fast into its former state." (This is precisely the stone of Sisyphus; and in this way one takes the earth, as the Indians do, as a place of atonement for ancient sins that can now no longer be remembered.) "An individual makes progress, but humanity constantly vacillates between fixed limits; regarded as a whole, however, it maintains in all periods of time roughly the same level of morality, the same measure of religion and irreligious, of virtue and vice, of happiness (?) and misery." He introduces these assertions by saying (p. 46): "Do you want to guess what sort of purpose providence has for humanity? Forge no hypotheses" (he had earlier called these "theory"); "just look around at what is actually happening, and if you can take an overview of the history of all past ages, look at what has happened from time immemorial. This is fact, this must have belonged to that purpose, must have been approved within the plan of wisdom or at least adopted along with it."

8:308

I am of another opinion. If it is a sight worthy of a divinity to see a virtuous man struggling with adversity and temptations to evil and yet holding out against them, it is a sight most unworthy, I shall not say of a divinity but even of the most common but well-disposed human being to see the human race from period to period taking steps upward toward virtue and soon after falling back just as deeply into vice and misery. To watch this tragedy for a while might be moving and instructive, but the curtain must eventually fall. For in the long run it turns into a farce; and even if the actors do not tire of it, because they are fools, the spectator does, when one or another act gives him sufficient grounds for gathering that the never-ending piece is forever the same. If it is merely a play, the punishment coming at the end can make up for his unpleasant feelings*u* by means of the outcome. But in real life,*v* to let countless vices pile one upon another (even with virtues intervening), so that some day there will be plenty to punish is, at least according to our concepts, even contrary to the morality of a wise creator and ruler of the world.

I shall therefore be allowed to assume that, since the human race is constantly advancing with respect to culture (as its natural end) it is also to be conceived as progressing toward what is better with respect to the moral end of its existence, and that this will indeed be *interrupted* from time to time but will never be *broken off.* I do not need to prove this presupposition; it is up to its adversary to prove [his] case. For I rest my case on my innate duty, the duty of every member of the series of generations – to which I (as a human being in general) belong and am yet not so good in the moral character*w* required of me as I ought to be and hence could be – so to influence posterity that it becomes always better (the possibility of this must, accordingly, also be assumed), and to do it in such a way that this duty may be legitimately*x* handed down from one member [in the series of] generations to another. It does not matter how many doubts may be raised against my hopes from history, which, if they were proved, could move me to desist from a task so apparently futile; as long as these doubts cannot be made quite certain I cannot exchange the duty (as something *liquidum*) for the rule of prudence not to attempt the impracticable (as something *illiquidum,* since it is merely hypothetical); and however uncertain I may always be and remain as to whether something better is to be hoped for the human race, this cannot infringe upon the maxim, and hence upon its presupposition, necessary for practical purposes, that it is practicable.

This hope for better times, without which an earnest desire to do something profitable for the general well-being*y* would never have warmed the human heart, has moreover always influenced the work of well-disposed people; and even the good Mendelssohn must have counted on it when he exerted himself so zealously for the enlightenment and welfare of the nation to which he belonged. For he could not reasonably hope to bring this about all by himself, without others after him continuing along the same path. Confronted by the sorry sight, not so much of those troubles that oppress human beings from natural causes as rather of those that they themselves inflict upon one another, the mind is nevertheless cheered up by the pros-

---

u *Empfindungen*
v *in der Wirklichkeit*
w *Beschaffenheit*
x *rechtmäßig*
y *Wohl*

pect that matters could become better in the future, and indeed with unselfish benevolence, since we shall be long in our graves and shall not harvest the fruits we have helped to sow. Empirical arguments[z] against the success of these resolutions, which are taken on hope, accomplish nothing here. For, that what has not succeeded up to now will therefore never succeed does not even justify abandoning a pragmatic or technical purpose (for example, that of flights with aerostatic balloons), still less a moral purpose that, if only it is not demonstratively impossible to effect it, becomes a duty. Besides, a good deal of evidence[a] can be put forward to show that in our age, as compared with all previous ages, the human race as a whole has actually made considerable moral progress (short-term checks can prove nothing to the contrary), and that the outcry about its incessantly increasing depravity comes from the very fact that when it reaches a higher level of morality it sees farther ahead, and its judgment about what one is as compared with what one ought to be, hence our self-reproach, becomes all the more severe the more levels of morality we have already climbed during the whole of the course of the world that we have become acquainted with.

If we now ask by what means this unending progress toward the better can be maintained and even accelerated, it is soon seen that this immeasurably distant success will depend not so much upon what *we* do (e.g., on the education we give the younger generation) and by what methods we should proceed in order to bring it about, but instead upon what human *nature* will do in and with us to *force* us onto a track we would not readily take of our own accord. For only from nature, or rather from *providence* (since supreme wisdom is required for the complete fulfillment of this end), can we expect an outcome that is directed to the whole and from it to the parts, whereas people in their *schemes* set out only from the parts and may well remain with them, and may be able to reach the whole, as something too great for them, in their ideas but not in their influence, especially since, with their mutually adverse schemes, they would hardly unite for it by their own free resolution.

Just as omnilateral violence and the need arising from it must finally bring a people to decide to subject itself to the coercion that reason itself prescribes to them as means, namely to public law, and to enter into a *civil*[b] *constitution,* so too must the need arising from the constant wars by which states in turn try to encroach upon or subjugate one another at last bring them, even against their will, to enter into a *cosmopolitan*[c] *constitution;* or else, if this condition[d] of universal peace is still more dangerous to freedom from

---

[z] *Beweisgründe*
[a] *Beweise*
[b] *staatsbürgerliche*
[c] *weltbürgerliche*
[d] *Zustand*

another quarter, by leading to the most fearful despotism (as has indeed happened more than once with states that have grown too large), this need must still constrain states to enter a condition that is not a cosmopolitan commonwealth under a single head but is still a rightful condition of *federation* in accordance with a commonly agreed upon *right of nations*.

For the advancing culture of states, along with their growing propensity to aggrandize themselves by cunning or violence at the expense of others, must multiply wars and give rise to higher and higher costs because of ever larger armies (remaining under pay), kept at the ready and in training and equipped with ever more numerous instruments of war; meanwhile the price of all necessities constantly rises, though a corresponding increase in the metals representing them cannot be hoped for; moreover, no peace lasts long enough for the savings during it to catch up with expenditures on costs for the next war, and the invention of a national debt against this, though certainly an ingenious expedient, is in the end a self-defeating one; hence impotence must eventually bring about what good will ought to have done but did not do: that each state becomes so organized internally that it is not the head of state, whom war really costs nothing (since he wages it at another's cost, namely that of the people), who has the decisive voice as to whether there is to be war or not, but instead the people, which pays for it (admittedly, this necessarily presupposes the realization of that idea of the original contract). For the people will not readily put itself in danger of personal poverty, which does not touch the head of state, out of a mere desire for aggrandizement or because of some supposed, merely verbal offense. And thus posterity too (to which no burdens not incurred by it will be shifted) could always progress to the better even in the moral sense, without love for posterity having to be the cause of this but only the self-love of each age, such progress being possible because every commonwealth, unable to harm another by force, must have recourse only to right and has grounds to hope that others similarly constituted will come to its assistance in this.

This is, however, only an opinion and a mere hypothesis; it is uncertain, like all judgments that want to assign for an intended effect not entirely within our control the only natural cause adequate to it; and even as such, it does not involve a principle for the subjects in an already existing state to enforce it (as has already been shown), but only for uncoercible heads of state. Although in the usual order of things it is not in the nature of the human being to relinquish his power by choice[e] it is still not impossible in pressing circumstances. Thus it can be considered an expression not unbefitting the moral wishes and hopes of people (once aware of their inability) to expect the circumstances required for these from *providence*, which will provide an outcome for the end of *humanity* as a whole species, to reach its

---

[e] *willkürlich*

final destination by the free use of its powers as far as they extend, to which end the ends of *human beings*, considered separately, are directly opposed. For, the very opposition of inclinations to one another, from which evil arises, furnishes reason a free play to subjugate them all and, in place of evil, which destroys itself, to establish the rule of good, which, once it exists, continues to maintain itself of its own accord.

∴

Nowhere does human nature appear less lovable than in the relations of entire peoples to one another. No state is for a moment secure from others in either its independence or its property. The will to subjugate one another or to diminish what belongs to another always exists, and arming for defence, which often makes peace more oppressive and more destructive of internal welfare than war itself, can never be relaxed. Now, the only possible remedy for this is a right of nations, based on public laws accompanied by power to which each state would have to submit (by analogy with civil right, or the right of a state, among individuals); for, an enduring universal peace by means of the so-called *balance of power in Europe* is a mere fantasy, like Swift's house that the builder had constructed in such perfect accord with all the laws of equilibrium that it collapsed as soon as a sparrow alighted upon it. But, it will be said, states will never submit to coercive laws of this kind; and a proposal for a universal state of nations*ᶠ* to whose power all individual states should voluntarily accommodate themselves so as to obey its laws – however good it may sound in the theory of an Abbé St. Pierre or of a Rousseau[12] – still does not hold in practice; and so it has always been ridiculed by great statesmen, and still more by heads of state, as an academic and childish idea emerging from the schools.

For my own part, I nevertheless put my trust in theory, which proceeds from the principle of right, as to what relations among human beings and states *ought to be*, and which commends to earthly gods the maxim always so to behave in their conflicts that such a universal state of nations will thereby be ushered in, and so to assume that it is possible (*in praxi*) and that it *can be;* but at the same time I put my trust (*in subsidium*) in the nature of things, which constrains one to go where one does not want to go (*fata volentem ducunt, nolentem trahunt*).*ᵍ* In the latter, account is also taken of human nature, in which respect for right and duty is still alive, so that I cannot and will not take it to be so immersed in evil that morally practical reason should not, after many unsuccessful attempts, finally triumph over evil and present human nature as lovable after all. Thus on the cosmopolitan level, too, it can be maintained: What on rational grounds holds for theory also holds for practice.

ᶠ Völkerstaat
ᵍ The fates lead the willing, drive the unwilling. Seneca *Epist. mor.* 18.4.

Toward perpetual peace

Introduction

In 1795 King Frederick William II of Prussia withdrew from the War of the First Coalition and, on April 5, concluded the separate Peace of Basel with the revolutionary government of France. In a letter of August 15 of the same year (12: 35) Kant offered the Königsberg publisher Nicolovius what may well be the most widely read of his informal works, *Toward Perpetual Peace*.

Projects for "perpetual peace," and criticisms of them, had been in the air since 1713, when the Abbé St. Pierre, a secretary at the congress preceding the Treaty of Utrecht, had published the first two volumes of his *Projet pour rendre la paix perpetuelle en Europe*. Among the more prominent of his defenders and critics were Leibniz, Voltaire, Frederick the Great, and Rousseau. As might be expected, Kant was aware of the debate. In a Reflection that Adickes dates from about 1755 Kant notes Bayle's view that, although "it is possible *in abstracto* to put the rules of Christianity into practice, this is not the case with regard to princes: it was impossible in connection with the Abbé St. Pierre's proposal" (6: 241; AK 16, #2116). As the present essay shows, Kant did not consider the idea of a league of nations impossible, but he did not rely for his evidence upon experience of how princes have behaved.

Two years later, in *The Metaphysics of Morals*, Kant would set forth systematically the grounds on which "morally practical reason pronounces in us its irresistible veto: There is to be no war, neither between you and me in a state of nature nor between us as states," which in their relation to one another are still in a state of nature (6: 354). On these grounds he concludes that it is our duty to work toward perpetual peace, the "final end of the doctrine of right within the limits of reason alone," and so toward its condition, a league of nations. In order for us to do so, it is enough that the impossibility of a universal and lasting peace, "the highest political good," cannot be demonstrated. Since Kant's purpose in *The Metaphysics of Morals* is limited to determining what our duties are, he need not discuss the subject further in that work. Thematically, *Toward Perpetual Peace* takes up where *The Doctrine of Right* ends.

Toward perpetual peace

A philosophical project

Toward perpetual peace

It may be left undecided whether this satirical inscription on a certain Dutch innkeeper's signboard picturing a graveyard[1] was to hold for human beings in general, or for heads of state in particular, who can never get enough of war, or only for philosophers, who dream that sweet dream. The author of the present treatise, however, lays down the following condition: the practical politician takes the stance of looking down with great self-satisfaction on the theoretical politician as an academic who, with his ineffectual ideas, poses no danger to a state, which must proceed on principles derived from experience, and who can be allowed to fire off all his skittle balls at once, without the *worldly-wise* statesman needing to pay heed to it; hence the latter must also behave consistently in case of a conflict with the former, by not suspecting danger to the state behind the opinions ventured and expressed publicly by the theorist; by this *clausula salvatoria*[a] the author of this treatise wants expressly to protect himself, in proper form, against any malicious interpretation.

Section I,

which contains the preliminary articles for perpetual peace among states.

1. "No treaty of peace shall be held to be such if it is made with a secret reservation of material for a future war."

For in that case it would be a mere truce, a suspension of hostilities, not *peace*, which means the end of all hostilities and to which it is already a suspicious pleonasm to attach the adjective *perpetual*. Causes for a future war, extant even if as yet unrecognized by the contracting parties themselves, are all annihilated by a peace treaty, no matter how acute and skilled the sleuthing by which they may be picked out of documents in archives. A mental reservation (*reservatio mentalis*) regarding old claims to be worked out only in the future – which neither party may mention just now because both are too exhausted to continue the war – with the ill will to make use of the first favorable opportunity for this end belongs to

---

[a] The little saving clause

jesuitical casuistry and is beneath the dignity of a ruler, just as readiness to engage in deductions of this sort is beneath the dignity of his minister, if the matter is appraised as it is in itself.

But if, according to enlightened concepts of political prudence, the true honor of a state is put in the continual increase of its power by whatever means, then that judgment will admittedly look academic and pedantic.

> 2. "No independently existing state (whether small or large) shall be acquired by another state through inheritance, exchange, purchase or donation."

For a state is not (like the land on which it resides) a belonging (*patrimonium*). It is a society of human beings that no one other than itself can command or dispose of. Like a trunk, it has its own roots; and to annex it to another state as a graft is to do away with its existence as a moral person and to make a moral person into a thing, and so to contradict the idea of the original contract, apart from which no right over a people can be thought.* Everyone knows into what danger the presumption that acquisition can take place in this way has brought Europe, the only part of the world in which it is known, in our times right up to the present: the presumption, namely, that states can marry each other, partly as a new kind of industry for making oneself predominant by family alliances even without expending one's forces, and partly as a way of extending one's possession of land. The hiring out of troops of one state to another against an enemy not common to both is also to be counted in this; for the subjects are thereby used and used up as things to be managed at one's discretion.

> 3. "Standing armies (*miles perpetuus*) shall in time be abolished altogether."

For they incessantly threaten other states with war by readiness to appear always prepared for war; they spur states on to outdo one another in the number of armed men, which knows no limit; and inasmuch as peace, by the costs related to it, finally becomes even more oppressive than a short war, a standing army is itself the cause of an offensive war, waged by a state in order to be relieved of this burden; in addition, being hired to kill or to be killed seems to involve a use of human beings as mere machines and tools in the hands of another (a state), and this cannot well be reconciled with the right of humanity in our own person. But it is quite different with military exercises undertaken voluntarily and periodically by the citizens of a state in order to secure themselves and their own country

---

*A hereditary kingdom is not a state that can be inherited by another state, but the right to govern it can be inherited by another physical person. In that case the state acquires a ruler, but the ruler as such (i.e. as one already possessing another kingdom) does not acquire the state.

against attacks from without. It would turn out the same with accumulation of a treasure: regarded by other states as a threat of war, it would force them to undertake preventive attacks (for of the three powers,[b] the *power of armies*, the *power of alliances* and the *power of money*, the last might well be the most reliable instrument of war), were it not for the difficulty of discovering the amount of it.

4. "No national debt shall be contracted with regard to the external affairs of a state."

This expedient of seeking help for the national economy from outside or within a state (for the improvement of roads, new settlements, establishing stores of food against years of crop failure, and so forth) incurs no suspicion. But as machinery by which powers oppose one another, a credit system of debts growing out of sight and yet always secured against present demand (since the demand is not made by all the creditors at once) – the ingenious invention of a commercial people in this century[2] – is a dangerous power of money, namely a treasury for carrying on war that exceeds the treasuries of all other states taken together and that can only be exhausted by the deficit in taxes that is inevitable at some time (but that is postponed for a long time because trade is stimulated by the reaction [of such loans] on industry and earnings). This facility in making war, combined with the inclination of those in power to do so, which seems to be implanted in human nature, is therefore a great hindrance to perpetual peace, and there would have to be a preliminary article forbidding it – all the more so because the bankruptcy of such a state, finally unavoidable, must entangle other states in the loss without their having deserved it, and this would be doing them a public wrong. Hence other states are at least justified in allying themselves against such a state and its pretensions.

8:346

5. "No state shall forcibly interfere in the constitution and government of another state."

For what can justify it in doing so? Perhaps the scandal that one state gives to the subjects of another state? It can much rather serve as a warning to them, by the example of the great troubles a people has brought upon itself by its lawlessness; and, in general, the bad example that one free person gives another (as *scandalum acceptum*) is no wrong to it. But it would be a different matter if a state, through internal discord, should split into two parts, each putting itself forward as a separate state and laying claim to the whole; in that case a foreign state could not be charged with interfering in the constitution of another state if it gave assistance to one of them (for this is anarchy). But as long as this internal conflict is not yet critical, such interference of foreign powers would be a

---

[b] *Mächten*

violation of the right of a people dependent upon no other and only struggling with its internal illness; thus it would itself be a scandal given and would make the autonomy of all states insecure.

> 6. "No state at war with another shall allow itself such acts of hostility as would have to make mutual trust impossible during a future peace; acts of this kind are employing *assassins* (*percussores*) or *poisoners* (*venefici*), *breach of surrender, incitement to treason* (*perduellio*) within the enemy state, and so forth."

These are dishonorable stratagems. For some trust in the enemy's way of thinking*ᶜ* must still remain even in the midst of war, since otherwise no peace could be concluded and the hostilities would turn into a war of extermination (*bellum internecinum*); war is, after all, only the regrettable expedient for asserting one's right by force in a state of nature (where there is no court that could judge with rightful force); in it neither of the two parties can be declared an unjust enemy (since that already presupposes a judicial decision), but instead the *outcome* of the war (as in a so-called judgment of God) decides on whose side the right is; but a punitive war (*bellum punitivum*) between states is not thinkable (since there is no relation of a superior to an inferior between them). From this it follows that a war of extermination, in which the simultaneous annihilation of both parties and with it of all right as well can occur, would let perpetual peace come about only in the vast graveyard of the human race. Hence a war of this kind, and so too the use of means that lead to it, must be absolutely forbidden. But that the means mentioned above unavoidably lead to it is clear from this: that those infernal arts, being mean in themselves, would not, if they came into use, be confined for long within the boundaries of war, as for example the use of spies (*uti exploratoribus*), in which use is made only of *others'* dishonesty (which can never be completely eradicated); instead, they would also be carried over into a condition of peace, so that its purpose would be altogether destroyed.

. .

Although the laws cited above are objectively, that is, in the intention of the ruler,*ᵈ* *laws of prohibition* only (*leges prohibitivae*), nevertheless some of them are of the *strict* kind (*leges strictae*), holding without regard for differing circumstances, that insist on his putting a stop to an abuse *at once* (such as numbers 1, 5, 6), but others (such as numbers 2, 3, 4) are laws that, taking into consideration the circumstances in which they are to be *applied, subjectively* widen his authorization (*leges latae*) and contain permissions, not to make exceptions to the rule of right, but to *postpone* putting

---

ᶜ *Denkungsart*
ᵈ *der Machthabenden*

these laws into effect, without however losing sight of the end; he may not postpone to a nonexistent date (*ad calendas graecas*, as Augustus used to promise) putting into effect the law, for example, to *restore* in accordance with number 2 the freedom of certain states deprived of it, and so not restore it; he is permitted only to delay doing so, lest implementing the law prematurely counteract its very purpose. For the prohibition here concerns only the *way of acquiring*, which from now on shall not hold, but not the *status of possession*,[e] which, though it does not have what is required in order to be called a right,[f] was nevertheless in its time (that of putative possession) taken to be legitimate according to the public opinion of every state at the time.*

* Whether, in addition to commands (*leges praeceptivae*) and prohibitions (*leges prohibitivae*), there could also be *permissive laws* (*leges permissivae*) of pure reason has hitherto been doubted, and not without grounds. For laws as such involve a ground of objective practical necessity, whereas permissions involve a ground of the practical contingency of certain actions; thus a *permissive law* would involve necessitation to an action such that one cannot be necessitated to do it, and, if the object of the law had the same meaning in both kinds of relation, this would be a contradiction. But in the permissive law here, the prohibition presupposed is directed only to the future way of acquiring a right (e.g., by inheritance), whereas the exemption from this prohibition, i.e., the permission, is directed to the present status of possession, which in the transition from the state of nature to the civil condition can continue as possession that, though not in conformity with rights,[g] is still *possession in good faith* (*possessio putativa*) in accordance with a permissive law of natural right, although a putative possession, as soon as it has been cognized as such, is prohibited in a state of nature, just as a similar way of acquiring is prohibited in the subsequent civil condition (after the transition has been made), and this authorization to continue in possession would not occur if such an alleged acquisition were to take place in the civil condition; for then, as soon as its nonconformity with rights were discovered, it would have to cease, as a wrong.

I wanted only to draw the attention of teachers of natural right to the concept of a *lex permissiva*, which reason presents of itself in its systematic divisions, especially since in civil (statutory) law use is often made of the concept, but with the following difference: the prohibitive law stands all by itself and the permission is not included in that law as a limiting condition (as it should be) but is thrown in among exceptions to it. Then it is said that this or that is prohibited, *except* for number 1, number 2, number 3, and so forth indefinitely, since permissions are added to the law only contingently, not in accordance with a principle but by groping about among cases that come up; for otherwise the conditions would have had to be introduced *into the formula of the prohibitive law*, and in this way it would have become at the same time a permissive law. It is therefore regrettable that the ingenious but still unsolved competition problem of the wise and astute Count von Windischgrätz,[3] which insisted on precisely that, was so soon abandoned. For the possibility of such a formula (similar to a mathematical formula) is the sole genuine touchstone of legislation that remains consistent, without which the so-called *ius certum* will always remain a pious wish. In that case we shall have merely *general* laws (which hold on *the whole*); but we shall have no universal laws (which hold *generally*), as the concept of a law nevertheless seems to require.

[e] *Besitzstand*
[f] *den erforderlichen Rechtstitel*
[g] *unrechtmäßiger*

Section II,

which contains the definitive articles for perpetual peace among states.

A condition of peace among men living near one another is not a state of nature (*status naturalis*), which is much rather a condition of war, that is, it involves the constant threat of an outbreak of hostilities even if this does not always occur. A condition of peace must therefore be *established*; for suspension of hostilities is not yet assurance of peace, and unless such assurance is afforded one neighbor by another (as can happen only in a *lawful* condition), the former, who has called upon the latter for it, can treat him as an enemy.*

FIRST DEFINITIVE ARTICLE FOR PERPETUAL PEACE

The civil constitution in every state shall be republican.

A constitution established, first on principles of the *freedom* of the members of a society (as individuals), second on principles of the *dependence* of all upon a single common legislation (as subjects), and third on the law of their *equality* (*as citizens of a state*) – the sole constitution that issues from the idea of the original contract, on which all rightful legislation of a people must be based – is a *republican* constitution.† The republican con-

---

* It is usually assumed that one may not behave with hostility toward another unless he has actively *wronged* me; and that is also quite correct if both are in a condition of *being under civil laws*. For by having entered into such a condition one affords the other the requisite assurance (by means of a superior having power over both). – But a human being (or a nation) in a mere state of nature denies me this assurance and already wrongs me just by being near me in this condition, even if not actively (*facto*) yet by the lawlessness of his condition (*statu iniusto*), by which he constantly threatens me; and I can coerce him either to enter with me into a condition of being under civil laws or to leave my neighborhood. Hence the postulate on which all the following articles are based is that all men who can mutually affect one another must belong to some civil constitution.

But any rightful constitution is, with regard to the persons within it,

(1) one in accord with the *right of citizens of a state*, of individuals within a people (*ius civitatis*),
(2) one in accord with the *right of nations*, of states in relation to one another (*ius gentium*),
(3) one in accord with the *right of citizens of the world*, insofar as individuals and states, standing in the relation of externally affecting one another, are to be regarded as citizens of a universal state of mankind (*ius cosmopoliticum*). This division is not made at will[h] but is necessary with reference to the idea of perpetual peace. For if only one of these were in a relation of physically affecting another and were yet in a state of nature, the condition of war would be bound up with this, and the aim here is just to be freed from it.

†*Rightful* (hence external) *freedom* cannot be defined, as it usually is, by the warrant to do whatever one wants provided one does no wrong to anyone. For what does *warrant* mean? The possibility of an action insofar as one thereby does no wrong to anyone. So the

[h] *willkürlich*

stitution is thus, as far as right is concerned, in itself that which every kind of civil constitution has as its original basis; the question now is only whether it is also the sole constitution that can lead toward perpetual peace.

Now, in addition to the purity of its origin – its having arisen from the pure source of the concept of right – the republican constitution does offer the prospect of the result wished for, namely perpetual peace; the ground of this is as follows. When the consent of the citizens of a state is required in order to decide whether there shall be war or not (and it cannot be otherwise in this constitution), nothing is more natural than that they will be very hesitant to begin such a bad game, since they would have to decide to take upon themselves all the hardships of war (such as themselves doing the fighting and paying the costs of the war from their own belongings, painfully making good the devastation it leaves behind, and finally – to make the cup of troubles overflow – a burden of debt that embitters peace itself, and

---

definition would go as follows: freedom is the possibility of actions whereby one does no wrong to anyone. One does no wrong to anyone (one may do what one wants) provided one does no wrong to anyone; hence it is an empty tautology. My external (rightful) *freedom* is, instead, to be defined as follows: it is the warrant to obey no other external laws than those to which I could have given my consent. Similarly, external (rightful) *equality* within a state is that relation of its citizens in which no one can rightfully bind another to something without also being subject to a law by which he in turn *can* be bound in the same way by the other. (There is no need to define the principle of *rightful* dependence, since it is already present in the concept of a state constitution as such.) The validity of these innate and inalienable rights belonging necessarily to humanity is confirmed and enhanced by the principle of rightful relations of a human being even to higher beings (if he thinks of them), inasmuch as he represents himself, in accord with the very same principles, as also a citizen of a state in a supersensible world. For, as regards my freedom, I have no obligation even with respect to divine laws that I can cognize by reason alone except insofar as I could have given my consent to them (since it is by the law of freedom of my own reason that I first make for myself a concept of the divine will). As regards the principle of equality with respect to the most sublime being in the world, except for God, that I might happen to think of (a great *Aeon*): if I do my duty in my post as that Aeon does his duty in his, there is no basis for mere obedience to duty belonging to me and the right to command to him. That this principle of *equality* is not (like the principle of freedom) also appropriate to our relation to God has its ground in this: that he is the only being to whom the concept of duty is inapplicable.

But as regards the right of equality of all citizens of a state as subjects, the answer to the question, whether a *hereditary nobility* is allowable, turns only on whether the *rank* granted by a state (of one subject being above another) would have to precede *merit*, or whether the latter would have to precede the former. Now it is obvious that if rank is connected with birth, it is quite uncertain whether merit (skill and fidelity in one's office) will follow; hence it will be just as if rank (being in command) were granted to a favorite without any merit, and the general will of a people in the original contract (which is yet the principle of all rights) will never decide upon this. For a nobleman is not necessarily a *noble* man. As for *nobility of office* (as the rank of a higher magistracy could be called, which must be acquired for oneself by merit), there rank adheres to a post, not as property to a person, and equality is not violated by it; for, when he retires from his office, he also lays down his rank and goes back among the people.

that can never be paid off because of new wars always impending); on the other hand, under a constitution in which subjects are not citizens of the state, which is therefore not republican, [deciding upon war] is the easiest thing in the world; because the head of state is not a member of the state but its proprietor[i] and gives up nothing at all of his feasts, hunts, pleasure palaces, court festivals, and so forth, he can decide upon war, as upon a kind of pleasure party, for insignificant cause, and can with indifference leave the justification of the war, for the sake of propriety, to the diplomatic corps, which is always ready to provide it.

∴

So that a republican constitution will not be confused with a democratic constitution (as usually happens), the following must be noted. The forms of a state (*civitas*) can be divided either according to the different persons who have supreme power within a state or according to the *way* a people *is governed* by its head of state, whoever this may be; the first is called, strictly speaking, the form of *sovereignty* (*forma imperii*), and only three such forms are possible: namely, either only *one*, or *some* in association, or *all* those together who constitute the civil society possess sovereign power (*autocracy, aristocracy,* and *democracy,* the power of a prince, the power of a nobility, and the power of a people). The second is the form of government (*forma regiminis*) and has to do with the way a state, on the basis of its civil constitution (the act of the general will by which a multitude becomes a people), makes use of its plenary power; and with regard to this, the form of a state is either *republican* or *despotic*. *Republicanism* is the political principle of separation of the executive power (the government) from the legislative power; despotism is that of the high-handed management of the state by laws the regent has himself given, inasmuch as he handles the public will as his private will. Of the three forms of state, that of *democracy* in the strict sense of the word is necessarily a *despotism* because it establishes an executive power in which all decide for and, if need be, against one (who thus does not agree), so that all, who are nevertheless not all, decide; and this is a contradiction of the general will with itself and with freedom.

This is to say that any form of government which is not *representative* is, strictly speaking, *without form*, because the legislator cannot be in one and the same person also executor of its will (any more than the universal of the major premise in a syllogism can also be the subsumption of the particular under it in the minor premise); and even if the other two state constitutions are always defective insofar as they leave room for this kind of government, in their case it is at least possible for them to adopt a kind of government in conformity with the *spirit* of a representative system, as

---

[i] *nicht Staatsgenoße, sondern Staatseigentümer*

Frederick II, for example, at least *said* that he was only the highest servant of the state,* whereas a democratic constitution makes this impossible because there everyone wants to be ruler. It can therefore be said that the smaller the number of persons exercising the power of a state (the number of rulers) and the greater their representation, so much the more does its constitution accord with the possibility of republicanism, and the constitution can hope by gradual reforms finally to raise itself to this. On this basis it is already harder in an aristocracy than in a monarchy to achieve this sole constitution that is perfectly rightful, but in a democracy it is impossible except by violent revolution. The kind of government,† however, is of incomparably greater concern to the people than is the form of state (though a good deal also depends on how adequate the latter is to the former's end). But if the kind of government is to be in conformity with the concept of right, it must have a representative system, in which alone a republican kind of government is possible and without which the government is despotic and violent (whatever the constitution may be). None of the ancient republics, so called, knew this system, and because of this they simply had to disintegrate into despotism, which under the rule of a single individual is still the most bearable of all.

8:353

SECOND DEFINITIVE ARTICLE FOR PERPETUAL PEACE

8:354

The right of nations shall be based on a *federalism* of free states.

Nations, as states, can be appraised as individuals, who in their natural condition (that is, in their independence from external laws) already

---

* The exalted epithets often bestowed on a ruler ("the divinely anointed," "the administrator of the divine will on earth and its representative") have often been censured as gross and dizzying flattery, but, it seems to me, without grounds. Far from making the ruler of a country arrogant, they would rather have to humble him in his soul if he is intelligent (as must be assumed) and make him reflect that he has taken on an office too great for a human being – namely the most sacred office that God has on earth, that of trustee of *the right of human beings* – and that he must always be concerned about having in some way offended against this "apple of God's eye."

8:353

† Mallet du Pan boasts,⁴ in his pompous but hollow and empty language, of having at last, after many years of experience, become convinced of the truth of Pope's well-known saying: "For forms of government let fools contest; whate'er is best administered is best." If this means that the best administered government is best administered, he has, as Swift expressed it, cracked a nut that rewarded him with a worm; but if it means that the best administered government is also the best government, i.e., the best constitution of a state, then it is quite false; for examples of good governments prove nothing about kinds of government. Who governed better than a Titus or a Marcus Aurelius, and yet one left a Domitian as his successor and the other a Commodus; and this could not have happened if the state had had a good constitution, since their unsuitability for this post was well known early enough and the ruler's power was also sufficient to exclude them.

wrong one another by being near one another; and each of them, for the sake of its security, can and ought to require the others to enter with it into a constitution similar to a civil constitution, in which each can be assured of its right. This would be a *league of nations*, which, however, need not be a state of nations. That would be a contradiction, inasmuch as every state involves the relation of a *superior* (legislating) to an *inferior* (obeying, namely the people); but a number of nations within one state would constitute only one nation, and this contradicts the presupposition (since here we have to consider the right of *nations* in relation to one another insofar as they comprise different states and are not to be fused into a single state).

Just as we now regard with profound contempt, as barbarous, crude, and brutishly degrading to humanity, the attachment of savages to their lawless freedom, by which they would rather struggle unceasingly than subject themselves to a lawful coercion to be instituted by themselves, thus preferring a mad freedom to a rational freedom, so, one would think, civilized peoples (each united into a state) must hasten to leave such a depraved condition, the sooner the better; but instead each *state* puts its majesty (for the majesty of a people is an absurd expression) just in its not being subject to any external lawful coercion at all, and the splendor of its chief consists in his being able, without even having to put himself in danger, to command many thousands to sacrifice themselves for a matter that is of no concern to them;* and the difference between the European and the American savages consists mainly in this: that whereas many tribes of the latter have been eaten up by their enemies, the former know how to make better use of those they have defeated than to make a meal of them, and would rather increase the number of their subjects, and so too the multitude of their instruments for even more extensive wars, by means of them.

In view of the malevolence of human nature, which can be seen unconcealed in the free relations of nations (whereas in a condition under civil laws it is greatly veiled by the government's constraint), it is surprising that the word *right* could still not be altogether banished as pedantic from the politics of war and that no state has yet been bold enough to declare itself publicly in favor of this view; for Hugo Grotius, Pufendorf, Vattel,[5] and the like (only sorry comforters) – although their code, couched philosophically or diplomatically, has not the slightest *lawful* force and cannot even have such force (since states as such are not subject to a common external constraint) – are always duly cited in *justification* of an offensive war, though there is no instance of a state ever having been moved to desist from its plan by arguments armed with the testimony of such important men. This hom-

---

* Thus a Bulgarian prince gave the following reply to the Greek emperor's benign offer to settle their dispute by a duel: "A smith who has tongs will not lift the glowing iron from the coals with his own hands."

age that every state pays the concept of right (at least verbally) nevertheless proves that there is to be found in the human being a still greater, though at present dormant, moral predisposition to eventually become master of the evil principle within him (which he cannot deny) and also to hope for this from others; for otherwise the word *right* would never be spoken by states wanting to attack one another, unless merely to make fun of it, as a certain Gallic prince defined right: "It is the prerogative nature has given the stronger over the weaker, that the latter should obey him."

The way in which states pursue their right can never be legal proceedings before an external court but can only be war; but right cannot be decided by war and its favorable outcome, *victory;* and by a *peace pact* a current war can be brought to an end but not a condition of war, of always finding pretexts for a new war (and this cannot straightaway be declared wrong, since in this condition each is judge in his own case); however, what holds in accordance with natural right for human beings in a lawless condition, "they ought to leave this condition," cannot hold for states in accordance with the right of nations (since, as states, they already have a rightful constitution internally and hence have outgrown the constraint of others to bring them under a more extended law-governed constitution in accordance with their concepts of right); yet reason, from the throne of the highest morally legislative power, delivers an absolute condemnation of war as a procedure for determining rights and, on the contrary, makes a condition of peace, which cannot be instituted or assured without a pact of nations among themselves, a direct duty; so there must be a league of a special kind, which can be called a *pacific league (foedus pacificum),* and what would distinguish it from a *peace pact (pactum pacis)* is that the latter seeks to end only *one* war whereas the former seeks to end *all war* forever. This league does not look to acquiring any power of a state but only to preserving and securing the *freedom* of a state itself and of other states in league with it, but without there being any need for them to subject themselves to public laws and coercion under them (as people in a state of nature must do). The practicability (objective reality) of this idea of a *federalism* that should gradually extend over all states and so lead to perpetual peace can be shown. For if good fortune should ordain that a powerful and enlightened people can form itself into a republic (which by its nature must be inclined to perpetual peace), this would provide a focal point of federative union for other states, to attach themselves to it and so to secure a condition of freedom of states conformably with the idea of the right of nations; and by further alliances of this kind, it would gradually extend further and further.

8:356

It is understandable for a people to say, "There shall be no war among us; for we want to form ourselves into a state, that is, to establish for ourselves a supreme legislative, executive, and judicial power, which settles our disputes peaceably." But if this state says, "There shall be no war between myself and other states, although I recognize[j] no supreme legislative power which secures my right to me and to which I secure its right," it is not understandable on what I want to base my confidence in my right, unless it is the surrogate of the civil social union, namely the free federalism that reason must connect necessarily with the concept of the right of nations if this is to retain any meaning at all.

The concept of the right of nations as that of the right *to go to* war is, strictly speaking, unintelligible (since it is supposed to be a right to determine what is right not by universally valid external laws limiting the freedom of each but by unilateral maxims through force); one would have to mean by it that it is quite right if human beings so disposed destroy one another and thus find perpetual peace in the vast grave that covers all the horrors of violence along with their authors. In accordance with reason there is only one way that states in relation with one another can leave the lawless condition, which involves nothing but war; it is that, like individual human beings, they give up their savage (lawless) freedom, accommodate themselves to public coercive laws, and so form an (always growing) *state of nations* (*civitas gentium*) that would finally encompass all the nations of the earth. But, in accordance with their idea of the right of nations, they do not at all want this, thus rejecting *in hypothesi* what is correct *in thesi;* so (if all is not to be lost) in place of the positive idea *of a world republic* only the *negative* surrogate of a *league* that averts war, endures, and always expands can hold back the stream of hostile inclination that shies away from right, though with constant danger of its breaking out.* (*Furor impius intus – fremit horridus ore cruento.* Virgil.)[k]

THIRD DEFINITIVE ARTICLE FOR PERPETUAL PEACE

"Cosmopolitan right shall be limited to conditions of universal *hospitality.*"

Here, as in the preceding articles, it is not a question of philanthropy but of *right*, so that *hospitality* (hospitableness) means the right of a foreigner

---

* At the end of a war, when peace is concluded, it would not be unfitting for a nation to proclaim, after the festival of thanksgiving, a day of atonement, calling upon heaven, in the name of the state, to forgive the great sin of which the human race continues to be guilty, that of being unwilling to acquiesce in any lawful constitution in relation to other nations but, proud of its independence, preferring instead to use the barbarous means of war (even though what is sought by war, namely the right of each state, is not decided by it). Festivals of thanksgiving during a war for a *victory* won, hymns that (in the style of the Israelites) are sung to the *Lord of Hosts*, stand in no less marked contrast with the moral idea of the father of human beings; for, beyond indifference to the way nations seek their mutual rights (which is regrettable enough), they bring in joy at having annihilated a great many human beings or their happiness.

[j] *erkenne*

[k] Within, impious rage – shall roar savagely with bloody mouth. *Aeneid* 1.294–6.

not to be treated with hostility because he has arrived on the land of another. The other can turn him away, if this can be done without destroying him, but as long as he behaves peaceably where he is,[l] he cannot be treated with hostility. What he can claim is not the *right to be a guest* (for this a special beneficent pact would be required, making him a member of the household for a certain time), but the *right to visit;* this right, to present oneself for society, belongs to all human beings by virtue of the right of possession in common of the earth's surface on which, as a sphere, they cannot disperse infinitely but must finally put up with being near one another; but originally no one had more right than another to be on a place on the earth. Uninhabitable parts of the earth's surface, seas and deserts, divide this community, but in such a way that *ships* and *camels* (*ships* of the desert) make it possible to approach one another over these regions belonging to no one[m] and to make use of the right to the *earth's surface*, which belongs to the human race in common, for possible commerce. The inhospitableness of the inhabitants of sea coasts (for example, the Barbary Coast) in robbing ships in adjacent seas or enslaving stranded seafarers, or that of the inhabitants of deserts (the Arabian Bedouins) in regarding approach to nomadic tribes as a right to plunder them, is therefore contrary to natural right; but this right to hospitality – that is, the authorization of a foreign newcomer – does not extend beyond the conditions which make it possible to *seek* commerce with the old inhabitants. In this way distant parts of the world can enter peaceably into relations with one another, which can eventually become publicly lawful and so finally bring the human race ever closer to a cosmopolitan constitution.

If one compares with this the *inhospitable* behavior of civilized, especially commercial, states in our part of the world, the injustice they show in *visiting* foreign lands and peoples (which with them is tantamount to *conquering* them) goes to horrifying lengths. When America, the negro countries, the Spice Islands, the Cape, and so forth were discovered, they were, to them, countries belonging to no one,[n] since they counted the inhabitants as nothing. In the East Indies (Hindustan), they brought in foreign soldiers under the pretext of merely proposing to set up trading posts, but with them oppression of the inhabitants, incitement of the various Indian states to widespread wars, famine, rebellions, treachery, and the whole litany of troubles that oppress the human race.

China* and Japan (*Nipon*), which had given such guests a try, have

---

* In order to write this great empire with the name by which it calls itself (namely *China*, not Sina or a name that sounds like it), one need only consult Georgii's *Alphabetum Tibetanum*, pp. 651–54, especially note b. According to the observation of Professor Fischer of Petersburg, it really has no determinate name by which it calls itself; but the most common one is

[l] *auf seinem Platz*
[m] *herrenlos*
[n] *die keinem angehörten*

therefore wisely [placed restrictions on them], the former allowing them access but not entry,*o* the latter even allowing access to only a single European people, the Dutch, but excluding them, like prisoners, from community with the natives. The worst of this (or, considered from the standpoint of a moral judge, the best) is that the commercial states*p* do not even profit from this violence; that all these trading companies are on the verge of collapse; that the Sugar Islands, that place of the cruelest and most calculated slavery, yield no true profit but serve only a mediate and indeed not very laudable purpose, namely, training sailors for warships and so, in turn, carrying on wars in Europe, and this for powers that make much ado of their piety and, while they drink wrongfulness like water, want to be known as the elect in orthodoxy.

Since the (narrower or wider) community of the nations of the earth has now gone so far that a violation of right on *one* place of the earth is felt in *all*, the idea of a cosmopolitan right is no fantastic and exaggerated way of representing right; it is, instead, a supplement to the unwritten code of the right of a state and the right of nations necessary for the sake of any

---

still the word *Kin,* namely *gold* (which the Tibetans express by *Ser*), so that the emperor is called King of *Gold* (i.e., of the most magnificent country in the world); it may well be that the word sounds like *Chin* in the empire itself, though (because of the guttural letter) it is pronounced *Kin* by the Italian missionaries. From this it can then be seen that what the Romans called the Land *of the Sers* was China but that silk was brought from there to Europe via *Greater Tibet* (presumably through *Lesser Tibet* and Bukhara, crossing Persia and so forth). This led to numerous reflections on the antiquity of this astonishing state as compared with that of Hindustan, and on its connection with *Tibet* and through this with Japan, although the name *Sina* or *Tschina,* which neighboring countries are supposed to give it, leads nowhere. Perhaps the ancient community between Europe and Tibet, which has never been rightly acknowledged, can also be explained from what Hesychius has kept open for us about it, namely from the hierophant's cry (*Konx Ompax*) in the Eleusinian Mysteries (cf. *Journey of the Younger Anacharsis,* Part V, p. 447 ff.). For, according to Georgii's *Alphabetum Tibetanum,* the word *Concioa* means *god,* and it markedly resembles *Konx,* and *Pah-cio* (ibid. p. 520), which the Greeks might easily have pronounced *pax,* means *promulgator legis,* the divinity pervading the whole of nature (also called *Cencresi,* p. 177). But *Om,* which La Croze translates as *benedictus, blessed,* can scarcely mean anything other than *beatific,* if applied to the deity (p. 507). Now since P. Francisco Orazio, who repeatedly asked the Tibetan *lamas* what they understood by god (*Concioa*), always received the answer, "*It is the gathering of all the holy ones*" (i.e., of the blessed souls, at last returned to divinity by being reborn as lamas after numerous migrations through all kinds of bodies, transformed into *Burchane,* i.e., beings worthy of adoration, p. 223), that mysterious name *Konx Ompax* could well designate that *holy (Konx), blessed (Om),* and *wise (Pax)* supreme being who pervades the whole world (nature personified) and, used in the Greek *mysteries,* may well have signified *monotheism* to the epopts, as opposed to the *polytheism* of the uninitiated masses, although P. Orazio suspected a kind of atheism behind it (loc. cit.). But how that mysterious word reached the Greeks across Tibet can be explained in the above way, which can also make plausible the early commerce of Europe with China across Tibet (perhaps even earlier than with Hindustan).[6]

o den Zugang, aber nicht den Eingang
p dieser

330

public rights of human beings and so for perpetual peace; only under this condition can we flatter ourselves that we are constantly approaching perpetual peace.

First supplement
On the guarantee of perpetual peace

What affords this *guarantee* (surety) is nothing less than the great artist nature (*natura daedala rerum*)*[q]* from whose mechanical course purposiveness shines forth visibly, letting concord arise by means of the discord between human beings even against their will; and for this reason nature, regarded as necessitation by a cause the laws of whose operation are unknown to us, is called *fate*, but if we consider its purposiveness in the course of the world as the profound wisdom of a higher cause directed to the objective final end of the human race and predetermining this course of the world, it is called *providence*,* which

---

* In the mechanism of nature, to which the human being (as a sensible being) belongs, there is evident a form lying at the basis of its existence, which we can make comprehensible to ourselves only if we ascribe it to the end of a creator of the world determining it in advance; we call its determination in advance (divine) *providence* in general; insofar as it is put in the *beginning* of the world, we call it *founding* providence (*providentia conditrix; semel iussit, semper parent* – Augustine);*[r]* but as put in the *course* of nature, to maintain this in accord with universal laws of purposiveness, we call it *ruling providence* (*providentia gubernatrix*); as [directing nature] further to particular ends not to be foreseen by the human being but only conjectured from the outcome, we call it *guiding* providence (*providentia directrix*); and finally, with respect to single events as divine ends, we no longer call it providence but *dispensation* (*directio extraordinaria*), although (since this in fact alludes to miracles, though the events are not called such), it is a foolish presumption for the human being to want to cognize an event as a dispensation; for it is absurd to conclude from a single event to a particular principle of the efficient cause (to conclude that this event is an end and not merely an indirect result, by a natural mechanism, of another end quite unknown to us), and it is full of self-conceit, however pious and humble such talk may sound. So too the division of providence (regarded *materialiter*), as directed to *objects* in the world, into *general* and *special* providence is false and self-contradictory (that, e.g., it is indeed concerned to preserve species of creatures but leaves individuals to chance); for it is called general in its purpose just because no single thing is thought to be excepted from it. Presumably, what was meant here is the division of providence (regarded *formaliter*) in terms of the way its purpose is carried out, namely into *ordinary* providence (e.g., the annual death and revival of nature with the changes of seasons) and *extraordinary* providence (e.g., the transporting of wood by ocean currents to Arctic coasts where it cannot grow, thus providing for the native inhabitants, who could not live without it); in the latter case, although we can very well explain to ourselves the physico-mechanical cause of these appearances (e.g., by the wooded river banks in temperate countries, where trees fall into the rivers and are carried farther afield by currents such as the Gulf Stream), we must still not overlook the teleological cause as well, which intimates the foresight of a wisdom in command of nature. But as for the concept, current in the schools, of a divine *intervention* or collaboration

[q] Nature the contriver of things. Lucretius *De rerum natura* 5.234.
[r] Providence the founder; once it has ordered, they always obey.

we do not, strictly speaking, *cognize* in these artifices of nature or even so much as *infer* from them but instead (as in all relations of the form of things to ends in general) only can and must *add it in thought*, in order to make for ourselves a concept of their possibility by analogy with actions of human art; but the representation of their relation to and harmony with the end that reason prescribes immediately to us (the moral end) is an idea, which is indeed transcendent for *theoretical* purposes but for practical purposes (e.g., with respect to the concept of the duty *of perpetual peace* and putting that mechanism of nature to use for it) is dogmatic and well founded as to its reality. Moreover, the use of the word *nature* when, as here, we have to do only with theory (not with religion) is more befitting the limitations of human reason (which must confine itself within the limits of possible experience with respect to the relation of effects to their causes) and more *modest* than is the expression of a *providence* cognizable for us, with which one presumptuously puts on the wings of Icarus in order to approach more closely the secret of its inscrutable purpose.

Now, before we determine more closely this affording of the guarantee, it will be necessary first to examine the condition" that nature has prepared for the persons acting on its great stage, which finally makes its assurance of peace necessary; only then shall we examine the way it affords this guarantee.

Its preparatory arrangement consists in the following: that it 1) has taken care that people should be able to live in all regions of the earth; 2) by *war* it has driven them everywhere, even into the most inhospitable

---

(*concursus*) toward an effect in the sensible world, this must be given up. For to want to pair what is disparate (*gryphes iungere equis*)' and to let what is itself the complete cause of alterations in the world *supplement* its own predetermining providence (which must therefore have been inadequate) during the course of the world is, *first*, self-contradictory. For example, to say that, *next to God*, the physician cured the illness, and was thus his assistant in it, is *in the first place* self-contradictory. For *causa solitaria non iuvat.*' God is the author of the physician together with all his medicines and so the effect must be ascribed *entirely* to him, if one wants to ascend all the way to that highest original ground, theoretically incomprehensible to us. Or one can also ascribe it *entirely* to the physician, insofar as we follow up this event as belonging to the order of nature and as explicable in terms of the order of nature, within the chain of causes in the world. *Second*, such a way of thinking also does away with all determinate principles for appraising an effect. But from a *morally practical* point of view (which is thus directed entirely to the supersensible), as, e.g., in the belief that God, by means incomprehensible to us, will make up for the lack of our own righteousness if only our disposition is genuine, so that we should never slacken in our striving toward the good, the concept of a divine *concursus* is quite appropriate and even necessary; but it is self-evident that no one must attempt to *explain* a good action (as an event in the world) by this *concursus*, which is a futile theoretical cognition of the supersensible and is therefore absurd.

' To couple griffins with horses. Virgil *Eclogues* 8.27.
' a single cause does not assist
" *Zustand*

regions, in order to populate these; 3) by war it has compelled them to enter into more or less lawful relations. That moss grows even in the cold wastes around the Arctic Ocean, which the *reindeer* can scrape from under the snow in order to be the nourishment, or also the draft animal, for the Ostiaks or Samoyeds; or that the sandy wastes contain salt for the *camel*, which seems as if created for traveling in them, so as not to leave them unused, is already wonderful. But the end shines forth even more clearly when we see that on the shore of the Arctic Ocean there are, besides fur-bearing animals, also seals, walruses, and whales, whose flesh gives the inhabitants food and whose blubber gives them warmth. But nature's foresight arouses most wonder by the driftwood it brings to these barren regions (without anyone knowing exactly where it comes from), without which material they could make neither their boats and weapons nor their huts to live in; there they have enough to do warring against animals, so that they live peaceably among themselves. What *drove* them *into* those regions, however, was presumably nothing other than war. But the first *instrument of war*, among all the animals the human being learned to tame and domesticate at the time the earth was being populated, was the *horse* (for the elephant belongs to a later time, namely the time of the luxury of already established states); so too, the art of cultivating certain kinds of grasses, called *grain*, whose original characteristics we can no longer cognize, and of diversifying and improving certain *types of fruits* by transplanting and grafting (perhaps in Europe only two species, the crab apple and the wild pear), could arise only in the condition of already established states, where there was secured ownership of land, after human beings, previously in the lawless freedom of *hunting*,* fishing, or pastoral life, had been driven to *agricultural* life; then *salt* and *iron* were discovered, perhaps the first articles, everywhere in demand, of a trade among various peoples, by which they were first brought into a *peaceable relation* to each other and so into understanding, community, and peaceable relations with one another, even with the most distant.

In taking care that people *could* live everywhere on the earth, nature at the same time despotically willed that they *should* live everywhere, even if against their inclination, and without this "should" even presupposing a concept of duty that would bind them to do so by means of a moral law;

8:364

---

* Of all ways of life, that of the *hunter* is undoubtedly most opposed to a civilized constitution; for families, having to separate, soon become strangers to one another and subsequently, being dispersed in extensive forests, also *hostile* since each needs a great deal of space for acquiring its food and clothing. The *prohibition of blood addressed to Noah* (Genesis 9:4–6) – which, often reiterated, was a condition later imposed by Jewish Christians upon the newly accepted Christians of heathen origin, though in a different connection (Acts 15, 20 and 21, 25) – seems to have been originally nothing other than a prohibition of the *hunter's way of life;* for in it cases must often come up in which raw flesh is eaten, and if the latter is forbidden so too is the former.

8:364

instead it chose war to achieve this end it has. That is to say, we see peoples whose unity of language enables us to recognize the unity of their descent, such as the Samoyeds on the Arctic Ocean on the one hand and on the other a people of similar language two hundred [German] miles distant in the Altaian Mountains, between whom another, namely a Mongolian people given to horsemanship and hence to war, has thrust itself and so driven the former part of the tribe far away from the latter, into the most inhospitable Arctic regions, where they would certainly not have spread of their own inclination;* in the same way the Finns in the northernmost regions of Europe, called Lapps, are now just as far separated from the Hungarians, to whom they are related in language, by Gothic and Samartian peoples who thrust themselves in between them; and what can have driven the Eskimos (a race quite distinct from all American races and perhaps descended from European adventurers of ancient times) into the north of America, and the Pesherae into the south all the way to Tierra del Fuego, if not war, which nature makes use of as a means to populate the earth everywhere. War itself, however, needs no special motive but seems to be engrafted onto human nature and even to hold as something noble, to which the human being is impelled by the drive to honor without self-seeking incentives, so that *military courage* is judged (by the American savages as well as by the European savages in the age of chivalry) to be of immediately great worth, not only *if* there is war (as would be reasonable) but also in order that *there may be war*, and war is often begun merely in order to display courage; hence an inner *dignity* is put in war itself, and even philosophers have eulogized it as a certain ennoblement of humanity, unmindful of the saying of a certain Greek, "War is bad in that it makes more evil people than it takes away." So much for what nature does *for its own end* with respect to the human race as a class of animals.

Now we come to the question concerning what is essential to the purpose of perpetual peace: what nature does for this purpose with reference to the end that the human being's own reason makes a duty for him, hence to the favoring of his *moral purpose*, and how it affords the guarantee that what man *ought* to do in accordance with laws of freedom but does not do, it is assured he *will* do, without prejudice to this freedom, even by a constraint of nature, and this in terms of all three relations of public right: the *right of a state*, the *right of nations* and *cosmopolitan right*. When I say of

---

* The question could be raised: if nature willed that these frozen shores not remain uninhabited, what will become of their inhabitants if (as we may expect) it some day ceases to bring them driftwood? For we may believe that, as culture progresses, the occupants of the temperate zones will make better use of the wood growing on the banks of their rivers than to let it fall into them and be swept out to sea. I reply: those who live on the Ob, the Yenisi, the Lena, and so forth will bring it to them by trade and will barter it for the animal products so abundant in the sea around the Arctic coasts, once it (nature) has first exacted peace among them.

nature, it *wills* that this or that happen, this does not mean, it lays upon us a *duty* to do it (for only practical reason, without coercion, can do that) but rather that nature itself *does* it, whether we will it or not (*fata volentem ducunt, nolentem trahunt*).[v]

1. Even if a people were not forced by internal discord to submit to the constraint of public laws, war would still force them from without to do so, inasmuch as by the natural arrangement discussed above each people would find itself in the neighborhood of another people pressing upon it, against which it must form itself internally into a *state* in order to be armed as a *power* against it. Now the *republican* constitution is the only one that is completely compatible with the right of human beings, but it is also the most difficult one to establish and even more to maintain, so much so that many assert it would have to be a state of *angels* because human beings, with their self-seeking inclinations, would not be capable of such a sublime form of constitution. But now nature comes to the aid of the general will grounded in reason, revered but impotent in practice, and does so precisely through those self-seeking inclinations, so that it is a matter only of a good organization of a state (which is certainly within the capacity of human beings), of arranging those forces of nature in opposition to one another in such a way that one checks the destructive effect of the other or cancels it, so that the result for reason turns out as if neither of them existed at all and the human being is constrained to become a good citizen even if not a morally good human being. The problem of establishing a state, no matter how hard it may sound, is *soluble* even for a nation of devils (if only they have understanding) and goes like this: "Given a multitude of rational beings all of whom need universal laws for their preservation but each of whom is inclined covertly to exempt himself from them, so to order this multitude and establish their constitution that, although in their private dispositions they strive against one another, these yet so check one another that in their public conduct the result is the same as if they had no such evil dispositions." Such a problem must be soluble. For the problem is not the moral improvement of human beings but only the mechanism of nature, and what the task requires one to know is how this can be put to use in human beings in order so to arrange the conflict of their unpeaceable dispositions within a people that they themselves have to constrain one another to submit to coercive law and so bring about a condition of peace in which laws have force. It can be seen even in actually existing states, still very imperfectly organized, that they are already closely approaching in external conduct what the idea of right prescribes, though the cause of this is surely not inner morality[w] (for it is not the case that a good state constitution is to be expected from inner

8:366

---

[v] The Fates lead the willing, drive the unwilling. Seneca *Epist. mor.* 18.4.
[w] *das Innere der Moralität*

morality; on the contrary, the good moral education^x of a people is to be expected from a good state constitution), and thus that reason can use the mechanism of nature, through self-seeking inclinations that naturally counteract one another externally as well, as a means to make room for its own end, the rule of right,^{y} and in so doing also to promote and secure peace within as well as without, so far as a state itself can do so. Here it is therefore said that nature *wills* irresistibly that right should eventually gain supremacy. What we here neglect to do eventually comes about of its own accord, though with great inconvenience. "If one bends the reed too hard it breaks; and he who wills too much wills nothing." Bouterwek.[7]

2. The idea of the right of nations presupposes the *separation* of many neighboring states independent of one another; and though such a condition is of itself a condition of war (unless a federative union of them prevents the outbreak of hostilities), this is nevertheless better, in accordance with the idea of reason, than the fusion of them by one power overgrowing the rest and passing into a universal monarchy, since as the range of government expands laws progressively lose their vigor, and a soulless despotism, after it has destroyed the seed of good, finally deteriorates into anarchy. Yet the craving of every state (or of its head) is to attain a lasting condition of peace in this way, by ruling the whole world where possible. But *nature wills* it otherwise. It makes use of two means to prevent peoples from intermingling and to separate them: differences of *language* and of *religion*,* which do bring with them the propensity to mutual hatred and pretexts for war but yet, with increasing culture and the gradual approach of human beings to greater agreement in principles, leads to understanding in a peace that is produced and secured, not as in such a despotism (in the graveyard of freedom), by means of a weakening of all forces, but by means of their equilibrium in liveliest competition.

Just as nature wisely separates states that the will of each state, and even on grounds of the right of nations, would like to unite under itself by cunning or force, so on the other hand it also unites nations that the concept of cosmopolitan right would not have secured against violence and war, and does so by means of their mutual self-interest. It is the *spirit of commerce,* which cannot coexist with war and which sooner or later takes

---

* *Different religions:* an odd expression! just as if one could also speak of different *morals*. There can indeed be historically different *creeds*,^{z} [to be found] not in religion but in the history of means used to promote it, which is the province of scholarship, and just as many different *religious books* (the Zendavesta, the Vedas, the Koran, and so forth), but there can be only one single *religion* holding for all human beings and in all times. Those can therefore contain nothing more than the vehicle of religion, what is contingent and can differ according to differences of time and place.

^{x} Bildung
^{y} der rechtlichen Vorschrift
^{z} Glaubesarten

hold of every nation. In other words, since the *power of money* may well be the most reliable of all the powers (means) subordinate to that of a state, states find themselves compelled (admittedly not through incentives of morality) to promote honorable peace and, whenever war threatens to break out anywhere in the world, to prevent it by mediation, just as if they were in a permanent league for this purpose; for, by the nature of things, great alliances for war can only rarely be formed and even more rarely succeed. In this way nature guarantees perpetual peace through the mechanism of human inclinations itself, with an assurance that is admittedly not adequate for *predicting* its future (theoretically) but that is still enough for practical purposes and makes it a duty to work toward this (not merely chimerical) end.

Second supplement
Secret article for perpetual peace

A secret article in negotiations of public right is *objectively*, that is, considered in terms of its content, a contradiction; but *subjectively*, appraised in terms of the quality of the person who dictates it, a secret can well be present in them, inasmuch as a person finds it prejudicial to his dignity to announce publicly that he is its author.

The sole article of this kind is contained in the following proposition: *The maxims of philosophers about the conditions[a] under which public peace is possible shall be consulted by states armed for war.*

But it seems to be humiliating for the legislative authority of a state, to which one must naturally ascribe the greatest wisdom, to seek from its *subjects* (philosophers) instructions about the principles of its conduct toward other states, and yet very advisable to do so. A state will therefore *invite their instruction tacitly* (thus making a secret of it), and this is tantamount to saying that it will *allow* them *to speak* freely and publicly about universal maxims of waging war and establishing peace (for that they will do of their own accord, if only they are not forbidden to do so); and the agreement of states with one another on this point requires no special arrangement of states among themselves for this purpose but is already present in obligation by universal (morally legislative) human reason. This does not mean, however, that a state must give the principles of philosophers precedence over the findings of lawyers (representatives of the power of the state), but only that they be given a *hearing*. A lawyer who has made his symbol the *scales* of right along with the *sword* of justice does not usually make use of the latter merely to keep all extraneous influences

[a] *Bedingungen*

away from the former, but when one side of the scales refuses to sink he puts the sword into it (*vae victis*);[b] and a lawyer who is not also a philosopher (at least in morality) is greatly tempted to do so, since his office is only to apply existing laws but not to investigate whether such laws themselves need to be improved, and he counts this rank of his faculty, which is in fact lower, as higher because it is accompanied by power (as is also the case with the other two faculties).[8] Beneath this allied power the philosophical faculty stands on its very low step. So it is said of philosophy, for example, that she is the *handmaiden* of theology (and likewise of the other two faculties). But it is not clear whether "she bears the torch before her mistress or carries the train behind."

That kings should philosophize or philosophers become kings is not to be expected, but it is also not to be wished for, since possession of power unavoidably corrupts the free judgment of reason. But that kings or royal peoples (ruling themselves by laws of equality) should not let the class of philosophers disappear or be silent but should let it speak publicly is indispensable to both, so that light may be thrown on their business; and, because this class is by its nature incapable of forming seditious factions or clubs, it cannot be suspected of spreading *propaganda*.

Appendix

I.
ON THE DISAGREEMENT BETWEEN MORALS AND POLITICS WITH A VIEW TO PERPETUAL PEACE

Morals is of itself practical in the objective sense, as the sum of laws commanding unconditionally, in accordance with which we *ought* to act, and it is patently absurd, having granted this concept of duty its authority, to want to say that one nevertheless *cannot* do it. For in that case this concept would of itself drop out of morals (*ultra posse nemo obligatur*);[c] hence there can be no conflict of politics, as doctrine of right put into practice, with morals, as theoretical doctrine of right (hence no conflict of practice with theory); for if there were, one would have to understand by the latter a general *doctrine of prudence,* that is, a theory of maxims for choosing the most suitable means to one's purposes aimed at advantage, that is, to deny that there is a [doctrine of] morals at all.

Politics says, "*Be ye wise as serpents*"; morals adds (as a limiting condition) "*and guileless as doves.*"[d] If both cannot coexist in one command, there

---
[b] woe to the vanquished
[c] no one is obligated beyond what he can do
[d] Matthew 10:16

is really a conflict of politics with morals; but if both ought nevertheless to be thoroughly united, then the concept of opposition is absurd, and the question of how that conflict is to be resolved cannot even be posed as a problem. Although the proposition *honesty is the best politics* contains a theory that is, unfortunately, very often contradicted by practice, the equally theoretical proposition *honesty is better than all politics* is raised infinitely above all objections and is indeed the indispensable condition of all politics. The tutelary god*e* of morals does not yield to Jupiter (the god of power); for Jupiter is still subject to fate, that is, reason is not sufficiently enlightened to survey the series of predetermining causes that would allow it to predict confidently the happy or unhappy results of human actions in accordance with the mechanism of nature (though it is sufficiently enlightened to hope they will be in conformity with its wish). But it throws enough light everywhere for us to see what we have to do in order to remain on the path of duty (in accordance with rules of wisdom), and thereby do toward the final end.

But now the practical man (for whom morals is mere theory), bases his despairing denial of our benign hope (even while granting *ought* and *can*) strictly on this: that he pretends to see in advance, from the nature of the human being, that *he is* never *going to will* what is required in order to realize that end leading toward perpetual peace. Admittedly, the volitions of *all individuals* to live in a lawful constitution in accordance with principles of freedom (the *distributive* unity of the will *of all*) is not adequate to this end; but there is still required for it this solution of a difficult problem, that *all together* will this condition (the *collective* unity of the united will), so that a whole of civil society comes to be; and since, accordingly, a uniting cause must be added to this variety of the particular volitions of all, in order to produce from them a common will, which no one of the all is capable of, in the *carrying out* of that idea (in practice) the only beginning of the rightful condition to be counted upon is that by *power*, on the coercion of which public right is afterward based; and (since we can scarcely allow for a moral disposition of the legislator such that, after the disorderly multitude has been united into a people, he will now leave the people to bring about a rightful constitution by its common will) it can be anticipated that in actual experience there will be great deviations from that idea (of theory).

8:371

It is then said that he who once has power in his hands will not let the people prescribe laws for him. A state that is once in possession [of the power] not to be subject to any external laws will not make itself dependent upon the tribunal of other states with respect to the way it is to pursue its right against them; and even a continent, if it feels itself superior to another that does not otherwise stand in its way, will not leave unused the means of strengthening its power by plundering or even conquering it; and so all the plans of theory for the right of a state, the right of

e Grenzgott

nations, and cosmopolitan right dissolve into ineffectual, impracticable ideals, whereas a practice that is based on empirical principles of human nature, one that does not consider it demeaning to draw instruction for its maxims from the way of the world, can alone hope to find a sure ground for its edifice of political prudence.

Admittedly, if there were no freedom and no moral law based upon it and everything that happens or can happen is instead the mere mechanism of nature, then politics (as the art of making use of this mechanism for governing human beings) would be the whole of practical wisdom, and the concept of right would be an empty thought. But if one finds it indispensably necessary to join the concept of right with politics, and even to raise it to the limiting condition of politics, it must be granted that the two can be united. I can indeed think of a *moral politician*, that is, one who takes the principles of political prudence in such a way that they can coexist with morals, but not of a *political moralist*, who frames a morals to suit the statesman's advantage.

A moral politician will make it his principle that, once defects that could not have been prevented are found within the constitution of a state or in the relations of states, it is a duty, especially for heads of state, to be concerned about how they can be improved as soon as possible and brought into conformity with natural right, which stands before us as a model in the idea of reason, even at the cost of sacrifices to their self-seeking [inclinations]. Since the severing of a bond of civil or cosmopolitan union even before a better constitution is ready to take its place is contrary to all political prudence, which agrees with morals in this, it would indeed be absurd to require that those defects be altered at once and violently; but it can be required of the one in power that he at least take to heart the maxim that such an alteration is necessary, in order to keep constantly approaching the end (of the best constitution in accordance with laws of right). A state can already *govern* itself in a republican way even though, by its present constitution, it possesses a despotic *ruling power*,[f] until the people gradually becomes susceptible to the influence of the mere idea of the authority of law (just as if it possessed physical power) and thus is found fit to legislate for itself (such legislation being originally based on right). Even if a constitution more in conformity with law were attained illegitimately, by the violence of a *revolution* engendered by a bad constitution, it could then not be held permissible to lead the people back to the old one, although during the revolution anyone who took part in it by violence or intrigue would be subject with right to the punishment of rebels. But as regards the external relations of states, it cannot be demanded of a state that it give up its constitution even though this is a despotic one (which is, for all that, the stronger kind in relation to

[f] *Herrschermacht*

external enemies), so long as it runs the risk of being at once devoured by other states; hence, as for that resolution, it must also be permitted to postpone putting it into effect until a more favorable time.*

Thus it may always be that despotizing*g* moralists (erring in practice) offend in various ways against political prudence (by measures prematurely adopted or recommended); yet when they offend against nature experience must gradually bring them onto a better course; but moralizing politicians, by glossing over political principles contrary to right on the pretext that human nature is not *capable* of what is good in accord with that idea, as reason prescribes it, *make* improvement *impossible* and perpetuate, as far as they can, violations of right.

Instead of the practice*h* of which these politically prudent men boast, they deal in *machinations*,*i* inasmuch as their only concern is to go along with the power now ruling (so as not to neglect their private advantage), and thereby to hand over the people and where possible the whole world, in the way of true lawyers (of the craft, not of *legislation*) when they go into politics. For since it is not their business to reason subtly about legislation itself but to carry out the present commands of the law of the land, to them whatever lawful constitution now exists must always be the best and, when this is altered from on high, the one following it, since everything is then in its proper mechanical order. But if this skill in turning their hand to everything gives them the illusion that they are also able to judge the principles of a *state's constitution* as such in accordance with concepts of right (hence á priori, not empirically); if they make much of their knowledge of *human beings* (which is admittedly to be expected, since they have to do with so many) but without knowing the *human being* and what can be made of him (for which a higher standpoint of anthropological observation is required), and equipped with these concepts approach the right of a state and the right of nations, as reason prescribes it, then they cannot make this transition except in the spirit of chicanery; for they follow their usual procedure (of a mechanism in accordance with despotically given coercive laws) even where concepts of reason admit only coercion through

8:374

---

* These are permissive laws of reason that allow a situation of public right afflicted with injustice to continue until everything has either of itself become ripe for a complete overthrow or has been made almost ripe by peaceful means; for some *rightful* constitution or other, even if it is only to a small degree in conformity with right, is better than none at all, which latter fate (anarchy) a *premature* reform would meet with. Thus political wisdom, in the condition in which things are at present, will make reforms in keeping with the ideal of public right its duty; but it will use revolutions, where nature of itself has brought them about, not to gloss over an even greater oppression, but as a call of nature to bring about by fundamental reforms a lawful constitution based on principles of freedom, the only kind that endures.

g *despotisirende*
h *Praxis*
i *Praktiken*

laws in accordance with principles of freedom, by which a state constitution that can continue valid[j] is first possible – a problem the supposedly practical man believes he can solve empirically, ignoring that idea, from experience of how the hitherto most lasting[k] constitutions were arranged, even though they were for the most part contrary to right. The maxims he makes use of for this (though he does not let them become known) amount, roughly, to the following sophistical maxims:

1. *Fac et excusa.* Seize any favorable opportunity for taking possession without any sanction to do so (whether of a right of a state over its people or of a right over a neighboring people); the justification can be presented much more easily and elegantly *after the fact*, and the violence glossed over (especially in the first case, where the supreme power within a state is also the legislative authority, which one must obey without reasoning subtly about it),[9] than if one were willing to devise convincing arguments in advance and to wait for counterarguments about them. Such audacity itself gives a certain semblance of inner conviction about the legitimacy of the deed, and the god *bonus eventus* is the best defense attorney afterward.

2. *Si fecisti, nega.* Whatever crime you have yourself committed, for example, so as to reduce your people to despair and hence to rebellion, deny that the guilt is *yours;* instead, maintain that your subjects' recalcitrance is to blame or, if you have seized a neighboring nation, human nature, since if a human being does not anticipate another in using force, the other can be surely counted upon to anticipate and seize him.

3. *Divide et impera.* That is, if there are certain privileged leaders in your nation who have chosen you to be merely their chief (*primus inter pares*),[l] set them at variance among themselves and at odds with the people; then come to the people's aid with the illusion of greater freedom, and all will be dependent upon your unconditional will. Or if you are dealing with external states, stirring up disagreement among them is a fairly sure means for you to subjugate them one after another by seeming to assist the weaker.

Certainly, no one is now taken in by these political maxims, for all of them are already generally known; nor is it the case that [politicians] are ashamed of them, as if their injustice were all too obvious. For, since great powers are never shamed before the judgment of the masses but only before one another, and, with regard to those principles, only their *failure* and not their becoming public can make those powers ashamed (since with respect to the morality of maxims they are all agreed among themselves), there is still left to them *political honor*, which they can count upon

---
[j] *eine zu Recht beständige Staatsverfassung*
[k] *am besten bestandene*
[l] first among equals

TOWARD PERPETUAL PEACE

with confidence, namely the honor of *augmenting their power*, in whatever way they may acquire it.*

From all these twistings and turnings by which an immoral[m] doctrine of prudence tries to bring a condition of peace among human beings out of the warlike condition of a state of nature, at least this much is clear: people can no more get away from the concept of right in their private relations than in their public relations, and they dare not openly base politics merely on the machinations of prudence and so disown all allegiance[n] to the concept of a public right (this is especially noticeable in the concept of the right of nations); instead they give it all the honor due it, even if they should think up a hundred pretexts and subterfuges to evade it in practice, and attribute to cunning force the authority of being the source and the bond of all right. In order to put an end to this sophistry (if not to the injustice glossed over by it) and to bring the false *representatives* of the powerful on earth to confess that they speak not on behalf of right but of force – the tone of which they adopt, as if it were for them to give orders – it will be well to expose the illusion with which they dupe themselves and others, to find the supreme principle from which the aim of perpetual peace issues, and to show that all the evil standing in its way arises from the fact that the political moralist begins where the moral politician correctly leaves off and, in thus subordinating principles to the end (i.e., putting the cart before the horse), frustrates his own purpose of bringing politics into agreement with morals.

8:376

---

* Even if it might be doubted whether there is, in *human beings* who live together within a state, a certain malevolence rooted in human nature, and instead of it the deficiency of a culture that has not yet progressed far enough (barbarism) might with some plausibility be cited as the cause of the unlawful appearances of their way of thinking, this malevolence is quite undisguisedly and irrefutably obvious in the external relation of *states* to one another. Within each state it is veiled by the coercion of civil laws, for the citizens' inclination to violence against one another is powerfully counteracted by a greater force, namely that of the government, and so not only does this give the whole a moral veneer (*causae non causae*) but also, by its checking the outbreak of unlawful inclinations, the development of the moral predisposition to immediate respect for right is actually greatly facilitated. For each now believes that he himself would indeed hold the concept of right sacred and follow it faithfully, if only he could expect every other to do likewise, and the government in part assures him of this; thereby a great step is taken *toward* morality (though it is not yet a moral step), toward being attached to this concept of duty even for its own sake, without regard for any return. But since each, with his good opinion of himself, still presupposes the evil disposition in all others, the judgment they mutually pronounce on one another is that they are all *in fact* of little worth (why this is so, since the *nature* of the human being as a free being cannot be blamed, need not be discussed). Since, however, respect for the concept of right, which the human being simply cannot renounce, most solemnly sanctions the theory of his capacity to become adequate to it, each sees that he, for his own part, must act in conformity with it, no matter how others may behave.

8:376

[m] *unmoralischen*
[n] *allen Gehorsam aufzukündigen*

In order to make practical philosophy consistent with itself, it is necessary first to decide the question, whether in problems of practical reason one must begin from its *material principle*, the *end* (as object of choice), or from its *formal* principle, that is, the principle (resting only on freedom in external relations) in accordance with which it is said: So act that you can will that your maxim should become a universal law (whatever the end may be).

The latter principle must undoubtedly take precedence; for, as a principle of right, it has unconditional necessity, whereas the former necessitates only if the empirical conditions of the proposed end, namely of its being realized, are presupposed; and even if this end (e.g., perpetual peace) were also a duty, it would still have to be derived from the formal principle of maxims for acting externally. Now the first principle, that of the *political moralist* (the problem of the right of a state, the right of nations, and cosmopolitan right), is a mere *technical problem* (*problema technicum*), whereas the second, as the principle of the *moral politician*, for whom it is a *moral problem* (*problema morale*), is far removed from the other in its procedure for leading to perpetual peace, which is now wished for not only as a natural good but also as a condition^o arising from acknowledgment of duty.

For the solution of the first problem, namely that of political prudence, much knowledge of nature is required in order to make use of its mechanism for the end proposed, and yet all this is uncertain with respect to its result concerning perpetual peace, whichever of the three divisions of public right one takes. Whether a people can better be kept obedient and also prosperous for a long period of time by severity or by the bait of vanity, whether by the supreme power of one individual or by several leaders united, perhaps even by an aristocracy of merit only or by the power of the people within it, is uncertain. History provides examples of the opposite [resulting] from all kinds of government (with the single exception of the truly republican one, which, however, can occur only to a moral politician). Still more uncertain is a *right of nations* supposedly established on statutes according to ministerial plans, which right is in fact only an empty word and rests on pacts that contain in the very act of their being concluded the secret reservation that they may be violated. On the other hand, the solution of the second problem, namely *that of political wisdom*, urges itself upon us of its own accord, so to speak, is clear to everyone, and puts all artifices to shame; moreover, it leads straight to the end, but with the reminder of prudence not to draw toward it precipitately by force but to approach it steadily as favorable circumstances arise.

It can therefore be said, "Seek ye first the kingdom of pure practical reason and its *justice*, and your end (the blessing of perpetual peace) will come

---

^o *Zustand*

to you of itself." For morals has in it the peculiarity – and indeed with respect to its principles of public right (hence with reference to a politics cognizable a priori) – that the less it makes conduct dependent upon the proposed end, the intended advantage whether natural or moral, so much the more does it harmonize with it on the whole; and this happens because it is just the general will given a priori (within a nation or in the relation of various nations to one another) that alone determines what is laid down as right among human beings; but this union of the will of all, if only it is acted upon consistently in practice, can also, in accordance with the mechanism of nature, be the cause bringing about the effect aimed at and providing the concept of right with efficacy. Thus it is, for example, a principle of moral politics that a people is to unite itself into a state in accordance with freedom and equality as the sole concepts of right, and this principle is not based upon prudence but upon duty. On the other hand political moralists, however subtly they reason about how the natural mechanism of a multitude of human beings entering into society would invalidate those principles and thwart their purpose, and also try to prove their contention against them by examples of badly organized constitutions of ancient and modern times (e.g., of democracies without a representative system), do not deserve a hearing, especially since such a pernicious theory itself produces the trouble it predicts, throwing human beings into one class with other living machines, which need only be aware that they are not free in order to become, in their own judgment, the most miserable of all beings in the world.

The proposition that has become proverbial, *fiat iustitia, pereat mundus*,[p] or in German, "let justice reign even if all the rogues in the world perish because of it," sounds rather boastful but it is true; it is a sturdy principle of right, which bars all the devious paths marked out by cunning or force, provided it is not misinterpreted and taken, as it might be, as permission to make use of one's own right with utmost rigor (which would conflict with ethical duty) but is taken instead as the obligation of those in power not to deny anyone his right or to encroach upon it out of disfavor or sympathy for others; and for this there is required, above all, a constitution organized in accordance with pure principles of right within a state, and then too the union of this state with other neighboring or even distant states for a lawful settlement of their disputes (by analogy with a universal state). This proposition means nothing other than that political maxims must not issue from the welfare and happiness of each state that is to be expected from following them, and so not from the end that each of them makes its object – (from "I will")[q] as the supreme (though empirical) principle of political wisdom – but must issue from the pure concept of duty of right (from "I ought,"[r] the

---

[p] do justice though the world perish
[q] *vom Wollen*
[r] *vom Sollen*

principle of which is given a priori by pure reason), whatever the natural consequences may be. The world will by no means perish by there coming to be fewer evil people. What is morally evil has the property, inseparable from its nature, of being at odds with itself in its aims and destructive of them (especially in relation to others similarly disposed), so that it clears the way for the (moral) principle of the good, even if progress is slow.

Thus there is *objectively* (in theory) no conflict at all between morals and politics. But *subjectively* (in the self-seeking propensity of human beings, which, however, because it is not based on maxims of reason, must still not be called practice), such conflict will remain; and it may always remain because it serves as the whetstone of virtue, whose true courage (according to the principle *tu ne cede malis, sed contra audientior ito*)[s] in the present case consists, not so much in resolutely standing up to the troubles and sacrifices one must thereby take upon oneself, but in looking straight in the face what is far more dangerous, the deceitful and treacherous but yet subtly reasoning principle in ourselves which pretends that the weakness of human nature justifies any transgression, and in overcoming its craftiness.

8:380

In fact the political moralist can say that regent and people or nation and nation do *each other* no wrong when they attack each other by force or fraud, though they do wrong generally in that they deny all respect to the concept of right,[10] which alone could found peace in perpetuity. For since one of them transgresses his duty toward the other, who is just as wrongfully disposed toward him, when the two destroy themselves it *happens* to both of them quite rightly, though in such a way that there is always enough of this race left to keep this game going to the most distant times, so that posterity may some day take a warning example from them. Providence is thus justified in the course of the world; for the moral principle in the human being never dies out, and reason, which is capable pragmatically of carrying out rightful ideas in accordance with that principle, grows steadily with advancing culture, but so too does the guilt for those transgressions. It seems that creation alone, namely that such a race of corrupt beings should have been put on earth at all, cannot be justified by any theodicy (if we assume that the human race never will be or can be better off);[11] but this standpoint for appraising matters is much too high for us, as if we could support for theoretical purposes our concepts (of the wisdom) of the supreme power inscrutable to us. To such desperate conclusions we are unavoidably driven if we do not assume that pure principles of right have objective reality, that is, that they can be carried out; and people within a state as well as states in their relations with one another must act in accordance with those principles, regardless of what objec-

---

[s] Do not yield to troubles, but press on more boldly. Virgil *Aeneid* 6.95.

tions empirical politics may bring against them. True politics can therefore not take a step without having already paid homage to morals, and although politics by itself is a difficult art, its union with morals is no art at all; for as soon as the two conflict with each other, morals cuts the knot that politics cannot untie. The right of human beings must be held sacred, however great a sacrifice this may cost the ruling power. One cannot compromise here and devise something intermediate, a pragmatically conditioned right (a cross between right and expediency); instead, all politics must bend its knee before right, but in return it can hope to reach, though slowly, the level where it will shine unfailingly.

II.
ON THE AGREEMENT OF POLITICS WITH MORALS IN ACCORD WITH THE TRANSCENDENTAL CONCEPT OF PUBLIC RIGHT

If I abstract from all the *matter* of public right as teachers of right usually think of it (from the various empirically given relations of individuals within a state or also of states to one another), I am still left with the *form of publicity*, the possibility of which is involved in every claim to a right, since without it there would be no justice (which can be thought only as *publicly known*) and so too no right, which is conferred only by justice.

Every claim to a right must have this capacity for publicity, and since one can very easily appraise whether it is present in a case at hand – that is, whether or not publicity is consistent with an agent's principles – it can yield a criterion to be found a priori in reason that is very easy to use; in case they are inconsistent we can cognize at once, as if by an experiment of pure reason, the falsity (illegitimacy) of the claim in question (*praetensio iuris*).

After abstracting in this way from everything empirical that the concept of the right of a state or the right of nations contains (such as the malevolence of human nature, which makes coercion necessary), one can call the following proposition the *transcendental formula* of public right.

"All actions relating to the rights of others are wrong if their maxim is incompatible with publicity."

This principle is not to be regarded as *ethical* only (belonging to the doctrine of virtue) but also as *juridical* (bearing upon the right of human beings). For a maxim that I cannot *divulge* without thereby defeating my own purpose, one that absolutely must *be kept secret* if it is to succeed and that I cannot *publicly acknowledge* without unavoidably arousing everyone's opposition to my project, can derive this necessary and universal, hence a priori foreseeable, resistance of everyone to me only from the injustice with which it threatens everyone. This principle is, moreover, only *negative*, that is, it serves only for cognizing by means of it what is *not right* toward others. It is, like an axiom, indemonstrably certain and is, besides, easy to apply, as can be seen from the following examples of public right.

1. *With regard to the right of a state* (*ius civitatis*), namely right within a state, a question arises here that many consider difficult to answer and that the transcendental principle of publicity quite easily resolves: "Is rebellion a legitimate means for a people to throw off the oppressive power of a so-called tyrant (*non titulo, sed exercitio talis*)?"[1] The rights of the people are injured, and no wrong is done to him (the tyrant) by his dethronement; there is no doubt about this. For all that, it is still in the highest degree wrong of the subjects to seek their right in this way, and they can not in the least complain about injustice if, having failed in this conflict, they have to suffer the most severe punishment.

A good deal of subtle reasoning can be done on both sides of this issue if one wants to settle it by a dogmatic deduction of grounds of right; but the transcendental principle of the publicity of public right can spare itself this prolixity. In accordance with it a people asks itself, before the establishment of the civil contract, whether it dares to make publicly known the maxim of its intention to rebel upon occasion. It is easily seen that if one wanted to make it a condition, in establishing a constitution for a state, that in certain cases force would be exercised against its head, the people would have to arrogate to itself a legitimate power over him. But in that case he would not be the head, or, if both were made conditions of establishing a state, no state at all would be possible, though the people's aim was to establish one. The wrongfulness of rebellion is therefore clear from this: that the maxim of rebellion, if one *publicly acknowledged it as* one's maxim, would make one's own purpose impossible. One would therefore have to keep it secret. But this would not be necessary on the part of the head of state. He can freely declare that he will punish any rebellion with the death of the ringleaders, even if they believe that he was the first to transgress the fundamental law; for if the head of state is aware of possessing *irresistible* supreme power (and this must be assumed to be the case in any civil constitution, since he who does not have enough power to protect each one among the people against the others does not have the right to command the people either), he need not be concerned that he will thwart his own purpose by acknowledging his maxim; but it is also quite consistent with this that, if the people's rebellion should succeed, that head of state would return to the status of a subject and must not start a rebellion for his restoration but also need not fear being called to account for his previous administration of the state.

2. *With regard to the right of nations.* Only under the presupposition of some kind of rightful condition (i.e., of that external condition in which a right can actually be assigned to human beings can we speak of a right of

---

[1] not the title, but the practices [of a tyrant]

nations; for, as a public right, it contains in its very concept the publication of a general will determining for each what is its own, and this *status iuridicus* must proceed from some kind of pact, which need not (like that from which a state arises) be based on coercive laws but may, if necessary, be a condition of *continuing free* association, like that of the federalism of various states discussed above. For apart from some kind of *rightful condition* that actually binds together various (natural or moral) persons, and so in a state of nature, the only kind of right there can be is private right. Here again there arises a conflict of politics with morals (the latter regarded as doctrine of right), where that criterion of publicity of maxims can likewise be easily applied, though only if the pact binds the states solely for the purpose of maintaining themselves in peace, among themselves and collectively toward other states, but certainly not for the sake of making acquisitions. Here the following cases of the antinomy between politics and morals arise, [which are presented] along with their resolution.

a) "If one of these states has promised another something, whether it be assistance or cession of certain territories or subsidies and the like, it may be asked whether, in a case where the welfare[u] of this state is at stake, it can release itself from keeping its word by regarding itself as a twofold person: first as a *sovereign,* accountable to no one within its state, but then in turn merely as the supreme *official of the state,* which must give an account to the state; from this would follow the conclusion that what it has bound itself to do in the first capacity it is released from in the second." But if a state (or its head) divulged this maxim of his, then every other would naturally either shun him or unite with others in order to oppose his pretensions, and this proves that politics, with all its cunning, would have to frustrate its own end on this footing (of openness), so that that maxim would have to be wrong.

b) "If a neighboring power that has grown to a formidable size (*potentia tremenda*)[v] arouses anxiety, may one assume that because it *can* oppress it is also going *to will* to do so, and does this give the less powerful a right to (united) attack upon it, even without first having been injured by it?" A state that was willing to *make known* its affirmative maxim about this would only bring on the trouble still more certainly and quickly. For the greater power would anticipate the smaller ones, and as for their uniting, that is only a feeble reed against someone who knows how to make use of *divide et impera.* This maxim of political prudence, declared publicly, thus necessarily thwarts its own purpose and is therefore unjust.[12]

c) "If a smaller state, by its location, separates the territory of a larger one, which needs this [continuous] territory for its preservation, is the latter not justified in subjugating the former and incorporating it?" It is

---

[u] *Heil*
[v] awesome power

easily seen that the larger state must not divulge such a maxim in advance; for, either smaller states would unite in good time or other powerful ones would do so in order to contest this booty, so that this maxim makes itself impracticable by its openness; this is a sign that it is unjust and can be so in a very high degree; for that an object of injustice is small does not prevent the injustice done to it from being very great.

3. *With regard to cosmopolitan right,* I pass over it in silence here; for, because of its analogy with the right of nations, its maxims are easy to state and to evaluate.

In the principle of the incompatibility of such maxims of the right of nations with publicity we have a good indication of the *disagreement* of politics with morals (as doctrine of right). But now we need to learn what the condition*ʷ* is under which its maxims agree with the right of nations. For it cannot be concluded, conversely, that maxims compatible with publicity are on that account also just, since one who has decisively superior power has no need to conceal its maxims. The condition under which a right of nations as such is possible is that a *rightful condition*ˣ already exists. For without this there is no public right, and any right that one may think of outside it (in a state of nature) is instead merely private right. Now we have seen above that a federative condition of states having as its only purpose the avoidance of war is the sole *rightful* condition compatible with the *freedom* of states. Thus the harmony of politics with morals is possible only within a federative union (which is therefore given a priori and is necessary by principles of right), and all political prudence has for its rightful basis the establishment of such a union in its greatest possible extent, without which end all its subtilizing is unwisdom and veiled injustice. Such a spurious politics has its *casuistry* to match the best Jesuit school – the *reservatio mentalis,* formulating public pacts in expressions that, as occasions arise, can be interpreted to one's advantage as one wants (e.g., the distinction of the *status quo de fait* and *de droit*); the *probabilismus,* subtly detecting evil intentions in others, or even making the likelihood of their possible superior power a rightful ground for undermining other, peaceful states; finally the *peccatum philosophicum* (*peccatillum, bagatelle*), taking the devouring of a *small* state to be an easily pardonable trifle if a much *larger* state gains by it, to the supposedly greater good of the world.*

---

* Precedents*ʸ* for such maxims can be found in Counsellor Garve's treatise "Über die Verbindung der Moral mit der Politik," 1788.¹³ This worthy scholar acknowledges at the very beginning that he is unable to give a satisfactory answer to this question. But to approve of their union while yet acknowledging that one cannot fully remove the objections that can be raised against it seems to grant a greater indulgence than might be advisable to those who are very much inclined to abuse it.

ʷ Bedingung
ˣ Zustand
ʸ Belege

The duplicity of politics with respect to morals, in making use of one or the other branch of it for its purposes, abets this. Both philanthropy and respect for the *rights* of the human being are duties: but the former is only *conditional* duty whereas the latter is *unconditional* duty, commanding absolutely, and whoever wants to give himself up to the sweet feeling of beneficence must first be completely assured that he has not transgressed this unconditional duty. Politics readily agrees with morals in the first sense (as ethics), in order to surrender the rights of human beings to their superiors; but with morals in the second meaning (as doctrine of right), before which it would have to bend its knee, it finds it advisable not to get involved in any pact at all, preferring to deny it any reality and to construe all duties as benevolence only; but this ruse of a furtive politics would still be easily thwarted by philosophy, publicizing those maxims it uses, if only politics would venture to let philosophers publicize their own maxims.

8:386

With this in view I propose another transcendental, and affirmative, principle of public right, the formula of which would be as follows:

"All maxims which *need* publicity (in order not to fail in their end) harmonize with right and politics combined."

For if they can attain their end only through publicity, they must conform with the universal end of the public (happiness), and to be in accord with this (to make the public satisfied with its condition) is the proper task of politics. But if this end is to be attainable *only* through publicity, that is, by the removal of all distrust toward the maxims of politics, such maxims must also be in accord with the right of the public, since only in this is the union of the ends of all possible. I must leave the further elaboration and discussion of this principle to another occasion; but that it is a transcendental formula can be seen from its exclusion of all empirical conditions (of the doctrine of happiness), as the matter of the law, and its having regard only for the form of universal lawfulness.

∴

If it is a duty to realize the condition of public right, even if only in approximation by unending progress, and if there is also a well-founded hope of this, then the *perpetual peace* that follows upon what have till now been falsely called peace treaties (strictly speaking, truces) is no empty idea but a task that, gradually solved, comes steadily closer to its goal (since the times during which equal progress takes place will, we hope, become always shorter).

The metaphysics of morals

Translator's note on the text of The metaphysics of morals

A. THE EDITION

The two parts of *The Metaphysics of Morals* were first published separately, the *Doctrine of Right* probably in January 1797 and the *Doctrine of Virtue* in August of that year. In the edition of 1798, Kant's revisions to the text were apparently limited to adding a parenthetical explanation of his term *Läsion* (Ak. 6:249) and an appendix in reply to Bouterwek's review of the *Doctrine of Right* published on February 18, 1797. A more extensively revised edition was published in 1803, during Kant's lifetime but without his cooperation.

With two exceptions to be noted later, the present translation is based on the text of *The Metaphysics of Morals* edited by Paul Natorp in Volume 6 (1907) of the Prussian Academy of the Sciences edition of Kant's works. Natorp's decision not to use the "improved" edition of 1803 is based on his conviction that such alterations in the *Doctrine of Virtue* as are improvements do not justify the use of a text in the production of which Kant was not involved. I have followed Natorp in relegating to notes any substantive emendations that clarify the text. I have also made use of his notes in identifying authors whose works Kant cites. Bouterwek's review is included in Volume 20 of the Academy edition.

It has long been recognized that the text of *The Doctrine of Right* is corrupt to the extent that paragraphs 4–8 in §6 do not belong there. On the history of this discovery, see Thomas Mautner, "Kant's Metaphysics of Morals: A Note on the Text," *Kant-Studien* 72 (1981): 356–9. Bernd Ludwig, in his recent *Philosophische Bibliothek* edition of the *Rechtslehre* (Hamburg, Meiner, 1986), proceeded on the hypothesis that this corruption of the text could have been far more extensive and could account for the obscurity of the work. More specifically, he suggested that the copyist misunderstood Kant's directions about deletions and insertions in the text, which had been put together from various manuscripts, and that Kant, who was by then working on the *Tugendlehre*, was unwilling to interrupt his work by reviewing the completed manuscript. Hence the manuscript delivered to the printer was not at all the text that Kant had in mind. As for Kant's failure to take notice of the published text, Ludwig cites Kant's general lack of interest in his completed works unless the occasion arose for examining them, and the cursory response to Bouterwek's question about *lädieren*.

However, Ludwig maintained that Kant's original text can be reconstructed on the basis of evidence within the published text itself, such as explicit assertions about its structure, implicit assertions about the sequence of particular passages, and indirect indications derived from general rules of exposition, such as defining a term before applying it. Ludwig gives a detailed account of his thesis in the Introduction to his edition of the *Rechtslehre* and in Part I of its companion volume *Kants Rechtslehre*, Volume 2 in Reinhard Brandt and Werner Stark, eds., *Kant Forschungen* (Hamburg, Meiner, 1988). His reconstruction of a part of the text is discussed in his article "The Right of a State" in Immanuel Kant's *Doctrine of Right, Journal of the History of Philosophy* 27, 3 (1990): 403–15. A list of the major changes his edition made in the text follows.

1) The "Table of the Division of the Doctrine of Right" (AK 6:210) is moved from the end of the Preface to the end of the "Introduction to the Doctrine of Right."
2) The sections of the "Introduction to the Metaphysics of Morals" are reordered II, I, IV, III.
3) In the section "*Philosophia Practica Universalis*," paragraph 14, followed by paragraph 16, is inserted after paragraph 8, and the block of paragraphs 9–13 and 15 is moved to follow paragraph 23.
4) The "Division of the Metaphysics of Morals" (AK:6 239 ff.) is removed from the "Introduction to the Doctrine of Right" and inserted in "On the Division of a Metaphysics of Morals," after AK 221. The final paragraph (AK 6:243) remains in the "Introduction to the Doctrine of Right," after the table inserted according to 1).
5) A title page, "Part I: Metaphysical First Principles of the Doctrine of Right," is inserted before the "Introduction to the Doctrine of Right."
6) §2 is inserted in place of paragraphs 4–8 in §6. Paragraphs 4–8 are deleted.
7) §3 is deleted.
8) §10, paragraph 4 is moved to §17 (which has become §16) as its third paragraph. Paragraph 5 is deleted.
9) §15 is deleted.
10) The "Remark" (AK 6:270) is moved to §11, as its conclusion.
11) §31, "Dogmatic Division of All Rights that Can Be Acquired by Contract," is inserted as a new §21a at the end of Section II, "On Contract Right" (AK 6:276).
12) A title page, "The Doctrine of Right, Part II: Public Right," is inserted after §40 (AK 6:306).
13) The order of §43 and §44 is reversed. The heading "Public

Right, Section I: The Right of a State" is moved to AK 6: 313, preceding §45, so that §43 and §44 are included in the twelve paragraphs forming the "Transition from What Is Mine or Yours in a State of Nature to What Is Mine or Yours in a Rightful Condition Generally."

14) §§45–9, 51 and 52, are reordered 45, 48, 46, 49, 47, 51, 52. §50 is made a new "Remark," F, and "Remarks" A–F are put at the end of "The Right of a State." The Akademie §47 (AK:6 315–16) is made a new §50.

As mentioned earlier, the present translation follows the Academy edition text except for two points, regarding which, after consultation with the General Editors of the Cambridge edition, Ludwig's emendations have been adopted. These are the points numbered (2) and (6) above. That is, the numbering of sections in the Introduction has been altered, and § 2 has been substituted for paragraphs 4–8 of § 6. Section 2 has been omitted, but the remaining sections have not been renumbered, and the five paragraphs of text in § 6 that have been replaced are given in a footnote.

As for the format of this translation, the standard conventions of the Cambridge edition have been followed: Kant's notes are indicated by asterisks and daggers and appear at the bottom of the page of text on which they appear. Translator's notes, dealing with matters of text and translation, are indicated by letters and also appear at the bottom of the page. I have translated only those Latin words or passages that are not mere repetitions of the German or that are identifiable quotations. Editorial footnotes, indicated by Arabic numerals, are to be found at the end of the work. All references to Kant's works are to the Academy edition. The pagination of the Academy edition of *The Metaphysics of Morals* is given in the margins of the present translation. Since most translators of Kant's works provide the Academy pagination, references to his other writings can be readily identified in the various translations available. The present translation is, essentially, the translation published in 1991 in the Cambridge Texts in German Philosophy series modified to conform with the editorial policy of The Cambridge Edition of the Works of Immanuel Kant in English Translation.

I am deeply indebted to Lewis White Beck, Douglas P. Dryer, and Raymond Geuss who read earlier versions of this translation and offered numerous very useful suggestions. I have incorporated much of their advice in the present translation. However, I am solely responsible for whatever errors remain.

B. THE TERMINOLOGY OF THE *RECHTSLEHRE*

The most serious problem of translation in *The Metaphysics of Morals* is the term *Recht*. Like the Latin *ius*, it has multiple meanings. Kant's predecessors distinguished four senses of *ius* or *Ius*. As referring to an action, *ius* is derived from *iustum* or *non iniustum* and means that the action is not contrary to justice (*iustitia*) taken in a strict and narrow sense, which was then specified as not depriving someone of what is his (*suum*). Second, it refers to the body of laws concerned with such actions, as distinguished from a law (*lex*) or laws of whatever kind, for example, "the law of love" as distinguished from justice. Third, it means a quality of a person, a "faculty" (*facultas*) by which he can have or do something without injustice, that is, in such a way that his action will be *iustum* or in accord with *Ius*. Finally, it means what has been decided by a court in cases of conflict about *ius* in the first three senses.

The German language can eliminate one of these four meanings; it has the word *Rechtens* for what has been decided by a court. For the rest, *Recht* can mean a system of what Kant calls external laws, such laws as can be given by someone other than the reason of those subject to them. As an adjective *recht* characterizes actions that conform with external laws; strictly speaking, such actions should be called *gerecht*, but when it is clear that the context of the discussion is *Recht* in the sense just specified Kant often uses *recht* instead. Finally, *Recht* can mean "a right." In addition, Kant uses a number of compound words (such as *Rechtspflicht* and *Rechtsgesetz*) and a number of adjectives derived from *Recht* (such as *rechtlich* and *rechtmässig*).

A translator faces several problems, most notably, how to translate *Recht* itself in the sense of a system of external laws and how to distinguish this from the other substantive use of *Recht*, "a right." Two possibilities were considered and rejected. First, *Recht* as a system of laws could have been translated as "law." For Kant there are two systems of laws, one comprising the subject matter of *Rechtslehre* and the other that of *Tugendlehre*. In order to distinguish the two systems, the first could have been capitalized, as is done in referring to a "Law faculty" or a "Law school." A number of considerations argued against this translation. I shall mention two. First, the only word available for *ein Recht* is "a right," and Kant, as might be expected, is not content to leave the various senses of *ius* merely associated by their common reference to one member of a division of laws. He argues, instead, for a conceptual connection of *das Recht* and *ein Recht*, which will determine the way in which "a right" will be used in the text. Not only does "Law" obscure the conceptual tie, by way of *recht*, between the two substantive senses of *Recht:* it is not always clear in which sense *Recht* is being used (on some occasions the indefinite article or the plural form points to "a right" or "rights," but this guidepost is often missing and sometimes misleading). Second, if *Recht* were translated as "Law," the adjectives derived from it would appropriately be translated as "legal," obscuring the distinction between a state of nature and civil society and Kant's argument for the moral necessity of living in a civil society.

A second possible translation of *Recht*, "justice," was also considered and rejected. In addition to the problem involved in "Law," "justice" suggests "fairness in the distribution of goods." Kant does use *Gerechtigkeit* (justice) and *austeilende Gerechtigkeit* (distributive justice), but the *Rechtslehre* is not a treatise on "social justice." Even if this connotation could be avoided, Kant's use of *Gerechtigkeit* would, it seems, make it implausible to distinguish "natural justice" from "legal justice."

Unfortunately, the English language has no word for *das Recht*, and a translator is naturally reluctant to introduce one. However, the considerations discussed in the preceding paragraphs seemed to warrant the use of "right" for a system of external laws. When it is impossible to maintain in English Kant's distinction between a body of laws and the rights people have in accordance with such laws, a note indicates the translation's deviation from the text. A primary objective of the present edition of Kant's works is to avoid, as far as possible, injecting the translator's interpretation into the text. A translator must, of course, do something with troublesome words or phrases; they cannot simply be left in German. In translating *das Recht* as "right" and calling attention to such derivatives as *rechtlich* when they occur, my intention is to indicate the common source of all these terms and their general relation, leaving the reader to determine more specific connections within the course of Kant's argument.

What Kant specifies as the subject matter of *Rechtslehre* determines the translation of a number of common words whose meaning would otherwise be indeterminate. The most important of these are discussed in notes as the word appears. More generally, the distinctions drawn in *The Metaphysics of Morals* require some modification of the terminology appropriate in other, perhaps theoretical, contexts. With a view to distinctions that would eventually be needed and to a plausible level of consistency in Kant's mature practical philosophy, these modifications were introduced earlier. Some notes in the present work are, accordingly, repetitions of what was said in notes to earlier works. As Kant's terminology comes into play, the reader may be interested to note that a number of words and phrases used metaphorically throughout his practical and even his theoretical writings are here assigned their literal meaning.

Introduction

If Kant's decision to write the *Critique of Practical* Reason was unexpected, the same cannot be said of *The Metaphysics of Morals*. In 1765 he wrote to Lambert that, through a misunderstanding, his investigation into the method proper to metaphysics was announced as the title of a forthcoming book; instead of discussing this method in the abstract he would write some short works, the material for which was at hand. The first of them would be "metaphysical first principles of natural philosophy and metaphysical first principles of practical philosophy" (10:56). Although Kant did, at the time, regard metaphysics as consisting of rational principles and its method as differing from that of mathematics, Hamann's account of the "metaphysics of morals" Kant was writing in 1767 described it as dealing "more with what man is than with what he ought to be." In May 1768 Kant mentioned in a letter to Herder that his "metaphysics of morals" should be completed by the end of the year. The insights he had gained into the nature and limits of human capacities and inclinations would enable him to set forth the basic principles as well as the method of moral philosophy (10:74).

The year 1768, however, was the eve of *The Forms and Principles of the Sensible and Intelligible World* and of a new conception of metaphysics as "pure" knowledge, comprising only concepts and principles not derived from experience. In 1770 Kant mentioned to Lambert his intention of using the winter to put in order and draw up his investigations in "pure moral philosophy, in which no empirical principles are to be found, and as it were metaphysics of morals" (10:97). Kant's increasing dissatisfaction with the results of his Inaugural Dissertation is documented in his letters to Marcus Herz between 1771 and 1773. In the first of them he spoke of quickly finishing his book "On the Boundaries of Sensibility and Reason" and including in it a sketch of what constitutes taste, metaphysics, and morals (10:123). In 1772 he said that his "critique of pure reason" would deal with the nature of both theoretical and practical knowledge insofar as it is purely intellectual. The first part, which would determine the sources of metaphysics, its method, and its limits, should be completed in about three months; he would then go on to "the pure principles of morality" (10:132). Toward the end of 1773 Kant wrote that he would be glad when he has completed his "transcendental philosophy, which is really a critique of pure reason," and would then go on to "metaphysics, which has only two parts: metaphysics of nature and metaphysics of morals." He would produce the latter first and looked forward to it with pleasure (10:145).

The *Critique of Pure Reason* was finally published in 1781. But the first of Kant's three major works in moral philosophy was not *The Metaphysics of Morals* but rather a short treatise, the *Groundwork of the Metaphysics of Morals* (1785), which laid its foundation. The "supreme principle" of moral philosophy should be exhibited in its purity, as having its source in reason alone, before being applied to human nature in *The Metaphysics of Morals*, which would set forth the entire system of human duties. Though the only foundation for a metaphysics of morals is a critique of pure practical reason, the final section of the *Groundwork* would serve the purpose. His next work in moral philosophy, however, was the *Critique of Practical Reason* (1788).

Kant's readers continued to await his metaphysics of morals. There was, apparently, reason to expect it in 1791; when it did not appear at the Book Fair in Berlin that year rumor had it that Frederick the Great's reactionary successor, Frederick William II, had forbidden Kant to write any more (11:173). The rumor was premature, and when the Cabinet Order came it was directed at Kant's philosophy of religion. The first part of *The Metaphysics of Morals*, "Metaphysical First Principles of the Doctrine of Right," was finally published early in 1797. Its second part, "Metaphysical First Principles of the Doctrine of Virtue," followed some six months later.

It need hardly be said that *The Metaphysics of Morals* has little resemblance to what Kant might have written thirty years earlier. Nothing like it could have been produced before the developments in his conception of metaphysics and of the basic principle of morals put forward respectively in the *Critique of Pure Reason* and the *Groundwork of the Metaphysics of Morals*. By 1785, however, Kant was apparently ready to apply the principle formulated in the *Groundwork* and anticipated no great difficulty in working out the system of human duties. The question may be raised why he postponed doing so for another twelve years. The delay could well be explained simply by the various projects in which he was, as usual, engaged. However, a contributing factor could have been unforeseen difficulties in working out the system.

The two parts of *The Metaphysics of Morals* comprise subsystems of duties, distinguished by the two kinds of moral laws that can be derived from the principle that unifies the parts into the whole system. The first part, *Rechtslehre*, has as its content the a priori principles on which external laws are based, such laws as can be prescribed by others as well as by the agent's own will. To such duties there correspond rights on the part of others, and a right is an authorization to use coercion. Kant therefore had to give an account of the rights that human beings have and can acquire, most notably rights to things or property rights. In a letter to Eberhard in October 1794, Schiller reported having heard that Kant was dissatisfied with his earlier view and would have something new to say on the difficult problem of property. Kant's Preface to the *Rechtslehre* notes that the section relevant to the problem of acquired rights, *Privatrecht*, has been worked over more thoroughly than some of the later sections: it is certainly the most original part of the work. The speed with which the second part of the system, ethics or *Tugendlehre*, followed would suggest that if there were unforeseen difficulties they had been resolved in the general introduction to *The Metaphysics of Morals* and in the *Rechtslehre*.

*The
metaphysics of morals*

*Part I
Metaphysical first principles
of the
doctrine of right*

Preface

The critique of *practical* reason was to be followed by a system, the metaphysics of **morals,** which falls into metaphysical and first principles of the *doctrine of right*[a] and metaphysical first principles of the *doctrine of virtue.* (This is a counterpart of the metaphysical first principles of *natural science,* already published.)[1] The Introduction that follows presents and to some degree makes intuitive the form which the system will take in both these parts.

For the **doctrine of right,** the first part of the doctrine of morals, there is required a system derived from reason which could be called the *metaphysics of right.* But since the concept of right is a pure concept that still looks to practice (application to cases that come up in experience), a *metaphysical system* of right would also have to take account, in its divisions, of the empirical variety of such cases, in order to make its division complete (as is essential in constructing a system of reason). But *what is empirical* cannot be divided completely, and if this is attempted (at least to approximate to it), empirical concepts cannot be brought into the system as integral parts of it but can be used only as examples in remarks. So the only appropriate title for the first part of *The Metaphysics of Morals* will be *Metaphysical First Principles of the Doctrine of Right;* for in the application of these principles to cases the system itself cannot be expected, but only approximation to it. Accordingly, it will be dealt with as in the (earlier) *Metaphysical First Principles of Natural Science:* namely, that right which belongs to the system outlined a priori will go into the text, while rights taken from particular cases of experience will be put into remarks, which will sometimes be extensive; for otherwise it would be hard to distinguish what is metaphysics here from what is empirical application of rights.[b]

Philosophic treatises are often charged with being obscure, indeed deliberately unclear, in order to affect an illusion of deep insight. I cannot

---

[a] On the term "right" (*Recht*) see Translator's Introduction. As for "doctrine," Kant concludes his Preface to the *Critique of Judgment* by noting that this critique concludes the critical part of his enterprise and that he will now proceed to the doctrinal [*doktrinal*] part, i.e., to the application of the principles established in the first two critiques in a metaphysics of nature and a metaphysics of morals (5:170). Compare *Groundwork of the Metaphysics of Morals* (4:387).
[b] *Rechtspraxis*

better anticipate or forestall this charge than by readily complying with a duty that Garve, a philosopher in the true sense of the word, lays down for all writers, but especially for philosophic writers. My only reservation is imposed by the nature of the science that is to be corrected and extended.

This wise man rightly requires (in his work entitled *Vermischte Aufsätze*, page 352 ff.)² that every philosophic teaching be capable of being made *popular* (that is, of being made sufficiently clear to the senses to be communicated to everyone) if the teacher is not to be suspected of being muddled in his own concepts. I gladly admit this with the exception only of the systematic critique of the faculty of reason*ᶜ* itself, along with all that can be established only by means of it; for this has to do with the distinction of the sensible in our cognition from that which is supersensible but yet belongs to reason. This can never become popular – no formal metaphysics can – although its results can be made quite illuminating for the healthy reason (of an unwitting metaphysician). Popularity (common language) is out of the question here; on the contrary, scholastic *precision* must be insisted upon, even if this is censured as hair-splitting (since it is the *language of the schools*); for only by this means can precipitate reason be brought to understand itself, before making its dogmatic assertions.

But if *pedants* presume to address the public (from pulpits or in popular writings) in technical terms that belong only in the schools, the critical philosopher is no more responsible for that than the grammarian is for the folly of those who quibble over words (*logodaedalus*). Here ridicule can touch only the man, not the science.

It sounds arrogant, conceited, and belittling of those who have not yet renounced their old system to assert that before the coming of the critical philosophy there was as yet no philosophy at all. – In order to decide about this apparent presumption, it need but be asked *whether there could really be more than one philosophy*. Not only have there been different ways of philosophizing and of going back to the first principles of reason in order to base a system, more or less successfully, upon them, but there had to be many experiments of this kind, each of which made its contribution to present-day philosophy. Yet since, considered objectively, there can be only one human reason, there cannot be many philosophies; in other words, there can be only one true system of philosophy from princi-

---

ᶜ Vernuftvermögens. In such compounds as *Vernunftvermögen, Erkenntnisvermögen, Begehrungsvermögen*, and so forth, *Vermögen* is translated as "faculty." In the present introductory material a note indicates where the word *Vermögen* by itself has been translated as "capacity" or "ability." Within the two parts of the *The Metaphysics of Morals*, where a right as well as a virtue is a *Vermögen*, the standard translation of *Vermögen* is "capacity" or "ability." In a different but related sense, usually made clear by the context, *Vermögen* is translated by "wealth" (or "resources" or "means").

ples, in however many different and even conflicting ways one has philosophized about one and the same proposition. So the *moralist* rightly says that there is only one virtue and one doctrine of virtue, that is, a single system that connects all duties of virtue by one principle; the *chemist*, that there is only one chemistry (Lavoisier's);[3] the *teacher of medicine*, that there is only one principle for systematically classifying diseases (Brown's).[4] Although the *new system* excludes all the others, it does not detract from the merits of earlier moralists, chemists, and teachers of medicine, since without their discoveries and even their unsuccessful attempts we should not have attained that unity of the true principle which unifies the whole of philosophy into one system. – So anyone who announces a system of philosophy as his own work says in effect that before this philosophy there was none at all. For if he were willing to admit that there had been another (and a true) one, there would then be two different and true philosophies on the same subject, which is self-contradictory. – If, therefore, the critical philosophy calls itself a philosophy before which there had as yet been no philosophy at all, it does no more than has been done, will be done, and indeed must be done by anyone who draws up a philosophy on his own plan.

The charge that one thing which essentially distinguishes the critical philosophy is not original to it but was perhaps borrowed from another philosophy (or from mathematics) would be *less* important but not altogether negligible. A reviewer in Tübingen[5] claims to have discovered that the definition of philosophy which the author of the *Critique of Pure Reason* gives out as his own, not inconsiderable, discovery had been put forth many years earlier by someone else in almost the same words.* I leave it to anyone to judge whether the words *intellectualis quaedam constructio* could have yielded the thought of *the presentation of a given concept in an a priori intuition*, which at once completely distinguishes philosophy from mathematics. I am sure that Hausen[6] himself would not have allowed his words to be interpreted in this way; for the possibility of an a priori intuition, and that space is an a priori intuition and not (as Wolff explains it)[7] a juxtaposition of a variety of items outside one another given merely to empirical intuition (perception), would already have frightened him off, since he would have felt that this was getting him entangled in far-reaching philosophic investigations. To this acute mathematician the presentation *made as it were by means of the*

6:208

---

* *Porro de actuali constructione hic non quaeritur, cum ne possint quidem sensibiles figurae ad rigorem definitionem effingi; sed requiritur cognitio eorum, quibus absolvitur formatio, quae intellectualis quaedam constructio est.* C. A. Hausen, *Elem. Mathes.*, Pars I, p. 86A (1734). [Moreover, what is in question here is not an actual construction, since sensible figures cannot be devised in accordance with the strictness of a definition; what is required is, rather, cognition of what goes to make up the figure, and this is, as it were, a construction made by the intellect.]

understanding meant nothing more than an (empirical) *drawing* of a *line* corresponding to a concept, in which attention is paid only to the rule and abstraction is made from unavoidable deviations in carrying it out, as can also be perceived in equalities constructed in geometry.

As far as the spirit of the critical philosophy is concerned, the *least* important consideration is the mischief that certain imitators of it have made by using some of its terms, which in the *Critique of Pure Reason* itself cannot well be replaced by more customary words, outside the *Critique* in public exchange of thoughts. This certainly deserves to be condemned, although in condemning it Nicolai[8] reserves judgment as to whether such terms can be entirely dispensed with in their own proper field, as though they were used everywhere merely to hide poverty of thought. – Meanwhile it is more amusing to laugh at an *unpopular pedant* than at an *uncritical ignoramus* (for, in fact, a metaphysician who clings obstinately to his own system, heedless of any critique, can be classed as an uncritical ignoramus, even though he willfully[d] *ignores* what he does not want to let spread since it does not belong to his older school of thought). But if it is true, as Shaftesbury asserts,[9] that a doctrine's ability to withstand *ridicule* is not a bad touchstone of its truth (especially in the case of a practical doctrine), then the critical philosophy's turn must finally come to laugh *last* and so laugh *best* when it sees the systems of those who have talked big for such a long time collapse like houses of cards one after another and their adherents scatter, a fate they cannot avoid.

Toward the end of the book I have worked less thoroughly over certain sections than might be expected in comparison with the earlier ones, partly because it seems to me that they can be easily inferred from the earlier ones and partly, too, because the later sections (dealing with public right) are currently subject to so much discussion, and still so important, that they can well justify postponing a decisive judgment for some time.

I hope to have the *Metaphysical First Principles of the Doctrine of Virtue* ready shortly.[10]

TABLE
of the Division of the Doctrine of Right

Part I
Private Right with Regard to External Objects
(The Sum of Laws that Do Not Need to Be Promulgated)

Chapter I
How to *Have* Something External as One's Own

Chapter II
How to *Acquire* Something External

---

[d] *willkürlich*

Division of External Acquisition

Section I
Property Right

Section II
Contract Right

Section III
Domestic Right

Episodic Section
Ideal Acquisition

Chapter III
Acquisition that Is Dependent Subjectively on a Court of Justice

Part II
Public Right
(The Sum of Laws that Need to Be Promulgated)

Chapter I
The Right of a State

Chapter II
The Right of Nations

Chapter III
Cosmopolitan Right

Introduction
to the metaphysics of morals

I.[e]
ON THE IDEA OF AND THE NECESSITY FOR A METAPHYSICS OF MORALS

It has been shown elsewhere that for natural science, which has to do with objects of outer sense, one must have a priori principles and that it is possible, indeed necessary, to prefix a system of these principles, called a metaphysical science of nature, to natural science applied to particular experiences, that is, to physics. Such principles must be derived from a priori grounds if they are to hold as universal in the strict sense. But physics (at least when it is a question of keeping its propositions free from error) can accept many principles as universal on the evidence of experience. So Newton assumed on the basis of experience the principle of the equality of action and reaction in the action of bodies upon one another, yet extended it to all material nature. Chemists go still further and base their most universal laws of the combination and separation of substances[f] by their own forces entirely on experience, and yet so trust to the universality and necessity of those laws that they have no fear of discovering an error in experiments made with them.

But it is different with moral laws. They hold as laws only insofar as they can be *seen* to have an a priori basis and to be necessary. Indeed, concepts and judgments about ourselves and our deeds and omissions signify nothing moral if what they contain can be learned merely from experience. And should anyone let himself be led astray into making something from that source into a moral principle, he would run the risk of the grossest and most pernicious errors.

If the doctrine of morals were merely the doctrine of happiness it would be absurd to seek a priori principles for it. For however plausible it may sound to say that reason, even before experience, could see the means for achieving a lasting enjoyment of the true joys of life, yet every-

---

[e] The following section was number II in AK. See above, Translator's Note to the text of *The Metaphysics of Morals*.
[f] *Materien*

thing that is taught a priori on this subject is either tautological or assumed without any basis. Only experience can teach what brings us joy. Only the natural drives for food, sex, rest, and movement, and (as our natural predispositions develop) for honor, for enlarging our cognition and so forth, can tell each of us, and each only in his particular way, in what he will *find* those joys; and, in the same way, only experience can teach him the means by which to *seek* them. All apparently a priori reasoning about this comes down to nothing but experience raised by induction to generality, a generality (*secundum principia generalis, non universalis*) still so tenuous that everyone must be allowed countless exceptions in order to adapt his choice[g] of a way of life to his particular inclinations and his susceptibility to satisfaction and still, in the end, to become prudent only from his own or others' misfortunes.

6:216

But it is different with the teachings of morality.[h] They command for everyone, without taking account of his inclinations, merely because and insofar as he is free and has practical reason. He does not derive instruction in its laws from observing himself and his animal nature or from perceiving the ways of the world, what happens and how we behave (although the German word *Sitten,* like the Latin *mores,* means only manners and customs). Instead, reason commands how we are to act even though no example of this could be found, and it takes no account of the advantages we can thereby gain, which only experience could teach us. For although reason allows us to seek our advantage in every way possible to us and can even promise us, on the testimony of experience, that it will probably be more to our advantage on the whole to obey its commands than to transgress them, especially if obedience is accompanied with prudence, still the authority of its precepts *as commands* is not based on these considerations. Instead it uses them (as counsels) only as a counterweight against inducements to the contrary, to offset in advance the error of biased scales in practical appraisal, and only then to insure that the weight of a pure practical reason's a priori grounds will turn the scales in favor of the authority of its precepts. If, therefore, a system of a priori cognition from concepts alone is called *metaphysics,* a practical philosophy, which has not nature but freedom of choice for its object, will presuppose and require a metaphysics of morals, that is, it is itself a *duty* to *have* such a metaphysics, and every human being also has it within himself, though as a rule only in an obscure way; for without a priori principles how could he

---

[g] *Wahl*

[h] *mit den Lehren der Sittlichkeit.* In 6:219 Kant distinguishes between the legality of an action and its *Moralität (Sittlichkeit)*; drawing the same distinction in 6:225 he uses *Sittlichkeit (moralitas)*. In the present context, however, it would seem that he continues to discuss what he has been calling *Sittenlehre,* i.e., the "doctrine of morals" or of duties generally. In 6:239 he refers to the metaphysics of morals in both its parts as *Sittenlehre (Moral)*.

believe that he has a giving of universal law within himself? But just as there must be principles in a metaphysics of nature for applying those highest universal principles of a nature in general to objects of experience, a metaphysics of morals cannot dispense with principles of application, and we shall often have to take as our object the particular *nature* of human beings, which is cognized only by experience, in order to *show* in it what can be inferred from universal moral principles. But this will in no way detract from the purity of these principles or cast doubt on their a priori source. – This is to say, in effect, that a metaphysics of morals cannot be based upon anthropology but can still be applied to it.

The counterpart of a metaphysics of morals, the other member of the division of practical philosophy as a whole, would be moral anthropology, which, however, would deal only with the subjective conditions in human nature that hinder people or help them in *fulfilling* the laws of a metaphysics of morals. It would deal with the development, spreading, and strengthening of moral principles (in education in schools and in popular instruction), and with other similar teachings and precepts based on experience. It cannot be dispensed with, but it must not precede a metaphysics of morals or be mixed with it; for one would then run the risk of bringing forth false or at least indulgent moral laws, which would misrepresent as unattainable what has only not been attained just because the law has not been seen and presented in its purity (in which its strength consists) or because spurious or impure incentives were used for what is itself in conformity with duty and good. This would leave no certain moral principles, either to guide judgment or to discipline the mind in observance of duty, the precepts of which must be given a priori by pure reason alone.

As for the higher division under which the division just mentioned falls, namely that of philosophy into theoretical and practical philosophy, I have already explained myself elsewhere (in the *Critique of Judgment*) and explained that practical philosophy can be none other than moral wisdom. Anything that is practical and possible in accordance with laws of nature (the distinctive concern of art)[i] depends for its precepts entirely upon the theory of nature: only what is practical in accordance with laws of freedom can have principles that are independent of any theory; for there is no theory of what goes beyond the properties of nature. Hence philosophy can understand by its practical part (as compared with its theoretical part) no *technically practical* doctrine but only a *morally practical* doctrine; and if the proficiency of choice in accordance with laws of freedom, in contrast to laws of nature, is also to be called *art* here, by this would have to be understood a kind of art that makes possible a system of freedom like a

---

[i] *Kunst*. In the *Groundwork of the Metaphysics of Morals* (4:415) Kant called such precepts those of "skill" (*Geschicklichkeit*).

II.^j
ON THE RELATION OF THE FACULTIES OF THE HUMAN MIND TO MORAL LAWS

system of nature, truly a divine art were we in a position also to carry out fully, by means of it, what reason prescribes and to put the idea of it into effect.

The *faculty of desire* is the faculty to be, by means of one's representations, the cause of the objects of these representations. The faculty of a being to act in accordance with its representations is called *life*.

First, pleasure or *displeasure*, susceptibility to which is called *feeling*, is always connected with desire^k or aversion; but the converse does not always hold, since there can be a pleasure that is not connected with any desire for an object but is already connected with a mere representation that one forms of an object (regardless of whether the object of the representation exists or not). *Second*, pleasure or displeasure in an object of desire does not always precede the desire and need not always be regarded as the cause of the desire but can also be regarded as the effect of it.

The capacity^l for having pleasure or displeasure in a representation is called *feeling* because both of these involve what is *merely subjective* in the relation of our representation and contain no relation at all to an object for possible cognition of it* (or even cognition of our condition). While even sensations, apart from the quality (of e.g., red, sweet and so forth) they have because of the nature of the subject, are still referred to an object as elements in our cognition of it, pleasure or displeasure (in what is red or sweet) expresses nothing at all in the object but simply a relation to the subject. For this very reason pleasure and displeasure cannot be explained more clearly in themselves; instead, one can only specify what results they have in certain circumstances, so as to make them recognizable in practice.

---

* One can characterize sensibility as the subjective aspect of our representations in general; for it is the understanding that first refers representations to an object, i.e., only it *thinks* something by means of them. What is subjective in our representations may be such that it can also be referred to an object for cognition of it (either in terms of its form, in which case it is called pure intuition, or in terms of its matter, in which case it is called sensation); in this case sensibility, as susceptibility to such a representation, is *sense*. Or else what is subjective in our representations cannot become *an element in our cognition* because it involves *only* a relation of the representation of the *subject* and nothing that can be used for cognition of an object; and then susceptibility to the representation is called *feeling*, which is the effect of a representation (that may be either sensible or intellectual) upon a subject and belongs to sensibility, even though the representation itself may belong to the understanding or to reason.

^j This section was numbered I in AK.
^k *Begehren*
^l *Fähigkeit*

That pleasure which is necessarily connected with desire (for an object whose representation affects feeling in this way) can be called *practical pleasure*, whether it is the cause or the effect of the desire. On the other hand, that pleasure which is not necessarily connected with desire for an object, and so is not at bottom a pleasure in the existence of the object of a representation but is attached only to the representation by itself, can be called merely contemplative pleasure or *inactive delight*. We call feeling of the latter kind of pleasure *taste*. Practical philosophy, accordingly, speaks of contemplative pleasure only *in passing*, not as if the concept *belonged within* it. As for practical pleasure, that determination of the faculty of desire which is caused and therefore necessarily *preceded* by such pleasure is called *desire*[m] in the narrow sense; habitual desire[n] is called *inclination;* and a connection of pleasure with the faculty of desire that the understanding judges to hold as a general rule (though only for the subject) is called an *interest*. So if a pleasure necessarily precedes a desire, the practical pleasure must be called an interest of inclination. But if a pleasure can only follow upon an antecedent determination of the faculty of desire it is an intellectual pleasure, and the interest in the object must be called an interest of reason; for if the interest were based on the senses and not on pure rational principles alone, sensation would then have to have pleasure connected with it and in this way be able to determine the faculty of desire. Although where a merely pure interest of reason must be assumed no interest of inclination can be substituted for it, yet in order to conform to ordinary speech we can speak of an inclination for what can be an object only of an intellectual pleasure as a habitual desire from a pure interest of reason; but an inclination of this sort would not be the cause but rather the effect of this pure interest of reason, and we could call it a *sense-free inclination (propensio intellectualis)*.

Concupiscence (lusting after something) must also be distinguished from desire itself, as a stimulus to determining desire. Concupiscence is always a sensible modification of the mind but one that has not yet become an act of the faculty of desire.

The faculty of desire in accordance with concepts, insofar as the ground determining it to action lies within itself and not in its object, is called a faculty to *do or to refrain from doing as one pleases*.[o] Insofar as it is joined with one's consciousness of the ability[p] to bring about its object by

---

[m] *Begierde*. Although it would be appropriate to translate *Begierde* by a word other than "desire," which has been used for *Begehren* and in *Begehrungsvermögen*, it is difficult to find a suitable word that has not been preempted. However, *Begierde*, as distinguished from *Neigung*, or "inclination," does not figure prominently in the present work.
[n] *Begierde*
[o] *nach Belieben*
[p] *des Vermögens*

one's action it is called *choice*;*q* if it is not joined with this consciousness its act is called a *wish*. The faculty of desire whose inner determining ground, hence even what pleases it,*r* lies within the subject's reason is called the *will*.*s* The will is therefore the faculty of desire considered not so much in relation to action (as choice is) but rather in relation to the ground determining choice to action. The will itself, strictly speaking, has no determining ground; insofar as it can determine choice, it is instead practical reason itself.

Insofar as reason can determine the faculty of desire as such, not only *choice* but also mere *wish* can be included under the will. That choice which can be determined by *pure reason* is called free choice. That which can be determined only by *inclination* (sensible impulse, *stimulus*) would be animal choice (*arbitrium brutum*). Human choice, however, is a choice that can indeed be *affected* but not *determined* by impulses, and is therefore of itself (apart from an acquired proficiency*t* of reason) not pure but can still be determined to actions by pure will. *Freedom* of choice is this independence from being *determined* by sensible impulses; this is the negative concept of freedom. The positive concept of freedom is that of the ability*u* of pure reason to be of itself practical. But this is not possible except by the subjection of the maxim of every action to the condition of its qualifying as universal law. For as pure reason applied to choice irrespective of its objects, it does not have within it the matter of the law; so, as a faculty of principles (here practical principles, hence a lawgiving faculty), there is nothing it can make the supreme law and determining ground of choice except the form, the fitness of maxims of choice to be universal law. And since the maxims of human beings, being based on subjective causes, do not of themselves conform with those objective principles, reason can prescribe this law only as an imperative that commands or prohibits absolutely.

6:214

In contrast to laws of nature, these laws of freedom are called *moral* laws. As directed merely to external actions and their conformity to law they are called *juridical* laws; but if they also require that they (the laws) themselves be the determining grounds of actions, they are *ethical* laws, and then one says that conformity with juridical laws is the *legality* of an action and conformity with ethical laws is its *morality*. The freedom to which the former laws refer can be only freedom in the *external* use of choice, but the freedom to which the latter refer is freedom in both the external and the internal use of choice, insofar as it is determined by laws

---

q *Willkür*
r *selbst das Belieben*
s *Wille*
t *Fertigkeit*
u *Vermögen*

of reason. In theoretical philosophy it is said that only objects of outer sense are in space, whereas objects of outer as well as of inner sense are in time, since the representations of both are still representations, and as such belong together to inner sense. So too, whether freedom in the external or in the internal use of choice is considered, its laws, as pure practical laws of reason for free choice generally, must also be internal determining grounds of choice, although they should not always be considered in this respect.

III.[v]
PRELIMINARY CONCEPTS OF THE METAPHYSICS OF MORALS
(*PHILOSOPHIA PRACTICA UNIVERSALIS*)

The concept of *freedom* is a pure rational concept, which for this very reason is transcendent for theoretical philosophy, that is, it is a concept such that no instance corresponding to it can be given in any possible experience, and of an object of which we cannot obtain any theoretical cognition; the concept of freedom cannot hold as a constitutive but solely as a regulative and, indeed, merely negative principle of speculative reason. But in reason's practical use the concept of freedom proves its reality by practical principles, which are laws of a causality of pure reason for determining choice independently of any empirical conditions (of sensibility generally) and prove a pure will in us, in which moral concepts and laws have their source.

On this concept of freedom, which is positive (from a practical point of view), are based unconditional practical laws, which are called *moral*. For us, whose choice is sensibly affected and so does not of itself conform to the pure will but often opposes it, moral laws are *imperatives* (commands or prohibitions) and indeed categorical (unconditional) imperatives. As such they are distinguished from technical imperatives (precepts of art), which always command only conditionally. By categorical imperatives certain actions are *permitted* or *forbidden*, that is, morally possible or impossible, while some of them or their opposites are morally necessary, that is, obligatory. For those actions, then, there arises the concept of a duty, observance or transgression of which is indeed connected with a pleasure or displeasure of a distinctive kind (moral *feeling*), although in practical laws of reason we take no account of these feelings (since they have nothing to do with the *basis* of practical laws but only with the subjective *effect* in the mind when our choice is determined by them, which can differ from one subject to another [without objectively, i.e., in the judgment of reason, at all adding to or detracting from the validity or influence of these laws]).

---
[v] This section was numbered IV in AK.

The following concepts are common to both parts of *The Metaphysics of Morals*.

Obligation is the necessity of a free action under a categorical imperative of reason.

An imperative is a practical rule by which an action in itself contingent is *made* necessary. An imperative differs from a practical law in that a law indeed represents an action as necessary but takes no account of whether this action already inheres by an *inner* necessity in the acting subject (as in a holy being) or whether it is contingent (as in the human being); for where the former is the case there is no imperative. Hence an imperative is a rule the representation of which *makes* necessary an action that is subjectively contingent and thus represents the subject as one that must be *constrained* (necessitated)[w] to conform with the rule. – A categorical (unconditional) imperative is one that represents an action as objectively necessary and makes it necessary not indirectly, through the representation of some *end* that can be attained by the action, but through the mere representation of this action itself (its form), and hence directly. No other practical doctrine can furnish instances of such imperatives than that which prescribes obligation (the doctrine of morals). All other imperatives are *technical* and are, one and all, conditional. The ground of the possibility of categorical imperatives is this: that they refer to no other property of choice (by which some purpose can be ascribed to it) than simply to its *freedom*.

That action is *permitted* (*licitum*) which is not contrary to obligation; and this freedom which is not limited by any opposing imperative, is called an authorization (*facultas moralis*). Hence it is obvious what is meant by *forbidden* (*illicitum*).

Duty is that action to which someone is bound. It is therefore the matter of obligation, and there can be one and the same duty (as to the action) although we can be bound to it in different ways.

A categorical imperative, because it asserts an obligation with respect to certain actions, is a morally practical *law*. But since obligation involves not merely practical necessity (such as a law in general asserts) but also *necessitation*, a categorical imperative is a law that either commands or prohibits, depending upon whether it represents as a duty the commission or omission of an action. An action that is neither commanded nor prohibited is merely *permitted*, since there is no law limiting one's freedom (one's authorization) with regard to it and so too no

---

[w] *genötigt* (*necessitiert*). Kant repeatedly gives *Zwang* (constraint) and *Nötigung* (necessitation) as synonyms. Although *Nötigung* is perhaps his favored term, I have often translated *Nötigung* by the more common English word "constraint."

duty. Such an action is called morally indifferent (*indifferens, adiaphoron, res merae facultatis*). The question can be raised whether there are such actions and, if there are, whether there must be permissive laws (*lex permissiva*), in addition to laws that command and prohibit (*lex praeceptiva, lex mandati* and *lex prohibitiva, lex vetiti*), in order to account for someone's being free to do or not to do something as he pleases. If so, the authorization would not always have to do with an indifferent action (*adiaphoron*); for, considering the action in terms of moral laws, no special law would be required for it.[11]

An action is called a *deed* insofar as it comes under obligatory laws and hence insofar as the subject, in doing it, is considered in terms of the freedom of his choice. By such an action the agent is regarded as the *author* of its effect, and this, together with the action itself, can be *imputed* to him, if one is previously acquainted with the law by virtue of which an obligation rests on these.

A *person* is a subject whose actions can be *imputed* to him. *Moral* personality is therefore nothing other than the freedom of a rational being under moral laws (whereas psychological personality is merely the ability[x] to be conscious of one's identity in different conditions of one's existence). From this it follows that a person is subject to no other laws than those he gives to himself (either alone or at least along with others).

A *thing* is that to which[y] nothing can be imputed. Any object of free choice which itself lacks freedom is therefore called a thing (*res corporalis*).

6:224   A deed is *right* or *wrong* (*rectum aut minus rectum*)[z] in general insofar as it conforms with duty or is contrary to it (*factum licitum aut illicitum*);[a] the duty itself, in terms of its content or origin, may be of any kind. A deed contrary to duty is called a *transgression* (*reatus*).

An *unintentional* transgression which can still be imputed to the agent is called a mere *fault* (*culpa*). An *intentional* transgression (i.e., one accompanied by consciousness of its being a transgression) is called a *crime* (*dolus*). What is right in accordance with external laws is called *just* (*iustum*); what is not, *unjust* (*iniustum*).[b]

A *conflict of duties* (*collisio officiourum s. obligationum*)[c] would be a relation between them in which one of them would cancel the other (wholly or in part). – But since duty and obligation are concepts that express the objective practical *necessity* of certain actions and two rules opposed to each other cannot be necessary at the same time, if it is a duty to act in

---

[x] *Vermögen*
[y] *Sache ist ein Ding*
[z] right or less right
[a] licit or illicit deed
[b] *gerecht . . . ungerecht*
[c] collision of duties or obligations

accordance with one rule, to act in accordance with the opposite rule is not a duty but even contrary to duty; so a *collision of duties* and obligations is inconceivable (*obligationes non colliduntur*).[d] However, a subject may have, in a rule he prescribes to himself, two *grounds* of obligation (*rationes obligandi*), one or the other of which is not sufficient to put him under obligation[e] (*rationes obligandi non obligantes*), so that one of them is not a duty. – When two such grounds conflict with each other, practical philosophy says, not that the stronger obligation takes precedence (*fortior obligatio vincit*)[f] but that the stronger *ground of obligation* prevails (*fortior obligandi ratio vincit*).[g]

Obligatory laws for which there can be an external lawgiving are called *external* laws (*leges externae*) in general. Those among them that can be recognized as obligatory a priori by reason even without external lawgiving are indeed external but *natural* laws, whereas those that do not bind without actual external lawgiving (and so without it would not be laws) are called *positive* laws. One can therefore contain only positive laws; but then a natural law would still have to precede it, which would establish the authority of the lawgiver (i.e., his authorization to bind others by his mere *choice*).

A principle that makes certain actions duties is a practical law. A rule that the agent himself makes his principle on subjective grounds is called his *maxim;* hence different agents can have very different maxims with regard to the same law.

The categorical imperative, which as such only affirms what obligation is, is: act upon a maxim that can also hold as a universal law. – You must therefore first consider your actions in terms of their subjective principles; but you can know whether this principle also holds objectively only in this way: that when your reason subjects it to the test of conceiving yourself as also giving universal law through it, it qualifies for such a giving of universal law.

The simplicity of this law in comparison with the great and various consequences that can be drawn from it must seem astonishing at first, as must also its authority to command without appearing to carry any incentive with it. But in wondering at an ability[h] of our reason to determine choice by the mere idea that a maxim qualifies for the *universality* of a practical law, one learns that just these practical (moral) laws first make known a property of choice, namely its freedom, which speculative reason

6:225

---

[d] obligations do not conflict
[e] *zur Verpflichtung nicht zureichend ist.* Although Kant apparently uses both *Verbindlichkeit* and *Verpflichtung* for "obligation," the latter seems at times to have the sense of "put under obligation" and to be closely related to *verbinden*, which I often translate as "to bind."
[f] the stronger obligation wins
[g] the stronger ground of obligation wins
[h] *Vermögen*

would never have arrived at, either on a priori grounds or through any experience whatever, and which, once reason has arrived at it, could in no way be shown theoretically to be possible, although these practical laws show incontestably that our choice has this property. It then seems less strange to find that these laws, like mathematical postulates, are *incapable of being proved* and yet *apodictic*, but at the same time to see a whole field of practical cognition open up before one, where reason in its theoretical use, with the same idea of freedom or with any other of its ideas of the supersensible, must find everything closed tight against it. – The conformity of an action with the law of duty is its *legality* (*legalitas*); the conformity of the maxim of an action with a law is the *morality* (*moralitas*) of the action. A *maxim* is a *subjective* principle of action, a principle which the subject himself makes his rule (how he wills to act). A principle of duty, on the other hand, is a principle that reason prescribes to him absolutely and so objectively (how he *ought* to act).

6:226   The supreme principle of the doctrine of morals is, therefore, act on a maxim which can also hold as a universal law. – Any maxim that does not so qualify is contrary to morals.

>Laws proceed from the will, *maxims* from choice. In man the latter is a free choice; the will, which is directed to nothing beyond the law itself, cannot be called either free or unfree, since it is not directed to actions but immediately to giving laws for the maxims of actions (and is, therefore, practical reason itself). Hence the will directs with absolute necessity and is itself *subject to* no necessitation. Only *choice* can therefore be called *free*.

>But freedom of choice cannot be defined – as some have tried to define it – as the ability to make a choice[i] for or against the law (*libertas indifferentiae*),[j] even though choice as a *phenomenon* provides frequent examples of this in experience. For we know freedom (as it first becomes manifest to us through the moral law) only as a *negative* property in us, namely that of not being *necessitated* to act through any sensible determining grounds. But we cannot present *theoretically* freedom as a *noumenon*, that is, freedom regarded as the ability[k] of the human being merely as an intelligence, and show how it can *exercise constraint* upon his sensible choice; we cannot therefore present freedom as a positive property. But we can indeed see that, although experience shows that the human being as a *sensible being* is able to choose[l] *in opposition to* as

---

[i] *das Vermögen der Wahl*
[j] liberty of indifference
[k] *Vermögen*
[l] *ein Vermögen zeigt . . . zu wählen*

well as *in conformity with* the law, his freedom as an *intelligible being* cannot be *defined*[m] by this, since appearances cannot make any supersensible object (such as free choice) understandable. We can also see that freedom can never be located in a rational subject's being able to choose in opposition to his (lawgiving) reason, even though experience proves often enough that this happens (though we still cannot comprehend how this is possible). – For it is one thing to accept a proposition (on the basis of experience) and another thing to make it the *expository principle*[n] (of the concept of free choice) and the universal feature for distinguishing it (from *arbitrio bruto s. servo*);[o] for the first does not maintain that the feature belongs *necessarily* to the concept, but the second requires this. – Only freedom in relation to the internal lawgiving of reason is really an ability;[p] the possibility of deviating from it is an inability. How can the former be defined[q] by the latter? It would be a definition that added to the practical concept the *exercise* of it, as this is taught by experience, a *hybrid definition* (*definitio hybrida*) that puts the concept in a false light.

6:227

A (morally practical) *law* is a proposition that contains a categorical imperative (a command). One who commands (*imperans*) through a law is the *lawgiver* (*legislator*). He is the author (*autor*) of the obligation in accordance with the law, but not always the author of the law. In the latter case the law would be a positive (contingent) and chosen[r] law. A law that binds us a priori and unconditionally by our own reason can also be expressed as proceeding from the will of a supreme lawgiver, that is, one who has only rights and no duties (hence from the divine will); but this signifies only the idea of a moral being whose will is a law for everyone, without his being thought as the author of the law.

Imputation (*imputatio*) in the moral sense[12] is the *judgment* by which

---

[m] As Kant notes in the *Critique of Pure Reason* A 730, B 758, the German language has only one word, *Erklärung*, to express "exposition," "explication," "declaration," and "definition." Despite the strictures he places upon "definition," he adds that "we need not be so stringent in our requirements as altogether to refuse to philosophic expositions [*Erklärungen*] the honorable title, definition." At the conclusion of the present paragraph he gives *definitio hybrida* as equivalent to *Bastarderklärung*. See also his use of *Definition* and *Erklärung* (or *definieren* and *erklären* in, e.g., 248–9, 260 and 286–7). Both in the *Doctrine of Right* and in the *Doctrine of Virtue*, where Kant is discussing the *Erklärung* of the concept of virtue, I have used "define" and "definition," indicating the German words in notes.

[n] *Erklärungsprinzip*

[o] animal or enslaved power of choice

[p] *Vermögen*

[q] *erklärt aus*

[r] *willkürlich*

someone is regarded as the author (*causa libera*)*ˢ* of an action, which is then called a *deed* (*factum*) and stands under laws. If the judgment also carries with it the rightful consequences of this deed, it is an imputation having rightful force (*imputatio iudiciaria s. valida*);*ᵗ* otherwise it is merely an imputation *appraising* the deed (*imputatio diiudicatoria*).*ᵘ* – The (natural or moral) person that is authorized to impute with rightful force is called a *judge* or a court (*iudex s. forum*).

If someone does *more* in the way of duty than he can be constrained*ᵛ* by law to do, what he does is *meritorious* (*meritum*); if what he does is just exactly what the law *requires*, he does *what is owed*ʷ (*debitum*); finally, if what he does is *less* than the law requires, it is morally *culpable*ˣ (*demeritum*). The *rightful* effect of what is culpable is *punishment* (*poena*); that of a meritorious deed is *reward* (*praemium*) (assuming that the reward, promised in the law, was the motive to it); conduct in keeping with what is owed has no rightful effect at all. – Kindly *recompense*ʸ (*remuneratio s. respensio*) stands in no *rightful relation*ᶻ to a deed.

The good or bad results of an action that is owed, like the results of omitting a meritorious action, cannot be imputed to the subject (*modus imputationis tollens*).*ᵃ*

The good results of a meritorious action, like the bad results of a wrongful*ᵇ* action, can be imputed to the subject (*modus imputationis ponens*).*ᶜ*

Subjectively, the degree to which an action *can be imputed* (*imputabilitas*) has to be assessed by the magnitude of the obstacles that had to be overcome. – The greater the natural obstacles (of sensibility) and the less the moral obstacle (of duty), so much the more merit is to be accounted for a *good deed*, as when, for example, at considerable self-sacrifice I rescue a complete stranger from great distress.

On the other hand, the less the natural obstacles and the greater the obstacle from grounds of duty, so much the more is a transgression to be imputed (as culpable). – Hence the state of mind of the subject, whether he committed the deed in a state of agitation or with cool deliberation, makes a difference in imputation, which has results.

ˢ free cause
ᵗ judiciary or valid imputation
ᵘ judging imputation
ᵛ *gezwungen werden kann*
ʷ *Schuldigkeit*
ˣ *Verschuldung*
ʸ *gütige Vergeltung*
ᶻ *Rechtsverhältniß*
ᵃ by way of taking away imputation
ᵇ *unrechtmäßig*
ᶜ by way of adding imputation

IV.[d]
ON THE DIVISION OF A METAPHYSICS OF MORALS*

In all lawgiving (whether it prescribes internal or external actions, and whether it prescribes them a priori by reason alone or by the choice of another) there are two elements: **first**, a law, which represents an action that is to be done as *objectively* necessary, that is, which makes the action a duty; and **second**, an incentive, which connects a ground for determining choice to this action *subjectively* with the representation of the law. Hence the second element is this: that the law makes duty the incentive. By the first the action is represented as a duty, and this is a merely theoretical cognition of a possible determination of choice, that is, of practical rules. By the second the obligation so to act is connected in the subject with a ground for determining choice generally.

All lawgiving can therefore be distinguished with respect to the incentive (even if it agrees with another kind with respect to the action that it makes a duty, e.g., these actions might in all cases be external). That lawgiving which makes an action a duty and also makes this duty the incentive is *ethical*. But that lawgiving which does not include the incentive of duty in the law and so admits an incentive other than the idea of duty itself is *juridical*. It is clear that in the latter case this incentive which is something other than the idea of duty must be drawn from *pathological*[e] determining grounds of choice, inclinations and aversions, and among these, from aversions; for it is a lawgiving, which constrains, not an allurement, which invites.

The mere conformity or nonconformity of an action with law, irrespective of the incentive to it, is called its *legality* (lawfulness); but that conformity in which the idea of duty arising from the law is also the incentive to the action is called its *morality*.

Duties in accordance with rightful[f] lawgiving can be only external

---

* A *deduction* of the division of a system, i.e., a proof that it is both complete and *continuous* – that is, that a transition from the concept divided to the members of the division takes place without a leap (*divisio per saltum*) in the entire series of subdivisions – is one of the most difficult conditions which the architect of a system has to fulfill. Even what the *highest divided concept* would be, the division of which are *right* and *wrong* (*aut fas aut nefas*) calls for reflection. This concept is the *act of free choice* in general. Teachers of ontology similarly begin with the concepts of *something* and *nothing*, without being aware that these are already members of a division for which the concept divided is missing. This concept can be only that of an *object* in general.

[d] This section was numbered III in AK.

[e] *von den pathologischen Bestimmungsgründen der Willkür.* See *Groundwork of the Metaphysics of Morals* (4:399, note j).

[f] *rechtlich.* The term is introduced here as, apparently, synonymous with "juridical" (*juridisch*).

duties, since this lawgiving does not require that the idea of this duty, which is internal, itself be the determining ground of the agent's choice; and since it still needs an incentive suited to the law, it can connect only external incentives with it. On the other hand, ethical lawgiving, while it also makes internal actions duties, does not exclude external actions but applies to everything that is a duty in general. But just because ethical lawgiving includes within its law the internal incentive to action (the idea of duty), and this feature must not be present in external lawgiving, ethical lawgiving cannot be external (not even the external lawgiving of a divine will), although it does take up duties which rest on another, namely an external, lawgiving by making them, *as duties,* incentives in its lawgiving.

It can be seen from this that all duties, just because they are duties, belong to ethics; but it does not follow that the *lawgiving* for them is always contained in ethics: for many of them it is outside ethics. Thus ethics commands that I still fulfill a contract I have entered into, even though the other party could not coerce[g] me to do so; but it takes the law (*pacta sunt servanda*) and the duty corresponding to it from the doctrine of right, as already given there. Accordingly the giving of the law that promises agreed to must be kept lies not in ethics but in *Ius.* All that ethics teaches is that if the incentive which juridical lawgiving connects with that duty, namely external constraint, were absent, the idea of duty by itself would be sufficient as an incentive. For if this were not the case, and if the lawgiving itself were not juridical so that the duty arising from it was not really a duty of right (as distinguished from a duty of virtue), then faithful performance (in keeping with promises made in a contract) would be put in the same class with actions of benevolence and the obligation to them, and this must not happen. It is no duty of virtue to keep one's promises but a duty of right, to the performance of which one can be coerced. But it is still a virtuous action (a proof of virtue) to do it even where no coercion may be *applied.*[h] The doctrine of right and the doctrine of virtue are therefore distinguished not so much by their different duties as by the difference in their lawgiving, which connects one incentive or the other with the law.

Ethical lawgiving (even if the duties might be external) is that which *cannot* be external; juridical lawgiving is that which can also be external. So it is an external duty to keep a promise made in a contract; but the command to do this merely because it is a duty, without regard for any

---

[g] *zwingen.* Kant uses *Zwang* (and *zwingen*) for both the constraint exercised upon one's choice by one's own will, through the thought of duty, and the constraint exercised by another's choice, through one's aversions. When *Zwang* (or *zwingen*) occurs in the context of right and without the modifier *äussere* (external), it is translated as "coercion" (or "to coerce"). *Äussere Zwang* is translated as "external constraint." If there is room for doubt regarding the context, the word is given in a note. See also 6:222, note a.

[h] *besorgt werden darf*

other incentive, belongs to *internal* lawgiving alone. So the obligation is assigned to ethics not because the duty is of a particular kind (a particular kind of action to which one is bound) – for there are external duties in ethics as well as in right – but rather because the lawgiving in this case is an internal one and can have no external lawgiver. For the same reason duties of benevolence, even though they are external duties (obligations to external actions), are still assigned to ethics because their lawgiving can be only internal. – Ethics has its special duties as well (e.g., duties to oneself), but it also has duties in common with right; what it does not have in common with right is only the kind of *obligation*. For what is distinctive of ethical lawgiving is that one is to perform actions just because they are duties and to make the principle of duty itself, wherever the duty comes from, the sufficient incentive for choice. So while there are many *directly ethical* duties, internal lawgiving makes the rest of them, one and all, indirectly ethical.

6:221

Introduction
to the doctrine of right

A.
WHAT THE DOCTRINE OF RIGHT IS.

The sum of those laws for which an external lawgiving is possible is called the *Doctrine of Right* (*Ius*). If there has actually been such lawgiving, it is the doctrine of *positive right*, and one versed in this, a jurist (*iurisconsultus*), is said to be *experienced in the law* (*Iurisperitus*) when he not only knows external laws but also knows them externally, that is, in their application to cases that come up in experience. Such knowledge can also be called *legal expertise* (*Iurisprudentia*), but without both together it remains mere *juridical science* (*Iurisscientia*). The last title belongs to *systematic* knowledge of the doctrine of natural right (*Ius naturae*), although one versed in this must supply the immutable principles for any giving of positive law.

B.
WHAT IS RIGHT?

Like the much-cited query "what is truth?" put to the logician, the question "what is right?" might well embarrass the *jurist* if he does not want to lapse into a tautology or, instead of giving a universal solution, refer to what the laws in some country at some time prescribe. He can indeed state what is laid down as right[i] (*quid sit iuris*), that is, what the laws in a certain place and at a certain time say or have said. But whether what these laws prescribed is also right, and what the universal criterion is by which one could recognize right as well as wrong (*iustum et iniustum*),[j] this would remain hidden from him unless he leaves those empirical principles behind for a while and seeks the sources of such judgments in reason

---

[i] *was Rechtens sei*. According to 23:262, what is laid down as right (*Rechtens, iuris est*) is what is right or wrong in accordance with positive laws.

[j] In 6:223–4 Kant used *gerecht* and *ungerecht*, *iustum* and *iniuatum*, for what is right or wrong in accordance with external laws, and *recht* and *unrecht* for what is right or wrong generally. Within *The Doctrine of Right* he uses simply *recht* and *unrecht*, although the context makes it clear that only external laws are under consideration. In the present passage the Academy edition capitalizes the words, as *Recht* and *Unrecht*.

alone, so as to establish the basis for any possible giving of positive laws (although positive laws can serve as excellent guides to this). Like the wooden head in Phaedrus's fable, a merely empirical doctrine of right is a head that may be beautiful but unfortunately it has no brain.

The concept of right, insofar as it is related to an obligation corresponding to it (i.e., the moral concept of right), has to do, *first*, only with the external and indeed practical relation of one person to another, insofar as their actions, as deeds,*^k* can have (direct or indirect) influence on each other. But, *second*, it does not signify the relation of one's choice to the mere wish (hence also to the mere need) of the other, as in actions of beneficence of callousness, but only a relation to the other's *choice*. *Third*, in this reciprocal relation of choice no account at all is taken of the *matter* of choice, that is, of the end each has in mind with the object he wants; it is not asked, for example, whether someone who buys goods from me for his own commercial use will gain by the transaction or not. All that is in question is the *form* in the relation of choice on the part of both, insofar as choice is regarded merely as *free*, and whether the action of one can be united with the freedom of the other in accordance with a universal law.

Right is therefore the sum of the conditions under which the choice of one can be united with the choice of another in accordance with a universal law of freedom.

C.
THE UNIVERSAL PRINCIPLE OF RIGHT.[l]

"Any action is *right* if it can coexist with everyone's freedom in accordance with a universal law, or if on its maxim the freedom of choice of each can coexist with everyone's freedom in accordance with a universal law."

If then my action or my condition[m] generally can coexist with the freedom of everyone in accordance with a universal law, whoever hinders me in it does me *wrong*;[n] for this hindrance (resistance) cannot coexist with freedom in accordance with a universal law.

6:231

---

[k] *als Facta*, perhaps "as facts." In 6:227 *factum* was given as the parenthetical equivalent of *Tat* or "deed." In some passages it is unclear whether *Tat* is to be taken as "fact" or as "deed" or as both.

[l] *Allgemeines Prinzip des Rechts*

[m] *Zustand*. Throughout the *Doctrine of Right*, *Zustand* is translated as "condition" except (1) where the familiar term "state of nature" is called for and (2) where it seems to require the translation "status," in Kant's discussion of rights to persons akin to rights to things. In the *Doctrine of Virtue*, where there is no occasion for mistaking "state" for *Staat*, "state" and "condition" are used interchangeably. In the few texts in which "condition" in the sense of *Zustand* and in the sense of *Bedingung* might be confused, the German word is provided in a note.

[n] *tut der mir Unrecht*

It also follows from this that it cannot be required that this principle of all maxims be itself in turn my maxim, that is, it cannot be required that *I make it the maxim* of my action; for anyone can be free so long as I do not impair his freedom by my *external action,* even though I am quite indifferent to his freedom or would like in my heart to infringe upon it. That I make it my maxim to act rightly is a demand that ethics makes on me.

Thus the universal law of right,*°* so act externally that the free use of your choice can coexist with the freedom of everyone in accordance with a universal law, is indeed a law that lays an obligation on me, but it does not at all expect, far less demand, that I *myself should* limit my freedom to those conditions*ᵖ* just for the sake of this obligation; instead, reason says only that freedom *is* limited to those conditions in conformity with the idea of it and that it may also be actively*ᵍ* limited by others; and it says this as a postulate that is incapable of further proof. – When one's aim is not to teach virtue but only to set forth what is *right,* one need not and should not represent that law of right as itself the incentive to action.

D.
RIGHT IS CONNECTED WITH AN AUTHORIZATION TO USE COERCION.

Resistance that counteracts the hindering of an effect promotes this effect and is consistent with it. Now whatever is wrong is a hindrance to freedom in accordance with universal laws. But coercion is a hindrance or resistance to freedom. Therefore, if a certain use of freedom is itself a hindrance to freedom in accordance with universal laws (i.e., wrong), coercion that is opposed to this (as a *hindering of a hindrance to freedom*) is consistent with freedom in accordance with universal laws, that is, it is right. Hence there is connected with right by the principle of contradiction an authorization to coerce someone who infringes upon it.

E.
A STRICT RIGHT CAN ALSO BE REPRESENTED AS THE POSSIBILITY OF A FULLY RECIPROCAL USE OF COERCION THAT IS CONSISTENT WITH EVERYONE'S FREEDOM IN ACCORDANCE WITH UNIVERSAL LAWS.

This proposition says, in effect, that right need not be conceived as made up of two elements, namely an obligation in accordance with a law and an

---

° *das allgemeine Rechtsgesetz*
ᵖ *Bedingungen*
ᵍ *tätlich,* perhaps "in fact"

authorization of him who by his choice puts another under obligation to coerce him to fulfill it. Instead, one can locate the concept of right directly in the possibility of connecting universal reciprocal coercion with the freedom of everyone. That is to say, just as right generally has as its object only what is external in actions, so strict right, namely that which is not mingled with anything ethical, requires only external grounds for determining choice; for only then is it pure and not mixed with any precepts of virtue. Only a completely external right can therefore be called *strict* (right in the narrow sense). This is indeed based on everyone's consciousness of obligation in accordance with a law; but if it is to remain pure, this consciousness may not and cannot be appealed to as an incentive to determine his choice in accordance with this law. Strict right rests instead on the principle of its being possible to use external constraint that can coexist with the freedom of everyone in accordance with universal laws. – Thus when it is said that a creditor has a right to require his debtor to pay his debt, this does not mean that he can remind the debtor that his reason itself puts him under obligation to perform this; it means, instead, that coercion which constrains everyone to pay his debts can coexist with the freedom of everyone, including that of debtors, in accordance with a universal external law. Right and authorization to use coercion therefore mean one and the same thing.

The law of a reciprocal coercion necessarily in accord with the freedom of everyone under the principle of universal freedom is, as it were, the *construction* of that concept, that is, the presentation of it in pure intuition a priori, by analogy with presenting the possibility of bodies moving freely under the law of the *equality of action and reaction*. In pure mathematics we cannot derive the properties of its objects immediately from concepts but can discover them only by constructing concepts. Similarly, it is not so much the *concept* of right as rather a fully reciprocal and equal coercion brought under a universal law and consistent with it, that makes the presentation of that concept possible. Moreover, just as a purely formal concept of pure mathematics (e.g., of geometry) underlies this dynamical concept, reason has taken care to furnish the understanding as far as possible with a priori intuitions for constructing the concept of right. – A right line (*rectum*), one that is straight, is opposed to one that is *curved* on the one hand and to one that is *oblique* on the other hand. As opposed to one that is curved, straightness is that *inner property* of a line such that there is only *one* line between two given points. As opposed to one that is oblique, straightness is that *position* of a *line* toward another intersecting or touching it such that there can be only *one* line (the perpendicular) which does not incline more to one side than to the other and which divides the space on both sides equally. Analogously to this, the doctrine of right wants to

6:233

be sure that *what belongs* to each[r] has been determined (with mathematical exactitude). Such exactitude cannot be expected in the doctrine of virtue, which cannot refuse some room for exceptions (*latitudinem*). – But without making incursions into the province of ethics, one finds two cases that lay claim to a decision about rights although no one can be found to decide them, and that belong as it were within the *intermundia* of Epicurus. – We must first separate these two cases from the doctrine of right proper, to which we are about to proceed, so that their wavering principles will not affect the firm basic principles of the doctrine of right.

APPENDIX TO THE INTRODUCTION TO THE DOCTRINE OF RIGHT.

On ambiguous[s] right. (*Ius aequivocum*.)

An authorization to use coercion is connected with any right in the *narrow* sense (*ius strictum*). But people also think of a right in a *wider* sense (*ius latium*), in which there is no law by which an authorization to use coercion can be determined. – There are two such true or alleged rights, *equity* and the *right of necessity*. The first admits a right without coercion, the second, coercion without a right. It can easily be seen that this ambiguity really arises from the fact that there are cases in which a right is in question but for which no judge can be appointed to render a decision.

I.
Equity.
(Aequitas.)

Equity (considered objectively) is in no way a basis for merely calling upon another to fulfill an ethical duty (to be benevolent and kind). One who demands something on this basis stands instead upon his *right*, except that he does not have the conditions that a judge needs in order to determine by how much or in what way his claim could be satisfied.[13] Suppose that the terms on which a trading company was formed were that the partners should share equally in the profits, but that one partner nevertheless *did* more than the others and so *lost* more when the company met with reverses. By *equity* he can demand more from the company than merely an equal share with the others. In accordance with proper (strict) right, however, his demand would be refused; for if one thinks of a judge

---

[r] *das Seine.* This term, which subsequently comes to the foreground, is often translated as "what is his," "an object that is his," "one's belongings," "what belongs to him." Similar expressions are used for *das Meine* and *das Deine.*
[s] or "equivocal," *zweideutigen*

in this case, he would have no definite particulars (*data*) to enable him to decide how much is due by the contract. Or suppose that a domestic servant is paid his wages at the end of a year in money that has depreciated in the interval, so that he cannot buy with it what he could have bought with it when he concluded the contract. The servant cannot appeal to his right to be compensated when he gets the same amount of money but it is of unequal value. He can appeal only on grounds of equity (a mute divinity who cannot be heard); for nothing was specified about this in the contract, and a judge cannot pronounce in accordance with indefinite conditions.

It also follows from this that a *court of equity* (in a conflict with others about their rights) involves a contradiction. Only where the judge's own rights are concerned, and he can dispose of the case for his own person, may and should he listen to equity, as, for example, when the crown itself bears the damages that others have incurred in its service and for which they petition it to indemnify them, even though it could reject their claim by strict right on the pretext that they undertook this service at their own risk.

6:235

The *motto* (*dictum*) of *equity* is "the strictest right is the greatest wrong" (*summum ius summa injuria*). But this ill cannot be remedied by way of what is laid down as right, even though it concerns a claim to a right; for this claim belongs only to the *court of conscience* (*forum poli*) whereas every question of what is laid down as right must be brought before *civil right* (*forum soli*).

II.
The right of necessity.[14]
(*Ius necessitatis.*)

This alleged right is supposed to be an authorization to take the life of another who is doing nothing to harm me, when I am in danger of losing my own life. It is evident that were there such a right the doctrine of right would have to be in contradiction with itself. For the issue here is not that of a *wrongful*[t] assailant upon my life whom I forestall by depriving him of his life (*ius inculpatae tutelae*),[u] in which case a recommendation[v] to show moderation (*moderamen*) belongs not to right but only to ethics. It is instead a matter of violence being permitted against someone who has used no violence against me.

It is clear that this assertion is not to be understood objectively, in terms of what a law prescribes, but only subjectively, as the verdict[w] that

---
[t] *ungerechten*
[u] right to blameless (self-)defense
[v] *Anempfehlung*
[w] *Sentenz*, perhaps "the sentence." Throughout *The Metaphysics of Morals* Kant seems to draw no clear or consistent distinction between a "sentence" and a "verdict" or "decision" of a court.

would be given by a court. In other words, there can be no *penal law* that would assign the death penalty to someone in a shipwreck who, in order to save his own life, shoves another, whose life is equally in danger, off a plank on which he had saved himself. For the punishment threatened by the law could not be greater than the loss of his own life. A penal law of this sort could not have the effect intended, since a threat of an ill that is still *uncertain* (death by a judicial verdict) cannot outweigh the fear of an ill that is *certain* (drowning). Hence the deed of saving one's life by violence is not to be judged *inculpable* (*inculpabile*) but only *unpunishable* (*impunibile*), and by a strange confusion jurists take this *subjective* impunity to be *objective* impunity (conformity with law).

The motto of the right of necessity says: "Necessity has no law" (*necessitas non habet legem*). Yet there could be no necessity that would make what is wrong conform with law.

One sees that in both appraisals of what is right (in terms of a right of equity and a right of necessity) the *ambiguity* (*aequivocatio*) arises from confusing the objective with the subjective basis of exercising the right (before reason and before a court). What someone by himself recognizes on good grounds as right will not be confirmed by a court, and what he must judge to be of itself wrong is treated with indulgence by a court; for the concept of right, in these two cases, is not taken in the same sense.

DIVISION OF THE DOCTRINE OF RIGHT.

A.
General division of duties of right.

One can follow Ulpian in making this division if a sense is ascribed to his formulae which he may not have thought distinctly in them but which can be explicated[x] from them or put into them. They are the following:

1) *Be an honorable human being* (*honeste vive*).[y] Rightful honor[z] (*honestas iuridica*) consists in asserting one's worth as a human being in relation to others, a duty expressed by the saying, "Do not make yourself a mere means for others but be at the same time an end for them." This duty will be explained later as obligation from the right of humanity in our own person (*Lex iusti*).[15]

2) *Do not wrong anyone* (*neminem laede*) even if, to avoid doing so, you should have to stop associating with others and shun all society (*Lex iuridica*).

3) (If you cannot help associating with others), *enter* into a society with them in which each can keep what is his (*suum cuique tribue*). — If

---
[x] *entwickelt*. See *Groundwork of the Metaphysics of Morals* (4:397, note d).
[y] *Sei ein rechtlicher Mensch* . . .
[z] *Die rechtliche Ehrbarkeit*

this last formula were translated "Give to each what is *his*," what it says would be absurd, since one cannot give anyone something he already has. In order to make sense it would have to read: "*Enter* a condition in which what belongs to each can be secured to him against everyone else" (*Lex iustitiae*).

So the above three classical formulae serve also as principles for dividing the system of duties of right into *internal* duties, *external* duties, and duties that involve the derivation of the latter from the principle of the former by subsumption.

B.
General division of rights.

1. As systematic *doctrines*, rights are divided into *natural right*, which rests only on a priori principles, and *positive* (statutory) right, which proceeds from the will of a legislator.
2. The highest division of rights, as (moral) *capacities*[a] for putting others under obligations (i.e., as a lawful basis, *titulum*, for doing so), is the division into *innate* and *acquired* right. An innate right is that which belongs to everyone by nature, independently of any act that would establish a right;[b] an acquired right is that for which such an act is required.

What is innately mine or yours can also be called what is *internally* mine or yours (*meum vel tuum internum*); for what is externally mine or yours must always be acquired.

There is only one innate right.

Freedom (independence from being constrained by another's choice), insofar as it can coexist with the freedom of every other in accordance with a universal law, is the only original right belonging to every man by virtue of his humanity. – This principle of innate freedom already involves the following authorizations, which are not really distinct from it (as if they were members of the division of some higher concept of a right): innate *equality*, that is, independence from being bound by others to more than

---

[a] *Vermögen*[16]
[b] *rechtliche Akt*. In 23:262, Kant defines a rightful action (*eine rechtliche Handlung, actus iuridicus*) as "someone's action from which a right of his arises." This involves complications. Strictly speaking an *Akt*, translated as "act," is not the same as an "action," *Handlung*, although actions are necessary but not sufficient conditions for acquiring rights; and a rightful act can also be one by which someone gives up a right (6:300). In any case, this translation is too narrow to cover all the contexts in which Kant uses *rechtliche Akt*. In the following paragraph it seems to mean, more generally, an act affecting rights. On the translation of *rechtliche*, see Translator's Introduction.

6:238 one can in turn bind them; hence a human being's quality of being *his own master* (*sui iuris*), as well as being a human being *beyond reproach* (*iusti*), since before he performs any act affecting rights[c] he has done no wrong to anyone; and finally, his being authorized to do to others anything that does not in itself diminish what is theirs, so long as they do not want to accept it – such things as merely communicating his thoughts to them, telling or promising them something, whether what he says is true and sincere or untrue and insincere (*veriloquium aut falsiloquium*); for it is entirely up to them whether they want to believe him or not.*

The aim in introducing such a division within the system of natural right (insofar as it is concerned with innate right) is that when a dispute arises about an acquired right and the question comes up, on whom does the burden of proof (*onus probandi*) fall, either about a controversial fact or, if this is settled, about a controversial right, someone who refuses to accept this obligation can appeal methodically to his innate right to freedom (which is now specified in its various relations), as if he were appealing to various bases for rights.

With regard to what is innately, hence internally, mine or yours, there are not several *rights;* there is only *one* right. Since this highest division consists of two members very unequal in content, it can be put in the prolegomena and the division of the doctrine of right can refer only to what is externally mine or yours.

6:239
DIVISION OF THE METAPHYSICS OF MORALS AS A WHOLE.

I.

All duties are either *duties of right* (*officia iuris*), that is, duties for which external lawgiving is possible, or *duties of virtue* (*officia virtutis s. ethica*),[f] for

---

* Telling an untruth intentionally, even though merely frivolously, is usually called a *lie* (*mendacium*) because it can also harm someone, at least to the extent that if he ingenuously repeats it others ridicule him as gullible. The only kind of untruth we want to call a lie, in the sense *bearing upon rights*,[d] is one that directly infringes upon another's right, e.g., the false allegation that a contract has been concluded with someone, made in order to deprive him of what is his (*falsiloquium dolosum*).[e] And this distinction between closely related concepts is not without basis; for when someone merely says what he thinks, another always remains free to take it as he pleases. But a rumor, having some basis, that this is a human being whose talk cannot be believed comes so close to the reproach of calling him a liar that the borderline separating what belongs to *Ius* from what must be assigned to ethics can only be drawn in just this way.

[c] *rechtlichen Akt*
[d] *im rechtlichen Sinne*
[e] deceitful falsehood
[f] duties of virtue or ethics

which external lawgiving is not possible. – Duties of virtue cannot be subject to external lawgiving simply because they have to do with an end which (or the having of which) is also a duty. No external lawgiving can bring about someone's setting an end for himself (because this is an internal act of the mind), although it may prescribe external actions that lead to an end without the subject making it his end.

But why is the doctrine of morals usually called (especially by Cicero) a doctrine of *duties* and not also a doctrine of *rights*, even though rights have reference to duties? – The reason is that we know our own freedom (from which all moral laws, and so all rights as well as duties proceed) only through the *moral imperative*, which is a proposition commanding duty, from which the capacity for putting others under obligation,[g] that is, the concept of a right, can afterwards be explicated.[h]

II.

In the doctrine of duties a human being can and should be represented in terms of his capacity for freedom, which is wholly supersensible, and so too merely in terms of his *humanity*, his personality independent of physical attributes (*homo noumenon*), as distinguished from the same subject represented as affected by physical attributes, *a human being* (*homo phaenomenon*). Accordingly right and end, related in turn to duty in this twofold property, yield the following divisions:

Division
in Accordance with the Objective Relation of Law to Duty

6:240

Perfect Duty

	1. The right of humanity in our own person		2. The right of human beings	
Duty to Oneself		(of right) Duty (of virtue)		Duty to Others
	3. The end of humanity in our own person		4. The end of human beings	

Imperfect Duty

[g] *Vermögen andere zu verpflichten*
[h] *entwickelt*

6.241

III.

The subjects between whom a relation of right to duty can be thought of (whether admissibly or not) can stand related to each other in different ways, and so a division can also be made from this point of view.

*Division
in Accordance with the Relation of the Subject Imposing Obligation to the Subject Put under Obligation.*

1.	2.
The relation in terms of rights of human beings toward beings that have neither rights nor duties.	The relation in terms of rights of human beings toward beings that have rights as well as duties.
Vacat[i]	*Adest*
For these are beings lacking reason, which can neither bind us nor by which we can be bound.	For this is a relation of human beings to human beings.
3.	4.
The relation in terms of rights of human beings toward beings that have only duties but no rights.	The relation in terms of rights of human beings toward a being that has only rights but no duties (God).
Vacat	*Vacat*
For these would be human beings without personality (serfs, slaves).	At least in philosophy, since such a being is not an object of possible experience.

So only in Number 2 is there found a *real* relation between right and duty. The reason that it is not to be found in Number 4 is that this would be a *transcendent* duty, that is, a duty for which no corresponding external subject imposing the obligation can *be given*, so that the relation here is only *ideal* from a theoretical point of view, that is, a relation to a thought-entity.[j] We ourselves *make* the concept of this being, but this concept is not altogether *empty;* instead it is fruitful in reference to ourselves and to maxims of internal morality, and so for an internal practical purpose,

---

[i] *Vacat* might be rendered "has no members," *Adest* "has members."
[j] *Gedankending*

inasmuch as our entire *immanent duty* (that which can be fulfilled) lies only in this relation that can merely be thought of.   6:242

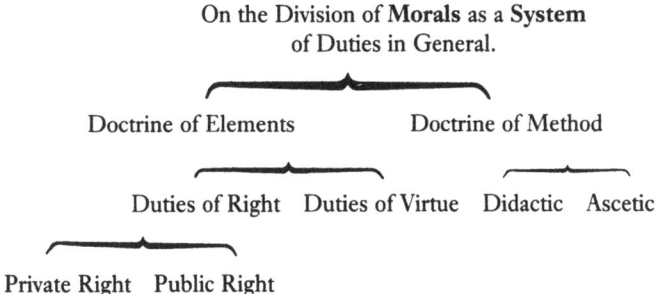

On the Division of **Morals** as a **System** of Duties in General.

Doctrine of Elements — Doctrine of Method

Duties of Right — Duties of Virtue — Didactic — Ascetic

Private Right — Public Right

and so on, everything that involves not only the contents of a scientific doctrine of morals but also its architectonic form, once its metaphysical first principles have traced out completely the universal principles for it.

The highest division of natural right cannot be the division (sometimes made) into *natural* and *social* right; it must instead be the division into natural and *civil* right, the former of which is called *private right* and the latter *public right*. For a *state of nature* is not opposed to a social but to a civil condition, since there can certainly be society in a state of nature, but no *civil* society (which secures what is mine or yours by public laws). This is why right in a state of nature is called private right.

*The
doctrine of right*

*Part I
Private right*

The universal doctrine of right
Part I
Private right
Concerning what is externally mine or yours[k]
in general

Chapter I
How to have something external as one's own.

§ 1.
That is *rightfully mine* (*meum iuris*) with which I am so connected that another's use of it without my consent would wrong me. The subjective condition of any possible use is *possession*.

But something *external* would be mine only if I may assume that I could be wronged by another's use of a thing even *though I am not in possession of it*. — So it would be self-contradictory to say that I have something external as my own if the concept of possession could not have different meanings, namely *sensible* possession and *intelligible* possession, and by the former could be understood *physical* possession but by the latter a *merely rightful* possession of the same object.

But the expression "an object is *external to me*" can mean either that it is an object merely *distinct* from me (the subject) or else that it is also to be found in *another location* (*positus*) in space or time. Only if it is taken in the first sense can possession be thought of as rational possession; if taken in the second sense it would have to be called empirical possession. — *Intelligible* possession (if this is possible) is possession of an object *without holding it* (*detentio*).

§ 3.[l]
Whoever wants to assert that he has a thing as his own must be in possession of an object, since otherwise he could not be wronged[m] by

---

[k] In the translation of the phrase *Mein und Dein* (*meum et tuum*), "and" has been changed to "or."

[l] § 2 is omitted here but replaces a portion of the text of § 6. See above, Translator's Note.

[m] *lädiert*. In 6:249 Kant gives *Abbruch an meiner Freiheit* . . . as a parenthetical explanation of *Läsion*.

another's use of it without his consent. For if something outside this object which is not connected with it by rights affects it, it would not be able to affect himself (the subject) and do him any wrong.

§ 4. *Exposition of the concept of external objects that are yours or mine.*

There can be only *three* external objects of my choice: 1) a (corporeal) *thing* external to me; 2) another's *choice* to perform a specific deed (*praestatio*); 3) another's *status*ⁿ in relation to me. These are objects of my choice in terms of the categories of *substance, causality,* and *community* between myself and external objects in accordance with laws of freedom.

a) I cannot call an object in *space* (a corporeal thing) mine unless, *even though I am not in physical possession of it*, I can still assert that I am actually in some other (hence not physical) possession of it. – So I shall not call an apple mine because I have it in my hand (possess it physically), but only if I can say that I possess it even though I have put it down, no matter where. In the same way, I shall not be able to say that the land on which I have lain down is mine because I am on it, but only if I can assert that it still remains in my possession even though I have left the place. For someone who tried in the first case (of empirical possession) to wrest the apple from my hand or to drag me away from my resting place would indeed wrong me with regard to what is *internally* mine (freedom); but he would not wrong me with regard to what is externally mine unless I could assert that I am in possession of the object even without holding it. I could not then call these objects (the apple and the resting place) mine.

b) I cannot call the *performance* of something by another's choice mine if all I can say is that it came into my possession *at the same time* that he promised it (*pactum re initum*),ᵒ but only if I can assert that I am in possession of the other's choice (to determine him to perform it) even though the time for his performing it is still to come. The other's promise is therefore included in my belongings and goods (*obligatio activa*), and I can count it as mine not merely if (as in the first case) I already have *what was promised* in my possession, but even though I do not possess it yet. So I must be able to think that I am in possession of this object independently of being limited by temporal conditions, and so independently of empirical possession.

c) I cannot call a *wife,* a *child,* a *servant,* or, in general, another person mine because I am now in charge of them as members of my household or have them within my restraining walls and in my

---
ⁿ *Zustand*
ᵒ having undertaken a compact regarding a thing

control and possession, but only if, although they have withdrawn from such constraint and I do not possess them (empirically), I can still say that I possess them merely by my will, hence *merely rightfully*, as long as they exist somewhere or at some time. Only if and insofar as I can assert this are they included in my belongings.

§ 5. Definition of the concept of external objects that are mine or yours.

The *nominal definition*[p] of what is externally mine – that which suffices only to *distinguish* the object from all others and arises from a complete and determinate *exposition* of the concept – would be: that outside me is externally mine which it could be a wrong (an infringement upon my freedom which can coexist with the freedom of everyone in accordance with a universal law) to prevent me from using as I please. – But the *real definition*[q] of this concept – that which also suffices for the *deduction* of it (cognition of the possibility of the object) – goes like this: something external is mine if I would be wronged by being disturbed in my use of it *even though I am not in possession of it* (not holding the object). – I must be in some sort of possession of an external object if it is to be called *mine*, for otherwise someone who affected this object against my will would not also affect me and so would not wrong me. So, in consequence of 4, *intelligible possession (possessio noumenon)* must be assumed to be possible if something external is to be mine or yours. Empirical possession (holding) is then only possession in *appearance (possessio phaenomenon)*, although the *object* itself that I possess is not here treated, as it was in the Transcendental Analytic, as an appearance but as a thing in itself; for there reason was concerned with theoretical cognition of the nature of things and how far it could extend, but here it is concerned with the practical determination of choice in accordance with laws of *freedom*, whether the object can be cognized through the senses or through the pure understanding alone, and *right* is a pure practical *rational concept* of choice under laws of freedom.

6:249

For the same reason it is not appropriate to speak of possessing a right to this or that object but rather of possessing it *merely rightfully;* for a right is already an intellectual possession of an object and it would make no sense to speak of possessing a possession.

§ 6. Deduction of the concept of merely rightful possession of an external object (possessio noumenon).

The question: how is it possible for *something external to be mine or yours?* resolves itself into the question: how is *merely rightful* (intelligible) *posses-*

---

[p] *Namenerklärung*
[q] *Sacherklärung*

sion possible? and this, in turn, into the third question: how is a *synthetic* a priori proposition about right possible?

All propositions about right[r] are a priori propositions, since they are laws of reason (*dictamina rationis*). An a priori proposition about right with regard to *empirical possession* is *analytic*, for it says nothing more than what follows from empirical possession in accordance with the principle of contradiction, namely, that if I am holding a thing (and so physically connected with it), someone who affects it without my consent (e.g., snatches an apple from my hand) affects and diminishes what is internally mine (my freedom), so that his maxim is in direct contradiction with the axiom of right.[17] So the proposition about empirical possession in conformity with rights does not go beyond the right of a person with regard to himself.

On the other hand, a proposition about the possibility of possessing a thing *external to myself,* which puts aside any conditions of empirical possession in space and time (and hence presupposes the possibility of *possessio noumenon*), goes beyond those limiting conditions; and since it affirms possession of something even without holding it, as necessary for the concept of something external that is mine or yours, *it is synthetic.* Reason has then the task of showing how such a proposition, which goes beyond the concept of empirical possession, is possible a priori.[18]

Postulate of practical reason with regard to rights.[s, 1]

It is possible for me to have any external object of my choice as mine, that is, a maxim by which, if it were to become a law, an object of choice would

---

[r] *Rechtssätze*
[s] The next three paragraphs originally numbered § 2, replace the following passage from AK:

In this way, for example, taking possession of a separate piece of land is an act of private choice, without being *unsanctioned* [*ohne doch eigenmächtig zu sein*]. The possessor bases his act on an innate *possession in common* [*Gemeinbesitze*] of the surface of the earth and on a general will corresponding *a priori* to it, which permits *private possession* on it (otherwise, unoccupied things would in themselves and in accordance with a law be made things that belong to no one). By being the first to take possession he originally acquires a definite piece of land [*bestimmten Boden*] and resists with right (*iure*) anyone else who would prevent him from making private use of it. Yet since he is in a state of nature, he cannot do so by legal proceedings [*von rechtswegen*] (*de iure*) because there does not exist any public law in this state.

Even if a piece of land were considered or declared to be *free,* that is, open to anyone's use, one could still not say that it is free by nature or *originally* free, prior to any act establishing a right; for that would again be a relation to things, namely to the land, which would refuse possession of itself to anyone; instead one would say that this land is free because of a prohibition on everyone to make use of it, and for this, possession of it in common is required, which cannot take place without a contract. But land that can be free only in this way must really be in the possession of all those (joined together) who forbid or suspend one another's use of it.

in itself (objectively) have to *belong to no one* (*res nullius*) is contrary to rights.*

For an object of my choice is something that I have the *physical* power to use. If it were nevertheless absolutely not within my *rightful* power to make use of it, that is, if the use of it could not coexist with the freedom of everyone in accordance with a universal law (would be wrong), then freedom would be depriving itself of the use of its choice with regard to an object of choice, by putting *usable* objects beyond any possibility of being *used;* in other words, it would annihilate them in a practical respect and make them into *res nullius*, even though in the use of things choice was formally consistent with everyone's outer freedom in accordance with universal laws. – But since pure practical reason lays down only formal laws as the basis for using choice and thus abstracts from its matter, that is, from other properties of the object *provided only that it is an object of choice*, it can contain no absolute prohibition against using such an object, since this would be a contradiction of outer freedom with itself. – But an object of my *choice* is that which I have the physical capacity to use as I please, that whose

---

This *original* community of land, and with it of things upon it (*communio fundi originaria*), 6:251 is an idea that has objective (rightfully practical) reality. This kind of community must be sharply distinguished from a *private community* (*communio primaeva*), which is a fiction;[19] for a primitive community would have to be one that was *instituted* and arose from a contract by which everyone gave up private possessions and, by uniting his possessions with those of everyone else, transformed them into a collective possession [*Gesammtbesitz*]; and history would have to give us proof of such a contract. But it is contradictory to claim that such a procedure is an *original* taking possession and that each human being could and should have based his separate possession upon it.

Residing [*Sitz*] on land (*sedes*) is to be distinguished from being in possession (*possessio*) of it, and *settling* or making a settlement [*Niederlassung, Ansiedelung*] (*incolatus*), which is a lasting private possession of a place dependent upon the presence of the subject on it, is to be distinguished from taking possession of land with the intention of some day acquiring it. I am not talking here about settling as a second act to establish a right, which can either follow upon taking possession or not take place at all; for settling of this kind would not be original possession but would be possession derived from others' consent.

Merely physical possession of land (holding it) is already a right to a thing, though certainly not of itself sufficient for regarding it as mine. Relative to others, since (as far as one knows) it is first possession, it is consistent with the principle of outer freedom and is also involved in original possession in common, which provides a priori the basis on which any private possession is possible. Accordingly, to interfere with the use of a piece of land by the first occupant of it is to wrong him. Taking first possession has therefore a rightful basis (*titulus possessionis*), which is original possession in common; and the saying "Happy are those who are in possession" (*beati possidentes*), because none is bound to certify his possession, is a basic principle of natural right, which lays down taking first possession as a rightful basis for acquisition on which every first possessor can rely.

t Rechtliches Postulat. On the translation of *rechtlich*, see Translator's Introduction.

u rechtswidrig. On the translation of *rechtswidrig* and its opposite, *rechtmässig*, see Translator's Introduction.

v Vermögen

use lies within my *power*[w] (*potentia*). This must be distinguished from having the same object under my control[x] (*in potestatem meam redactum*), which presupposes not merely a *capacity* but also an *act* of choice. But in order to *think of* something simply as an object of my choice it is sufficient for me to be conscious of having it within my power. – It is therefore an a priori presupposition of practical reason to regard and treat any object of my choice as something which could objectively be mine or yours.

This postulate can be called a permissive law (*lex permissiva*) of practical reason, which gives us an authorization that could not be got from mere concepts of right as such, namely to put all others under an obligation, which they would not otherwise have, to refrain from using certain objects of our choice because we have been the first to take them into our possession. Reason wills that this hold as a principle, and it does this as *practical* reason, which extends itself a priori by this postulate of reason.[y]

In an a priori *theoretical* principle, namely, an a priori intuition would have to underlie the given concept (as was established in the *Critique of Pure Reason*); and so something would have to be *added to* the concept of possession of an object. But with this practical principle the opposite procedure is followed and all conditions of intuition which establish empirical possession must be *removed* (disregarded), in order to *extend* the concept of possession beyond empirical possession and to be able to say: it is possible for any external object of my choice to be reckoned as rightfully mine if I have control of it (and only insofar as I have control of it) without being in possession of it.

The possibility of this kind of possession, and so the deduction of the concept of nonempirical possession, is based on the postulate of practical reason with regard to rights: "that it is a duty of right to act towards others so that what is external (usable) could also become someone's," together with the exposition of the concept of an external object that belongs to someone, since that concept rests simply on that of *nonphysical* possession. There is, however, no way of proving of itself the possibility of nonphysical possession or of having any insight into it (just because it is a rational concept for which no corresponding intuition can be given); its possibility is instead an immediate consequence of the postulate referred to. For if it is necessary to act in accordance with that principle of right, its intelligible condition (a merely rightful possession) must then also be possible. – No one need be surprised that *theoretical* principles about external objects that are mine or yours get lost in the intelligible and represent no extension of cognition, since no theoretical deduction can be given for the possibility of the concept of freedom on which they are based. It can only be inferred

---

[w] *in meiner Macht*
[x] *in meiner Gewalt*
[y] The text cited in note *s* replaces text originally found here.

from the practical law of reason (the categorical imperative), as a fact of reason.

§ 7. *Application to objects of experience of the principle that it is possible for something external to be mine or yours.*

The concept of merely rightful possession is not an empirical concept (dependent upon conditions of space and time) and yet it has practical reality, that is, it must be applicable to objects of experience, cognition of which is dependent upon those conditions. – The way to proceed with the concept of a right with respect to such objects, so that they can be external objects which are mine or yours, is the following. Since the concept of a right is simply a rational concept, it cannot be applied *directly* to objects of experience and to the concept of empirical *possession*, but must first be applied to the understanding's pure concept of *possession* in general. So the concept to which the concept of a right is directly applied is not that of *holding* (*detentio*), which is an empirical way of thinking of possession, but rather the concept of *having*,[20] in which abstraction is made from all spatial and temporal conditions and the object is thought of only as *under my control* (*in potestate mea positum esse*). So too the expression *external* does not mean existing in a *place other* than where I am, or that my decision and acceptance are occurring at a different time from the making of the offer; it means only an object *distinct* from me. Now, practical reason requires me, by its law of right, to apply mine or yours to objects not in accordance with sensible conditions but in abstraction from them, since it has to do with a determination of choice in accordance with laws of freedom, and it also requires me to think of possession of them in this way, since only a *concept of the understanding* can be subsumed under concepts of right. I shall therefore say that I possess a field even though it is in a place quite different from where I actually am. For we are speaking here only of an intellectual relation to an object, insofar as I have it *under my control* (the understanding's concept of possession independent of spatial determinations), and the object is *mine* because my will to use it as I please does not conflict with the law of outer freedom. Here practical reason requires us to think of possession *apart from* possession of this object of my choice in appearance (holding it), to think of it not in terms of empirical concepts but of concepts of the understanding, those that can contain a priori conditions of empirical concepts. Upon this is based the validity of such a concept of possession (*possessio noumenon*), as a *giving of law* that holds for everyone; for such lawgiving is involved in the expression "this external object is *mine*," since by it an obligation is laid upon all others, which they would not otherwise have, to refrain from using the object.

6:253

So the way to have something external as what is mine consists in a merely rightful connection of the subject's will with that object in accor-

6:254

dance with the concept of intelligible possession, independently of any relation to it in space and time. – It is not because I occupy a place on the earth with my body that this place is something external which is mine (for that concerns only my outer *freedom*, hence only possession of myself, not a thing external to me, so that it is only an internal right). It is mine if I still possess it even though I have left it for another place; only then is my external right involved. And anyone who wants to make my continuous occupation of this place by my person the condition of my having it as mine must either assert that it is not at all possible to have something external as mine (and this conflicts with the postulate 2) or else require that in order to have it as mine I be in two places at once. Since this amounts to saying that I am to be in a place and also not be in it, he contradicts himself.

This can also be applied to the case of my having accepted a promise. For my having and possession in what was promised is not annulled by the promisor's saying at one time "this thing is to be yours" and then at a later time saying of the same thing "I now will that it not be yours." For in such intellectual relations it is as if the promisor had said, without any time between the two declarations of his will, "this is to be yours" and also "this is not to be yours," which is self-contradictory.

The same holds of the concept of rightful possession of a person, as included in the subject's belongings (his wife, child, servant). This domestic community and the possession of their respective status vis-à-vis one another by all its members is not annulled by their being authorized to separate from one another and go to different *places;* for what connects them is a relation *in terms of rights*, and what is externally mine or yours here is based, as in the preceding cases, entirely on the assumption that purely rational possession without holding each other is possible.

Rightfully practical reason is forced into a critique of itself in the concept of something external which is mine or yours, and this by an antinomy of propositions concerning the possibility of such a concept; that is, only by an unavoidable dialectic in which both thesis and antithesis make equal claims to the validity of two conditions that are inconsistent with each other is reason forced, even in its practical use (having to do with rights), to make a distinction between possession as appearance and possession that is thinkable merely by the understanding.

The *thesis* says: *It is possible* to have something external as mine even though I am not in possession of it.

The *antithesis* says: *It is not possible* to have something external as mine unless I am in possession of it.

Solution: Both propositions are true, the first if I understand, by the word "possession", empirical possession (*possessio phaenomenon*), the second if I understand by it purely intelligible possession (*possessio noumenon*). – But we cannot see how intelligible possession is possible and so how it is possible for something external to be mine or yours, but must infer it from the postulate of practical reason. With regard to this postulate it is particularly noteworthy that practical reason *extends* itself without intuitions and without even needing any that are a priori, merely by *leaving out* empirical conditions, as it is justified in doing by the law of freedom. In this way it can lay down *synthetic* a priori propositions about right, the proof of which (as will soon be shown) can afterwards be adduced, in a practical respect, in an analytic way.

§ 8. It is possible to have something external as one's own only in a rightful condition, under an authority giving laws publicly, that is, in a civil condition.

When I declare (by word or deed), I will that something external is to be mine, I thereby declare that everyone else is under obligation to refrain from using that object of my choice, an obligation no one would have were it not for this act of mine to establish a right. This claim involves, however, acknowledging that I in turn am under obligation to every other to refrain from using what is externally his; for the obligation here arises from a universal rule having to do with external rightful relations. I am therefore not under obligation to leave external objects belonging to others untouched unless everyone else provides me assurance that he will behave in accordance with the same principle with regard to what is mine. This assurance does not require a special act to establish a right, but is already contained in the concept of an obligation corresponding to an external right, since the universality, and with it the reciprocity, of obligation arises from a universal rule. – Now, a unilateral will cannot serve as a coercive law for everyone with regard to possession that is external and therefore contingent, since that would infringe upon freedom in accordance with universal laws. So it is only a will putting everyone under obligation, hence only a collective general (common) and powerful will, that can provide everyone this assurance. – But the condition of being under a general external (i.e., public) lawgiving accompanied with power is the civil condition. So only in a civil condition can something external be mine or yours.

6:256

Corollary: If it must be possible, in terms of rights, to have an external object as one's own, the subject must also be permitted to constrain everyone else with whom he comes into conflict about whether an external object is his or another's to enter along with him into a civil constitution.

§ 9. In a state of nature something external can actually be mine or yours but only **provisionally.**

When people are under a civil constitution, the statutory laws obtaining in this condition cannot infringe upon *natural right,* (i.e., that right which can be derived from a priori principles for a civil constitution); and so the rightful principle "whoever acts on a maxim by which it becomes impossible to have an object of my choice as mine wrongs me," remains in force. For a civil constitution is just the rightful condition, by which what belongs to each is only secured, but not actually settled and determined.[z] – Any guarantee, then, already presupposes what belongs to someone (to whom it secures it). Prior to a civil constitution (or in *abstraction* from it) external objects that are mine or yours must therefore be assumed to be possible, and with them a right to constrain everyone with whom we could have any dealings to enter with us into a constitution in which external objects can be secured as mine or yours. – Possession in anticipation of and preparation for the civil condition, which can be based only on a law of a common will, possession which therefore accords with the *possibility* of such a condition, is *provisionally rightful* possession, whereas possession found in an *actual* civil condition would be *conclusive* possession. – Prior to entering such a condition, a subject who is ready for it resists with right those who are not willing to submit to it and who want to interfere with his present possession; for the will of all others except for himself, which proposes to put him under obligation to give up a certain possession, is merely *unilateral*, and hence has as little lawful force in denying him possession as he has in asserting it (since this can be found only in a general will), whereas he at least has the advantage of being compatible with the introduction and establishment of a civil condition. – In summary, the way to have something external as one's own *in a state of nature* is physical possession which has in its favor the rightful *presumption* that it will be made into rightful possession through being united with the will of all in a public lawgiving, and in anticipation of this holds *comparatively* as rightful possession.

In accordance with the formula *Happy is he who is in possession* (*beati possedentes*), this prerogative of right arising from empirical possession does not consist in its being unnecessary for the possessor, since he is presumed to be an *honest man*, to furnish proof that his possession is in conformity with right (for this holds only in disputes about rights). This prerogative arises, instead, from the capacity[a] anyone has, by the postulate of practical reason, to have an external object of his choice as his own. Consequently, any holding of an external object is a condition whose conformity with right is based on that postulate by a previous act of will; and so long as this condition does not conflict with another's earlier possession of the same object he is provisionally justified, in accordance with the law of outer freedom, in preventing anyone who does not want to enter with him into a condition of public lawful

---

[z] *eigentlich aber nicht ausgemacht und bestimmt wird*
[a] *Vermögen*

freedom from usurping the use of that object, in order to put to his own use, in conformity with the postulate of reason, a thing that would otherwise be annihilated practically.

Chapter II.
How to acquire something external.

6:258

§ 10. General principle of external acquisition.
I acquire something when I bring it about (*efficio*) that it becomes *mine*. – Something external is originally mine which is mine without any act that establishes a right to it. But that *acquisition* is original which is not derived from what is another's.

Nothing external is originally mine, but it can indeed be *acquired* originally, that is, without being derived from what is another's. – A condition of community (*communio*) of what is mine and yours can never be thought to be original but must be acquired (by an act that establishes an external right), although possession of an external object can originally be only possession in common. Even if one thinks (problematically) of an *original* community (*communio mei et tui originaria*), it must still be distinguished from a *primitive* community (*communio primaeva*), which is supposed to have been instituted in the earliest *time* of relations of rights among human beings and cannot be based, like the former, on principles but only on history. Although primitive, it would always have to be thought to be acquired and derived (*communio derivata*).

The principle of external acquisition is as follows: that is mine which I bring under my *control* (in accordance with the law of outer *freedom*); which, as an object of my choice, is something that I have the capacity to use (in accordance with the postulate of practical reason); and which, finally, I *will* to be mine (in conformity with the idea of a possible united *will*).

The aspects,[b] (*attendenda*) of *original* acquisition are therefore: 1) *Apprehension* of an object that belongs to no one; otherwise it would conflict with another's freedom in accordance with universal laws. This *apprehension* is taking possession of an object of choice in space and time, so that the possession in which I put myself is *possessio phaenomenon*. 2) *Giving a sign* (*declaratio*) of my possession of this object and of my act of choice to exclude everyone else from it. 3) *Appropriation* (*appropriatio*), as the act of a general will (in idea) giving an external law through which everyone is bound to agree with my choice. – The validity of this last aspect of acquisition, on which rests the conclusion "this external object is *mine*," that is,

6:259

---
[b] *Momente*

the conclusion that my possession holds as possession *merely by right* (*possessio noumenon*), is based on this: since all these acts *have to do with a right* and so proceed from practical reason, in the question of what is laid down as right abstraction can be made from the empirical conditions of possession, so that the conclusion, "the external object is mine," is correctly drawn from sensible to intelligible possession.

Original acquisition of an external object of choice is called *taking control*[c] of it (*occupatio*), and only corporeal things (substances) can be acquired originally. When it takes place, what it requires as the condition of empirical possession is priority in time to anyone else who wants to take control of the object (*qui prior tempore potior iure*).[d] As original, it is only the result of a *unilateral* choice, for if it required a bilateral choice the acquisition would be derived from the contract of two (or more) persons and so from what is another's. – It is not easy to see how an act of choice of that kind could establish what belongs to someone. – However, if an acquisition is *first* it is not therefore *original*. For the acquisition of a public rightful condition by the union of the will of all for giving universal law would be an acquisition such that none could precede it, yet it would be derived from the particular wills of each and would be *omnilateral*, whereas original acquisition can proceed only from a unilateral will.

Division of the acquisition of something external that is mine or yours.

1. In terms of the *matter* (the object), I acquire either a corporeal *thing* (substance), or another's *performance* (causality), or another *person* himself, that is the status of that person, insofar as I get a right to make arrangements about him[e] (deal with him).

2. In terms of the *form* (the kind of acquisition), it is either a *right to a thing*[f] (*ius reale*), or a *right against a person*[g] (*ius personale*), or a *right to a person akin to a right to a thing*[h] (*ius realiter personale*), that is, possession (though not use) of another person as a thing.

3. In terms of the *basis* of the acquisition *in right*[i] (*titulus*), something external is acquired through the act of a *unilateral*, *bilateral* or *omnilateral* choice (*facto, pacto, lege*). Although this is not, strictly

---

[c] *Bemächtigung*. In the case of land, "occupying it" would be the appropriate translation. However, Kant also uses *Bemächtigung* in the context of rights to things generally and of rights against persons akin to rights to things.
[d] who is first in time has the stronger right
[e] *über denselben zu verfügen. Verfügung* is used in 6:314, and the phrase *über . . . verfügen* is used in 6:313 and again in 6:330, where it is followed by (*disponieren*).
[f] *Sachenrecht*
[g] *persönaliches Recht*
[h] *dinglich-persönliches Recht*
[i] *Rechtsgrunde*

speaking, a special member of the division of rights, it is still an aspect of the way acquisition is carried out.

SECTION I
ON PROPERTY RIGHT.[j]

§ 11. *What is a right to a thing?*[k]

The usual exposition of a *right to a thing* (*ius reale, ius in re*), that "it is a right *against every possessor of it*," is a correct nominal definition. – But what is it that enables me to recover an external object from anyone who is holding it and to constrain him (*per vindicationem*) to put me in possession of it again? Could this external rightful relation of my choice be a *direct* relation to a corporeal thing? Someone who thinks that his right is a direct relation to things rather than to persons would have to think (though only obscurely) that since there corresponds to a right on one side a duty on the other, an external thing always remains *under obligation* to the first possessor even though it has left his hands; that, because it is already under obligation to him, it rejects anyone else who pretends to be the possessor of it. So he would think of my right as if it were a *guardian spirit* accompanying the thing, always pointing me out to whoever else wanted to take possession of it and protecting it against any incursions by them. It is therefore absurd to think of an obligation of a person to things or the reverse, even though it may be permissible, if need be, to make this rightful relation perceptible by picturing it and expressing it in this way.

So the real definition would have to go like this: *a right to a thing* is a right to the private use of a thing of which I am in (original or instituted) possession in common[l] with all others. For this possession in common is the only condition under which it is possible for me to exclude every other possessor from the private use of a thing (*ius contra quemlibet huius rei possessorem*)[m] since, unless such a possession in common is assumed, it is inconceivable how I, who am not in possession of the thing, could still be wronged by others who are in possession of it and are using it. – By my unilateral choice I cannot bind another to refrain from using a thing, an obligation he would not otherwise have; hence I can do this only through the united choice of all who possess it in common. Otherwise I would have to think of a right to a thing as if the thing had an obligation to me, from which my right against every other possessor of it is then derived; and this is an absurd way of representing it.

---

[j] *Sachenrecht*. Kant introduces the term "property" (*Eigentum, dominium*), a full right to a thing, in his concluding remark to this section, 6:270.
[k] *Sachenrecht*
[l] *Gesammtbesitz*
[m] right against whoever is possessor of the thing

By the term "property right" (*ius reale*) should be understood not only a right to a thing (*ius in re*) but also the *sum* of all the laws having to do with things being mine or yours. – But it is clear that someone who was all alone on the earth could really neither have nor acquire any external thing as his own, since there is no relation whatever of obligation between him, as a person, and any other external object, as a thing. Hence, speaking strictly and literally, there is also no (direct) right to a thing. What is called a right to a thing is only that right someone has against a person who is in possession of it in common[n] with all others (in the civil condition).

§ 12. First acquisition of a thing can be only acquisition of land.

Land (understood as all habitable ground) is to be regarded as the *substance* with respect to whatever is movable upon it, while the existence of the latter is to be regarded only as *inherence*. Just as in a theoretical sense accidents cannot exist apart from a substance, so in a practical sense no one can have what is movable on a piece of land as his own unless he is assumed to be already in rightful possession of the land.

For suppose that the land belonged to no one: I could then remove every movable thing on it from its place and take it for myself until they were all gone, without thereby infringing upon the freedom of anyone else who is not now holding it; but whatever can be destroyed, a tree, a house and so forth, is movable (at least in terms of its matter), and if a thing that cannot be moved without destroying its form is called *immovable*, then by what is mine or yours with regard to that is understood not its substance but what adheres to it, which is not the thing itself.

§ 13. Any piece of land[o] can be acquired originally, and the possibility of such acquisition is based on the original community[p] of land in general.

The first proposition rests on the postulate of practical reason (§ 2). The proof of the second proposition is as follows.

All human beings are originally (i.e., prior to any act of choice that establishes a right) in a possession of land that is in conformity with right, that is, they have a right to be wherever nature or chance (apart from their will) has placed them. This kind of possession (*possessio*) – which is to be distinguished from residence (*sedes*), a chosen and therefore an acquired *lasting* possession – is a possession *in common*[q] because the spherical surface of the earth unites all the places on its surface; for if its surface were

---

[n] *im gemeinsamen Besitz*
[o] *Ein jeder Boden*
[p] *Gemeinschaft*
[q] *ein gemeinsamer Besitz*

an unbounded plane, people could be so dispersed on it that they would not come into any community with one another, and community would not then be a necessary result of their existence on the earth. – The possession by all human beings on the earth which precedes any acts of theirs that would establish rights (as constituted by nature itself) is an *original possession in common*[r] (*communio possessionis originaria*), the concept of which is not empirical and dependent upon temporal conditions, like that of a supposed *primitive possession in common* (*communio primaeva*), which can never be proved. Original possession in common is, rather, a practical rational concept which contains a priori the principle in accordance with which alone people can use a place on the earth in accordance with principles of right.

§ *14. In original acquisition, the act required to establish a right is taking control (occupatio).* 6:263

The only condition under which *taking possession* (*apprehensio*), beginning to hold (*possessionis physicae*) a corporeal thing in space, conforms with the law of everyone's outer freedom (hence a priori) is that of *priority* in time, that is, only insofar as it is the *first* taking possession (*prior apprehensio*), which is an act of choice. But the will that a thing (and so too a specific, separate place[s] on the earth) is to be mine, that is, appropriation of it (*appropriatio*), in original acquisition can be only *unilateral* (*voluntas unilateralis s. propria*).[t] Acquisition of an external object of choice by a unilateral will is *taking control* of it. So original acquisition of an external object, and hence too of a specific and separate piece of land, can take place only through taking control of it (*occupatio*).

No insight can be had into the possibility of acquiring in this way, nor can it be demonstrated by reasons;[u] its possibility is instead an immediate consequence of the postulate of practical reason. But the aforesaid will can justify an external acquisition only in so far as it is included in a will that is united a priori (i.e., only through the union of the choice of all who can come into practical relations with one another) and that commands absolutely. For a unilateral will (and a bilateral but still *particular* will is also unilateral) cannot put everyone under an obligation that is in itself contingent; this requires a will that is *omnilateral*, that is united not contingently but a priori and therefore necessarily, and because of this is the only will that is lawgiving. For only in accordance with this principle of the will is it possible for the free choice of each to accord with the freedom of

---

[r] *Gesammtbesitz*
[s] *bestimmter abgeteilter*
[t] unilateral or proper will
[u] *durch Gründe dartun*

all, and therefore possible for there to be any right, and so too possible for any external object to be mine or yours.

§ 15. *Something can be acquired conclusively only in a civil constitution; in a state of nature it can also be acquired, but only provisionally.*

A civil constitution, though its realization is subjectively contingent, is still objectively necessary, that is, necessary as a duty. With regard to such a constitution and its establishment there is therefore a real law of natural right[v] to which any external acquisition is subject.

The *empirical title* of acquisition was taking physical possession (*apprehensio physica*), based on the original community of land. Since there is only possession in *appearance* to put under possession in accordance with rational concepts of right, a title to take intellectual possession (setting aside all empirical conditions of space and time) must correspond to this empirical title of acquisition. This intellectual title is the basis of the proposition: "What I bring under my control in accordance with laws of outer freedom and will to become mine becomes mine."

But the *rational title* of acquisition can lie only in the idea of a will of all united a priori (necessarily to be united), which is here tacitly assumed as a necessary condition (*conditio sine qua non*); for a unilateral will cannot put others under an obligation they would not otherwise have. – But the condition in which the will of all is actually united for giving law is the civil condition. Therefore something external can be *originally* acquired only in conformity with the idea of a civil condition, that is, with a view to it and to its being brought about, but prior to its realization (for otherwise acquisition would be derived). Hence *original* acquisition can be only *provisional*. – *Conclusive* acquisition takes place only in the civil condition.

Still, that provisional acquisition is true acquisition; for, by the postulate of practical reason with regard to rights, the possibility of acquiring something external in whatever condition people may live together (and so also in a state of nature) is a principle of private right, in accordance with which each is justified in using that coercion which is necessary if people are to leave the state of nature and enter into the civil condition, which can alone make any acquisition conclusive.

The question arises, how far does authorization to take possession of a piece of land extend? As far as the capacity[w] for controlling it extends, that is, as far as whoever wants to appropriate it can defend it – as if the land were to say, if you cannot protect me you cannot command me. This is how the dispute over whether the sea is *free* or

---

[v] *wirkliches Rechtsgesetz der Natur*
[w] *Vermögen*

closed also has to be decided; for example, as far as a cannon shot can reach no one may fish, haul up amber from the ocean floor, and so forth, along the coast of a territory that already belongs to a certain state. – Moreover, in order to acquire land is it necessary to develop it (build on it, cultivate it, drain it, and so on)? No. For since these forms (of specification) are only accidents, they make no object of direct possession and can belong to what the subject possesses only insofar as the substance is already recognized as his. When first acquisition is in question, developing land is nothing more than an external sign of taking possession, for which many other signs that cost less effort can be substituted. – Furthermore, may one party interfere with another in its *act* of taking possession, so that neither enjoys the right of priority and the land remains always free, belonging to no one? Not *entirely;* since one party can prevent another from taking possession only by being on adjacent land, where it itself can be prevented from being, *absolute* hindrance would be a contradiction. But *with respect to* a certain piece of land (lying between the two), leaving it unused, as *neutral* territory to separate the two parties, would still be consistent with the right of taking control. In that case, however, this land really belongs to both in common[x] and is not something *belonging to no one* (*res nullius*), just because it is *used* by both to keep them apart. – Again, can anyone have a thing as his own on land no part of which belongs to someone? Yes, as in Mongolia where, since all the land belongs to the people, the use of it belongs to each individual, so that anyone can leave his pack lying on it or recover possession of his horse if it runs away, since it is his. On the other hand, it is only by means of a *contract* that anyone can have a movable thing as his on land that belongs to another. – Finally, can two neighboring peoples (or families) resist each other in adopting a certain use of land, for example, can a hunting people resist a pasturing people or a farming people, or the latter resist a people that wants to plant orchards, and so forth? Certainly, since as long as they keep within their boundaries the way they want to *live* on their land is up to their own discretion (*res merae facultatis*).

Lastly, it can still be asked whether, when neither nature nor chance but just our own will brings us into the neighborhood of a people that holds out no prospect of a civil union with it, we should not be authorized to found colonies, by force if need be, in order to establish a civil union with them and bring these human beings (savages) into a rightful condition (as with the American Indians, the Hottentots and the inhabitants of New Holland); or (which is not much better), to found colonies by fraudulent purchase of their land, and so become owners of their land, making use of our superiority without regard for their first posses-

[x] *gemeinschaftlich*

sion. Should we not be authorized to do this, especially since nature itself (which abhors a vacuum) seems to demand it, and great expanses of land in other parts of the world, which are now splendidly populated, would have otherwise remained uninhabited by civilized people or, indeed, would have to remain forever uninhabited, so that the end of creation would have been frustrated? But it is easy to see through this veil of injustice (Jesuitism), which would sanction any means to good ends. Such a way of acquiring land is therefore to be repudiated.

The indeterminacy, with respect to quantity as well as quality, of the external object that can be acquired makes this problem (of the sole, original external acquisition) the hardest of all to solve. Still, there must be some original acquisition or other of what is external, since not all acquisition can be derived. So this problem cannot be abandoned as insoluble and intrinsically impossible. But even if it is solved through the original contract, such acquisition will always remain only provisional unless this contract extends to the entire human race.

§ *16. Exposition of the concept of original acquisition of land.*
All human beings are originally in *common possession*[y] of the land of the entire earth (*communio fundi originaria*) and each has by nature the *will* to use it (*lex iusti*) which, because the choice of one is unavoidably opposed by nature to that of another, would do away with any use of it if this will did not also contain the principle for choice by which a *particular possession* for each on the common land could be determined (*lex iuridica*). But the law which is to determine for each what land is mine or yours[z] will be in accordance with the axiom of outer freedom only if it proceeds from a will that is united *originally* and a priori (that presupposes no rightful act[a] for its union). Hence it proceeds only from a will in the civil condition (*lex iustitiae distributivae*), which alone determines what is *right*, what is *rightful*, and what is *laid down as right*.[b] – But in the former condition, that is, before the establishment of the civil condition but with a view to it, that is, *provisionally*, it is a *duty* to proceed in accordance with the principle of external acquisition. Accordingly, there is also a rightful *capacity*[c] of the will to bind everyone to recognize the act of taking possession and of appropriation as valid, even though it is only unilateral. Therefore provisional acquisition of land, together with all its rightful consequences, is possible.

Provisional acquisition, however, needs and gains the favor[d] of a law

---

[y] *Gesammt-Besitz*
[z] *das austeilende Gesetz des Mein und Dein eines jeden am Boden*
[a] *rechtlichen Akt.* See 6:237, note b.
[b] *was recht, was rechtlich und was Rechtens ist*
[c] *rechtliches Vermögen*
[d] *Gunst*

(*lex permissiva*) for determining the limits of possible rightful possession. Since this acquisition precedes a rightful condition and, as only leading to it, is not yet conclusive, this favor does not extend beyond the point at which *others* (participants) consent to its establishment. But if they are opposed to entering it (the civil condition), and as long as their opposition lasts, this favor carries with it all the effects of acquisition in conformity with right, since leaving the state of nature is based upon duty.

§ *17. Deduction of the concept of original acquisition.*

We have found the *title* of acquisition in an original community of land, and therefore of external possession subject to spatial conditions. We have found the *manner of acquisition* in the empirical conditions of taking possession (*apprehensio*), joined with the will to have the external object as one's own. Now we still need to explicate* from principles of pure practical reason with regard to rights *acquisition* itself, that is, the external mine or yours, which follows from the two elements given; that is, we need to explicate intelligible possession (*possessio noumenon*) of an object from that which is contained in the concept of it.

The *concept belonging to right*ᶠ of what is *externally* mine or yours, so far as this is a *substance*, cannot mean, as far as the term *external to me* is concerned, in another *place* than where I am, for it is a rational concept; instead, since only a pure concept of the understanding can be subsumed under a rational concept, the term can mean merely something *distinct* from me. And this rational concept cannot signify the concept of empirical possession (a continual taking possession, as it were), but only that of *having an external object under my control* (the connection of the object with me insofar as this is the subjective condition of its being possible for me to use it), which is a pure concept of the understanding. Now, if these sensible conditions of possession, as a relation of a person to *objects* that have no obligation, are left out or disregarded (abstracted from), possession is nothing other than a relation of a person to persons, all of whom are *bound*, with regard to the use of the thing, by the *will* of the first person, insofar as his will conforms with the axiom of outer freedom, with the *postulate* of his capacity to use external objects of choice, and with the *lawgiving* of the will of allᵍ thought as a united a priori. This, then, is *intelligible possession* of a thing, that is, possession by mere right, even though the object (the thing I possess) is a sensible object.

The first working, enclosing, or, in general, *transforming* of a piece of land can furnish no title of acquisition to it; that is, possession of an

6:268

ᵉ *entwickeln*
ᶠ *Rechtsbegriff*
ᵍ *allgemeinen Geseztgebung*

accident can provide no basis for rightful possession of the substance. What is mine or yours must instead be derived from ownership[h] of the substance in accordance with this rule (*accessorium sequitur suum principale*),[i] and whoever expends his labor on land that was not already his has lost his pains and toil to who was first. This is so clear of itself that it is hard to assign any other cause for that opinion, which is so old and still so widespread, than the tacit prevalent deception of personifying things and of thinking of a right to things as being a right *directly* against them, as if someone could, by the work he expends upon them, put things under an obligation to serve him and no one else; for otherwise people would probably not have passed so lightly over the question that naturally arises (already noted above), "How is a right to a thing possible?" For a right against every possessor of a thing means only an authorization on the part of someone's particular choice to use an object, insofar as this authorization can be thought as contained in a synthetic general will and as in accord with the law of this will.

As for corporeal things on land that is already mine, if they do not otherwise belong to another they belong *to me* without my needing a particular act establishing a right in order to make them mine (not *facto* but *lege*), for they can be regarded as accidents inhering in the substance (*iure rei meae*).[j] Anything else that is so connected with a thing of mine that another cannot separate it from what is mine without changing this also belongs to me (e.g., gold plating, mixing some stuff belonging to me with other materials, alluvium, or also, a change in a riverbed adjoining my land and the resulting extension of my land, and so forth). Whether land that extends beyond dry land can be acquired – that is, whether a tract of the ocean floor can be acquired (the right to fish off my shore, to bring up amber and so forth) – must be decided in accordance with the same principles. My *possession* extends as far as I have the mechanical ability,[k] from where I *reside*, to secure my land against encroachment by others (e.g., as far as cannon reach from the shore), and up to this limit the sea is closed (*mare clausum*). But since it is not possible to *reside* on the high seas themselves, possession also cannot extend to them and the open seas are free (*mare liberum*). But the owner of a shore cannot include, in his right to acquire, what is unintentionally *washed up on shore*, whether human beings or things belonging to them, since this is not wronging him (not a deed at all), and though a thing has been cast up on land which belongs to someone, it cannot be

---

[h] *Eigentum*
[i] accessory [possession] following on his principal
[j] my right in the thing
[k] *Vermögen*

treated as a *res nullius*.¹ On the other hand, a river can be originally acquired by someone who is in possession of both banks, as far as his possession of the banks extends; he can acquire the river just as he can acquire any dry land subject to the conditions mentioned above.

An external object which in terms of its substance belongs to someone is his *property* (*dominium*), in which all rights in this thing inhere (as accidents of a substance) and which the owner (*dominus*) can, accordingly, dispose of as he pleases (*ius disponendi de re sua*).ᵐ But from this it follows that an object of this sort can be only a corporeal thing (to which one has no obligation). So someone can be his own master (*sui iuris*) but cannot be the owner *of himself* (*sui dominus*) (cannot dispose of himself as he pleases) – still less can he dispose of others as he pleases – since he is accountable to the humanity in his own person. This is not, however, the proper place to discuss this point, which has to do with the right of humanity, not that of human beings. It is mentioned only incidentally, for a better understanding of what was discussed a little earlier. – Furthermore, there can be two complete owners of one and the same thing, without its being both mine and yours in common; they may only be possessors in common of what *belongs to only one of them as his*. This happens when one of the so-called joint owners (*condomini*) has only full possession without use, while the other has all the use of the thing along with possession of it. So the one who has full possession without use (*dominus directus*)ⁿ only restricts the other (*dominus utilis*)ᵒ to some continual performance without thereby limiting his use of the thing.

SECTION II.
ON CONTRACT RIGHT.ᵖ

§ 18.

6:271

My possession of another's choice, in the sense of my capacityᵠ to determine it by my own choice to a certain deed in accordance with laws of freedom (what is externally mine or yours with respect to the causality of another), is *a* right (of which I can have several against the same person or against others); but there is only a single sum (system) of laws, *contract right*, in accordance with which I can be in this sort of possession.

A right against a person can never be acquired originally and on one's

---

¹ thing belonging to no one
ᵐ right to dispose of the thing which is his
ⁿ *Vom persönlichen Recht*
ᵒ *Vermögen*
ᵖ *eigenmächtig*
ᵠ direct owner

own initiative[r] (for then it would not conform to the principle of the consistency of my choice with the freedom of everyone, and would therefore be wrong). So too, I cannot acquire a right against another through a deed of his that is *contrary to right* (*facto iniusto alterius*);[s] for even if he has wronged me and I have a right to demand compensation from him, by this I will still only preserve what is mine undiminished but will not acquire more than what I previously had.

Acquisition through another's deed to which I determine him in accordance with laws of right is, accordingly, always derived from what is his; and this derivation, as an act that establishes a right, cannot take place through a *negative* act of the other, namely his *abandoning* or *renouncing* what is his (*per derelictionem aut renunciationem*); for by such an act this would only cease to belong to one or the other, but nothing would be acquired. This derivation can take place only by *transferring* (*translatio*), which is possible only through a common will by means of which the object is always under the control of one or the other, since as one gives up his share in this common undertaking[t] the object becomes the other's through his acceptance of it (and so by a positive act of choice). – Transfer of the *property* of one to another is *alienation*. An act of the united choice of two persons by which anything at all that belongs to one passes to the other is a *contract*.

§ 19.

For every contract there are two *preparatory* and two *constitutive* rightful acts of choice. The first two (of *negotiating*) are *offering* (*oblatio*) and *assent* (*approbatio*) to it; the two others (of *concluding*) are *promise* (*promissum*) and *acceptance* (*acceptatio*). – For an offering cannot be called a promise apart from a preliminary judgment that what is offered (*oblatum*) would be *acceptable* to the promisee. This is indicated by the first two declarations, but by them alone nothing is as yet acquired.

But what belongs to the promisor does not pass to the promisee (as acceptant) by the *separate* will of either but only by the *united will* of both, and consequently only insofar as both wills are declared *simultaneously*. But this cannot take place by empirical acts of declaration, which must necessarily *follow* each other in time and are never simultaneous. For if I have promised and the other now wants to accept, I can still during the interval (however short it may be) regret having promised, since I am still free before he accepts; and because of this the one who accepts it, for his part, can consider himself as not bound to his counterdeclaration after the promise. – The external formalities (*solemnia*) in concluding a contract (shaking hands, or breaking a straw, *stipula*, held by both persons), and all

---

[r] owner of the use
[s] *Gemeinschaft*
[t] act unjustly to another

the confirmations back and forth of the declarations they have made, manifest the perplexity of the contracting parties as to how and in what way they are going to represent their declarations as existing *simultaneously*, at the same moment, although they can only be successive. They still do not succeed in this since their acts can only follow each other in time, so that when one act *is* the other is either *not yet* or is *no longer*.

Only a transcendental deduction of the concept of acquisition by contract can remove all these difficulties. It is true that in an external relation of *rights* my taking possession of another's choice (and his taking possession of mine in turn), as the basis for determining it to a deed, is first thought of empirically, by means of a declaration and counterdeclaration of the choice of each in time; this is the sensible condition of taking possession, in which both acts required for establishing the right can only follow one upon another. Since, however, that relation (as a rightful relation) is purely intellectual, that possession is represented through the will, which is a rational capacity*u* for giving laws, as intelligible possession (*possessio noumenon*) in abstraction from those empirical conditions, as what is mine or yours. Here both acts, promise and acceptance, are represented not as following one upon another but (as if it were *pactum re initum*) as proceeding from a single *common* will (this is expressed by the word *simultaneously*); and the object (*promissum*) is represented, by omitting empirical conditions, as acquired in accordance with a principle of pure practical reason.

6:273

> That this is the true and the only possible deduction of the concept of acquisition by contract is sufficiently confirmed by the painstaking but always futile efforts of those who investigate rights (e.g., Moses Mendelssohn in his *Jerusalem*)[21] to produce a proof of its possibility. – The question was, *why ought* I to keep my promise? for *that I ought* to keep it everyone readily grasps. But it is absolutely impossible to furnish a proof of this categorical imperative, just as it is impossible for a geometer to prove by means of inferences based on reason alone*v* that in order to make a triangle he must take three lines (an analytic proposition), two of which together must be greater than the third (a synthetic proposition, but both propositions are a priori). That I ought to keep my promise is a postulate of pure reason (pure as abstracting from all sensible conditions of space and time in what concerns the concept of right). The theory that it is possible to abstract from those conditions without giving up possession of the promise is itself the deduction of the concept of acquisition by contract, just as was the case in the preceding Section for the theory of acquisition of external things by taking control of them.

u *Vernunftvermögen*
v *Vernunftschlüße*, which could also be translated "syllogisms"

§ 20.

By a contract I acquire something external. But what is it that I acquire? Since it is only the causality of another's choice with respect to a performance he has promised me, what I acquire directly by a contract is not an external thing but rather his deed, by which that thing is brought under my control so that I make it mine. – By a contract I therefore acquire another's promise (not what he promised), and yet something is added to my external belongings; I have become *enriched*[w] (*locupletior*)[x] by acquiring an active obligation on the freedom and the means[y] of the other. – This *right* of mine is, however, only a right *against a person*, namely a right against a *specific* physical person, and indeed a right to act upon his causality (his choice) to *perform* something for me; it is not a *right to a thing*, a right against that *moral person* which is nothing other than the idea of the *choice of all united* a priori, by which alone I can acquire *a right against every possessor of the thing*, which is what constitutes any right to a thing.

> Transfer by contract of what is mine takes place in accordance with the law of continuity (*lex continui*), that is, possession of the object is not interrupted for a moment during this act; for otherwise I would acquire, in this condition, an object as something that has no possessor (*res vacua*), hence would acquire it originally, and this contradicts the concept of contract. – Because of this continuity, however, that which transfers what is mine to the other is not one of the two separate wills (*promittentis et acceptantis*),[z] but their united will. So the transfer does not take place in such a way that the promisor first abandons (*derelinquit*) his possession for the other's advantage, or renounces (*renunciat*) his right, and the other immediately takes it up, or the reverse. Transfer is therefore an act in which an object belongs, for a moment, to both together, just as when a stone that has been thrown reaches the apex of its parabolic path it can be regarded as, for just a moment, simultaneously rising and falling, and so first passing from its rising motion to its falling.

§ 21.

In a contract by which a thing is acquired, it is not acquired by *acceptance* (*acceptatio*) of the promise, but only by *delivery* (*traditio*) of what was promised. For any promise has to do with a *performance*, and if what is promised is a thing, the performance can be discharged only by an act in which the promisor puts the promisee in possession of the thing, that is, delivers it to him. So before the thing is delivered and received, the performance has

---

[w] *vermögender*
[x] *Vermögen*
[y] richer
[z] promising and accepting

not yet taken place: the thing has not yet passed from one to the other and so has not been acquired by the promisee. Hence the right that arises from a contract is only a right against a person, and becomes a right to a *thing* only by delivery of the thing.

A contract that is immediately followed by delivery (*pactum re initum*) excludes any interval between its being concluded and its being discharged and requires no further separate act by which what belongs to one is transferred to the other. But if a (definite or indefinite) time for delivering the thing is allowed between the conclusion and the discharge of the contract, the question arises whether the thing already belongs to the acceptor by the contract, prior to its being delivered, and his right is a right to the thing, or whether a separate contract having to do only with its being delivered must be added, so that the right acquired by mere acceptance is only a right against a person and becomes a right to a thing only by its being delivered. – That the latter is really the case is clear from the following.

If I conclude a contract about a thing that I want to acquire, for example, a horse, and at the same time put it in my stable or otherwise in my physical possession, it is then mine (*vi pacti re initi*),*ᵃ* and my right is a *right to the thing*. But if I leave it in the seller's hands, without making any separate arrangements with him as to who is to be in physical possession of the thing (*holding* it) before I take possession of it (*apprehensio*), and so before the change of possession, then this horse is not yet mine, and what I have acquired is only a right against a specific person, namely the seller, *to put me in possession* (*poscendi traditionem*), which is the subjective condition of its being possible for me to use it as I please. My right is only a right against a person, to require of the seller *performance* (*praestatio*) of his promise to put me in possession of the thing. Now if a contract does not include delivery *at the same time* (as *pactum re initum*), so that some time elapses between its being concluded and my taking possession of what I am acquiring, during this time I cannot gain possession without exercising a separate act to establish that right, namely a *possessory act* (*actum possessorium*), which constitutes a separate contract. This contract consists in my saying that I shall send for the thing (the horse) and the seller's agreeing to it. For it is not a matter of course that the seller will take charge, at his own risk, of something for another's use; this instead requires a separate contract, by which the one who is alienating a thing still remains its owner *for a specified time* (and must bear any risk that might affect it). Only if the one who is acquiring the thing delays beyond this time can the seller regard him as its owner and the thing as delivered to him.

6:276

ᵃ by force of starting the contract regarding a thing

Before this possessory act all that has been acquired through the contract is therefore a right against a person, and the promisee can acquire an external thing only by its being delivered.

SECTION III.
ON RIGHTS TO PERSONS AKIN TO RIGHTS TO THINGS.[b]

§ 22.

This right is that of possession of an external object *as a thing* and use of it *as a person*. – What is mine or yours in terms of this right is what is mine or yours *domestically*, and the relation of persons in the domestic condition is that of a community of free beings who form a society of members of a whole called a *household* (of persons standing in *community* with one another) by their affecting one another in accordance with the principle of outer freedom (*causality*). – Acquisition of this status, and within it, therefore takes place neither by a deed on one's own initiative (*facto*) nor by a contract (*pacto*) alone but by law (*lege*); for, since this kind of right is neither a right to a thing nor merely a right against a person but also possession of a person, it must be a right lying beyond any rights to things and any rights against persons. That is to say, it must be the right of humanity in our own person, from which there follows a natural permissive law, by the favor of which this sort of acquisition is possible for us.

§ 23.

In terms of the object, acquisition in accordance with this principle is of three kinds: a *man* acquires a *wife*;[c] a *couple* acquires *children*; and a *family* acquires *servants*. – Whatever is acquired in this way is also inalienable and the right of possessors of these objects is the *most personal* of all rights.

On the right of domestic society

Title I: Marriage right.

§ 24.

Sexual union (*commercium sexuale*) is the reciprocal use that one human being makes of the sexual organs and capacities of another (*usus membrorum*

---

[b] *Von dem dingliche Art persönlichen Recht.* As in Sections I and II, the heading here suggests "the sum of laws" having to do with such possession. However, this third member of the division of rights is an innovation on Kant's part, and there is no English term for it corresponding to "property" and "contract." At the beginning and at the end of Section III, accordingly, I have sometimes used "rights" in contexts that would call for "right."

[c] *Weib*

et facultatum sexualium alterius).[d] This is either a *natural* use (by which procreation of a being of the same kind is possible) or an *unnatural* use, and unnatural use takes place either with a person of the same sex or with an animal of a nonhuman species. Since such transgressions of laws, called unnatural (*crimina carnis contra naturam*)[e] or also unmentionable vices, do wrong to humanity in our own person, there are no limitations or exceptions whatsoever that can save them from being repudiated completely.

Natural sexual union takes place either in accordance with mere animal *nature* (*vaga libido, venus volgivaga, fornicatio*)[f] or in accordance with *law*. — Sexual union in accordance with law is *marriage* (*matrimonium*), that is, the union of two persons of different sexes for lifelong possession of each other's sexual attributes. — The end of begetting and bringing up children may be an end of nature, for which it implanted the inclinations of the sexes for each other; but it is not *requisite* for human beings who marry to make this their end in order for their union to be compatible with rights, for otherwise marriage would be dissolved when procreation ceases.

Even if it is supposed that their end is the pleasure of using each other's sexual attributes, the marriage contract is not up to their discretion but is a contract that is necessary by the law of humanity, that is, if a man and a woman want to enjoy each other's sexual attributes they *must* necessarily marry, and this is necessary in accordance with pure reason's laws of right.

§ 25.

For the natural use that one sex makes of the other's sexual organs is *enjoyment*, for which one gives itself up to the other. In this act a human being makes himself into a thing, which conflicts with the right of humanity in his own person. There is only one condition under which this is possible: that while one person is acquired by the other *as if it were a thing*, the one who is acquired acquires the other in turn; for in this way each reclaims itself and restores its personality. But acquiring a member of a human being is at the same time acquiring the whole person, since a person is an absolute unity. Hence it is not only admissible for the sexes to surrender to and accept each other for enjoyment under the condition of marriage, but it is possible for them to do so *only* under this condition. That this *right against a person* is also *akin to a right to a thing* rests on the fact that if one of the partners in a marriage has left or given itself into someone else's possession, the other partner is justified, always and without question, in bringing its partner back under its control, just as it is justified in retrieving a thing.

---

[d] use of the sexual members and faculties of another
[e] carnal crimes against nature
[f] illicit sexual love, illicit sexual desire of the masses, fornication

§ 26.

For the same reasons, the relation of the partners in a marriage is a relation of *equality* of possession, equality both in their possession of each other as persons (hence only in *monogamy*, since in polygamy the person who surrenders herself gains only a part of the man who gets her completely, and therefore makes herself into a mere thing), and also equality in their possession of material goods. As for these, the partners are still authorized to forgo the use of a part, though only by a separate contract.

For this reason it follows that neither concubinage nor hiring a person for enjoyment on one occasion (*pactum fornicationis*)[g] is a contract that could hold in right. As for the latter, everyone will admit that a person who has concluded such a contract could not rightfully be held to the fulfillment of her promise if she regrets it. So, with regard to the former, a contract to be a *concubine* (as *pactum turpe*)[h] also comes to nothing; for this would be a contract to *let* and *hire* (*locatio-conductio*) a member for another's use, in which, because of the inseparable unity of members in a person, she would be surrendering herself as a thing to the other's choice. Accordingly, either party can cancel the contract with the other as soon as it pleases without the other having grounds for complaining about any infringement of its rights. – The same considerations also hold for a morganatic marriage, which takes advantage of the inequality of estate of the two parties to give one of them domination over the other; for in fact morganatic marriage is not different, in terms of natural right only, from concubinage and is no true marriage. – If the question is therefore posed, whether it is also in conflict with the equality of the partners for the law to say of the husband's relation to the wife, he is to be your master (he is the party to direct,[i] she to obey): this cannot be regarded as conflicting with the natural equality of a couple if this dominance is based only on the natural superiority of the husband to the wife in his capacity to promote the common interest of the household, and the right to direct that is based on this can be derived from the very duty of unity and equality with respect to the *end*.

§ 27.

A marriage contract is *consummated* only *by conjugal sexual intercourse* (*copula carnalis*). A contract made between two persons of opposite sex, either with a tacit understanding to refrain from sexual intercourse or with

---

[g] pact of fornication
[h] wrongful pact
[i] *er der befehlende . . . Teil*

awareness that one or both are incapable of it, is a *simulated contract*, which institutes no marriage and can also be dissolved by either of them who pleases. But if incapacity appears only afterwards, that right cannot be forfeited through this accident for which no one is at fault.

Acquisition of a wife or of a husband therefore takes place neither *facto* (by intercourse) without a contract preceding it nor *pacto* (by a mere marriage contract without intercourse following it) but only *lege*, that is, as the rightful consequence of the obligation not to engage in sexual union except through *possession* of each other's person, which is realized only through the use of their sexual attributes by each other.

6:280

The right of domestic society

Title II: Parental right.

§ 28.

Just as there arose from one's duty to oneself, that is, to the humanity in one's own person, a right (*ius personale*) of both sexes to acquire each other as persons *in the manner of things* by marriage, so there follows from *procreation* in this community a duty to preserve and care for its *offspring;* that is, children, as persons, have by their procreation an original innate (not acquired) right to the care of their parents until they are able to look after themselves, and they have this right directly by law (*lege*), that is, without any special act being required to establish this right.

For the offspring is a *person*, and it is impossible to form a concept of the production of a being endowed with freedom through a physical operation.* So from a *practical point of view* it is a quite correct and even

---

* No concept can be formed of how it is possible for *God to create* free beings, for it seems as if all their future actions would have to be predetermined by that first act, included in the chain of natural necessity and therefore not free. But that such beings (we human beings) are still free the categorical imperative proves for morally practical purposes, as through an authoritative decision of reason without its being able to make this relation of cause to effect comprehensible for theoretical purposes, since both are supersensible. – All that one can require of reason here would be merely to prove that there is no contradiction in the concept of a *creation of free beings*, and it can do this if it shows that the contradiction arises only if, along with the category of causality, the *temporal condition*, which cannot be avoided in relation to sensible objects (namely, that the ground of an effect precedes it), is also introduced in the relation of supersensible beings. As for the supersensible, if the causal concept is to obtain objective reality for theoretical purposes, the temporal condition would have to be introduced here too. But the contradiction vanishes if the pure category (without a schema put under it) is used in the concept of creation with a morally practical and therefore nonsensible intent.

If the philosophic jurist reflects on the difficulty of the problem to be resolved and the necessity of solving it to satisfy principles of right in this matter, he will not hold this investigation, all the way back to the first elements of transcendental philosophy in a metaphysics of morals, to be unnecessary pondering that gets lost in pointless obscurity.

necessary idea to regard the act of procreation as one by which we have brought a person into the world without his consent and on our own initiative, for which deed the parents incur an obligation to make the child content with his condition so far as they can. – They cannot destroy their child as if he were something they had *made* (since a being endowed with freedom cannot be a product of this kind) or as if he were their property, nor can they even just abandon him to chance, since they have brought not merely a worldly being but a citizen of the world into a condition which cannot now be indifferent to them even just according to concepts of right.

§ 29.

From this duty there must necessarily also arise the right of parents to *manage* and develop the child, as long as he has not yet mastered the use of his members or of his understanding: the right not only to feed and care for him but to educate him, to develop him both *pragmatically*, so that in the future he can look after himself and make his way in life, and *morally*, since otherwise the fault for having neglected him would fall on the parents. They have the right to do all this until the time of his emancipation (*emancipatio*), when they renounce their parental right to direct him as well as any claim to be compensated for their support and pains up till now. After they have completed his education, the only obligation (to his parents) with which they can charge him is a mere duty of virtue, namely the duty of gratitude.

From a child's personality it also follows that the right of parents is not just a right to a thing, since a child can never be considered as the property of his parents, so that their right is not alienable (*ius personalissimum*).[j] But this right is also not just a right against a person, since a child still belongs to his parents as what is theirs (is still in their *possession* like a thing and can be brought back even against his will into his parents' possession from another's possession). It is, instead, a right to a person *akin to a right to a thing.*

From this it is evident that, in the doctrine of right, there must necessarily be added to the headings rights to things and rights against persons the heading *rights to persons akin to rights to things;* the division made up till now has not been complete. For when we speak of the rights of parents to children as part of their household, we are referring not merely to the children's duty to return when they have run away but to the parents' being justified in taking control of them and impounding them as things (like domestic animals that have gone astray).

[j] most personal right

THE METAPHYSICS OF MORALS

On the right of domestic society

Title III: Right of a head of the household.[k]

§ 30.

The children of a household, who together with their parents formed a *family*, reach their *majority* (*maiorennes*) without any contract to withdraw from their former dependence, merely by attaining the ability to support themselves (which happens partly as a natural coming of age in the general course of nature, partly in keeping with their particular natural qualities). In other words, they become their own masters (*sui iuris*) and acquire this right without any special act to establish it and so merely by law (*lege*). – Just as they are not in debt to their parents for their education, so the parents are released in the same way from their obligation to their children, and both children and parents acquire or reacquire their natural freedom. The domestic society that was necessary in accordance with law is not dissolved.

Both parties can now maintain what is actually the same household but with a different form of obligation, namely, as the connection of the head of the household with servants (male or female servants of the house). What they maintain is the same domestic society but it is now a society *under the head of the household* (*societas herelis*),[l] formed by a contract through which the head of the household establishes a domestic society with the children who have not attained their majority or, if the family has no children, with other free persons (members of the household). This would be a society of unequals (one party *being in command* or being its head, the other *obeying*, i.e., serving) (*imperantis et subiecti domestici*).[m]

6:283

Servants are included in what belongs to the head of a household and, as far as the form (the *way of his being in possession*)[n] is concerned, they are his by a right that is like a right to a thing; for if they run away from him he can bring them back in his control by his unilateral choice. But as far as the matter is concerned, that is, what *use* he can make of these members of his household, he can never behave as if he owned them (*dominus servi*); for it is only by a contract that he has brought them under his control, and a contract by which one party would completely renounce its freedom for the other's advantage would be self-contradictory, that is, null and void, since by it one party would cease to be a person and so would have no duty to keep the contract but would recognize only force. (The right of ownershhip with regard to someone who has forfeited his personality by a crime is not under consideration here.)

[k] *Das Hausherren-Recht*
[l] household society
[m] domestic ruler and subject
[n] *Besitzstand.* See 6:306.

431

The contract of the head of a household with servants can therefore not be such that his *use* of them would amount to using them up; and it is not for him alone to judge about this, but also for the servants (who, accordingly, can never be serfs); so the contract cannot be concluded for life but at most only for an unspecified time, within which one party may give the other notice. But children (even those of someone who has become a slave through his crime) are at all times free. For everyone is born free, since he has not yet committed a crime; and the cost of educating him until he comes of age cannot be accounted against him as a debt that he has to pay off. For the slave would have to educate his children if he could, without charging them with the cost of their education, and if he cannot the obligation devolves on his possessor.

6:284 So we see here again, as in the two preceding headings, that there is a right to persons akin to a right to things (of the head of the house over servants); for he can fetch servants back and demand them from anyone in possession of them, as what is externally his, even before the reasons that may have led them to run away and their rights have been investigated.

Dogmatic division
of all rights that can be acquired by contract

§ *31.*

A metaphysical doctrine of right can be required to enumerate a priori the members of a division (*divisio logica*) in a complete and determinate way, and to establish thereby a true *system* of them. Instead of providing a system, any *empirical division* is merely *fragmentary* (*partitio*), and leaves it uncertain whether there are not additional members that would be needed to fill out the entire sphere of the concept divided. – A division in accordance with an a priori principle (in contrast with empirical divisions) can be called *dogmatic.*

Every contract consists in itself, that is, considered *objectively*, of two acts that establish a right, a promise and its acceptance. Acquisition through acceptance is not a *part* of a contract (unless the contract is a *pactum re initum*, which requires delivery) but the rightfully necessary *result* of it. – But considered *subjectively* – that is, as to whether this rationally necessary result (the *acquisition* that *ought* to occur) will actually *result* (be the *natural* result) – accepting the promise still gives me no *guarantee* that it will actually result. Since this guarantee belongs externally to the modality of a contract, namely *certainty* of acquisition by means of a contract, it is an additional factor serving to complete the means for achieving the acquisition that is the purpose of a contract. – For this, three persons are involved: a *promisor,* an *acceptor,* and a *guarantor.* The acceptor, indeed, gains nothing more with regard to the object by means of the guarantor and his separate contract with the promisor, but he still gains the means of coercion for obtaining what is his.

In accordance with these principles of logical (rational) division there are, strictly speaking, only three simple and *pure* kinds of contract. There are innumerable mixed and empirical kinds of contract, which add, to the principles of what is mine or yours in accordance only with laws of reason, statutory and conventional ones; but they lie beyond the sphere of the metaphysical doctrine of right, which is all that should be considered here.

Every contract has for its purpose either A. *unilateral* acquisition (a gratuitous contract) or B. acquisition *by both parties* (an onerous contract), or no acquisition but only C. *guaranteeing what belongs to someone* (this contract can be gratuitous on one side but can still be onerous on the other side).

A. A *gratuitous* contract (*pactum gratuitum*) is:
  a) *Keeping* goods on trust (*depositum*),
  b) *Lending* a thing (*commodatum*),
  c) *Making a gift* (*donatio*).
B. Onerous contracts.
I. A contract to *alienate* something (*permutatio late sic dicta*).*º*
  a) *Barter* (*permutatio stricte sic dicta*).*ᵖ* Goods for goods.
  b) *Buying and selling* (*emtio venditio*). Goods for money.
  c) *Loan for Consumption* (*mutuum*). Lending a thing on the condition of its being returned only in kind (e.g., grain for grain, or money for money).
II. A contract to *let* and *hire* (*locatio conductio*).
  α. *Lending a thing of mine* to another for his use (*locatio rei*). Insofar as the contract is onerous, a *payment of interest* may also be added (*pactum usurarium*) if repayment can be made only in kind.
  β. A contract of *letting of work* on hire (*locatio operae*), that is, granting another the use of my powers for a specified price (*merces*). By this contract the worker is hired help (*mercennarius*).
  γ. A *contract empowering an agent* (*mandatum*). Carrying on another's affairs in his place and *in his name*. If someone carries on another's affairs in place of him but not also in his name, this is called *carrying on his affairs* without being *commissioned* to do so (*gestio negotii*); but when this is done in the other's name we speak of a *mandate*. As a contract of hiring this is an onerous contract (*mandatum onerosum*).

º changing (ownership) broadly speaking
ᵖ changing (ownership) strictly speaking

C. *Contracts providing security* (*cautio*).
   a) A joint *giving and taking of a pledge* (*pignus*).
   b) *Assuming liability* for another's promise (*fideiussio*).
   c) *Personally vouching for a person's performance* of something (*praestatio obsidis*).

In this table of all the ways of *transferring* (*translatio*) what belongs to another are to be found concepts of objects or instruments of transfer which [seem]*q* to be entirely empirical and, even in terms of their possibility, have no proper place in a *metaphysical* doctrine of right, in which division must be made in accordance with a priori principles, abstracting from the matter that is exchanged (which could be conventional) and considering only the form. Such, for example, is the concept of *money*, in contrast to all other alienable things, namely *goods*, under the heading of *buying and selling*, as well as the concept of a *book*. – But it will be shown that the concept of money, as the greatest and most useful means human beings have for *exchange* of things, called *buying and selling* (commerce), and so too the concept of a book, as the greatest means for exchanging thoughts, can still be resolved into pure intellectual relations. So the table of pure contracts need not be made impure by anything empirical mixed into it.

I.

WHAT IS MONEY?

Money is a thing that can be *used* only by being *alienated*. This is a good nominal *definition*[r] of it (as given by Achenwall);[22] that is to say, it is sufficient for distinguishing this kind of object of choice from any other, though it tells us nothing about the possibility of such a thing. Still, from the nominal definition one can see this much: *first*, that the alienation of money in exchange is intended not as a gift but for *reciprocal* acquisition (by a *pactum onerosum*); and *second*, that money *represents* all goods, since it is conceived as a universally accepted mere *means* of commerce (within a nation), having no value in itself, as opposed to things which are *goods* (i.e., which have value in themselves and are related to the particular needs of one or another in the nation).

A bushel of grain has the greatest direct value as a means for satisfying human needs. It can be used as fodder for animals, which nourish us, transport us, and work in place of us; by means of it, furthermore, the human population is increased and preserved, and in turn not only raises

---

q The structure of the sentence, *welche ganz empirisch zu sein und . . . nicht Platz haben*, seems to require this addition.

r *Namenerklärung*

these natural products again but also helps to satisfy our needs with the products of art, by building houses, making clothes, providing the enjoyments we seek and, in general, all the conveniences that form the goods of industry.*s* By contrast, the value of money is only indirect. One cannot enjoy money itself or make immediate use of it in any way. Yet it is still a means which, among all things, has the greatest usefulness.

On this basis a preliminary *real definition* of money can be given: it is the universal *means by which men exchange their industriousness*[t] *with one another.* Thus a nation's wealth, insofar as it is acquired by means of money, is really only the sum of the industry with which human beings pay one another and which is represented by the money in circulation within it.

The thing to be called money must, therefore, have cost as much *industry* to produce or to obtain from other human beings as the *industry* by which those goods (natural or artificial products) are acquired for which that industry is exchanged. For if it were easier to procure the stuff called money than goods, more money would then come into the market than goods for sale; and since the seller would have to have expended more industry for his goods than the buyer, who got the money more readily, industry in producing goods, and therefore trade in general, would diminish and be curtailed, along with the productive industry*u* which results in the nation's wealth. – Hence bank notes and promissory notes cannot be regarded as money, though they can substitute for it temporarily; for they cost almost no industry to produce and their value is based solely on the opinion that they will continue as before to be convertible into *hard cash;* but if it is eventually discovered that there is not enough hard cash for which they can be readily and securely exchanged, this opinion suddenly collapses and makes failure of payment inevitable. – So the productive industry of those who work the gold and silver mines in Peru or New Mexico, especially in view of the industry vainly expended in searches for deposits that are so often unsuccessful, is apparently still greater than that expended on the manufacture of goods in Europe; and this excess of industry would be discontinued from not being paid, letting those countries soon sink into poverty, if the Europeans did not increase their industry proportionately through being stimulated by those very materials, so that the luxuries they offer constantly stimulate in others a desire for mining. In this way industry always keeps pace with industry.*v*

But how is it possible that what were at first only goods finally became

6:288

---

s *Industrie*
t *Fleiß.* In view of what Kant regards as his direct quotation from Adam Smith (6:289), one would expect him to use *Arbeit,* "labor," rather than *Fleiß,* "industriousness" or "diligence." However, in "translating" Smith's sentence into German Kant uses *Fleiß.* In the remainder of this passage "industry" is used in the sense of "industriousness."
u *Erwerbfleiß*
v *so dass immer Fleiß gegen Fleiß in Concurrenz kommen*

money? This would happen if a powerful, opulent *ruler* who at first used a material for the adornment and splendor of his attendants (his court) came to levy taxes on his subjects in this material (as goods) (e.g., gold, silver, copper, or a kind of beautiful seashell, *cowries;* or as in the Congo a kind of matting called *makutes,* in Senegal iron ingots, or on the Coast of Guinea even black slaves), and in turn paid with this same material those his demand moved to industry in procuring it, in accordance with exchange regulations with them and among them (on a market or exchange). – In this way only (so it seems to me) could a certain merchandise have become a lawful means of exchange of the industry of subjects with one another, and thereby also become the wealth of the nation, that is, *money.*

The intellectual concept under which the empirical concept of money falls is therefore the concept of a thing which, in the circulation of possessions (*permutatio publica*), determines the *price* of all other things (goods), among which even the sciences belong, insofar as they would not otherwise be taught to others. The amount of money in a nation therefore constitutes its wealth (*opulentia*). For the price (*pretium*) of a thing is the judgment of the public about its *value* (*valor*) in proportion to that which serves as the universal means to represent reciprocal exchange of *industry* (its circulation). – Accordingly, where there is a great deal of trade, neither *gold* nor copper is regarded as strictly money but only as merchandise, since there is too little gold and too much copper for them to be easily put into circulation and yet available in sufficiently small parts, as is necessary for the exchange of merchandise, or a mass of it, in the smallest purchase. *Silver* (more or less alloyed with copper) is, accordingly, taken as the proper material for money and the measure for reckoning prices in the great trade of the world; other metals (even more so, nonmetallic materials) can be found as money only in a nation where there is little trade. – But when the first two metals are not only weighed but also stamped, that is, provided with a sign indicating how much they are to be worth, they are lawful money, that is, *coinage.*

"Money is therefore" (according to Adam Smith) "that material thing the alienation of which is the means and at the same time the measure of the industry by which human beings and nations carry on trade with one another."[23] – This definition*w* brings the empirical concept of money to an intellectual concept by looking only to the *form* of what each party provides in return for the other in onerous contracts (and abstracting from their matter), thereby bringing it to the concept of right in the exchange of what is mine or yours generally (*commutatio late sic dicta*),*x* so as to present the table above as a dogmatic division a priori, which is appropriate to the metaphysics of right as a system.

---

w *Erklärung*
x exchange broadly speaking

II.
WHAT IS A BOOK?

A book is a writing (it does not matter, here, whether it is written in hand or set in type, whether it has few or many pages), which represents a discourse that someone delivers to the public by visible linguistic signs. – One who *speaks* to the public in his own name is called the *author* (*autor*). One who, through a writing, discourses publicly in another's (the author's) name is a *publisher*. When a publisher does this with the author's permission, he is the legitimate publisher; but if he does it without the author's permission, he is an illegitimate publisher, that is, an *unauthorized publisher*.[y] The sum of all the reproductions of the original writing (the copies) is an *edition*.

Unauthorized publishing of books[z] is forbidden as a matter of right[a]

A *writing* is not an immediate sign of a *concept* (as is, for example, an etching which represents a certain person in a *portrait*, or a work in plaster that is a *bust*). It is rather a *discourse* to the public; that is, the author *speaks* publicly through the publisher. – But the *publisher* speaks (through his foreman, *operarius*, the printer), not in his own name (for he would then pass himself off as the author), but in the name of the author; and so he is entitled to do this only when the author *gives him a mandate* (*mandatum*). – Now it is true that an unauthorized publisher also speaks, by an edition on his own initiative,[b] in the name of the author, but he does so without having been given a mandate by the author (*gerit se mandatarium absque mandato*).[c] He therefore commits the crime of stealing the profits from the publisher who was appointed by the author (who is therefore the only legitimate one), profits the legitimate publisher could and would have derived from the use of his right (*furtum usus*). So *unauthorized publishing of books is forbidden as a matter of right*.

Why does unauthorized publishing, which strikes one even at first glance as unjust, still have an appearance of being rightful? Because *on the one hand* a book is a corporeal *artifact* (*opus mechanicum*)[d] that can be reproduced (by someone in legitimate possession of a copy of it), so that

---

[y] *Nachdrucker*

[z] Or "publishing books without having been empowered by the author." To translate *Büchernachdruck* as "literary piracy" would seem inconsistent with the "appearance of being rightful" which Kant says it has. The language used here is similar to that of his essay "*Von der Unrechtmässigkeit des Büchernachdrucks*," see this volume, pp. 23–35.

[a] *von rechtswegen verboten*. The term *von rechtswegen* was used earlier (6:250), apparently in the sense of "by legal proceedings."

[b] *durch seinen eigenmächtigen Verlag*

[c] acts as if he has a mandate without having a mandate

[d] mechanical work

there is a *right to a thing* with regard to it. *On the other hand* a book is also a mere *discourse* of the publisher to the public, which the publisher may not repeat publicly without having a mandate from the author to do so (*praestatio operae*), and this is a *right against a person*. The error consists in mistaking one of these rights for the other.

There is another case, under contracts to let and hire (B,II,α), in which the confusion of a right against a person with a right to a thing is material for disputes, that of *renting to a tenant* (*ius incolatus*). – The question arises, whether an owner who has leased his house (or land) to someone and sells it to someone else before the lease expires is bound to attach to the contract of sale the condition that the lease is to continue, or whether one can say that purchase breaks a lease (though notice is to be given the lessee, the time being determined by custom). – On the first alternative the house actually had an *encumbrance* (*onus*) on it, a right to this thing that the lessee had acquired in it (the house). This can indeed take place (by entering this encumbrance in the land register, as included in the contract to lease); but then this would not be a mere contract to lease, but one to which another contract had had to be added (one to which few landlords would agree). So the saying "Purchase breaks a lease" is valid, that is, a full right to a thing (property) outweighs any right against a person that cannot exist together with it. But it is still left open for the lessee to complain, on the basis of his right against a person, that he is to be compensated for any damages arising from the breaking of the contract.

Episodic chapter.
On ideal acquisition of an external object of choice.

§ 32.

I call acquisition *ideal* if it involves no causality in time and is therefore based on a mere *idea* of pure reason. It is nonetheless *true*, not imaginary, acquisition, and the only reason I do not call it real is that the act of acquiring is not empirical, since the subject acquires from another who either *does not yet* exist (only the possibility that he may exist is admitted) or who has *ceased to exist*, or when the subject *no longer exists*, so that coming into possession is merely a practical idea of reason. – There are three kinds of such acquisition: 1) by *prolonged possession*, 2) by *inheritance*, and 3) by *merit surviving death* (*meritum immortale*), that is, the claim to a good reputation after death. All three can, indeed, take effect only in a public rightful condition, but they are not *based* only on its constitution and the chosen[c] statues in it: they are also conceivable a priori in the state of

---
[c] *willkürlichen*

nature and must be conceived as prior to such statutes, in order that the laws in the civil constitution may afterwards be adapted to them (*sunt iuris naturae*).

I.
ACQUISITION BY PROLONGED POSSESSION.[f]

§ 33.

I acquire another's property merely by *long possession of it* (*usucapio*), not because I may legitimately *presume* that he consents to my acquiring it (*per consensum praesumtum*), nor because I can assume that, since he does not contradict me, he *has given it up* (*rem derelictam*), but because, even if there should be someone who was the true owner and as such laid claim to it (a claimant) I may still *exclude* him merely by virtue of my long possession, ignore his existence up to now, and carry on as if he existed up to the time of my possession only as a thought-entity, even if I should later learn of his reality as well as that of his claim. – Although this way of acquiring is called acquisition by prescription[g] (*per praescriptionem*), this is not altogether correct, since exclusion of claims is to be regarded only as a result of acquisition: acquisition must have come first. – It has now to be proved that it is possible to acquire something in this way.

Someone who does not exercise a continuous *possessory act* (*actus possessorius*) with regard to an external thing, as something that is his, is rightly regarded as someone who does not exist at all (as its possessor). For he cannot complain of being wronged as long as he does nothing to justify his title of possessor; and even if later on, when another has already taken possession of it, he declares himself its possessor, all he is saying is that he was once its owner, not that he still is and that his possession has remained uninterrupted without a continuous rightful act. – Hence if someone does not use a thing for a long time, only a rightful possessory act, and indeed one that is continuously maintained and documented, can guarantee that it is his.

For suppose that failure to perform this possessory act did not result in another's being able to base a firm right (*possessio irrefragabilis*) on his lawful possession in good faith (*possessio bonae fidei*) and regard himself as having acquired the thing that is in his possession. Then no acquisition at all would be conclusive (guaranteed); all acquisition would be only provisional (up to the present), since investigation of the past cannot reach all the way back to the first possessor and his act of acquisition. – The presumption on which prolonged possession (*usucapio*) is based is therefore not merely in *conformity with right* (permitted, *iusta*) as a *conjecture* but

6:292

---
[f] *Ersitzung.* See note 24.
[g] Or "superannuation of claims," *Verjährung*

is also in accord with rights (*praesumtio iuris et de iure*) as an assumption in terms of coercive laws (*suppositio legalis*). Whoever fails to document his possessory act has lost his claim to the present possessor, and the length of time during which he failed to do it (which cannot and need not be specified) is put forward only to support the certainty of his omission. That a hitherto unknown possessor could always get something back (recover it) when his possessory act has been interrupted (even through no fault of his own) contradicts the above postulate of practical reason with regard to rights (*dominia rerum incerta facere*).[h]

If he is a member of a commonwealth, that is, lives in the civil condition, the state (representing him) can indeed preserve his possession for him, although it was interrupted as private possession, and a present possessor need not prove his title of acquisition by tracing it back to the first possessor or basing it on prolonged possession. In the state of nature, however, prolonged possession is in conformity with right not, strictly speaking, for acquiring a thing but for maintaining possession of it without an act establishing the right; and this immunity from claims is also usually called acquisition. – Prescription[i] of an earlier possessor therefore belongs to natural right (*est iuris naturae*).

II.
INHERITANCE.

(*Acquisitio haereditatis.*)

§ 34.

Inheritance is transfer (*translatio*) of the belongings and goods of someone who is dying to a survivor by agreement of the wills of both. – Acquisition by the *heir* (*haeredis instituti*) and leaving by the *testator* (*testatoris*), that is, this change of belongings, takes place in one moment, namely the moment at which the testator ceases to exist (*articulo mortis*). It is therefore not, strictly speaking, a transfer (*translatio*) in the empirical sense, since this assumes two acts following each other, namely the acts by which one person first leaves his possessions and the other then comes into them. Instead it is an ideal acquisition. – Now inheritance in the state of nature cannot be conceived of without a *last will* (*dispositio ultimae voluntatis*). Whether this is a *contract of inheritance* (*pactum successorium*) or a *unilateral disposition to the heir* (*testamentum*) amounts to the question, whether and how it is possible for belongings to pass from one to the other precisely at the moment at which the subject ceases to exist. The question of how it is possible to acquire by inheritance must accordingly be investigated apart

---

[h] to act on uncertain ownerships of things
[i] *Präscription*

from the many ways in which it can be carried out (which are found only in a commonwealth).

"It is possible to acquire something through disposition to the heir." For the testator, Caius, promises and in his last will declares to Titius, who knows nothing of this promise, that upon his death his belongings are to pass to Titius. As long as he lives, Caius therefore remains sole owner of his belongings. Now it is true that by a unilateral will alone nothing can pass to the other person; for this there is required, besides the promise, acceptance (*acceptatio*) by the other party and a simultaneous will (*voluntas simultanea*), which is still lacking here; for, as long as Caius is alive, Titius cannot explicitly accept, so as to acquire by his acceptance, since Caius has promised only on the occasion of his death (otherwise the property would for a moment be common property, and this is not the testator's will). – Titius, however, still tacitly acquires a proprietary right[j] to the legacy as a right to a thing: namely, he has the exclusive right to accept it (*ius in re iacente*), so that the legacy at the moment of death is called *haereditas iacens*. Now, since every human being would necessarily accept such a right (since he can always gain but never lose by it), and so accepts tacitly, and since Titius, after Caius's death, is in this situation, he can acquire the bequest by acceptance of the promise, and the bequest has not become altogether ownerless (*res nullius*) in the meantime but only *vacant* (*res vacua*). For Titius alone has the right to make the choice as to whether or not he wants to make the belongings left to him his own.

Accordingly, testaments are also valid in accordance with mere natural right (*sunt iuris naturae*). This assertion, however, is to be taken as meaning that testaments are fit for and worth being introduced and sanctioned in the civil condition (if this makes its appearance some day). For only the civil condition (the general will in it) confirms possession of a legacy while it hovers between acceptance and rejection and strictly speaking belongs to no one.

III.
LEAVING BEHIND A GOOD REPUTATION AFTER ONE'S DEATH.

6:295

(*Bona fama defuncti.*)

§ 35.

It would be absurd to think that someone who has died can still possess something after his death (and so when he no longer exists), if what he left behind were a thing. But a *good reputation* is an innate external belonging, though an ideal one only, which clings to the subject as a person, a being

---

[j] *eigentümliches Recht*

of such a nature that I can and must abstract from whether he ceases to be entirely at his death or whether he survives as a person; for in the context of his rights in relation to others, I actually regard every person simply in terms of his humanity, hence as *homo noumenon*. So any attempt to stain someone's reputation by falsehood after his death is suspect, because it is at least ungenerous to spread reproaches against one who is absent and cannot defend himself, unless one is quite certain of them. Nevertheless, a well-founded accusation against him is still in order (so that the principle *de mortuis nihil nisi bene*^{k} is incorrect).

For someone to acquire by an irreproachable life and the death that ends it a (negatively) good name, which continues to be his when he no longer exists as *homo phaenomenon;* for those who survive him (relatives or strangers) to be also authorized by right to defend him (for unproved charges are dangerous to them as well, since they could get similar treatment when they die); for someone to be able to acquire such a right is, I say, a phenomenon as strange as it is undeniable, a phenomenon of reason giving law a priori which extends its commands and prohibitions even beyond the limits of life. – If anyone spreads it abroad that someone who has died committed a crime which in his lifetime would have made him dishonorable or only contemptible, whoever can produce proof that this charge is an intentional untruth and a lie can then publicly declare the one who spread the evil gossip a calumniator and so take away his honor. He could not do this unless he could rightly assume that the dead man was wronged by it, even though he is dead, and that this defense brings him satisfactions even though he no longer exists.* An apologist need not prove his authorization to play the role of apologist for the dead, for everyone inevitably arrogates this to himself as belonging not merely to duty of virtue (duty regarded ethically) but to the right of humanity as

---

* But one is not to draw from this any visionary conclusions about presentiments of a future life or about unseen relations to disembodied souls. For what is under discussion here does not go beyond the purely moral and rightful relations to be found among human beings during life as well. These are relations in which human beings stand as intelligible beings, insofar as one *logically puts aside,* that is, *abstracts from,* everything physical (i.e., everything belonging to their existence in space and time); but one does not remove them from this nature of theirs and let them become spirits, in which condition they would feel the injury of those who slander them. – Someone who, a hundred years from now, falsely repeats something evil about me injures me right now; for in a relation purely of rights, which is entirely intellectual, abstraction is made from any physical conditions (of time), and whoever robs me of my honor (a slanderer) is just as punishable as if he had done it during my lifetime – punishable, however, not by a criminal court but only by public opinion, which, in accordance with the right of retribution, inflicts on him the same loss of the honor he diminished in another. – Even a *plagiarism* that a writer perpetrates on a dead person, though it does not indeed stain the dead person's honor but only steals a part of it from him, is still avenged with right, as having wronged him (robbed the human being).

^{k} speak nothing but good about the dead

such; and the strain on the dead person need not have been prejudicial to any particular person, such as his friends and relatives, to justify such censure. – It is therefore indisputable that there is a basis for such an ideal acquisition and for someone's right after his death against those who survive him, even though no deduction of its possibility can be given.

Chapter III
On acquisition that is dependent subjectively upon the decision of a public court of justice.

§ 36.

If by natural right is understood only nonstatutory right, hence simply right that can be cognized a priori by everyone's reason, natural right will include not only the *justice* that holds among persons in their exchanges with one another (*iustitia commutativa*) but also distributive justice (*iustitia distributiva*), insofar as it can be cognized a priori in accordance with the principle of distributive justice how its decisions (*sententia*) would have to be reached.

The moral person that administers justice is a *court* (*forum*) and its administration of justice is a *judgment* (*iudicium*). All this is here thought out a priori only in accordance with conditions of right, without taking account of how such a constitution is to be actually set up and organized (*statutes*, hence empirical principles, belong to an actual constitution).

So the question here is not merely what is *right in itself,* that is, how every human being has to judge about it on his own, but what is right before a court, that is, what is laid down as right. And here there are *four* cases in which two different and opposing judgments can result and persist side by side, because they are made from two different points of view, both of which are true: one in accordance with private right, the other in accordance with the idea of public right. These cases are: 1) A *contract to make a gift* (*pactum donationis*). 2) A *contract to lend a thing* (*commodatum*). 3) *Recovering* something (*vindicatio*). 4) *Taking an oath* (*iuramentum*).

> It is a common fault (*vitium subreptionis*) of experts on right to *misrepresent*, as if it were also the objective principle of what is right in itself, that rightful principle which a court is authorized and indeed bound to adopt for its own use (hence for a subjective purpose) in order to pronounce and judge what belongs to each as his right, although the latter is very different from the former. – It is therefore of no slight importance to recognize this specific distinction and to draw attention to it.

A.

§ 37. *On a contract to make a gift.*

In accordance with *private right*, this contract (*donatio*), by which I *alienate without remuneration* (*gratis*) what is mine, a thing of mine (or my right), involves a relation of myself, the donor (*donans*), to another, the recipient (*donatorius*), by which what is mine passes to the recipient by his acceptance of it (*donum*). – But it is not to be presumed that I intend by this contract to be coerced to keep my promise and so also to give up my *freedom* gratuitously and, as it were, to throw myself away (*nemo suum iactare praesumitur*).[1] Yet this is what would happen in accordance with right in the civil condition, where the one who is to receive my gift can *coerce* me to carry out my promise. So, if the matter were to come before a court, that is, in accordance with public right, it would either have to be presumed that the donor consented to this coercion, which is absurd, or else the court in its judgment (verdict) simply takes no account of whether the donor did or did not want to reserve his freedom to go back on his promise, but takes account only of what is certain, namely, the promise and the promisee's acceptance of it. So even if, as can well be supposed, the promisor thought that he could not be bound to keep his promise should he regret having made it before it is time to fulfill it, the court assumes that he would have had to make this reservation expressly, and that if he did not he could be coerced to fulfill his promise. The court adopts this principle because otherwise its verdict on rights would be made infinitely more difficult or even impossible.

B.

§ 38. *On a contract to lend a thing.*

In this contract (*commodatum*) by which I permit someone to use without compensation something of mine, if the parties to the contract agree that *this very same thing* is to be brought under my control again, the borrower (*commodatarius*) cannot presume that the thing's owner (*commodans*) also assumes every risk (*casus*) of possible loss of the thing, or of what makes it useful, that might arise from its having been put into the borrower's possession. For it is not a matter of course that the owner, in addition to granting the borrower the use of his thing (such loss to himself as is inseparable from parting with it), has also issued the borrower a *guarantee* against any damage that could arise from his having let it out of his custody. A separate contract would have to be made about that. So the question can only be: on which of the two, the lender or the borrower, is it incumbent to attach expressly to a contract to lend the condition about

---

[1] no one is presumed to throw away what is his

assuming the risk for possible damage to the thing? or, if no such condition is attached, who can be *presumed* to have *agreed* to guarantee the lender's property (by the return of it, or its equivalent, to him)? Not the lender, for it cannot be presumed that he has gratuitously agreed to more than the mere use of the thing (that is, that he has also undertaken to guarantee the property). It is, rather, the borrower, because in taking on this guarantee he performs nothing more than is already contained in the contract.

Suppose, for example, that having been caught in the rain I go into a house and ask to borrow a coat, which is then, say, permanently stained when someone carelessly pours discoloring material from a window, or is stolen from me when I go into another house and take it off. Everyone would find it absurd to say that I need do nothing more than return the coat as it is, or that I have only to report that the theft occurred and that it was at most a matter of courtesy for me to commiserate with the owner over his loss, since he could demand nothing on the basis of his right. – But no one would think it absurd if, in requesting to use something, I also ask its owner beforehand to take on himself the risk of any mischance that might happen to it while it is in my hands, because I am poor and unable to compensate him for the loss. No one will find this superfluous and ridiculous, except, perhaps, when the lender is known to be a rich and considerate man, since it would then be almost insulting him not to presume that he would generously remit my debt in this case.

Now if (as the nature of a contract to lend involves) nothing is stipulated in it about a possible mischance (*casus*) that might affect the thing, so that agreement about this can only be presumed, a contract to lend is an uncertain contract (*pactum incertum*) with regard to what is mine and what is yours by it. Consequently, the judgment about this, that is, the decision as to who must bear the misfortune, cannot be made from the conditions of the contract itself; it can be decided only as it would be decided *before a court*, which always considers only what is certain in the case (which is here the possession of the thing as property). So the judgment in the *state of nature*, that is, in terms of the intrinsic character of the matter, will go like this: the damage resulting from mischance to a thing loaned falls on the *borrower* (*casum sentit commodatarius*).[m] But in the *civil condition*, and so before a court, the verdict will come out: the damage falls on the *lender* (*casum sentit dominus*).[n] This verdict will indeed be given on different grounds from the decree of sound reason alone, since a public judge cannot get involved in presumptions as to what the one party or the other may have thought. He can consider only that whoever has not attached a separate contract stipulating that he is free from any damages to the thing

6:300

[m] the case is borne by the borrower
[n] the case is borne by the lender

lent must himself bear them. — Hence the difference between the judgment that a court must make and that which each is justified in making for himself by his private reason is a point that is by no means to be overlooked in amending judgments about rights.[o]

C.
ON RECOVERY (REPOSSESSION) OF SOMETHING LOST

(*vindicatio.*)

§ 39.

It is clear from the foregoing that something of mine that continues to exist remains mine even though I am not continuously holding it; that it does not of itself cease to be mine apart from some act by which I give up my right to it (*derelictionis vel alienationis*);[p] and that I have a right to this thing (*ius reale*) and therefore a right against *whoever* holds it, not merely a right against a specific person (*ius personale*). But the question now is whether this right must also be regarded *by everyone else* as ownership that continues of itself, *if I have only not renounced* it, when the thing is in another's possession.

Suppose that someone has lost a thing (*res amissa*) and that someone else takes it *in good faith* (*bona fide*), as a supposed find. Or suppose that I get a thing by its being formally alienated by someone possessing it who represents himself as its owner although he is not. Since I cannot acquire a thing from someone who *is not its owner* (*a non domino*), the question arises whether I am excluded by the real owner from any right to this thing and left with only a personal right against the illegitimate possessor. — The latter is obviously the case if acquisition is judged merely in accordance with the intrinsic grounds that justify it (in the state of nature), not in accordance with what is appropriate for a court.

It must be possible for whatever can be alienated to be acquired by someone or other. The legitimacy of acquisition, however, rests entirely on the form in accordance with which what is possessed by another is transferred to me and accepted by me, that is, on the formalities of the act of exchange (*commutatio*) between the possessor of the thing and the one acquiring it, by which a right is established; I may not ask how the possessor obtained possession of it, since this would already be an offense (*quilibet praesumitur bonus, donec etc.*). Suppose, now, that it later turns out that the possessor was not the owner but that someone else was. I cannot then say that the owner could straightaway take the thing from me (as he

---
[o] *in Berichtigung der Rechtsurteile*
[p] abandonment or alienation

could from anyone else who might be holding it). For I have stolen nothing from him, but have, for example, bought a horse offered for sale in the public market in conformity with the law (*titulo emti venditi*). The title of acquisition on my part is indisputable since I (as buyer) am not bound or even authorized to search the other's (the seller's) title of possession – this investigation would go on to infinity in an ascending series. If the purchase is formally correct, I become not just the *putative* but the *true* owner of the horse.

But against this, the following argument arises with regard to rights. Any acquisition from one who is not the owner of a thing (*a non domino*) is null and void. I can derive no more from another than what he legitimately has. Even though, in buying a stolen horse for sale in the market, I proceed quite correctly as far as the form of acquisition (*modus acquierendi*) is concerned, my title of acquisition is still defective, since the horse did not belong to the one who actually sold it. I may well be its possessor *in good faith* (*possessor bona fidei*), but I am still only its putative owner (*dominus putativus*) and the true owner has a right to *recover* it (*rem suam vindicandi*).

If one asks what is to be laid down as right *in itself* (in the state of nature) in the acquisition of external things in accordance with principles of justice in people's exchanges with one another (*iustitia commutativa*), then one must answer as follows. If someone intends to acquire an external thing in this way it is in fact necessary for him to investigate whether the thing he wants to acquire does not already belong to someone else; that is to say, even if he has strictly observed the formal conditions for deriving the thing from what belongs to another (has bought the horse on the market in the proper way), as long as he remains ignorant as to whether someone else (other than the seller) is the true owner of it, the most he could have acquired is only a *right against a person* with regard to the thing (*ius ad rem*), so that if someone comes forth who can document his previous ownership of it, nothing is left to the alleged new owner but to have legitimately enjoyed the use of it up to this moment as its possessor in good faith. – Since it is largely impossible to discover who was absolutely first (the original owner) in the series of putative owners deriving their right from each other, no trade in external things, no matter how well it may agree with the formal conditions of this kind of justice (*iustitia commutativa*), can guarantee a secure acquisition.

Here again reason giving laws with regard to rights comes forth with a principle of *distributive justice*, of adopting as its guiding rule for the legitimacy of possession, not the way it would be judged *in itself* by the private will of each (in the state of nature), but the way it would be judged before a *court* in a condition brought about by the united will of all (in a civil condition). In a civil condition, conformity with the formal conditions of acquisition, which of themselves establish only a right against a person,

6:302

is postulated as an adequate substitute for the material grounds (which establish derivation from what belonged to a previous alleged owner); and what is *in itself* a right against a person, *when brought before a court*, holds as a right to a thing. A horse, for example, that someone puts up for sale in a public market regulated by police ordinances becomes my property if all the rules of buying and selling are strictly observed (but in such a way that the true owner retains the right to put forward a claim against the seller on the ground of his earlier, unforfeited possession of it); and what would otherwise be my right against a person is converted into a right to a thing, in accordance with which I can take (recover) it as mine wherever I find it, without having to get involved in how the seller obtained it.

So it is only for the sake of a court's verdict (*in favorem iustitiae distributivae*) that a right to a thing is taken and treated not *as it is in itself* (as a right against a person) but as it can be *most readily* and surely *judged* (as a right to a thing), and yet in accordance with a pure a priori principle. – On this principle various statutory laws (ordinances) are subsequently based, the primary purpose of which is to set up conditions under which alone a way of acquiring is to have rightful force, conditions *such that a judge* can assign to each what is his *most readily and with least hesitation*. For example, in the saying "Purchase breaks a lease," what is a right to a thing (the lease) in accordance with the nature of the contract, that is, in itself, holds as a mere right against a person; and conversely, as in the case discussed above, what is in itself only a right against a person holds as a right to a thing. In such cases the question is what principles a court in the civil condition should rely on in order to proceed most surely in its verdicts about the rights belonging to each.

D.
ON ACQUIRING GUARANTEES BY OATH.[25]
(*Cautio iuratoria.*)

§ 40.

No other reason could be given which could bind human beings as a matter of right[q] to *believe* and acknowledge that there are gods than that they could thereby swear an oath and be constrained to be truthful in what they say and faithful in keeping their promises by their fear of an all-seeing, almighty power whose vengeance they would have solemnly called down upon themselves in case their declarations were false. That in requiring oaths one does not count on morality in these two respects but only on blind superstition is clear from this: that one does not expect any guarantee *merely* from their *solemn* declarations before a court in matters of rights, even though every-

---

[q] *rechtlich*

one clearly sees the duty to be truthful in a case having to do with what is most sacred of all among human beings (the right of human beings). So mere fairy tales are the incentive in taking oaths, as, for example, according to Marsden's testimony, the Rajangs, a pagan people of Sumatra, swear by the bones of their dead ancestors even though they do not believe that there is a life after death; or as the Negroes of Guinea take an oath on their *fetish*, such as a bird's feather, calling upon it to break their neck, and so forth. They believe that an invisible power, whether it has understanding or not, already has by its nature this magical power that will come into play by their invocations. – This sort of belief is called religion but should strictly be called superstition. It is, however, indispensable for the administration of justice since, without counting on it, a *court* would not be sufficiently in a position to ascertain facts kept secret and give the right verdict. A law binding a people to take oaths is therefore obviously laid down only on behalf of the judicial authority.

But now the question is, what basis is there for the obligation that someone before a court is supposed to have, to accept another's oath as a proof, valid for right, of the truth of his testimony, which puts an end to all dispute? That is to say, what binds me as a matter of right to believe that another (who swears an oath) has any religion, so as to make my rights dependent upon his oath? So, too, can I be bound to take an oath? Both are wrong in themselves.

Yet with reference to a court, and so in the civil condition, if one admits that there is no other means than an oath for getting at the truth in certain cases, one must assume that everyone has a religion, so that it can be used as an expedient (*in casu necessitatis*) for the purpose of proceedings about rights *before a court*, which regards this spiritual coercion (*tortura spiritualis*) as a handy means, in keeping with the human propensity to superstition, for uncovering secrets and considers itself authorized to use it because of this. – But the legislative authority acts in a way that is fundamentally wrong in conferring authorization to do this on the judicial authority, since even in the civil condition coercion to take oaths is contrary to human freedom, which must not be lost.

6:305

An oath of office is usually *promissory*, an oath, namely, that the official earnestly *resolves* to fulfill his post in conformity with his duties. If it were changed into an *assertoric* oath – if, that is, the official was bound, say at the end of a year (or more), to swear that he had faithfully fulfilled his office during that time – this would arouse his conscience more than an oath he takes as a promise; for having taken a promissory oath, he can always make the excuse to himself later on that with the best of intentions he did not foresee the difficulties which he experienced only later, during the administration of his office. Moreover, he would be more concerned about being accused of failing in his duty if an observer is going to look at the sum of his offenses than if they are merely censured one after the other (and the earlier ones have been forgotten). – But a court can certainly not demand swearing to a *belief* (*de credulitate*). For in the first place it involves a self-contradiction; this thing intermediate between opinion and knowledge is the sort of thing that one can dare to bet on but certainly not to swear to. Second, a judge who requires swearing to a belief from a party in order to find out something relevant to his purpose, even if this purpose is the common good, commits a grave offense against the conscientiousness of the person taking the oath, partly by the thoughtlessness to which the oath misleads him and by which the judge defeats his own purpose, partly by the pangs of conscience a human being must feel, when he can find a certain matter very likely today, considered from a certain point of view, but quite unlikely tomorrow, when he considers it from a different point of view. A judge therefore wrongs one whom he constrains to take such an oath.

Transition from what is mine or yours
in a state of nature to what is mine or yours
in a rightful condition generally

§ *41.*

A rightful condition is that relation of human beings among one another that contains the conditions under which alone everyone is able to *enjoy* his rights, and the formal condition under which this is possible in accordance with the idea of a will giving laws for everyone[r] is called public justice. With reference to either the possibility or the actuality or the necessity of possession of objects (the matter of choice) in accordance with laws, public justice can be divided into *protective justice* (*iustitia tutatrix*), *justice in acquiring from one another* (*iustitia commutativa*), and *distributive justice* (*iustitia distributiva*). – In these the law says, *first*, merely what conduct is intrinsically *right*[s] in terms of its form (*lex iusti*); *second*, what [objects] are capable of being covered externally by law, in terms of their matter, that is, what way of being in possession is *rightful*[t] (*lex iuridica*); *third*, what is the decision of a court in a particular case in accordance with the given law under which it falls, that is, what is *laid down as right*[u] (*lex iustitiae*). Because of this a court is itself called the *justice* of a country, and whether such a thing exists or does not exist is the most

---

[r] *eines allgemein gesetzgebenden Willens*
[s] *recht*
[t] *dessen Besitzstand rechtlich ist*
[u] *Rechtens*

important question that can be asked about any arrangements having to do with rights.

A condition that is not rightful, that is, a condition in which there is no distributive justice, is called a state of nature (*status naturalis*). What is opposed to a state of nature is not (as Achenwall thinks) a condition that is *social* and that could be called an artificial condition (*status artificialis*), but rather the *civil* condition (*status civilis*), that of a society subject to distributive justice. For in the state of nature, too, there can be societies compatible with rights (e.g., conjugal, paternal, domestic societies in general, as well as many others); but no law, "You ought to enter this condition," holds a priori for these societies, whereas it can be said of a *rightful* condition that all human beings who could (even involuntarily)[v] come into relations of rights with one another *ought* to enter this condition.

The first and second of these conditions can be called the condition of *private right*, whereas the third and last can be called the condition of *public right*. The latter contains no further or other duties of human beings among themselves than can be conceived in the former state; the matter of private right is the same in both. The laws of the condition of public right, accordingly, have to do only with the rightful form of their association (constitution), in view of which these laws must necessarily be conceived as public.

The *civil union* (*unio civilis*) cannot itself be called a *society*, for between the *commander*[w] (*imperans*) and the *subject* (*subditus*) there is no partnership. They are not fellow-members: one is *subordinated to*, not *coordinated with* the other; and those who are coordinate with one another must for this very reason consider themselves equals since they are subject to common laws. The civil union *is* not so much a society but rather *makes* one.

6:307

§ 42.

From private right in the state of nature there proceeds the postulate of public right: when you cannot avoid living side by side with all others,[x] you ought to leave the state of nature and proceed with them into a rightful

---

[v] *unwillkürlich*

[w] *Befehlshaber*. Kant has not yet discussed the relation of the legislative, executive, and judicial authorities in a state. When he does so, in 6:316, the *(Ober)befehlshaber* is associated with the executive authority. Here, however, as in § 47, Kant is apparently using the word simply in the sense of "a superior in general."

[x] Grammatically, the relation of "with all others" to the rest of the sentence is ambiguous: the phrase could modify "proceed." My reasons for the above translation are, first, Kant's thesis of "original possession in common" of the earth's habitable surface by the whole human race and, second, the fact that the heading of § 41 indicates that § 42 is part of the transition from Private Right to the whole of Public Right. As Kant has said (6:266), until "the original contract" extends to the whole human race, acquisition will always remain provisional.

condition, that is, a condition of distributive justice. – The ground of this postulate can be explicated[y] analytically from the concept of *right* in external relations, in contrast with *violence* (*violentia*).

No one is bound to refrain from encroaching on what another possesses if the other gives him no equal assurance that he will observe the same restraint toward him. No one, therefore, need wait until he has learned by bitter experience of the other's contrary disposition; for what should bind him to wait till he has suffered a loss before he becomes prudent, when he can quite well perceive within himself the inclination of human beings generally to lord it over others as their master (not to respect the superiority of the rights of others when they feel superior to them in strength or cunning)? And it is not necessary to wait for actual hostility; one is authorized to use coercion against someone who already, by his nature, threatens him with coercion. (*Quilibet praesumitur malus, donec securitatem dederit oppositi.*)[z]

Given the intention to be and to remain in this state of externally lawless freedom, men do *one another* no wrong at all when they feud among themselves; for what holds for one holds also in turn for the other, as if by mutual consent (*uti partes de iure suo disponunt, ita ius est.*)[a] But in general they do wrong in the highest degree* by willing to be and to remain in a condition that is not rightful, that is, in which no one is assured of what is his against violence.

---

* This distinction between what is merely formally wrong and what is also materially wrong has many applications in the doctrine of right. An enemy who, instead of honorably carrying out his surrender agreement with the garrison of a besieged fortress, mistreats them as they march out or otherwise breaks the agreement, cannot complain of being wronged if his opponent plays the same trick on him when he can. But in general they do wrong in the highest degree, because they take away any validity from the concept of right itself and hand everything over to savage violence, as if by law, and so subvert the right of human beings as such.

[y] *entwickeln*
[z] He is presumed evil who threatens the safety of his opposite.
[a] The party who displaces another's right has the same right himself.

The doctrine of right

Part II
Public right

Public right

Section I.
The right of a state.

§ 43.

The sum of the laws which need to be promulgated generally in order to bring about a rightful condition is *public right*. – Public *right is therefore a system of laws for a people, that is, a multitude of human beings, or for a multitude of peoples, which, because they affect one another, need a rightful condition under a will uniting them*, a *constitution* (*constitutio*), so that they may enjoy what is laid down as right. – This condition of the individuals within a people in relation to one another is called a *civil* condition (*status civilis*), and the whole of individuals in a rightful condition, in relation to its own members is called a *state* (*civitas*). Because of its form, by which all are united through their common interest in being in a rightful condition, a state is called a *commonwealth* (*res publica latius sic dicta*).[b] In relation to other peoples, however, a state is called simply a *power* (*potentia*) (hence the word *potentate*). Because the union of the members is (presumed to be) one they inherited, a state is also called a nation (*gens*). Hence, under the general concept of public right we are led to think not only of the right of a state but also of a *right of nations* (*ius gentium*).[c] Since the earth's surface is not unlimited but closed, the concepts of the right of a state and of a right of nations lead inevitably to the idea of a *right for a state of nations* (*ius gentium*) or *cosmopolitan right* (*ius cosmopoliticum*). So if the principle of outer freedom limited by law is lacking in any one of these three possible forms of rightful condition, the framework of all the others is unavoidably undermined and must finally collapse.

§ 44.

It is not experience from which we learn of the maxim of violence in human beings and of their malevolent tendency to attack one another before external legislation[d] endowed with power appears, thus it is not

---

[b] republic in the broad sense

[c] The English terms "municipal law" and "international law" might be used here, if it were kept in mind that Kant's concern is only with a priori principles. However, given the meaning of *Recht* specified in AK 6: 229, it seems preferable to continue using this term throughout: *das öffentliche Recht* or "public right."

[d] Although Kant continues to use *Gesetzgebung* and *Gesetzgeber*, which were translated in Private Right as "lawgiving" and "lawgiver," he is now discussing a condition in which there are positive laws. Hence "legislation" and "legislator" seem appropriate.

some deed*ᵉ* that makes coercion through public law necessary. On the contrary, however well disposed and law-abiding human beings might be, it still lies a priori in the rational idea of such a condition (one that is not rightful) that before a public lawful condition is established individual human beings, peoples and states can never be secure against violence from one another, since each has its own right to do *what seems right and good to it* and not to be dependent upon another's opinion about this. So, unless it wants to renounce any concepts of right, the first thing it has to resolve upon is the principle that it must leave the state of nature, in which each follows its own judgment, unite itself with all others (with which it cannot avoid interacting), subject itself to a public lawful external coercion, and so enter into a condition in which what is to be recognized as belonging to it is determined *by law* and is allotted to it by adequate *power* (not its own but an external power); that is, it ought above all else to enter a civil condition.

It is true that the state of nature need not, just because it is natural, be a state of *injustice* (*iniustus*), of dealing with one another only in terms of the degree of force each has. But it would still be a state *devoid of justice* (*status iustitia vacuus*), in which when rights are *in dispute* (*ius controversum*), there would be no judge competent to render a verdict having rightful force. Hence each may impel the other by force to leave this state and enter into a rightful condition; for although each can acquire something external by taking control of it or by contract in accordance with its *concepts of right*, this acquisition is still only *provisional* as long as it does not yet have the sanction of public law, since it is not determined by public (distributive) justice and secured by an authority putting this right into effect.

If no acquisition were cognized as rightful even in a provisional way prior to entering the civil condition, the civil condition itself would be impossible. For in terms of their form, laws concerning what is mine or yours in the state of nature contain the same thing that they prescribe in the civil condition, insofar as the civil condition is thought of by pure rational concepts alone. The difference is only that the civil condition provides the conditions under which these laws are put into effect (in keeping with distributive justice). – So if external objects were not even *provisionally* mine or yours in the state of nature, there would also be no duties of right with regard to them and therefore no command to leave the state of nature.

§ 45.

A *state* (*civitas*) is a union of a multitude of human beings under laws of right. Insofar as these are a priori necessary as laws, that is, insofar as they

---

ᵉ Factum

follow of themselves from concepts of external right as such (are not statutory), its form is the form of a state as such, that is, of *the state in idea*, as it ought to be in accordance with pure principles of right. This idea serves as a norm (*norma*) for every actual union into a commonwealth (hence serves as a norm for its internal constitution).*f*

Every state contains three *authorities* within it,*g* that is, the general united will consists of three persons (*trias politica*): the *sovereign authority* (sovereignty)*h* in the person of the legislator; the *executive authority* in the person of the ruler (in conformity to law); and the *judicial authority* (to award to each what is his in accordance with the law) in the person of the judge (*potestas legislatoria, rectoria et iudiciaria*). These are like the three propositions in a practical syllogism: the major premise, which contains the *law* of that will; the minor premise, which contains the *command* to behave in accordance with the law, that is, the principle of subsumption under the law; and the conclusion, which contains the *verdict* (sentence), what is laid down as right in the case at hand.

§ 46.

The legislative authority can belong only to the united will of the people. For since all right is to proceed from it, it *cannot* do anyone wrong by its law. Now when someone makes arrangements about *another*, it is always possible for him to do the other wrong; but he can never do wrong in what he decides upon with regard to himself (for *volenti non fit iniuria*).*i* Therefore only the concurring and united will of all, insofar as each decides the same thing for all and all for each, and so only the general united will of the people, can be legislative.

6:314

The members of such a society who are united for giving law (*societas civilis*), that is, the members of a state, are called *citizens of a state* (*cives*). In terms of rights, the attributes of a citizen, inseparable from his essence (as a citizen), are: lawful *freedom*, the attribute of obeying no other law than that to which he has given his consent; civil *equality*, that of not recogniz-

---

f (*also im Inneren*)

g Or "powers" [*Gewalten*]. In §43 and §44 Kant used *Macht* (*potentia*), which was translated as "power." He now begins to use *Gewalt* (*potestas*). But once he distinguishes the three "powers" or "authorities" within a state, it is only the executive authority that has "power" in one sense, i.e., it is the authority which exercises coercion.

h *Herrschergewalt* (*Souveränität*). In this initial distinction of the three authorities within a state Kant specifies that "sovereignty" belongs to the legislative authority. Subsequently he introduces, without explanation, such a variety of terms that it is not always clear which of the three authorities is under discussion. I have used "sovereign," without noting the word used, only when Kant specifies *Souverän*. When "sovereign" is used for *Herrscher* or *Beherrscher*, a note is provided. Otherwise I have used the more general "head of state," except for passages that might indicate that one (physical) person has both legislative and executive authority.

i no wrong is done to someone who consents

ing among the *people* any superior with the moral capacity[j] to bind him as a matter of right in a way that he could not in turn bind the other; and third, the attribute of civil *independence*, of owing his existence and preservation to his own rights and powers as a member of the commonwealth, not to the choice of another among the people. From his independence follows his civil personality, his attribute of not needing to be represented by another where rights are concerned.

The only qualification for being a citizen is being fit to vote. But being fit to vote presupposes the independence of someone who, as one of the people, wants to be not just a part of the commonwealth but also a member of it, that is, a part of the commonwealth acting from his own choice in community with others. This quality of being independent, however, requires a distinction between *active* and *passive* citizens, though the concept of a passive citizen seems to contradict the concept of a citizen as such. – The following examples can serve to remove this difficulty: an apprentice in the service of a merchant or artisan; a domestic servant (as distinguished from a civil servant); a minor (*naturaliter vel civiliter*); all women and, in general, anyone whose preservation in existence (his being fed and protected) depends not on his management of his own business but on arrangements made by another (except the state). All these people lack civil personality and their existence is, as it were, only inherence. – The woodcutter I hire to work in my yard; the blacksmith in India, who goes into people's houses to work on iron with his hammer, anvil and bellows, as compared with the European carpenter or blacksmith who can put the products of his work up as goods for sale to the public; the private tutor, as compared with the school teacher; the tenant farmer as compared with the leasehold farmer, and so forth; these are mere underlings[k] of the commonwealth because they have to be under the direction or protection of other individuals, and so do not possess civil independence.

This dependence upon the will of others and this inequality is, however, in no way opposed to their freedom and equality *as human beings*, who together make up a people; on the contrary, it is only in conformity with the conditions of freedom and equality that this people can become a state and enter into a civil constitution. But not all persons qualify with equal right to vote within this constitution, that is, to be citizens and not mere associates in the state. For from their being able to demand that all others treat them in accordance with the laws of natural freedom and equality as *passive* parts of the state it does not

---

[j] *Vermögen*
[k] *Handlanger*

follow that they also have the right to manage the state itself as *active* members of it, the right to organize it or to cooperate for introducing certain laws. It follows only that, whatever sort of positive laws the citizens might vote for, these laws must still not be contrary to the natural laws of freedom and of the equality of everyone in the people corresponding to this freedom, namely that anyone can work his way up from this passive condition to an active one.

§ 47.

All those three authorities in a state are dignities,[l] and since they arise necessarily from the idea of a state as such, as essential for the establishment (constitution) of it, they are *civic dignities*. They comprise the relation of a *superior* over all (which, from the viewpoint of laws of freedom, can be none other than the united people itself) to the multitude of that people severally as *subjects*, that is, the relation of a *commander*[m] (*imperans*) to *those who obey* (*subditus*). – The act by which a people forms itself into a state is the *original contract*. Properly speaking, the original contract is only the idea of this act, in terms of which alone we can think of the legitimacy of a state. In accordance with the original contract, everyone (*omnes et singuli*) within a *people* gives up his external freedom in order to take it up again immediately as a member of a commonwealth, that is, of a people considered as a state (*universi*). And one cannot say: the human being in a state has sacrificed a *part* of his innate outer freedom for the sake of an end, but rather, he has relinquished entirely his wild, lawless freedom in order to find his freedom as such undiminished, in a dependence upon laws, that is, in a rightful condition, since this dependence arises from his own lawgiving will.

§ 48.

Accordingly, the three authorities in a state are, *first*, coordinate with one another (*potestates coordinatae*) as so many moral persons, that is, each complements the others to complete the constitution of a state (*complementum ad sufficientiam*).[n] But, *second*, they are also *subordinate* (*subordinatae*) to one another, so that one of them, in assisting another, cannot also usurp its function; instead, each has its own principle, that is, it indeed commands in its capacity[o] as a particular person, but still under the condition of the will of a superior. *Third*, through the union of both each subject is apportioned his rights.[26]

It can be said of these authorities, regarded in their dignity, that the will

6:316

---

[l] *Würden*
[m] *Gebeitenden*
[n] complement to sufficiency
[o] *Qualität*

of the *legislator* (*legislatoris*) with regard to what is externally mine or yours is *irreproachable* (*irreprehensibel*); that the executive power of the *supreme ruler* (*summi rectoris*) is *irresistible;* and that the verdict of the highest *judge* (*supremi iudicis*) is *irreversible* (cannot be appealed).

§ *49.*

The *ruler* of a state (*rex, princeps*) is that (moral or natural) person to whom the executive authority (*potestas executoria*) belongs. He is the *agent* of the state, who appoints the magistrates and prescribes to the people rules in accordance with which each of them can acquire something or preserve what is his in conformity with the law (through subsumption of a case under it). Regarded as a moral person, he is called the *directorate,* the government. His *directives* to the people, and to the magistrates and their superior (the minister) whom he charges with *administering the state* (*gubernatio*), are ordinances or *decrees* (not laws); for they are directed to decisions in particular cases and are given as subject to being changed. A *government* that was also legislative would have to be called a *despotic* as opposed to a *patriotic* government; but by a patriotic government is understood not a *paternalistic* one (*regimen paternale*), which is the most despotic of all (since it treats citizens as children), but one *serving the native land* (*regimen civitatis et patriae*). In it the state (*civitas*) does treat its subjects as members of one family but it also treats them as citizens of the state, that is, in accordance with laws of their own independence: each is in possession of himself and is not dependent upon the absolute will of another alongside him or above him.

So a people's sovereign[p] (legislator) cannot also be its *ruler,* since the ruler is subject to the law and so is put under obligation through the law by *another,* namely the sovereign.[q] The sovereign can also take the ruler's authority away from him, depose him, or reform his administration. But it cannot *punish* him (and the saying common in England, that the king, i.e., the supreme executive authority, can do no wrong, means no more than this); for punishment is, again, an act of the executive authority, which has the supreme capacity to *exercise coercion* in conformity with the law, and it would be self-contradictory for him to be subject to coercion.

Finally, neither the head of state nor its ruler can *judge,* but can only appoint judges as magistrates. A people judges itself through those of its fellow citizens whom it designates as its representatives for this by a free choice and, indeed, designates especially for each act. For a verdict (a sentence) is an individual act of public justice (*iustitiae distributativae*) performed by an administrator of the state (a judge or court) upon a subject, that is, upon someone belonging to the people; and so this act is

[p] *Beherrscher*
[q] *Souverän*

invested with no authority to assign (allot) to a subject what is his. Since each individual among a people is only passive in this relationship (to the authorities), if either the legislative or the executive authority were to decide in a controversial case what belongs to him, it might do him a wrong, since it would not be the people itself doing this and pronouncing a verdict of *guilty* or *not guilty* upon a fellow citizen. But once the facts in a lawsuit have been established, the court has judicial authority to apply the law, and to render to each what is his with the help of the executive authority. Hence only the *people* can give a judgment upon one of its members, although only indirectly, by means of representatives (the jury) whom it has delegated. – It would also be beneath the dignity of the head of state to play the judge, that is, to put himself in a position where he could do wrong and so have his decision appealed (*a rege male informato ad regem melius informandum*).[r]

There are thus three distinct authorities (*potestas legislatoria, executoria, iudiciaria*) by which a state (*civitas*) has its autonomy, that is, by which it forms and preserves itself in accordance with laws of freedom. – A state's *well-being* consists in their being united (*salus rei publicae suprema lex est*).[s] But the well-being of a state must not be understood as the *welfare* of its citizens and their *happiness;* for happiness can perhaps come to them more easily and as they would like it to in a state of nature (as Rousseau asserts) or even under a despotic government. By the well-being of a state is understood, instead, that condition in which its constitution conforms most fully to principles of right; it is that condition which reason, *by a categorical imperative*, makes it obligatory for us to strive after.

GENERAL REMARK

On the effects with regard to rights that follow from the nature of the civil union.

A.

A people should not *inquire* with any practical aim in view into the origin of the supreme authority to which it is subject, that is, a subject *ought not to reason subtly* for the sake of action[t] about the origin of this authority, as a right that can still be called into question (*ius controversum*) with regard to the obedience he owes it. For, since a people must be regarded as already united under a general legislative will in order to judge with rightful force

---

[r] from a king badly instructed to a king to be better instructed
[s] The well-being of the commonwealth is the supreme law. The saying seems to stem from Cicero *De Legibus* 3.8, *Salus populi suprema lex esto.*
[t] *werktätig vernünfteln*

about the supreme authority*ᵘ* (*summum imperium*), it cannot and may not judge otherwise than as the present head of state (*summus imperans*) wills it to. – Whether a state began with an actual contract of submission (*pactum subiectionis civilis*) as a fact, or whether power came first and law arrived only afterwards, or even whether they should have followed in this order: for a people already subject to civil law these subtle reasonings are altogether pointless and, moreover, threaten a state with danger. If a subject, having pondered over the ultimate origin of the authority now ruling,*ᵛ* wanted to resist this authority, he would be punished, got rid of, or expelled (as an outlaw, *exlex*) in accordance with the laws of this authority, that is, with every right. – A law that is so holy (inviolable) that it is already a crime even to call it in doubt *in a practical way*, and so to suspend its effect for a moment, is thought as if it must have arisen not from human beings but from some highest, flawless lawgiver; and that is what the saying "All authority is from God" means. This saying is not an assertion about the *historical basis* of the civil constitution; it instead sets forth an idea as a practical principle of reason: the principle that the presently existing legislative authority ought to be obeyed, whatever its origin.

Now, from this principle follows the proposition: the sovereign*ʷ* has only rights against his subjects and no duties (that he can be coerced to fulfill).*ˣ* – Moreover, even if the organ of the sovereign, the *ruler*, proceeds contrary to law, for example, if he goes against the law of equality in assigning the burdens of the state in matters of taxation, recruiting and so forth, subjects may indeed oppose this injustice by *complaints* (*gravamina*) but not by resistance.

Indeed, even the constitution cannot contain any article that would make it possible for there to be some authority in a state to resist the supreme commander*ʸ* in case he should violate the law of the constitution, and so to limit him.²⁷ For, someone who is to limit the authority in a state must have even more power*ᶻ* than he whom he limits, or at least as much power as he has; and, as a legitimate commander*ᵃ* who directs the subjects to resist, he must also be able to *protect* them and to render a judgment having rightful force in any case that comes up; consequently he has to be able to command resistance publicly. In that case, however, the supreme commander*ᵇ* in a state is not the supreme commander; instead, it is the

---

ᵘ *Staatsgewalt*
ᵛ *jetzt herrschenden*
ʷ *Herrscher*
ˣ *keine (Zwangs-) Pflichten*
ʸ *obersten Befehlshaber*
ᶻ *Macht*
ᵃ *rechtmässiger Gebieter*
ᵇ *obersten Befehlshaber*

one who can resist him, and this is self-contradictory. In that case the sovereign behaves through its minister as also the ruler and so as a despot; and the illusion that allows us to think of the people, through its deputies, as the limiting authority (though it has, properly speaking, only legislative authority) cannot conceal the despotism, so that it does not come to light from the measures the minister takes. The people, in being represented by its deputies (in parliament), has, in these guardians of its freedom and rights, men who have a lively interest in positions for themselves and their families, in the army, the navy and the civil service, that depend on the minister, and who are always ready to play into the government's hands (instead of resisting its encroachments; besides, a public declaration of resistance requires unanimity in a people which has been prepared in advance, and this cannot be permitted in time of peace). – Hence a so-called moderate constitution, as a constitution for the inner rights of a state, is an absurdity. Instead of belonging to right it is only a principle of prudence, not so much to make it more difficult for a powerful transgressor of the people's rights to exercise at will his influence[c] upon the government as to disguise his influence under the illusion of an opposition permitted to the people.

Therefore a people cannot offer any resistance to the legislative head of a state which would be consistent with right, since a rightful condition is possible only by submission to its general legislative will. There is, therefore, no right to *sedition* (*seditio*), still less to *rebellion* (*rebellio*), and least of all is there a right against the head of a state as an individual person (the monarch), *to attack his person* or even his life (*monarchomachismus sub specie tyrannicidii*)[d] on the pretext that he has abused his authority (*tyrannis*). – Any attempt whatsoever at this is *high treason* (*proditio eminens*), and whoever commits such treason must be punished by nothing less than death for attempting *to destroy his fatherland* (*parricida*). – The reason a people has a duty to put up with even what is held to be an unbearable abuse of supreme authority is that its resistance to the highest legislation can never be regarded as other than contrary to law, and indeed as abolishing the entire legal constitution. For a people to be authorized to resist, there would have to be a public law permitting it to resist, that is, the highest legislation would have to contain a provision that it is not the highest and that makes the people, as subject, by one and the same judgment sovereign over him to whom it is subject. This is self-contradictory, and the contradiction is evident as soon as one asks who is to be the judge in this dispute between people and sovereign (for, considered in terms of rights, these are always two distinct moral

---

[c] *seine willkürlichen Einflüße*
[d] murder of a monarch under the guise of tyrannicide

persons). For it is then apparent that the people wants to be the judge in its own suit.*

* The *dethronement* of a monarch can still be thought of as if he had *voluntarily* laid aside the crown and abdicated his authority, giving it back to the people, or as if, without any attack on the highest person, he had relinquished his authority and been reduced to the rank of a private person. Because of this the people who extorted this from him has at least the pretext of a *right of necessity* (*casus necessitatis*) in favor of its crime. But it never has the least right to punish him, the head of state, because of his previous administration, since everything he did, in his capacity as head of state, must be regarded as having been done in external conformity with rights, and he himself, as the source of the law, can do no wrong. Of all the atrocities involved in overthrowing a state by rebellion, the *assassination* of the monarch is not itself the worst, for we can still think of the people as doing it from fear that if he remained alive he could marshal his forces and inflict on them the punishment they deserve, so that their killing him would not be an enactment of punitive justice but merely a dictate of self-preservation. It is the formal *execution* of a monarch that strikes horror in a soul filled with the idea of human rights, a horror that one feels repeatedly as soon as and as often as one thinks of such scenes as the fate of Charles I or Louis XVI. But how are we to explain this feeling, which is not aesthetic feeling (sympathy, an effect of imagination by which we put ourselves in the place of the sufferer) but moral feeling resulting from the complete overturning of all concepts of right? It is regarded as a crime that remains forever and can never be expiated (*crimen immortale, inexpiabile*), and it seems to be like what theologians call the sin that cannot be forgiven either in this world or the next. The explanation of this phenomenon in the human mind seems to arise from the following reflections upon itself, which throw light on the principles of political rights themselves.

Any transgression of the law can and must be explained only as arising from a maxim of the criminal (to make such a crime his rule); for if we were to derive it from a sensible impulse, he would not be committing it as a *free* being and it could not be imputed to him. But how it is possible for the subject to form such a maxim contrary to the clear prohibition of lawgiving reason absolutely cannot be explained, since only what happens in accordance with the mechanism of nature is capable of being explained. Now the criminal can commit his misdeed either on a maxim he has taken as an objective rule (as holding universally) or only as an exception to the rule (exempting himself from it occasionally). In the *latter* case he *only deviates* from the law (though intentionally); he can at the same time detest his transgression and, without formally renouncing obedience to the law, only want to evade it. In the *first* case, however, he rejects the authority of the law itself, whose validity he still cannot deny before his own reason, and makes it his rule to act contrary to the law. His maxim is therefore opposed to the law not by way of *default* only (*negative*) but by *rejecting* it (*contrarie*) or, as we put it, his maxim is *diametrically* opposed to the law, as contradictory to it (hostile to it, so to speak). As far as we can see, it is impossible for a human being to commit a crime of this kind, a formally evil (wholly pointless) crime; and yet it is not to be ignored in a system of morals (although it is only the idea of the most extreme evil).

The reason for horror at the thought of the formal execution of a monarch *by his people* is therefore this: that while his *murder* is regarded as only an *exception* to the rule that the people makes its maxim, his *execution* must be regarded as a complete *overturning* of the principles of the relation between a sovereign and his people (in which the people, which owes its existence only to the sovereign's legislation, makes itself his master), so that violence is elevated above the most sacred rights brazenly and in accordance with principle. Like a chasm that irretrievably swallows everything, the execution of a monarch seems to be a crime from which the people cannot be absolved, for it is as if the state commits suicide. There is, accordingly, reason for assuming that the agreement to execute the monarch actually origi-

A change in a (defective) constitution, which may certainly be necessary at times, can therefore be carried out only through *reform* by the sovereign itself, but not by the people, and therefore not by *revolution;* and when such a change takes place this reform can affect only the *executive authority*, not the legislative. – In what is called a limited constitution, the constitution contains a provision that the people can legally *resist* the executive authority and its representatives (the minister) by means of its representatives (in parliament). Nevertheless, no active resistance (by the people combining at will;*e* to coerce the government to take a certain course of action, and so itself performing an act of executive authority) is permitted, but only *negative* resistance, that is, a *refusal* of the people (in parliament) to accede to every demand the government puts forth as necessary for administering the state. Indeed, if these demands were always complied with, this would be a sure sign that the people is corrupt, that its representatives can be bought, that the head of the government is ruling despotically through his minister, and that the minister himself is betraying the people.

Moreover, once a revolution has succeeded and a new constitution has been established, the lack of legitimacy with which it began and has been implemented cannot release the subjects from the obligation to comply with the new order of things as good citizens, and they cannot refuse honest obedience to the authority that now has the power. A dethroned monarch (who survives the upheaval) cannot be held to account, still less be punished, for what he previously carried out, provided he returns to the estate*f* of a citizen and prefers peace for himself and the state to the risk of running away in order to engage in the adventure of trying, as a claimant,*g* to get his throne back, whether by covertly inciting a counter-revolution or by the assistance of other powers. But if he prefers the latter course, his right to do so cannot be challenged since the insurrection that dispossessed him was unjust. But do other powers have the right to band together in an alliance on behalf of this deposed monarch, merely so as not to let that crime perpetrated by the people go unavenged and persist as a scandal for all states? Are they therefore authorized and called upon to restore by force the old constitution in any other state where the presently

6:321
6:322

6:323

---

nates not from what is supposed to be a rightful principle but from fear of the state's vengeance upon the people if it revives at some future time, and that these formalities are undertaken only to give that deed the appearance of punishment, and so of a *rightful procedure* (such as murder would not be). But this disguising of the deed miscarries; such a presumption on the people's part is still worse than murder, since it involves a principle that would have to make it impossible to generate again a state that has been overthrown.

e *der willkürlichen Verbindung*
f *Stand*
g Or "pretender," *Prätendent*

existing constitution has come about *by revolution?* These questions belong to the right of nations.

B.

Can the sovereign*ʰ* be regarded as the supreme proprietor*ⁱ* (of the land) or must he be regarded only as the one who has supreme command over the people by law? Since the land is the ultimate condition that alone makes it possible to have external things as one's own, and the first right that can be acquired is to possession and use of such things, all such rights must be derived from the sovereign as *lord of the land*, or better, as the supreme proprietor of it (*dominus territorii*). The people, the multitude of subjects, also belong to him (they are his people). But they belong to him not as if he owned them (by a right to things); they instead belong to him as their supreme commander*ʲ* (by a right against persons). – This supreme proprietorship is, however, only an idea of the civil union that serves to represent in accordance with concepts of right the necessary union of the private property of everyone within the people under a general public possessor, so that determination of the particular property of each is in accordance with the necessary formal principle of *division* (division of land), instead of with principles of *aggregation* (which proceeds empirically from the parts to the whole). In accordance with concepts of right, the supreme proprietor cannot have any land at all as his private property (for otherwise he would make himself a private person). All land belongs only to the people (and indeed to the people taken distributively, not collectively), except in the case of a nomadic people under a sovereign,*ᵏ* with whom there is no private ownership of land. – The supreme commander*ˡ* can therefore have no *domains*, that is, no estates for his private use (for maintaining his court). For if he did, it would then be up to his own discretion how far they should be extended, so that the state would run the risk of seeing all ownership of land in the hands of the government and all subjects as *serfs* (*glebae adscripti*), possessors only of what is the property of another, and therefore deprived of all freedom (*servi*). – One can say of the lord of the land that *he possesses nothing* (of his own) except himself; for if he had something of his own alongside others in the state, a dispute could arise between them and there would be no judge to settle it. But one can also say that *he possesses everything*, since he has the right of command over the people, to whom all external things belong (*divisim*) (the right to assign to each what is his).

ʰ *Beherrscher*
ⁱ Or "supreme owner," *Obereigentümer*
ʲ *Oberbefehlshaber*
ᵏ *nomadisch-beherrschtes*
ˡ *Oberbefehlshaber*

From this it follows that within a state there can also be no corporation, estate or order which, as owner of land, can pass it on in accordance with certain statutes to succeeding generations for their exclusive use (in perpetuity). The state can repeal such statutes at any time, provided it compensates those who are left. A *knightly order* (whether a corporation or merely a rank of individual persons who enjoy special honors) or a *clerical order*, called the church, can never acquire from those privileges with which they are favored ownership in land to pass on to their successors; they can acquire only use of it up to the present. The estates of a knightly order can be revoked without scruple (though under the condition mentioned above) if public opinion has ceased to favor *military honors* as a means for safeguarding the state against indifference in defending it. The holdings of the church can be similarly revoked if public opinion has ceased to want masses for souls, prayers and a multitude of clerics appointed for this as the means for saving the people from eternal fire. Those affected by such reforms cannot complain of their property being taken from them, since the reason for their possession hitherto lay only in the *people's opinion* and also had to hold as long as that lasted. But as soon as this opinion lapses, and even lapses only in the judgment of those who by their merit have the strongest claim to guide judgment, the supposed property has to cease, as if by an appeal of the people to the state (*a rege male informato ad regem melius informandum*).[m]

6:325

On this originally acquired ownership of land rests, again, the right of the supreme commander,[n] as supreme proprietor (lord of the land), to *tax* private owners of land, that is, to require payment of taxes on land, excise taxes and import duties, or to require the performance of services (such as providing troops for military service). This must, however, be done in such a way that the people taxes itself, since the only way of proceeding in accordance with principles of right in this matter is for taxes to be levied by those deputized by the people, even in case of forced loans (deviating from previously existing law), which it is permissible to exact by the right of majesty in case the state is in danger of dissolution.

On this supreme proprietorship also rests the right to administer the state's economy, finances and police. Police provide for public *security*, *convenience* and *decency;* for, the government's business of guiding the people by laws is made easier when the feeling for decency (*sensus decori*), as negative taste, is not deadened by what offends the moral sense, such as begging, uproar on the streets, stenches and public prostitution (*venus volgivaga*).[o]

A third right also belongs to the state for its preservation, that of *inspec-*

---

[m] from a king badly informed to a king better informed
[n] *Oberbefehlshaber*
[o] illicit sexual love of the masses

tion (*ius inspectionis*), so that no association (of political or religious fanatics) that could affect the *public* well-being of society (*publicum*) remains concealed. Instead, no association can refuse to disclose its constitution when the police demand it. But the police are not authorized to search anyone's private residence except in a case of necessity, and in every particular case they must be warranted to do so by a higher authority.

C.

To the supreme commander[p] there belongs *indirectly*, that is, insofar as he has taken over the duty of the people, the right to impose taxes on the people for its own preservation, such as taxes to support organizations providing for the *poor, foundling homes* and *church organizations*, usually called charitable or pious institutions.

The general will of the people has united itself into a society which is to maintain itself perpetually; and for this end it has submitted itself to the internal authority of the state in order to maintain those members of the society who are unable to maintain themselves.[q] For reasons of state the government is therefore authorized to constrain the wealthy[r] to provide the means of sustenance to those who are unable to provide for even their most necessary natural needs. The wealthy have acquired an obligation to the commonwealth, since they owe their existence to an act of submitting to its protection and care, which they need in order to live; on this obligation the state now bases its right to contribute what is theirs to maintaining their fellow citizens. This can be done either by imposing a tax on the property or commerce of citizens, or by establishing funds and using the interest from them, not for the needs of the state (for it is rich), but for the needs of the people. (Since we are speaking here only of the right of the state against the people) it will do this by way of coercion, by public taxation, nor merely by *voluntary* contributions, some of which are made for gain (such as lotteries, which produce more poor people and more danger to public property than there would otherwise be, and which should therefore not be permitted). The question arises whether the care of the poor should be provided for by *current contributions* – collected not by begging, which is closely akin to robbery, but by legal levies – so that each generation supports its own poor, or instead by *assets* gradually accumulated and by *pious* institutions generally (such as widows' homes, hospitals, and the like). – Only the first arrangement, which no one who has to live can withdraw from, can be considered in keeping with the right of a state; for even if current contributions increase with the number of the

---

[p] *Oberbefehlshaber*
[q] *die es selbst nicht vermögen*
[r] *die Vermögenden*

poor, this arrangement does not make poverty a means of acquisition for the lazy (as is to be feared of religious institutions) and so does not become an *unjust* burdening of the people by government.

As for maintaining those children abandoned because of poverty or shame, or indeed murdered because of this, the state has a right to charge the people with the duty of not knowingly letting them die, even though they are an unwelcome addition to the population.[s] Whether this should be done by taxing elderly unmarried people of both sexes generally (by which I mean *wealthy* unmarried people), since they are in part to blame for there being abandoned children, in order to establish foundling homes, or whether it can be done rightly in another way (it would be hard to find another means for preventing this) is a problem which has not yet been solved in such a way that the solution offends against neither rights nor morality.

As for *churches*, they must be carefully distinguished from religion, which is an inner disposition lying wholly beyond the civil power's sphere of influence. (As institutions for public *divine worship* on the part of the people, to whose opinion or conviction they owe their origin) churches become a true need of a state, the need for a people to regard themselves as subjects of a supreme *invisible* power to which they must pay homage and which can often come into very unequal conflict with the civil power. So a state does have a right with regard to churches. It does not have the right to legislate the internal constitutions of churches or to organize them in accordance with its own views, in ways it deems advantageous to itself, that is, to prescribe to the people or command beliefs and forms of divine worship (*ritus*) (for this must be left entirely to the teachers and directors the people itself has chosen). A state has only a *negative* right to prevent public teachers from exercising an influence on the *visible* political commonwealth that might be prejudicial to public peace. Its right is therefore that of policing, of not letting a dispute arising within a church or among different churches endanger civil harmony. For the supreme authority to say that a church should have a certain belief, or to say which it should have or that it must maintain it unalterably and may not reform itself, are interferences by it which are *beneath its dignity;* for in doing this, as in meddling in the quarrels of the schools, it puts itself on a level of equality with its subjects (the monarch makes himself a priest), and they can straightaway tell him that he understands nothing about it. The supreme authority especially has no right to prohibit internal reform of churches, for what the whole people cannot decide upon for itself the legislator also cannot decide for the people. But no people can decide never to make further progress in its insight (enlightenment) regarding beliefs, and so never to reform its churches, since this would be opposed

6:327

---

[s] Or "the wealth [resources] of the state," *Staatsvermögen*

to the humanity in their own persons and so to the highest right of the people. So no supreme authority can decide on this for the people. – But as for the expenses of maintaining churches: for the very same reason these cannot be charged to the state but must rather be charged to the part of the people who profess one or another belief, that is, only to the congregation.

D.

The rights of the supreme commander[†] of a state also include: 1) the distribution of *offices*, which are salaried administrative positions; 2) the distribution of *dignities*, which are eminent estates without pay, based on honor alone, that is, a division of rank into the higher (destined to command) and the lower (which, though free and bound only by public law, is still destined to obey the former); and 3) besides these (relatively beneficent) rights, the *right to punish* as well.

With regard to civil offices, the question arises whether the sovereign, once having given someone an office, has a right to take it away as he pleases (if the official has not committed a crime). I say, no. For the head of state can never make a decision about a civil official which the united will of the people would not make. Now the people (which has to bear the costs incurred from appointing an official) undoubtedly wants him to be competent for the position he is assigned to; and this he can be only after he has spent sufficiently long time in preparation and training, time he could have spent in training for another position that would have supported him. If the head of state had this right, offices would be filled as a rule by people who had not acquired the skill requisite for them and the mature judgment achieved by practice, and this would be contrary to the intention of the state, which also requires that everyone be able to rise from lower to higher offices (which would otherwise fall into the hands of sheer incompetence). Hence civil officials must be able to count on lifelong support.

Among *dignities*, not just those attached to an office but also that which makes its possessors members of a higher estate even without any special services on their part, is that of the *nobility*, which is distinct from the civil estate of the people and is transmitted to male descendants and by them to a wife born as a commoner, though if a woman born into the nobility marries a commoner she does not pass this rank on to her husband but herself reverts to the mere civil rank (of the people). – Now the question is whether the sovereign is entitled to establish a nobility, insofar as it is an estate intermediate between himself and the rest of the citizens that *can be inherited*. What this question comes down to is not whether it would be

---

[†] *obersten Befehlshabers*

prudent for the sovereign to do this, with a view to his own or the people's advantage, but only whether it would be in accord with the rights of the people for it to have an estate of persons above it who, while themselves subjects, are still *born* rulers[u] (or at least privileged) with respect to the people. – The answer to this question comes from the same principle as the reply to the preceding one: "What a people (the entire mass of subjects) cannot decide with regard to itself and its fellows, the sovereign can also not decide with regard to it." Now an *hereditary* nobility is a rank that precedes merit and also provides no basis to hope for merit, and is thus a thought-entity without any reality. For if an ancestor had merit he could still not bequeath it to his descendants: they must acquire it for themselves, since nature does not arrange things in such a way that talent and will, which make meritorious service to the state possible, are also *hereditary*. Since we cannot admit that any human being would throw away his freedom, it is impossible for the general will of the people to assent to such a groundless prerogative, and therefore for the sovereign to validate it. – The anomaly of subjects who want to be more than citizens of the state, namely born officials (a born professor, perhaps) may have crept into the machinery of government from older times (feudalism, which was organized almost entirely for war). The only way the state can then gradually correct this mistake it has made, of conferring hereditary privileges contrary to right, is by letting them lapse and not filling vacancies in these positions. So it has a provisional right to let these titled positions of dignity continue until even in public opinion the division into sovereign, nobility and commoners has been replaced by the only natural division into sovereign and people.

Certainly no human being in a state can be without any dignity, since he at least has the dignity of a citizen. The exception is someone who has lost it by his own *crime*, because of which, though he is kept alive, he is made a mere tool of another's choice (either of the state or of another citizen). Whoever is another's tool (which he can become only by a verdict and right)[v] is a *bondsman*[w] (*servus in sensu stricto*) and is the *property* (*dominium*) of another, who is accordingly not merely his *master* (*herus*) but also his *owner* (*dominus*) and can therefore alienate him as a thing, use him as he pleases (only not for shameful purposes) and *dispose of his powers*,

6:330

---

[u] *Befehlshaber*
[v] *Urteil und Recht*
[w] *Leibeigener*, technically, "serf." In 6:241 Kant classed *Leibeigene* and *Sklaven* together: they would be "human beings without personality." In 6:324 he used *grunduntertänig* (*glebae adscripti*) – as in the present passage he uses *Gutsuntertan* (*glebae adscriptus*) – and called serfs *servi*. Here too he refers to a *Leibeigener* as *servus in sensu stricto* or simply *servus*. In 6:333, a criminal is said to have reduced himself to the status of a slave, *Sklavenstand*. I shall henceforth reserve "serf" for *Gutsuntertan* and "slave" for *Sklave* and use the more general "bondsman" for *Leibeigener*.

though not of his life and members. No one can bind himself to this kind of dependence, by which he ceases to be a person, by a contract, since it is only as a person that he can make a contract. Now it might seem that someone could put himself under obligation to another person, by a contract to let and hire (*locatio conductio*), to perform services (in return for wages, board or protection) that are permissible in terms of their quality but *indeterminate* in terms of their quantity, and that he thereby becomes just a subject (*subiectus*), not a bondsman (*servus*). But this is only a deceptive appearance. For if the master is authorized to use the powers of his subject as he pleases, he can also exhaust them until his subject dies or is driven to despair (as with the Negroes on the Sugar Islands); his subject will in fact have given himself away, as property, to his master, which is impossible. – Someone can therefore hire himself out only for work that is determined as to its kind and its amount, either as a day laborer or as a subject living on his master's property. In the latter case he can make a contract, for a time or indefinitely, to perform services by working on his master's land in exchange for the use of it instead of receiving wages as a day laborer, or to pay rent (a tax) specified by a lease in return for his own use of it, without thereby making himself a *serf* (*glebae adscriptus*), by which he would forfeit his personality. Even if he has become a *personal* subject by his crime, his subjection cannot be *inherited*, because he has incurred it only by his own guilt. Nor can a bondsman's offspring be claimed as a bondsman because he has given rise to the expense of being educated; for parents have an absolute natural duty to educate their children and, in case the parents are in bondage, their masters take over this duty along with possession of their subjects.

E.

On the right to punish and to grant clemency.

I.

The *right to punish* is the right a ruler has against a subject to inflict pain upon him because of his having committed a crime. The head of a state can therefore not be punished; one can only withdraw from his dominion. – A transgression of public law that makes someone who commits it unfit to be a citizen is called a *crime* simply (*crimen*) but is also called a public crime (*crimen publicum*);[28] so the first (private crime) is brought before a civil court, the latter before a criminal court. – *Embezzlement*, that is, misappropriation of money or goods entrusted for commerce, and fraud in buying and selling, when committed in such a way that the other could detect it,[x] are

---

[x] *bei sehenden Augen des Anderen*

private crimes. On the other hand, counterfeiting money or bills of exchange, theft and robbery, and the like are public crimes, because they endanger the commonwealth and not just an individual person. – They can be divided into crimes arising from a *mean* character (*indolis abiectae*) and crimes arising from a *violent* character (*indolis violentae*).

Punishment by a court (*poena forensis*) – this is distinct from *natural punishment* (*poena naturalis*), in which vice punishes itself and which the legislator does not take into account – can never be inflicted merely as a means to promote some other good for the criminal himself or for civil society. It must always be inflicted upon him only *because he has committed a crime*. For a human being can never be treated merely as a means to the purposes of another or be put among the objects of rights to things: his innate personality protects him from this, even though he can be condemned to lose his civil personality. He must previously have been found *punishable* before any thought can be given to drawing from his punishment something of use for himself or his fellow citizens. The law of punishment is a categorical imperative, and woe to him who crawls through the windings of eudaimonism in order to discover something that releases the criminal from punishment or even reduces its amount by the advantage it promises, in accordance with the Pharisaical saying, "It is better for *one* man to die than for an entire people to perish." For if justice goes, there is no longer any value in human being's living on the earth. – What, therefore, should one think of the proposal to preserve the life of a criminal sentenced to death if he agrees to let dangerous experiments be made on him and is lucky enough to survive them, so that in this way physicians learn something new of benefit to the commonwealth? A court would reject with contempt such a proposal from a medical college, for justice ceases to be justice if it can be bought for any price whatsoever.

But what kind and what amount of punishment is it that public justice makes its principle and measure? None other than the principle of equality (in the position of the needle on the scale of justice), to incline no more to one side than to the other. Accordingly, whatever undeserved evil you inflict upon another within the people, that you inflict upon yourself. If you insult him, you insult yourself; if you steal from him, you steal from yourself; if you strike him, you strike yourself; if you kill him, you kill yourself. But only the *law of retribution* (*ius talionis*) – it being understood, of course, that this is applied by a court (not by your private judgment) – can specify definitely the quality and the quantity of punishment; all other principles are fluctuating and unsuited for a sentence of pure and strict justice because extraneous considerations are mixed into them. – Now it would indeed seem that differences in social rank would not allow the principle of retribution, of like for like,[y] but even when this is not possible

---

[y] *Gleiches mit Gleichem*

in terms of the letter, the principle can always remain valid in terms of its effect if account is taken of the sensibilities of the upper classes. – A fine, for example, imposed for a verbal injury has no relation to the offense, for someone wealthy might indeed allow himself to indulge in a verbal insult on some occasion; yet the outrage he has done to someone's love of honor can still be quite similar to the hurt done to his pride if he is constrained by judgment and right not only to apologize publicly to the one he has insulted but also to kiss his hand, for instance, even though he is of a lower class. Similarly, someone of high standing given to violence could be condemned not only to apologize for striking an innocent citizen socially inferior to himself but also to undergo a solitary confinement involving hardship; in addition to the discomfort he undergoes, the offender's vanity would be painfully affected, so that through his shame like would be fittingly repaid with like. – But what does it mean to say, "If you steal from someone, you steal from yourself"? Whoever steals makes the property of everyone else insecure and therefore deprives himself (by the principle of retribution) of security in any possible property. He has nothing and can also acquire nothing; but he still wants to live, and this is now possible only if others provide for him. But since the state will not provide for him free of charge, he must let it have his powers for any kind of work it pleases (in convict or prison labor) and is reduced to the status of a slave for a certain time, or permanently if the state sees fit. – If, however, he has committed murder he must *die*. Here there is no substitute that will satisfy justice. There is no *similarity* between life, however wretched it may be, and death, hence no likeness between the crime and the retribution unless death is judicially carried out upon the wrongdoer, although it must still be freed from any mistreatment that could make the humanity in the person suffering it into something abominable. – Even if a civil society were to be dissolved by the consent of all its members (e.g., if a people inhabiting an island decided to separate and disperse throughout the world), the last murderer remaining in prison would first have to be executed, so that each has done to him what his deeds deserve and blood guilt does not cling to the people for not having insisted upon this punishment; for otherwise the people can be regarded as collaborators in this public violation of justice.

This fitting of punishment to the crime, which can occur only by a judge imposing the death sentence in accordance with the strict law of retribution, is shown by the fact that only by this is a sentence of death pronounced on every criminal in proportion to his *inner wickedness* (even when the crime is not murder but another crime against the state that can be paid for only by death). – Suppose that some (such as Balmerino[29] and others) who took part in the recent Scottish rebellion believed that by their uprising they were only performing a duty they owed the House of Stuart, while others on the contrary were out for their private interests;

and suppose that the judgment pronounced by the highest court had been that each is free to make the choice between death and convict labor. I say that in this case the man of honor would choose death, and the scoundrel convict labor. This comes along with the nature of the human mind; for the man of honor is acquainted with something that he values even more highly than life, namely *honor*, while the scoundrel considers it better to live in shame than not to live at all (*animam praeferre pudori. Iuven.*).[z] Since the man of honor is undeniably less deserving of punishment than the other, both would be punished quite proportionately if all alike were sentenced to death; the man of honor would be punished mildly in terms of his sensibilities and the scoundrel severely in terms of his. On the other hand, if both were sentenced to convict labor the man of honor would be punished too severely and the other too mildly for his vile action. And so here too, when sentence is pronounced on a number of criminals united in a plot, the best equalizer before justice is *death*. – Moreover, one has never heard of anyone who was sentenced to death for murder complaining that he was dealt with too severely and therefore wronged; everyone would laugh in his face if he said this. – If his complaint were justified it would have to be assumed that even though no wrong is done to the criminal in accordance with the law, the legislative authority of the state is still not authorized to inflict this kind of punishment and that, if it does so, it would be in contradiction with itself.

6:334

Accordingly, every murderer – anyone who commits murder, orders it, or is an accomplice in it – must suffer death; this is what justice, as the idea of judicial authority, wills in accordance with universal laws that are grounded a priori. – If, however, the number of accomplices (*correi*) to such a deed is so great that the state, in order to have no such criminals in it, could soon find itself without subjects; and if the state still does not want to dissolve, that is, to pass over into the state of nature, which is far worse because there is no external justice at all in it (and if it especially does not want to dull the people's feeling by the spectacle of a slaughterhouse), then the sovereign must also have it in his power, in this case of necessity (*casus necessitatis*), to assume the role of judge (to represent him) and pronounce a judgment that decrees for the criminals a sentence other than capital punishment, such as deportation, which still preserves the population.[30] This cannot be done in accordance with public law but it can be done by an executive decree that is, by an act of the right of majesty which, as clemency, can always be exercised only in individual cases.

In opposition to this the Marchese Beccaria,[31] moved by overly compassionate feelings of an affected humanity (*compassibilitas*), has put forward his assertion that any capital punishment is wrongful because it could not be contained in the original civil contract; for if it were, everyone in a

6:335

---

[z] "Preferring a life of shame," Juvenal *Satires* 3.8.83.

people would have to have consented to lose his life in case he murdered someone else (in the people), whereas it is impossible for anyone to consent to this because no one can dispose of his own life. This is all sophistry and juristic trickery.

No one suffers punishment because he has willed *it* but because he has willed a *punishable action;* for it is no punishment if what is done to someone is what he wills, and it is impossible *to will* to be punished. – Saying that I will to be punished if I murder someone is saying nothing more than that I subject myself together with everyone else to the laws, which will naturally also be penal laws if there are any criminals among the people. As a colegislator in dictating the *penal law,* I cannot possibly be the same person who, as a subject, is punished in accordance with the law; for as one who is punished, namely as a criminal, I cannot possibly have a voice in legislation (the legislator is holy). Consequently, when I draw up a penal law against myself as a criminal, it is pure reason in me (*homo noumenon*), legislating with regard to rights, which subjects me, as someone capable of crime and so as another person (*homo phaenomenon*), to the penal law, together with all others in a civil union. In other words, it is not the people (each individual in it) that dictates capital punishment but rather the court (public justice), and so another than the criminal; and the social contract contains no promise to let oneself be punished and so to dispose of oneself and one's life. For, if the authorization to punish had to be based on the offender's *promise,* on his *willing* to let himself be punished, it would also have to be left to him to find himself punishable and the criminal would be his own judge. – The chief point of error (πρωτον ψευδος) in this sophistry consists in its confusing the criminal's own judgment (which must necessarily be ascribed to his *reason*) that he has to forfeit his life with a resolve on the part of his *will* to take his own life, and so in representing as united in one and the same person the judgment upon a right[a] and the realization of that right.[b]

There are, however, two crimes deserving of death, with regard to which it still remains doubtful whether *legislation* is also authorized to impose the death penalty. The feeling of honor leads to both, in one case the *honor of one's sex,* in the other *military honor,* and indeed true honor, which is incumbent as duty on each of these two classes of people. The one crime is a mother's *murder of her child (infanticidium maternale)*; the other is *murdering a fellow soldier (commilitonicidium)* in a *duel.* – Legislation cannot remove the disgrace of an illegitimate birth any more than it can wipe away the stain of suspicion of cowardice from a subordinate officer who fails to respond to a humiliating affront with a force of his own rising above fear of death. So it seems that in these two cases people find themselves in the state of nature, and that these acts of *killing (homocidium),* which would then not have to be

[a] *Rechtsbeurteilung*
[b] *Rechtsvollziehung*

called murder (*homocidium dolosum*), are certainly punishable but cannot be punished with death by the supreme power. A child that comes into the world apart from marriage is born outside the law (for the law is marriage) and therefore outside the protection of the law. It has, as it were, stolen into the commonwealth (like contraband merchandise), so that the commonwealth can ignore its existence (since it was not right[c] that it should have come to exist in this way), and can therefore also ignore its annihilation; and no decree can remove the mother's shame when it becomes known that she gave birth without being married. – So too, when a junior officer is insulted he sees himself constrained by the public opinion of the other members of his estate to obtain satisfaction for himself and, as in the state of nature, *punishment* of the offender not by law, taking him before a court, but by a *duel*, in which he exposes himself to death in order to prove his military courage, upon which the honor of his estate essentially rests. Even if the duel should involve *killing* his opponent, the killing that occurs in this fight which takes place in public and with the consent of both parties, though reluctantly, cannot strictly be called *murder* (*homocidium dolosum*). – What, now, is to be laid down as right in both cases (coming under criminal justice)? – Here penal justice finds itself very much in a quandary. Either it must declare by law that the concept of honor (which is here no illusion) counts for nothing and so punish with death, or else it must remove from the crime the capital punishment appropriate to it, and so be either cruel or indulgent. The knot can be undone in the following way: the categorical imperative of penal justice remains (unlawful killing of another must be punished by death); but the legislation itself (and consequently also the civil constitution), as long as it remains barbarous and undeveloped, is responsible for the discrepancy between the incentives of honor in the people (subjectively) and the measures that are (objectively) suitable for its purposes. So the public justice arising from the state becomes an *injustice* from the perspective of the justice arising from the people.

II.

Of all the rights of a sovereign, the *right to grant clemency* to a criminal (*ius aggratiandi*), either by lessening or entirely remitting punishment, is the slipperiest one for him to exercise; for it must be exercised in such a way as to show the splendor of his majesty, although he is thereby doing injustice in the highest degree. – With regard to crimes of *subjects* against one another it is absolutely not for him to exercise it; for here failure to punish (*impunitas criminis*) is the greatest wrong against his subjects. He can make use of it, therefore, only in case of a wrong done *to himself*

---

[c] *billig*

(*crimen laesae maiestatis*). But he cannot make use of it even then if his failure to punish could endanger the people's security. – This right is the only one that deserves to be called the right of majesty.

On the relation with regard to rights of a citizen to his native land and to foreign countries.

§ 50.

A *country* (*territorium*) whose inhabitants are citizens of it simply by its constitution, without their having to perform any special act to establish the right (and so are citizens by birth), is called their *native land*. A country of which they are not citizens apart from this condition is called a foreign *country*. If a foreign country forms part of a larger realm it is called a *province* (in the sense in which the Romans used this word), which must respect the land of the state that rules it as the *mother country* (*regio domina*); for a province is not an integral part of the realm (*imperii*), a place of *residence* for fellow-citizens, but only a possession of it, a *secondary house*[d] for them.

1) *A subject* (regarded also as a citizen) has the right to emigrate, for the state could not hold him back as its property. But he can take out of it with him only his movable belongings, not his fixed belongings, as he would be doing if he were authorized to sell the land he previously possessed and take with him the money he got for it.

2) The *lord of the land* has the right to encourage *immigration* and settling by foreigners (colonists), even though his native subjects might look askance at this, provided that their private ownership of land is not curtailed by it.

3) He also has the right to *banish* a subject to a province outside the country, where he will not enjoy any of the rights of a citizen, that is, to *deport* him, if he has committed a crime that makes it harmful to the state for his fellow citizens to associate with him.

4) He also has the right to *exile* him altogether (*ius exilii*), to send him out into the wide world, that is, entirely outside his country (in Old German, this is called *Elend* [misery]). Since the lord of the land then withdraws all protection from him, this amounts to making him an outlaw within his boundaries.

---

[d] *Unterhauses*. Some editors suggest that this is a typographical error for *Untertans*, in which case the phrase would mean only that the mother country possesses the province as a subject. If *Unterhauses* is not a typographical error, Kant may mean that the citizens of the mother country are not, by birth, citizens of the province of the ruling state. See 6:338 and 6:348. A province is a "foreign country" (*Ausland*), as far as the "mother country" or ruling state is concerned.

§ 51.

The three authorities in a state, which arise from the concept of a *commonwealth* as such (*res publica latius dicta*), are only the three relations of the united will of the people, which is derived a priori from reason. They are a pure idea of a head of state, which has objective practical reality. But this head of state (the sovereign) is only a *thought-entity* (to represent the entire people) as long as there is no physical person to represent the supreme authority in the state and to make this idea effective on the people's will. Now, the relation of this physical person to the people's will can be thought of in three different ways: either that *one* in the state has command over all; or that *several*, equal among themselves, are united in command over all the others; or that *all* together have command over each and so over themselves as well. In other words, the *form of a state* is either *autocratic, aristocratic* or *democratic*. (The expression *monarchical*, in place of *autocratic*, is not suitable for the concept intended here; for a *monarch* is one who has the *highest* authority, whereas an *autocrat*, who *rules by himself*, has *all* the authority. The autocrat is the sovereign, whereas the monarch merely represents the sovereign.) – It is easy to see that the autocratic form of state is the *simplest*, namely the relation of one (the king) to the people, so that only one is legislator. The aristocratic form of state is already *composed* of two relations: the relation of the nobility (as legislator) to one another, to constitute the sovereign, and then the relation of this sovereign to the people. But the democratic form of state is the most composite of all, since it involves the following relations: first, it unites the will of all to form a people; then it unites the will of the citizens to form a commonwealth; then it sets this *sovereign*, which is itself the united will of the citizens, over the commonwealth.* It is true that, with regard to the administration of right within a state, the simplest form is also the best. With regard to right itself, however, this form of state is the most dangerous for a people, in view of how conducive it is to despotism. It is indeed the most reasonable maxim to simplify the mechanism of unifying a nation by coercive laws, that is, when all the members of the nation are passive and obey *one* who is over them; but in that case none who are subjects are also *citizens of the state*. As for the consolation with which the people is supposed to be content – that monarchy (strictly speaking here, autocracy) is the best constitution *when the monarch is good* (i.e., when he not only intends what is good but also has insight into it) – this is one of those wise remarks that are tautologous. It says nothing more than that the best constitution is the one by which the administrator of the state is made into the best ruler, that is, that the best constitution is that which is best.

---

* I shall not mention the adulterations of these forms that arise from invasion by powerful unauthorized people (*oligarchy* and *ochlocracy*), or the so-called mixed constitutions, since this would take us too far afield.

§ 52.

It is *futile* to inquire into the *historical documentation*ᵉ of the mechanism of government, that is, one cannot reach back to the time at which civil society began (for savages draw up no record of their submission to law; besides, we can already gather from the nature of uncivilized human beings that they were originally subjected to it by force). But it is *culpable* to undertake this inquiry with a view to possibly changing by force the constitution that now exists. For this transformation would have to take place by the people acting as a mob, not by legislation; but insurrection in a constitution that already exists overthrows all civil rightful relations and therefore all right, that is, it is not change in the civil constitution but dissolution of it. The transition to a better constitution is not then a metamorphosis but a palingenesis, which requires a new social contract on which the previous one (now annulled) has no effect. – But it must still be possible, if the existing constitution cannot well be reconciled with the idea of the original contract, for the sovereign to change it, so as to allow to continue in existence that form which is essentially required for a people to constitute a state. Now this change cannot consist in a state's reorganizing itself from one of the three forms into another, as, for example, aristocrats agreeing to submit to autocracy or deciding to merge into a democracy, or the reverse, as if it rested on the sovereign's free choiceᶠ and discretion which kind of constitution it would subject the people to. For even if the sovereign decided to transform itself into a democracy, it could still do the people a wrong, since the people itself could abhor such a constitution and find one of the other forms more to its advantage.

The different forms of states are only the *letter* (*littera*) of the original legislation in the civil state, and they may therefore remain as long as they are taken, by old and long-standing custom (and so only subjectively), to belong necessarily to the machinery of the constitution. But the *spirit* of the original contract (*anima pacti originarii*) involves an obligation on the part of the constituting authority to make the *kind of government* suited to the idea of the original contract. Accordingly, even if this cannot be done all at once, it is under obligation to change the kind of government gradually and continually so that it harmonizes *in its effect* with the only constitution that accords with right, that of a pure republic, in such a way that the old (empirical) statutory forms, which served merely to bring about the *submission* of the people, are replaced by the original (rational) form, the only form which makes *freedom* the principle and indeed the condition for any exercise of *coercion*, as is required by a rightful constitution of a state in the strict sense of the word. Only it will finally lead to what is literally a state. – This is the only constitution of a state that lasts, the constitution in which

ᵉ *Geschichtsurkunde*
ᶠ *freien Wahl*

law itself rules and depends on no particular person. It is the final end of all public right, the only condition in which each can be assigned *conclusively* what is his; on the other hand, so long as those other forms of state are supposed to represent literally just so many different moral persons invested with supreme authority, no absolutely rightful condition of civil society can be acknowledged, but only *provisional* right within it.

Any true republic is and can only be a *system representing* the people, in order to protect its rights in its name, by all the citizens united and acting through their delegates (deputies). But as soon as a person who is head of state (whether it be a king, nobility, or the whole of the population, the democratic union) also lets itself be represented, then the united people does not merely *represent* the sovereign: it *is* the sovereign itself. For in it (the people) is originally found the supreme authority from which all rights of individuals as mere subjects (and in any event as officials of the state) must be derived; and a republic, once established, no longer has to let the reins of government out of its hands and give them over again to those who previously held them and could again nullify all new institutions by their absolute choice.

A powerful ruler in our time[32] therefore made a very serious error in judgment when, to extricate himself from he embarrassment of large state debts, he left it to the people to take this burden on itself and distribute it as it saw fit; for then the legislative authority naturally came into the people's hands, not only with regard to the taxation of subjects but also with regard to the government, namely to prevent it from incurring new debts by extravagance or war. The consequence was that the monarch's sovereignty[g] wholly disappeared (it was not merely suspended) and passed to the people, to whose legislative will the belongings of every subject became subjected. Nor can it be said that in this case one must assume a tacit but still contractual promise of the National Assembly not to make itself the sovereign but only to administer this business of the sovereign and, having attended to it, return the reins of government into the monarch's hands; for such a contract is in itself null and void. The right of supreme legislation in a commonwealth is not an alienable right but the most personal of all rights. Whoever has it can control the people only through the collective will of the people; he cannot control the collective will itself, which is the ultimate basis of any public contract. A contract that would impose obligation on the people to give back its authority would not be incumbent upon the people as the legislative power, yet would still be binding upon it; and this is a contradiction, in accordance with the saying "No one can serve two masters."[h]

6:342

[g] *Herrschergewalt*
[h] Matthew 6:24

Public right
Section II.
The right of nations.

§ 53.

As natives of a country, those who constitute a nation can be looked upon analogously to descendants of the same *ancestors* (*congeniti*) even though they are not. Yet in an intellectual sense and from the perspective of rights, since they are born of the same mother (the republic) they constitute as it were one family (*gens, natio*), whose members (citizens of the state) are of equally high birth and do not mix with those who may live near them in a state of nature, whom they regard as inferior; the latter (savages), however, for their own part consider themselves superior because of the lawless freedom they have chosen, even though they do not constitute states but only tribes. The right of *states* in relation to one another (which in German is called, not quite correctly, the *right of nations*, but should instead be called the right of states, *ius publicum civitatum*) is what we have to consider under the title the right of nations. Here a state, as a moral person, is considered as living in relation to another state in the condition of natural freedom and therefore in a condition of constant war. The rights of states consist, therefore, partly of their right *to go to* war, partly of their right *in* war, and partly of their right to constrain each other to leave this condition of war and so form a constitution that will establish lasting peace, that is, its right *after* war. In this problem the only difference between the state of nature of individual human beings and of families (in relation to one another) and that of nations is that in the right of nations we have to take into consideration not only the relation of one state toward another as a whole, but also the relation of individual persons of one state toward the individuals of another, as well as toward another state as a whole. But this difference from the rights of individuals in a state of nature makes it necessary to consider only such features as can be readily inferred from the concept of a state of nature.

§ 54.

The elements of the right of nations are these: 1) states, considered in external relation to one another, are (like lawless savages) by nature in a nonrightful condition. 2) This nonrightful condition is a *condition* of war (of the right of the stronger), even if it is not a condition of actual war and actual attacks being constantly made (hostilities). Although no state is wronged by another in this condition (insofar as neither wants anything better), this condition is in itself still wrong in the highest degree, and states neighboring upon one another are under obligation to leave it. 3) A league of nations in accordance with the idea of an original social contract is necessary, not in order to meddle in one another's internal dissensions but to protect against attacks from without. 4) This alliance must, however, involve no sovereign authority (as in a civil constitution), but only an *association* (federation); it must be an alliance that can be renounced at any time and so must be renewed from time to time. This is a right *in subsidium* of another and original right, to avoid getting involved in a state of actual war among the other members (*foedus Amphictyonum*).33

§ 55.

As regards the original right that free states in a state of nature have to go to war with one another (in order, perhaps, to establish a condition more closely approaching a rightful condition), the first question that arises is: what right has a state *against its own subjects* to use them for war against other states, to expend their goods and even their lives in it, or to put them at risk, in such a way that whether they shall go to war does not depend on their own judgment, but they may be sent into it by the supreme command of the sovereign?

It might seem that this right can be easily proved, namely from the right to do what one wants with what belongs to one (one's property). Anyone has an incontestable property in anything the substance of which he has himself *made*. – What follows, then, is the deduction, as a mere jurist would draw it up.

There are various *natural products* in a country that must still be considered *artifacts* (*artefacta*) of the state as far as the *abundance* of natural products of a certain kind is concerned, since the country would not have yielded them in such abundance had there not been a state and an orderly, powerful government, but the inhabitants had been in a state of nature. – Whether from lack of food or from the presence of predatory animals in the country where I live, hens (the most useful kind of fowl), sheep, swine, cattle and so forth would either not exist at all or at best would be scarce unless there were a government in this country, which secures the inhabitants in what they acquire and possess. – This holds true of the human population as well, which can only be small, as it is in the American wilderness, even if we attribute to these people the greatest industry (which they do not have). The inhabitants would be very scarce since they could not take their attendants and spread out on a land that is always in danger of being laid waste by men or by wild and predatory beasts. There would therefore not be adequate sustenance for such a great abundance of human beings as now live in a country. – Now just as we say that since vegetables (e.g., potatoes) and domestic animals are, as regards their abundance, a human *product*, which he can use, wear out or destroy (kill), it seems we can also say that since most of his subjects are his own product, the supreme authority in a state, the sovereign, has the right to lead them into war as he would take them on a hunt, and into battles as on a pleasure trip.

While such an argument for this right (which may well be present obscurely in the monarch's mind) holds with regard to animals, which can be one's *property*, it simply cannot be applied to human beings, especially as citizens of a state. For they must always be regarded as colegislating members of a state (not merely as means, but also as ends in themselves), and must therefore give their free assent, through their representatives, not only to waging war in general but also to each particular declaration of war. Only under this limiting condition can a state direct them to serve in a way full of danger to them.

We shall therefore have to derive this right from the *duty* of the sovereign to the people (not the reverse); and for this to be the case the people will have to be regarded as having given its vote to go to war. In this capacity it is, although passive (letting itself be disposed of), also active and represents the sovereign itself.

§ 56.

In the state of nature among states, the *right to go to war* (to engage in hostilities) is the way in which a state is permitted to prosecute its right against another state, namely by its own *force*, when it believes it has been wronged by the other state; for this cannot be done in the state of nature by a lawsuit (the only means by which disputes are settled in a rightful condition). – In addition to active violations (first aggression, which is not the same as first hostility) it may be *threatened*. This includes another state's being the first to undertake *preparations*, upon which is based the right of *prevention* (*ius praeventionis*), or even just the *menacing* increase in another state's *power* (by its acquisition of territory) (*potentia tremenda*).[i] This is a wrong to the lesser power merely by the *condition* of the *superior power*, before any deed on its part, and in the state of nature an attack by the lesser power is indeed legitimate.[34] Accordingly, this is also the basis of the right to a balance of power among all states that are contiguous and could act on one another.

As for *active violations* which give a *right to go to war*, these include *acts of retaliation* (*retorsio*), a state's taking it upon itself to obtain satisfaction for an offense committed against its people by the people of another state, instead of seeking compensation (by peaceful methods) from the other state. In terms of formalities, this resembles starting a war without first renouncing peace (without a *declaration of war*); for if one wants to find a right in a condition of war, something analogous to a contract must be assumed, namely, *acceptance* of the declaration of the other party that both want to seek their right in this way.

---

[i] awesome power

§ 57. 6:347

The greatest difficulty in the right of nations has to do precisely with right during a war; it is difficult even to form a concept of this or to think of law in this lawless state without contradicting oneself (*inter arma silent leges*).ʲ Right during a war would, then, have to be the waging of war in accordance with principles that always leave open the possibility of leaving the state of nature among states (in external relation to one another) and entering a rightful condition.

No war of independent states against each other can be a *punitive war* (*bellum punitivum*). For punishment occurs only in the relation of a superior (*imperantis*) to those subject to him (*subditum*), and states do not stand in that relation to each other. – Nor, again, can any war be either a *war of extermination* (*bellum internecinum*) or of *subjugation* (*bellum subiugatorium*), which would be the moral annihilation of a state (the people of which would either become merged in one mass with that of the conqueror or reduced to servitude).ᵏ The reason there cannot be a war of subjugation is not that this extreme measure a state might use to achieve a condition of peace would in itself contradict the right of a state; it is rather that the idea of the right of nations involves only the concept of an antagonism in accordance with principles of outer freedom by which each can preserve what belongs to it, but not a way of acquiring, by which one state's increase of power could threaten others.

A state against which war is being waged is permitted to use any means of defense except those that would make its subjects unfit to be citizens; for it would then also make itself unfit to qualify, in accordance with the right of nations, as a person in the relation of states (as one who would enjoy the same rights as others). Means of defense that are not permitted include: using its own subjects as spies; using them or even foreigners as assassins or poisoners (among whom so-called snipers, who lie in wait to ambush individuals, might well be classed); or using them merely for spreading false reports – in a word, using such underhanded means as would destroy the trust requisite to establishing a lasting peace in the future.

In war it is permissible to exact supplies and contributions from a 6:348 defeated enemy, but not to plunder the people, that is, not to force individual persons to give up their belongings (for that would be robbery, since it was not the conquered people that waged the war; rather, the state under whose rule they lived waged the war *through the people*). Instead, receipts should be issued for everything requisitioned, so that in the peace that follows the burden imposed on the country or province can be divided proportionately.

ʲ In time of war the laws are silent. Cicero *Pro Milone* 4.10.
ᵏ *Knechtschaft*

§ 58.

The right of a state *after a war*, that is, at the time of the peace treaty and with a view to its consequences, consists in this: the victor lays down the conditions on which it will come to an agreement with the vanquished and hold *negotiations* for concluding peace. The victor does not do this from any right he pretends to have because of the wrong his opponent is supposed to have done him; instead, he lets this question drop and relies on his own force. The victor can therefore not propose compensation for the costs of the war since he would then have to admit that his opponent had fought an unjust war. While he may well think of this argument he still cannot use it, since he would then be saying that he had been waging a punitive war and so, for his own part, committing an offense against the vanquished. Rights after a war also include a right to an exchange of prisoners (without ransom), without regard for their being equal in number.

A defeated state or its subjects do not lose their civil freedom through the conquest of their country, so that the state would be degraded to a colony and its subjects to bondage; for if they did the war would have been a *punitive war*, which is self-contradictory. – A *colony* or province is a people that indeed has its own constitution, its own legislation, and its own land, on which those who belong to another state are only foreigners even though this other state has supreme *executive* authority over the colony or province. – The state having that executive authority is called the *mother state*, and the daughter state, though ruled by it, still governs itself (by its own parliament, possibly with a viceroy presiding over it) (*civitas hybrida*).[1] This was the relation Athens had with respect to various islands and that Great Britain now has with regard to Ireland.

Still less can *bondage* and its legitimacy be derived from a people's being overcome in war, since for this one would have to admit that a war could be punitive. Least of all can hereditary bondage be derived from it; hereditary bondage as such is absurd since guilt from someone's crime cannot be inherited.

The concept of a peace treaty already contains the provision that an *amnesty* goes along with it.

§ 59.

The right to peace is 1) the right to be at peace when there is a war in the vicinity, or the right to *neutrality*; 2) the right to be assured of the continuance of a peace that has been concluded, that is, the right to a *guarantee*; 3) the right to an *alliance* (confederation) of several states for their common *defense* against any external or internal attacks, but not a league for attacking others and adding to their own territory.

---

[1] hybrid state

§ 60.

There are no limits to the rights of a state against an *unjust enemy* (no limits with respect to quantity or degree, though there are limits with respect to quality); that is to say, an injured state may not use *any* means *whatever* but may use those means that are allowable to any degree that it is able to, in order to maintain what belongs to it. – But what is an *unjust enemy* in terms of the concepts of the right of nations, in which – as is the case in a state of nature generally – each state is judge in its own case? It is an enemy whose publicly expressed will (whether by word or deed) reveals a maxim by which, if it were made a universal rule, any condition of peace among nations would be impossible and, instead, a state of nature would be perpetuated. Violation of public contracts is an expression of this sort. Since this can be assumed to be a matter of concern to all nations whose freedom is threatened by it, they are called upon to unite against such misconduct in order to deprive the state of its power to do it. But they are not called upon *to divide its territory among themselves* and to make the state, as it were, disappear from the earth, since that would be an injustice against its people, which cannot lose its original right to unite itself into a commonwealth, though it can be made to adopt a new constitution that by its nature will be unfavorable to the inclination of war.

It is *pleonastic*, however, to speak of an unjust enemy in a state of nature; for a state of nature is itself a condition of injustice. A just enemy would be one that I would be doing wrong by resisting; but then he would also not be my enemy.

6:350

§ 61.

Since a state of nature among nations, like a state of nature among individual human beings, is a condition that one ought to leave in order to enter a lawful condition, before this happens any rights of nations, and anything external that is mine or yours which states can acquire or retain by war, are merely *provisional*. Only in a universal *association of states* (analogous to that by which a people becomes a state) can rights come to hold *conclusively* and a true *condition of peace* come about. But if such a state made up of nations were to extend too far over vast regions, governing it and so too protecting each of its members would finally have to become impossible, while several such corporations would again bring on a state of war. So *perpetual peace*, the ultimate goal of the whole right of nations, is indeed an unachievable idea. Still, the political principles directed toward perpetual peace, of entering into such alliances of states, which serve for continual *approximation* to it, are not unachievable. Instead, since continual approximation to it is a task based on duty and therefore on the right of human beings and of states, this can certainly be achieved.

Such an *association* of several *states* to preserve peace can be called a *permanent congress of states*, which each neighboring state is at liberty to join. Something of this kind took place (at least as regards the formalities of the right of nations for the sake of keeping the peace) in the first half of the present century, in the assembly of the States General at the Hague. The ministers of most of the courts of Europe and even of the smallest republics lodged with it their complaints about attacks being made on one of them by another. In this way they thought of the whole of Europe as a single confederated state which they accepted as arbiter, so to speak, in their public disputes. But later, instead of this, the right of nations survived only in books; it disappeared from cabinets or else, after force had already been used, was relegated in the form of a deduction to the obscurity of archives.

By a *congress* is here understood only a voluntary[m] coalition of different states which can be *dissolved* at any time, not a federation (like that of the American states) which is based on a constitution and can therefore not be dissolved. – Only by such a congress can the idea of a public right of nations be realized, one to be established for deciding their disputes in a civil way, as if by a lawsuit, rather than in a barbaric way (the way of savages), namely by war.

[m] *willkürliche*

Public right
Section III.
Cosmopolitan right.35

§ 62.

This rational idea of a *peaceful*, even if not friendly, thoroughgoing community of all nations on the earth that can come into relations affecting one another is not a philanthropic (ethical) principle but a principle *having to do with rights*. Nature has enclosed them all together within determinate limits (by the spherical shape of the place they live in, a *globus terraqueus*)." And since possession of the land, on which an inhabitant of the earth can live, can be thought only as possession of a part of a determinate whole, and so as possession of that to which each of them originally has a right, it follows that all nations stand *originally* in a community of land, though not of *rightful* community of possession (*communio*) and so of use of it, or of property in it; instead they stand in a community of possible physical *interaction* (*commercium*), that is, in a thoroughgoing relation of each to all the others of *offering to engage in commerce* with any other,° and each has a right to make this attempt without the other being authorized to behave toward it as an enemy because it has made this attempt. – This right, since it has to do with the possible union of all nations with a view to certain universal laws for their possible commerce, can be called *cosmopolitan right* (*ius cosmopoliticum*).

Although the seas might seem to remove nations from any community with one another, they are the arrangements of nature most favoring their commerce by means of navigation; and the more *coastlines* these nations have in the vicinity of one another (as in the Mediterranean), the more lively their commerce can be. However, visiting these coasts, and still more settling there to connect them with the mother country, provides the occasion for troubles and acts of violence in one place on our globe to be felt all over it. Yet this possible abuse cannot annul the right of citizens of the world *to try to* establish community with all and, to this end, to *visit* all regions of the earth. This is not, however, a right to *make a settlement* on the land of another nation (*ius incolatus*);*ᵖ* for this, a specific contract is required.

The question arises, however: in newly discovered lands, may a nation undertake to *settle* (*accolatus*)*ᵍ* and take possession in the neighborhood of a people that has already settled in the region, even without its consent?

" globe of earth and water
° Kant moves between *Wechselwirkung*, i.e., interaction, intercourse, or "commerce" in a very general sense, and *Verkehr*, which he used in his discussion of contracts to signify exchange of property, "commerce" in a more specific sense.
ᵖ right to inhabit
ᵍ dwell near, as a neighbor

If the settlement is made so far from where that people resides that there is no encroachment on anyone's use of his land, the right to settle is not open to doubt. But if these people are shepherds or hunters (like the Hottentots, the Tungusi, or most of the American Indian nations) who depend for their sustenance on great open regions, this settlement may not take place by force but only by contract, and indeed by a contract that does not take advantage of the ignorance of those inhabitants with respect to ceding their lands. This is true despite the fact that sufficient specious reasons to justify the use of force are available: that it is to the world's advantage, partly because these crude peoples will become civilized (this is like the pretext by which even Büsching[36] tries to excuse the bloody introduction of Christianity into Germany), and partly because one's own country will be cleaned of corrupt men, and they or their descendants will, it is hoped, become better in another part of the world (such as New Holland). But all these supposedly good intentions cannot wash away the stain of injustice in the means used for them. Someone may reply that such scruples about using force in the beginning, in order to establish a lawful condition, might well mean that the whole earth would still be in a lawless condition; but this consideration can no more annul that condition of right[r] than can the pretext of revolutionaries within a state, that when constitutions are bad it is up to the people to reshape them by force and to be unjust once and for all so that afterwards they can establish justice all the more securely and make it flourish.

Conclusion

If someone cannot prove that a thing is, he can try to prove that it is not. If (as often happens) he cannot succeed in either, he can still ask whether he has any *interest* in assuming one or the other (as an hypothesis), either from a theoretical or from a practical point of view. An assumption is adopted from a theoretical point of view in order merely to explain a certain phenomenon (such as, for astronomers, the retrograde motion and stationary state of the planets). An assumption is adopted from a practical point of view in order to achieve a certain end, which may be either a *pragmatic* (merely technical end)[s] or a *moral* end, that is, an end such that the maxim of adopting it is itself a duty. — Now it is evident that what would be made our duty in this case is not the *assumption* (*suppositio*) that this end can be realized, which would be a judgment about it that is merely theoretical and, moreover, problematic; for there can be no obligation to do this (to believe something). What is incumbent upon us as a

---

[r] *Rechtsbedingung*
[s] *Kunstzweck*

duty is rather to act in conformity with the idea of that end, even if there is not the slightest theoretical likelihood that it can be realized, as long as its impossibility cannot be demonstrated either.

Now morally practical reason pronounces in us its irresistible *veto: there is to be no war*, neither war between you and me in the state of nature nor war between us as states, which, although they are internally in a lawful condition, are still externally (in relation to one another) in a lawless condition; for war is not the way in which everyone should seek his rights. So the question is no longer whether perpetual peace is something real or a fiction, and whether we are not deceiving ourselves in our theoretical judgment when we assume that it is real. Instead, we must act as if it is something real, though perhaps it is not; we must work toward establishing perpetual peace and the kind of constitution that seems to us most conducive to it (say, a republicanism of all states, together and separately) in order to bring about perpetual peace and put an end to the heinous waging of war, to which as their chief aim all states without exception have hitherto directed their internal arrangements. And even if the complete realization of this objective always remains a pious wish, still we are certainly not deceiving ourselves in adopting the maxim of working incessantly toward it. For this is our duty, and to admit that the moral law within us is itself deceptive would call forth in us the wish, which arouses our abhorrence, rather to be rid of all reason and to regard ourselves as thrown by one's principles into the same mechanism of nature as all the other species of animals.

6:355

It can be said that establishing universal and lasting peace constitutes not merely a part of the doctrine of right but rather the entire final end of the doctrine of right within the limits of mere reason; for the condition of peace is alone that condition in which what is mine and what is yours for a multitude of human beings is secured under *laws* living in proximity to one another, hence those who are united under a constitution; but the rule for this constitution, as a norm for others, cannot be derived from the experience of those who have hitherto found it most to their advantage; it must, rather, be derived a priori by reason from the ideal of a rightful association of human beings under public laws as such. For all examples (which only illustrate but cannot prove anything) are treacherous, so that they certainly require a metaphysics. Even those who ridicule metaphysics admit its necessity, though carelessly, when they say for example, as they often do, "the best constitution is that in which power belongs not to human beings but to the laws." For what can be more metaphysically sublimated than this very idea, which even according to their own assertion has the most confirmed objective reality, as can also be easily shown in actually occurring cases? The attempt to realize this idea should not be made by way of revolution, by a leap, that is, by violent overthrow of an already existing defective constitution (for there would then be an intervening moment in which any rightful condition would be annihilated). But if it is attempted and carried out by gradual reform in accordance with firm principles, it can lead to continual approximation to the highest political good, perpetual peace.

Appendix
Explanatory remarks
on
The metaphysical first principles of the doctrine of right

I take the occasion for these remarks chiefly from the review of this book in the *Göttingen Journal* (No.28, 18 Feb. 1797).[37] In this review the book was examined with insight and rigor, but also with appreciation and "the hope that those first principles will be a lasting gain for the science." I shall use this review as a guide for my criticism as well as for some elaboration of this system.

My astute critic takes exception to a definition at the very beginning of the *Introduction* to the *Doctrine of Right*. What is meant by the faculty of desire? It is, the text says, the capacity[t] to be by means of one's representations the cause of the objects of these representations. – To this exposition he objects "that it comes to nothing as soon as one abstracts from the *external* conditions of the result of desire. – But the faculty of desire is something even for an idealist, even though the external world is nothing for him." *I reply:* but are there not also intense but still consciously futile longings (e.g., Would to God that man were still alive!), which are *devoid of any deed* but not *devoid of any result*, since they still work powerfully within the subject himself (make him ill), though not on external things? A desire, as a *striving* (*nisus*) to be a *cause* by means of one's representations, is still always causality, at least within the subject, even when he sees the inadequacy of his representations for the effect he envisages. – The misunderstanding here amounts to this: that since consciousness of one's capacity *in general* is (in the case mentioned) also consciousness of one's *incapacity*[u] with respect to the external world, the definition is not applicable to an idealist. Since, however, all that is in question here is the relation of a cause (a representation) to an effect (a feeling) in general, the causality of a representation (whether the causality is external or internal) with regard to its object must unavoidably be thought in the concept of the faculty of desire.

---

[t] *Vermögen*
[u] *seines Vermögen uberhaupt . . . seines Unvermögens*

I.
LOGICAL PREPARATION FOR A RECENTLY PROPOSED CONCEPT OF A RIGHT.

If philosophers versed in right want to rise or venture all the way to metaphysical first principles of the doctrine of right (without which all their juridical science[v] would be merely statutory), they cannot be indifferent to assurance of the completeness of their *division* of concepts of rights, since otherwise that science would not be a *rational system* but merely an aggregate hastily collected. – For the sake of the form of the system, the *topic* of principles must be complete, that is, the *place* for a concept (*locus communis*) must be indicated, the place that is left open for this concept by the synthetic form of the division. Afterwards one may also show that one or another concept which might be put in this place would be self-contradictory and falls from this place.

Up to now jurists have admitted two commonplaces: that of a right to *things* and that of a right against *persons*. By the mere form of joining these two concepts together into one, two more places are opened up for concepts, as members of an a priori division: that of a right to a thing akin to a right against a person and that of a right to a person akin to a right to a thing. It is therefore natural to ask whether we have to add some such new concept and whether we must come across it in the complete table of division, even if it is only problematic. There can be no doubt that this is the case. For a merely logical division (which abstracts from the content of cognition, from the object) is always a *dichotomy*, for example, any right is either a right to a thing or not a right to a thing. But the division in question here, namely the metaphysical division, might also be a fourfold division; for besides the two simple members of the division, two further relations might have to be added, namely those of the conditions limiting a right, under which one right enters into combination with the other. This possibility requires further investigation. – The concept of a *right to a thing akin to a right against a person* drops out without further ado, since no right of a *thing* against a *person* is conceivable. Now the question is whether the reverse of this relation is just as inconceivable or whether this concept, namely that of a *right to a person akin to a right to a thing*, is a concept that not only contains no self-contradiction but also belongs necessarily (as given a priori in reason) to the concept of what is externally mine or yours, that of not *treating* persons in a similar way to *things* in all

---

[v] *Rechtswissenschaft*. See 6:229, where Kant seemed to say that only systematic knowledge of natural right is a true science. When coupled with that passage, his use here of *erhaben oder versteigen*, which I have translated as "rise or venture," might be a suggestion that some philosophic jurists have got out of their element in attempting to discuss the issues at hand.

respects, but still of *possessing* them as things and dealing with them as things in many relations.

2.
JUSTIFICATION OF THE CONCEPT OF A RIGHT TO A PERSON AKIN TO A RIGHT TO A THING.

Put briefly and well, the definition of a right to a person akin to a right to a thing is this: "It is the right of a human being to have a *person* other than himself as *his own.*"* I take care to say "a *person*"; for while it is true that someone can have as his own another *human being* who by his crime has forfeited his personality (become a bondsman), this right to a thing is not what is in question here.

We must now examine whether this concept, this "new phenomenon in the juristic sky," is a *stella mirabilis*" (a phenomenon never seen before, growing into a star of the first magnitude but gradually disappearing again, perhaps to return at some time) or merely a *shooting star.*

3.
EXAMPLES.

To have something external as one's own means to possess it rightfully; but possessing something is the condition of its being possible to use it. If this condition is thought as merely physical, possession is called *holding.* – That I am legitimately holding something is not of itself sufficient for saying that the object is mine or for making it mine. But if I am authorized, for whatever reason, to insist upon holding an object that has escaped from my control or been torn from it, this concept of a right is a *sign* (as an effect is a sign of its cause) that I consider myself authorized to treat this object and to use it as *what is mine,* and consider myself as also in intelligible possession of it.

What is one's own here does not, indeed, mean what is one's own in the sense of property in the person of another (for a human being cannot have property in himself, much less in another person), but means what is one's own in the sense of usufruct (*ius utendi fruendi*),ˣ to make direct use

---

* I do not say here "to have a person as mine" (using the adjective), but "to have a person as *what is mine,* to *meum,*" (using the substantive). For I can say "this is *my father,*" and that signifies only my physical relation (of connection) to him in a general way, e.g., I *have* a father; but I cannot say "I have him as *what is mine.*" However, if I say "my wife" this signifies a special, namely a rightful, relation of the possessor to an object as a *thing* (even though the object is also a person). Possession (*physical* possession), (*manipulatio*) something as a thing, even if this must, in another respect, be treated at the same time as a person.

" wondrous star, or supernova
ˣ right of the use of the fruits

of a person *as of* a thing, as a means to my end, but still without infringing upon his personality.

But this end, as the condition under which such use is legitimate, must be morally necessary. A man cannot desire a woman in order to *enjoy* her as a thing, that is, in order to take immediate satisfaction in merely animal intercourse with her, nor can a woman give herself to him for this without both renouncing their personalities (in carnal or bestial cohabitation), that is, this can be done only under the condition of *marriage*. Since marriage is a reciprocal giving of one's very person into the possession of the other, it must *first* be concluded, so that neither is dehumanized through the bodily use that one makes of the other.

Apart from this condition carnal enjoyment is *cannibalistic* in principle (even if not always in its effect). Whether something is consumed by mouth and teeth, or whether the woman is consumed by pregnancy and the perhaps fatal delivery resulting from it, or the man by exhaustion of his sexual capacity from the woman's frequent demands upon it, the difference is merely in the manner of enjoyment. In this sort of use by each of the sexual organs of the other, each is actually a *consumable* thing (*res fungibilis*)[y] with respect to the other, so that if one were to make oneself such a thing by *contract*, the contract would be contrary to law (*pactum turpe*).[z]

6:360

Similarly, a man and a woman cannot beget a child as their joint *work* (*res artificialis*) and without both of them incurring an obligation toward the child and toward each other to maintain it. This is, again, acquisition of a human being *as of* a thing, but only formally so (as befits a right to a person that is only akin to a right to a thing). Parents* have a right against every possessor (*ius in re*)[a] of their child who has been removed from their control. Since they also have a right to constrain it to carry out and comply with any of their directions that are not contrary to a possible lawful freedom (*ius ad rem*),[b] they also have a right against a person against the child.

Finally, when their duty to provide for their children comes to an end as they reach maturity, parents still have a right to use them as members of the household subject to their direction, for maintaining the household, until they leave. This is a duty of parents toward them which follows from the natural limitation of the parents' right. Up until this time children are indeed members of the household and belong to the *family;* but from now

---

* In written German *Ältern* means *Seniores* and *Eltern* means *Parentes*. Although the two words cannot be distinguished in speech, they are very different in meaning.
[y] a thing on which a right to other things is based
[z] wrongful compact
[a] right in the thing
[b] right to the thing

on they belong to the *service* of the family (*famulatus*), so that the head of the house cannot add them to what is his (as his domestics) except by contract. – In the same way, the head of a house can also make the service of those *outside the family* his own in terms of a right to them akin to a right to a thing and acquire them as domestics (*famulatus domesticus*) by a contract. Such a contract is not just a contract to *let and hire* (*locatio conductio operae*),^c but a giving up of their persons into the possession of the head of the house, a lease (*locatio conductio personae*).^d What distinguishes such a contract from letting and hiring is that the servant agrees *to do whatever is permissible* for the welfare of the household, instead of being commissioned for a specifically determined job, whereas someone who is hired for a specific job (an artisan or day laborer) does not give himself up as part of the other's belongings and so is not a member of the household. – Since he is not in the rightful possession of another who puts him under obligation to perform certain services, even if he lives in the other's house (*inquilinus*), the head of the house cannot *take possession* of him as a thing (*via facti*); he must instead insist upon the laborer's doing what he promised in terms of a right against a person, as something he can command by rightful proceedings (*via iuris*). – So much for the clarification and defense of a strange type of right which has recently been added to the doctrine of natural law, although it has always been tacitly in use.

4.
ON CONFUSING A RIGHT TO A THING WITH A RIGHT AGAINST A PERSON.

I have also been censured for heterodoxy in natural private right for the proposition that *sale breaks a lease* (*The Doctrine of Right*, 31, p. 129 [AK. 6:290]).

It does seem at first glance to conflict with all rights arising from a contract that someone could give notice to someone leasing his house before the period of residence agreed upon is up and, so it seems, break his promise to the lessee, provided he grants him the time for vacating it that is customary by the civil laws where they live. – But if it can be proved that the lessee knew or must have known, when he contracted to lease it, that the promise made to him by the *lessor*, the owner, naturally (without its needing to be stated expressly in the contract) and therefore tacitly included the condition, *as long as the owner does not sell the house during this time* (or does not have to turn it over to his creditors if he should become bankrupt), then the lessor has not broken his promise, which was already a conditional one in terms of reason, and the lessee's

---
^c let and hire of a work
^d let and hire of a person

right was not encroached upon if he was given notice before the lease expired.

For the right a lessee has by a contract to lease is a right *against a person*, to something a certain person has to perform for another (*ius ad rem*); it is not a right against *every* possessor of a thing (*ius in re*), not a right to a *thing*.

A lessee could, indeed, secure himself in his *contract to lease* and produce a right to a thing as regards the house; he could, namely, have this right only to the lessor's house *registered* (entered in the land registry), as attached to the land. Then he could not be turned out of his lease, before the time settled upon had expired, by the owner's giving notice or even by his death (his natural death or also his civil death, bankruptcy). If he does not do this, perhaps because he wanted to be free to conclude a lease on better terms elsewhere or because the owner did not want to encumber his house with such an *onus*, it may be concluded that, as regards the time for giving notice, each of the parties was aware that he had made a contract subject to the tacit condition that it could be dissolved if this became convenient (except for the period of grace for vacating, as determined by civil law). Certain rightful consequences of a *bare* contract to lease give further confirmation of one's authorization to break a lease by sale; for if a lessor dies, no obligation to continue the lease is ascribed to his heir, since this is an obligation only on the part of a certain person and ceases with his death (though the legal time for giving notice must still be taken into account in this case). Neither can the right of a lessee, as such, pass to his heir without a separate contract; nor, as long as both parties are alive, is a lessee authorized to sublet to anyone without an explicit agreement.

5.
FURTHER DISCUSSION OF THE CONCEPT OF THE RIGHT TO PUNISH.

The mere idea of a civil constitution among *human beings* carries with it the concept of punitive justice belonging to the supreme authority. The only question is whether it is a matter of indifference to the legislator what kinds of punishment are adopted, as long as they are effective measures for eradicating crime (which violates the security a state gives each in his possession of what is his), or whether the legislator must also take into account respect for the humanity in the person of the wrongdoer (i.e., respect for the species) simply on grounds of right. I said that the *ius talionis*[c] is by its form always the principle for the right to punish since it alone is the principle determining this idea a priori (not derived from experience of which measures would be most effective for eradicating

---
[c] right of retaliation

crime).* – But what is to be done in the case of crimes that cannot be punished by a return for them because this would be either impossible or itself a punishable crime against *humanity* as such, for example, rape as well as pederasty or bestiality? The punishment for rape and pederasty is castration (like that of a white or black eunuch in a seraglio), that for bestiality, permanent expulsion from civil society, since the criminal has made himself unworthy of human society. – *Per quod quis peccat, per idem punitur et idem.*[f] – The crimes mentioned are called unnatural because they are perpetrated against humanity itself. To inflict *whatever* punishments *one chooses*[g] for these crimes would be literally contrary to the concept of *punitive justice*. For the only time a criminal cannot complain that a wrong is done him is when he brings his misdeed[h] back upon himself, and what is done to him in accordance with penal law is what he has perpetrated on others, if not in terms of its letter at least in terms of its spirit.

6.
ON A RIGHT FROM PROLONGED POSSESSION.

"A right based on *prolonged possession* (*Usucapio*) should, according to p. 131 ff. [AK. 6:291 ff.]), be established by natural right. For unless one admits that an *ideal acquisition*, as it is here called, is established by possession in good faith, no acquisition at all would be conclusively secured. (Yet Kant himself admits only provisional acquisition in the state of nature, and because of this insists on the juristic necessity of a civil constitution. – I assert that I am the *possessor* of something *in good faith*, however, only against someone who cannot prove that he was *possessor* of the same thing *in good faith* before me and has not ceased by his will to be its possessor.)" – This is not the question here. The question is whether I can also *assert* that I am the owner even if someone should come forward claiming to be the *earlier* true owner of the thing, but where it was *abso-*

---

* In every punishment there is something that (rightly) offends the accused's feeling of honor, since it involves coercion that is unilateral only, so that his dignity as a citizen is suspended, at least in this particular case; for he is subjected to an external duty to which he, for his own part, may offer no resistance. A man of nobility or wealth who has to pay a fine feels the loss of his money less than the humiliation of having to submit to the will of an inferior. *Punitive justice* (*iustitia punitiva*) must be distinguished from *punitive prudence*, since the argument for the former is *moral*, in terms of being *punishable* (*quia peccatum est*) while that for the latter is *merely pragmatic* (*ne peccetur*) and based on experience of what is most effective in eradicating crime; and punitive justice has an entirely different *place* in the topic of concepts of right, *locus iusti*; its place is not that of the *conducibilis*, of what is *useful* for a certain purpose, nor that of the mere *honesti*, which must be sought in ethics.

[f] One who commits a sin is punished through it and in the same way.
[g] *Willkürlich Strafen*
[h] *Übeltat*

lutely impossible to learn of his existence as its possessor and of his being in possession as its owner. This occurs if the claimant has not (whether by his own fault or not) given any publicly valid sign of his uninterrupted possession, for example, by recording it in the registry or by voting as undisputed owner in civil assemblies.

For the question here is, who ought to prove his legitimate acquisition? This obligation (*onus probandi*)[i] cannot be imposed on the possessor, since he has been in possession of it as far back as his confirmed history reaches. In accordance with principles of right, the one who claims to be the earlier owner of the thing is cut completely out of the series of successive possessors by the interval during which he has given no civilly valid sign of his ownership. This failure to perform any public possessory act makes him a claimant without a title. (Against his claim it can be said here, as in theology, *conservatio est continua creatio*).[j] Even if a claimant who had not previously appeared should later come forward supplied with documents he found, there would be room for doubt, in his case again, whether a still earlier claimant could appear at some future time and base his claim on earlier possession. – Finally acquiring something by *prolonged possession* of it (*acquirere per usucaptionem*)[k] does not depend at all on the *length of time* one has possessed it. For it is absurd to suppose that a wrong becomes a right because it has continued for a long time. Far from a right in a thing being based on use of it, *use* of it (however long) presupposes a right in it. Therefore *prolonged possession* (*usucapio*), regarded as acquisition of a thing by long use of it, is a self-contradictory concept. Prescription[l] as a means of conserving possession (*conservatio possessionis per praescriptionem*) is no less self-contradictory, although it is a distinct concept as far as the argument for appropriation is concerned.[38] That is to say, a negative basis, that is, the entire *non-use* of one's right, not even that which is necessary to show oneself as possessor, is taken to be an *abandonment* of this right (*derelictio*), a rightful act, that is, the use of one's right against another, so as to acquire the object of the earlier possessor by excluding it (*per praescriptionem*) from his claim; and this involves a contradiction.

I therefore acquire without giving proof and without any act establishing my right. I have no need for proof; instead I acquire by law (*lege*). What follows? *Public* immunity from claims, that is, *security in my possession* by law, since I do not need to produce proof, and take my stand on my uninterrupted possession. But that any *acquisition* in a state of nature is only provisional has no bearing on the question of the security of *possession* of what is acquired, which must precede acquisition.

6:365

---

[i] burden of proof
[j] conservation is continuous creation
[k] to acquire by *usucapio*, i.e., by prolonged possession
[l] Or "superannuation of claims," *Verjährung der Ansprüche*

7.
ON INHERITANCE.

As for the right of inheritance, this time the acuteness of the reviewer has failed to find him the nerve of the proof of my assertion. – I did not say (p. 135 [AK 6:294]) that every human being necessarily accepts any *thing offered* him which he can only gain and not lose by accepting (for there are indeed no such things). I said, rather, that everyone always in fact accepts, unavoidably and tacitly but still validly, the *right to accept the offer* at the same moment, namely when the nature of the matter involves the absolute impossibility of the offer being retracted, the moment of the testator's death; for then the promisor cannot withdraw it and the promisee, without needing to do any act to establish the right, is at the same moment the accepter, not of the legacy promised but of the right to accept or refuse it. When the will is opened he sees that he had already at that moment, before accepting the legacy, become richer than he was before, since he had acquired the exclusive *authorization to accept* and this is already an enriching circumstance. – Although a civil condition is presupposed in order for someone who no longer exists to make *something belong to another*, this transfer of possession by one who is dead does not alter the possibility of acquiring in accordance with universal principles of natural right, even though a civil constitution is the necessary basis for applying these principles to the case at hand. – That is to say, something left unconditionally to my free choice*ᵐ* to accept or refuse is called a *res iacens*. If the owner of something offers it to me gratuitously (promises that it will be mine), for example, when he offers me a piece of furniture of the house I am about to move from, I have the exclusive right to accept his offer (*ius in re iacente*)*ⁿ* so long as he does not withdraw it (and if he dies in the meantime this is impossible), that is, I alone can accept it or refuse it as I please; and I do not get this exclusive right to make the choice through any special rightful act of declaring that I will to have this right. I acquire it without any such act (*lege*). – So I can indeed declare that I will *not to have the thing* (because accepting it might involve me in unplesantness with others), but I cannot will to have the exclusive choice of *whether it is to belong to me or not*; for I have this right (to accept or refuse) immediately from the offer, without my declaring my acceptance of it, since if I could refuse even to have this choice I would be choosing not to choose, which is a contradiction. Now this right to choose passes to me at the moment of the testator's death, and by his testament (*institutio haeredis*) I acquire, not yet his belongings and goods, but nevertheless *merely rightful* (intelligible) possession of his belongings or a part of them, which I can now refuse to accept to the advantage of others.

ᵐ freien Wahl
ⁿ right in a thing cast aside

Consequently this possession is not interrupted for a moment; succession passes instead in a continuous series from the dying man to his appointed heirs by their acceptance. The proposition *testamenta sunt iuris naturae*[o] is thus established beyond any doubt.

8.
ON THE RIGHT OF A STATE WITH REGARD TO PERPETUAL FOUNDATIONS FOR ITS SUBJECTS.

A *foundation* (*sanctio testamentaria beneficii perpetui*) is an institution that has been voluntarily established, and confirmed by a state, for the benefit of certain members of it who succeed one another until they have all died out. – It is called *perpetual* if the statute for maintaining it is bound up with the constitution of the state itself (for a state must be regarded as perpetual). Those who are to benefit from a foundation are either the *people* generally, or a part of them united by certain special principles, or a certain *estate*, or a *family* and its descendants continuing in perpetuity. An example of the first kind is a *hospital*; of the second, a *church*; of the third, an *order* (spiritual or secular); and of the fourth, an estate that is *entailed*.

It is said that such corporations and their *right* of succession cannot be annulled, since it became by a *bequest* the property of the heirs appointed, so that annulling such a constitution (*corpus mysticum*)[p] would amount to depriving someone of his belongings.

A.

Those institutions for the benefit of the poor, invalids and the sick[q] which have been set up at the expense of the state (foundations and hospitals) can certainly not be done away with. But if the intention of the testator's will rather than its letter is to have priority, circumstances can arise in time which make it advisable to nullify such a foundation at least in terms of its form. – So it has been found that the poor and the sick (except for patients in mental hospitals) are cared for better and more economically when they are helped with certain sums of money (proportioned to the needs of the time), with which they can board where they want, with relatives or acquaintances, than when – as in the hospital at Greenwich – they are provided splendid institutions, serviced by expensive personnel, which severely limit their freedom. – It cannot be said then that the state is depriving the people, which is entitled to the benefits of this foundation, of what is theirs; the state is instead promoting this by choosing wiser means for preserving it.

---

[o] testaments are by right of nature
[p] mystical body
[q] *Die wohltätige Anstalt*

B.

The clergy which does not propagate itself carnally (the Catholic clergy) possesses, with the favor of the state, estates and the subjects attached to them. These belong to a spiritual state (called a church), to which the laity, for the salvation of their souls, have given themselves by their bequests as its property.[r] And so the clergy, as a special estate, has possessions which can be bequeathed by law from one generation to the next, and which are adequately documented by papal bulls. – But may one assume that this relation to the laity can be directly taken from the clergy by the absolute power of the secular state? Would this not amount to depriving someone by force of what is his, as the unbelievers of the French republic are attempting to do?

The question here is whether the church can belong to the state or the state belong to the church; for two supreme authorities cannot without contradiction be subordinate one to the other. – It is evident that only the *first constitution (politico-hierarchica)* could subsist by itself, since every civil constitution is of *this* world because it is an earthly authority (of human beings) that, along with its results, can be confirmed in experience. Even if we concede to believers, whose *kingdom* is in heaven and the *other world*, a constitution relating to that world (*hierarchico-politica*), they must submit to the sufferings of this era under the higher authority of men[s] of this world. – Hence only the first constitution is to be found.

Religion (in appearance), as belief in the dogmas of a church and in the power of priests, who are the aristocrats of such a constitution though it can also be monarchical (papal), can neither be imposed upon a people nor taken away from them by any civil authority; nor can a citizen be excluded from the service of the state and the advantages this brings him because his religion is different from that of the court (as Great Britain has done with the Irish nation).

In order to partake of the grace a church promises to show believers even after their death, certain devout and believing souls establish foundations in perpetuity, by which certain estates of theirs are to become the property of a church after their death; and the state may pledge itself to fealty to a church regarding this or that foundation, or indeed all of them,[t] so that these people may have the prayers, indulgences, and penances by which the servants of the church appointed for this (clergy) promise that

---

[r] *welchem die Weltliche durch Vermächtnisse . . . sich als ihr Eigentum hingegeben haben*[39]
[s] *Menschen*
[t] *an diesem oder jenem Teil, oder gar ganz.* Perhaps "in this or that respect, or indeed entirely." The remainder of the sentence is grammatically defective. Natorp suggests that the passage "so that . . . fare well in the other world" may have been written in the margin for insertion earlier in the sentence, after "believing souls." In that case, it would be the intention of these souls, not of the state, to improve their lot in the next world.

they will fare well in the other world. But such a foundation, supposedly instituted in perpetuity, is not at all established in perpetuity; the state can cast off this burden a church has laid upon it when it wants to. – For a church itself is an institution built merely upon belief, so that when the illusion arising from this opinion disappears through popular enlightenment, the fearful authority of the clergy based on it also falls away and the state, with full right, takes control of the property the church has arrogated to itself, namely the land bestowed on it through bequests. However, the feudal tenants of the institution that hitherto existed have the right to demand compensation as long as they live.

Even perpetual foundations for the poor, and educational institutions, cannot be founded in perpetuity and be a perpetual encumbrance on the land because they have a certain character specified by the founder in accordance with his ideas; instead the state must be free to adapt them to the needs of the time. – No one need be surprised that it becomes more and more difficult for this idea to be carried out in all its details (e.g., that poor students must supplement by singing for alms an inadequate educational fund beneficently established); for if the one who sets up the foundation is somewhat ambitious as well as good-natured, he does not want someone else to alter it in accordance with his concepts; he wants to be immortalized in it. That, however, does not change the nature of the matter itself and the right, indeed the duty, of a state to alter any foundation if it is opposed to the preservation of the state and its progress to the better. Such a foundation, therefore, can never be regarded as established in perpetuity.

C.

The nobility of a country that is not under an aristocratic but a monarchical constitution is an institution that may be permitted for a certain period of time and may even be necessary by circumstances. But it cannot be asserted that this estate can be established in perpetuity, and that the head of a state should not be authorized to annul this preeminence of estate entirely, or that if he does this he has deprived his (noble) subjects of what was *theirs*, of what belonged to them by inheritance. A nobility is a temporary fraternity authorized by the state, which must go along with the circumstances of the time and not infringe upon the universal right of human beings which has been suspended for so long. – For the rank of nobleman in a state is not only dependent upon the constitution itself; it is only an accident of the constitution, which can exist only by inherence in a state (a nobleman as such is conceivable only in a state, not in the state of nature). Accordingly, when a state alters its constitution, someone who thereby loses his title and precedence cannot say that he was deprived of what was his, since he could call it his only under the condition that this form of state continued; but a state has the right to alter its form (e.g., to reform itself into a republic). – Orders and the privilege of bearing certain signs of them, therefore, give no *perpetual* right of possession.

D.

Finally, as regards the *foundation of entailed estates*, in which someone possessed of goods arranges his inheritance so that the next of kin in the series of successive heirs should always be lord of the estate (by analogy with a state having a hereditary monarchy, where the *lord of the land* is determined in this way): not only can such a foundation be annulled at any time with the consent of all male relatives and need not last in perpetuity – as if the right of inheritance were attached to the land – and it cannot be said that letting an entailment terminate violates the foundation and the will of the original lord who established it, its founder; but a state also has a right and indeed a duty in this matter: as reasons for reforming itself gradually become apparent, not to let such a federative system of its subjects, as if they were viceroys (analogous to dynasties and satrapies), revive when it has once become extinct.

Conclusion

Finally, the reviewer has made the following remark about the ideas I presented under the heading of public right, with regard to which, as he says, space does not permit him to express himself: "So far as we know, no philosopher has yet admitted that most paradoxical of all paradoxical propositions: the proposition that the mere *idea* of sovereignty should constrain me to obey as my lord whoever has set himself up as my lord, without my asking who has given him the right to command me. Is there to be no difference between saying that one ought to recognize sovereignty and supreme authority and saying that one ought to hold a priori as his lord this or that person, whose existence is not even given a priori?" – Now, granting the *paradox* here, I at least hope that, once the matter is considered more closely, I cannot be convicted of *heterodoxy*. I hope, rather, my astute and careful reviewer, who criticizes with moderation (and who, despite the offense he takes, "regards these metaphysical first principles of a doctrine of right on the whole as a gain for the science") will not regret having taken them under his protection against the obstinate and superficial condemnation of others, at least as an attempt not unworthy of a second examination.

That one who finds himself in possession of supreme commanding and legislative authority over a people must be obeyed; that obedience to him is so rightfully unconditional that even to *investigate* publicly the title by which he acquired his authority, and so to cast doubt upon it with a view to resisting him should this title be found deficient, is already punishable; that there is a categorical imperative, *Obey the authority who has power over you* (in whatever does not conflict with inner morality) – this is the offensive proposition called in question. – But what seems to shock the reviewer's reason is not only this principle, which makes an actual deed*^a (taking control) the condition and the basis for a right, but also that the *mere idea* of sovereignty over a people constrains me, as belonging to that people, to obey without previously investigating the right that is claimed (*The Doctrine of Right* § 49).

Every actual deed (fact) is an object in *appearance* (to the senses). On the other hand, what can be represented only by pure reason and must be counted among *ideas*, to which no object given in experience can be adequate – and a perfectly *rightful constitution* among human beings is of this sort – is the thing in itself.

If then a people united by laws under an authority exists, it is given as an object of experience in conformity with the idea of the unity of a people *as such* under a powerful supreme will, though it is indeed given only in appearance, that is, a rightful constitution in the general sense of the term exists. And even though this constitution may be afflicted with great defects and gross faults and be in need eventually of important improvements, it is still absolutely unpermitted and culpable to resist it. For if the people should hold that it is justified in opposing force to this constitution, however faulty, and to the supreme authority, it would think that it had the right to put force in place of the supreme legislation that prescribes all rights, which would result in a supreme will that destroys itself.

6:372

The *idea* of a civil constitution as such, which is also an absolute command that practical reason, judging according to concepts of right, gives to every people, is *sacred* and irresistible. And even if the organization of a state should be faulty by itself, no subordinate authority in it may actively resist its legislative supreme authority; the defects attached to it must instead be gradually removed by reforms the state itself carries out. For otherwise, if a subject acts on the contrary maxim (of proceeding by unsanctioned choice), a good constitution can come into being only by blind chance. – The command "Obey the authority that has power over you" does not inquire how it came to have this power (in order perhaps to undermine it); for the authority which already exists, under which you live, is already in possession of legislative authority, and though you can

---

^a *Factum*. The following paragraph begins *Ein jedes Factum* (*Tatsache*). Since what is in question is, first, someone's actually taking control or seizing power, and second, an actually existing constitution, the difficulties noted above regarding the translation of *Factum* as "fact" or "deed," and of *Gewalt* as "authority" or "power" become acute.

indeed reason publicly about its legislation, you cannot set yourself up as an opposing legislator.

Unconditional submission of the people's will (which in itself is not united and is therefore without law) to a *sovereign* will (uniting all by means of *one* law) is a *deed* that can begin only by seizing supreme power[v] and so first establishing public right. – To permit any resistance to this absolute power[w] (resistance that would limit that supreme power) would be self-contradictory; for then this supreme power (which may be resisted), would not be the lawful supreme power which first determines what is to be publicly right or not. This principle is already present a priori in the *idea* of a civil constitution as such, that is, in a concept of practical reason; and although no example in experience is *adequate* to be put under this concept, still none must contradict it as a norm.

[v] *Tat, die nur durch Bemächtigung der obsersten Gewalt anheben kann*
[w] *Machtvollkommenheit*

The
metaphysics of morals

Part II
Metaphysical first principles
of the
doctrine of virtue

Preface

A *philosophy* of any subject (a system of rational cognition from concepts) requires a system of *pure rational* concepts independent of any conditions of intuition, that is, a *metaphysics*. – The only question is whether every *practical* philosophy, as a doctrine of duties, and so too the *doctrine of virtue* (ethics), also needs *metaphysical first principles*, so that it can be set forth as a genuine science (systematically) and not merely as an aggregate of precepts sought out one by one (fragmentarily). – No one will doubt that the pure doctrine of right needs metaphysical first principles; for it has to do only with the *formal condition* of choice that is to be limited in external relations in accordance with laws of freedom, without regard for any *end* (the matter of choice). Here the doctrine of duties is, accordingly, a mere *scientific doctrine* (*doctrina scientiae*).*

But in this philosophy (the doctrine of virtue) it seems directly contrary to the idea of it to go all the way back to *metaphysical first principles*, so as to make the concept of duty, though purified of anything empirical (any feeling), the incentive. For what sort of concept can be made of the force and herculean strength needed to subdue the vice-breeding inclinations if virtue is to borrow its weapons from the arsenal of metaphysics, a speculative subject that few know how to handle? Hence all doctrine of virtue,[x] in lecture halls, from pulpits, or in popular books, also becomes ridiculous if it is decked out in scraps of metaphysics. – But it is not useless, much less ridiculous, to investigate in metaphysics the first grounds of the doctrine of virtue; for someone, as a philosopher, has to go to the first grounds of this concept of duty, since otherwise neither certitude nor purity can be

---

*Someone *versed in practical philosophy* is not thereby a *practical philosopher*. A practical philosopher is one who makes the *final end of reason* the principle *of his actions* and joins with this such knowledge as is necessary for it. Since this knowledge aims at action it need not be spun out into the finest threads of metaphysics, unless it has to do with a duty of right. In that case *what is mine* and *what is yours* must be determined on the scales of justice exactly, in accordance with the principle that action and reaction are equal, and so with a precision analogous to that of mathematics; but this is not necessary when it has to do with a mere duty of virtue. For what counts in the latter case is not merely knowing *what* it is one's duty to do (because of the ends all human beings have by their nature this is easily stated); it is primarily the inner principle of the will, namely that consciousness of this duty be also the *incentive* to actions. This is what is required in order to say, of someone who joins with his knowledge this principle of wisdom, that he is a *practical philosopher*.

[x] Or, perhaps, "teaching of virtue," *aller Tugendlehren*

expected anywhere in the doctrine of virtue. In that case a popular teacher can indeed be content to rely on a certain *feeling* which, because of the results expected from it, is called *moral,* insofar as he insists that the following lesson be taken to heart, as the touchstone for deciding whether or not something is a duty of virtue: "How could a maxim such as yours harmonize with itself if everyone, in every case, made it a universal law?" But if it were mere feeling that made it our duty even to use this proposition as the touchstone, this duty would not be dictated by reason but would be taken to be a duty only instinctively, and hence blindly.

But in fact no moral principle is based, as people sometimes suppose, on any *feeling* whatsoever. Any such principle is really an obscurely thought *metaphysics* that is inherent in every human being because of his rational predisposition, as a teacher will readily grant if he experiments in questioning his pupil *socratically* about the imperative of duty and its application to moral appraisal of his actions. – The way the teacher *presents* this (his technique) should not always be metaphysical nor his terms scholastic, unless he wants to train his pupil as a philosopher. But his *thought* must go all the way back to the elements of metaphysics, without which no certitude or purity can be expected in the doctrine of virtue, nor indeed any moving force.

If one departs from this principle and begins with pathological or pure aesthetic or even moral *feeling* (with what is subjectively rather than objectively practical); if, that is, one begins with the matter of the will, the *end,* instead of with the form of the will, the *law,* in order to determine duties on this basis, then there will indeed be no *metaphysical first principles* of the doctrine of virtue, since feeling, whatever may arouse it, always belongs to the *order of nature.* – But then the doctrine of virtue, being corrupted at its source, is corrupted alike in schools, lecture halls and so forth. For the kind of incentive by which, as means, one is led to a good purpose (that of fulfilling every duty) is not a matter of indifference. – Hence, no matter how *metaphysics* may disgust the supposed teachers of wisdom who discourse on duty as *oracles* or *geniuses,* those same people who oppose metaphysics still have an indispensable duty to go back to its principles even in the doctrine of virtue and, before they teach, to become pupils in the classroom of metaphysics.

∴

After it has been made so clear that the principle of duty is derived from pure reason, one cannot help wondering how this principle could be reduced again to a *doctrine of happiness,* though in such a way that a certain *moral* happiness not based on empirical causes – a self-contradictory absurdity[40] – has been thought up as the end. – It happens in this way. When a thoughtful human being has overcome incentives to vice and is aware of having done his often bitter duty, he finds himself in a state that could well be called happiness, a state of contentment and peace of soul in which virtue is its own reward. – Now a *eudaimonist* says: this delight, this happiness is really his motive for acting virtuously. The concept of duty does not determine his will *directly;* he is moved to do his duty only *by means of* the happiness he anticipates. – But since he can expect this reward of virtue only from consciousness of having done his duty, it is clear that the latter must have come first, that is, he must find himself under obligation to do his duty before he thinks that happiness will result from his observance of duty and without thinking of this. A eudaimonist's *etiology* involves him in a *circle;* that is to say, he can hope to be *happy* (or inwardly blessed) only if he is conscious of having fulfilled his duty, but he can be moved to fulfill his duty only if he foresees that he will be made happy by it. – But there is also a *contradiction* in this subtle reasoning. For on the one hand he ought to fulfill his duty without first asking what effect this will have on his happiness, and so on *moral* grounds; but on the other hand he can recognize that something is his duty only by whether he can count on gaining happiness by doing it, and so in accordance with a *pathological* principle, which is the direct opposite of the moral principle.

6:378

In another place (the *Berliner Monatsschrift*)[41] I have, I think, reduced the distinction between *pathological pleasure* and *moral pleasure* to its simplest terms. Pleasure that must precede one's observance of the law in order for one to act in conformity with the law is pathological and one's conduct follows the *order of nature;* but pleasure that must be *preceded* by the law in order to be felt is in the *moral order.* – If this distinction is not observed, if *eudaimonism* (the principle of happiness) is set up as the basic principle instead of *eleutheronomy* (the principle of the freedom of internal lawgiving), the result is the *euthanasia* (easy death) of all morals.

The cause of these errors is as follows. People who are accustomed merely to explanations by natural sciences[y] will not get into their heads the categorical imperative from which these laws proceed dictatorially, even though they feel themselves compelled irresistably by it. Being unable to *explain* what lies entirely beyond that sphere (*freedom* of choice), however exalting is this very prerogative of the human being, his capacity for such an *idea,* they are stirred by the proud claims of speculative reason, which makes its power so strongly felt in other fields, to band together in a general *call to arms,* as it were, to defend the omnipotence of theoretical reason. And so now, and perhaps for a while longer, they assail the moral concept of freedom and, wherever possible, make it suspect; but in the end they must give way.

[y] *physiologische Erklärungen*

Introduction
to the doctrine of virtue

In ancient times "ethics" signified the *doctrine of morals* (*philosophia moralis*) in general, which was also called the *doctrine of duties*. Later on it seemed better to reserve the name "ethics" for one part of moral philosophy, namely for the doctrine of those duties that do not come under external laws (it was thought appropriate to call this, in German, the *doctrine of virtue*). Accordingly, the system of the doctrine of duties in general is now divided into the system of the *doctrine of right* (*ius*), which deals with duties that can be given by external laws, and the system of the *doctrine of virtue* (*Ethica*), which treats of duties that cannot be so given; and this division may stand.

I.
DISCUSSION OF THE CONCEPT OF A DOCTRINE OF VIRTUE.

The very *concept of duty* is already the concept of a *necessitation* (constraint) of free choice through the law. This constraint may be an *external constraint* or a *self-constraint*. The moral *imperative* makes this constraint known through the categorical nature of its pronouncement (the unconditional ought). Such constraint, therefore, does not apply to rational beings as such (there could also be *holy* ones) but rather to *human beings*, rational *natural* beings, who are unholy enough that pleasure can induce them to break the moral law, even though they recognize its authority; and even when they do obey the law, they do it *reluctantly* (in the face of opposition from their inclinations), and it is in this that such *constraint* properly consists.* – But since the human being is still a *free* (moral) being, when

---

* Yet if a human being looks at himself objectively (under the aspect of *humanity* in his own person), as his pure practical reason determines him to do, he finds that *as a moral being* he is also holy enough to break the inner law *reluctantly;* for there is no human being so depraved as not to feel an opposition to breaking it and an abhorrence of himself in the face of which he has to constrain himself [to break the law]. – Now it is impossible to explain the phenomenon that at this parting of the ways (where the beautiful fable places Hercules between virtue and sensual pleasure) the human being shows more propensity to listen to his inclinations than to the law. For we can explain what happens only by deriving it from a cause in accordance with laws of nature, and in so doing we would not be thinking of choice as free. – But it is this self-constraint in opposite directions and its unavoidability that makes known the inexplicable property of *freedom* itself.

the concept of duty concerns the internal determination of his will (the incentive) the constraint that the concept of duty contains can be only self-constraint (through the representation of the law alone); for only so can that *necessitation* (even if it is external) be united with the freedom of his choice. Hence in this case the concept of duty will be an ethical one.

Impulses of nature, accordingly, involve *obstacles* within the human being's mind to his fulfillment of duty and (sometimes powerful) forces opposing it, which he must judge that he is capable of resisting and conquering by reason not at some time in the future but at once (the moment he thinks of duty): he must judge that he *can* do what the law tells him unconditionally that he *ought* to do.

Now the capacity[z] and considered resolve to withstand a strong but unjust opponent is *fortitude* (*fortitudo*) and, with respect to what opposes the moral disposition *within us*, **virtue** (*virtus, fortitudo moralis*). So the part of the general doctrine of duties that brings inner, rather than outer, freedom under laws is a *doctrine of virtue*.

The doctrine of right dealt only with the *formal* condition of outer freedom (the consistency of outer freedom with itself if its maxim were made universal law), that is, with **right**. But ethics goes beyond this and provides a *matter* (an object of free choice), an **end** of pure reason which it represents as an end that is also objectively necessary, that is, an end that, as far as human beings are concerned, it is a duty to have. – For since the sensible inclinations of human beings tempt them to ends (the matter of choice) that can be contrary to duty, lawgiving reason can in turn check their influence only by a moral end set up against the ends of inclination, an end that must therefore be given a priori, independently of inclinations.

An *end* is an object of the choice (of a rational being), through the representation of which choice is determined to an action to bring this object about. – Now, I can indeed be constrained by others to perform *actions* that are directed as means to an end, but I can never be constrained by others *to have an end:* only I myself can *make* something my end. – But if I am under obligation to make my end something that lies in concepts of practical reason, and so to have, besides the formal determining ground of choice (such as right contains), a material one as well, an end that could be set against the end arising from sensible impulses, this would be the concept of an *end that is in itself a duty*. But the doctrine of this end would not belong to the doctrine of right but rather to ethics, since *self-constraint* in accordance with (moral) laws belongs to the concept of ethics alone.

For this reason ethics can also be defined as the system of the *ends* of pure practical reason. – Ends and duties distinguish the two divisions of the doctrine of morals in general. That ethics contains duties that one

6:381

---

[z] *Vermögen*

cannot be constrained by others (through natural[a] means) to fulfill follows merely from its being a doctrine of *ends*, since *coercion* to ends (to have them) is self-contradictory.

That ethics is a *doctrine of virtue* (*doctrina officiorum virtutis*)[b] follows, however, from the above exposition of virtue when it is connected with the kind of obligation whose distinctive feature was just pointed out. – That is to say, determination to an *end* is the only determination of choice the very concept of which excludes the possibility of constraint *through natural means* by the *choice* of another. Another can indeed *coerce* me *to do* something that is not my end (but only a means to another's end), but not to *make this my end;* and yet I can have no end without making it an end for myself. To have an end that I have not myself made an end is self-contradictory, an act of freedom which is yet not free. – But it is no contradiction to set an end for myself that is also a duty, since I constrain myself to it and this is altogether consistent with freedom.* – But how is such an end possible? That is the question now. For that the concept of a thing is possible (not self-contradictory) is not yet sufficient for assuming the possibility of the thing itself (the objective reality of the concept).

II.
DISCUSSION OF THE CONCEPT OF AN END THAT IS ALSO A DUTY.[c]

One can think of the relation of end to duty in two ways: one can begin with the end and seek out the *maxim* of actions in conformity with duty or, on the other hand, one can begin with the maxim of actions in conformity with duty and seek out the end that is also a duty. – The *doctrine of right* takes the first way. What end anyone wants to set for his action is left to his free choice. The maxim of his action, however, is determined a priori, namely, that the freedom of the agent could coexist with the freedom of every other in accordance with a universal law.

But *ethics* takes the opposite way. It cannot begin with the ends that a human being may set for himself and in accordance with them prescribe

---

* The less a human being can be constrained by natural means and the more he can be constrained morally (through the mere representation of duty), so much the more free he is. Suppose, for example, one so firm of purpose and strong of soul that he cannot be dissuaded from a pleasure he intends to have, no matter how others may reason with him about the harm he will do himself by it. If such a one gives up his plan immediately, though reluctantly, at the thought that by carrying it out he would omit one of his duties as an official or neglect a sick father, he proves his freedom in the highest degree by being unable to resist the call of duty.

[a] *physisch*. "Natural" is also used to translate *physisch* in discussions of one's natural happiness, one's natural welfare, and one's natural perfection (as distinguished in each case from its moral counterpart).

[b] doctrine of duties of virtue

[c] *von einem Zweck, der zugleich Pflicht ist*. For an elaboration of this phrase, see 6:385.

the maxims he is to adopt, that is, his duty; for that would be to adopt maxims on empirical grounds, and such grounds yield no concept of duty, since this concept (the categorical ought) has its root in pure reason alone. Consequently, if maxims were to be adopted on the basis of those ends (all of which are self-seeking), one could not really speak of the concept of duty. – Hence in ethics the *concept of duty* will lead to ends and will have to establish *maxims* with respect to ends we *ought* to set ourselves, grounding them in accordance with moral principles.

Setting aside the question of what sort of end is in itself a duty and how such an end is possible, we have here only to show that a duty of this kind is called a *duty of virtue* and why it is called by this name. 6:383

To every duty there corresponds *a* right in the sense of an *authorization* to do something (*facultas moralis generatim*); but it is not the case that to every duty there correspond *rights* of another to coerce someone (*facultas iuridica*). Instead, such duties are called, specifically, *duties of right*. – Similarly, to every ethical *obligation* there corresponds the concept of virtue, but not all ethical duties are thereby duties of virtue. Those duties that have to do not so much with a certain end (matter, object of choice) as merely with *what is formal* in the moral determination of the will (e.g., that an action in conformity with duty must also be done *from duty*) are not duties of virtue. Only *an end that is also a duty* can be called a **duty of virtue**. For this reason there are several duties of virtue (and also various virtues), whereas for the first kind of duty only one (virtuous disposition) is thought, which however holds for all actions.

What essentially distinguishes a duty of virtue from a duty of right is that external constraint to the latter kind of duty is morally possible, whereas the former is based only on free self-constraint. – For finite *holy* beings (who could never be tempted to violate duty) there would be no doctrine of virtue but only a doctrine of morals, since the latter is autonomy of practical reason whereas the former is also *autocracy* of practical reason, that is, it involves consciousness of the *capacity*[d] to master one's inclinations when they rebel against the law, a capacity which, though not directly perceived, is yet rightly inferred from the moral categorical imperative. Thus human morality in its highest stage can still be nothing more than virtue, even if it be entirely pure (quite free from the influence of any incentive other than that of duty). In its highest stage it is an ideal (to which one must continually approximate), which is commonly personified poetically by the *sage*.

But virtue is not to be defined[e] and valued merely as an *aptitude*[f] and (as the prize essay of Cochius, the court-chaplain,[42] puts it) a long-standing

---

[d] *des Vermögens*
[e] *zu erklären*
[f] *Fertigkeit*

habit[g] of morally good actions acquired by practice. For unless this aptitude results from considered, firm, and continually purified principles, then, like any other mechanism of technically practical reason, it is neither armed for all situations nor adequately secured against the changes that new temptations could bring about.

Remark.

Virtue = +a is opposed to *negative lack of virtue* (moral weakness = 0) as its *logical opposite* (*contradictorie oppositum*); but it is opposed to vice = +a as its *real opposite* (*contrarie s. realiter oppositum*);[h] and it is not only unnecessary but even improper to ask whether great *crimes* might not require more strength of soul than do great *virtues*. For by strength of soul we mean strength of resolution in a human being as a being endowed with freedom, hence his strength insofar as he is in control of himself (in his senses) and so in the state of *health* proper to a human being. But great crimes are paroxysms, the sight of which makes one whose soul is healthy shudder. The question would therefore come to something like this: whether a human being in a fit of madness could have more physical strength than when he is sane. This one can admit without attributing more strength of soul to him, if by soul is meant the vital principle of man in the free use of his powers; for, since the basis of great crimes is merely the force of inclinations that *weaken* reason, which proves no strength of soul, the above question would be tantamount to whether someone could show more strength during an attack of sickness than when he is healthy. This can be straightway denied, since health consists in the balance of all his bodily forces, while lack of health is a weakening in the system of these forces; and it is only by reference to this system that absolute health can be appraised.

III.
ON THE BASIS FOR THINKING OF AN END THAT IS ALSO A DUTY.

An **end** is an *object* of free choice, the representation of which determines it to an action (by which the object is brought about). Every action, therefore, has its end; and since no one can have an end without *himself* making the object of his choice into an end, to have any end of action whatsoever is an act of *freedom* on the part of the acting subject, not an effect of *nature*. But because this act which determines an end is a practi-

---

[g] *Gewohnheit*
[h] Contrary or really opposed. Compare Kant's 1763 essay on negative quantities in natural science, AK 2:167–204, and *Critique of Pure Reason* A 264–65/B/320–1.

cal principle that prescribes the end itself (and so prescribes unconditionally), not the means (hence not conditionally), it is a categorical imperative of pure practical reason, and therefore an imperative which connects a *concept of duty* with that of an end in general.

Now, there must be such end and a categorical imperative corresponding to it. For since there are free actions there must also be ends to which, as their objects, these actions are directed. But among these ends there must be some that are also (i.e., by their concept) duties. – For were there no such ends, then all ends would hold for practical reason only as means to other ends; and since there can be no action without an end, a *categorical* imperative would be impossible. This would do away with any doctrine of morals.[i]

So it is not a question here of ends the human being *does adopt* in keeping with the sensible impulses of his nature, but of objects of free choice under its laws, which he *ought to make* his ends. The study of the former type of ends can be called the technical (subjective) doctrine of ends; it is really the pragmatic doctrine of ends, containing the rules of prudence in the choice of one's ends. The study of the latter type of ends, however, must be called the moral (objective) doctrine of ends. But this distinction is superfluous here, since the doctrine of morals is already clearly distinguished in its concept from the doctrine of nature (in this case, anthropology) by the fact that anthropology is based on empirical principles, whereas the moral doctrine of ends, which treats of duties, is based on principles given a priori in pure practical reason.

IV.
WHAT ARE THE ENDS THAT ARE ALSO DUTIES?

They are *one's own perfection* and *the happiness of others.*

Perfection and happiness cannot be interchanged here, so that *one's own happiness* and *the perfection of others* would be made ends that would be in themselves duties of the same person.

For *his own happiness* is an end that every human being has (by virtue of the impulses of his nature), but this end can never without self-contradiction be regarded as a duty. What everyone already wants unavoidably, of his own accord, does not come under the concept of *duty*, which is *constraint* to an end adopted reluctantly. Hence it is self-contradictory to say that he is *under obligation* to promote his own happiness with all his powers.

So too, it is a contradiction for me to make another's *perfection* my end and consider myself under obligation to promote this. For the *perfection* of another human being, as a person, consists just in this: that he *himself* is

6:386

---

[i] *Sittenlehre*

able[j] to set his end in accordance with his own concepts of duty; and it is self-contradictory to require that I do (make it my duty to do) something that only the other himself can do.

V.
CLARIFICATION OF THESE TWO CONCEPTS.

A.
One's own perfection

The word *perfection* is open to a good deal of misinterpretation. Perfection is sometimes understood as a concept belonging to transcendental philosophy, the concept of the *totality* of the manifold which, taken together, constitutes a thing. – Then again, as a concept belonging to *teleology*, it is taken to mean the harmony of a thing's properties with an *end*. Perfection in the first sense could be called *quantitative* (material) perfection, and in the second, *qualitative* (formal) perfection. The quantitative perfection of a thing can be only one (for the totality of what belongs to a thing is one). But one thing can have several qualitative perfections, and it is really qualitative perfection that is under discussion here.

When it is said that it is in itself a duty for a human being to make his end the perfection belonging to a human being as such (properly speaking, to humanity), this perfection must be put in what can result from his *deeds*, not in mere *gifts* for which he must be indebted to nature; for otherwise it would not be a duty. This duty can therefore consist only in *cultivating* one's *faculties* (or natural predispositions),[k] the highest of which is *understanding*, the faculty of concepts and so too of those concepts that have to do with duty. At the same time this duty includes the cultivation of one's *will* (moral cast of mind),[l] so as to satisfy all the requirements of duty. 1) A human being has a duty to raise himself from the crude state of his nature, from his animality (*quoad actum*), more and more toward humanity, by which he alone is capable of setting himself ends; he has a duty to diminish his ignorance by instruction and to correct his errors. And it is not merely that technically practical reason *counsels* him to do this as a means to his further purposes (of art); morally practical reason *commands* it absolutely and makes this end his duty, so that he may be worthy of the humanity that dwells within him. 2) A human being has a duty to carry the cultivation of his *will* up to the purest virtuous disposition, in which the *law* becomes also the incentive to his actions that conform with duty and

---
[j] *vermögend ist*
[k] *seines Vermögens (oder der Naturanlage)*
[l] *sittlicher Denkungsart*

he obeys the law from duty. This disposition is inner morally practical perfection. Since it is a feeling of the effect that the lawgiving will within the human being exercises on his capacity to act in accordance with his will, it is called *moral feeling*, a special *sense* (*sensus moralis*), as it were. It is true that moral sense is often misused in a visionary way, as if (like Socrates' daimon) it could precede reason or even dispense with reason's judgment. Yet it is a moral perfection, by which one makes one's object every particular end that is also a duty.

B.
The happiness of others

Since it is unavoidable for human nature to wish for and seek happiness, that is, satisfaction with one's state, so long as one is assured of its lasting, this is not an end that is also a duty. – Some people, however, make a distinction between moral happiness (which consists in satisfaction with one's person and one's own moral conduct, and so with what one *does*) and natural happiness (which consists in satisfaction with what nature bestows, and so with what one *enjoys* as a gift from without). Although I refrain here from censuring a misuse of the word happiness (that already involves a contradiction), it must be noted that the former kind of feeling belongs only under the preceding heading, namely perfection. – For, someone who is said to feel happy in the mere consciousness of his rectitude already possesses the perfection which was explained there as that end which is also a duty.

6:388

When it comes to my promoting happiness as an end that is also a duty, this must therefore be the happiness of *other* human beings, *whose* (permitted) *end I thus* make *my own end as well*. It is for them to decide what they count as belonging to their happiness; but it is open to me to refuse them many things that *they* think will make them happy but that I do not, as long as they have no right to demand them from me as what is theirs. But time and again an alleged *obligation* to attend to my *own* (natural) happiness is set up in competition with this end, and my natural and merely subjective end is thus made a duty (an objective end). Since this is often used as a specious objection to the division of duties made above (in IV), it needs to be set right.

Adversity, pain, and want are great temptations to violate one's duty. It might therefore seem that prosperity, strength, health, and well-being in general, which check the influence of these, could also be considered ends that are duties, so that one has a duty to promote *one's own* happiness and not just the happiness of others. – But then the end is not the subject's happiness but his morality, and happiness is merely a means for removing obstacles to his morality – a *permitted* means, since no one else has a right to require of me that I sacrifice my ends if these are not immoral. To seek prosperity for its own sake is not directly a duty, but indirectly it can well be a duty, that of warding off poverty insofar as this is a great temptation to vice. But then it is not my happiness but the preservation of my moral integrity that is my end and also my duty.

VI.
ETHICS DOES NOT GIVE LAWS FOR *ACTIONS* (*IUS* DOES THAT), BUT ONLY FOR *MAXIMS* OF ACTIONS.

The concept of duty stands in immediate relation to a *law* (even if I abstract from all ends, as the matter of the law). The formal principle of duty, in the categorical imperative "So act that the maxim of your action could become a universal *law*," already indicates this. Ethics adds only that this principle is to be thought as the law of *your* own will and not of will in general, which could also be the will of others; in the latter case the law would provide a duty of right, which lies outside the sphere of ethics. – Maxims are here regarded as subjective principles which merely *qualify* for a giving of universal law, and the requirement that they so qualify is only a negative principle (not to come into conflict with a law as such). – How can there be, beyond this principle, a law for the maxims of actions?

Only the concept of an *end* that is also a duty, a concept that belongs exclusively to ethics, establishes a law for maxims of actions by subordinating the subjective end (that everyone has) to the objective end (that everyone ought to make his end). The imperative "You ought to make this or that (e.g., the happiness of others) your end" has to do with the matter of choice (an object). Now, no free action is possible unless the agent also intends an end (which is the matter of choice). Hence, if there is an end that is also a duty, the only condition that maxims of actions, as means to ends, must contain is that of qualifying for a possible giving of universal law. On the other hand, the end that is also a duty can make it a law to have such a maxim, although for the maxim itself the mere possibility of agreeing with a giving of universal law is already sufficient.

For maxims of actions can be *arbitrary*,[m] and are subject only to the limiting condition of being fit for a giving of universal law, which is the formal principle of actions. A *law*, however, takes arbitrariness[n] away from actions, and this distinguishes it from any *recommendation* (where all that one requires is to know the most suitable means to an end).

---

[m] *willkürlich*
[n] *das Willkürliche*

VII.
ETHICAL DUTIES ARE OF *WIDE* OBLIGATION, WHEREAS DUTIES OF RIGHT ARE OF *NARROW* OBLIGATION.

This proposition follows from the preceding one; for if the law can prescribe only the maxim of actions, not actions themselves, this is a sign that it leaves a playroom (*latitudo*) for free choice in following (complying with) the law, that is, that the law cannot specify precisely in what way one is to act and how much one is to do by the action*°* for an end that is also a duty. – But a wide duty is not to be taken as permission to make exceptions to the maxim of actions but only as permission to limit one maxim of duty by another (e.g., love of one's neighbor in general by love of one's parents), by which in fact the field for the practice of virtue is widened. – The wider the duty, therefore, the more imperfect is a man's obligation to action; as he, nevertheless, brings closer to *narrow* duty (duties of right) the maxim of complying with wide duty (in his disposition), so much the more perfect is his virtuous action.

Imperfect duties alone are, accordingly, *duties of virtue.*^p Fulfillment of them is *merit* (*meritum*) = +a; but failure to fulfill them^q is not in itself *culpability* (*demeritum*) = −a) but rather mere *deficiency in moral worth* = 0, unless the subject should make it his principle not to comply with such duties. It is only the strength of one's resolution, in the first case, that is properly called *virtue* (*virtus*); one's weakness, in the second case, is not so much *vice* (*vitium*) as rather mere *want of virtue*, lack of moral strength (*defectus moralis*). (As the word "*Tugend*"^r comes from "*taugen*"^s so "*Untugend*"^t comes from "*zu nichts taugen.*"^u) Every action contrary to duty is called a *transgression* (*peccatum*). It is when an intentional transgression has become a principle that it is properly called a *vice* (*vitium*).

Although there is nothing meritorious in the conformity of one's actions with right (in being an honest human being), the conformity with right of one's maxims of such actions, as duties, that is, **respect** for right,

---

° d.i. nicht bestimmt angegeben könne, wie und wie viel durch die Handlung

p Die unvollkommenen Pflichten sind also allein Tugendpflichten.

q ihre Übertretung, literally, "transgression of them." In discussing duties of virtue, notably duties of love, Kant sometimes refers to "neglect" of them, e.g., Vernachlässigung (6:432), Pflichtvergessenheit (6:432), Verabsäumung (6:464). Transgression of a duty of virtue is failure to adopt a maxim of promoting an end that is also a duty. More generally, when Übertretung occurs with "of a duty" or "of a law," I have sometimes translated it as "violating" a duty or "breaking" a law.

r "virtue"

s "to be fit for"

t "lack of virtue"

u "not to be fit for anything," or, colloqurelly, to be worthless or a "do-nothing"

is *meritorious*. For one thereby *makes* the right of humanity, or also the right of human beings, one's *end* and in so doing widens one's concept of duty beyond the concept of what is *due* (*officium debiti*), since another can indeed by his right require of me actions in accordance with the law, but not that the law be also my incentive to such actions. The same holds true of the universal ethical command, "act in conformity with duty *from* duty." To establish and quicken this disposition in oneself is, as in the previous case, *meritorious*, since it goes beyond the law of duty for actions and makes the law itself also the incentive.

But for this very reason these duties, too, must be counted as duties of wide obligation. With respect to them (and, indeed, in order to bring wide obligation as close as possible to the concept of narrow obligation), there is a subjective principle of ethical *reward*, that is, a receptivity to being rewarded in accordance with laws of virtue: the reward, namely, of a moral pleasure that goes beyond mere contentment with oneself (which can be merely negative) and which is celebrated in the saying that, through consciousness of this pleasure, virtue is its own reward.

If this merit is a human being's merit in relation to other human beings for promoting what all human beings recognize as their natural end (for making their happiness his own), it could be called *sweet merit;* for consciousness of it produces a moral enjoyment in which men are inclined by sympathy *to revel*. But *bitter merit*, which comes from promoting the true well-being of others even when they fail to recognize it as such (when they are unappreciative and ungrateful), usually yields no such return. All that it produces is *contentment* with oneself, although in this case the merit would be greater still.

VIII.
EXPOSITION OF DUTIES OF VIRTUE AS WIDE DUTIES.

1. One's own perfection as an end that is also a duty.

a) *Natural* perfection is the *cultivation* of any *capacities* whatever[v] for furthering ends set forth by reason. That this is a duty and so in itself an end, and that the cultivation of our capacities, even without regard for the advantage it affords us, is based on an unconditional (moral) imperative rather than a conditional (pragmatic) one, can be shown in this way. The capacity to set oneself an end – any end whatsoever – is what characterizes humanity (as distinguished from animality). Hence there is also bound up with the end of humanity in our own person the rational will, and so the duty, to make ourselves worthy of humanity by culture in general, by procuring or promoting the *capacity* to realize all sorts of

---

[v] *aller Vermögen überhaupt*

possible ends, so far as this is to be found in the human being himself. In other words, the human being has a duty to cultivate the crude predispositions of his nature, by which the animal is first raised into the human being. It is therefore a duty in itself.

But this duty is a merely ethical one, that is, a duty of wide obligation. No rational principle prescribes specifically[w] *how* far one should go in cultivating one's capacities (in enlarging or correcting one's capacity for understanding, i.e., in acquiring knowledge or skill[x]). Then too, the different situations in which human beings may find themselves make a human being's choice[y] of the occupation for which he should cultivate his talents very much a matter for him to decide as he chooses.[z] – With regard to natural perfection, accordingly, there is no law of reason for actions but only a law for maxims of actions, which runs as follows: "Cultivate your powers of mind and body so that they are fit to realize any ends you might encounter," however uncertain you are which of them could sometime become yours.

b) The *cultivation of morality* in us. The greatest perfection of a human being is to do his duty *from duty* (for the law to be not only the rule but also the incentive of his actions). – At first sight this looks like a *narrow* obligation, and the principle of duty seems to prescribe with the precision and strictness of a law not only the *legality* but also the *morality* of every action, that is, the disposition. But in fact the law, here again, prescribes only the *maxim of the action*, that of seeking the basis of obligation solely in the law and not in sensible impulse (advantage or disadvantage), and hence not the *action itself*. – For a human being cannot see into the depths of his own heart so as to be quite certain, in even a *single* action, of the purity of his moral intention and the sincerity of his disposition, even when he has no doubt about the legality of the action. Very often he mistakes his own weakness, which counsels him against the venture of a misdeed, for virtue (which is the concept of strength); and how many people who have lived long and guiltless lives may not be merely *fortunate* in having escaped so many temptations? In the case of any deed it remains hidden from the agent himself how much pure moral content there has been in his disposition.

Hence this duty too – the duty of assessing the worth of one's actions not by their legality alone but also by their morality (one's disposition) – is of only *wide* obligation. The law does not prescribe this inner action in the human mind but only the maxim of the action, to strive with all one's might that the thought of duty for its own sake is the sufficient incentive of every action conforming to duty.

[w] *bestimmt*
[x] *Kunstfähigkeit*
[y] *Wahl*
[z] *sehr willkürlich*

2. The happiness of others as an end that is also a duty.

a) *Natural welfare.* *Benevolence* can be unlimited, since nothing need be done with it. But it is more difficult to *do good,*[a] especially if it is to be done not from affection (love) for others but from duty, at the cost of forgoing the satisfaction of concupiscence and of active injury to it in many cases.[b] – The reason that it is a duty to be beneficent is this: since our self-love cannot be separated from our need to be loved (helped in case of need) by others as well, we therefore make ourselves an end for others; and the only way this maxim can be binding is through its qualification as a universal law, hence through our will to make others our ends as well. The happiness of others is therefore an end that is also a duty.

But I ought to sacrifice a part of my welfare to others without hope of return, because this is a duty, and it is impossible to assign determinate limits to the extent of this sacrifice. How far it should extend depends, in large part, on what each person's true needs are in view of his sensibilities, and it must be left to each to decide this for himself. For, a maxim of promoting others' happiness at the sacrifice of one's own happiness, one's true needs, would conflict with itself if it were made a universal law. Hence this duty is only a *wide* one; the duty has in it a latitude for doing more or less, and no specific limits can be assigned to what should be done. – The law holds only for maxims, not for determinate actions.

b) The happiness of others also includes their *moral well-being* (*salubritas moralis*), and we have a duty, but only a negative one, to promote this. Although the *pain* one feels from the pangs of conscience has a moral source it is still a natural effect, like grief, fear, or any other state of suffering. To see to it that another does not deservedly suffer this inner reproach is not *my* duty but *his affair;* but it is my duty to refrain from doing anything that, considering the nature of a human being, could tempt him to do something for which his conscience could afterwards pain him, to refrain from what is called giving scandal. – But this concern for others' moral contentment does not admit of determinate limits being assigned to it, so that the obligation resting on it is only a wide one.

IX.
WHAT IS A DUTY OF VIRTUE?

Virtue is the strength of a human being's maxims in fulfilling his duty. – Strength of any kind can be recognized only by the obstacles it can over-

---

[a] *Wohltun.* In 6:450 ff. Kant discusses the difference between the duty of benevolence, *Wohlwollen,* and the duty of beneficence, *Wohltun.* Except in that passage I have often translated *Wohltun* and its cognates by such expressions as "to do good," "to help," "a favor."
[b] *mit Aufopferung und Kränkung mancher Concupiscenz*

come, and in the case of virtue these obstacles are natural inclinations, which can come into conflict with the human being's moral resolution; and since it is the human being *himself* who puts these obstacles in the way of his maxims, virtue is not merely a self-constraint (for then one natural inclination could strive to overcome another), but also a self-constraint in accordance with a principle of inner freedom, and so through the mere representation of one's duty in accordance with its formal law.

All duties involve a concept of *constraint* through a law. *Ethical* duties involve a constraint for which only internal lawgiving is possible, whereas duties of right involve a constraint for which external lawgiving is also possible. Both, therefore, involve constraint, whether it be self-constraint or constraint by another. Since the moral capacity[c] to constrain oneself can be called virtue, action springing from such a disposition (respect for law) can be called virtuous (ethical) action, even though the law lays down a duty of right; for it is the *doctrine of virtue* that commands us to hold the right of human beings sacred.

But what it is virtuous to do is not necessarily a *duty of virtue* strictly speaking. What it is virtuous to do may concern only *what is formal* in maxims, whereas a duty of virtue has to do with their matter, that is to say, with an end that is thought as also a duty. – But since ethical obligation to ends, of which there can be several, is only *wide* obligation – because it involves a law only for *maxims* of actions, and an end is the matter (object) of choice – there are many different duties, corresponding to the different ends prescribed by the law, which are called *duties of virtue* (*officia honestatis*) just because they are subject only to free self-constraint, not constraint by other human beings, and because they determine an end that is also a duty.

6:395

Like anything *formal*, virtue as the will's conformity with every duty, based on a firm disposition, is merely one and the same. But with respect to the *end* of actions that is also a duty, that is, what one *ought* to make one's *end* (what is material), there can be several virtues; and since obligation to the maxim of such an end is called a duty of virtue, there are many duties of virtue.

The supreme principle of the doctrine of virtue is: act in accordance with a maxim of *ends* that it can be a universal law for everyone to have. – In accordance with this principle a human being is an end for himself as well as for others, and it is not enough that he is not authorized to use either himself or others merely as means (since he could then still be indifferent to them); it is in itself his duty to make the human being as such his end.

This basic principle of the doctrine of virtue, as a categorical imperative, cannot be proved, but it can be given a deduction from pure practical

[c] *Vermögen*

reason. – What, in the relation of a human being to himself and others, *can* be an end *is* an end for pure practical reason; for, pure practical reason is a faculty of ends generally, and for it to be indifferent to ends, that is, to take no interest in them, would therefore be a contradiction, since then it would not determine maxims for actions either (because every maxim of action contains an end) and so would not be practical reason. But pure reason can prescribe no ends a priori without setting them forth as also duties, and such duties are then called duties of virtue.

X.
THE SUPREME PRINCIPLE OF THE DOCTRINE OF RIGHT[43] WAS *ANALYTIC;* THAT OF THE DOCTRINE OF VIRTUE IS *SYNTHETIC.*

It is clear in accordance with the principle of contradiction that, if external constraint checks the hindering of outer freedom in accordance with universal laws (and is thus a hindering of the hindrances to freedom), it can coexist with ends as such. I need not go beyond the concept of freedom to see this; the end that each has may be whatever he wills. – The supreme *principle of right* is therefore an analytic proposition.

But the principle of the doctrine of virtue goes beyond the concept of outer freedom and connects with it, in accordance with universal laws, an *end* that it makes a *duty.* This principle is therefore synthetic. – Its possibility is contained in the deduction (IX).

When, instead of constraint from without, *inner* freedom comes into play, the capacity[d] for self-constraint not by means of other inclinations but by pure practical reason (which scorns such intermediaries), the concept of duty is extended beyond outer freedom, which is limited only by the formal provision of its compatibility with the freedom of all. This extension beyond the concept of a duty of right takes place through *ends* being laid down, from which right abstracts altogether. – In the moral imperative and the presupposition of freedom that is necessary for it are found the *law,* the *capacity* (to fulfill the law), and the *will* determining the maxim; these are all the elements that make up the concept of a duty of right. But in the imperative that prescribes a *duty of virtue* there is added not only the concept of self-constraint but that of an *end,* not an end that we have but one that we ought to have, one that pure practical reason therefore has within itself. The highest, unconditional end of pure practical reason (which is still a duty) consists in this: that virtue be its own end and, despite the benefits it confers on human beings, also its own reward. Virtue so shines as an ideal that it seems, by human standards, to eclipse

[d] *Vermögen*

holiness itself, which is never tempted to break the law.* Nevertheless, this is an illusion arising from the fact that, having no way to measure the degree of a strength except by the magnitude of the obstacles it could overcome (in us, these are inclinations), we are led to mistake the *subjective* conditions by which we assess the magnitude for the *objective* conditions of the magnitude itself. Yet in comparison with *human ends*, all of which have their obstacles to be contended with, it is true that the worth of virtue itself, as its own end, far exceeds the worth of any usefulness and any empirical ends and advantages that virtue may still bring in its wake.

It is also correct to say that the human being is under obligation *to virtue* (as moral strength). For while the capacity[c] (*facultas*) to overcome all opposing sensible impulses can and must be simply *presupposed* in man on account of his freedom, yet this capacity as *strength* (*robur*) is something he must acquire; and the way to acquire it is to enhance the moral *incentive* (the thought of the law), both by contemplating the dignity of the pure rational law in us (*contemplatione*) and by *practicing* virtue (*exercitio*).

XI.
IN ACCORDANCE WITH THE PRINCIPLES SET FORTH ABOVE, THE SCHEMA OF DUTIES OF VIRTUE CAN BE DIAGRAMMED IN THE FOLLOWING WAY:

What Is Material in Duties of Virtue

	1. *My own end* which is also my duty (My own *perfection*) 3. The *law* which is also the incentive On which the *morality*	2. *The end of others,* the promotion of which is also my duty (The *happiness* of others) 4. The *end* which is also the incentive On which the *legality*

Internal Duty of Virtue / External Duty of Virtue

of every free determination of the will is based

What Is Formal in Duties of Virtue

---

* Man with all his faults
  Is better than a host of angels without will. Haller[44]

[c] *Vermögen*

6:399

XII.
CONCEPTS OF WHAT IS PRESUPPOSED ON THE PART OF FEELING BY THE MIND'S RECEPTIVITY [f] TO CONCEPTS OF DUTY AS SUCH.

There are certain moral endowments such that anyone lacking them could have no duty to acquire them. – They are *moral feeling, conscience, love* of one's neighbor, and *respect* for oneself (*self-esteem*).[g] There is no obligation to have these because they lie at the basis of morality, as *subjective* conditions of receptiveness to the concept of duty, not as objective conditions of morality. All of them are natural predispositions of the mind (*praedispositio*) for being affected by concepts of duty, antecedent predispositions on the side of *feeling*.[h] To have these predispositions cannot be considered a duty; rather, every human being has them, and it is by virtue of them that he can be put under obligation. – Consciousness of them is not of empirical origin; it can, instead, only follow from consciousness of a moral law, as the effect this has on the mind.

a.
Moral feeling.

This is the susceptibility to feel pleasure or displeasure merely from being aware that our actions are consistent with or contrary to the law of duty. Every determination of choice proceeds *from the representation of a possible action to* the deed through the feeling of pleasure or displeasure, taking an interest in the action or its effect. The state of *feeling*[i] here (the way in which inner sense is affected) is either *pathological* or *moral*. – The former is that feeling which precedes the representation of the law; the latter, that which can only follow upon it.

Since any consciousness of obligation depends upon moral feeling to make us aware of the constraint present in the thought of duty, there can be no duty to have moral feeling or to acquire it; instead every human being (as a moral being) has it in him originally. Obligation with regard to

---

[f] *Ästhetische Vorbegriffe der Empfänglichkeit des Gemüts Achtung.* Although I have translated *Achtung* throughout as "respect," it should be noted that Kant gives two different Latin equivalents: *reverentia* in the context of one's feeling for the moral law and for oneself as the source of the law (e.g., 6:402), and *observantia aliis praestanda* in the context of duties of virtue to others (e.g., 6:452).

[g] *Achtung für sich selbst (Selbstschätzung).*

[h] *ästhetisch*

[i] *ästhetische Zustand*

moral feeling can be only to *cultivate* it and to strengthen it through wonder at its inscrutable source. This comes about by its being shown how it is set apart from any pathological stimulus and is induced most intensely in its purity by a merely rational representation.

6:400

It is inappropriate to call this feeling a moral *sense*, for by the word "sense" is usually understood a theoretical capacity for perception*ʲ* directed toward an object, whereas moral feeling (like pleasure and displeasure in general) is something merely subjective, which yields no cognition. – No human being is entirely without moral feeling, for were he completely lacking in receptivity to it he would be morally dead; and if (to speak in medical terms) the moral vital force could no longer excite this feeling, then humanity would dissolve (by chemical laws, as it were) into mere animality and be mixed irretrievably with the mass of other natural beings. – But we no more have a special *sense* for what is (morally) good and evil than for *truth*, although people often speak in this fashion. We have, rather, a *susceptibility* on the part of free choice to be moved by pure practical reason (and its law), and this is what we call moral feeling.

b.
Conscience.

So too, conscience is not something that can be acquired, and we have no duty to provide ourselves with one; rather, every human being, as a moral being, *has* a conscience within him originally. To be under obligation to have a conscience would be tantamount to having a duty to recognize duties. For, conscience is practical reason holding the human being's duty before him for his acquittal or condemnation in every case that comes under a law. Thus it is not directed to an object but merely to the subject (to affect moral feeling by its act), and so it is not something incumbent on one, a duty, but rather an unavoidable fact.*ᵏ* So when it is said that a certain human being *has* no conscience, what is meant is that he pays no heed to its verdict. For if he really had no conscience, he could not even conceive of the duty to have one, since he would neither impute anything to himself as conforming with duty nor reproach himself with anything as contrary to duty.

6:401

I shall here pass over the various divisions of conscience and note only that, as follows from what has been said, an *erring* conscience is an absurdity. For while I can indeed be mistaken at times in my objective judgment as to whether something is a duty or not, I cannot be mistaken in my subjective judgment as to whether I have submitted it to my practical reason (here in its role as judge) for such a judgment; for if I could be

ʲ Wahrnehmungsvermögen
ᵏ Tatsache

mistaken in that, I would have made no practical judgment at all, and in that case there would be neither truth nor error. *Unconscientiousness* is not lack of conscience but rather the propensity to pay no heed to its judgment. But if someone is aware that he has acted in accordance with his conscience, then as far as guilt or innocence is concerned nothing more can be required of him. It is incumbent upon him only to enlighten his *understanding* in the matter of what is or is not duty; but when it comes, or has come, to a deed, conscience speaks involuntarily[1] and unavoidably. Therefore, to act in accordance with conscience cannot itself be a duty; for if it were, there would have to be yet a second conscience in order for one to become aware of the act of the first.

The duty here is only to cultivate one's conscience, to sharpen one's attentiveness to the voice of the inner judge and to use every means to obtain a hearing for it (hence the duty is only indirect).

c.
Love of human beings.

Love is a matter of *feeling*, not of willing, and I cannot love because I *will* to, still less because I *ought* to (I cannot be constrained to love); so a *duty to love* is an absurdity. But *benevolence* (*amor benevolentiae*), as conduct,[m] can be subject to a law of duty. However, unselfish benevolence toward human beings is often (though very inappropriately) also called *love;* people even speak of love which is also a duty for us when it is not a question of another's happiness but of the complete and free surrender of all one's ends to the ends of another (even a supernatural) being. But every duty is *necessitation*, a constraint, even if this is to be self-constraint in accordance with a law. What is done from constraint, however, is not done from love.

6:402 To *do good* to other human beings insofar as we can is a duty, whether one loves them or not; and even if one had to remark sadly that our species, on closer acquaintance, is not particularly lovable, that would not detract from the force of this duty. – But *hatred of them* is always *hateful*, even when it takes the form merely of completely avoiding them (separatist misanthropy), without active hostility toward them. For benevolence always remains a duty, even toward a misanthropist, whom one cannot indeed love but to whom one can still do good.

But to hate vice in human beings is neither a duty nor contrary to duty; it is, rather, a mere feeling of aversion to vice, a feeling neither affected by the will nor affecting it. *Beneficence* is a duty. If someone practices it often and succeeds in realizing his beneficent intention, he eventually comes

---

[1] *unwillkürlich*
[m] *als ein Tun*

actually to love the person he has helped. So the saying "you ought to *love* your neighbor as yourself" does not mean that you ought immediately (first) to love him and (afterwards) by means of this love do good to him. It means, rather, *do good* to your fellow human beings, and your beneficence will produce love of them in you (as an aptitudeⁿ of the inclination to beneficence in general).

Hence only the love that is *delight*^o (*amor complacentiae*) is direct. But to have a duty to this (which is a pleasure joined immediately to the representation of an object's existence), that is, to have to be constrained to take pleasure in something, is a contradiction.

d.
Respect.

Respect (*reverentia*) is, again, something merely subjective, a feeling of a special kind, not a judgment about an object that it would be a duty to bring about or promote. For, such a duty, regarded as a duty, could be represented to us only through the *respect* we have for it. A duty to have respect would thus amount to being put under obligation to duties. – Accordingly it is not correct to say that a human being has a *duty of self-esteem;* it must rather be said that the law within him unavoidably forces from him *respect* for his own being, and this feeling (which is of a special kind) is the basis of certain duties, that is, of certain actions that are consistent with his duty to himself. It cannot be said that he *has* a duty of respect toward himself, for he must have respect for the law within himself in order even to think of any duty whatsoever.

6:403

XIII.
GENERAL PRINCIPLES OF THE METAPHYSICS OF MORALS IN HANDLING A *PURE* DOCTRINE OF VIRTUE.

First. For any one duty only *one* ground of obligation can be found; and if someone produces two or more proofs for a duty, this is a sure sign either that he has not yet found a valid proof or that he has mistaken two or more different duties for one.

For any moral proof, as philosophical, can be drawn only by means of rational knowledge *from concepts* and not, as in mathematics, by the construction of concepts. Mathematical concepts allow a number of proofs for one and the same proposition because in a priori *intuition* there can be

---
ⁿ *Fertigkeit*
^o *Liebe des Wohlgefallens*

IMMANUEL KANT

several ways of determining the properties of an object, all of which lead back to the same ground. – If, for example, someone wants to draw a proof for the duty of truthfulness first from the *harm* a lie does to other human beings and then also from the *worthlessness* of a liar and his violation of respect for himself, what he has proved in the first case is a duty of benevolence, not of truthfulness, and so a duty other than the one for which proof was required. – But it is a highly unphilosophical expedient to resort to a number of proofs for one and the same proposition, consoling oneself that the multitude of reasons makes up for the inadequacy of any one of them taken by itself; for this indicates trickery and insincerity. When different insufficient reasons are *juxtaposed*, one does not compensate for the deficiency of the others for certainty or even for probability.

6:404　Proofs must *proceed* by ground and consequent in *a single series* to a sufficient ground; only in this way can they be demonstrative. – Yet the former method is the usual device of rhetoric.

Second. The distinction between virtue and vice can never be sought in the *degree* to which one follows certain maxims; it must rather be sought only in the specific *quality* of the maxims (their relation to the law). In other words, the well-known principle (Aristotle's) which locates virtue in the *mean* between two vices is false.* Let good management, for instance, consist in the *mean* between two vices, prodigality and avarice: as a virtue, it cannot be represented as arising either from a gradual diminution of prodigality (by saving) or from an increase of spending on the miser's part – as if these two vices, moving in opposite directions, met in good management. Instead, each of them has its distinctive maxim, which necessarily contradicts the maxim of the other.

---

*The formulae commonly used in the language of classical ethics: [1] *medio tutissimus ibis;* [2] *omne nimium vertitur in vitium;* [3] *est modus in rebus,* etc.; [4] *medium tenuere beati;* [5] *insani sapiens nomen habeat,*[p] etc., contain a superficial wisdom which really has no determinate principles. For who will specify for me this mean between the two extremes? What distinguishes *avarice* (as a vice) from thrift (as a virtue) is not that avarice carries thrift *too far* but that avarice has an *entirely different* principle (maxim), that of putting the end of economizing not in *enjoyment* of one's means but merely in *possession* of them, while denying oneself any enjoyment from them. In the same way, the vice of *prodigality* is not to be sought in an excessive enjoyment of one's means but in the bad maxim which makes the use of one's means the sole end, without regard for preserving them.

[p] [1] You will travel most safely in the middle of the road (Ovid *Metamorphoses* 2.137); [2] Too much of anything becomes vice; [3] There is a certain measure in our affairs and finally fixed limits, beyond which or short of which there is no place for right (Horace *Satires* 1.1.105–06), quotation supplemented in view of Kant's note to 6:433; [4] Happy are those who keep to the mean; [5] It is a foolish wisdom, equivalent to wickedness, that seeks to be virtuous beyond the proper measure (Horace *Epistles* 1.6.15), quotation supplemented in view of 6:409 and 6:433 n.

For the same reason, no vice whatever can be defined*q* in terms of *going further* in carrying out certain aims than there is any purpose in doing (e.g., *Prodigalitas* **est excessus** *in consumendis opibus*)*r* or of not going as far as is needed in carrying them out (e.g., *Avaritia* **est defectus** etc.).*s* Since this does not specify the *degree*, although it makes the conformity or nonconformity of conduct with duty depend entirely on it, this cannot serve as a definition.*t*

Third. Ethical duties must not be determined in accordance with the capacity to fulfill the law that is ascribed to human beings; on the contrary, their moral capacity must be estimated by the law, which commands categorically, and so in accordance with our rational knowledge of what they ought to be in keeping with the idea of humanity, not in accordance with the empirical knowledge we have of them as they are. These three maxims for scientific treatment of a doctrine of virtue are opposed to the following ancient dicta:

1) There is only one virtue and one vice.
2) Virtue is the observance of the middle way between opposing vices.*u*
3) Virtue (like prudence) must be learned from experience.

6:405

On virtue in general.

Virtue signifies a moral strength of the will. But this does not exhaust the concept; for such strength could also belong to a *holy* (superhuman) being, in whom no hindering impulses would impede the law of its will and who would thus gladly do everything in conformity with the law. Virtue is, therefore, the moral strength of a *human being's* will in fulfilling his *duty*, a moral *constraint* through his own lawgiving reason, insofar as this constitutes itself an authority *executing* the law.*v* – Virtue itself, or possession of it, is not a duty (for then one would have to be put under obligation to duties); rather, it commands and accompanies its command with a moral constraint (a constraint possible in accordance with laws of inner freedom). But because this constraint is to be irresistible, strength is required, in a degree which we can assess only by the magnitude of the obstacles that the human being himself furnishes through his inclinations. The vices, the brood of dispositions opposing the law, are the monsters he

---

q *erklärt*
r prodigality is *excess* in consuming one's means
s avarice is deficiency etc.
t *Erklärung*
u The first edition has *Meinungen*, "opinions," which seems to be a simple mistake for *Lastern*, "vices."
v *einer das Gesetz ausführenden Gewalt*

has to fight. Accordingly this moral strength, as *courage* (*fortitudo moralis*), also constitutes the greatest and the only true honor that man can win in war and is, moreover, called *wisdom* in the strict sense, namely practical wisdom, since it makes the *final end* of his existence on earth its own end. – Only in its possession is he "free," "healthy," "rich," "a king," and so forth and can suffer no loss by chance or fate, since he is in possession of himself and the virtuous man cannot lose his virtue.

Any high praise for the ideal of humanity in its moral perfection can lose nothing in practical reality from examples to the contrary, drawn from what human beings now are, have become, or will presumably become in the future; and *anthropology*, which issues from merely empirical cognition, can do no damage to *anthroponomy*, which is laid down by a reason giving laws unconditionally. And while virtue (in relation to human beings, not to the law) can be said here and there to be meritorious and to deserve to be rewarded, yet in itself, since it is its own end it must also be regarded as its own reward.

Considered in its complete perfection, virtue is therefore represented not as if a human being possesses virtue but rather as if virtue possesses him; for in the former case it would look as if he still had a choice (for which he would need yet another virtue in order to choose virtue in preference to any other goods offered him). – To think of several virtues (as one unavoidably does) is nothing other than to think of the various moral objects to which the will is led by the one principle of virtue, and so too with regard to the contrary vices. The expression that personifies both is an aesthetic device which still points to a moral sense. – So an aesthetic of morals, while not indeed part of the metaphysics of morals, is still a subjective presentation of it in which the feelings that accompany the constraining power of the moral law (e.g., disgust, horror, etc., which make moral aversion sensible) make its efficacy felt, in order to get the better of *merely* sensible incitements.

XIV.
ON THE PRINCIPLE THAT DISTINGUISHES THE DOCTRINE OF VIRTUE FROM THE DOCTRINE OF RIGHT.

This distinction, on which the main division of the *doctrine of morals* as a whole also rests, is based on this: that the concept of **freedom**, which is common to both, makes it necessary to divide duties into duties of *outer freedom* and duties of *inner freedom*, only the latter of which are ethical. – Hence inner freedom must first be treated in a preliminary remark (*discursus praeliminaris*), as the condition of all *duties of virtue*, (just as conscience was treated earlier, as the condition of all duties as such).

Remark
On the **doctrine of virtue** *in accordance with the principle of inner* **freedom**

An *aptitude*[w] (*habitus*) is a facility[x] in acting and a subjective perfection of *choice*. – But not every such *facility* is a *free* aptitude (*habitus libertatis*); for if it is a *habit*[y] (*assuetudo*), that is, a uniformity in action that has become a *necessity* through frequent repetition, it is not one that proceeds from freedom, and therefore not a moral aptitude. Hence virtue cannot be *defined* as an aptitude for free actions in conformity with law unless there is added "to determine oneself to act through the thought of the law," and then this aptitude is not a property of choice but of the *will*, which is a faculty of desire that, in adopting a rule, also gives it as a universal law. Only such an aptitude can be counted as virtue.

But two things are required for inner freedom: being one's own *master*[z] in a given case (*animus sui compos*), and *ruling* oneself[a] (*imperium in semetipsum*), that is, subduing one's affects and *governing* one's passions.[b] – In these two states one's *character* (*indoles*) is noble (*erecta*); in the opposite case it is mean (*indoles abiecta, serva*).

XV.
VIRTUE REQUIRES, IN THE FIRST PLACE, GOVERNING ONESELF

Affects and *passions*[45] are essentially different from each other. Affects belong to *feeling* insofar as, preceding reflection, it makes this impossible or more difficult. Hence an affect is called *precipitate* or *rash* (*animus praeceps*), and reason says, through the concept of virtue, that one should *get hold of* oneself. Yet this weakness in the use of one's understanding coupled with the strength of one's emotions is only a *lack of virtue* and, as it were, something childish and weak, which can indeed coexist with the best will. It even has one good thing about it: that this tempest quickly subsides. Accordingly a propensity to an affect (e.g., *anger*) does not enter into kinship with vice so readily as does a passion. A *passion* is a sensible *desire* that has become a lasting inclination (e.g., *hatred*, as opposed to anger). The calm with which one gives oneself up to it permits reflection

6:408

---
[w] *Fertigkeit*
[x] *Leichtigkeit*
[y] *Angewohnheit*
[z] *seiner selbst . . . Meister . . . zu sein*
[a] *über sich selbst Herr zu sein*
[b] *seine Affekten zu zähmen und seine Leidenschaften zu beherrschen*

and allows the mind to form principles upon it and so, if inclination lights upon something contrary to the law, to brood upon it, to get it rooted deeply, and so to take up what is evil (as something premeditated) into its maxim. And the evil is then *properly* evil,[c] that is, a true *vice*.

Since virtue is based on inner freedom it contains a positive command to a human being, namely to bring all his capacities and inclinations under his (reason's) control and so to rule over himself, which goes beyond forbidding him to let himself be governed by his feelings and inclinations (the duty of *apathy*); for unless reason holds the reins of government in its own hands, his feelings and inclinations play the master over him.

XVI.
VIRTUE NECESSARILY PRESUPPOSES *APATHY* (REGARDED AS STRENGTH).

The word "apathy" has fallen into disrepute, as if it meant lack of feeling and so subjective indifference with respect to objects of choice; it is taken for weakness. This misunderstanding can be prevented by giving the name "*moral apathy*" to that absence of affects which is to be distinguished from indifference because in cases of moral apathy feelings arising from sensible impressions lose their influence on moral feeling only because respect for the law is more powerful than all such feelings together. – Only the apparent strength of someone feverish lets a lively sympathy even for *what is good* rise into an affect, or rather degenerate into it. An affect of this kind is called *enthusiasm*, and the *moderation* that is usually recommended even for the practice of virtue is to be interpreted as referring to it (*insani sapiens nomen habeat[;] aequus iniqui* – **ultra quam satis est** *virtutem si petat ipsam. Horat.*);[d] for otherwise it is absurd to suppose that one could be *too wise, too virtuous*. An affect always belongs to sensibility, no matter by what kind of object it is aroused. The true strength of virtue is a *tranquil mind* with a considered and firm resolution to put the law of virtue into practice. That is the state of *health* in the moral life, whereas an affect, even one aroused by the thought of *what is good*, is a momentary, sparkling phenomenon that leaves one exhausted. – But that the human being can be called fantastically virtuous who allows *nothing to be morally indifferent* (*adiaphora*) and strews all his steps with duties, as with mantraps; it is not indifferent to him whether I eat meat or fish, drink beer or wine, supposing that both

---

[c] *ein qualificiertes Böse. Qualificiert* is used throughout the discussion of vices opposed to duties of love (6:458–61) and is translated as "proper."
[d] The wise man has the name of being a fool, the just man of being iniquitous, if he seeks virtue *beyond what is sufficient.* Horace *Epistles* 1.6.15.

agree with me. Fantastic virtue is a concern with petty details*e* which, were it admitted into the doctrine of virtue, would turn the government of virtue into tyranny.

Remark

Virtue is always *in progress* and yet always starts *from the beginning*. – It is always in progress because, considered *objectively*, it is an ideal and unattainable, while yet constant approximation to it is a duty. That it always starts from the beginning has a *subjective* basis in human nature, which is affected by inclinations because of which virtue can never settle down in peace and quiet with its maxims adopted once and for all but, if it is not rising, is unavoidably sinking. For, moral maxims, unlike technical ones, cannot be based on habit*f* (since this belongs to the natural constitution of the will's determination); on the contrary, if the practice of virtue were to become a habit the subject would suffer loss to that *freedom* in adopting his maxims which distinguishes an action done from duty.

XVII.
CONCEPTS PRELIMINARY TO THE DIVISION OF THE DOCTRINE OF VIRTUE

6:410

This principle of division must **first,** in terms of what is *formal*, contain all the conditions that serve to distinguish a part of the doctrine of morals in general from the doctrine of right and to do so in terms of its specific form. It does this by laying it down 1) that duties of virtue are duties for which there is no external lawgiving; 2) that since a law must yet lie at the basis of every duty, this law in ethics can be a law of duty given, not for actions, but only for the maxims of actions; 3) that (as follows in turn from this) ethical duty must be thought as *wide*, not as narrow, duty.

The principle of division must **secondly,** in terms of what is *material*, present the doctrine of virtue not merely as a doctrine of duties generally but also as a *doctrine of ends*, so that a human being is under obligation to regard himself, as well as every other human being, as his end. These are usually called duties of self-love and of love for one's neighbor; but then these words are used inappropriately, since there can be no direct duty to love, but instead to do that*g* by which one makes oneself and others one's end.

Third, with regard to the distinction of the material from the formal in

---

e Mikrologie
f Gewohnheit
g zu Handlungen, literally, "to actions"

the principle of duty (of conformity with law from conformity with ends),[h] it should be noted that not every *obligation of virtue*[i] (*obligatio ethica*) is a duty of virtue (*officium ethicum s. virtutis*); in other words, respect for law as such does not yet establish an end as a duty, and only such an end is a duty of virtue. – Hence there is only *one* obligation of virtue, whereas there are *many* duties of virtue; for there are indeed many objects that it is also our duty to have as ends, but there is only one virtuous disposition, the subjective determining ground to fulfill one's duty, which extends to duties of right as well although they cannot, because of this, be called duties of virtue. – Hence all the *divisions* of ethics will have to do only with duties of virtue. Viewed in terms of its formal principle, ethics is the science of how one is under obligation[j] without regard for any possible external lawgiving.

Remark

But, it will be asked, why do I introduce a division of ethics into a *Doctrine of Elements* and a *Doctrine of Method*, when no such division was needed in the doctrine of right? – The reason is that the doctrine of right has to do only with narrow duties, whereas ethics has to do with wide duties. Hence the doctrine of right, which by its nature must determine duties strictly (precisely), has no more need of general directions (a method) as to how to proceed in judging than does pure mathematics; instead, it certifies its method by what it does.[k] – But ethics, because of the latitude it allows in its imperfect duties, unavoidably leads to questions that call upon judgment to decide how a maxim is to be applied in particular cases, and indeed in such a way that judgment provides another (subordinate) maxim (and one can always ask for yet another principle for applying this maxim to cases that may arise). So ethics falls into a casuistry, which has no place in the doctrine of right.

Casuistry is, accordingly, neither a *science* nor a part of a science; for in that case it would be dogmatics, and casuistry is not so much a doctrine about how *to find* something as rather a practice in how *to seek* truth. So it is *woven into ethics* in a *fragmentary* way, not systematically (as dogmatics would have to be), and is added to ethics only by way of scholia to the system.

On the other hand, the *Doctrine of Method* of morally practical reason, which deals not so much with judgment as with reason and its *exercise* in both the *theory* and the *practice* of its duties, belongs to ethics in particular. The *first* exercise of it consists in *questioning* the pupil about what he already knows of concepts of duty, and may be called the

---

[h] *der Gesetzmäßigkeit von der Zweckmäßigkeit*
[i] *Tugendverpflichtung*
[j] *von der Art . . . verbindlich zu sein*
[k] *sie durch die Tat wahr macht*

erotetic method. If he knows this because he has previously been told it, so that now it is drawn merely from his memory, the method is called the *catechistic* method proper; but if it is assumed that this is already present naturally in the pupil's reason and needs only to be developed¹ from it, the method is called that of *dialogue* (Socratic method). Catechizing, as exercise in theory, has *ascetics* for its practical counterpart. Ascetics is that part of the doctrine of method in which is taught not only the concept of virtue but also how to put into practice and cultivate the *capacity for* as well as the will to virtue.ᵐ

In accordance with these principles we shall set forth the system in two parts: the *doctrine* of the *elements of ethics* and the *doctrine* of the *methods of ethics*. Each part will have its divisions. In the first part, these will be made in accordance with the different *subjects* to whom human beings are under obligation; in the second part, in accordance with the different *ends* that reason puts them under obligation to have, and with their receptivity to these ends.

XVIII.

The division that practical reason lays out to establish a system of its concepts in an *ethics* (the architectonic division) can be made in accordance with principles of two kinds, taken either singly or together. One sets forth *in terms of its matter* the *subjective* relation between a being that is under obligation and the being that puts him under obligation; the other sets forth in a system *in terms of its form* the *objective* relation of ethical laws to duties generally. – The *first* division is that of the *beings* in relation to whom ethical obligation can be thought; the *second* would be the division of the *concepts* of pure ethically practical reason which have to do with the duties of those beings. These concepts are, accordingly, required for ethics only insofar as it is to be a *science*, and so are required for the methodic arrangement of all the propositions found on the basis of the first division.

*First division of ethics
in accordance with the distinction of subjects and their laws.*

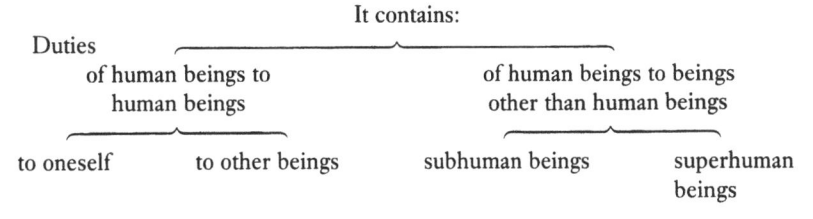

It contains:

Duties

of human beings to human beings	of human beings to beings other than human beings
to oneself — to other beings	subhuman beings — superhuman beings

¹ *entwickelt*
ᵐ *das Tugendvermögen sowohl als der Wille dazu*

IMMANUEL KANT

Second division of ethics
in accordance with principles of a system of pure practical reason.

```
                        Ethical
           ┌───────────────┴───────────────┐
   Doctrine of Elements            Doctrine of Methods
   ┌───────┴───────┐                ┌──────┴───────┐
Dogmatics      Casuistry        Catechizing      Ascetics
```

Because the latter division has to do with the form of the science, it must precede the first, as the ground plan of the whole.

I.
Doctrine of the elements of ethics

Doctrine of the elements of ethics
Part I
On duties to oneself as such
Introduction

§ 1. The concept of a duty to oneself contains (at first glance) a contradiction.

If the I *that imposes obligation* is taken in the same sense as the I *that is put under obligation,*ⁿ a duty to oneself is a self-contradictory concept. For the concept of duty contains the concept of being passively constrained (I am *bound*). But if the duty is a duty to myself, I think of myself as *binding* and so as actively constraining (I, the same subject, am imposing obligation). And the proposition that asserts a duty to myself (I *ought* to bind myself) would involve being bound to bind myself (a passive obligation that was still, in the same sense of the relation, also an active obligation), and hence a contradiction. – One can also bring this contradiction to light by pointing out that the one imposing obligation (*auctor obligationis*) could always release the one put under obligation (*subiectum obligationis*) from the obligation (*terminus obligationis*), so that (if both are one and the same subject) he would not be bound at all to a duty he lays upon himself. This involves a contradiction.

§ 2. Nevertheless, a human being has duties to himself.

For suppose there were no such duties: then there would be no duties whatsoever, and so no external duties either. – For I can recognize that I am under obligation to others only insofar as I at the same time put myself under obligation, since the law by virtue of which I regard myself as being under obligation proceeds in every case from my own practical reason; and in being constrained by my own reason, I am also the one constraining myself.*

§ 3. Solution of this apparent antinomy.

When a human being is conscious of a duty to himself, he views himself, as the subject of duty, under two attributes: first as a *sensible being*, that is, as a

---

* So when it is a question, for example, of vindicating my honor or of preserving myself, I say "I owe it to myself." Even in what concerns duties of less importance – those having to do only with what is meritorious rather than necessary in my compliance with duty – I speak in the same way, for example "I owe it to myself to increase my fitness for social intercourse and so forth (to cultivate myself)."

ⁿ *das verpflichtende Ich . . . dem verpflichteten*

human being (a member of one of the animal species), and secondly as an *intelligible being* (not merely as a being that has reason, since reason as a theoretical faculty[o] could well be an attribute[p] of a living corporeal being). The senses cannot attain this latter aspect of a human being; it can be cognized only in morally practical relations, where the incomprehensible property of *freedom* is revealed by the influence of reason on the inner lawgiving will.

Now the human being as a *natural being* that has reason (*homo phaenomenon*) can be determined by his reason, as a *cause*, to actions in the sensible world, and so far the concept of obligation does not come into consideration. But the same human being thought in terms of his *personality*, that is, as a being endowed with *inner freedom* (*homo noumenon*), is regarded as a being that can be put under obligation and, indeed, under obligation to himself (to the humanity in his own person). So the human being (taken in these two different senses) can acknowledge a duty to himself without falling into contradiction (because the concept of a human being is not thought in one and the same sense).

§4. On the principle on which the division of duties to oneself is based.

The division can be made only with regard to objects of duty, not with regard to the subject that puts himself under obligation. The subject that is bound, as well as the subject that binds, is always the *human being only;* and though we may, in a theoretical respect, distinguish soul and body from each other, as natural characteristics of a human being, we may not think of them as different substances putting him under obligation, so as to justify a division of duties to the *body* and duties to the *soul* – Neither experience nor inferences of reason[q] give us adequate grounds for deciding whether the human being has a soul (in the sense of a substance dwelling in him, distinct from the body and capable of thinking independently of it, that is, a spiritual substance), or whether life may not well be, instead, a property of matter. And even if the first alternative be true, it is still inconceivable that he should have a duty to a *body* (as a subject imposing obligation), even to a human body.

1) The only *objective* division of duties to oneself will, accordingly, be the division into what is **formal** and what is **material** in duties to oneself. The first of these are *limiting* (negative) duties; the second, *widening* (positive duties to oneself). Negative duties *forbid* a human being to act contrary to the **end** of his nature and so have to do merely with his moral *self-preservation;* positive duties, which *command* him to make a certain object of

---

[o] *nach ihrem theoretischen Vermögen*
[p] *Qualität*
[q] *Schlüsse der Vernunft*

choice his end, concern his *perfecting* of himself. Both of them belong to virtue, either as duties of omission (*sustine et abstine*) or as duties of commission (*viribus concessis utere*), but both belong to it as duties of virtue. The first belong to the moral **health** (*ad esse*) of a human being as object of both his outer senses and his inner sense, to the *preservation* of his nature in its perfection (as *receptivity*). The second belong to his moral *prosperity* (*ad melius esse, opulentia moralis*), which consists in possessing a *capacity* sufficient for all his ends, insofar as this can be acquired; they belong to his *cultivation* (active perfecting) of himself. – The first principle of duty to oneself lies in the dictum "live in conformity with nature" (*naturae convenienter vive*), that is, *preserve* yourself in the perfection of your nature; the second, in the saying "*make yourself more perfect* than mere nature has made you" (*perfice te ut finem, perfice te ut medium*).'

2) There will be a *subjective* division of a human being's duties to himself, that is, one in terms of whether the subject of duty (the human being) views himself both as an **animal** (natural) and a moral being or **only as a moral** being.

There are impulses of nature having to do with man's **animality**. Through them nature aims at a) his self-preservation, b) the preservation of the species, and c) the preservation of his capacity to enjoy life, though still on the animal level only.' – The vices that are here opposed to his duty to himself are *murdering himself*, the unnatural use of his *sexual inclination*, and such *excessive consumption of food and drink* as weakens his capacity for making purposive use of his powers.

But a human being's duty to himself as a moral being *only* (without taking his animality into consideration) consists in what is *formal* in the consistency of the maxims of his will with the *dignity* of humanity in his person. It consists, therefore, in a prohibition against depriving himself of the *prerogative* of a moral being, that of acting in accordance with principles, that is, inner freedom, and so making himself a plaything of the mere inclinations and hence a thing. – The vices contrary to this duty are **lying, avarice,** and **false humility** (servility). These adopt principles that are directly contrary to his character as a moral being (in terms of its very form), that is, to inner freedom, the innate dignity of a human being, which is tantamount to saying that they make it one's basic principle to have no basic principle and hence no character, that is, to throw oneself away and make oneself an object of contempt. – The virtue that is opposed to all these vices could be called *love of honor* (*honestas interna, iustum sui aestimium*), a cast of mind' far removed from *ambition* (*ambitio*) (which can be quite mean). But it will appear prominently later on, under this name.

' perfect yourself as an end, perfect yourself as a means
' The second edition emends the preceding passage to read: "c) the preservation of the subject's capacity to use his powers purposefully and to enjoy . . . "
' *Denkungsart*

The doctrine of virtue
Part I
Doctrine of the elements of ethics
Book I
Perfect duties to oneself

Chapter I.
Man's duty to himself as an animal being.

§ 5.

The *first*, though not the principal, duty of a human being to himself as an animal being is *to preserve himself* in his animal nature.

The contrary of this is willful[a] *physical death* or killing oneself (*autochiria*), which can be thought as either total, suicide (*suicidium*), or only partial, mutilating oneself. Mutilating oneself can in turn be either *material, depriving* oneself of certain integral, organic *parts*, that is, maiming oneself, or *formal, depriving* oneself (permanently or temporarily) of one's *capacity* for the natural (and so indirectly for the moral) *use* of one's powers.

Since this chapter deals only with negative duties and so with duties of omission, the articles about duties must be directed against the *vices* opposed to duties to oneself.

CHAPTER I
ARTICLE I.
ON KILLING ONESELF.

§ 6.

Willfully *killing* oneself[b] can be called **murdering oneself** (*homocidium dolosum*) only if it can be proved that it is in general a crime committed either against one's own person or also, through one's killing oneself, against another (as when a pregnant person takes her life).

---

[a] *willkürliche*
[b] *Die willkürliche Entleibung seiner selbst*

a) Killing oneself is a crime (murder). It can also be regarded as a violation of one's duty to other people (the duty of spouses to each other, of parents to their children, of a subject to his superior[w] or to his fellow citizens, and finally even as a violation of duty to God, as his abandoning the post assigned him in the world without having been called away from it). But since what is in question here is only a violation of duty to oneself, the question is whether, if I set aside all those relations, a human being is still bound to preserve his life simply by virtue of his quality as a person and whether he must acknowledge in this a duty (and indeed a strict duty) to himself.

It seems absurd to say that a human being could wrong himself[x] (*volenti non fit iniuria*).[y] Hence the Stoic thought it a prerogative of his (the sage's) personality to depart from life at his discretion (as from a smoke-filled room) with peace of soul, free from the pressure of present or anticipated ills, because he could be of no more use in life. – But there should have been in this very courage, this strength of soul not to fear death and to know of something that the human being can value even more highly than his life, a still stronger motive for him not to destroy himself, a being with such powerful authority over the strongest sensible incentives, and so not to deprive himself of life.

A human being cannot renounce his personality as long as he is a subject of duty, hence as long as he lives; and it is a contradiction that he should be authorized to withdraw from all obligation, that is, freely to act as if no authorization were needed for this action. To annihilate the subject of morality in one's own person is to root out the existence of morality itself from the world, as far as one can, even though morality is an end in itself. Consequently, disposing of oneself as a mere means to some discretionary end is debasing humanity in one's person (*homo noumenon*), to which the human being (*homo phaenomenon*) was nevertheless entrusted for preservation.

To deprive oneself of an integral part or organ (to maim oneself) – for example, to give away or sell a tooth to be transplanted into another's mouth, or to have oneself castrated in order to get an easier livelihood as a singer, and so forth – are ways of partially murdering oneself. But to have a dead or diseased organ amputated when it endangers one's life, or to have something cut off that is a part but not an organ of the body, for example, one's hair, cannot be counted as a crime against one's own

---

[w] *Obrigkeit*
[x] *sich selbst beleidigen könne.* In discussing perfect duties to oneself, as well as imperfect duties of respect to others, Kant often uses the terminology of *The Doctrine of Right*, as, e.g., in the preceding paragraph he called killing oneself a *Verbrechen*, which in *The Doctrine of Right* was a "crime" (*crimen*). Given the context in which these terms were introduced, however, it does not always seem advisable to translate them precisely as they were used in speaking of rights.
[y] no one is wronged willingly

person – although cutting one's hair in order to sell it is not altogether free from blame.

Casuistical questions

Is it murdering oneself to hurl oneself to certain death (like Curtius) in order to save one's country? – or is deliberate*ᶻ* martyrdom, sacrificing oneself for the good of all humanity, also to be considered an act of heroism?

Is it permitted to anticipate by killing oneself the unjust death sentence of one's ruler – even if the ruler permits this (as did Nero with Seneca)? Can a great king who died recently[46] be charged with a criminal intention for carrying a fast-acting poison with him, presumably so that if he were captured when he led his troops into battle he could not be forced to agree to conditions of ransom harmful to his state? – for one can ascribe this purpose to him without having to presume that mere pride lay behind it.

A man who had been bitten by a mad dog already felt hydrophobia coming on. He explained, in a letter he left, that, since as far as he knew the disease was incurable, he was taking his life lest he harm others as well in his madness (the onset of which he already felt). Did he do wrong?

Anyone who decides to be vaccinated against smallpox puts his life in danger, even though he does it *in order to preserve his life;* and, insofar as he himself brings on the disease that endangers his life, he is in a far more doubtful situation, as far as the law of duty is concerned, than is the sailor, who at least does not arouse the storm to which he entrusts himself. Is smallpox inoculation, then, permitted?

ARTICLE II.
ON DEFILING ONESELF BY LUST.

§ 7.

Just as love of life is destined by nature to preserve the person, so sexual love is destined by it to preserve the species; in other words, each of these is a *natural end,* by which is understood that connection of a cause with an effect in which, although no understanding is ascribed to the cause, it is still thought by analogy with an intelligent cause, and so as if it produced human beings on purpose. What is now in question is whether a person's use of his sexual capacity is subject to a limiting law of duty with regard to the person himself or whether he is authorized to direct the use of his sexual attributes to mere animal pleasure, without having in view the preservation of the species, and would not thereby be acting contrary to a duty to himself. – In the doctrine of right it was shown that the human being cannot make use of *another* person to get this pleasure apart from a special limitation by a contract establishing the right, by which two per-

---

ᶻ vorsetzliche

sons put each other under obligation. But the question here is whether the human being is subject to a duty to himself with regard to this enjoyment, violation of which is a *defiling* (not merely a debasing)[a] of the humanity in his own person. The impetus to this pleasure is called carnal lust (or also simply lust). The vice engendered through it is called lewdness; the virtue with regard to this sensuous impulse is called chastity, which is to be represented here as a duty of the human being to himself. Lust is called *unnatural* if one is aroused to it not by a real object but by his imagining it, so that he himself creates one, contrapurposively;[b] for in this way imagination brings forth a desire contrary to nature's end, and indeed to an end even more important than that of love of life itself, since it aims at the preservation of the whole species and not only of the individual.

6:425

That such an unnatural use (and so misuse) of one's sexual attribute is a violation of duty *to oneself,* and indeed one contrary to morality in its highest degree, occurs to everyone immediately, with the thought of it, and stirs up an aversion to this thought to such an extent that it is considered indecent even to call this vice by its proper name. This does not occur with regard to murdering oneself, which one does not hesitate in the least to lay before the world's eyes in all its horror (in a *species facti*).[c] In the case of unnatural vice it is as if the human being in general felt ashamed of being capable of treating his own person in such a way, which debases him beneath the beasts, so that when even the permitted bodily union of the sexes in marriage (a union which is in itself merely an animal union) is to be mentioned in polite society, this occasions and requires much delicacy to throw a veil over it.

But it is not so easy to produce a rational proof that unnatural, and even merely unpurposive,[d] use of one's sexual attribute is inadmissible as being a violation of duty to oneself (and indeed, as far as its unnatural use is concerned, a violation in the highest degree). – The *ground of proof* is, indeed, that by it the human being surrenders his personality (throwing it away), since he uses himself merely as a means to satisfy an animal impulse. But this does not explain the high degree of violation of the humanity in one's own person by such a vice in its unnaturalness, which seems in terms of its form (the disposition it involves) to exceed even murdering oneself. It consists, then, in this: that someone who defiantly casts off life as a burden is at least not making a feeble surrender to animal impulse in throwing himself away; murdering oneself requires courage, and in this disposition there is still always room for respect for the humanity in one's own person. But unnatural lust, which is complete abandon-

---

[a] *eine Schändung (nicht bloß Abwürdigung)*
[b] *zweckwidrig*
[c] *'Species facti* is the totality of those features of a deed that belong essentially to its imputability. See A. G. Baumgarten, *Initia philosophiae practicae primae*, included in 19:62.
[d] *unzweckmäßigen*

ment of oneself to animal inclination, makes the human being not only an object of enjoyment but, still further, a thing that is contrary to nature, that is, a *loathsome* object, and so deprives him of all respect for himself.

Casuistical questions

Nature's end in the cohabitation of the sexes is procreation, that is, the preservation of the species. Hence one may not, at least, act contrary to that end. But is it permitted to engage in this practice (even within marriage) *without taking this end into consideration?*

If, for example, the wife is pregnant or sterile (because of age or sickness), or if she feels no desire for intercourse, is it not contrary to nature's end, and so also contrary to one's duty to oneself, for one or the other of them, to make use of their sexual attributes – just as in unnatural lust? Or is there, in this case, a permissive law of morally practical reason, which in the collision of its determining grounds makes permitted something that is in itself not permitted (indulgently, as it were), in order to prevent a still greater violation? – At what point can the limitation of a wide obligation be ascribed to *purism* (a pedantry regarding the fulfillment of duty, as far as the wideness of the obligation is concerned), and the animal inclinations be allowed a latitude, at the risk of forsaking the law of reason?

Sexual inclination is also called "*love*" (in the narrowest sense of the word) and is, in fact, the strongest possible sensible pleasure[e] in an object. – It is not merely *sensitive* pleasure,[f] as in objects that are pleasing in mere reflection on them (receptivity to which is called taste). It is rather pleasure from the *enjoyment* of another person, which therefore belongs to the *faculty of desire* and, indeed, to its highest stage, passion. But it cannot be classed with either the love that is delight[g] or the love of benevolence (for both of these, instead, deter one from carnal enjoyment). It is a unique kind of pleasure (*sui generis*), and this ardor has nothing in common with moral love properly speaking, though it can enter into close union with it under the limiting conditions of practical reason.

ARTICLE III.
ON STUPEFYING ONESELF BY THE EXCESSIVE USE OF FOOD OR DRINK.

§ 8.

Here the reason for considering this kind of excess a vice is not the harm or bodily pain (diseases) that a human being brings on himself by it; for

---
[e] *Sinnenlust*
[f] *sinnliche Lust*
[g] *zur Liebe des Wohlgefallens*

then the principle by which it is to be counteracted would be one of well-being[h] and comfort (and so of happiness), and such a principle can establish only a rule of prudence, never a duty – at least not a direct duty.

Brutish excess in the use of food and drink is misuse of the means of nourishment that restricts or exhausts our capacity to use them intelligently. *Drunkenness* and *gluttony* are the vices that come under this heading. A human being who is drunk is like a mere animal, not to be treated as a human being. When stuffed with food he is in a condition in which he is incapacitated, for a time, for actions that would require him to use his powers with skill and deliberation. – It is obvious that putting oneself in such a state violates a duty to oneself. The first of these debasements, below even the nature of an animal, is usually brought about by fermented drinks, but it can also result from other narcotics, such as opium and other vegetable products. They are seductive because, under their influence, people dream for a while that they are happy and free from care, and even imagine that they are strong; but dejection and weakness follow and, worst of all, they create a need to use the narcotics again and even to increase the amount. Gluttony is even lower than that animal enjoyment of the senses, since it only lulls the senses into a passive condition and, unlike drunkenness, does not even arouse imagination to an *active* play of representations; so it approaches even more closely the enjoyment of cattle.

Casuistical questions 6:428

Can one at least justify, if not eulogize, a use of wine bordering on intoxication, since it enlivens the company's conversation and in so doing makes them speak more freely? – Or can it even be granted the merit of promoting what Horace praises in Cato: *virtus eius incaluit mero?*[i] – The use of opium and spirits for enjoyment is closer to being a base act than the use of wine, since they make the user silent, reticent and withdrawn by the dreamy euphoria they induce. They are therefore permitted only as medicines. – But who can determine the *measure* for someone who is quite ready to pass into a state in which he no longer has clear eyes for *measuring?* Mohammedanism, which forbids wine altogether, thus made a very bad choice in permitting opium to take its place.[j]

Although a banquet is a formal invitation to excess in both food and drink, there is still something in it that aims at a moral end, beyond mere

---

[h] *Wohlbefindens*
[i] His virtue was enkindled by unmixed wine. Kant is quoting, from memory, Horace *Odes* 3.21.11.
[j] In the second edition, the sentence "The use of opium . . . only as medicines" follows the sentence "But who can determine . . . for *measuring?*"

physical well-being:*k* it brings a number of people together for a long time to converse with one another. And yet the very number of guests (if, as Chesterfield says, it exceeds the number of the muses) allows for only a little conversation (with those sitting next to one); and so the arrangement is at variance with that end, while the banquet remains a temptation to something immoral, namely intemperance, which is a violation of one's duty to oneself – not to mention the physical harm of overindulgence, which could perhaps be cured by a doctor. How far does one's moral authorization to accept these invitations to intemperance extend?

Chapter II.
The human being's duty to himself merely as a moral being.

This duty is opposed to the vices of *lying, avarice* and *false humility* (servility).

6:429

I.
ON LYING.

§ 9.

The greatest violation of a human being's duty to himself regarded merely as a moral being (the humanity in his own person) is the contrary of truthfulness, *lying (aliud lingua promptum, aliud pectore inclusum gerere).*[l] In the doctrine of right an intentional untruth is called a lie only if it violates another's right; but in ethics, where no authorization is derived from harmlessness, it is clear of itself that no intentional untruth in the expression of one's thoughts can refuse this harsh name. For, the dishonor (being an object of moral contempt) that accompanies a lie also accompanies a liar like his shadow. A lie can be an external lie (*mendacium externum*) or also an internal lie. – By an external lie a human being makes himself an object of contempt in the eyes of others; by an internal lie he does what is still worse: he makes himself contemptible in his own eyes and violates the dignity of humanity in his own person. And so, since the harm that can come to others from lying is not what distinguishes this vice (for if it were, the vice would consist only in violating one's duty to others), this harm is not taken into account here. Neither is the harm that a liar brings upon himself; for then a lie, as a mere error in prudence, would conflict with the pragmatic maxim, not the moral maxim, and it could not be considered a violation of duty at all. – By a lie a human being throws

---

k Wohlleben

l To have one thing shut up in the heart and another ready on the tongue. Sallust *The War with Catiline* 10.5.

away and, as it were, annihilates his dignity as a human being. A human being who does not himself believe what he tells another (even if the other is a merely ideal person) has even less worth than if he were a mere thing; for a thing, because it is something real and given, has the property of being serviceable so that another can put it to some use. But communication of one's thoughts to someone through words that yet (intentionally) contain the contrary of what the speaker thinks on the subject is an end that is directly opposed to the natural purposiveness of the speaker's capacity to communicate his thoughts, and is thus a renunciation by the speaker of his personality, and such a speaker is a mere deceptive appearance of a human being, not a human being himself. – *Truthfulness* in one's declarations is also called *honesty*[m] and, if the declarations are promises, *sincerity*;[n] but, more generally, truthfulness is called *rectitude*.[o]

Lying (in the ethical sense of the word), intentional untruth as such, need not be *harmful* to others in order to be repudiated; for it would then be a violation of the rights of others. It may be done merely out of frivolity or even good nature;[p] the speaker may even intend to achieve a really good end by it. But his way of pursuing this end is, by its mere form, a crime of a human being against his own person and a worthlessness that must make him contemptible in his own eyes. 6:430

It is easy to show that the human being is actually guilty of many **inner** lies, but it seems more difficult to explain how they are possible; for a lie requires a second person whom one intends to deceive, whereas to deceive oneself on purpose seems to contain a contradiction.

The human being as a moral being (*homo noumenon*) cannot use himself as a natural being (*homo phaenomenon*) as a mere means (a speaking machine), as if his natural being were not bound to the inner end (of communicating thoughts), but is bound to the condition of using himself as a natural being in agreement with the declaration (*declaratio*) of his moral being and is under obligation to himself to *truthfulness*. – Someone tells an inner lie, for example, if he professes belief in a future judge of the world, although he really finds no such belief within himself but persuades himself that it could do no harm and might even be useful to profess in his thoughts to one who scrutinizes hearts a belief in such a judge, in order to win his favor in case he should exist. Someone also lies if, having no doubt about the existence of this future judge, he still flatters himself that he inwardly reveres his law, though the only incentive he feels is fear of punishment.

Insincerity is mere lack of *conscientiousness*, that is, of purity in one's professions before one's *inner* judge, who is thought of as another person

---

[m] *Ehrlichkeit*
[n] *Redlichkeit*
[o] *Aufrichtigkeit*
[p] *Gutmütigkeit*, perhaps "kindness"

when conscientiousness is taken quite strictly; then if someone, from self-love, takes a wish for the deed because he has a really good end in mind, his inner lie, although it is indeed contrary to his duty to himself, gets the name of a frailty, as when a lover's wish to find only good qualities in his beloved blinds him to her obvious faults. – But such insincerity in his declarations, which a human being perpetrates upon himself, still deserves the strongest censure, since it is from such a rotten spot (falsity, which seems to be rooted in human nature itself) that the ill of untruthfulness spreads into his relations with other human beings as well, once the highest principle of truthfulness has been violated.

Remark

It is noteworthy that the Bible dates the first crime, through which evil entered the world, not from *fratricide* (Cain's) but from the first *lie* (for even nature rises up against fratricide), and calls the author of all evil a liar from the beginning and the father of lies. However, reason can assign no further ground for the human propensity to *hypocrisy*[q] (*esprit fourbe*), although this propensity must have been present before the lie; for, an act of freedom cannot (like a natural effect) be deduced and explained in accordance with the natural law of the connection of effects with their causes, all of which are appearances.

Casuistical questions

Can an untruth from mere politeness (e.g., the "your obedient servant" at the end of a letter) be considered a lie? No one is deceived by it. – An author asks one of his readers "How do you like my work?" One could merely seem to give an answer, by joking about the impropriety of such a question. But who has his wit always ready? The author will take the slightest hesitation in answering as an insult. May one, then, say what is expected of one?

If I say something untrue in more serious matters,[r] having to do with what is mine or yours, must I answer for all the consequences it might have? For example, a householder has ordered his servant to say "not at home" if a certain human being asks for him. The servant does this and, as a result, the master slips away and commits a serious crime, which would otherwise have been prevented by the guard sent to arrest him. Who (in accordance with ethical principles) is guilty in this case? Surely the servant, too, who violated a duty to himself by his lie, the results of which his own conscience imputes to him.

[q] *Gleisnerei*
[r] *in wirklichen Geschäften*

II.
ON AVARICE.

§ 10.

By avarice in this context I do not mean *greedy avarice*[s] (acquiring the means to good living in excess of one's true needs), for this can also be viewed as a mere violation of one's duty (of beneficence) *to others;* nor, again, do I mean *miserly avarice,*[t] which is called *stinginess* or niggardliness when it is shameful but which can still be mere neglect of one's duties of love to others. I mean, rather, restricting *one's own* enjoyment of the means to good living so narrowly as to leave one's own true needs unsatisfied. It is really this kind of avarice, which is contrary to duty *to oneself,* that I am referring to here.[u]

In the censure of this vice, one example can show clearly[v] that it is incorrect to define any virtue or vice in terms of mere **degree,** and at the same time prove the uselessness of the *Aristotelian* principle that virtue consists in the middle way between two vices.

If I regard *good management* as the mean between prodigality and avarice and suppose this mean to be one of degree, then one vice would pass over into the (*contrarie*) opposite vice only through the *virtue;* and so virtue would be simply a diminished, or rather a vanishing, vice. The result, in the present case, would be that the real duty of virtue would consist in making no use at all of the means to good living.

If a vice is to be distinguished from a virtue, the difference one must cognize and explain is not a difference in the *degree* of practicing moral maxims but rather in the objective *principle* of the maxims. – The *maxim* of *greedy* avarice (prodigality) is to get and maintain[w] all the means to good living *with the intention of enjoyment.* – The maxim of *miserly* avarice, on the other hand, is to acquire as well as maintain all the means to good living, but *with no intention of enjoyment* (i.e., in such a way that one's end is only possession, not enjoyment).

Hence the distinctive mark of the latter vice is the principle of possessing means for all sorts of ends, but with the reservation of being unwilling

---

[s] *habsüchtigen Geiz*
[t] *kargen Geiz*
[u] In place of the passage "nor, again, do I mean *miserly avarice,*" the second edition has "I mean, rather, *miserly avarice,* which is called stinginess or niggardliness when it is shameful; and I am concerned with this kind of avarice, not as consisting in mere neglect of one's duties of love to others, but as a restricting of one's own use of the means for living well so narrowly as to leave one's true needs unsatisfied, and so as contrary to one's duty *to oneself.*" In fact, only two kinds of avarice, prodigality and miserliness, are in question.
[v] *kann man ein Beispiel der Unrichtigkeit aller Erklärungen deutlich machen und zugleich die Unbrauchbarkeit . . . dartun*
[w] The second edition omits "and maintain."

6:433 to use them for oneself, and so depriving oneself of the comforts necessary to enjoy life; and this is directly contrary to duty to oneself with regard to the end.* Accordingly, prodigality and miserliness are not distinguished from each other by degree; they are rather distinguished specifically, by their opposed maxims.

Casuistical questions

Selfishness (*solipsismus*) is the basis both of the greed (insatiability in acquiring wealth) that aims at sumptuous living and of niggardliness (painful 6:434 anxiety about waste); and it may seem that both of them – prodigality as well as miserliness – are to be repudiated merely because they end in poverty, though in the case of prodigality this result is unexpected and in the case of miserliness it is chosen[x] (one wills to live like a pauper). And so, since we are here speaking only of duty to oneself, it may be asked whether either prodigality or miserliness should be called a vice at all, or whether both are not mere imprudence and so quite beyond the bounds of one's duty to oneself. But miserliness is not just mistaken thrift, but rather

---

* The proposition, one ought not to do too much or too little of anything, says in effect nothing, since it is a tautology. What does it mean "to do too much"? Answer: to do more than is good. What does it mean "to do too little"? Answer: to do less than is good. What does it mean to say "I *ought* (to do or to refrain from something)"? Answer: that it is not good (that it is contrary to duty) to do more or less than is good. If that is the wisdom in search of which we should go back to the ancients (Aristotle), as to those who were nearer the fountainhead – *virtus consistit in medio, medium tenuere beati, est modus in rebus, sunt certi denique fines, quos citraque nequit consistere rectum* – then we have made a bad choice in turning to its oracle. Between truthfulness and lying (which are *contradictorie oppositis*) there is no mean; but there is indeed a mean between candor and reticence (which are *contrarie oppositis*), since one who declares his thoughts can say only what is true without telling the *whole truth*. Now it is quite natural to ask the teacher of virtue to point out this mean to me. But this he cannot do; for both duties of virtue have a latitude in their application (*latitudinem*), and judgment can decide what is to be done only in accordance with rules of prudence (pragmatic rules), not in accordance with rules of morality (moral rules). In other words, what is to be done cannot be decided after the manner of *narrow* duty (*officium strictum*), but after the manner of *wide* duty (*officium latum*). Hence one who complies with the basic principles of virtue can, it is true, commit a *fault* (*peccatum*) in putting these principles into practice, by doing more or less than prudence prescribes. But insofar as he adheres strictly to these basic principles he cannot practice a *vice* (*vitium*), and Horace's verse, *insani sapiens nomen habeat aequus iniqui,* **ultra quam satis est** *virtutem si petat ipsam,* is utterly false, if taken literally. In fact, *sapiens* here means only a *judicious* man (*prudens*), who does not think fantastically of virtue in its perfection. This is an ideal which requires one to approximate to this end but not to attain it completely, since the latter requirement surpasses man's powers and introduces a lack of sense (fantasy) into the principle of virtue. For really to be *too virtuous* – that is, to be too attached to one's duty – would be almost equivalent to making a circle too round or a straight line too straight. [For a translation of these Latin quotations see the page of this translation corresponding to 6:404 n.]

[x] *willkürliche*

slavish subjection of oneself to the goods that contribute to happiness,[y] which is a violation of duty to oneself since one ought to be their master. It is opposed to *liberality* of mind (*liberalitas moralis*) generally (not to generosity, *liberalitas sumptuosa*, which is only an application of this to a special case), that is, opposed to the principle of independence from everything except the law, and is a way in which the subject defrauds himself. But what kind of a law is it that the internal lawgiver itself does not know how to apply? Ought I to economize on food or only in my expenditures on external things? in old age, or already in youth? Or is thrift as such a virtue?

III.
ON SERVILITY.

§ 11.

In the system of nature, a human being (*homo phaenomenon, animal rationale*) is a being of slight importance and shares with the rest of the animals, as offspring of the earth, an ordinary value (*pretium vulgare*). Although a human being has, in his understanding, something more than they and can set himself ends, even this gives him only an *extrinsic* value for his usefulness (*pretium usus*); that is to say, it gives one man a higher value than another, that is, a *price* as of a commodity in exchange with these animals as things, though he still has a lower value than the universal medium of exchange, money, the value of which can therefore be called preeminent (*pretium eminens*).

But a human being regarded as a *person*, that is, as the subject of a morally practical reason, is exalted above any price; for as a person (*homo noumenon*) he is not to be valued merely as a means to the ends of others or even to his own ends, but as an end in itself, that is, he possesses a *dignity* (an absolute inner worth) by which he exacts *respect* for himself from all other rational beings in the world. He can measure himself with every other being of this kind and value himself on a footing of equality with them.

Humanity in his person is the object of the respect which he can demand from every other human being, but which he must also not forfeit. Hence he can and should value himself by a low as well as by a high standard, depending on whether he views himself as a sensible being (in terms of his animal nature) or as an intelligible being (in terms of his moral predisposition). Since he must regard himself not only as a person generally but also as a *human being*, that is, as a person who has duties his own reason lays upon him, his insignificance as a *human animal* may not infringe upon his consciousness of his dignity as a *rational human being*, and he should not disavow the moral self-esteem of such a being, that is,

6:435

---

[y] *die Glücksgüter*

he should pursue his end, which is in itself a duty, not abjectly, not in a *servile spirit* (*animo servili*) as if he were seeking a favor, not disavowing his dignity, but always with consciousness of his sublime moral predisposition (which is already contained in the concept of virtue). And this *self-esteem* is a duty of the human being to himself.

The consciousness and feeling of the insignificance of one's moral worth *in comparison with the* **law** is *humility* (*humilitas moralis*). A conviction of the greatness of one's moral worth, but only from failure to compare it with the law, can be called *moral arrogance* (*arrogantia moralis*). – Waiving any claim to moral worth in oneself, in the belief that one will thereby acquire a borrowed worth, is morally false *servility* (*humilitas spuria*).

Humility *in comparing oneself with other human beings* (and indeed with any finite being, even a seraph) is no duty; rather, trying to equal or surpass others in this respect, believing that in this way one will get an even greater inner worth, is *ambition* (*ambitio*), which is directly contrary to one's duty to others. But belittling one's own moral worth merely as a means to acquiring the favor of another, whoever it may be (hypocrisy and flattery[z])* is false (lying) humility, which is contrary to one's duty to oneself since it degrades one's personality.

True humility follows unavoidably from our sincere and exact comparison of ourselves with the moral law (its holiness and strictness). But from our capacity[a] for internal lawgiving and from the (natural) human being's feeling himself compelled to revere the (moral) human being within his own person, at the same time there comes *exaltation* of the highest self-esteem, the feeling of his inner worth (*valor*), in terms of which he is above any price (*pretium*) and possesses an inalienable dignity (*dignitas interna*), which instills in him respect for himself (*reverentia*).

§ *12.*

This duty with reference to the dignity of humanity within us, and so to ourselves, can be recognized, more or less, in the following examples.

Be no man's lackey. – Do not let others tread with impunity on your rights. – Contract no debt for which you cannot give full security. – Do not accept favors you could do without, and do not be a parasite or a flatterer or (what really differs from these only in degree) a beggar. Be thrifty, then, so that you will not become destitute. – Complaining and whining, even crying out in bodily pain, is unworthy of you, especially if you are aware of

---

* "*Heucheln*," properly "*häuchlen*" ["to dissemble"], seems to be derived from "*Hauch*," a moaning "breath" interrupting one's speech (a sigh). "*Schmeicheln*" ["to flatter"] seems to stem from "*Schmiegen*" ["to bend"] which, as a habit, is called "*Schmiegeln*" ["cringing"] and finally, in High German, "*Schmeicheln*."

[z] *Heuchelei und Schmeichelei*
[a] *Fähigkeit*

having deserved it; thus a criminal's death may be ennobled (its disgrace averted) by the resoluteness with which he dies. – Kneeling down or prostrating oneself on the ground, even to show your veneration for heavenly objects, is contrary to the dignity of humanity, as is invoking them in actual images;[b] for you then humble yourself, not before an *ideal* represented to you by your own reason, but before an *idol* of your own making.

Casuistical questions

Is not the human being's feeling for his sublime vocation, that is, his *elation of spirit* (*elatio animi*) or esteem for himself, so closely akin to *self-conceit* (*arrogantia*), the very opposite of true *humility* (*humilitas moralis*), that it would be advisable to cultivate humility even in comparing ourselves with other human beings, and not only with the law? Or would not this kind of self-abnegation instead strengthen others' verdict on us to the point of despising our person, so that it would be contrary to our duty (of respect) to ourselves? Bowing and scraping before a human being seems in any case to be unworthy of a human being.

Preferential tributes of respect in words and manners even to those who have no civil authority – reverences, obeisances (compliments) and courtly phrases marking with the utmost precision every distinction in rank, something altogether different from courtesy (which is necessary even for those who respect each other equally) – the *Du, Er, Ihr*, and *Sie*, or *Ew. Wohledeln, Hochedeln, Hochedelgeborenen, Wohlgeborenen* (*ohe, iam satis est!*)[c] as forms of address, a pedantry in which the Germans seem to outdo any other people in the world (except possibly the Indian castes): does not all this prove that there is a widespread propensity to servility in human beings? (*Hae nugae in seria ducunt.*)[d] But one who makes himself a worm cannot complain afterwards if people step on him.

Chapter II.

SECTION I.

On the Human Being's Duty to Himself as His Own Innate Judge.

§ 13.

Every concept of duty involves objective constraint through a law (a moral imperative limiting our freedom) and belongs to practical under-

---

[b] *in gegenwärtigen Bildern*
[c] Stay, that's enough! Horace *Satires* 1.5.12.
[d] These trifles lead to serious things.

standing, which provides a rule. But the internal *imputation* of a *deed*, as a case falling under a law (*in meritum aut demeritum*), belongs to the *faculty of judgment* (*iudicium*), which, as the subjective principle of imputing an action, judges with rightful force whether the action as a deed (an action coming under a law) has occurred or not. Upon it follows the conclusion of *reason* (the verdict), that is, the connecting of the rightful result with the action (condemnation or acquittal). All of this takes place before a *tribunal* (*coram iudicio*), which, as a moral person giving effect to the law, is called a *court* (*forum*). – Consciousness of an *internal court* in the human being ("before which his thoughts accuse or excuse one another") is **conscience**.

Every human being has a conscience and finds himself observed, threatened, and, in general, kept in awe (respect coupled with fear) by an internal judge; and this authority watching over the law in him is not something that he himself (voluntarily)[e] *makes*, but something incorporated in his being. It follows him like his shadow when he plans to escape. He can indeed stun himself or put himself to sleep by pleasures and distractions, but he cannot help coming to himself or waking up from time to time; and when he does, he hears at once its fearful voice. He can at most, in extreme depravity, bring himself to *heed* it no longer, but he still cannot help *hearing* it.

Now, this original intellectual and (since it is the thought of duty) moral predisposition called *conscience* is peculiar in that, although its business is a business of a human being with himself, one constrained by his reason sees himself constrained to carry it on as at the bidding *of another person*. For the affair here is that of trying *a case* (*causa*) before a court. But to think of a human being who is *accused* by his conscience as *one and the same person* as the judge is an absurd way of representing a court, since then the prosecutor would always lose. – For all duties a human being's conscience will, accordingly, have to think of *someone other* than himself (i.e., other than the human being as such) as the judge of his actions, if conscience is not to be in contradiction with itself. This other may be an actual person or a merely ideal person that reason creates for itself.*

---

*A human being who accuses and judges himself in conscience must think of a dual personality in himself, a doubled self which, on the one hand, has to stand trembling at the bar of a court that is yet entrusted to him, but which, on the other hand, itself administers the office of judge that it holds by innate authority. This requires clarification, if reason is not to fall into self-contradiction. – I, the prosecutor and yet the accused as well, am the same *human being* (*numero idem*). But the human being as the subject of the moral lawgiving which proceeds from the concept of freedom and in which he is subject to a law that he gives himself (*homo noumenon*) is to be regarded as another (*specie diversus*) from the human being as a sensible being endowed with reason, though only in a practical respect – for there is no theory about the causal relation of the intelligible to the sensible – and this specific differ-

[e] *willkürlich*

Such an ideal person (the authorized judge of conscience) must be a scrutinizer of hearts, since the court is set up *within* the human being. But he must also *impose all obligation,* that is, he must be, or be thought as, a person in relation to whom all duties whatsoever are to be regarded as also his commands; for conscience is the inner judge of all free actions. – Now since such a moral being must also have all power (in heaven and on earth) in order to give effect to his laws (as is necessarily required for the office of judge), and since such an omnipotent moral being is called **God**, conscience must be thought of as the subjective principle of being accountable to God for all one's deeds. In fact the latter concept is always contained (even if only in an obscure way) in the moral self-awareness of conscience.

This is not to say that a human being is entitled, through the idea to which his conscience unavoidably guides him, to *assume* that such a supreme being *actually exists* outside himself – still less that he is *bound* by his conscience to do so. For the idea is not given to him *objectively*, by theoretical reason, but only *subjectively*, by practical reason, putting itself under obligation to act in keeping with this idea; and through using practical reason, but *only in following out the analogy* with a lawgiver for all rational beings in the world, human beings are merely pointed in the direction of thinking of conscientiousness (which is also called *religio*) as accountability to a holy being (morally lawgiving reason) distinct from us yet present in our inmost being, and of submitting to the will of this being, as the rule of justice. The concept of religion is here for us only "a principle of estimating all our duties as divine commands."

1) In a case involving conscience (*causa conscientiam tangens*), the human being thinks of conscience as *warning* him (*praemonens*) before he makes his decision. In cases where conscience is the sole judge (*casibus conscientiae*), being most scrupulous (*scrupulositas*) where the concept of duty (something moral in itself) is concerned cannot be considered hair-splitting (a concern with petty details), nor can a real violation be considered a pecadillo (*peccatillium*) and be left to the advice of a conscience that speaks at will[h] (according to the principle *minima non curat praetor*).[i] Hence ascribing a *wide* conscience to someone amounts to calling him *unconscientious*.

---

ence is that of the faculties (higher and lower) of the human being that characterize him. The first is the prosecutor, against whom the accused is granted a legal adviser (defense counsel). When the proceedings are concluded the internal judge, as a person *having power*, pronounces the sentence of happiness or misery, as the moral results of the deed. Our reason cannot pursue further his power (as ruler of the world) in this function; we can only revere his unconditional *iubeo*[f] or *veto*[g]

[f] I command
[g] I forbid
[h] *willkürlich*
[i] the praetor is not concerned about trifles

2) When the deed has been done the *prosecutor* first comes forward in conscience, but along with him comes a *defense counsel* (advocate); and their dispute cannot be settled amicably (*per amicabilem compositionem*) but must rather be decided with all the rigor of right. Upon this follows

3) The verdict of conscience upon the human being, *acquitting* or *condemning* him with rightful force, which concludes the case.[47] It should be noted that when conscience acquits him it can never decide on a *reward* (*praemium*), something gained that was not his before, but can bring with it only *rejoicing* at having escaped the danger of being found punishable. Hence the blessedness found in the comforting encouragement of one's conscience is not *positive* (joy) but merely *negative* (relief from preceding anxiety); and this alone is what can be ascribed to virtue, as a struggle against the influence of the evil principle in a human being.

SECTION II.

On the **First Command** of All Duties to Oneself.

§ 14.

This command is "*know*[j] (scrutinize, fathom) *yourself*," not in terms of your natural perfection (your fitness or unfitness for all sorts of discretionary[k] or even commanded ends) but rather in terms of your moral perfection in relation to your duty. That is, know your heart – whether it is good or evil, whether the source of your actions is pure or impure, and what can be imputed to you as belonging originally to the *substance* of a human being or as derived (acquired or developed)[l] and belonging to your moral *condition*.

Moral cognition of oneself, which seeks to penetrate into the depths (the abyss) of one's heart which are quite difficult to fathom, is the beginning of all human wisdom. For in the case of a human being, the ultimate wisdom, which consists in the harmony of a being's will with its final end, requires him first to remove the obstacle within (an evil will actually present in him) and then to develop the original predisposition to a good will within him, which can never be lost. (Only the descent into the hell of self-cognition can pave the way to godliness.)

§ 15.

This moral cognition of oneself will, first, dispel *fanatical* contempt for oneself as a human being (for the whole human race), since this contradicts itself. – It is only through the noble predisposition to the good in us,

---
[j] *Erkenne*
[k] *beliebigen*
[l] *erworben oder zugezogen*

which makes the human being worthy of respect, that one can find one who acts contrary to it contemptible (the human being himself, but not the humanity in him). – But such cognition will also counteract that *egotistical* self-esteem which takes mere wishes – wishes that, however ardent, always remain empty of deeds – for proof of a good heart. (*Prayer,* too, is only a wish declared inwardly before someone who knows hearts.) Impartiality in appraising oneself in comparison with the law, and sincerity in acknowledging to oneself one's inner moral worth or lack of worth are duties to oneself that follow directly from this first command to cognize oneself.

6:442

EPISODIC SECTION

On an **amphiboly** in **moral concepts of reflection**, taking what is a human being's duty to himself for a duty to other beings

§ 16.

As far as reason alone can judge, a human being has duties only to human beings (himself and others), since his duty to any subject is moral constraint by that subject's will. Hence the constraining (binding) subject must, *first,* be a person; and this person must, *secondly,* be given as an object of experience, since the human being is to strive for the end of this person's will and this can happen only in a relation to each other of two beings that exist (for a mere thought-entity cannot be the *cause* of any result in terms of ends). But from all our experience we know of no being other than a human being that would be capable[m] of obligation (active or passive). A human being can therefore have no duty to any beings other than human beings; and if he thinks he has such duties, it is because of an *amphiboly* in his *concepts of reflection,* and his supposed duty to other beings is only a duty to himself. He is led to this misunderstanding by mistaking his duty *with regard to* other beings for a duty *to* those beings.

This supposed duty can be referred to objects *other than persons* or to objects that are indeed persons, but quite *imperceptible* ones (who cannot be presented to the outer senses). – The first (*nonhuman*) objects can be mere inorganic matter (minerals), or matter organized for reproduction though still without sensation (plants), or the part of nature endowed with sensation and choice (animals). The second (*superhuman*) objects can be thought as spiritual beings (angels, God). – It must now be asked whether there is a relation of duty between human beings and beings of these two kinds, and what relation there is between them.

---

[m] *fähig*

§ 17.

A propensity to wanton destruction of what is *beautiful* in inanimate nature (*spiritus destructionis*) is opposed to a human being's duty to himself; for it weakens or uproots that feeling in him which, though not of itself moral, is still a disposition[n] of sensibility that greatly promotes morality or at least prepares the way for it: the disposition, namely, to love something (e.g., beautiful crystal formations, the indescribable beauty of plants) even apart from any intention to use it.

With regard to the animate but nonrational part of creation, violent and cruel treatment of animals is far more intimately opposed to a human being's duty to himself, and he has a duty to refrain from this; for it dulls his shared feeling of their suffering and so weakens and gradually uproots a natural predisposition that is very serviceable to morality in one's relations with other people. The human being is authorized to kill animals quickly (without pain) and to put them to work that does not strain them beyond their capacities (such work as he himself must submit to). But agonizing physical experiments for the sake of mere speculation, when the end could also be achieved without these, are to be abhorred. – Even gratitude for the long service of an old horse or dog (just as if they were members of the household) belongs *indirectly* to a human being's duty *with regard to* these animals; considered as a *direct* duty, however, it is always only a duty of the human being *to* himself.

§ 18.

Again, we have a duty *with regard to* what lies entirely beyond the limits of our experience but whose possibility is met with in our ideas, for example, the idea of God; it is called the *duty of religion,* the duty "of recognizing all our duties *as* (*instar*) divine commands." But this is not consciousness of a duty *to God*. For this idea proceeds entirely from our own reason and we ourselves make it, whether for the theoretical purpose of explaining to ourselves the purposiveness in the universe as a whole or also for the purpose of serving as the incentive in our conduct. Hence we do not have before us, in this idea, a given being to whom we would be under obligation; for in that case its reality would first have to be shown (disclosed) through experience. Rather, it is a duty of the human being to himself to apply this idea, which presents itself unavoidably to reason, to the moral law in him, where it is of the greatest moral fruitfulness. In this **(practical)** sense it can therefore be said that to have religion is a duty of the human being to himself.

---

[n] *Stimmung*

THE METAPHYSICS OF MORALS

Duties to oneself
Book II.
On a human being's imperfect duties to himself (with regard to his end).

SECTION I.

A human being's duty to himself to develop and increase his **natural perfection,** that is, for a pragmatic purpose.⁰

§ 19.

A human being has a duty to himself to cultivate (*cultura*) his natural powers (powers of spirit, mind, and body), as means to all sorts of possible ends. – He owes it to himself (as a rational being) not to leave idle and, as it were, rusting away the natural predispositions and capacities*ᵖ* that his reason can some day use. Even supposing that he could be satisfied with the innate scope of his capacities for his natural needs, his reason must first show him, by principles, that this meager scope of his capacities is *satisfactory;* for, as a being capable*ᵍ* of ends (of making objects his ends), he must owe the use of his powers not merely to natural instinct but rather to the freedom by which he determines their scope. Hence the basis on which he should develop his capacities (for all sorts of ends) is not regard for the *advantages* that their cultivation can provide; for the advantage might (according to Rousseau's principles) turn out on the side of his crude natural needs. Instead, it is a command of morally practical reason and a *duty* of a human being to himself to cultivate his capacities (some among them more than others, insofar as people have different ends), and to be in a pragmatic respect a human being equal to the end of his existence.

Powers of spirit are those whose exercise is possible only through reason. They are creative to the extent that their use is not drawn from experience but rather derived a priori from principles, of the sort to be found in mathematics, logic, and the metaphysics of nature. The latter two are also included in philosophy, namely theoretical philosophy, which does not then mean wisdom, as the word itself would suggest, but only science. However, theoretical philosophy can help to promote the end of wisdom.

Powers of soulʳ are those which are at the disposal of understanding and the rule it uses to fulfill whatever purposes one might have, and because of

6:445

⁰ *in pragmatischer Absicht*
ᵖ *Naturanlage und Vermögen*
ᵍ *fähig*
ʳ *Seelenkräfte*

this experience is their guide. They include memory, imagination and the like, on which can be built learning, taste (internal and external embellishment) and so forth, which furnish instruments for a variety of purposes.

Finally, cultivating the *powers of the body* (gymnastics in the strict sense) is looking after the *basic stuff* (the matter) in a human being, without which he could not realize his ends. Hence the continuing and purposive invigoration of the animal in him is an end of a human being that is a duty to himself.

§ 20.

Which of these natural perfections should take *precedence*, and in what proportion one against the other it may be a human being's duty to himself to make these natural perfections his end, are matters left for him to choose in accordance with his own rational reflection about what sort of life he would like to lead and whether he has the powers necessary for it (e.g., whether it should be a trade, commerce, or a learned profession). For, quite apart from the need to maintain himself, which in itself cannot establish a duty, a human being has a duty to himself to be a useful member of the world, since this also belongs to the worth of humanity in his own person, which he ought not to degrade.

But a human being's duty to himself regarding his *natural* perfection is only a *wide* and imperfect duty; for while it does contain a law for the maxim of actions, it determines nothing about the kind and extent of actions themselves but allows a latitude for free choice.

SECTION II.

On a human being's duty to himself to increase his **moral** perfection, that is, for a moral purpose only.[s]

§ 21.

First, this perfection consists subjectively in the *purity* (*puritas moralis*) of one's disposition to duty, namely, in the law being by itself alone the incentive, even without the admixture of aims derived from sensibility, and in actions being done not only in conformity with duty but also *from duty*. – Here the command is "be holy." *Secondly*, as having to do with one's entire moral end, such perfection consists objectively in fulfilling all one's duties and in attaining completely one's moral end with regard to oneself. Here the command is "be perfect." But a human being's striving after this end always remains only a progress from *one* perfection to another. "If there be any virtue, and if there be any praise, strive for it."[48]

[s] *in bloss sittlicher Absicht*

§ 22.

This duty to oneself is a *narrow* and perfect one in terms of its quality; but it is wide and imperfect in terms of its degree, because of the *frailty* (*fragilitas*) of human nature.

It is a human being's duty to *strive* for this perfection, but not to *reach* it (in this life), and his compliance with this duty can, accordingly, consist only in continual progress. Hence while this duty is indeed narrow and perfect *with regard to* its object (the idea that one should make it one's end to realize), *with regard to* the subject it is only a wide and imperfect duty to himself.

The depths of the human heart are unfathomable. Who knows himself well enough to say, when he feels the incentive to fulfill his duty, whether it proceeds entirely from the representation of the law or whether there are not many other sensible impulses contributing to it that look to one's advantage (or to avoiding what is detrimental) and that, in other circumstances, could just as well serve vice? – But with regard to perfection as a moral end, it is true that in its idea (objectively) there is only *one* virtue (as moral strength of one's maxims); but in fact (subjectively) there is a multitude of virtues, made up of several different qualities,[1] and it would probably be impossible not to find in it some lack of virtue, if one wanted to look for it (though, because of those virtues, such other qualities are not usually called vices). But a sum of virtues such that our cognition of ourselves can never adequately tell us whether it is complete or deficient can be the basis only of an imperfect duty to be perfect.

All duties to oneself regarding the end of humanity in our own person, are, therefore, only imperfect duties.

---

[1] *von heterogener Beschaffenheit*

Doctrine of the elements of ethics
Part II.
Duties of virtue to others.

Chapter I.
On duties to others merely as human beings.

SECTION I.
ON THE DUTY OF LOVE TO OTHER HUMAN BEINGS.

Division

§ 23.

The chief division can be that into duties to others by performing which you also put others under obligation and duties to others the observance of which does not result in obligation on the part of others. – Performing the first is *meritorious* (in relation to others); but performing the second is fulfilling a duty *that is owed.* – *Love* and *respect* are the feelings that accompany the carrying out of these duties. They can be considered separately (each by itself) and can also exist separately (one can *love* one's neighbor though he might deserve but little *respect,* and can show him the respect necessary for every human being regardless of the fact that he would hardly be judged worthy of love). But they are basically always united by the law into one duty, only in such a way that now one duty and now the other is the subject's principle, with the other joined to it as accessory. – So we shall acknowledge that we are under obligation to help someone poor; but since the favor we do implies that his well-being depends on our generosity, and this humbles him, it is our duty to behave as if our help is either merely what is due him or but a slight service of love, and to spare him humiliation and maintain his respect for himself.

§ 24.

In speaking of laws of duty (not laws of nature) and, among these, of laws for human beings' external relations with one another, we consider ourselves in a moral (intelligible) world where, by analogy with the physical world, *attraction* and *repulsion* bind together rational beings (on earth). The principle of **mutual love** admonishes them constantly to *come closer*

THE METAPHYSICS OF MORALS

to one another; that of the **respect** they owe one another, to keep themselves *at a distance* from one another; and should one of these great moral forces fail, "then nothingness (immorality), with gaping throat, would drink up the whole kingdom of (moral) beings like a drop of water" (if I may use Haller's words, but in a different reference).

§ 25.

In this context, however, **love** is not to be understood as *feeling*,[u] that is, as pleasure in the perfection of others; love is not to be understood as *delight* in them (since others cannot put one under obligation to have feelings). It must rather be thought as the maxim of *benevolence* (practical love), which results in beneficence.

The same holds true of the **respect** to be shown to others. It is not to be understood as the mere *feeling* that comes from comparing our own *worth* with another's (such as a child feels merely from habit toward his parents, a pupil toward his teacher, or any subordinate toward his superior). It is rather to be understood as the *maxim* of limiting our self-esteem by the dignity of humanity in another person, and so as respect in the practical sense (*observantia aliis praestanda*).

Moreover, a duty of free respect toward others is, strictly speaking, only a negative one (of not exalting oneself above others) and is thus analogous to the duty of right not to encroach upon what belongs to anyone.[v] Hence, although it is a mere duty of virtue, it is regarded as *narrow* in comparison with a duty of love, and it is the latter that is considered a *wide* duty.

The duty of love for one's neighbor can, accordingly, also be expressed as the duty to make others' *ends* my own (provided only that these are not immoral). The duty of respect for my neighbor is contained in the maxim not to degrade any other to a mere means to my ends (not to demand that another throw himself away in order to slave[w] for my end).

By carrying out the duty of love to someone I put another under obligation; I make myself deserving from him. But in observing a duty of respect I put only myself under obligation; I keep myself within my own bounds so as not to detract anything from the worth that the other, as a human being, is authorized to put upon himself.

On the duty of love in particular

§ 26.

Since the love of human beings (philanthropy) we are thinking of here is practical love, not the love that is delight in them, it must be taken as

---

[u] *ästhetisch*
[v] *niemanden des Seine zu schmälern*
[w] *Fröhnen*

active benevolence, and so as having to do with the maxim of actions. – Someone who finds satisfaction in the well-being (*salus*) of human beings considered simply as human beings for whom it is *well* when things go well for every other, is called a *friend of humanity* in general (a philanthropist). Someone for whom it is well only when things go badly for others is called an *enemy of humanity* (a misanthropist in the practical sense). Someone who is indifferent to how things go for others if only they go well for himself is *selfish* (*solipsista*). – But someone who avoids other human beings because he can find no *delight* in them, though he indeed *wishes* all of them *well*, would be *shy* of them (a misanthropist in terms of his sensibility),[x] and his turning away from them could be called anthropophobia.

§ 27.

In accordance with the ethical law of perfection "love your neighbor as yourself," the maxim of benevolence (practical love of human beings) is a duty of all human beings toward one another, whether or not one finds them worthy of love. – For, every morally practical relation to human beings is a relation among them represented by pure reason, that is, a relation of free actions in accordance with maxims that qualify for a giving of universal law and so cannot be selfish (*ex solipsismo prodeuntes*). I want everyone else to be benevolent toward me (*benevolentiam*); hence I ought also to be benevolent toward everyone else. But since all *others* with the exception of myself would not be *all*, so that the maxim would not have within it the universality of a law, which is still necessary for imposing obligation, the law making benevolence a duty will include myself, as an object of benevolence, in the command of practical reason. This does not mean that I am thereby under obligation to love myself (for this happens unavoidably, apart from any command, so there is no obligation to it); it means instead that lawgiving reason, which includes the whole species (and so myself as well) in its idea of humanity as such,[y] includes me as giving universal law along with all others in the duty of mutual benevolence, in accordance with the principle of equality, and *permits* you to be benevolent to yourself on the condition of your being benevolent to every other as well; for it is only in this way that your maxim (of beneficence) qualifies for a giving of universal law, the principle on which every law of duty is based.

§ 28.

Now the benevolence present in love for all human beings is indeed the greatest in its *extent*, but the smallest in its *degree;* and when I say that I take an interest in this human being's well-being only out of my love for

---

[x] *ästhetischer Misanthrop*
[y] In the first edition the phrase *nicht der Mensch* ("not the human being") occurs here. It is omitted in the second edition.

all human beings, the interest I take is as slight as an interest can be. I am only not indifferent with regard to him.

Yet one human being is closer to me than another, and in benevolence I am closest to myself. How does this fit in with the precept "love your *neighbor* (your fellow-human being) as yourself"? If one is closer to me than another (in the duty of benevolence) and I am therefore under obligation to greater benevolence to one than to the other but am admittedly closer to myself (even in accordance with duty) than to any other, then it would seem that I cannot, without contradicting myself, say that I ought to love every human being as myself, since the measure of self-love would allow for no difference in degree. – But it is quite obvious that what is meant here is not merely benevolence in *wishes*, which is, strictly speaking, only taking delight in the well-being of every other and does not require me to contribute to it (everyone for himself, God for us all); what is meant is, rather, active, practical benevolence (beneficence), making the well-being and happiness of others my *end*. For in wishing I can be *equally* benevolent to everyone, whereas in acting I can, without violating the universality of the maxim, vary the degree greatly in accordance with the different objects of my love (one of whom concerns me more closely than another).

Division of duties of love

They are duties of A) *beneficence*, B) *gratitude*, and C) *sympathy*.

A.
On the duty of beneficence.
§ 29.

Providing for oneself to the extent necessary just to find satisfaction in living (taking care of one's body, but not to the point of effeminacy)[z] belongs among duties to oneself. The contrary of this is depriving oneself (slavishly) of what is essential to the cheerful enjoyment of life, by *avarice*, or depriving oneself (fanatically) of enjoyment of the pleasures of life by exaggerated *discipline* of one's natural inclinations. Both of these are opposed to a human being's duty to himself.

But beyond *benevolence* in our wishes for others (which costs us nothing) how can it be required as a duty that this should also be practical, that is, that everyone who has the means to do so should be *beneficent* to those in need? – Benevolence is satisfaction in the happiness (well-being) of others; but beneficence is the maxim of making others' happiness one's end, and the duty to it consists in the subject's being constrained by his reason to adopt this maxim as a universal law.

---

[z] *Weichlichkeit*

It is not obvious that any such law is to be found in reason. On the contrary, the maxim "Everyone for himself, God (fortune) for us all" seems to be the most natural one.

§ 30.

To be beneficent, that is, to promote according to one's means the happiness of others in need, without hoping for something in return, is everyone's duty.

For everyone who finds himself in need wishes to be helped by others. But if he lets his maxim of being unwilling to assist others in turn when they are in need become public, that is, makes this a universal permissive law, then everyone would likewise deny him assistance when he himself is in need, or at least would be authorized to deny it. Hence the maxim of self-interest would conflict with itself if it were made a universal law, that is, it is contrary to duty. Consequently the maxim of common interest, of beneficence toward those in need, is a universal duty of human beings, just because they are to be considered fellow human beings, that is, rational beings with needs, united by nature in one dwelling place so that they can help one another.

§ 31.

Someone who is *rich* (has abundant means for the happiness of others, i.e., means in excess of his own needs) should hardly even regard beneficence as a meritorious duty on his part, even though he also puts others under obligation by it. The satisfaction he derives from his beneficence, which costs him no sacrifice, is a way of reveling in moral feelings. He must also carefully avoid any appearance of intending to bind the other by it; for if he showed that he wanted to put the other under an obligation (which always humbles the other in his own eyes), it would not be a true benefit that he rendered him. Instead, he must show that he is himself put under obligation by the other's acceptance or honored by it, hence that the duty is merely something that he owes, unless (as is better) he can practice his beneficence in complete secrecy. – This virtue is greater when the benefactor's means are limited and he is strong enough quietly to take on himself the hardship he spares the other; then he is really to be considered morally rich.

Casuistical questions

How far should one expend one's resources in practicing beneficence? Surely not to the extent that he himself would finally come to need the beneficence of others. How much worth has beneficence extended with a cold hand (by a will to be put into effect at one's death)? – If someone who exercises over another (a serf of his estate) the greater power permitted by the law of the hand *robs* the other of his freedom to make himself happy in accordance with his own choices, can he, I say, consider himself the other's benefactor because he looks after him paternalistically in accordance with *his own* concepts of happiness? Or is not the injustice of depriving someone of his freedom something so contrary to duty of right as such that one who willingly consents to submit to this condition, counting on his master's beneficence, commits the greatest rejection of his own humanity, and that the master's utmost concern for him would not really be beneficence at all? Or could the merit of such beneficence be so great as to outweigh the right of human beings? – I cannot do good to anyone in accordance with *my* concepts of happiness (except to young children and the insane), thinking to benefit him by forcing a gift upon him; rather, I can benefit him only in accordance with *his* concepts of happiness.

Having the resources to practice such beneficence as depends on the goods of fortune is, for the most part, a result of certain human beings being favored through the injustice of the government, which introduces an inequality of wealth that makes others need their beneficence. Under such circumstances, does a rich man's help to the needy, on which he so readily prides himself as something meritorious, really deserve to be called beneficence at all?

B.
On the duty of gratitude.

Gratitude consists in *honoring* a person because of a benefit he has rendered us. The feeling connected with this judgment is respect for the benefactor (who puts one under obligation), whereas the benefactor is viewed as only in a relation of love toward the recipient. – Even mere heartfelt *benevolence* on another's part, without physical results, deserves to be called a duty of virtue; and this is the basis for the distinction between *active* and merely *affective*[a] gratitude.

6:455

§ 32.

Gratitude is a duty. It is not a merely *prudential* maxim of encouraging the other to show me further beneficence by acknowledging my obligation to him for a favor he has done (*gratiarum actio est ad plus dandum invitatio*),[b] for I would then be using my acknowledgment merely as a means to my further purposes. Gratitude is, rather, direct constraint in accordance with a moral law, that is, a duty.

But gratitude must also be considered, in particular, a *sacred* duty, that is, a duty the violation of which (as a scandalous example) can destroy the moral incentive to beneficence in its very principle. For, a moral object is

---

[a] *affektionellen*
[b] an action of gratitude is an invitation to more of the same

sacred if the obligation with regard to it cannot be discharged completely by any act in keeping with it (so that one who is under obligation always remains under obligation). Any other duty is an *ordinary* duty. – But one cannot, by any repayment of a kindness received, *rid* oneself of the obligation for it, since the recipient can never win away from the benefactor his *priority* of merit, namely having been the first in benevolence. – But even mere heartfelt benevolence, apart from any such act (of beneficence), is already a basis of obligation to gratitude. – A grateful disposition of this kind is called *appreciativeness*.

§ 33.

As far as the *extent*[c] of this gratitude is concerned, it reaches not only to one's contemporaries but also to one's predecessors, even to those one cannot identify with certainty. It is for this reason, too, that it is thought improper not to defend the ancients, who can be regarded as our teachers, from all attacks, accusations, and disdain, insofar as this is possible. But it is a foolish mistake to attribute preeminence in talents and good will to the ancients in preference to the moderns just because of their antiquity, as if the world were steadily declining in accordance with laws of nature from its original perfection, and to despise everything new in comparison with antiquity.

But the *intensity*[d] of gratitude, that is, the degree of obligation to this virtue, is to be assessed by how useful the favor was to the one put under obligation and how unselfishly it was bestowed on him. The least degree is to render *equal* services to the benefactor if he can receive them (if he is still living) or, if he cannot, to render them to others; it involves not regarding a kindness received as a burden one would gladly be rid of (since the one so favored stands a step lower than his benefactor, and this wounds his pride), but taking even the occasion for gratitude as a moral kindness, that is, as an opportunity given one to unite the virtue of gratitude with love of man, to combine the *cordiality*[e] of a benevolent disposition with *sensitivity*[f] to benevolence (attentiveness to the smallest degree of this disposition in one's thought of duty), and so to cultivate one's love of human beings.

C.
Sympathetic feeling is generally a duty.
§ 34.

Sympathetic joy and *sadness* (*sympathia moralis*) are sensible feelings of pleasure or displeasure (which are therefore to be called "aesthetic") at

---

[c] *Extension*
[d] *Intension*
[e] *Innigkeit*
[f] *Zärtlichkeit*

another's state of joy or pain (shared feeling, sympathetic feeling). Nature has already implanted in human beings receptivity to these feelings. But to use this as a means to promoting active and rational benevolence is still a particular, though only a conditional, duty. It is called the duty of *humanity* (*humanitas*) because a human being is regarded here not merely as a rational being but also as an animal endowed with reason. Now, humanity can be located either in the *capacity*[g] and the *will* to *share in others' feelings* (*humanitas practica*) or merely in the *receptivity*, given by nature itself, to the feeling of joy and sadness in common with others (*humanitas aesthetica*). The first is *free*, and is therefore called *sympathetic* (*communio sentiendi liberalis*); it is based on practical reason. The second is *unfree* (*communio sentiendi illiberalis, servilis*); it can be called *communicable* (since it is like receptivity to warmth or contagious diseases), and also compassion,[h] since it spreads naturally among human beings living near one another. There is obligation only to the first.

6:457

It was a sublime way of thinking that the Stoic ascribed to his wise men when he had him say "I wish for a friend, not that he might help *me* in poverty, sickness, imprisonment, etc., but rather that I might stand by *him* and rescue a human being." But the same wise man, when he could not rescue his friend, said to himself "what is it to me?" In other words, he rejected compassion.

In fact, when another suffers and, although I cannot help him, I let myself be infected by his pain (through my imagination), then two of us suffer, though the trouble really (in nature) affects only *one*. But there cannot possibly be a duty to increase the ills in the world and so to do good *from compassion*. This would also be an insulting kind of beneficence, since it expresses the kind of benevolence one has toward someone unworthy, called *pity;* and this has no place in people's relations with one another, since they are not to make a display of their worthiness to be happy.

§ 35.

But while it is not in itself a duty to share the sufferings (as well the joys) of others, it is a duty to sympathize actively in their fate; and to this end it is therefore an indirect duty to cultivate the compassionate natural (aesthetic)[i] feelings in us, and to make use of them as so many means to sympathy based on moral principles and the feeling appropriate to them. – It is therefore a duty not to avoid the places where the poor who lack the most basic necessities are to be found but rather to seek them out, and not to shun sickrooms or debtors' prisons and so forth in order to avoid

---

[g] *Vermögen*
[h] Or "imparted suffering." The words translated as "sympathetic," "communicable," and "compassion" are, respectively, *teilnehmend, mitteilend,* and *Mitleidenschaft.*
[i] *ästhetische*

sharing painful feelings one may not be able to resist. For this is still one of the impulses that nature has implanted in us to do what the representation of duty alone might not accomplish.[j]

Casuistical questions

Would it not be better for the well-being of the world generally if human morality were limited to duties of right, fulfilled with the utmost conscientiousness, and benevolence were considered morally indifferent? It is not so easy to see what effect this would have on human happiness. But at least a great moral adornment, benevolence,[k] would then be missing from the world. This is, accordingly, required by itself, in order to present the world as a beautiful moral whole in its full perfection, even if no account is taken of advantages (of happiness).

Gratitude is not, strictly speaking, love toward a benefactor on the part of someone he has put under obligation, but rather *respect* for him. For universal love of one's neighbor can and must be based on equality of duties, whereas in gratitude the one put under obligation stands a step lower than his benefactor. Is it not this, namely pride, that causes so much ingratitude? seeing someone above oneself and feeling resentment at not being able to make oneself fully his equal (as far as relations of duty are concerned)?

On the vices of hatred for human beings, directly (contrarie) opposed to love of them.

§ 36.

They comprise the loathsome family of *envy, ingratitude,* and *malice.* – In these vices, however, hatred is not open and violent but secret and veiled, adding meanness to one's neglect of duty to one's neighbor, so that one also violates a duty to oneself.

a) *Envy* (*livor*) is a propensity to view the well-being of others with distress, even though it does not detract from one's own. When it breaks forth into action (to diminish their well-being) it is called envy *proper;* otherwise it is merely *jealousy* (*invidentia*). Yet envy is only an indirectly malevolent disposition, namely a reluctance to see our own well-being overshadowed by another's because the standard we use to see how well off we are is not the intrinsic worth of our own well-being but how it compares with that of others. – Accordingly one speaks, too, of *enviable* harmony and happiness in a marriage or family and so forth, just as if envying someone were permitted in many cases. Movements of envy are therefore present in human nature, and only when they break out do they

---
[j] *für sich allein nicht ausrichten würde*[49]
[k] *Menschenliebe*

constitute the abominable vice of a sullen passion that tortures oneself and aims, at least in terms of one's wishes, at destroying others' good fortune. This vice is therefore contrary to one's duty to oneself as well as to others.

b) When *ingratitude* toward one's benefactor extends to hatred of him it is called *ingratitude proper*, but otherwise mere *unappreciativeness*. It is, indeed, publicly judged to be one of the most detestable vices; and yet human beings are so notorious for it that it is not thought unlikely that one could even make an enemy by rendering a benefit. – What makes such a vice possible is misunderstanding one's duty to oneself, the duty of not needing and asking for others' beneficence, since this puts one under obligation to them, but rather preferring to bear the hardships of life oneself than to burden others with them and so incur indebtedness (obligation); for we fear that by showing gratitude we take the inferior position of a dependent in relation to his protector, which is contrary to real self-esteem (pride in the dignity of humanity in one's own person). Hence gratitude is freely shown to those who must *unavoidably* have preceded us in conferring benefits (to the ancestors we commemorate or to our parents); but to contemporaries it is shown only sparingly and indeed the very opposite of it is shown, in order to hide this relation of inequality. – But ingratitude is a vice that shocks humanity, not merely because of the *harm* that such an example must bring on people in general by deterring them from further beneficence (for with a genuine moral disposition they can, just by scorning any such return for their beneficence, put all the more inner moral worth on it), but because ingratitude stands love of human beings on its head, as it were, and degrades absence of love into an authorization to hate the one who loves.

c) *Malice*, the direct opposite of sympathy, is likewise no stranger to human nature; but when it goes so far as to help bring about ills or evil it makes hatred of human beings visible and appears in all its hideousness as *malice proper*. It is indeed natural that, by the laws of imagination (namely, the law of contrast), we feel our own well-being and even our good conduct more strongly when the misfortune of others or their downfall in scandal is put next to our own condition, as a foil to show it in so much the brighter light. But to rejoice immediately in the existence of such *enormities* destroying what is best in the world as a whole, and so also to wish for them to happen, is secretly to hate human beings; and this is the direct opposite of love for our neighbor, which is incumbent on us as a duty. – It is the *haughtiness* of others when their welfare is uninterrupted, and their *self-conceit* in their good conduct (strictly speaking, only in their good fortune in having so far escaped temptations to public vice) – both of which an egotist accounts to his merit – that generate this malevolent joy, which is directly opposed to one's duty in accordance with the principle of sympathy (as expressed by Terence's honest Chremes): "I am a human being; whatever befalls human beings concerns me too."[50]

6:460

The sweetest form of malice is the *desire for revenge*.[1] Besides, it might even seem that one has the greatest right, and even the obligation (as a desire for justice), to make it one's end to harm others without any advantage to oneself.

Every deed that violates a human being's right deserves punishment, the function of which is to *avenge*[m] a crime on the one who committed it (not merely to make good the harm that was done). But punishment is not an act that the injured party can undertake on his private authority but rather an act of a court distinct from him, which gives effect to the law of a *supreme authority* over all those subject to it; and when (as we must in ethics) we regard human beings as in a rightful condition but *in accordance only with laws of reason* (not civil laws), then no one is authorized to inflict punishment and to avenge[n] the wrongs sustained by them except him who is also the supreme moral lawgiver; and he alone (namely God) can say "Vengeance[o] is mine; I will repay." It is, therefore, a duty of virtue not only to refrain from repaying another's enmity with hatred out of mere revenge but also not even to call upon the judge of the world for vengeance, partly because a human being has enough guilt of his own to be greatly in need of pardon and partly, and indeed especially, because no punishment, no matter from whom it comes, may be inflicted out of hatred. – It is therefore a duty of human beings to be *forgiving* (*placabilitas*). But this must not be confused with *meek toleration* of wrongs (*mitis iniuriarum patientia*), renunciation of rigorous means (*rigorosa*) for preventing the recurrence of wrongs by others; for then a human being would be throwing away his rights and letting others trample on them, and so would violate his duty to himself.

Remark. If vice is taken in the sense of a basic principle (a vice proper), then any vice, which would make human nature itself detestable, is *inhuman* when regarded objectively. But considered subjectively, that is, in terms of what experience teaches us about our species, such vices are still *human*. As to whether, in vehement revulsion, one could call some of these vices *devilish*, and so too the virtues opposed to them *angelic*, both of these concepts are only ideas of a maximum used as a standard for comparing degrees of morality; in them one assigns a human being his place in *heaven* or *hell*, without making of him an intermediate sort of being who occupies neither one place nor the other. The question may remain open here whether Haller did not hit upon it better with his "an ambiguous hybrid of angel and beast." But dividing something composite into two heterogeneous things yields no

---

[1] *Rachbegierde*
[m] *wodurch . . . gerächt . . . wird*
[n] *rächen*
[o] *Rache*

definite concept at all, and can lead us to none in ordering beings whose class distinctions are unknown to us. The first comparison (of angelic virtue and devilish vice) is an exaggeration. The second – although human beings do, alas, also fall into *brutish* vices – does not justify attributing to them a predisposition to these vices *belonging to their species,* any more than the stunting of some trees in a forest is a reason for making them a special *kind* of plant.

SECTION II.
ON DUTIES OF VIRTUE TOWARD OTHER HUMAN BEINGS ARISING FROM THE RESPECT DUE THEM.

6:462

§ 37.

Moderation in one's demands generally, that is, willing restriction of one's self-love in view of the self-love of others, is called *modesty.* Lack of *such moderation* (lack of modesty) as regards one's worthiness to be *loved* by others is called *egotism* (*philautia*). But lack of modesty in one's claims to be **respected** by others is *self-conceit* (*arrogantia*). The *respect* that I have for others or that another can require from me (*observantia aliis praestanda*) is therefore recognition of a *dignity* (*dignitas*) in other human beings, that is, of a worth that has no price, no equivalent for which the object evaluated (*aestimii*) could be exchanged. – Judging something to be worthless is contempt.

§ 38.

Every human being has a legitimate claim to respect from his fellow human beings and is *in turn* bound to respect every other. Humanity itself is a dignity; for a human being cannot be used merely as a means by any human being (either by others or even by himself) but must always be used at the same time as an end. It is just in this that his dignity (personality) consists, by which he raises himself above all other beings in the world that are not human beings and yet can be used, and so over all *things*. But just as he cannot give himself away for any price (this would conflict with his duty of self-esteem), so neither can he act contrary to the equally necessary self-esteem of others, as human beings, that is, he is under obligation to acknowledge, in a practical way, the dignity of humanity in every other human being. Hence there rests on him a duty regarding the respect that must be shown to every other human being.

§ 39.

6:463

To be *contemptuous* of others (*contemnere*), that is, to deny them the respect owed to human beings in general, is in every case contrary to duty; for they are human beings. At times one cannot, it is true, help inwardly *looking down* on some in comparison with others (*despicatui habere*); but the outward manifestation of this is, nevertheless, an offense.[p] – What is *dangerous* is no object of contempt, and so neither is a vicious man; and if my superiority to his attacks justifies my saying that I despise him, this means only that I am in no danger from him, even though I have prepared no defense against him, because he shows himself in all his depravity. Nonetheless I cannot deny all respect to even a vicious man as a human being; I cannot withdraw at least the respect that belongs to him in his quality as a human being, even though by his deeds he makes himself unworthy of it. So there can be disgraceful punishments that dishonor humanity itself (such as quartering a man, having him torn by dogs, cutting off his nose and ears). Not only are such punishments more painful than loss of possessions and life to one who loves honor (who claims the respect of others, as everyone must); they also make a spectator blush with shame at belonging to a species that can be treated that way.

> *Remark.* On this is based a duty to respect a human being even in the logical use of his reason, a duty not to censure his errors by calling them absurdities, poor judgment and so forth, but rather to suppose that his judgment must yet contain some truth and to seek this out, uncovering, at the same time, the deceptive illusion (the subjective ground that determined his judgment which, by an oversight, he took for objective), and so, by explaining to him the possibility of his having erred, to preserve his respect for his own understanding. For if, by using such expressions, one denies any understanding to someone who opposes one in a certain judgment, how does one want to bring him to understand that he has erred? – The same thing applies to the censure of vice, which must never break out into complete contempt and denial of any moral worth to a vicious human being; for on this supposition he could never be improved, and this not consistent with the idea of a *human being,* who as such (as a moral being) can never lose entirely his predisposition to the good.

§ 40.

Respect for the law, which in its subjective aspect is called moral feeling, is identical with consciousness of one's duty. This is why showing respect for a human being as a moral being (holding his duty in highest esteem) is also a duty that others have toward him and a right to which he cannot renounce his claim. – This claim is called *love of honor,* and its manifestation in external conduct, *respectability* (*honestas externa*). An offense against respectability is called *scandal,* an example of disregarding respectability that might lead others to follow it. To *give* scandal is quite contrary to duty.

---

[p] *Beleidigung*

But to *take* scandal at what is merely unconventional (*paradoxon*) but otherwise in itself good is a delusion (since one holds what is unusual to be impermissible as well), an error dangerous and destructive to virtue. – For a human being cannot carry his giving an example of the respect due others so far as to degenerate into blind imitation (in which custom, *mos*, is raised to the dignity of a law), since such a tyranny of popular mores would be contrary to his duty to himself.

§ 41.

Failure to fulfill mere duties of love is *lack of virtue* (*peccatum*). But failure to fulfill the duty arising from the *respect* owed to every human being as such is a *vice* (*vitium*). For no one is wronged if duties of love are neglected; but a failure in the duty of respect infringes upon one's lawful claim. – The first violation is opposed to duty as its *contrary* (*contrarie oppositum virtutis*). But what not only adds nothing moral but even abolishes the worth of what would otherwise be to the subject's good is *vice.*

For this reason, too, duties to one's fellow human beings arising from the respect due them are expressed only negatively, that is, this duty of virtue will be expressed *only indirectly* (through the prohibition of its opposite).

On vices that violate duties of respect for other human beings.

These vices are A) *arrogance,* B) *defamation,* and C) *ridicule.*

A.
Arrogance.
§ 42.

Arrogance (*superbia* and, as this word expresses it, the inclination to be always *on top*) is a kind of *ambition* (*ambitio*) in which we demand that others think little of themselves in comparison with us. It is, therefore, a vice opposed to the respect that every human being can lawfully claim.

It differs from **pride proper** (*animus elatus*), which is *love of honor,* that is, a concern to yield nothing of one's human dignity in comparison with others (so that the adjective "*noble*" is usually added to "pride" in this sense); for arrogance demands from others a respect it denies them. – But *pride* itself becomes a fault and an offense when it, too, is merely a demand upon others to concern themselves with one's importance.

Arrogance is, as it were, a solicitation on the part of one seeking honor for followers, whom he thinks he is entitled to treat with contempt. It is obvious that this is *unjust* and opposed to the respect owed to human beings as such; that it is *folly,* that is, frivolity in using means to something so related to them as not to be worth being taken as an end; that someone arrogant is even a *conceited ass*,[q] that is, that he shows an offensive lack of understanding in using such means as must bring about, on the part of others, the exact opposite of his end (for the more he shows that he is trying to obtain respect, the more everyone denies it to him). – But it might not be so readily noticed that someone arrogant is always *mean* in the depths of his soul. For he would not demand that others think little of themselves in comparison with him unless he knew that, were his fortune suddenly to change, he himself would not find it hard to grovel and to waive any claim to respect from others.

B.
Defamation.
§ 43.

By defamation (*obtrectatio*) or backbiting I do not mean *slander* (*contumelia*), a *false* defamation to be taken before a court; I mean only the immediate inclination, with no particular aim in view, to bring into the open something prejudicial to respect for others. This is contrary to the respect owed to humanity as such; for every scandal given weakens that respect, on which the impulse to the morally good rests, and so far as possible makes people skeptical about it.

The intentional *spreading* (*propalatio*) of something that detracts from another's honor – even if it is not a matter of public justice, and even if what is said is true – diminishes respect for humanity as such, so as finally to cast a shadow of worthlessness over our race itself, making misanthropy (shying away from human beings) or contempt the prevalent cast of mind, or to dull one's moral feeling by repeatedly exposing one to the sight of such things and accustoming one to it. It is, therefore, a duty of virtue not to take malicious pleasure in exposing the faults of others so that one will be thought as good as, or at least not worse than, others, but rather to throw the veil of philanthropy[r] over their faults, not merely by softening our judgments but also by keeping these judgments to ourselves; for examples of respect that we give others can arouse their striving to deserve it. – For this reason, a mania for spying on the morals of others (*allotrio-episcopia*) is by itself already an offensive inquisitiveness on the part of anthropology, which everyone can resist with right as a violation of the respect due him.

C.
Ridicule.
§ 44.

Wanton faultfinding and *mockery*, the propensity to expose others to laughter, to make their faults the immediate object of one's amusement, is a

---

[q] The distinction between being "foolish" and being "a conceited ass" is, as in *Anthropology from a Pragmatic Point of View* (7:210), that between *Torheit* and *Narrheit*.
[r] *Menschenliebe*

kind of malice. It is altogether different from *banter*, from the familiarity among friends in which one makes fun of their peculiarities that only seem to be faults but are really marks of their pluck in sometimes departing from the rule of fashion (for this is not derision). But holding up to ridicule a person's real faults, or supposed faults as if they were real, in order to deprive him of the respect he deserves, and the propensity to do this, a mania for *caustic* mockery (*spiritus causticus*), has something of fiendish joy in it; and this makes it an even more serious violation of one's duty of respect for other human beings.

This must be distinguished from a jocular, even if derisive, brushing aside with contempt an insulting attack of an adversary (*retorsio iocosa*), by which the mocker (or, in general, a malicious but ineffectual adversary) is himself made the laughing stock. This is a legitimate defense of the respect one can require from him. But when the object of his mockery is really no object for wit but one in which reason necessarily takes a moral interest, then no matter how much ridicule the adversary may have uttered and thereby left himself open to laughter it is more befitting the dignity of the object and respect for humanity either to put up no defense against the attack or to conduct it with dignity and seriousness.

> *Remark.* It will be noticed that under the above heading virtues were not so much commended as rather the vices opposed to them censured. But this is already implicit in the concept of the respect we are bound to show other human beings, which is only a *negative* duty. I am not bound to *revere*[s] others (regarded merely as human beings), that is, to show them *positive* high esteem.[t] The only reverence[u] to which I am bound by nature is reverence for law as such (*revere legem*); and to revere[v] the law, but not to revere other human beings in general (*reverentia adversus hominem*) or to perform some act of reverence for them, is a human being's universal and unconditional duty toward others, which each of them can require as the respect originally owed others (*observantia debita*).

6:468

The different forms of respect to be shown to others in accordance with differences in their qualities or contingent relations – differences of age, sex, birth, strength or weakness, or even rank and dignity, which depend in part on arbitrary arrangements – cannot be set forth in detail and classified in the *metaphysical* first principles of a doctrine of virtue, since this has to do only with its pure rational principles.

---

[s] *verehren*

[t] *Hochachtung*

[u] *Achtung*

[v] *verehren*. Kant may well have in mind the duty not to give scandal. However, the second edition changes this sentence to read "To obey the law also with regard to other men, but not to . . ."

Chapter II.
On ethical duties of human beings toward one another with regard to their **condition**.

§ 45.

These (duties of virtue) do not really call for a special chapter in the system of pure ethics; since they do not involve principles of obligation for human beings as such toward one another, they cannot properly constitute a *part* of the *metaphysical* first principles of a doctrine of virtue. They are only rules modified in accordance with differences of the *subjects* to whom the principle of virtue (in terms of what is formal) is *applied* in cases that come up in experience (the material). Hence, like anything divided on an empirical basis, they do not admit of a classification that could be guaranteed to be complete. Nevertheless, just as a passage from the metaphysics of nature to physics is needed – a transition having its own special rules – something similar is rightly required from the metaphysics of morals: a transition which, by applying the pure principles of duty to cases of experience, would *schematize* these principles, as it were, and present them as ready for morally practical use. How should one behave, for example, toward human beings who are in a state of moral purity or depravity? toward the cultivated or the crude? toward men of learning or the ignorant, and toward the learned insofar as they use their science as members of polite society or outside society, as specialists in their field (scholars)? toward those whose learning is pragmatic or those in whom it proceeds more from spirit and taste? How should people be treated in accordance with their differences in rank, age, sex, health, prosperity or poverty and so forth? These questions do not yield so many different *kinds* of ethical *obligation*[w] (for there is only *one,* that of virtue as such), but only so many different ways of *applying* it (corollaries). Hence they cannot be presented as sections of ethics and members of the *division* of a system (which must proceed a priori from a rational concept), but can only be appended to the system. Yet even this application belongs to the complete presentation of the system.

Conclusion of the elements of ethics
On the most intimate union of love with respect in
friendship

§ 46.

Friendship (considered in its perfection) is the union of two persons through equal mutual love and respect. – It is easy to see that this is an

---

[w] *Arten der ethischen Verpflichtung*

ideal of each participating and sharing sympathetically in the other's well-being through the morally good will that unites them, and even though it does not produce the complete happiness of life, the adoption of this ideal in their disposition toward each other makes them deserving of happiness; hence human beings have a duty of friendship. – But it is readily seen that friendship is only an idea (though a practically necessary one) and unattainable in practice, although striving for friendship (as a maximum of good disposition toward each other) is a duty set by reason, and no ordinary duty but an honorable one. For in his relations with his neighbor how can a human being ascertain whether one of the elements requisite to this duty (e.g., benevolence toward each other) is *equal* in the disposition of each of the friends? Or, even more difficult, how can he tell what relation there is in the same person between the feeling from one duty and that from the other (the feeling from benevolence and that from respect)? And how can he be sure that if the *love* of one is stronger, he may not, just because of this, forfeit something of the other's *respect*, so that it will be difficult for both to bring love and respect subjectively into that equal balance required for friendship? – For love can be regarded as attraction and respect as repulsion, and if the principle of love bids friends to draw closer, the principle of respect requires them to stay at a proper distance from each other. This limitation on intimacy, which is expressed in the rule that even the best of friends should not make themselves too familiar with each other, contains a maxim that holds not only for the superior in relation to the inferior but also in reverse. For the superior, before he realizes it, feels his pride wounded and may want the inferior's respect to be put aside for the moment, but not abolished. But once respect is violated, its presence within is irretrievably lost, even though the outward marks of it (manners) are brought back to their former course.

6:470

Friendship thought as attainable in its purity or completeness (between Orestes and Pylades, Theseus and Pirithous) is the hobby horse of writers of romances. On the other hand Aristotle says: My dear friends, there is no such thing as a friend! The following remarks may draw attention to the difficulties in perfect friendship.

From a moral point of view it is, of course, a duty for one of the friends to point out the other's faults to him; this is in the other's best interests and is therefore a duty of love. But the latter sees in this a lack of the respect he expected from his friend and thinks that he has either already lost or is in constant danger of losing something of his friend's respect, since he is observed and secretly criticized by him; and even the fact that his friend observes him and finds fault with him[x] will seem in itself offensive.

---

[x] The context of "even the fact" would make *gemeistert* (finds fault with) seem to be a misprint for *gemustert* (examines).

How one wishes for a friend in need (one who is, of course, an active friend, ready to help at his own expense)! But still it is also a heavy burden to feel chained to another's fate and encumbered with his needs. – Hence friendship cannot be a union aimed at mutual advantage but must rather be a purely moral one, and the help that each may count on from the other in case of need must not be regarded as the end and determining ground of friendship – for in that case one would lose the other's respect – but only as the outward manifestation of an inner heartfelt benevolence, which should not be put to the test since this is always dangerous; each is generously concerned with sparing the other his burden and bearing it all by himself, even concealing it altogether from his friend, while yet he can always flatter himself that in case of need he could confidently count on the other's help. But if one of them accepts a favor from the other, then he may well be able to count on equality in love, but not in respect; for he sees himself obviously a step lower in being under obligation without being able to impose obligation in turn. – Although it is sweet to feel in possession of each other that approaches fusion into one person, friendship is something so delicate (*teneritas amicitiae*) that it is never for a moment safe from interruptions if it is allowed to rest on feelings, and if this mutual sympathy and self-surrender are not subjected to principles or rules preventing excessive familiarity and limiting mutual love by requirements of respect. Such interruptions are common among uncultivated people, although they do not always result in a split (for the rabble fight and make up). Such people cannot part with each other, and yet they cannot be at one with each other since they need quarrels in order to savor the sweetness of being united in reconciliation. – But in any case the love in friendship cannot be an affect; for emotion is blind in its choice, and after a while it goes up in smoke.

§ 47.

Moral friendship (as distinguished from friendship based on feeling)[y] is the complete confidence of two persons in revealing their secret judgments and feelings to each other, as far as such disclosures are consistent with mutual respect.

The human being is a being meant for society (though he is also an unsociable one), and in cultivating the social state he feels strongly the need to *reveal* himself to others (even with no ulterior purpose). But on the other hand, hemmed in and cautioned by fear of the misuse others may make of his disclosing his thoughts, he finds himself constrained *to lock up* in himself a good part of his judgments (especially those about other people). He would like to discuss with someone what he thinks about his associates, the government, religion and so forth, but he cannot risk it:

[y] *ästhetischen*

partly because the other person, while prudently keeping back his own judgments, might use this to harm him, and partly because, as regards disclosing his faults, the other person may conceal his own, so that he would lose something of the other's respect by presenting himself quite candidly to him.

If he finds someone intelligent[z] – someone who, moreover, shares his general outlook on things – with whom he need not be anxious about this danger but can reveal himself with complete confidence, he can then air his views. He is not completely alone with his thoughts, as in a prison, but enjoys a freedom he cannot have with the masses, among whom he must shut himself up in himself. Every human being has his secrets and dare not confide blindly in others, partly because of a base cast of mind in most human beings to use them to one's disadvantage and partly because many people are indiscreet or incapable of judging and distinguishing what may or may not be repeated. The necessary combination of qualities is seldom found in one person (*rara avis in terris, nigroque simillima cygno*),[a] especially since the closest friendship requires that a judicious and trusted friend be also bound not to share the secrets entrusted to him with anyone else, no matter how reliable he thinks him, without explicit permission to do so.

This (merely moral friendship) is not just an ideal but (like black swans) actually exists here and there in its perfection. But that (pragmatic) friendship, which burdens itself with the ends of others, although out of love, can have neither the purity nor the completeness requisite for a precisely determinant maxim; it is an ideal of one's wishes, which knows no bounds in its rational concept but which must always be very limited in experience.

A *friend of human beings*[b] as such (i.e., of the whole race) is one who takes an effective[c] interest in the well-being of all human beings (rejoices with them) and will never disturb it without heartfelt regret. Yet the expression "a *friend* of human beings" is somewhat narrower in its meaning than "one who merely loves human beings" (a *philanthropist*).[d] For the former includes, as well, thought and consideration for the *equality* among them, and hence the idea that in putting others under obligation by his beneficence he is himself under obligation, as if all were brothers under one *father* who wills the happiness of all. – For, the relation of a protector, as a benefactor, to the one he protects, who owes him gratitude, is indeed a relation of mutual love, but not of friendship, since the respect owed by each is not equal. Taking to heart the duty of being benevolent as a friend

6:473

---

[z] *der Verstand hat*
[a] A bird that is rare on earth, quite like a black swan. Juvenal *Satires* 2.6.165.
[b] *Menschenfreund*
[c] *ästhetisch*
[d] *Menschenliebenden (Philanthrop)*

of human beings (a necessary humbling of oneself) serves to guard against the pride that usually comes over those fortunate enough to have the means for beneficence.

Appendix.
On the virtues of social intercourse
(*virtutes homileticae*).

§ 48.

It is a duty to oneself as well as to others not to *isolate* oneself (*separatistam agere*) but to use one's moral perfections in social intercourse (*officium commercii, sociabilitas*). While making oneself a fixed center of one's principles, one ought to regard this circle drawn around one as also forming part of an all-inclusive circle of those who, in their disposition, are citizens of the world – not exactly in order to promote as the end what is best for the world*ᵉ* but only to cultivate what leads indirectly to this end: to cultivate a disposition of reciprocity – agreeableness, tolerance, mutual love and respect (affability and propriety, *humanitas aesthetica et decorum*) and so to associate the graces with virtue. To bring this about is itself a duty of virtue.

These are, indeed, only *externals* or by-products (*parerga*), which give a beautiful illusion resembling virtue that is also not deceptive since everyone knows how it must to be taken. *Affability, sociability, courtesy, hospitality,* and *gentleness* (in disagreeing without quarreling) are, indeed, only tokens; yet they promote the feeling for virtue itself by a striving to bring this illusion as near as possible to the truth. By all of these, which are merely the manners one is obliged to show in social intercourse, one binds others too; and so they still promote a virtuous disposition by at least making virtue fashionable.*ᶠ*

But the question arises whether one may also keep company with those who are vicious. One cannot avoid meeting them, without leaving the world; and besides, our judgment about them is not competent. – But if the vice is a scandal, that is, a publicly given example of contempt for the strict laws of duty, which therefore brings dishonor with it, then even though the law of the land does not punish it, one must break off the association that existed or avoid it as much as possible, since continued association with such a person deprives virtue of its honor and puts it up for sale to anyone who is rich enough to bribe parasites with the pleasures of luxury.

ᵉ das Weltbeste
ᶠ beliebt

II.

Doctrine of the methods of ethics

Doctrine of the methods of ethics

Section I.
Teaching ethics[g]

§ 49.

The very concept of virtue already implies that virtue must be acquired (that it is not innate); one need not appeal to anthropological knowledge based on experience to see this. For a human being's moral capacity would not be virtue were it not produced by the *strength* of his resolution in conflict with powerful opposing inclinations. Virtue is the product of pure practical reason insofar as it gains ascendancy over such inclinations with consciousness of its supremacy (based on freedom).

That virtue can and must be *taught* already follows from its not being innate; a doctrine of virtue is therefore *something that can be taught.*[h] But since one does not acquire the power to put the rules of virtue into practice merely by being taught how one ought to behave in order to conform with the concept of virtue, the Stoics meant only that virtue cannot be *taught* merely by concepts of duty or by exhortations (by paraenesis), but must instead by *exercised* and cultivated by efforts to combat the inner enemy within the human being (asceticism); for one cannot straightway do all that one *wants* to do, without having first tried out and exercised one's powers. But the *decision* to do this must be made all at once and completely, since a disposition (*animus*) to surrender at times to vice, in order to break away from it gradually, would itself be impure and even vicious, and so could bring about no virtue (which is based on a single principle).

§ 50.

As for the method of teaching (for every scientific doctrine must be treated *methodically*; otherwise is would be set forth *chaotically*), this too must be *systematic* and not *fragmentary* if the doctrine of virtue is to be presented as a *science.* But it can be set forth either by *lectures*, when all those to whom it is directed merely *listen*, or else by *questions*, when the teacher asks his pupils what he wants to teach them. And this erotetic method is, in turn, divided into the method of **dialogue** and that of **catechism**, depending on whether the teacher addresses his questions to

---

[g] *Die ethische Didaktik.* In the "second division of ethics," 6:413, this was called "Catechizing," although in 6:411 two methods, catechizing and dialogue, were distinguished.
[h] *eine Doktrin*

the pupil's reason or just to his memory. For if the teacher wants to question his pupil's reason he must do this in a dialogue in which teacher and pupil question and answer each other *in turn*. The teacher, by his questions, guides his young pupil's course of thought merely by presenting him with cases in which his predisposition for certain concepts will develop (the teacher is the midwife of the pupil's thoughts). The pupil, who thus sees that he himself can think, responds with questions of his own about obscurities in the propositions admitted or about his doubts regarding them, and so provides occasions for the *teacher* himself to *learn* how to question skillfully, according to the saying *docendo discimus*.[i] (For logic has not yet taken sufficiently to heart the challenge issued to it, that it should also provide rules to direct one in *searching* for things, i.e., it should not limit itself to giving rules for *conclusive* judgments but should also provide rules for *preliminary* judgments (*iudicia praevia*), by which one is led to thoughts. Such a theory can be a guide even to the mathematician in his discoveries, and moreover he often makes use of it.)

§ 51.

For the beginning pupil the first and most essential instrument for *teaching*[j] the doctrine of virtue is a moral *catechism*. This must precede a religious catechism; it cannot be interwoven, merely as an interpolation, in the teachings of religion but must rather be presented separately, as a self-subsistent whole; for, it is only by pure moral principles that a transition from the doctrine of virtue to religion can be made, since otherwise the professions of religion would be impure. – For their own part, even the worthiest and most eminent theologians have hesitated to draw up a catechism for teaching statutory religion (which they would personally answer for), though one would have thought this the least that could be expected from the vast treasury of their learning.

But a pure *moral* catechism, as the basic teaching of duties of virtue, involves no such scruple or difficulty since (as far as its content is concerned) it can be developed from ordinary human reason, and (as far as its form is concerned) it needs only to be adapted to rules of teaching suited for the earliest instruction. The formal principle of such instruction does not, however, permit Socratic *dialogue* as the way of teaching for this purpose, since the pupil has no idea what questions to ask; and so the teacher alone does the questioning. But the answer which he methodically draws from the pupil's reason must be written down and preserved in definite words that cannot easily be altered, and so be committed to the pupil's *memory*. So the way of teaching by catechism differs from both the *dogmatic* way (in which only the teacher speaks) and the way of *dialogue* (in which both teacher and pupil question and answer each other).

[i] by teaching we learn
[j] *doktrinale Instrument*

§ 52.

The *experimental* (technical) means for cultivating virtue is *good* example on the part of the teacher (his exemplary conduct) and *cautionary* example in others, since, for a still undeveloped human being, imitation is the first determination of his will to accept maxims that he afterwards makes for himself. – To form a habit is to establish a lasting inclination apart from any maxim, through frequently repeated gratifications of that inclination; it is a mechanism of sense rather than a principle of thought (and one that is easier to *acquire* than *to get rid of* afterwards). – As for the power of examples* (good or bad) that can be held up to the propensity for imitation or warning, what others give us can establish no maxim of virtue. For, a maxim of virtue consists precisely in the subjective autonomy of each human being's practical reason and so implies that the law itself, not the conduct of other human beings, must serve as our incentive. Accordingly, a teacher will not tell his naughty pupil: take an example from that good (orderly, diligent) boy! For this would only cause him to hate that boy, who puts him in an unfavorable light. A good example (exemplary conduct) should not serve as a model but only as a proof that it is really possible to act in conformity with duty. So it is not comparison with any other human being whatsoever (as he is), but with the *idea* (of humanity), as he ought to be, and so comparison with the law, that must serve as the constant standard of a teacher's instruction.

Remark
Fragment of a moral catechism.

The teacher elicits from his pupil's reason, by questioning, what he wants to teach him; and should the pupil not know how to answer the question, the teacher, guiding his reason, suggests the answer to him.

1. Teacher: What is your greatest, in fact your whole, desire in life?
Pupil: (is silent)
Teacher: That *everything* should *always* go the way you would like it to.
2. Teacher: What is such a condition called?
Pupil: (is silent)
Teacher: It is called *happiness* (continuous well-being, enjoyment of life, complete satisfaction with one's condition).

---

*"Instance" [*Beispiel*], a German word, is commonly used as synonymous with "example" [*Exempel*], but the two words really do not have the same meaning. To take something as an *example* and to bring forward an *instance* to clarify an expression are altogether different concepts. An example is a particular case of a *practical* rule, insofar as this rule represents an action as practicable or impracticable, whereas an *instance* is only a particular (*concretum*), represented in accordance with concepts as contained under a universal (*abstractum*), and is a presentation of a concept merely for theory.

3. Teacher: Now, if it were up to you to dispose of all happiness (possible in the world), would you keep it all for yourself or would you share it with your fellow human beings?

Pupil: I would share it with others and make them happy and satisfied too.

4. Teacher: Now that proves that you have a good enough *heart;* but let us see whether you have a good *head* to go along with it. – Would you really give a lazy fellow soft cushions so that he could pass his life away in sweet idleness? Or would you see to it that a drunkard is never short of wine and whatever else he needs to get drunk? Would you give a swindler a charming air and manner to dupe other people? And would you give a violent man audacity and strong fists so that he could crush other people? Each of these things is a means that somebody wishes for in order to be happy in his own way.

Pupil: No, I would not.

5. Teacher: You see, then, that even if you had all happiness in your hands and, along with it, the best will, you still would not give it without consideration to anyone who put out his hand for it; instead you would first try to find out to what extent each was worthy of happiness. But as for yourself, would you at least have no scruples about first providing yourself with everything that you count in your happiness?

Pupil: I would have none.

Teacher: But doesn't it occur to you to ask, again, whether you yourself are worthy of happiness?

Pupil: Of course.

Teacher: Now the force in you that strives only toward happiness is *inclination;* but that which limits your inclination to the condition of your first being worthy of happiness is your *reason;* and your capacity to restrain and overcome your inclinations by your reason is the freedom of your will.

6. Teacher: As to how you should set about sharing in happiness and also becoming at least not unworthy of it, the rule and instruction in this lies in your *reason* alone. This amounts to saying that you need not learn this rule for your conduct from experience or be taught it by others. Your own reason teaches you what you have to do and directly commands you to do it. Suppose, for example, that a situation arises in which you could get a great benefit for yourself or your friend by making up a subtle *lie* that would harm no one: What does your reason say about it?

Pupil: That I ought not to lie, no matter how great the benefits to myself and my friend might be. Lying is *mean* and makes a human being *unworthy* of happiness. – Here is an unconditional necessitation through a command (or prohibition) of reason, which I must obey; and in the face of it all my inclinations must be silent.

Teacher: What do we call this necessity, which reason lays directly upon a human being, of acting in conformity with its law? 6:482

Pupil: It is called *duty*.

Teacher: So a human being's observance of his duty is the universal and sole condition of his worthiness to be happy, and his worthiness to be happy is identical with his observance of duty.

7. Teacher: But even if we are conscious of such a good and active will in us, by virtue of which we consider ourselves worthy (or at least not unworthy) of happiness, can we base on this a sure hope of sharing in happiness?

Pupil: No, not on this alone. For it is not always within our power to provide ourselves with happiness, and the course of nature does not of itself conform with merit. Our good fortune in life (our welfare in general) depends, rather, on circumstances that are far from all being in our control. So our happiness always remains a wish that cannot become a hope, unless some other power is added.

8. Teacher: Has reason, in fact, any grounds of its own for assuming the existence of such a power, which apportions happiness in accordance with a human being's merit or guilt, a power ordering the whole of nature and governing the world with supreme wisdom? that is, any grounds for believing in God?

Pupil: Yes. For we see in the works of nature, which we can judge, a wisdom so widespread and profound that we can explain it to ourselves only by the inexpressibly great art of a creator of the world. And with regard to the moral order, which is the highest adornment of the world, we have reason to expect a no less wise regime, such that if we do not make ourselves *unworthy of happiness*, by violating our duty, we can also hope to *share* in happiness.

In this catechism, which must be carried out through all the articles of virtue and vice, the greatest care must be taken to base the command of duty not on the advantages or disadvantages that follow from observing it, whether for the one it is to put under obligation or even for others, but quite purely on the moral principle. Only casual mention should be made of advantages and disadvantages, as of a supplement which could really be dispensed with but which is serviceable, merely as an instrument, for the taste of those who are weak by nature. It is the *shamefulness* 6:483 of vice, not its *harmfulness* (to the agent himself), that must be emphasized above all. For unless the dignity of virtue is exalted above everything else in actions, the concept of duty itself vanishes and dissolves into mere pragmatic precepts, since a human being's consciousness of his own nobility then disappears and he is for sale and can be bought for a price that the seductive inclinations offer him.

Now when this is wisely and carefully developed out of a human being's own reason, with regard for the differences in age, sex and rank which he gradually encounters, then there is still something that must come at the end, which moves the soul inwardly and puts him in a position in which he can look upon himself only with the greatest wonder at the original predisposition dwelling within him, the impression of which is never erased. – When, namely, at the end of his instruction his duties are once more, by way of summary, recounted in their order (recapitulated); and when, in the case of each of them, his attention is drawn to the fact that none of the pains, hardships, and sufferings of life – not even the threat of death – which may befall him because he faithfully attends to his duty can rob him of consciousness of being their master and superior to them all, then the question is very close to him: what is it in you that can be trusted to enter into combat with all the forces of nature within you and around you and to conquer them if they come into conflict with your moral principles? Although the solution to this question lies completely beyond the capability[k] of speculative reason, the question arises of itself; and if he takes it to heart, the very incomprehensibility in this cognition of himself must produce an exaltation in his soul which only inspires it the more to hold its duty sacred, the more it is assailed.

In this catechistic moral instruction it would be most helpful to the pupil's moral development to raise some casuistical questions in the analysis of every duty and to let the assembled children test their understanding by having each say how he would solve the tricky problem put to him. – The advantage of this is not only that it is a *cultivation of reason* most suited to the capacity of the undeveloped (since questions about what one's duty is can be decided far more easily than speculative questions), and so is the most appropriate way to sharpen the understanding of young people in general. Its advantage lies especially in the fact that it is natural for a human being to *love* a subject which he has, by his own handling, brought to a science (in which he is now proficient); and so, by this sort of practice, the pupil is drawn without noticing it to an *interest* in morality.

But it is most important in this education not to present the moral catechism mixed with the religious one (to combine them into one) or, what is worse yet, to have it follow upon the religious catechism. On the contrary, the pupil must always be brought to a clear insight into the moral catechism, which should be presented with the utmost diligence and thoroughness. For otherwise the religion that he afterwards

---

[k] *das Vermögen der speculativen Vernunft*

professes will be nothing but hypocrisy; he will acknowledge duties out of fear and feign an interest in them that is not in his heart.

Section II.
Ethical ascetics.

§ 53.

The rules for practicing virtue (*exercitiorum virtutis*) aim at a frame of mind that is both *valiant* and *cheerful*[l] in fulfilling its duties (*animus strenuus et hilaris*). For, virtue not only has to muster all its forces to overcome the obstacles it must contend with; it also involves sacrificing many of the joys of life, the loss of which can sometimes make one's mind gloomy and sullen. But what is not done with pleasure but merely as compulsory service has no inner worth for one who attends to his duty in this way and such service is not loved by him; instead, he shirks as much as possible occasions for practicing virtue.

With regard to the principle of a vigorous, spirited, and valiant practice of virtue, the cultivation of virtue, that is, moral *ascetics*, takes as its motto the *Stoic* saying: accustom yourself *to put up with* the misfortunes of life that may happen and *to do without* its superfluous pleasures (*assuesce incommodis et descuesce commoditatibus vitae*).[m] This is a kind of *regimen*[n] for keeping a human being healthy. But *health* is only a negative kind of well-being: it cannot itself be felt. Something must be added to it, something which, though it is only moral, affords an agreeable enjoyment to life. This is the ever-cheerful heart, according to the idea of the virtuous *Epicurus*. For who should have more reason for being of a cheerful spirit, and not even finding it a duty to put himself in a cheerful frame of mind and make it habitual, than one who is aware of no intentional transgression in himself and is secured against falling into any? (*hic murus aheneus esto* etc., *Horat.*)[o] On the other hand monkish ascetics, which from superstitious fear or hypocritical loathing of oneself goes to work with self-torture and mortification of the flesh, is not directed to virtue but rather to fantastically purging oneself of sin by imposing punishments on oneself. Instead of morally *repenting* sins (with a view to improving), it wants to do *penance* by punishments chosen and inflicted by oneself. But such punishment is a contradiction (because punishment must always be imposed by another); moreover, it cannot produce the cheerfulness that accompanies virtue, but much rather brings with

6:485

---
[l] *gehen auf die zwei Gemütsstimmungen hinaus, wackeren und fröhlichen Gemuts . . . zu sein*
[m] accustom yourself to the inconveniences and disaccustom yourself to the conveniences of life
[n] *Diätetik*
[o] let this be our wall of bronze, etc. Horace *Epistles* 1.1.60.

it secret hatred for virtue's command. – Ethical gymnastics, therefore, consists only in combatting natural impulses sufficiently to be able to master them when a situation comes up in which they threaten morality; hence it makes one valiant and cheerful in the consciousness of one's restored freedom. To *repent* of something and to impose a *penance* on oneself (such as a fast) not for hygienic but for pious considerations are, morally speaking, two very different precautionary measures. To repent of a past transgression when one recalls it is unavoidable and, in fact, it is even a duty not to let this recollection disappear; but doing penance, which is cheerless, gloomy, and sullen, makes virtue itself hated and drives adherents away from it. Hence the training (discipline) that a human being practices on himself can become meritorious and exemplary only through the cheerfulness that accompanies it.

Conclusion
Religion*ᵖ* as the doctrine of duties to God lies beyond the bounds of pure moral philosophy

Protagoras of Abdera began his book with the words: "*As for whether there are gods or not, I do not know what to say.*"* For this the Athenians drove him off his land and from the city and burned his books before the public assembly. (Quintilian, *Institutio Oratoria,* Book 3, Chapter I)⁵¹ – In doing this the Athenian judges, as human beings, did him a great *wrong*. But as *officials of the state* and judges they proceeded quite *rightly* and consistently; for how could someone swear an oath unless it had been decreed publicly and lawfully, *on high authority* (*de par le Senat*), that there are gods?†

But granting this belief and admitting that *religion* is an integral part of the general *doctrine of duties,* the problem now is to determine the bound-

---

* "*De diis, neque ut sint, neque ut non sint, habeo dicere.*"
†Later on, however, a great and wise moral lawgiver completely forbade the taking of oaths as something absurd and, at the same time, almost bordering on blasphemy; however, from a political point of view people still maintain that this device is quite indispensable as a means serving the administration of public justice, and liberal interpretations of that prohibition have been thought up in order to soften it. – Although it would be absurd to swear in earnest that there is a God (because one must already have postulated this in order to be able to take an oath at all), the question still remains: whether an oath would not be possible and valid if someone swears only in case there is a God (like Protagoras, deciding nothing about it)? – In fact, every oath that has been taken both sincerely and circumspectly may well have been taken in just this sense. – For if someone is willing simply to swear that God exists, his offer, it might seem, involves no risk for him, whether he believes in God or not. If there is a God (the deceiver will say), then I have hit the mark; if there is no God, then neither is there anyone to call me to account, and by such an oath I run no risk. – But *if there is a God*, then is there no danger of being caught in a lie deliberately told just in order to deceive him?
ᵖ *Religionslehre*

aries of the *science* to which it belongs. Is it to be considered a part of ethics (for what is in question here cannot be the rights of human beings against one another), or must it be regarded as lying entirely beyond the bounds of a purely philosophic morals?

The *formal aspect* of all religion, if religion is defined[q] as "the sum of all duties *as* (*instar*) divine commands," belongs to philosophic morals, since this definition expresses only the relation of reason to the *idea* of God which reason makes for itself; and this does not yet make a duty of religion into a duty *to* (*erga*) God, as a being existing outside our idea, since we still abstract from his existence. – The ground on which a human being is to think of all his duties in keeping with this *formal aspect* of religion (their relation to a divine will given a priori) is only subjectively logical. That is to say, we cannot very well make obligation (moral constraint) intuitive for ourselves without thereby thinking of *another*'s will, namely God's (of which reason in giving universal laws is only the spokesman). – But this duty *with regard to God* (properly speaking, with regard to the idea we ourselves make of such a being) is a duty of a human being to himself, that is, it is not objective, an obligation to perform certain services for another, but only subjective, for the sake of strengthening the moral incentive in our own lawgiving reason.

But as for the *material* aspect of religion, the sum of duties *to* (*erga*) God, that is, the service to be performed for him (*ad praestandum*), this would be able to contain special duties as divine commands which do not proceed only from reason giving universal laws, so that they would be cognizable by us only empirically, not a priori, and would therefore belong only to revealed religion. They would therefore also have to assume the existence of such a being, not merely the idea of him for practical purposes, and to assume it not at will[r] but rather as something that could be set forth as given directly (or indirectly) in experience. But such a religion would still comprise no part of a *purely philosophic morals*, no matter how well grounded it might otherwise be.

So *religion* as the doctrine of duties *to* God lies entirely beyond the bounds of purely philosophic ethics, and this serves to justify the author of the present ethical work for not having followed the usual practice of bringing religion, conceived in that sense, into ethics, in order to make it complete.

6:488

We can indeed speak of a "Religion *within the Boundaries* of Mere Reason"[52] which is not, however, derived *from* reason alone but is also based on the teachings of history and revelation, and considers only the *harmony* of pure practical reason with these (shows that there is no conflict between them). But in that case as well religion is not *pure;* it is rather

[q] *erklärt*
[r] *willkürlich*

religion applied to a history handed down to us,[s] and there is no place for it in an *ethics* that is pure practical philosophy.

Concluding remark.

All moral relations of rational beings, which involve a principle of the harmony of the will of one with that of another, can be reduced to *love* and *respect;* and, insofar as this principle is practical, in the case of love the basis for determining one's will can be reduced to another's *end*, and in the case of respect, to another's *right.* – If one of these is a being that has only rights and no duties to the other (God) so that the other has only duties and no rights against him, then the principle of the moral relation between them is *transcendent.* (On the other hand, the moral relation of human beings to human beings, whose wills limit one another, has an *immanent* principle.)

The divine end with regard to the human race (in creating and guiding it) can be thought only as proceeding from *love*, that is, as the *happiness* of human beings. But the principle of God's will with regard to the *respect* (awe) due[t] him, which limits the effects of love, that is, the principle of God's right, can be none other than that of *justice.* To express this in human terms, God has created rational beings from the need, as it were, to have something outside himself which he could love or by which he could also be loved.

But in the judgment of our own reason, the claim that divine *justice* makes upon us is not only as great but even greater (because the principle is a limiting one), and the claim is that of *punitive* justice. – For, there is no place for *reward* (*praemium, remuneratio gratuita*) in justice toward beings who have only duties and no rights in relation to another, but only in His love and beneficence (*benignitas*) toward them;[53] still less can a claim to compensation (*merces*) be made by such beings, and *compensatory justice*[u] (*iustitia brabeutica*) in the relation of God to human beings is a contradiction.

But in the idea of an exercise of justice by a being who is above any interference with his ends there is something that cannot well be reconciled with the relation of human beings to God: namely, the concept of a *wrong*[v] that could be done to the infinite and inaccessible ruler of the world; for what is in question here is not human beings' violations of each other's rights, on which God, as the punishing judge, passes sentence, but of a violation supposed to be done to God himself and his right. The concept of this is *transcendent*, that is, it lies entirely beyond

---

[s] *auf eine vorliegende Geschichte angewandt*
[t] *der schuldigen Achtung (Ehrfurcht)*
[u] *belohnende Gerechtigkeit*
[v] *Läsion*

the concept of any punitive justice for which we can bring forward any instance (i.e., any instance among human beings) and involves extravagant[w] principles that cannot be brought into accord with those we would use in cases of experience and that are, accordingly, quite empty for our practical reason.

Here the idea of divine punitive justice is personified. There is no particular judging being that exercises it (for then this being would come into conflict with principles of right); instead it is *justice* – as if it were a substance (otherwise called *eternal* justice) which, like the *fate* (destiny) of the ancient philosophical poets, is above even Jupiter – that pronounces on rights in accordance with an iron, inevitable necessity which we cannot penetrate further. – Now some instances of this.

Punishment (according to Horace)[54] does not let the criminal out of its sight as he strides proudly before it; rather, it keeps limping after him until it catches him. – Blood innocently shed cries out for vengeance. – Crime cannot remain unavenged; if punishment does not strike the criminal, then his descendants must suffer it, or if it does not befall him during his lifetime, then it must take place in a life after death,* which is accepted and readily believed in expressly so that the claim of eternal justice may be settled. – I will not allow *bloodguilt* to come upon my land by granting pardon to an evil, murdering duellist for whom you intercede, a wise ruler once said. – *Guilt for sins* must be expiated, even if a completely innocent person should have to offer himself to atone for it (in which case the suffering he took upon himself could not properly be called punishment, since he himself had committed no crime). All of this makes it clear that this judgment of condemnation is not attributed to a *person* administering justice (for the person could not pronounce in this way without doing others wrong), but rather that *justice* by itself, as a transcendent principle ascribed to a supersensible subject, determines the right of this being. All of this conforms, indeed, with the *formal aspect* of this principle, but it conflicts with the *material aspect* of it, the *end*, which is always the *happiness* of human beings. – For, in view of the eventual multitude of criminals who keep the register of their guilt running on and on, punitive justice would make the *end* of creation consist not in the creator's *love* (as one must yet think it to be) but rather in the strict observance of his *right* (it would make

6:490

---

* It is not even necessary to bring the hypothesis of a future life into this, in order to present that threat of punishment as completely fulfilled. For a human being, considered in terms of his morality, is judged as a supersensible object by a supersensible judge, not under conditions of time; only his existence is relevant here. His life on earth – be it short or long or even everlasting – is only his existence in appearance, and the concept of justice does not need to be determined more closely since belief in a future life does not, properly speaking, come first, so as to let the effect of criminal justice upon it be seen; on the contrary, it is from the necessity of punishment that the inference to a future life is drawn.

[w] *überschwengliche*

God's right itself, located in his *glory*,[x] the end). But since the latter (justice) is only the condition limiting the former (benevolence), this seems to contradict principles of practical reason, by which the creation of a world must have been omitted if it would have produced a result so contrary to the intention of its author, which can have only love for its basis.

From all this it is clear that in ethics, as pure practical philosophy of internal lawgiving, only the moral relations of *human beings to human beings* are comprehensible by us. The question of what sort of moral relation holds between God and the human being goes completely beyond the bounds of ethics and is altogether incomprehensible for us. This, then, confirms what was maintained above: that ethics cannot extend beyond the limits of human beings' duties to one another.

TABLE
OF THE DIVISION OF ETHICS.
I. DOCTRINE OF THE ELEMENTS OF ETHICS.
Part I. On a Human Being's *Duties to Himself.*

Book I.
On a Human Being's *Perfect Duties* to Himself.

Chapter I.
On a Human Being's Duties to Himself as an *Animal Being.*

Chapter II.
On a Human Being's Duties to Himself Merely as a *Moral* Being.

Section I.
On a Human Being's Duties to Himself as His Own Innate *Judge.*

Section II.
On the First Command of All Duties to Oneself.

Episodic Section.
On an Amphiboly in Moral *Concepts of Reflection* with Regard to Duties to Oneself.

Book II.
On a Human Being's *Imperfect* Duties to Himself with Regard to His End.

Section I.
On the Duty to Oneself to Develop and Increase One's Natural Perfection.

Section II.
On the Duty to Oneself to Increase One's Moral Perfection.

DOCTRINE OF THE ELEMENTS OF ETHICS.
Part II.
On Ethical *Duties to Others.*

---

[x] *das Ehre Gottes*

Chapter I.
On Duties to Others *Merely as Human Beings.*

Section I.
On the *Duty of Love* to Other Human Beings.

Section II.
On the *Duty of Respect* for Others.

Chapter II.
On Duty to Others in Accordance with *Differences in Their Condition.*
On the Most Intimate Union of Love with Respect in Friendship.

II. DOCTRINE OF THE METHODS OF ETHICS.

Section I.
Teaching Ethics.

Section II.
Ethical Ascetics.

Conclusion of the Entire Ethics.

On a supposed right to lie from philanthropy

Introduction

In 1796 Benjamin Constant, a French politician and author, published a pamphlet entitled *Des réactions politiques*. The following year a translation was published in the journal *Frankreich im Jahr 1797*, apparently edited by Karl Friedrich Cramer. In a note Cramer said that Constant had told him that Kant was the "German philosopher" he referred to as holding a view about lying that would make society impossible. Granting that he had "somewhere or other" put forward the view, Kant undertook to refute the "French philosopher's" conclusion that it would make civil society impossible. Kant's reply was published in the September issue of the *Berliner Blätter*, founded by Biester after publication of the *Berlinische Monatsschrift* had been discontinued. (See Biester's letters to Kant of August 5 and September 20, 1797, 12:191-2 and 200-1.)

In *The Doctrine of Right*, published in January 1797, Kant had included, in everyone's innate right to freedom, one's being authorized to communicate one's thoughts to others, to tell or promise them something "whether what he says is true and sincere or untrue and insincere; for it is entirely up to them whether they want to believe him or not." Contractual rights are acquired by the two acts of promising and accepting; only then does failure to fulfill one's promise deprive another of what is his. However, Kant later distinguished between "what is only formally wrong and what is also materially wrong," a distinction that "has many applications in the doctrine of right." In general, people do not wrong one another by doing what would make civil society impossible, but they nevertheless do wrong "in the highest degree" by making the concept of right inapplicable, and with it the concept of a right as distinguished from force. Relying on this distinction, Kant argues that lying is always wrong in the context of right, as distinguished from virtue. Drawing upon his conception of legal imputation of the consequences of one's actions, he maintains, further, that one would be legally responsible for the unforeseen results of a lie.

On a supposed right to lie from philanthropy

On a supposed right to lie from philanthropy*a*

In the journal *Frankreich im Jahr 1797*, Part VI, No. 1, "On Political Reactions" by Benjamin Constant contains the following (p. 123).

"The moral principle 'it is a duty to tell the truth' would, if taken unconditionally and singly, make any society impossible. We have proof of this in the very direct consequences drawn from this principle by a German philosopher, who goes so far as to maintain that it would be a crime to lie to a murderer who asked us whether a friend of ours whom he is pursuing has taken refuge in our house."*

The French philosopher rebuts this principle as follows (p. 124): "It is a duty to tell the truth. The concept of duty is inseparable from the concept of right. A duty is that on the part of one being which corresponds to the rights of another. Where there are no rights, there are no duties. To tell the truth is therefore a duty, but only to one who has a right to the truth. But no one has a right to a truth that harms others."

The πρωτον ψευδος*b* here lies in the proposition "*To tell the truth is a duty, but only to one who has a right to the truth.*"

It is to be noted, first, that the expression "to have a right to the truth" is meaningless. One must instead say one has a right to his own *truthfulness (veracitas)*, that is, to the subjective truth in his person.4 For to have a right to a truth objectively would be tantamount to saying that, as in the case with what is yours or mine generally, it is a matter of one's *will* whether a given proposition is to be true or false; and this would give rise to an extraordinary logic.

Now the *first question* is whether someone, in cases where he cannot evade an answer of "yes" or "no," has the *authorization* (the right) to be untruthful. The *second question* is whether he is not, indeed, bound to be

---

*"J. D. Michaelis of Göttingen1 put forward this extraordinary opinion earlier than Kant. The author of this paper himself told me that the philosopher spoken of in this passage is Kant." K. F. Cramer†2

†I hereby grant that I actually said this somewhere or other, though I cannot now recall where.3

a aus Menschenliebe
b original falsity

untruthful in a certain statement which he is compelled[c] to make by an unjust constraint,[d] in order to prevent a threatened misdeed to himself or to another.

Truthfulness in statements that one cannot avoid is a human being's duty to everyone,* however great the disadvantage to him or to another that may result from it; and although I indeed do no wrong to him who unjustly compels me to make the statement if I falsify it, I nevertheless do wrong in the most essential part of duty *in general* by such falsification, which can therefore be called a lie (though not in a jurist's sense); that is, I bring it about, as far as I can, that statements (declarations) in general are not believed, and so too that all rights which are based on contracts come to nothing and lose their force; and this is a wrong inflicted upon humanity generally.

Thus a lie, defined merely as an intentionally untrue declaration to another, does not require what jurists insist upon adding for their definition, that it must harm another (*mendacium est falsiloquium in praeiudicium alterius*).[e] [5]For it always harms another, even if not another individual, nevertheless humanity generally, inasmuch as it makes the source of right unusable.

Such a well-meant lie *can*, however, also become by an *accident* (*casus*) punishable in accordance with civil laws; but what escapes being punishable merely by accident can be condemned as wrong even in accordance with external laws. That is to say, if you have *by a lie* prevented someone just now bent on murder from committing the deed, then you are legally[f] accountable for all the consequences that might arise from it. But if you have kept strictly to the truth, then public justice can hold nothing against you, whatever the unforeseen consequences might be.[6] It is still possible that, after you have honestly answered "yes" to the murderer's question as to whether his enemy is at home, the latter has nevertheless gone out unnoticed, so that he would not meet the murderer and the deed would not be done; but if you had lied and said that he is not at home, and he has actually gone out (though you are not aware of it), so that the murderer encounters him while going away and perpetrates his deed on him, then you can by right[g] be prosecuted as the author[h] of his death. For if you had

---

*I here prefer not to sharpen this principle to the point of saying: "Untruthfulness is a violation of duty to oneself." For this belongs to ethics, but what is under discussion here is a duty of right. The doctrine of virtue looks, in this transgression, only to *worthlessness*, reproach for which a liar draws upon himself.

[c] *nötigt*
[d] *ungerechter Zwang*
[e] a lie is speaking falsely in prejudice to another
[f] *auf rechtliche Art*
[g] *mit Recht*
[h] *Urheber*

ON A SUPPOSED RIGHT TO LIE FROM PHILANTHROPY

told the truth to the best of your knowledge, then neighbors might have come and apprehended the murderer while he was searching the house for his enemy and the deed would have been prevented. Thus one *who tells a lie*, however well disposed he may be, must be responsible for its consequences even before a civil court and must pay the penalty for them, however unforeseen they may have been; for truthfulness is a duty that must be regarded as the basis of all duties to be grounded on contract, the law of which is made uncertain and useless if even the least exception to it is admitted.

To be *truthful* (honest) in all declarations is therefore a sacred command of reason prescribing unconditionally, one not to be restricted by any conveniences.[i]

In this connection Constant makes a well-considered and also correct remark about the decrying of principles so strict that they allegedly lose themselves in impracticable ideas and are thus to be repudiated. "Every time," he says (at the bottom of p. 123), "that a principle proved to be true seems inapplicable, this is because we do not know the *intermediary principle*,[j] which contains the means of application." He adduces (p. 121) the doctrine of *equality* as the first link in the formation of the social chain: "namely, (p. 122) that no human being can be bound except through laws to the formation of which he has contributed. In a very closely knit society this principle can be applied in an immediate way and needs no intermediary principle in order to become a common one. But in a very large society one must add a new principle to the principle that we have here put forward. This intermediary principle is that individuals can contribute to the formation of laws either in their own person or through *representatives*. One who wanted to apply the *first* principle to a large society without adopting the intermediary one in order to do so would inevitably bring about its ruin. But this circumstance, which would only testify to the ignorance or incompetence[k] of the legislator, would prove nothing against the principle." He concludes (p. 125) with these words: "A principle recognized as true must therefore never be abandoned, however apparent is the danger present in it."[l] (And yet the good man himself had abandoned the unconditional principle of truthfulness because of the danger to society it brought with it, since he could discover no intermediary principle that would serve to prevent this danger, and here there is actually no such principle to be inserted.)

8:428

If we are going to keep the names of persons as they were specified here, "the French philosopher" confused an action by which someone

---

[i] *Convenienzen*
[j] *mittlern Grundsatz*
[k] *Ungeschicklichkeit*
[l] *wie anscheinend auch Gefahr dabei sich befindet*

harms (*nocet*) another by telling a truth he cannot avoid admitting with an action by which he *wrongs* (*laedit*) another. It was merely an *accident* (*casus*) that the truthfulness of the statement harmed the resident of the house, not a free *deed* (in the juridical sense). For, from one's right to require another to lie to one's advantage would follow a claim opposed to all lawfulness. Every individual, however, has not only a right but even the strictest duty to truthfulness in statements that he cannot avoid, though they may harm himself or others. Thus in telling the truth he himself does not, strictly speaking, *do* the harm to the one who suffers by it; instead, an accident *causes* the harm. For he is not at all free to choose*ᵐ* in the matter, because truthfulness (if he must speak) is an unconditional duty. The "German philosopher" will therefore not take as his principle the proposition (p. 124), "To tell the truth is a duty but only to someone who *has a right to the truth*," first because the principle is not clearly formulated, inasmuch as truth is not a possession the right to which could be granted to one but denied to another; but he will not do so mainly because the duty of truthfulness (the only matter under discussion here) makes no distinction between persons to whom one has this duty and those to whom one can exempt oneself from it, since it is, instead, an *unconditional duty*, which holds in all relations.

Now, in order to progress from a *metaphysics* of right (which abstracts from all conditions of experience) to a principle of *politics* (which applies these concepts to cases of experience) and, by means of this, to the solution of a problem of politics in keeping with the universal principle of right, a philosopher will give 1) an *axiom*, that is, an apodictically certain proposition that issues immediately from the definition of external right (consistency of the *freedom* of each with the freedom of everyone in accordance with a universal law); 2) a *postulate* (of external public *law*, as the united will of all in accordance with the principle of *equality*, without which there would be no freedom of everyone); 3) a *problem* of how it is to be arranged that in a society, however large, harmony in accordance with the principles of freedom and equality is maintained (namely, by means of a representative system); this will then be a principle of *politics*, the arrangement and organization of which will contain decrees, drawn from experiential cognition of human beings, that have in view only the mechanism for administering right and how this can be managed appropriately."ⁿ Right must never be accommodated to politics, but politics must always be accommodated to right.

The author says, "A proposition recognized as true (to which I add, recognized a priori, hence apodictically) must never be abandoned, however apparent is the danger present in it." But here one must understand

---

ᵐ wählen
ⁿ zweckmäßig

not the danger of *harming* (contingently) but of *doing wrong* generally, as would happen if I make the duty of truthfulness, which is altogether unconditional and constitutes the supreme rightful condition in statements,⁷ into a conditional duty subordinate to other considerations and, though by a certain lie I in fact*°* wrong no one, I nevertheless violate the principle of right with respect to all unavoidable necessary statements *in general* (I do wrong formally though not materially);⁸ and this is much worse than committing an injustice to someone or other, since such a deed does not always presuppose in the subject a principle of doing so.*ᵖ*

Someone who is not indignant at another's question as to whether he is going to be truthful in the statement he is about to make – indignant at the suspicion it expresses that he might be a liar – but asks permission to think about possible exceptions is already a liar (*in potentia*); for he shows that he does not recognize truthfulness as a duty in itself but reserves for himself exceptions to a rule that by its essence does not admit of exceptions, since in doing so it would directly contradict itself.

All practical principles of right*ᵍ* must contain strict truth, and here the so-called intermediary principles can contain only the closer determination of their application to cases that come up (in accordance with rules of politics), but never exceptions from those principles; for exceptions would nullify the universality on account of which alone they are called principles.

° *in der Tat*
ᵖ *einen Grundsatz dazu*
ᵍ *rechtlich-praktische Grundsätze*

On turning out books
Two letters
to
Mr. Friedrich Nicolai
from Immanuel Kant

Introduction

Friedrich Nicolai (1733–1811) was a publisher, satirical novelist, and popular enlightenment philosopher of empiricist sympathies who attacked Kant and his philosophy for its forbidding style of writing and its use of abstruse terminology (see *Metaphysics of Morals*, editorial note 8.) In 1796, after Nicolai had ridiculed Schiller for his use of Kantian jargon, Kant alluded to Nicolai's criticisms in *Metaphysics of Morals* (6:208–209), insisting that they do not apply to the critical philosophy itself. Shortly thereafter, in his novel *Leben und Meinungen Sempronius Gundiberts* (1798), Nicolai responded by explicitly directing his satires at Kant himself. On the title page appeared the phrase "The ridiculous despotism," drawn from Kant (*Critique of Pure Reason*, B xxxv) but now directed back at him. In the novel the terminology of *a priori* and *a posteriori* was employed both playfully and contemptuously, and variants of it were devised for purposes of ridicule.

In the same year, Nicolai also published a posthumous volume of *Vermischten Schriften* by the conservative writer Justus Möser (1720–1794), containing an uncompleted fragment of an essay on "Theory and Practice," directed polemically against Kant's essay on the same topic. When Kant condemns as unjust some existing social and political arrangements (in particular, the political privileges of the hereditary nobility), Möser dismisses this as the irresponsible work of a ridiculous "theorist" who is out of touch with "practical" reality. This too angered Kant, and the philosopher held Nicolai as well as Möser responsible for the attempt to make a laughingstock of him.

The two open letters contained in "On Turning Out Books" (*Über die Buchmacherei*) contain both a reply to the Möser fragment and an aggressive attack on Nicolai's activities as a writer and publisher. The tone of Kant's polemic is generally humorous, but the humor is biting and contemptuous, and we may be surprised at the degree of bitterness displayed in it. Nicolai, however, apparently made enemies easily; some of the attacks on him by F. H. Jacobi are far nastier than Kant's. It is noteworthy in this connection that Kant does not fail to accompany his attack on Nicolai with an explicit defense of freedom of the press, insisting that he is not engaged in anything wrongful or illegal.

Probably of greatest philosophical interest is the first of the two letters, containing Kant's reply to Möser's attempt to frame a literary counterexample to Kant's claim that a people could not consent to impose on itself a political constitution involving a hereditary aristocracy. It sheds light on the meaning of Kant's "ideal" social contract theory, and the use of the idea of a social contract as a criterion for the natural justice or injustice of laws and political arrangements. Also of interest, however, are Kant's harsh words in the second letter about the harmful effects on the process of enlightenment of the commercialization of writing and public communication.

These two letters were first published in pamphlet form by Kant's Königsberg publisher Nicolovius in 1798, but almost simultaneously in Leipzig and Jena in the fourth volume of a collection of his shorter writings.

I am grateful to Paul Guyer for helpful suggestions on the translation.

On turning out books
Two letters
to
Mr. Friedrich Nicolai
from Immanuel Kant

FIRST LETTER 8:433

To Mr. Friedrich Nicolai, the author

The learned relics of the excellent Möser (who often also painted in the comic-burlesque) fell into the hands of his friend of many years, Mr. Friedrich Nicolai. There was a part of a fragmentary treatise by Möser with the heading: *On Theory and Practice*, which was communicated to the latter in manuscript, and as Mr. Nicolai assumed that Möser himself would have communicated it if he had brought it entirely to an end, and in this connection it was remarked that Möser had been not only a royalist but also, if one would so call it, an aristocrat, or a defender of hereditary nobility, to the wonderment and annoyance of many recent politicians in Germany. – Among other things, it has been asserted (since Kant's *Metaphysical First Principles of Right*, first edition, page 192[1]) that a people would never, on the basis of a free and considered decision, concede such a hereditary principle. Against this, Möser, in his well known whimsical manner, composed a narrative in which persons in very high offices step forward as *equal to viceroys but really as true subjects of the state*, and twelve cases were introduced: in the first six, the sons of deceased officials are *passed over*, which stands badly with the subjects; in the case of the latter six, on the contrary, they are *chosen*, which the people finds to be better; – from which it is clearly evident that a whole people can *indeed* resolve upon its own hereditary subjection under higher fellow subjects, and further evident that the latter is useful *practice*, so that this airy *theory*, like so many others, will be blown away like chaff for the amusement of his readers.

It is always thus with the maxim *calculated* for the advantage of the people: however prudent the people may think itself to have become through experience, if it *would choose* for itself a subordinate ruler, then in so doing it can and will often hatefully *miscalculate*, because the method of experience for being prudent (the pragmatic principle has hardly any other guidance than to become prudent through harm. – Here, however, it is now a matter of an administration[a] which is secure and prescribed by *reason*, which does not want to know what the people *will* choose, in order to satisfy its existing aims, but instead how it unconditionally *ought* to choose, whether that is conducive to these aims or not (the moral principle); i.e., the question is what and how, if a people is called upon to choose, it must decide according to the *principle of right*. For this whole problem is to be judged (in the *Metaphysical First Principles of the Doctrine of Right*, p. 192), as a question belonging to the *doctrine of right*: whether the sovereign is *entitled* to found a middle estate between itself and the remaining citizens of the state; and here the verdict is then that the people will not and cannot rationally resolve on such a subordinate authority, because otherwise it would

8:434

---

[a] *Leitung*

be subject to the whims and crotchets of a subject that itself needs to be governed, which contradicts itself. – Here the principle of judgment is not empirical but rather a principle a priori, like all propositions whose assertion at the same time carries *necessity* with it, which also alone yields *judgments of reason* (as distinct from judgments of the understanding). An *empirical doctrine of right*, on the contrary, if it is to be counted as philosophy and not as belonging to a statutory lawbook, is a self-contradiction.*

Now that is *good*; but, as the old aunties like to say in the style of a fairy tale, it is not *overly good*.[b] Fiction now takes another course.

That is, after the people in the six following regimes[c] had, to the general joy, chosen the son of his predecessor, then as the visionary story further tells us, partly through the simple progress of *enlightenment* gradually taking place during this time, partly also because every government is burdensome for the people, which the exchange of the old for something new promises directly to alleviate, there arose *demagogues* among the people, and then it was decreed as follows:

Namely, in the *seventh* regime the people to be sure elect the son of the previous duke. The latter, however, had already progressed with the age in culture and luxury, and had little desire to maintain the prosperity of the people through good economy, but to enjoy it all the more. Hence he let the old castle deteriorate, so as to erect pleasure houses and hunting lodges for festive enjoyments and chasing wild game, for his own indulgence and taste and that of the people. The splendid theater and the old silver table service was transformed, the former into a great ballroom, the latter into a more tasteful porcelain, under the pretext that as money the silver promises a better course of trade in the land. – In the *eighth*, the hereditary government, well established and confirmed by the people, found it even more advisable to abolish, with the consent of the people, the right of primogeniture prevailing by custom up to then; for it seemed evident to it that the first born was not for that reason at the same time the wisest born. – In the *ninth*, the people[d] will find it better to establish certain provincial councils with revolving personnel than to institute a

---

*According to the principle of eudaimonia (the doctrine of happiness), in which no necessity and universal validity are to be found (since it remains to each individual to determine what he, according to his inclination, will count toward his happiness), the people will, to be sure, be permitted to choose such a hereditary regime for its constitution; – but according to the eleutheronomical[2] principle (of which the doctrine of right is a part) it will establish no *subordinate* external legislator, because it considers itself thereby as legislative and at the same time as subject to these laws, and hence practice (in matters of pure reason) must always be arranged according to theory. – It is *unjust* to decree thus, even if it might be customary and in many cases even useful to the state; which latter, however, is never certain.
[b] *allzugut*
[c] *Gouvernements*
[d] The text in AK is apparently flawed at this point; perhaps some words are missing.

government by the old, remaining*c* councillors, who in the end commonly play at being despots – and happier too; and not to recognize the suggested hereditary pastor, since thereby the clergy must perpetuate itself as the *guild of obscurantists*. – In the *tenth*, as in the *eleventh*, they say, the disgust at misalliances is a caprice of the old feudal constitution to the disadvantage of those ennobled by nature, and it is rather a proof of the sprouting of noble feelings among the people if – as is inevitable with progress in enlightenment – it thinks talent and a good way of thinking superior to hereditary rank in deciding what should play the role of exemplar – – just as in the *twelfth* one will smile at the good-naturedness of the old aunt in doing homage*f* to the young, immature*g* child who is presumably destined to be duke even before he understands what that means; but to make this into a principle of state would be an absurd presumption. And thus the whims of the people, if it is allowed that it might decide to give itself a hereditary regime*h* which still remains a subject, are transformed into deformities which are so very much opposed to its aim (its happiness) that the proper saying will be: *Turpiter atrum desinit in piscem mulier formosa superne.**i*

8:436

Therefore, every constitution grounded on the happiness principle, even if one can safely allege a priori that the people will prefer it to every other, can be *parodied* into ridicule; and if one turns up the other side of the coin, then of the choice of the people that wants to give itself a master, one can say the same as what that Greek said about marriage: "Whatever you may do, you will regret it."*j*

Mr. Friedrich Nicolai, therefore, has come to misfortune with his interpretation and defense in the alleged concern of another (namely, Möser). – It will surely go better for him, however, when we see him occupied with his own.

SECOND LETTER

To Mr. Friedrich Nicolai, the publisher

The *turning out of books* is not an insignificant branch of business in a commonwealth whose culture has already progressed quite far, and where

---

*c**bleibenden*
*f*There seems to be a verb left out of this sentence; we follow Maier's suggestion that *zu huldigen* might have been intended (AK 8:520).
*g**unmündigen*
*h**Gouverneur*
i"What ends shamefully and vilely as a fish is a woman beautifully formed above." Horace, *Epistles* 2.3.3-4.
*j*According to Maier (AK 8:520), the reference is to Ioannes Stobaeus, *Anthology* (Hense edition, 2.520.7). But the same saying is ascribed by Diogenes Laertius (2.33) to Socrates.

reading has become a nearly indispensable and general need. – This part of *industry* in a country, however, thereby reaps uncommon gains if it is carried on *in the manner of a factory*, which, however, cannot happen unless by means of a **publisher** capable of *judging* the taste of the public and *paying* for the skill of every manufacturer who is to be employed. – Yet as a stimulus to his publishing trade, he does not need to take into account the inner worth and content of the commodities he publishes, but only the market *to* which, and the fashion*[k]* of the day *for* which, the in any case ephemeral products of the printing press are brought into lively currency, and can achieve a swift, even if not an enduring, turnover of inventory.

An experienced connoisseur of the turning out of books, will not, as a publisher, simply wait for ardent and skilled writers to offer their wares for sale; as the manager of a factory, he contrives the material as well as the fashion,*[l]* which – whether by its novelty or even the scurrilousness of its wit, so that the reading public gets something to gape at and ridicule – which, I say, will meet with the greatest demand, or in any case, will also incur the quickest depreciation; here it is not asked who, or how many, might have worked on a text to which such bantering*[m]* is devoted – even if it is not, indeed, well suited to it – since the reproach to such a text will not fall to the account of the publisher, but touches only those hired to turn out such books.[3]

Anyone who carries on such a public business in manufacturing and trade, compatible with the freedom of the people, is always a good citizen, whomever it may annoy. For self-seeking, when it does not contravene the police laws, is no crime; and Mr. Nicolai profits in this quality at least more safely than in the quality of an author, because what is contemptible in the distortions of his offering *Sempronius Gundibert* and its harlequin consorts does not touch the one who puts on the show,*[n]* but only the one who plays the role of the fool*[o]* in it.

. .

But how is it, then, with the troublesome question about *theory* and *practice* as it touches on the *authorship* of Mr. Friedrich Nicolai, which really occasioned the present criticism,*[p]* and which also stands in the closest connection to it? – The case just now presented of *prudence in publication*, as opposed to *soundness of publication* (of the superiority of illusion over

---

[k]Liebhaberei
[l]Façon
[m]Persiflieren
[n]der die Bude aufschlägt, literally, "the one who opens the booth." Kant is apparently likening the satirical authors whose work Nicolai publishes to the clowns presented by an impresario in a common form of street theater.
[o]Narren
[p]Censur

truth), can be finally judged in accordance with the same principles as those used in Möser's fiction; only instead of the word *practice,*[q] which signifies an open and honest treatment of a problem, one uses the term *practices*[r] (with emphasis on the penultimate syllable), and therefore seeks to make all theory seem childish and ridiculous in the eyes of a businessman; and following the principle: "The world wants to be deceived, – therefore let it be deceived!"[4] such practices, will also not fail to achieve their end.

What is proved, however, by the complete ignorance and incapacity of these mocking imitation philosophers to condemn judgments of reason, is this: that they appear not to comprehend at all what is really meant by cognition a priori (ingeniously[s] called by them "cognition from beforehand"[t]) as distinct from empirical cognition. The *Critique of Pure Reason*, to be sure, has said often and clearly enough that they are propositions asserted with consciousness of their inner *necessity* and absolute (apodictic) *universality*,[5] hence not, once again, recognized as dependent on experience, so that in themselves they could be not *one way* or *another*, because otherwise the division of judgments in accordance with that farcical example would turn out: "Brown were Pharaoh's cows, yet also of other colors."[6] But no one is blinder than he who *will* not see,[7] and this unwillingness has here an interest, namely that the strangeness of the spectacle, where things are removed from their natural places and represented standing on their head, draws many curiosity seekers to it, and through the crowd of viewers (for at least a short time), it revives the market and does not allow the industrial trade in the literary business to die down for too long; but then this too has its utility, even if not precisely an intended one, namely that the farce, which in the end becomes disgusting, afterward prepares the way for labors in the sciences which are all the more serious and well-grounded.

I. Kant

[q] *Praxis*
[r] *Praktiken*, tricks or machinations; emphasizing the penultimate syllable emphasizes the contrast with *Praxis*, and perhaps also the term's connotation of *dishonest* practices.
[s] *sinnreich*
[t] *Vonvornerkenntnis*

Editorial notes

Kant's review of Schulz

1. *selbstdenkenden.* Compare *Groundwork of the Metaphysics of Morals* (4:388).
2. Joseph Priestley's case against free will was presented in *The Doctrine of Philosophical Necessity Illustrated* (1777). For further discussion of Priestley see the *Critique of Practical Reason* (5:98).
3. In 1782 Martin Ehlers, professor of philosophy in Kiel, published a treatise entitled *Über die Lehre von der menschlichen Freiheit und über die Mittel, zu einer hohen Stufe moralischer Freiheit zu gelangen.*

What is enlightenment?

1. Compare *The Doctrine of Right* (6:327–8).
2. One of the sayings with which Frederick the Great was credited (or charged) was "It is not a monarch's duty to lead his subjects to heaven. Each of them must get there as best he can."
3. On Anton Friedrich Büsching, see *The Doctrine of Right* (6:353 n).

On the wrongfulness of unauthorized publication of books

1. For the sake of consistency I have retained, as far as possible, the vocabulary used in translating Kant's discussion of this subject in *The Doctrine of Right* (6:289–90). What is provided there (in Kant's division of contracts, 6:285) but missing from the present essay is the useful term "mandate" (*mandatum*) for *Vollmacht*. Although "authorized" is used for *Befugnis* and "unauthorized publication" for *Nachdruck*, the context makes it clear that in the latter case authorization is used in the sense of an author's empowering a publisher to deliver his discourse to the public.
2. In *The Doctrine of Right* Kant does not speak of a "positive" or affirmative (*bejahendes*) right against a person as distinguished from the "negative" (*verneinende*) right, involved in ownership, to prevent others from interfering with one's use of one's property. On the distinction between a property right or right to a thing (*Recht in einer Sache, ius reale, ius in re*) and a right against a person (*persönliche Recht, ius personale*), see 6:260, 271–4.
3. Philipp Daniel Lippert's *Daktyliothek* was first published in Latin in 1755–6 as *Dactyliotheca universalis* and later appeared in German as well.

EDITORIAL NOTES TO PAGES 46-115

Groundwork of The metaphysics of morals

1   Christian Wolff's *Philosophia Practica Universalis* was published in two volumes in 1738-9. Kant himself uses *"Philosophia practica universalis"* as the subtitle of Section III of his Introduction *to The Metaphysics of Morals* (6:221-8), the title of which is "Concepts Preliminary to the Metaphysics of Morals" and in which he discusses concepts common to both *The Doctrine of Right* and *The Doctrine of Virtue.*

2   Kant did plan to publish a work having this title; he apparently did not, however, intend to write a work entitled *Critique of Practical Reason.* I take it that he is here referring to subject matter rather than titles, and I have therefore capitalized neither. However, since a sharp distinction should be drawn between the proposed book that he calls "a metaphysics of morals" and the "metaphysics of morals" to which Section II of the *Groundwork* makes the "transition," I have marked the distinction by retaining his definite or indefinite article in the case of the former while omitting it in the case of the latter.

3   On the sense of *Verstand, Witz,* and *Urteilskraft* that is relevant in this context, see *Anthropology from a Pragmatic Point of View* (7:196-201). On "character" in the general sense in which the word is used in this sentence, see ibid., 7:249, 291-6.

4   Johann Georg Sulzer (1720-79), who in 1775 became director of the philosophic division of the Berlin Academy. He was best known for his writings in aesthetics, especially his *Allgemeine Theorie der Schönen Künste.*

5   *Weltklugheit,* or prudence regarding the world. Compare pragmatic *Weltkenntniss* in 7:120; also 271 ff.

6   In his *Inquiry into the Original of Our Ideas of Beauty and Virtue* (1725) and *Essay on the Nature and Conduct of the Passions and Affections and Illustrations upon the Moral Sense* (1728), Francis Hutcheson maintained that we make moral distinctions and are motivated to virtuous actions not through reason but through a moral sense, by means of which benevolence pleases us.

Review of Hufeland

1   This imposing list begins with the names of several authors of classical works in philosophy, natural right and law: Hugo Grotius (1583-1645), Thomas Hobbes (1588-1679), Samuel Pufendorf (1632-1694), Christian Thomasius (1655-1728), and (later) Christian Wolff (1679-1754). (On Hobbes, see *Theory and Practice* 8:289-307; for references to Grotius and Pufendorf, see *Toward Perpetual Peace* 8:355 and editorial note 5 and *Metaphysics of Morals,* editorial notes 16, 19, and 21. For references to Wolff, see *Groundwork* 4:390, *Metaphysics of Morals* 6:208, and *Critique of Practical Reason,* editorial note 7.) Then the list proceeds to some important names in seventeenth and eighteenth century legal studies: Heinrich Cocceji (1644-1719), his son Samuel Cocceji (1679-1755), Nicolaus Hieronymus Gundling (1671-1729), Georg Beyer (1665-1714), Gottlieb Samuel Treuer (1683-1743), and Heinrich Köhler (1685-1737). This is followed by long list of contempo-

rary German philosophers and legal scholars. Gottfried Achenwall (1719–1772) was the author of a textbook in natural law used by Kant (see *Theory and Practice* 8:301–302 and *Metaphysics of Morals* 6:286n and editorial note 22); other scholars of law and natural right were Justus Claproth (1728–1805), Johann Jacob Schmauss (1690–1757), Ludwig Julius Friedrich Höpfner (1743–1797), and Johann August Schlettwein (1731–1802). Many of the philosophers listed belonged to the "popular philosophers" of the German Enlightenment: Johann Georg Feder (1740–1821), Christian Garve (1742–1798), Johann August Eberhard (1739–1809), Ernst Platner (1744–1818), Moses Mendelssohn (1729–1786), and Christian Georg Selle (1748–1800) (Concerning Feder, see *Critique of Practical Reason*, editorial notes 1, 3, and 6. Concerning Garve, see *Critique of Practical Reason*, editorial note 6, p. 287, *Theory and Practice* 8:278–289, *Toward Perpetual Peace* 8:385n and editorial note 13, and *Metaphysics of Morals* editorial note 2. Concerning Mendelssohn, see *What Is Enlightenment?* 8:42, *Critique of Practical Reason* editorial notes 12 and 13, *Theory and Practice* 8:307–312, and *Metaphysics of Morals* 6:273n and editorial notes 5 and 35. Concerning Eberhard, see *Metaphysics of Morals* editorial notes 5 and 21.) The other figures listed are J. G. Sulzer (1720–1779), Johann Friedrich Flatt (1759–1827), Johann Georg Hamann (1730–1788), Johann August Heinrich Ulrich (1746–1813), and Johann Friedrich Zöllner (1753–1804). Sulzer was Director of the Berlin Academy in 1775 (see above pp. 64–65 and *Groundwork* editorial note 4). Flatt was a Wolffian critic of Kant (see *Critique of Practical Reason* 5:8n and editorial note 1 and *Metaphysics of Morals* 6:207). Hamann was an influential figure on the German counter-enlightenment (see *Toward Perpetual Peace* editorial note 6). Regarding Ulrich, see above pp. 119–131. Regarding Zöllner, see above p. 13.

2   This account directly contrasts Hufeland's approach to grounding practical laws with Kant's own, as it was soon to be presented in the *Critique of Practical Reason* (5:21, 26–27, 33–35, 57–59).

3   We are unable to locate any text in which Hobbes says anything of the kind (cf. the comment of Heinrich Maier, AK 8:482).

4   What Kant has to say about compensation is to be found in his discussion of the right of contract (*Metaphysics of Morals* 6:297, 299–303).

5   For Kant's views on imputation, see *Metaphysics of Morals* 6:224, 228.

Critique of practical reason

1   The review was by Johann Friedrich Flatt in the *Tübinger gelehrte Anzeigen*, May 13, 1786. Flatt is, again, the "reviewer from Tübingen" referred to in *The Metaphysics of Morals* (6:207). The review was in the spirit of Gottlieb August Tittel's *Über Herrn Kants Moralreform* (1786), which asked "Is the entire Kantian reform of moral philosophy to limit itself to a new formula?" Tittel made further criticisms relevant to Kant's remarks in the Preface to the *Critique of Practical Reason*, e.g., that a proposition "so common and well known" could be made so obscure, requiring one to put a human being in two worlds, and censured his terminology, in effect charging him with (in Kant's words, "putting new patches on an old garment" (10). In a letter to

EDITORIAL NOTES TO PAGES 143–174

Kant of June 11, 1786, the editor of the *Berlinische Monatsschrift*, Johann Erich Biester, referred to Tittel as "the feeble shadow of a feeble (F)eder" (10:457) and suggested that their attacks were not sufficiently important to warrant a reply. On Feder, see notes 3 and 6.

2   The reviewer was H. A. Pistorius in *Allgemeine deutsche Bibliothek*. Although the review was anonymous, a letter to Kant from Daniel Jenisch of May 14, 1787, identified Pistorius as the author (AK 10:486). The section of the *Critique* entitled "On the Concept of an Object of Pure Practical Reason" is Kant's reply to this particular concern of Pistorius. Kant's primary concern, however, is with the more fundamental problem, raised by Pistorius, about the consistency of theoretical and practical reason (AK 5:8).

3   Kant's reference is to Johann Georg Feder, the author of *Über Raum und Caußalität zur Prüfung der Kantischen Philosophie*, Göttingen 1789. In a letter of June 25, 1787, to Christian Gottfried Schutz Kant says that he expects to send his *Critique of Practical Reason* to the publisher the following week and adds "this will be better than any controversy with Feder and Abel (the first of whom maintains that there is no a priori cognition at all)" (10:490).

4   In his *Enquiry concerning Human Understanding*, Section IV, Hume maintains that the propositions of mathematics are, in Kant's terms, analytic. In *A Treatise of Human Nature* I, III, I, he had considered the propositions of geometry synthetic and empirical. However, Kant apparently had no direct access to the *Treatise*.

5   William Cheselden (1688–1752) reported his patient's reaction to an operation that restored his vision in *Philosophical Transactions*, 1728. His report could have become known to Kant either through Kästner's *Vollständigem Lehrbegriff der Optik* of 1755 or through its repetition by Herder in 1769.

6   This note, like the comparable note in the *Prolegomena to Any Future Metaphysics* (4:375 n), is apparently directed against Feder, the editor who had revised Christian Garve's review of the *Critique of Pure Reason*. This review, which appeared in the supplement to the *Göttingische gelehrte Anzeigen* of January 19, 1782, was cited in the *Prolegomena* as "A Specimen of a Judgment of the Critique prior to Its Examination" (4:372–80).

7   Epicurus and the Stoics are discussed elsewhere in the *Critique*, especially in the Dialectic. Kant's references to moralists not otherwise mentioned are as follows: (a) Michel de Montaigne (1533–92), essayist and skeptical philosopher, whose most important philosophical essay, "Apology for Raimond Sebond," stressed human stupidity and immorality; (b) Bernard Mandeville (1670–1733), author of *The Fable of the Bees; or Private Vices, Public Benefits*; (c) Francis Hutcheson (1694–1746), a leading proponent of the "moral sense" or "moral sentiment" theory; (d) Christian Wolff (1697–1754), prolific writer and systematizer of rationalist philosophy, known as the "preceptor of Germany" (for further references to Wolff in this volume, see *Groundwork of the Metaphysics of Morals* [4:390] and *The Metaphysics of Morals* [6:208]); (e) Christian August Crusius (1715–75), professor of theology in Leipzig, who, before his interests turned exclusively to theology, was one of the best known Pietist philosophers and critics of Wolffianism.

8   Kant's reference is to the *Groundwork of the Metaphysics of Morals*, Section III.

9 Bernard de Fontenelle (1657–1757), man of letters, historian of science, and popular philosopher, was considered a forerunner of the Enlightenment.
10 Joseph Priestley (1733–1804), *The Doctrine of Philosophical Necessity Illustrated*, London 1777. On the "fatalism" involved in transcendental realism, see Kant's review of Schulz's *Attempt at a Doctrine of Morals for All Men* and Kraus's review of Ulrich's *Eleutheriology*, both of which are included in this volume. Kant's discussion of punishment (5:37–38 above) is echoed in his review of Schulz's book.
11 A. von Vaucason's automata attracted considerable attention when they were first exhibited in Paris in 1738. Materialists sometimes used them to illustrate their theory of man as a machine.
12 Moses Mendelssohn, *Morgenstunden* (1785), ch. 11. In view of the controversy about Lessing's Spinozism, in which Mendelssohn defended Lessing against Jacobi, Kant's reference to the "otherwise acute Mendelssohn" could be taken as a warning that the consequence of his rejecting transcendental idealism is Spinozism.
13 Thomas Wizenmann (1759–87), a friend of Jacobi, entered the controversy between Mendelssohn and Jacobi (see note 12) with his *Die Resultate der Jacobi'schen und Mendelssohn'schen Philosophie kritisch untersucht von einem Freywilligen*, published anonymously in 1786. In commenting on the controversy in his essay "What Does It Mean to Orient Oneself in Thinking?" (1786) Kant mentioned the "acute author of the *Resultate*." In the following year Wizenmann replied with an essay *An den Herrn Professor Kant von dem Verfasser der Resultate Jacobi'schen und Mendelssohn'schen Philosophie kritisch untersucht von einem Freywilligen*.
14 Phalaris, tyrant of Agrigentum, invented a method of executing people by burning them to death in a brass bull.

Theory and practice

1 Possibly a reference to Edmund Burke's *Reflections on the Revolution in France* (1790), which had been translated into German by Friedrich Gentz in 1793. Although Burke's remarks are relevant to Part II of Kant's essay, he uses the quotation from Virgil cited by Kant.
2 On Garve, see *The Metaphysics of Morals* (6:206, n).
3 See *The Metaphysics of Morals* (6:223).
4 In Kant's division of contracts, this appears as *locatio operae*, a type of contract to let and hire as distinguished from a contract to alienate something. See *The Doctrine of Right* (6:285).
5 On Achenwall, see *The Metaphysics of Morals* (6:286 n).
6 In 1354 Duke John III, in a charter granted to Brabant, promised to maintain the integrity of the duchy and not to wage war, make treaties, or impose taxes without consulting his subjects represented by the municipalities. Before entering Brussels, the capital, a duke of Brabant had to swear to abide by the contract. In case he should violate it, the subjects were released from their duty of obedience.
7 Heinrich Maier, the Academy editor, considers it unlikely that Danton

would have said this and suggests that either Kant or a newspaper report attributed to him what had been said by someone else, perhaps Robespierre.
8   The so-called Glorious Revolution in which, after James II had been overthrown and fled to France, Parliament legislated the accession to the throne of his eldest, Protestant daughter, Mary, and her husband, William III of Orange, and restricted the monarchy to the Protestant successors of James I. A dispute arose, between Whigs and Tories, as to whether James II had forfeited the throne by violating the original contract or by abdicating.
9   On Mendelssohn, see *The Doctrine of Right* (6:273 n).
10 On the distinction between these two senses of "love," see *The Doctrine of Virtue* (6:402, 449).
11 Gotthold Ephraim Lessing, writer and dramatist, published his *Die Erziehung des Menschengeschlechts* in 1780.
12 On the Abbé St. Pierre's *Projet pour rendre la paix perpetuelle en Europe*, see the translator's introduction to *Toward Perpetual Peace*. In 1761 Rousseau published his *Extrait de projet de paix perpetuelle de M. l'Abbé de Saint-Pierre*, in which he praised the project of a European alliance for peace and pointed out its advantages for both sovereigns and subjects. If it is nevertheless not carried out, the reason will be, not that it is chimerical, but that people are foolish and that it would be a kind of stupidity to be wise in the midst of fools. In his *Jugement sur le paix perpetuelle*, written about the same time but withheld from publication, he maintained that, although the project was good, such an alliance could be realized only by force and through revolutions, the cost of which would be too high. In an essay of 1784, "Idea for a Universal History from a Cosmopolitan Point of View" (8:24), Kant noted that the idea of a league of nations put forward by the Abbé St. Pierre and by Rousseau had been ridiculed as fantastic, "perhaps because they believed that its realization was imminent."

Toward perpetual peace

1   The story of this sign can be traced to a remark of Leibniz in his Preface to *Codex Iuris gentium Diplomaticus* (Hanover, 1693).
2   Presumably, the English.
3   Joseph Niklas, Imperial Count of Windischgrätz (1744–1802), proposed as a problem for scholarly competition, how to formulate contracts in such a way that they could not be given more than one interpretation, so that disputes about transfer of property would be impossible and lawsuits about such contracts could not arise.
4   Jacques Mallet du Pan (1749–1800), a writer of Swiss birth and opponent of the French Revolution. At the end of his treatise *Considérations sur la Révolution de France et sur les causes qui en prolongent la durée* (1793) he speaks of a maxim that has guided him for fifteen years and that an English poet has presented in a couplet. The verse quoted is from Alexander Pope's *Essay on Man* 3, 303–4. The reference to Jonathan Swift is to his *Tale of a Tub:* "Wisdom is a hen, whose cackling we must value and consider, because it is attended with an egg; but then lastly, it is a nut, which, unless you

choose with judgment, may cost you a tooth, and pay you with nothing but a worm."

5 Hugo Grotius (1583–1645), Samuel Pufendorf (1632–94), and Emmerich de Vattel (1714–67) were the most renowned exponents of natural right theory in early modern times. Their chief works were, respectively, *De iure belli et pacis* (1625), *De iure naturae et gentium* (1672), and *Le droit des gens* (1758).

6 *Alphabetum Tibetanum missionum apostolicarum commodo editum . . . Studio et labore Fr. Augustini Antonii Georgii eremitae Augustinui (1762)*, also cited in *Religion within the Boundaries of Mere Reason* (6:108 n). The other references in this note are to Johann Eberhard Fischer, *Quaestiones Petropolitanae, (III) De variis nominibus imperii Sinarium* (1770); the Greek dictionary compiled by the grammarian Hesychius in the 5th or 6th century A.D.; Abbé Jean Jacques Barthelemy, *Voyâge du jeune Anacharsis en Grèce, dans le milieu du quatrième siècle avant l'âge vulgaire* (1788); Matherin Veyissiere de La Croze, a Benedictine monk, and Pater Francisco Orazio della Penna, a missionary who lived in Lhasa, are cited by Georgi as Kant's note indicates. Kant's long note may have been occasioned by one of his disputes with Johann Georg Hamann. After Hamann had published his *Fragmente einer apokryphischen Sibylle über apokalyptische Mysterien* (1779), Kant, according to a letter from Hamann to Herder of April 18, 1783, wrote to Hamann arguing that the word was of Tibetan origin, a view that Hamann considered mistaken.

7 Friedrich Bouterwek (1766–1828), professor of philosophy in Göttingen. See his letter to Kant of August 25, 1793 (11:431–2; see also 13:345).

8 On the relation of the "lower faculty" (philosophy) to the three "higher faculties" (theology, law, and medicine), see *The Conflict of the Faculties* (7: 21–9).

9 Compare *The Doctrine of Right* (6:318).

10 Compare *The Doctrine of Right* (6:307–8).

11 Compare *The Doctrine of Right* (6:490).

12 Compare, however, *The Doctrine of Right* (6:346).

13 On Christian Garve, to whom Part I of "On the Common Saying: That May Be Correct in Theory but It Is of No Use in Practice," is directed, see *The Metaphysics of Morals* (6:207 n).

The metaphysics of morals

1 *Metaphysische Anfangsgründe der Naturwissenshaft* (1785).

2 Christian Garve (1742–98) was professor of philosophy at Leipzig. Part I of Kant's essay "On the Common Saying: That May Be True in Theory but It Does Not Apply in Practice" (1793), which deals with the relation of theory to practice in moral philosophy in general, is a reply to some objections raised by Garve in his *Versuche über verschiedene Gegenstände aus der Moral und Literatur*. Kant's reference to Garve in the present context is topical, since in his *Vermischte Aufsätze* (1796) Garve complains about the mischief that "various authors of the Kantian school" (though not Kant himself) have been making in popular philosophy.

3 Antoine Laurent Lavoisier (1743–94), whose discovery of the role of oxygen

EDITORIAL NOTES TO PAGES 367-392

in combustion and influence in establishing the nomenclature of chemistry earned him the title of principal architect of the new science of chemistry.

4 On the system of the controversial Scottish physician John Brown (1735–88), see my introduction to the translation of Kant's *Rektoratsrede*, "On Philosophers' Medicine of the Body," in Lewis W. Beck, ed., *Kant's Latin Writings* (New York and Bern, Peter Lang, 1986; revised edition, 1992).

5 According to Natorp (5:505–7) the reviewer from Tübingen was probably the same Johann Friedrich Flatt to whom Kant refers in his Preface to the *Critique of Practical Reason* (5:8 n). In reviewing a mathematical dissertation by J. C. Yelin, Flatt remarked that, since everything must now be expressed in Kantian language, the author calls the construction of a quantity *eine Darstellung durch reine Anschauung*, and went on to use the text Kant cites from Hausen as proof that only the terminology, not the concept, is new. As might be expected, Kant was annoyed with Flatt's recurrent theme that his cardinal distinctions had already been made in substance by other writers. Compare Kant's reply, in 1790, to a similar charge by Johann August Eberhard, *On a Recent Discovery according to Which Any New Critique of Pure Reason Has Been Made Superfluous by an Earlier One* (8:187–251).

6 Christian Hausen (1693–1745) was professor of mathematics at Leipzig.

7 See Christian Wolff, *Ontology* § 588.

8 See Walter Strauss, *Friedrich Nicolai und die kritische Philosophie: ein Beitrag zur Geschichte der Aufklärung* (Stuttgart, Kohlhammer, 1927). In 1796 Nicolai, in his *Beschreibung einer Reise durch Deutschland und die Schweiz im Jahre 1781*, ridiculed the use to which Schiller and his followers had put Kantian terminology. Despite Kant's warning that this criticism should not be extended to the critical philosophy itself, Nicolai did just that with his publication of *Leben und Meinungen Sempronius Gundiberts* (1798), which called forth Kant's *Über die Buchmacherei: Zwei Briefe an Herrn Friedrich Nicolai* (8:431–8).

9 Anthony Ashley Cooper, third Earl of Shaftesbury (1651–1713). The reference is to his *Characteristics of Men, Manners, Opinions, Times*, Treatise II, "*Sensus communis*, an Essay on the Freedom of Wit and Humour" (1709), Section I: "Truth ... may bear all Lights: and one of those principal Lights ... is Ridicule itself. ... So much, at least, is allow'd by All, who at any time appeal to this Criterion."

10 That *The Doctrine of Right* was written and published before *The Doctrine of Virtue* accounts for the title page (6:203) and table of contents (6:210) in the Academy edition.

11 On permissive laws see "Toward Perpetual Peace" (8:347 n, 373 n).

12 Compare Kant's discussion, in *The Doctrine of Virtue*, of conscience (6:400–1) and of one's duty to oneself as judge of oneself (6:437–40).

13 Compare 296–300.

14 For further discussion of "the right of necessity," see "Theory and Practice" (8:300 n).

15 On the basis of the concluding sentence of § A and the diagram on 6:240, one would expect this explanation within *The Doctrine of Virtue*'s discussion of perfect duties to oneself. No such explanation is provided, although the

virtue contrary to at least some of the vices discussed there is called, in 6:420, *Ehrliebe* (*honestas interna, iustum sui aestimium*). See also the use of *Ehrlichkeit* with regard to lying, 6:429. What all these terms have in common is the practical affirmation of one's dignity as a person. Their source may well be the Stoic *honestum*. There are occasional references to "the right of humanity in one's own person" in 23:276 and 390. Within *The Doctrine of Right*, however, "the right [or right] of humanity" seems to be a limiting condition on the rights of others.

16   A right, as a *Vermögen*, might be called a "faculty" in an unusual sense. Kant's predecessors in the natural right tradition, most notably Hugo Grotius, had conceptually distinguished but sometimes verbally conflated *potestas* and *facultas*. A moral power is one's title to do what is not unjust. In accordance with the law of nature, every human being has his original *suum*, which includes his life, limbs, and liberty. Since it is right for him to use and to consume what he needs, and wrong for anyone to interfere with him, he has moral power to use force in defense of what is originally his. But a right in the derivative sense of a moral faculty involves an extension of one's *suum* and has to be acquired. Because all human beings are equal with respect to the original *suum*, it is necessary that others transfer to him, by express or at least tacit consent, a part of what is theirs, i.e., control over their actions and, indirectly, over things (*De Iure Belli ac Pacis Libri Tres*, I,I,x,7 and I,Ii,i,5). In view of Kant's distinction between Grotius's historical "primitive community" and his own rational "original community" (6:251, 258) he may be rejecting Grotius's distinction between *potestas* and *facultas* in favor of his own distinction between innate and acquired rights. However, the relation is too tenuous to warrant translating *Vermögen* in the sense of a right as "faculty." On Kant's distinction between authorization to do something (*facultas moralis generatim*) and authorization to use coercion (*facultas iuridica*) see 6:383.

17   In his essay "On a Supposed Right to Lie from Philanthropy" Kant says that a metaphysics of right requires "1) an axiom, that is, an apodictically certain proposition that issues immediately from the definition of external right (consistency of the freedom of each with the freedom of everyone in accordance with a universal law)" (8:349). He goes on to add that it requires "2) a postulate (of external public law)."

18   It is generally agreed that the following five paragraphs, which I have enclosed in brackets, do not belong here. On the history of this discovery, see Thomas Mautner, "Kant's Metaphysics of Morals: A Note on the Text," *Kant-Studien* 72 (1981): 356–9. For further discussion of the state of the text, see Translator's Introduction. According to Ludwig's reconstruction of the text, § 2 should be inserted in place of the five paragraphs bracketed.

19   Although Kant does not mention Hugo Grotius by name, he is presumably thinking here, as in 6:258, of Grotius's theory (adopted by others in the natural right tradition) of how people moved from a primitive common possession of goods, in which each could rightly use what he needed, to the institution of private property. See *De Iure Belli ac Pacis Libri Tres*, II. 1–2.

20   In 23:325, Kant points out that in the critical philosophy "having" (*habere*) is a predicable, or derivative concept, of the category of causality.

EDITORIAL NOTES TO PAGES 423–459

21 Moses Mendelssohn, *Gesammelte Schriften* (Hildesheim, H. A. Gerstenberg, 1972), pp. 255–362. Kant is probably referring to Mendelssohn's view that "a contract is nothing other than one party's relinquishing his right and the other party's accepting it" (p. 279). By this, the first party's "perfect right" to something he does not need for his preservation (his right to use coercion) becomes an "imperfect right" (a right to request or petition). The terminology of "perfect" and "imperfect" rights seems to have originated with Samuel Pufendorf, as an emendation of Grotius's distinction between "faculties" and "aptitudes." Although Kant rejects the distinction, in the *Doctrine of Virtue* he uses the language of what is "owed" or "due" with regard to duties of respect.

22 Gottfried Achenwall's *Ius Naturae* was one of the texts Kant used for the course on natural right that he gave at least twelve times during his teaching career. Achenwall's text, with Kant's comments on it, is included in 19:3.

23 Adam Smith says merely, "It is in this manner that money has become in all civilized nations the universal instrument of commerce, by the intervention of which goods of all kinds are bought and sold, or exchanged for one another." *The Wealth of Nations*, Bk. I, Ch. IV (Middlesex and New York, Penguin Books, 1970), p. 131. He does, however, develop in Chapter V the notion that labor determines the value of all goods.

24 The distinction between "long possession" or "usucaption" (*Ersitzung, usucapio*) and "superannuation of claims" or "prescription" (*Verjährung, praescriptio*) discussed here has a long history. In Roman Law, acquiring ownership (*dominium*) of a thing by *usucapio* was originally available only under the *ius civile*, for Roman citizens, and *praescriptio* had to be devised as an analogous procedure for provincials or foreigners. It did not confer ownership but enabled the possessor to bar a claimant's right of action against him if he could show that he had been possessor in good faith for the prescribed period of time. But before the code of Justinian, prescription had come to extinguish the claimant's title instead of merely barring his action; and when Justinian abolished the distinction between Italian and provincial land (which had belonged to the Roman people or to the emperor), prescription by 30 years' possession gave ownership to a possessor in good faith, even if the thing had originally been stolen. See R. W. Leage, *Roman Private Law* (London, Macmillan and Co., 1930), pp. 159–71.

25 Kant seems to be thinking here of "the decisory oath," which would decide a fact at issue in a case. This was one of the devices of civil procedure designed to protect the judge from threats by the wealthy and the powerful. "The decisory oath worked in the following way: Party A could put Party B on his oath as to a fact at issue that was within Party B's knowledge. If Party B refused to swear, the fact was taken as conclusively proved against him. If Party B swore, the fact was taken as conclusively proved in his favor." John Henry Merryman, *The Civil Law Tradition* (Stanford, Stanford University Press, 1969), p. 126.

26 Natorp suggests that a fairly extensive portion of the text may be missing here, in which "first," "second," and "third" occurred twice and the first occurrence of "third" got replaced by the second. In any case, the "third" point here seems to concern the relation of the judicial authority to the

legislative and the executive authorities, not another relation parallel to coordination and subordination.

27 Although Kant goes on to call a "moderate" [*gemässigte*] constitution *ein Unding* (an "absurdity" in the sense, apparently, of a logical impossibility), it would seem from 6:322 that the absurdity consists in supposing that a parliament representing the people can *actively* resist the highest executive authority. I take it that his references to a "moderate" and to a "limited" [*eingeschränkte*] constitution are both directed at the British Constitution. Compare "Theory and Practice" 8:303.

28 Natorp suggests that, here again, something is apparently missing from the text, regarding the first kind of crime.

29 Arthur Elphinstone, 6th Baron Balmerino, who took part in the attempt of 1745–6 to put Prince Charles Edward Stuart on the British throne, was captured in the defeat of the Scottish forces at Culloden and subsequently beheaded.

30 Kant is apparently referring to deportation to a province as distinguished from exile. See below, 6:338.

31 Cesare Bonesana, Marchese Beccaria, whose influential *Dei delitti e della pene* (1764) argued for a reform of the harsh penal codes of the time. Kant's interest in Beccaria may well have arisen from Beccaria's reliance on a text from Rousseau's *Social Contract*, which had been published in 1762: "All laws must be regarded as if they proceeded from the unanimous will of the people."

32 In 1789 Louis XVI convoked the Estates General, which transformed itself into the National Assembly and then, as the Constituent Assembly, adopted a new constitution in 1791.

33 An amphictyonic league, in Greek history, was an association of neighboring states or tribes for the protection of and in the interests of a common religious center. When capitalized, the Amphictyonic League refers to the Delphic Amphictyony, formed to protect the temple of Apollo at Delphi and to direct the Pythian games.

34 In "Toward Perpetual Peace," however, Kant reaches the opposite conclusion by using his "principle of publicity" (8:384).

35 Part III of "Theory and Practice," directed against Moses Mendelssohn, is concerned with Cosmopolitan Right, as Part II, directed against Hobbes, is concerned with The Right of a State. In "Toward Perpetual Peace" (8:368), Kant maintains that "the spirit of commerce" is a driving force in human nature and, since commerce and war are incompatible, one of the forces by which nature can be viewed as working toward peace.

36 Anton Friedrich Büsching (1724–93) was a well-known geographer and theologian.

37 The appendix was added in the 1798 edition of *The Doctrine of Right* in reply to a review by Friedrich Bouterwek (reprinted in 20: 445–53). Kant's quotations are not always accurate.

38 *Zueignung.* In 6:259 *Zueignung* (*appropriatio*) was said to be the third of the *Momente* (*attendenda*) in original acquisition. As Kant pointed out (6:291), ideal acquisition can take effect only in civil society. In the remainder of the paragraph the text seems to be corrupt.

EDITORIAL NOTES TO PAGES 502–611

39 In the context of the discussion, one would have expected Kant to say that laymen have given their estates and the feudal subjects attached to them to a church. So too, at the beginning of the next paragraph when Kant raises the question of whether the church "can belong to" (*als das Seine angehören können*) the state or the state to the church, the kind of right involved would seem to require a distinction between the estates of a church and a church as a body of believers (6:327).

40 The primary sense of *Glück*, a component of the German word for "happiness" [*Glückseligkeit*], is "luck" or "fortune." See also 6:387.

41 Natorp suggests that Kant's reference is to Part I of "Theory and Practice," which was first published in the *Berliner Monatsschrift* in 1793. Another possibility, suggested by Vorländer, is "On a Recently Prominent Elevated Tone in Philosophy," which appeared in that journal in 1796.

42 Leonhard Cochius's "*Untersuchung über die Neigungen*" was the prize essay of the Berlin Academy for 1767.

43 I.e., the principle enunciated in § D, 6:231.

44 Here, and again in 6:461, Kant cites or refers to Albrecht Haller's poem "*Über die Ursprung des Übels*," and on 6:449 refers to his poem "*Über die Ewigkeit.*" Natorp's notes give the relevant portions of the poems.

45 On the affects and passions see *Anthropology from a Pragmatic Point of View* (7:251–82), *The Conflict of the Faculties*, Part III (7:95–116), and the *Rektoratsrede*, referred to in note 4 above.

46 Frederick the Great.

47 *der den Beschluss macht.* It both concludes the case and is the conclusion [*Schluss*] of the practical syllogism discussed above, 6:438.

48 The quotations in this paragraph are taken from 1 Peter 1:16, Matthew 5:48, and Philippians 4:8.

49 See also Kant's assertion, in "The End of All Things" (1784), 8:337–38, that if one considers not only what ought to be done but whether it actually will be done, love is an indispensable supplement to the imperfection of human nature, since unless it is added one could not count on very much being done.

50 Terence *The Self-Tormentor* 1.125.

51 Natorp suggests that the reference is probably to Cicero *On the Nature of the Gods* 1.23.63.

52 *Religion within the Boundaries of Mere Reason* (1793), AK 6.

53 It seems inappropriate to speak of a "reward" [*Belohnung*] as having a place in love and beneficence. Perhaps Kant is referring to a reward that "was promised in the law" (6:227).

54 *Odes* 3.2.31–2.

On a supposed right to lie from philanthropy

1 Johann David Michaelis (1717–91), a renowned biblical scholar, was professor of theology in Göttingen and a colleague of C. F. Stäudlin, whose invitation elicited from Kant the treatise that became Part I of *The Conflict of the Faculties* and to whom Kant dedicated the book. See Kant's reference to Michaelis in this work (7:343).

EDITORIAL NOTES TO PAGES 611-627

2 Karl Friedrich Cramer, whose role in Kant's reply to Constant is noted in the translator's introduction, was dismissed from his position as professor of Greek and oriental languages at the University of Kiel because of his outspoken sympathy for the French Revolution.

3 Heinrich Meier, editor of the Academy edition of this essay, states that no such place is to be found in Kant's previous works.

4 Kant might be referring to "the Right of Humanity" in one's own person mentioned in *The Doctrine of Right* (6:237–8, 240).

5 Compare *The Doctrine of Right* (6:238).

6 See *The Metaphysics of Morals* (6:227–8).

7 See *The Doctrine of Virtue* (6:429).

8 See *The Doctrine of Virtue* (6:238).

On turning out books

1 AK 6:329, cf. *Perpetual Peace* 8:350–351. The only statement of this argument that could have been known to Möser (who died in 1794) is found in Kant's 1793 essay on theory and practice (AK 8:292–294).

2 that is, the principle of the law of freedom ("eleutheros" = freedom, "nomos" = law). Kant elsewhere uses the term "eleutheronomy" to characterize his own view in contrast to "eudaimonism" (*Metaphysics of Morals* 6:378).

3 Here, and in the reference to Nicolai in the heading of this letter as "publisher" rather than as "author," Kant seems to be suggesting that *Sempronius Gundibert* was not really, or at least not solely, Nicolai's work (cf. AK 8:520).

4 *Die Welt will betrogen sein, so werde sie dann betrogen!* is an old German proverb.

5 Cf. *Critique of Pure Reason* Axv, A1–2, B3, A24, A25/B41, A47/B64, A91/B123–124, A196/B241.

6 Cf. Genesis 30:32 and 41:3.

7 "Who is blinder than he who will not see?" Andrew Boorde, *Breviary of Health* (1547).

Glossary

German–English

Abbruch tun	infringe upon
Absicht	purpose, intention, aim
absondern	abstract, separate, set aside
Achtung	respect (*reverentia*)
Affekt	emotion
Afterrenden	defamation
Akt	act (cf. *Handlung*)
allgemein	universal, general (*universalis, generalis*)
allgemeine Gesetzgebung	giving universal law(s)
Allgemeingültigkeit	universal validity
anerkennen	recognize, acknowledge
Anfangsgründe	first principles
Angeklagte	accused
angenehm	agreeable
Angewohnheit	habit (*assuetudo*)
Ankläger	prosecutor
Anlage	predisposition, constitution
Anleihe	loan
Annehmung	assumption, adoption
Anschauung	intuition (*intuitus*)
Anspruch	claim
Antrieb	impulse
Anwendung	application
Art	way, species, kind
Aufbewahrung	keeping
auffordern	require
Aufforderung	requirement, demand
Aufstand	sedition
ausführen	carry out, fulfill
ausführende Gewalt	executive authority
ausübende Gewalt	executive authority
Auswahl	selection
Bedeutung	significance, signification, meaning (cf. *Sinn*)

641

GLOSSARY

Bedingung — condition
Bedürfnis — need
Befehl — order
Befehlshaber — commander (*imperans*), executive authority
Befriedigung — satisfaction
Befugnis — authorization, warrant
Begebenheit — occurrence, event
Begehrungsvermögen — faculty of desire
Begierde — desire
Begnädigung — pardon
begreifen — comprehend
Begriff — concept (*conceptus*)
beharrlich — persisting, abiding
Beharrlichkeit — persistence, perseverance
Beherrscher — ruler
Beispiel — example, instance
bekennen — acknowledge
Beleidigung — offense, insult
Belieben (nach) — at (one's) discretion
beliebig — discretionary
Bemächtigung — taking control (*occupatio*)
Bemerkung — observation (cf. *Anmerkung*)
Benutzung — utilization
berechtigen — justify, entitle
Beschaffenheit — constitution, property, characteristics, nature (cf. *Eigenschaft, Natur*)
Beschiedenheit — modesty
Besitz — possession
besonder — particular, special
beständig — constant
bestimmen — determine
Bestimmung — determination, vocation (*determinatio*)
Bestimmungsgrund — motive, determining ground
Beurteilung — appraisal
Bewegungsgrund — motive
Beweis — proof
Beziehung — relation, reference (cf. *Verhältnis*)
Bild — image
Bildung — education, formation (cf. *Ausbildung*)
billig — equitable, fair
billigen — approve
Billigkeit — equity (*aequitas*)
Boden — land (*fundus*) (cf. *Land*, country)
Böse — evil (cf. *Übel*)
brauchbar — usable
bürgerlich — civil (*civilis*)

GLOSSARY

Darstellung	presentation, exhibition, display
dartun	establish (cf. *aufstellen*)
Dauer	duration
Demut	humility
Denkungsart	way of thinking, frame of mind, cast of mind
Deutlichkeit	distinctness, clarity
Ding	thing
Ehrbegierde	ambition (*ambitio*)
ehrlich	honest, honorable
Ehrliebe	love of honor
Eifersucht	jealousy
eigen	proper
Eigendünkel	self-conceit
Eigenliebe	self-love
Eigenschaft	property
Eigentum	property
Eigentümer	owner, proprietor (*dominus*)
eigentümlich	peculiar
einsehen	have insight into
Einsicht	insight
Einwilligung	consent
Empfänglichkeit	receptivity
Empfindung	feeling, sensation
Endabsicht	final purpose
Endzweck	final end
eng	narrow (*strictum*)
entäussern	divest
Entschließung	decision
entwickeln	develop, explicate (*explicare*)
Erfahrung	experience
erhaben	sublime
erkennen	cognize, recognize
Erkenntnis	cognition (*cognitio*)
Erklärung	definition, explanation, explication, declaration
Erlaubnis	permission
Erlaubnisgesetz	permissive law
Erläuterung	illustration, elucidation
Erscheinung	appearance
erweisen	prove, demonstrate
Erwerbung	acquisition
ewig	eternal, perpetual
Fertigkeit	aptitude (cf. *Leichtigkeit*)
Folge	result

GLOSSARY

Folgerung	consequence
Fortschritt	progress, advance
fremd	extraneous, not belonging to, foreign, another
Gastfreiheit	hospitality
Gattung	genus, species, race
Gebieter	commander
Gebot	command
Gebrauch	use, employment (cf. *Benutzung*)
Gedankending	thought-entity (*ens rationis*)
gefallen	like, please (v.r.)
Gefühl	feeling
Gegenstand	object
Geist	spirit, mind
Gelehrte	scholar
Gelehrtheit	scholarship, learning
Gelindigkeit	gentleness
Gemeinbesitz	possession in common
Gemeinschaft	community (*communio*, interaction) (*commercio*)
Gemeinwesen	commonwealth, community
Gemüt	mind
Gemütsart	character (*indoles*)
Genuss	enjoyment
Gerechtigkeit	justice, righteousness
Gerichtshof	court, tribunal
Gesammtbesitz	collective possession
Geschäft	concern, business, practical affairs
Geschicklichkeit	skill
Gesetzgeber	legislator, lawgiver
Gesetzgebung	legislation, lawgiving
Gesetzmäßigkeit	lawfulness, conformity with law
Gesinde	servants
Gesinnung	disposition
Gesprächigkeit	sociability
gewahr	aware
Gewalt	control, authority, force
Gewissenlosigkeit	unconscientiousness
Glück	(good) fortune, luck
Glückseligkeit	happiness
Grad	degree
Grenze	bound(ary)
Grund	ground
Grundsatz	principle (cf. *Prinzip*)
Gültigkeit	validity

GLOSSARY

Handlung	act(ion)
Hang	propensity
Heil	well-being
Heiligkeit	holiness
herrenlos	belonging to no one (*res nullius*)
Herrschaft	dominion
Herrschergewalt	sovereignty, sovereign (cf. *Souveränität*)
hervorbringen	produce, bring forth
hinreichend	sufficient
Hochmut	arrogance
Hochschätzung	esteem
Höflichkeit	courtesy
Inbegriff	sum total
Inhabung	holding (*detentio*)
Keim	germ
kennen	know, have cognizance of, be acquainted with
Kenntnis	knowledge
klar	clear
Klugheit	prudence (*prudentia*)
Kraft	power, force
Kritik	critique, criticism
Kultur	culture, cultivation
Kunst	art
lädieren	wrong
Langmut	patience
Läsion	infringement, wrong
Laster	vice
Legalität	legality
Lehre	doctrine, teaching
Leibeigener	bondsman
Leidenschaft	passion
Leistung	performance
Leitfaden	guide, clue
Lust	pleasure (*voluptas*) (cf. *Vergnügen*)
Macht	power (*in potentia mea*), might
Mann	man
Mannigfaltigkeit	manifold
Mäßigkeit	moderation
Materie	matter

GLOSSARY

Meine (Deine, Seine)	what is mine (yours, one's), what belongs to me; *etwas als das Seine haben*, to have as one's own
meinen	hold or express opinion(s), opine
Meinung	opinion, estimation
Mensch	human being
Menschenliebe	philanthropy, benevolence, love of humanity
Menschheit	humanity
menschlich	human
Menschlichkeit	humanity
Merkmal	mark (*nota*)
mißbilligen	disapprove
Missfallen	dislike
Mitfreude	sympathetic joy
Mitleid	(sympathetic) sadness, pity
Mitleidenschaft	compassion
Moral	morals, moral philosophy
Moralität	morality
Mündigkeit	majority
Narr	conceited ass
Naturrecht	natural right
Nebenzweck	incidental end
Neid	envy
Neigung	inclination
nötigen	necessitate
Nötigung	constraint, necessitation
Notwendigkeit	necessity
Oberbefehlshaber	supreme commander, supreme ruler
Oberhaupt	head
oberst	supreme
Object	object
Obliegenheit	(something) incumbent upon (one)
Obrigkeit	authority
Offenbarung	revelation
öffentlich	public
peremptorisch	conclusive, peremptory
Pflicht	duty
pflichtmäßig	in conformity with duty
pflichtwidrig	contrary to duty
Prinzip	principle (cf. *Grundsatz*)
Probierstein	touchstone
provisorisch	provisional

GLOSSARY

Qualität	quality, capacity, role
Rache	vengeance
Ratschluß	decree (*decretum*)
Recht	right (n.) (*ius*)
Rechtens	laid down as right
rechtlich	rightful, honorable, having to do with rights, by right, etc.
rechtmäßig	in conformity with right, in accord with right, legitimate
Rechtsanspruch	verdict, sentence
Rechtsgesetz	principle of right
rechtskräftig	having rightful force
Rechtspflicht	duty of right
rechtwidrig	contrary to right
Regent	ruler
Regierer	governor
Regierung	government, governance
Reich	kingdom
Schadenfreude	malice
schätzen	value, estimate
Schein	illusion
Scherz	banter
schlimm	bad
Schluß	inference (cf. *Vernunftschluss, Verstandeschluss*)
schmälern	diminish, detract from
Schmerz	pain
Schranke	limit(ation)
Schuld	guilt
schuldig	owed (*debitum*)
Schwärmerei	enthusiasm
Selbständigkeit	self-sufficiency, independence
Selbstentleibung	killing oneself, suicide
Selbstliebe	self-love
Selbstmord	murdering oneself
Selbstschätzung	self-esteem
Selbstsucht	self-seeking, selfishness
Selbsttätigkeit	spontaneity
Selbstzufriedenheit	self-contentment
Seligkeit	blessedness
sichern	secure, assure, guarantee
Sinn	sense, meaning
Sinnlichkeit	sensibility
Sitten	morality, manners

GLOSSARY

Sittlichkeit	morals
Souveränität	sovereignty
Spottsucht	mockery
stiften	institute, establish
Stolz	pride
strafbar	punishable
Strafgesetz	penal law
sträflich	culpable
Streit	conflict
Tat	deed
Tatigkeit	activity
Tausch	barter
Teilnehmung	sympathy
Tierheit	animality
Tor	fool
Trieb	drive, impulse
Triebfeder	incentive
Tugend	virtue
Tugendpflicht	duty of virtue
Übel	ill, ill-being, troubles (cf. *Böse*)
übereinstimmen	agree
Übergabe	delivery
Überlegung	reflection
Übermut	arrogance, haughtiness
Überredung	persuasion
Übertretung	transgression
Überzeugung	conviction
unerforschlich	inscrutable
ungereimt	absurd
Unlauterkeit	impurity
Unlust	displeasure, aversion (*taedium*)
Unparteilichkeit	impartiality
unrecht	wrong
Unredlichkeit	dishonesty
Unschuld	innocence
Unsterblichkeit	immortality
Unterlassung	omission, neglect
Unterschied	difference, distinction
Untersuchung	investigation
Untugend	lack of virtue
Urheber	author
Ursache	cause (*causa*)
ursprünglich	original
Urteilskraft	(faculty of) judgment

GLOSSARY

verabscheuen	abhor
verachten	be contemptuous of
Verachtung	contempt
Veränderung	alteration
verantwortlich	accountable, responsible
verbinden	bind, obligate
Verbindung	combination (*conjunctio*), alliance
Verbot	prohibition
Verbrechen	crime
Verdienst	merit
Verehrung	reverence
Vereinigung	unification, union
Verfassung	constitution
verfügen	dispose
Vergehen	transgression
Verhältnis	relation, relationship
Verhöhnung	ridicule
Verknüpfung	connection
Verleihen	lending
Verletzung	violation
Verleumdung	slander
Vermögen	capacity, faculty, power, wealth, means, resources
Vernunft	reason
vernünftelnd	rationalizing, sophistical
Verpflichtung	obligation
Verschenkung	gift
Verschuldung	fault (*culpa*), culpability (*demeritum*)
Verstand	understanding (*intellectus*)
Volk	people, nation
Völlerei	gluttony
vollkommen	perfect (v.)
Vollkommenheit	perfection (*perfectio*)
vollständig	complete
Voraussetzung	presupposition
Vorschrift	precept
Vorsehung	providence (*providentia*)
vorsetzlich	intentional
vorstellen	represent
Vorstellung	representation (*repraesentatio*)
wählen	choose
Wahn	delusion
Wahrnehmung	perception
Wahrscheinlichkeit	probability
Wechsel	change

GLOSSARY

wechselseitig	reciprocal
Weib	wife
weit	wide (*latum*)
weltbürgerlich	cosmopolitan
Wert	worth, value
Widerstand	resistance
Wille	will (*voluntas*)
Willkür	(power of) choice (*arbitrium*)
willkürlich	arbitrary, voluntary, chosen
wirklich	actual, real
Wirkung	effect, operation
Wissen	knowing, knowledge (*scientia*)
Wissenschaft	science (*scientia*)
Wohl(sein)	well-being
Wohlfahrt	welfare
Wohlgefallen	delight
Wohltätigkeit	beneficence
Wohltun	beneficence
Wohlwollen	benevolence
wollen	will
Wollen	volition
Würde	dignity
Würdigkeit	worthiness
zufällig	contingent
Zufriedenheit	satisfaction, contentment
Zugänglichkeit	affability
zurechnen	impute
Zusammenhang	connection
Zusammensetzung	composition, synthesis
Zustand	state, condition
Zwang	coercion, constraint
Zweck	end
zweckmäßig	purposive, appropriate, suitable
Zweckmäßigkeit	purposiveness

English–German

abiding	beharrlich
abstract	absondern
absurd	ungereimt
accused	Angeklägte
acknowledge	bekennen
acquisition	Erwerbung
act	Akt
action	Handlung
activity	Tätigkeit

GLOSSARY

actual	wirklich
affability	Zugänglichkeit
agree	übereinstimmen
agreeable	angenehm
alteration	Veränderung
ambition	Ehrbegierde (*ambitio*)
animality	Tierheit
appearance	Erscheinung
application	Anwendung
appraisal	Beurteilung
approve	billigen
aptitude	Fertigkeit
arbitrary	willkürlich
arrogance	Hochmut, Übermut
art	Kunst
assumption	Annehmung
author	Urheber
authority	Gewalt, Obrigkeit
authorization	Befugnis
aversion	Unlust
aware	gewahr
bad	schlimm, schlecht
barter	Tausch
beneficence	Wohltätigkeit, Wohltun
benevolence	Wohlwollen
bind	verbinden
blessedness	Seligkeit
bondsman	Leibeigener
bound(ary)	Grenze
cancel	aufheben
capacity	Vermögen
cause	Ursache
change	Wechsel
character	Character, Gemütsart
characteristic	Beschaffenheit
choice (power of)	Willkür
choose	wählen
civil	bürgerlich
claim	Anspruch
clear	klar, deutlich
clue	Leitfaden
coercion	Zwang
cognition	Erkenntnis
cognize	erkennen
collective possession	Gesammtbesitz

GLOSSARY

combination — Verbindung
command — Gebot, Befehl
commander — Befehlshaber (*imperans*), Gebieter
common possession — Gemeinbesitz
commonwealth — Gemeinwesen
compassion — Mitleidenschaft
complacency — Behaglichkeit
complete — vollständig
completion — Vollendung
composition — Zusammensetzung
comprehend — begreifen
conceited ass — Narr
concept — Begriff
concern — Beschäftigung, Geschäft
conclusive (possession) — peremptorisch
condition — Bedingung, Zustand
conflict — Streit
connection — Verknüpfung
consent — Einwilligung
consequence — Folgerung
constant — beständig
constitution — Verfassung, Beschaffenheit
constraint — Nötigung, Zwang
contempt — Verachtung
contentment — Zufriedenheit
control — Gewalt
conviction — Überzeugung
cosmopolitan — weltbürgerlich
country — Land
court — Gerichtshof
courtesy — Höflichkeit
crime — Verbrechen
criticism — Kritik
culpability — Verschuldung (*demeritum*)
culpable — sträflich, cf. strafbar

declaration — Erklärung
decree — Ratschluß (*decretum*)
deed — Tat
defamation — Afterreden
definition — Erklärung, Definition
degree — Grad
delight — Wohlgefallen
delivery — Übergabe
delusion — Wahn
desire — Begierde
determination — Bestimmung

GLOSSARY

determine	bestimmen
develop	entwickeln
difference	Unterschied
dignity	Würde
diminish	schmälern
disapprove	mißbilligen
discretion	Belieben
discretionary	beliebig
dishonesty	Unredlichkeit
dislike	Mißfallen
display	darstellen
displeasure	Unlust
dispose	verfügen
disposition	Gesinnung
distinctness	Deutlichkeit
doctrine	Lehre
domain	Umfang
domestic right	dinglich-persönliches Recht
dominion	Herrschaft
duration	Dauer
duty	Pflicht
education	Bildung, Ausbildung, Erziehung
effect	Wirkung
emotion	Affekt
employment	Gebrauch
end	Zweck
enjoyment	Genuß
enthusiasm	Schwärmerei
entitle	berechtigen
envy	Neid
equitable	billig
equity	Billigkeit
establish	dartun
esteem	Hochschätzung
event	Ereignis
evil	Böse
example	Beispiel
executive	ausübende, ausführende
exhibition	Darstellung
experience	Erahrung
explanation	Erklärung
explicate	entwickeln
explication	Erklärung
fair	billig
faith	Glaube

653

GLOSSARY

fault	Verschuldung (*culpa*)
feeling	Gefühl, Empfindung
final end	Endzweck
final purpose	Endabsicht
fool	Tor
force	Kraft
general	allgemein
gentleness	Gelindigkeit
genus	Gattung
germ	Keim
gift	Verschenkung
gluttony	Völlerei
good fortune	Glück
government	Regierung
ground	Grund
guide	Leitfaden
guilt	Schuld
habit	Angewohnheit
happiness	Glückseligkeit
haughtiness	Übermut
head	Oberhaupt
holding	Inhabung
holiness	Heiligkeit
honest	ehrlich
honor	Ehre
honorable	rechtlich (*honestas*), ehrlich
hospitality	Gastfreiheit
human	menschlich
human being	Mensch
humanity	Menschheit, Menschlichkeit, Humanität
ill	Übel
illusion	Schein, Illusion
image	Bild
immortality	Unsterblichkeit
impartiality	Unparteilichkeit
impulse	Trieb, Antrieb
impurity	Unlauterkeit
impute	zurechnen
incentive	Triebfeder
inclination	Neigung
incumbent (upon)	Obliegenheit
independence	Selbständigkeit
inference	Schluß

GLOSSARY

infringe	lädieren, Abbruch tun
infringement	Läsion
innocence	Unschuld
insight	Einsicht
instance	Beispiel
institute	stiften
insult	Beleidigung
intention	Absicht, Vorsatz
intentional	vorsetzlich
interaction	Wechselwirkung
intuition	Anschauung (*intuitus*)
jealousy	Eifersucht
judgment	Urteil, Urteilskraft
justice	Gerechtigkeit
killing oneself	Selbstentleibung
kind	Art
kingdom	Reich
know	wissen, kennen
knowledge	Wissen, Kenntnis
land	Boden (*fundus*)
lawfulness	Gesetzmäßigkeit
lawgiver	Gesetzgeber
learning	Gelehrtheit
legality	Legalität
legislation	Gesetzgebung
legislator	Gesetzgeber
lending	Verleihen
life conduct	Lebenswandel
like	gefallen (v.r.)
limit(ation)	Schranke, Einschränkung
loan	Anleihe
love	Liebe
luck	Glück
majority	Mündigkeit
malice	Schadenfreude
manifold	Mannigfaltigkeit
mark	Merkmal (*nota*)
matter	Materie
meaning	Sinn, Bedeutung
merit	Verdienst
might	Macht
mind	Gemüt, Geist
mockery	Spottsucht

GLOSSARY

moderation	Mäßigkeit
morality, morals	Sitten, Sittlichkeit, Moral, Moralität
motive	Bewegungsgrund, Bestimmungsgrund
murdering oneself	Selbstmord
narrow	eng
nation	Volk
natural right	Naturrecht
nature	Natur, Beschaffenheit
necessitate	Nötigen
necessity	Notwendigkeit
need	Bedürfnis
object	Gegenstand, Object
obligation	Verpflichtung, Verbinding
occurrence	Begebenheit
omission	Unterlassung
operation	Wirkung
opinion	Meinung
original	ursprünglich
owed	schuldig (*debitum*)
owner	Eigentümer
pain	Schmerz
particular	besonder
passion	Leidenschaft
patience	Langmut
penal law	Strafgesetz
people	Volk
perception	Wahrnehmung
perfect	vollkommen
perfection	Vollkommenheit
permission	Erlaubnis
permissive law	Erlaubnisgesetz
perpetual	ewig
persistence	Beharrlichkeit
persisting	beharrlich
persuasion	Überredung
philanthropy	Menschenliebe
pity	Mitleid
please	gefallen (v.r.)
pleasure	Lust
possession	Besitz
power	Gewalt, Macht, Kraft
precept	Vorschrift
predisposition	Anlage
presentation	Darstellung

GLOSSARY

presupposition	Voraussetzung
pride	Stolz
principle	Grundsatz, Prinzip
probability	Wahrscheinlichkeit
problem	Aufgabe, Problem
progress	Fortschritt
prohibition	Verbot
proof	Beweis
propensity	Hang
property	Eigenschaft, Eigentum
proprietor	Eigentümer
prove	beweisen, erweisen
prudence	Klugheit
public	öffentlich
punishable	strafbar, cf. sträflich
purpose	Absicht
purposiveness	Zweckmäßigkeit
quality	Qualität
rationalize	vernünfteln
real	wirklich, real
reason	Vernunft
receptivity	Empfänglichkeit
reciprocal	wechselseitig
recognize	anerkennen, erkennen
reconcile	versöhnen
reference	Verweisung, Beziehung
reflection	Überlegung
relation	Beziehung, Verhältnis
represent	vorstellen
representation	Vorstellung
resistance	Widerstand
resolve	auflösen
respect	Achtung
result	Folge
revelation	Offenbarung
ridicule	Verhöhnung
right (n.)	Recht
rightful	rechtlich
ruler	Regent, Beherrscher
satisfaction	Befriedigung, Zufriedenheit
scholar	Gelehrte
scholarship	Gelehrsamkeit
science	Wissenschaft
scripture	Schrift

GLOSSARY

sedition	Aufstand
selection	Auswahl
self-conceit	Eigendünkel
self-contentment	Selbstzufriedenheit
selfishness	Selbstsucht
self-love	Eigenliebe, Selbstliebe
self-seeking	Selbstsucht
self-sufficiency	Selbständigkeit
sensation	Empfindung
sense(s)	Sinn(e)
sensibility	Sinnlichkeit
separate	absondern
servants	Gesinde
set aside	absondern
significance	Bedeutung
signification	Bedeutung
skill	Geschicklichkeit
slander	Verleumdung
sociability	Gesprächigkeit
solve	auflösen
sophistical	vernünftelnd
soul	Seele
sovereignty	Souveränitat, Herrschergewalt
species	Art, Species, Gattung
spontaneity	Selbsttätigkeit
state	Zustand
sublime	erhaben
suicide	Selbstentleibung
sum total	Inbegriff
supreme	oberst
supreme commander	Oberbefehlshaber
sympathetic sadness	Mitleid
sympathy	Teilnehmung
synthesis	Synthesis, Zusammensetzung
task	Aufgabe
teaching	Lehre
thing	Ding, Sache
touchstone	Probierstein
transgression	Übertretung
troubles	Übel
unconscientiousness	Gewissenlosigkeit
understanding	Verstand
union	Vereinigung
universal	allgemein

GLOSSARY

universal validity	Allgemeingültigkeit
use	Gebrauch
validity	Gültigkeit
vengeance	Rache
verdict	Rechtsspruch, Ausspruch
vice	Laster
violation	Verletzung
virtue	Tugend
vocation	Bestimmung
volition	Wollen
voluntary	willkürlich, freiwillig
way	Art, Weise
welfare	Wohlfahrt
well-being	Wohl, Wohlergehen, Heil
wife	Weib
will	Wille
worth	Wert
worthiness	Würdigkeit
wrong	unrecht (tun)

Index of names

Abdera, 598
Achenwall, G., 115, 299–300, 434, 630, 632, 637
Adickes, E., 313
Anacharsis, 634
Anaxagoras, 252
Aristotle, 532–3, 555–6, 585
Augustus, 321

Balmerino, *see* Elphinstone, A.
Barthelemy, J., 634
Baumgarten, A. G., 549
Bayle, P., 313
Beccaria, C., 475–6, 638
Beck, L. W., xv, xxvi, 357, 635
Beiser, F. C., xxvi
Beyer, G., 115, 629
Biester, J. E., 25, 275–6, 607, 631
Boleyn, A., 264
Boorde, A., 640
Bouterwek, F., 336, 356, 492–506, 634, 638
Brabant, 632
Brandt, R., 356
Brown, J., 367, 635
Burke, E., 275, 632
Büsching, A. F., 190, 628, 638
Byrd, B. S., xi

Cain, 554
Catiline, 552
Cato, 551
Charles I (of England), 464
Charles V (Holy Roman Emperor), 161
Cheselden, W., 147, 631
Chesterfield, Lord, 552
Chremes, 577
Cicero, 287, 395, 461
Claproth, J., 115, 630
Cocceji, H., 115, 629
Cocceji, S., 115, 629
Cochius, L., 515, 639
Commodus, 325
Constant, B., 607–15, 639–40
Cramer, K. F., 607, 640
Crusius, C. A., 172, 631
Curtius, 548

Danton, G. J., 301, 632–3
Diogenes Laertius, 625
Domitian, 325
Dryer, D. P., 357

Eberhard, J. A., 115, 362, 630, 635
Ehlers, M., 9, 628
Elphinstone, A., 474, 638
Epicurus, 158, 172–3, 229–33, 237, 241–2, 253, 390, 597, 631

Feder, J. G., 115, 630, 631
Fischer, J. E., 329, 634
Flatt, J. F., xxv–xxvi, 115, 143, 367, 630, 635
Fontenelle, B., 202, 632
Francis I (of France), 161
Frederick II (the Great, of Prussia), xxvii, xxx, 3, 13, 18, 21, 313, 324–5, 361, 548, 628, 639
Frederick William II (of Prussia), xxvii–xxviii, 3, 13, 313, 361

Garve, C., xxviii, 13, 115, 275–6, 281–90, 350, 366, 630, 631, 632, 634
Geismann, G., xi
Gentz, F., 632
Georgius, A., 329–30, 634
Geuss, R., 357
Gregor, M. J., xi
Grotius, H., 115, 326, 629, 634, 636–7
Gundibert, S., 619, 626, 635, 640
Gundling, N. H., 115, 629
Guyer, P., xxvi, xxxiii, 113, 620

Haller, V. A., 527, 578, 639
Hamann, J. G., 39, 115, 630, 634
Hausen, C. A., 367, 635
Henrich, D., xv
Henry VIII (of England), 264
Herder, J. G., xxi–xxii, 631, 634
Herz, M., 360
Heschyius, 634
Hippocrates, 303
Hobbes, T., xxviii, 115, 116, 275–6, 290, 302, 629, 630
Höpfner, L. J. F., 115, 630

INDEX OF NAMES

Horace, 17, 141, 532, 536, 551, 559, 597, 601, 625
Hufeland, G., 113–17, 629–30
Hume, D., 146–7, 180–5
Hutcheson, F., xiv, xviii, 91, 172, 629, 631

Jacobi, F. H., 619, 632
Jacobs, B., xxx
James I (of England), 633
James II (of England), 633
Jenisch, D., 631
John III, Duke of Brabant, 632
Justinian, 637
Juvenal, 266–8

Kant I: early writings on moral theory, xiii–xvi; mature moral theory, xx–xxvii; moral convictions, xiii, xvii–xx; philosophy of religion xxviii–xxx; political theory, xxvii–xxx.
Kästner, J., 631
Kohler, H., 115, 629
Konx Ompax, 330
Kraus, C. J., 121–31, 632

LaCroze, F., 330, 634
Lambert, J. H., 360
Lavoisier, A., 367, 634–5
Leage, R. W., 637
Leibniz, G. W., 217–18, 268, 313, 317, 633
Lessing, G. E., 632, 633
Lippert, P. D., 34, 628
Louis XVI (of France), 464, 481
Lucretius, 331
Ludwig, B., 355–7

Maier, H., 625, 630, 632–3, 640
Mallet du Pan, J., 325, 633
Mandeville, B., 172, 631
Marcus Aurelius, 325
Mary II (of England), 633
Mautner, T., 355, 636
McCarthy, T., xi
Mendelssohn, M., xiii, xxviii, 13, 22, 115, 221, 275–6, 304–6, 423, 630, 632, 637
Menzer, P., 121
Merryman, J., 637
Michaelis, J. D., 639
Mohammed, 237, 551
Montaigne, M., 172, 631
Möser, J., 619, 623–5, 627, 640

Natorp, P., 136, 198, 355, 635, 639
Nero, 548
Newton, I., 370
Nicolai, F., 368, 617–27, 635, 640

Orazio, F., 330
Orestes, 585
Ovid, 532

Paton, H, J., xxiii
Paulsen, F., xxx
Penna, F., 634
Phaedrus, 387
Phalaris, 267, 632
Pirithous, 585
Pistorius, H. A., xxvi, 136, 631
Platner, E., 115, 630
Plato, 253
Pope, A., 325, 633
Priestley, J., 9, 628, 632
Protagoras, 598
Pufendorf, S., 115, 326, 629, 634
Pylades, 585

Quintilian, 598

Rehberg, A. W., 275
Robespierre, M., 633
Rosen, A., xix
Rousseau, J.-J., xiii, xvii–xix, xxi, xxvii–xxviii, xxix, 309, 313, 461, 565, 633, 638

Sallust, 552
Schiller, F., 362, 619
Schilpp, P. A., xvi–xvii
Schlettwein, J. A., 115, 630
Schmauß, J. J., 115, 630
Schmucker, J., xvi
Schneewind, J., xix
Schulz, J. H., 3–10, 121, 628, 632
Schulze, J., xx
Schütz, C. G., 136, 631
Siep, L., xxx
Sebond, R., 631
Selle, C. G., 115, 630
Seneca, 335, 548
Shaftesbury, 635
Smith, A., 435, 436, 637
Socrates, 58, 510, 539, 592, 625
Spinoza, B., 221
Stark, W., 356
Stäudlin, C. F., 639
Stobaeus, 625
St.-Pierre, Abbé de, xxix, 309, 313, 633
Strauss, W., 635
Strum, A., xxx
Stuart, Prince Charles, 638
Sulzer, J. G., 64–5, 115, 629, 630
Swift, J., 309, 325, 633

Terence, 577, 639
Theseus, 585

662

INDEX OF NAMES

Thomasius, C., 115, 629
Tieftrunk, J. H., 25
Tittel, G. A., xxvi, 630
Titus, 325
Treuer, G. S., 115, 629
Tunguses, 490

Ulpian, xxxi–xxxii, 392–393
Ulrich, J. A. H., 115, 121–31, 630, 632

Vaihinger, H., 121
Vattel, E., 326, 634
Vaucanson, A., 221, 632
Virgil, 281, 304, 328, 332, 346, 632

Voltaire, 203, 313
Vorländer, K., 639

Ward, K., xvii
William III (of England), 633
Windischgrätz, J., 321, 633
Wizenmann, T., xxvi, 255, 632
Wolff, C., 46, 115, 172, 367, 629, 631, 635
Wöllner, J. C., xxvii, 3

Yelin, J. C., 635

Zöllner, J. F., 13, 115, 630

Index of subjects

a priori, 61–4, 145–7, 180–2, 627
acquisition, 638; by contract, 424–5; by inheritance, 440–1, 500–1; by judgment in court, 443–52; by prolonged possession, 439–40, 498–99, 637; ideal, 438; original, 411–12, 418–21; right of, 411–21
administration, 325
aesthetic, 212, 534; *see also* feeling
affects, 535–6
agriculture, 333
ambition, 545, 558
America, 417, 483, 490
animality, 189, 242, 518, 545
antagonism, 76
anthropology, xxx–xxxi, 44–6, 64–6, 76, 90, 372, 534, 582
anthropomorphism, 245, 249
antinomy, 163, 224–5; of practical reason, 231–6
apathy, moral, 536–7
appropriation, 411
aristocracy, 470–2, 503–4, 623–5
armies, standing, 318–19
arrogance, 49, 209, 558, 579, 581–2
art, works of, 34
ascetics, ethical, 597–8
assassins, 320
Athens, 486, 598
atonement, 601
author (of book), 25–35
author (of obligation), 96, 381, 543
authorities, in a state, 458–61
autonomy, 81–6, 88–9, 92, 97–8, 166, 173–5, 243
avarice, 545, 555–7

balance of power, 309
barter, 433
beatitude, 235
beneficence, 53–4, 75, 90, 101, 167–8, 196, 245, 530, 571–3
benevolence, 206, 570–1
bestiality, 427
books, 25–35, 617–27, 640
Brussels, 632
buying and selling, 433

cash, 435
casuistry, 538
catechism, moral, 538, 540, 592–5
categories, 141–2, 249; deduction of, 253–4; of freedom, 145, 192–4
causality, 97–100, 126–31, 168–9, 180–6, 222–5, 229
celibacy, clerical, 502
character, 54, 473, 535
chemistry, 214, 367, 634–5
China, 329–30, 634
choice, 375–6, 405
Christianity, 242–3
church, 19, 468–70, 501–3, 639
citizen, 285; active and passive, 458; of the world, 281
clemency, 477–8
clergy, 19, 502
coercion, 388–90; right of, 116
colonialism, 329–31, 417–18, 486, 489–92
commerce, spirit of, 336
common possession, original, 411, 415–16
communication, freedom of, 302
concept, problematic, 142–3
concubinage, 428
conscience, 218–19, 529–30, 559–62
constitution, 304, 322–5, 638; change of, 463–5; civil, 296–7; constitutions, division of, 479
contempt, 579
contentment, 234–5; *see also* self-contentment
contract, 421–6, 443–52, 607, 637; division of, 433–4; gratuitous, 433; original, 20, 296–7, 302–3, 480, 623–5; right of, 495
cosmological ideas, 247
counsels, 69–71
court, 443–52
crime, 378, 472–3
critique, xvi, xxv–xxvi, 47, 141–3
culture, 307–9, 522–3, 596
custom, 146, 181
Cynicism, 242

death penalty, 474–7, 638
debt, national, 319

INDEX OF SUBJECTS

deduction, 173–80
deed, 378, 382
defamation, 582
deposit, stolen, 151–2, 288
despotism, 301, 324
dialectic, 60, 149, 223, 226–8
dignities, in state, 470–2
dignity, xvii–xx, 22, 60, 84–5, 88, 197–8, 262, 557–8
dinner parties, 551–2
disposition, 233, 239
drunkenness, 550–2
duels, 476–7
duties: division of, xxxi–xxxiii, 73–5, 383–5, 395–7, 527, 527–40, 544–5, 602–3; conflict of, 378–9; indirect, 54, 519–20; internal and external, 527; of right, 394–5; of virtue, xxxii–xiii, 394–5, 512–28; perfect and imperfect, 73–5, 194, 521, 635; proof of, 531–2; regarding animals, 563–4; to God, 396, 563–4; to nonpersons, 396; to oneself, 266, 543–5; antinomy of, 543–4; wide and narrow, 75, 80–1, 382, 521–2
duty, 52–6, 61–3, 84, 88, 169–71, 205, 209, 254, 280, 282, 286–9, 371, 377–8, 395, 512–18, 524–7, 595

education, moral, 209, 261–9, 305, 538–9, 591–7
eleutheronomy, 511, 624–5, 640
embezzlement, 472–3
empiricism, 143–7, 181–6, 197
end, 78–87, 115–17, 513–18, 534, 537; final, 282; in itself, 78, 210–11; of creation, 601–2
England, 460, 486, 501–2, 633
enlightenment, xiii, xxii, 13–22
entailment, 472, 504
enthusiasm, 10, 208–9, 239, 536
envy, 576
epopts, 330
equality, xvii–xix, 614; civil, xix, 291, 292–4, 322–3, 457
equity, 390–1; no court of, 391
eudaimonism, 155–60, 172, 370–1, 510–11, 624–5, 640
evil, 187–5, 242, 335, 343, 347
examples, moral, 63, 71, 263, 593
executive authority, 457; *see also* ruler
exile, 478

fact of reason, 164–166
faculty of desire, 143–4, 176, 186–8, 233–4, 373, 492; higher and lower, 156–8
faith, 254–7
fatalism, 9–10, 127, 219–22
fate, 601

fault, 378
federation, 326–8, 337, 482–3, 487–8
feeling, xiv–xvi, 55, 198–202, 213–14, 373–4; moral, xiv–xvi, xviii, 91, 172, 204, 285–6, 519, 528–9, 629, 631
folly, 581
forgiveness, 578
formal principles, 160–4, 167, 172–3, 344
formula of autonomy, xxiii–xxiv, 81, 86–7
formula of humanity as end in itself, xxiii–xxiv, xxxi–xxxii, 79–81, 245–6; *see also* humanity
formula of kingdom of ends, xvi, xxiii–xxiv, 83–7
formula of law of nature, xxiii, xxxi, 73–6, 175–6, 195–8
formula of universal law, xxiii–xxiv, xxxi, 56–7, 73–6
foundations, perpetual, 468–70, 501–4
France, xxix–xxx, 502, 633
freedom, xv, 7–10, 43, 94–108, 125–31, 139–42, 148–9, 162–6, 173–5, 174, 177–8, 180–6, 193, 197, 198, 215–25, 231, 246–7, 248–50, 259, 268–70, 286–7, 374–5, 376, 457, 628, 632; civil, 22; external, 7–8, 17–22, 290–2, 302–4, 322–3, 393–4, 480, 614; idea of, 97; inner, 268, 634–5, 544; lawless, 328; laws of, 403; negative concept, 94, 166–7; of indifference, 380–1; of the pen, 302; positive concept, 95, 135–6, 166–7
friendship, 584–8; moral, 586–8

general will, 292, 409–10, 415–16, 423, 457–9, 468
genius, 270
gift, 433, 444
Germany, 490
gluttony, 550–2
God, 8, 91–2, 140–1, 145–7, 172–3, 185, 192, 198, 206–8, 220–1, 239, 240–1, 246–7, 248–50, 254, 259, 283, 325, 332, 595, 599–602; attributes, 245, 252; existence of, 239–47; glory of, 245, 602; kingdom of, 243–4, 250; love of, 207–8; use of idea in science, 250–2; worship of, 245
Golden Rule, 80
good, 49–50, 143–4, 186–98, 284–5
good will, 49–56, 77, 92, 95
government, representative, *see* republic
gratitude, 573–4
Greenwich, 501
Guinea, 449

Hague, 488
happiness, xxii, 9, 49–54, 59, 68–72, 90,

665

INDEX OF SUBJECTS

happiness (*cont.*)
　97, 158–60, 167–8, 171, 189, 197, 214–15, 228, 231, 237, 240–2, 244–6, 256, 265, 281–9, 294, 297–300, 370–1, 593–4; moral, 510–11, 522, 524; of others, 517–18, 519–20, 524
haughtiness, 577
heteronomy, 83–93, 89–91, 166, 172–4
highest good, 140, 175, 192, 227–46, 247, 249, 255, 282–5
hiring, contract of, 433
history, xx–xxii, *see also* progress, historical
holiness, 145, 206, 210, 238–9, 243, 245–6; *see also* will, holy
honor, 476–7, 545, 581–2
Hottentots, 417, 490
human nature, 39, 76, 95; *see also* anthropology
humanity, xvii–xx, 79–81, 197, 210, 305, 512, 522–3, 567; right of, 80, 393, 427, 498; *see also* formula of humanity
humiliation, 203–4
humility, 545, 558–9
Hungary, 324
hypocrisy, 261

idea, 96, 99, 178, 248–50, 296, 593
ill, 187–93
illusion, 255
immortality, 140–1, 145–7, 238–9, 246–7, 248–50, 282–3, 289, 601
imperative, 66–70, 145, 154, 165, 377–9, 522–3; apodictic, 68, 380; assertoric, 68–70; categorical, xiii–xiv, 39, 67, 82, 92, 380; hypothetical, 67–70, 89, 92; pragmatic, 69–71; technical, 68
imputation, 117, 381–2, 607, 612–13
incentive, 78, 198–211
inclination, 49–55, 76–7, 79, 101, 235, 257–8, 374
independence of citizens, 291, 294–6, 322–3, 458
India, 330, 458
indifference, moral, 536
infanticide, 476–7
ingratitude, 576–7
inheritance, 438, 440–1, 500–1; of states, 318
injustice, general, xix–xx, 573
innocence, 59–60
intelligible world, *see* noumenal world
interest, 67, 82, 96, 105, 204, 236–8
intuition, 367
Ireland, 486, 502

jealousy, 576
judgment, 268–9; practical, 194–8
judicial authority, 457, 460–1

justice, 245, 344–6, 359, 456, 620; commutative, 477, 450; distributive, 447, 450, 456; divine, 600–1; punitive, 472–7, 600; retributive, 473–4; *see also* right

kingdom of ends, 83–8, 175; *see also* formula of kingdom of ends
kingdom of God, 243–4

land, property in, 405, 414–15
law, 55–6, 72, 153–4, 193, 358, 381; moral, 133–5, 261, 377–80, 520; of nature, 275; permissive, 20–1, 406; practical, 153, 160–8; public, 409; universal, 56–8, 81–5, 106
laws: apodictic, 62; classification of, 320–1; external, 379; moral, 370–6; of freedom, 375–7
league of nations, 326–8, 337, 482–3, 487–8
lease, 443, 448, 496–7
legality, 62, 198, 205, 261, 380
legislation, 383–5; political, 295, 297–9, 321, 458–60
legislator, 379, 381
legislative authority, 457–60
letter and spirit, 198
life, 50–1, 144, 373
loan, 433, 444–5
logic, 43–4, 212
love, 55, 75, 202, 245, 530–1, 550, 601, 639; duties of, 568–71

malice, 576–7
man of affairs, 281, 289, 337–47
mandate, 29–35, 433, 437–8, 628
marriage, 426–9, 495, 550; morganatic, 428
material principles, 155–60, 162–3, 167, 172–3, 344
materialism, 632
mathematics, 126, 181–3, 367, 389–90, 531–2, 635
maxim, 55–6, 73–5, 76, 153–4, 193, 204, 520; legislative form, 160–4
maxims, political, 342–3
mechanism, 217–19; of nature, 331–7
metaphysics, xiii, xv, xxv, 43–4, 135–6, 509
metaphysics of morals, xvi, xxv, 44–8, 63–6, 360–2, 370–3, 584
Metaphysics of Morals, xxx–xxxiii; terminology in, 357–9; textual emendations, 355–7, 636
method, 261–2
military, 19, 467, 476–7
misology, 51
mockery, 582–3
modesty, 579

INDEX OF SUBJECTS

money, 434–6, 637
moral feeling, *see* feeling
moral philosophy, popular, 39–40, 48, 63–6
moral politician, 340, 344–6
morality, 371
motive, 78
murder, 474–6
mysticism, 197, 237

nature, 7, 66, 98–108
necessitation, 377–8
necessity, 9–10, 102, 391–2, 632
New Holland, 417, 490
New Mexico, 435
noumenal world, 98–101, 103–7, 174–5, 179–86, 196–7, 216–22, 543–4, 547

oath, 448–50
object, 228; of desire, 155–60, 162–3; of practical reason, 232; of pure practical reason, 186–94
obligation, xiv–xv, 9–10, 46, 267, 377; wide and narrow, 521–4; *see also* duties
occupation, 415–16
opium, 551
ought, 9–10, 66, 101, 154; and can, 163–4; *see also* imperative

paederasty, 427
paralogisms, 246
passion, 535–6
paternalism, 291–2
peace, 487–8; perpetual, xxviii–xxix, 308–9, 313–51, 487, 490–2, 633, 635, 638
penance, 597–8
perfection, 90–2, 116–17, 172–3, 253, 631; moral, 523, 566–7; natural, 74–5, 522–3, 565–6; one's own, 518–19, 544–5
permission, 377, 406
personality, 79, 101, 194, 210, 269–70, 378, 557
Peru, 435
philanthropy, 587
philosophy, 337–8, 366–8; division of, 43; popular moral, 63–4, 77; theoretical and practical, xxvi, 372–3
physics, 43–4, 251–2
pleasure, 155–60, 186–93, 202, 204, 373–4, 511
pledge, 434, 448–50
police, 467
political moralist, 340, 344–6
politics, 614–15
popularity, 63–4, 366
possession: conclusive, 416–17; empirical, 402–3; noumenal, 403–7; physical, 402–3, 407–9; provisional, 418–19; right of, 407–11, 494
possibility, logical and real, 248–50
postulates of practical reason, 238–46
poverty, 435, 468–9, 501–3
precepts, 70–1, 193
prescription, 439, 499, 637
price, 77, 84, 558
principles, 153–4; of morality, 47–8; practical, 211–14; *see also* formal principles, material principles
privacy, 582
private use of reason, 18–22
progress: historical, xxx, 276, 304–9; moral, 238–9
promise, 57, 72, 74, 80, 154, 394, 422–4
property, 31–5, 295, 321, 421; in land, 405, 418–21, 466; transfer of, 422–6, 434, 435; *see also* possession
prostitution, 428
providence, 308, 331–7
prudence, 57, 69–71, 154, 169–70, 342–4; *see also* happiness, self-love
public communication, 17–22, 30–5
publication, 25–35, 617–27, 640; right of, 29–35, 437–8; unauthorized, 29–35, 437–8
publicity, principle of, 347–50
punishment, 170–1, 189, 472–8, 497–8, 600–2, 638
purposiveness, natural, 331–7

rationalism, 197
reason, 7–10, 99; common, 213; need of, 254–7; practical, 148–9, 236–8, 247–58; public use of, 18–22; pure, 179, 211–15; speculative, 141–43, 148–9, 236–8, 247–54
rebellion, 297–304, 458–66, 504–6, 638
reform, 341
regicide, 463
regulative principles, 179
religion, xxi, xxvii–xxviii, 13–22, 242–5, 245, 336, 564, 592, 598–600, 639
republic, 322–5, 340, 481, 491
reputation, right of, 441–3
res nullius, 404–5, 421
respect, 55–6, 58, 200–11, 269–71, 531; duties of, 568–9, 579–83; for law, 580; for oneself, 269, 559
revenge, 153
reverence, 206, 583
revolution, xxix–xxx, 18, 275–6, 465, 632
rhetoric, 532
ridicule, 582–3, 635
right, 29–35, 357–9, 365, 386–90, 514, 623–5; acquired, 393; against a person, 421–6; ambiguous, 390–2; antinomy

INDEX OF SUBJECTS

right (*cont.*)
 of, 408–9; as faculty, 393, 636; coercive, 116–17, 388–90; constitutional, 117; cosmopolitan, 322, 328–31, 334, 336–7, 350, 455, 489–92; division of, 392–7; domestic, 292–3, 402–3, 426–34, 495; fungible, 495; innate, 291, 293, 393–4; natural, 115–17, 393, 628–9; of acquisition, 411–21; of compensation, 117; of equity, 390–1; of hospitality, 328–31; of humanity, 80, 393, 427, 498; of marriage, 426–9, 495; of necessity, 299, 391–2; of possession, 401–11; conclusive, 410–11; provisional, 409–10; of recovery, 446–8; over servants, 431–2; parental, 426, 429–30, 495; postulate of private, 404–7; postulate of public, 451–2; principle of, 290–1, 293, 298, 322–3, 387–8, 526–7, 614–15; private, 397, 399–451; public, 290–1, 351, 397, 451–2, 453–92, 455; to a thing, 413–14; to land, 414–15; to persons akin to things, 426–34, 493–7
right, of a state, 281, 290–304, 322, 334–5, 348, 356, 455–81
right, of nations, 281, 304–9, 322, 325–8, 334, 336–7, 348–50, 455, 482–9
ruler, 298–303, 337–8, 451, 460–82

sanctification, 239
scandal, 524, 580–1
schema, 195
scholar, 18–22, 33, 262
Scotland, 474–5, 638
sedition, 463
self-conceit, 199–201, 204, 263, 577, 579
self-contempt, 77, 170, 562–3
self-contentment, 171, 205, 234–5
self-defense, 391–2
self-esteem, 531
self-knowledge, 567; duty of, 562–3
self-love, 8, 61–2, 77, 90, 155–6, 159–60, 168–70, 171, 199–200, 201–2, 287–9, 556, 579
serf, 466, 471, 472
servants, 426, 431–2, 458
servility, 545, 557–9
sex, 426–9, 495, 548–50
skepticism, 182–5, 222
sovereignty, 294, 458–66, 504–6
spies, 320, 485
starry heavens and moral law, 269–70
state, political, 455–72; form of, 479; of nations, 309, 326; origin of, 461–6, 480
state of nature, 397, 450–2, 456, 461, 487–8

statesman, 281, 317, 337–47
stipulation, 422–3
Stoicism, 145, 172, 188–90, 209, 229–30, 232–3, 242, 533, 575, 591, 631
subject, rights of, 302–4
sublime, 234
Sugar Islands, 472
suicide, 73–4, 80, 175, 196, 546–8, 549
supererogation, 208–9, 263, 266
superstition, 249
syllogism, practical, 212–13
sympathy, xix–xx, 53–4, 75, 207–9, 235; duty of, 574–6

talents, 74–5
taste, public, 626, 640
taxation, 319, 468–9
teleology, 50–1
temperament, 54
theological morals, 172–3, 241
theology: natural, 250; rational, 252–3
theory and practice, xxviii, 275–81
thing, 79, 378, 413
Tibet, 330
time, 215–22
treaty, 317–18, 326–8, 351, 486–7, 632
truthfulness, xxix, 45, 57, 72, 80, 89–90, 168, 171–2, 175, 189, 196, 394, 545, 552–4, 594–5, 607–15, 636, 639–40
turnspit, freedom of, 218
typic, 194–8
tyrannicide, 463

understanding, common, 40, 59, 98, 135–6

vengeance, 578
vice, 533–4, 578–9, 581
virtue, xxxii–xxxiii, 8, 208, 229, 231, 233–4, 242, 264, 512–16, 524–7, 530–9; as habit, 537; as mean, 532–3, 555–6; principle of, 526–7
virtues, social, 588
voting, 295–6

war, xxviii–xxix, 297, 307–9, 313, 317–21, 324–8, 332–3, 482–8, 632
wealth, 571–3
welfare, public, 294, 468–9, 501–3
well-being, 49–50, 187–93, 239
will, 66, 94–5, 100
will: good, 49–56, 77, 92, 95; holy, 67, 88, 165, 515, 533, 566, *see also* holiness
wine, 551
wisdom, 145, 227, 242, 245, 253, 271, 289–90, 337, 509, 534, 633
woe, 188